HOLT SCIENCE & TECHNOLOGY

Astronomy

HOLT, RINEHART AND WINSTON
A Harcourt Classroom Education Company
Austin • New York • Orlando • Atlanta • San Francisco • Boston • Dallas • Toronto • London

ANNOTATED TEACHER'S EDITION

Acknowledgments

Chapter Writers

Kathleen Meehan Berry
Science Chairman
Canon-McMillan School District
Canonsburg, Pennsylvania

Robert H. Fronk, Ph.D.
Chair of Science and Mathematics Education Department
Florida Institute of Technology
West Melbourne, Florida

Mary Kay Hemenway, Ph.D.
Research Associate and Senior Lecturer
Department of Astronomy
The University of Texas
Austin, Texas

Kathleen Kaska
Life and Earth Science Teacher
Lake Travis Middle School
Austin, Texas

Peter E. Malin, Ph.D.
Professor of Geology
Division of Earth and Ocean Sciences
Duke University
Durham, North Carolina

Karen J. Meech, Ph.D.
Associate Astronomer
Institute for Astronomy
University of Hawaii
Honolulu, Hawaii

Robert J. Sager
Chair and Professor of Earth Sciences
Pierce College
Lakewood, Washington

Lab Writers

Kenneth Creese
Science Teacher
White Mountain Junior High School
Rock Springs, Wyoming

Linda A. Culp
Science Teacher and Dept. Chair
Thorndale High School
Thorndale, Texas

Bruce M. Jones
Science Teacher and Dept. Chair
The Blake School
Minneapolis, Minnesota

Shannon Miller
Science and Math Teacher
Llano Junior High School
Llano, Texas

Robert Stephen Ricks
Special Services Teacher
Department of Classroom Improvement
Alabama State Department of Education
Montgomery, Alabama

James J. Secosky
Science Teacher
Bloomfield Central School
Bloomfield, New York

Academic Reviewers

Mead Allison, Ph.D.
Assistant Professor of Oceanography
Texas A&M University
Galveston, Texas

Alissa Arp, Ph.D.
Director and Professor of Environmental Studies
Romberg Tiburon Center
San Francisco State University
Tiburon, California

Paul D. Asimow, Ph.D.
Assistant Professor of Geology and Geochemistry
Department of Physics and Planetary Sciences
California Institute of Technology
Pasadena, California

G. Fritz Benedict, Ph.D.
Senior Research Scientist and Astronomer
McDonald Observatory
The University of Texas
Austin, Texas

Russell M. Brengelman, Ph.D.
Professor of Physics
Morehead State University
Morehead, Kentucky

John A. Brockhaus, Ph.D.
Director—Mapping, Charting, and Geodesy Program
Department of Geography and Environmental Engineering
United States Military Academy
West Point, New York

Michael Brown, Ph.D.
Assistant Professor of Planetary Astronomy
Department of Physics and Astronomy
California Institute of Technology
Pasadena, California

Wesley N. Colley, Ph.D.
Postdoctoral Fellow
Harvard-Smithsonian Center for Astrophysics
Cambridge, Massachusetts

Andrew J. Davis, Ph.D.
Manager—ACE Science Data Center
Physics Department
California Institute of Technology
Pasadena, California

Peter E. Demmin, Ed.D.
Former Science Teacher and Department Chair
Amherst Central High School
Amherst, New York

James Denbow, Ph.D.
Associate Professor
Department of Anthropology
The University of Texas
Austin, Texas

Roy W. Hann, Jr., Ph.D.
Professor of Civil Engineering
Texas A&M University
College Station, Texas

Frederick R. Heck, Ph.D.
Professor of Geology
Ferris State University
Big Rapids, Michigan

Richard Hey, Ph.D.
Professor of Geophysics
Hawaii Institute of Geophysics and Planetology
University of Hawaii
Honolulu, Hawaii

John E. Hoover, Ph.D.
Associate Professor of Biology
Millersville University
Millersville, Pennsylvania

Robert W. Houghton, Ph.D.
Senior Staff Associate
Lamont-Doherty Earth Observatory
Columbia University
Palisades, New York

Steven A. Jennings, Ph.D.
Assistant Professor
Department of Geography & Environmental Studies
University of Colorado
Colorado Springs, Colorado

Eric L. Johnson, Ph.D.
Assistant Professor of Geology
Central Michigan University
Mount Pleasant, Michigan

John Kermond, Ph.D.
Visiting Scientist
NOAA–Office of Global Programs
Silver Spring, Maryland

Zavareh Kothavala, Ph.D.
Postdoctoral Associate Scientist
Department of Geology and Geophysics
Yale University
New Haven, Connecticut

Karen Kwitter, Ph.D.
Ebenezer Fitch Professor of Astronomy
Williams College
Williamstown, Massachusetts

Valerie Lang, Ph.D.
Project Leader of Environmental Programs
The Aerospace Corporation
Los Angeles, California

Philip LaRoe
Professor
Helena College of Technology
Helena, Montana

Julie Lutz, Ph.D.
Astronomy Program
Washington State University
Pullman, Washington

Printed in the United States of America

ISBN 0-03-064796-7

2 3 4 5 6 7 032 05 04 03 02

Acknowledgments (cont.)

Duane F. Marble, Ph.D.
Professor Emeritus
Department of Geography and Natural Resources
Ohio State University
Columbus, Ohio

Joseph A. McClure, Ph.D.
Associate Professor
Department of Physics
Georgetown University
Washington, D.C.

Frank K. McKinney, Ph.D.
Professor of Geology
Appalachian State University
Boone, North Carolina

Joann Mossa, Ph.D.
Associate Professor of Geography
University of Florida
Gainesville, Florida

LaMoine L. Motz, Ph.D.
Coordinator of Science Education
Department of Learning Services
Oakland County Schools
Waterford, Michigan

Barbara Murck, Ph.D.
Assistant Professor of Earth Science
Erindale College
University of Toronto
Mississauga, Ontario, Canada

Hilary Clement Olson, Ph.D.
Research Associate
Institute for Geophysics
The University of Texas
Austin, Texas

Andre Potochnik
Geologist
Grand Canyon Field Institute
Flagstaff, Arizona

John R. Reid, Ph.D.
Professor Emeritus
Department of Geology and Geological Engineering
University of North Dakota
Grand Forks, North Dakota

Gary Rottman, Ph.D.
Associate Director
Laboratory for Atmosphere and Space Physics
University of Colorado
Boulder, Colorado

Dork L. Sahagian, Ph.D.
Professor
Institute for the Study of Earth, Oceans, and Space
University of New Hampshire
Durham, New Hampshire

Peter Sheridan, Ph.D.
Professor of Chemistry
Colgate University
Hamilton, New York

David Sprayberry, Ph.D.
Assistant Director for Observing Support
W.M. Keck Observatory
California Association for Research in Astronomy
Kamuela, Hawaii

Lynne Talley, Ph.D.
Professor
Scripps Institution of Oceanography
University of California
La Jolla, California

Glenn Thompson, Ph.D.
Scientist
Geophysical Institute
University of Alaska
Fairbanks, Alaska

Martin VanDyke, Ph.D.
Professor of Chemistry, Emeritus
Front Range Community College
Westminister, Colorado

Thad A. Wasklewicz, Ph.D.
Assistant Professor of Geography
University of Memphis
Memphis, Tennessee

Hans Rudolf Wenk, Ph.D.
Professor of Geology and Geophysical Sciences
University of California
Berkeley, California

Lisa D. White, Ph.D.
Associate Professor of Geosciences
San Francisco State University
San Francisco, California

Lorraine W. Wolf, Ph.D.
Associate Professor of Geology
Auburn University
Auburn, Alabama

Charles A. Wood, Ph.D.
Chairman and Professor of Space Studies
University of North Dakota
Grand Forks, North Dakota

Safety Reviewer

Jack Gerlovich, Ph.D.
Associate Professor
School of Education
Drake University
Des Moines, Iowa

Teacher Reviewers

Barry L. Bishop
Science Teacher and Dept. Chair
San Rafael Junior High School
Ferron, Utah

Yvonne Brannum
Science Teacher and Dept. Chair
Hine Junior High School
Washington, D.C.

Daniel L. Bugenhagen
Science Teacher and Dept. Chair
Yutan Junior & Senior High School
Yutan, Nebraska

Kenneth Creese
Science Teacher
White Mountain Junior High School
Rock Springs, Wyoming

Linda A. Culp
Science Teacher and Dept. Chair
Thorndale High School
Thorndale, Texas

Alonda Droege
Science Teacher
Pioneer Middle School
Steilacom, Washington

Laura Fleet
Science Teacher
Alice B. Landrum Middle School
Ponte Vedra Beach, Florida

Susan Gorman
Science Teacher
Northridge Middle School
North Richland Hills, Texas

C. John Graves
Science Teacher
Monforton Middle School
Bozeman, Montana

Janel Guse
Science Teacher and Dept. Chair
West Central Middle School
Hartford, South Dakota

Gary Habeeb
Science Mentor
Sierra–Plumas Joint Unified School District
Downieville, California

Dennis Hanson
Science Teacher and Dept. Chair
Big Bear Middle School
Big Bear Lake, California

Norman E. Holcomb
Science Teacher
Marion Local Schools
Maria Stein, Ohio

Tracy Jahn
Science Teacher
Berkshire Junior-Senior High School
Canaan, New York

David D. Jones
Science Teacher
Andrew Jackson Middle School
Cross Lanes, West Virginia

Howard A. Knodle
Science Teacher
Belvidere High School
Belvidere, Illinois

Michael E. Kral
Science Teacher
West Hardin Middle School
Cecilia, Kentucky

Kathy LaRoe
Science Teacher
East Valley Middle School
East Helena, Montana

Scott Mandel, Ph.D.
Director and Educational Consultant
Teachers Helping Teachers
Los Angeles, California

Kathy McKee
Science Teacher
Hoyt Middle School
Des Moines, Iowa

Michael Minium
Vice President of Program Development
United States Orienteering Federation
Forest Park, Georgia

Jan Nelson
Science Teacher
East Valley Middle School
East Helena, Montana

Dwight C. Patton
Science Teacher
Carroll T. Welch Middle School
Horizon City, Texas

Joseph Price
Chairman—Science Department
H. M. Brown Junior High School
Washington, D.C.

Terry J. Rakes
Science Teacher
Elmwood Junior High School
Rogers, Arkansas

Steven Ramig
Science Teacher
West Point High School
West Point, Nebraska

Helen P. Schiller
Science Teacher
Northwood Middle School
Taylors, South Carolina

Bert J. Sherwood
Science Teacher
Socorro Middle School
El Paso, Texas

Larry Tackett
Science Teacher and Dept. Chair
Andrew Jackson Middle School
Cross Lanes, West Virginia

Walter Woolbaugh
Science Teacher
Manhattan Junior High School
Manhattan, Montana

Alexis S. Wright
Middle School Science Coordinator
Rye Country Day School
Rye, New York

Gordon Zibelman
Science Teacher
Drexel Hill Middle School
Drexel Hill, Pennsylvania

J Astronomy

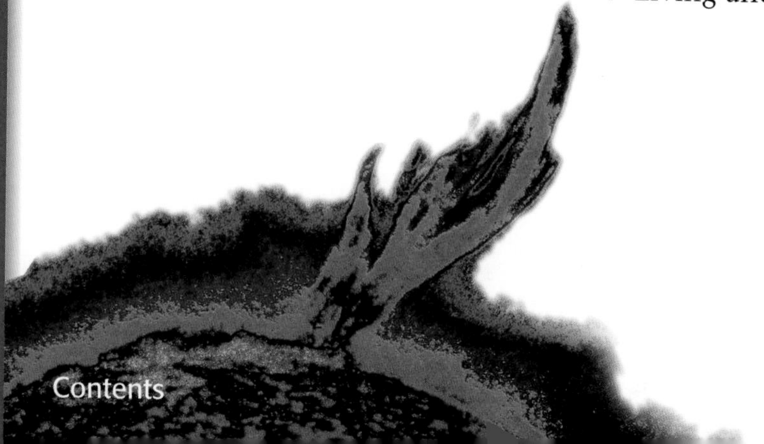

Skills Development

Process Skills

QuickLabs

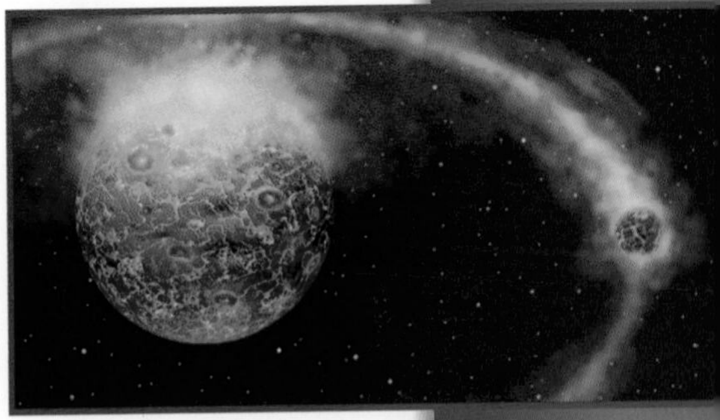

Chapter Labs

Skills Development

Research and Critical Thinking Skills

Apply

Feature Articles

Mathematics

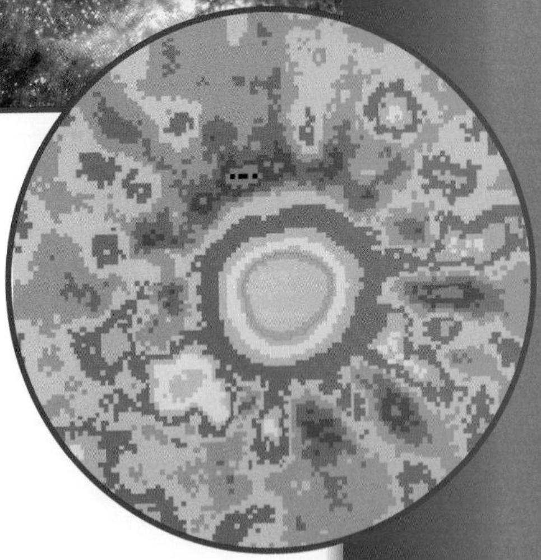

Connections

Program Scope and Sequence

Selecting the right books for your course is easy. Just review the topics presented in each book to determine the best match to your district curriculum.

	A MICROORGANISMS, FUNGI, AND PLANTS	B ANIMALS
CHAPTER 1	**It's Alive!! Or, Is It?** ❑ Characteristics of living things ❑ Homeostasis ❑ Heredity and DNA ❑ Producers, consumers, and decomposers ❑ Biomolecules	**Animals and Behavior** ❑ Characteristics of animals ❑ Classification of animals ❑ Animal behavior ❑ Hibernation and estivation ❑ The biological clock ❑ Animal communication ❑ Living in groups
CHAPTER 2	**Bacteria and Viruses** ❑ Binary fission ❑ Characteristics of bacteria ❑ Nitrogen-fixing bacteria ❑ Antibiotics ❑ Pathogenic bacteria ❑ Characteristics of viruses ❑ Lytic cycle	**Invertebrates** ❑ General characteristics of invertebrates ❑ Types of symmetry ❑ Characteristics of sponges, cnidarians, arthropods, and echinoderms ❑ Flatworms versus roundworms ❑ Types of circulatory systems
CHAPTER 3	**Protists and Fungi** ❑ Characteristics of protists ❑ Types of algae ❑ Types of protozoa ❑ Protist reproduction ❑ Characteristics of fungi and lichens	**Fishes, Amphibians, and Reptiles** ❑ Characteristics of vertebrates ❑ Structure and kinds of fishes ❑ Development of lungs ❑ Structure and kinds of amphibians and reptiles ❑ Function of the amniotic egg
CHAPTER 4	**Introduction to Plants** ❑ Characteristics of plants and seeds ❑ Reproduction and classification ❑ Angiosperms versus gymnosperms ❑ Monocots versus dicots ❑ Structure and functions of roots, stems, leaves, and flowers	**Birds and Mammals** ❑ Structure and kinds of birds ❑ Types of feathers ❑ Adaptations for flight ❑ Structure and kinds of mammals ❑ Function of the placenta
CHAPTER 5	**Plant Processes** ❑ Pollination and fertilization ❑ Dormancy ❑ Photosynthesis ❑ Plant tropisms ❑ Seasonal responses of plants	
CHAPTER 6		
CHAPTER 7		

Life Science

C CELLS, HEREDITY, & CLASSIFICATION	D HUMAN BODY SYSTEMS & HEALTH	E ENVIRONMENTAL SCIENCE
Cells: The Basic Units of Life ❑ Cells, tissues, and organs ❑ Populations, communities, and ecosystems ❑ Cell theory ❑ Surface-to-volume ratio ❑ Prokaryotic versus eukaryotic cells ❑ Cell organelles	**Body Organization and Structure** ❑ Homeostasis ❑ Types of tissue ❑ Organ systems ❑ Structure and function of the skeletal system, muscular system, and integumentary system	**Interactions of Living Things** ❑ Biotic versus abiotic parts of the environment ❑ Producers, consumers, and decomposers ❑ Food chains and food webs ❑ Factors limiting population growth ❑ Predator-prey relationships ❑ Symbiosis and coevolution
The Cell in Action ❑ Diffusion and osmosis ❑ Passive versus active transport ❑ Endocytosis versus exocytosis ❑ Photosynthesis ❑ Cellular respiration and fermentation ❑ Cell cycle	**Circulation and Respiration** ❑ Structure and function of the cardiovascular system, lymphatic system, and respiratory system ❑ Respiratory disorders	**Cycles in Nature** ❑ Water cycle ❑ Carbon cycle ❑ Nitrogen cycle ❑ Ecological succession
Heredity ❑ Dominant versus recessive traits ❑ Genes and alleles ❑ Genotype, phenotype, the Punnett square and probability ❑ Meiosis ❑ Determination of sex	**The Digestive and Urinary Systems** ❑ Structure and function of the digestive system ❑ Structure and function of the urinary system	**The Earth's Ecosystems** ❑ Kinds of land and water biomes ❑ Marine ecosystems ❑ Freshwater ecosystems
Genes and Gene Technology ❑ Structure of DNA ❑ Protein synthesis ❑ Mutations ❑ Heredity disorders and genetic counseling	**Communication and Control** ❑ Structure and function of the nervous system and endocrine system ❑ The senses ❑ Structure and function of the eye and ear	**Environmental Problems and Solutions** ❑ Types of pollutants ❑ Types of resources ❑ Conservation practices ❑ Species protection
The Evolution of Living Things ❑ Adaptations and species ❑ Evidence for evolution ❑ Darwin's work and natural selection ❑ Formation of new species	**Reproduction and Development** ❑ Asexual versus sexual reproduction ❑ Internal versus external fertilization ❑ Structure and function of the human male and female reproductive systems ❑ Fertilization, placental development, and embryo growth ❑ Stages of human life	**Energy Resources** ❑ Types of resources ❑ Energy resources and pollution ❑ Alternative energy resources
The History of Life on Earth ❑ Geologic time scale and extinctions ❑ Plate tectonics ❑ Human evolution	**Body Defenses and Disease** ❑ Types of diseases ❑ Vaccines and immunity ❑ Structure and function of the immune system ❑ Autoimmune diseases, cancer, and AIDS	
Classification ❑ Levels of classification ❑ Cladistic diagrams ❑ Dichotomous keys ❑ Characteristics of the six kingdoms	**Staying Healthy** ❑ Nutrition and reading food labels ❑ Alcohol and drug effects on the body ❑ Hygiene, exercise, and first aid	

Scope and Sequence *(continued)*

	F INSIDE THE RESTLESS EARTH	G EARTH'S CHANGING SURFACE
CHAPTER 1	**Minerals of the Earth's Crust** ❏ Mineral composition and structure ❏ Types of minerals ❏ Mineral identification ❏ Mineral formation and mining	**Maps as Models of the Earth** ❏ Structure of a map ❏ Cardinal directions ❏ Latitude, longitude, and the equator ❏ Magnetic declination and true north ❏ Types of projections ❏ Aerial photographs ❏ Remote sensing ❏ Topographic maps
CHAPTER 2	**Rocks: Mineral Mixtures** ❏ Rock cycle and types of rocks ❏ Rock classification ❏ Characteristics of igneous, sedimentary, and metamorphic rocks	**Weathering and Soil Formation** ❏ Types of weathering ❏ Factors affecting the rate of weathering ❏ Composition of soil ❏ Soil conservation and erosion prevention
CHAPTER 3	**The Rock and Fossil Record** ❏ Uniformitarianism versus catastrophism ❏ Superposition ❏ The geologic column and unconformities ❏ Absolute dating and radiometric dating ❏ Characteristics and types of fossils ❏ Geologic time scale	**Agents of Erosion and Deposition** ❏ Shoreline erosion and deposition ❏ Wind erosion and deposition ❏ Erosion and deposition by ice ❏ Gravity's effect on erosion and deposition
CHAPTER 4	**Plate Tectonics** ❏ Structure of the Earth ❏ Continental drifts and sea floor spreading ❏ Plate tectonics theory ❏ Types of boundaries ❏ Types of crust deformities	
CHAPTER 5	**Earthquakes** ❏ Seismology ❏ Features of earthquakes ❏ P and S waves ❏ Gap hypothesis ❏ Earthquake safety	
CHAPTER 6	**Volcanoes** ❏ Types of volcanoes and eruptions ❏ Types of lava and pyroclastic material ❏ Craters versus calderas ❏ Sites and conditions for volcano formation ❏ Predicting eruptions	

Earth Science

H WATER ON EARTH

The Flow of Fresh Water
- ❑ Water cycle
- ❑ River systems
- ❑ Stream erosion
- ❑ Life cycle of rivers
- ❑ Deposition
- ❑ Aquifers, springs, and wells
- ❑ Ground water
- ❑ Water treatment and pollution

Exploring the Oceans
- ❑ Properties and characteristics of the oceans
- ❑ Features of the ocean floor
- ❑ Ocean ecology
- ❑ Ocean resources and pollution

The Movement of Ocean Water
- ❑ Types of currents
- ❑ Characteristics of waves
- ❑ Types of ocean waves
- ❑ Tides

I WEATHER AND CLIMATE

The Atmosphere
- ❑ Structure of the atmosphere
- ❑ Air pressure
- ❑ Radiation, convection, and conduction
- ❑ Greenhouse effect and global warming
- ❑ Characteristics of winds
- ❑ Types of winds
- ❑ Air pollution

Understanding Weather
- ❑ Water cycle
- ❑ Humidity
- ❑ Types of clouds
- ❑ Types of precipitation
- ❑ Air masses and fronts
- ❑ Storms, tornadoes, and hurricanes
- ❑ Weather forecasting
- ❑ Weather maps

Climate
- ❑ Weather versus climate
- ❑ Seasons and latitude
- ❑ Prevailing winds
- ❑ Earth's biomes
- ❑ Earth's climate zones
- ❑ Ice ages
- ❑ Global warming
- ❑ Greenhouse effect

J ASTRONOMY

Observing the Sky
- ❑ Astronomy
- ❑ Keeping time
- ❑ Mapping the stars
- ❑ Scales of the universe
- ❑ Types of telescope
- ❑ Radioastronomy

Formation of the Solar System
- ❑ Birth of the solar system
- ❑ Planetary motion
- ❑ Newton's Law of Universal Gravitation
- ❑ Structure of the sun
- ❑ Fusion
- ❑ Earth's structure and atmosphere

A Family of Planets
- ❑ Properties and characteristics of the planets
- ❑ Properties and characteristics of moons
- ❑ Comets, asteroids, and meteoroids

The Universe Beyond
- ❑ Composition of stars
- ❑ Classification of stars
- ❑ Star brightness, distance, and motions
- ❑ H-R diagram
- ❑ Life cycle of stars
- ❑ Types of galaxies
- ❑ Theories on the formation of the universe

Exploring Space
- ❑ Rocketry and artificial satellites
- ❑ Types of Earth orbit
- ❑ Space probes and space exploration

Scope and Sequence *(continued)*

	K INTRODUCTION TO MATTER	L INTERACTIONS OF MATTER
CHAPTER 1	**The Properties of Matter** ❑ Definition of matter ❑ Mass and weight ❑ Physical and chemical properties ❑ Physical and chemical change ❑ Density	**Chemical Bonding** ❑ Types of chemical bonds ❑ Valence electrons ❑ Ions versus molecules ❑ Crystal lattice
CHAPTER 2	**States of Matter** ❑ States of matter and their properties ❑ Boyle's and Charles's laws ❑ Changes of state	**Chemical Reactions** ❑ Writing chemical formulas and equations ❑ Law of conservation of mass ❑ Types of reactions ❑ Endothermic versus exothermic reactions ❑ Law of conservation of energy ❑ Activation energy ❑ Catalysts and inhibitors
CHAPTER 3	**Elements, Compounds, and Mixtures** ❑ Elements and compounds ❑ Metals, nonmetals, and metalloids (semiconductors) ❑ Properties of mixtures ❑ Properties of solutions, suspensions, and colloids	**Chemical Compounds** ❑ Ionic versus covalent compounds ❑ Acids, bases, and salts ❑ pH ❑ Organic compounds ❑ Biomolecules
CHAPTER 4	**Introduction to Atoms** ❑ Atomic theory ❑ Atomic model and structure ❑ Isotopes ❑ Atomic mass and mass number	**Atomic Energy** ❑ Properties of radioactive substances ❑ Types of decay ❑ Half-life ❑ Fission, fusion, and chain reactions
CHAPTER 5	**The Periodic Table** ❑ Structure of the periodic table ❑ Periodic law ❑ Properties of alkali metals, alkaline-earth metals, halogens, and noble gases	
CHAPTER 6		

Physical Science

M FORCES, MOTION, AND ENERGY

Matter in Motion
- ❑ Speed, velocity, and acceleration
- ❑ Measuring force
- ❑ Friction
- ❑ Mass versus weight

Forces in Motion
- ❑ Terminal velocity and free fall
- ❑ Projectile motion
- ❑ Inertia
- ❑ Momentum

Forces in Fluids
- ❑ Properties in fluids
- ❑ Atmospheric pressure
- ❑ Density
- ❑ Pascal's principle
- ❑ Buoyant force
- ❑ Archimedes' principle
- ❑ Bernoulli's principle

Work and Machines
- ❑ Measuring work
- ❑ Measuring power
- ❑ Types of machines
- ❑ Mechanical advantage
- ❑ Mechanical efficiency

Energy and Energy Resources
- ❑ Forms of energy
- ❑ Energy conversions
- ❑ Law of conservation of energy
- ❑ Energy resources

Heat and Heat Technology
- ❑ Heat versus temperature
- ❑ Thermal expansion
- ❑ Absolute zero
- ❑ Conduction, convection, radiation
- ❑ Conductors versus insulators
- ❑ Specific heat capacity
- ❑ Changes of state
- ❑ Heat engines
- ❑ Thermal pollution

N ELECTRICITY AND MAGNETISM

Introduction to Electricity
- ❑ Law of electric charges
- ❑ Conduction versus induction
- ❑ Static electricity
- ❑ Potential difference
- ❑ Cells, batteries, and photocells
- ❑ Thermocouples
- ❑ Voltage, current, and resistance
- ❑ Electric power
- ❑ Types of circuits

Electromagnetism
- ❑ Properties of magnets
- ❑ Magnetic force
- ❑ Electromagnetism
- ❑ Solenoids and electric motors
- ❑ Electromagnetic induction
- ❑ Generators and transformers

Electronic Technology
- ❑ Properties of semiconductors
- ❑ Integrated circuits
- ❑ Diodes and transistors
- ❑ Analog versus digital signals
- ❑ Microprocessors
- ❑ Features of computers

O SOUND AND LIGHT

The Energy of Waves
- ❑ Properties of waves
- ❑ Types of waves
- ❑ Reflection and refraction
- ❑ Diffraction and interference
- ❑ Standing waves and resonance

The Nature of Sound
- ❑ Properties of sound waves
- ❑ Structure of the human ear
- ❑ Pitch and the Doppler effect
- ❑ Infrasonic versus ultrasonic sound
- ❑ Sound reflection and echolocation
- ❑ Sound barrier
- ❑ Interference, resonance, diffraction, and standing waves
- ❑ Sound quality of instruments

The Nature of Light
- ❑ Electromagnetic waves
- ❑ Electromagnetic spectrum
- ❑ Law of reflection
- ❑ Absorption and scattering
- ❑ Reflection and refraction
- ❑ Diffraction and interference

Light and Our World
- ❑ Luminosity
- ❑ Types of lighting
- ❑ Types of mirrors and lenses
- ❑ Focal point
- ❑ Structure of the human eye
- ❑ Lasers and holograms

HOLT SCIENCE & TECHNOLOGY

Components Listing

Effective planning starts with all the resources you need in an easy-to-use package for each short course.

Directed Reading Worksheets Help students develop and practice fundamental reading comprehension skills and provide a comprehensive review tool for students to use when studying for an exam.

Study Guide Vocabulary & Notes Worksheets and Chapter Review Worksheets are reproductions of the Chapter Highlights and Chapter Review sections that follow each chapter in the textbook.

Science Puzzlers, Twisters & Teasers Use vocabulary and concepts from each chapter of the Pupil's Editions as elements of rebuses, anagrams, logic puzzles, daffy definitions, riddle poems, word jumbles, and other types of puzzles.

Reinforcement and Vocabulary Review Worksheets Approach a chapter topic from a different angle with an emphasis on different learning modalities to help students that are frustrated by traditional methods.

Critical Thinking & Problem Solving Worksheets Develop the following skills: distinguishing fact from opinion, predicting consequences, analyzing information, and drawing conclusions. Problem Solving Worksheets develop a step-by-step process of problem analysis including gathering information, asking critical questions, identifying alternatives, and making comparisons.

Math Skills for Science Worksheets Each activity gives a brief introduction to a relevant math skill, a step-by-step explanation of the math process, one or more example problems, and a variety of practice problems.

Science Skills Worksheets Help your students focus specifically on skills such as measuring, graphing, using logic, understanding statistics, organizing research papers, and critical thinking options.

LAB ACTIVITIES

ALL LABS ARE CLASSROOM TESTED & APPROVED

Datasheets for Labs These worksheets are the labs found in the *Holt Science & Technology* textbook. Charts, tables, and graphs are included to make data collection and analysis easier, and space is provided to write observations and conclusions.

Whiz-Bang Demonstrations Discovery or Making Models experiences label each demo as one in which students discover an answer or use a scientific model.

Calculator-Based Labs Give students the opportunity to use graphing-calculator probes and sensors to collect data using a TI graphing calculator, Vernier sensors, and a TI CBL 2™ or Vernier Lab Pro interface.

EcoLabs and Field Activities Focus on educational outdoor projects, such as wildlife observation, nature surveys, or natural history.

Inquiry Labs Use the scientific method to help students find their own path in solving a real-world problem.

Long-Term Projects and Research Ideas Provide students with the opportunity to go beyond library and Internet resources to explore science topics.

ASSESSMENT

Chapter Tests Each four-page chapter test consists of a variety of item types including Multiple Choice, Using Vocabulary, Short Answer, Critical Thinking, Math in Science, Interpreting Graphics, and Concept Mapping.

Performance-Based Assessments Evaluate students' abilities to solve problems using the tools, equipment, and techniques of science. Rubrics included for each assessment make it easy to evaluate student performance.

TEACHER RESOURCES

Lesson Plans Integrate all of the great resources in the *Holt Science & Technology* program into your daily teaching. Each lesson plan includes a correlation of the lesson activities to the National Science Education Standards.

Teaching Transparencies Each transparency is correlated to a particular lesson in the Chapter Organizer.

Concept Mapping Transparencies, Worksheets, and Answer Key
Give students an opportunity to complete their own concept maps to study the concepts within each chapter and form logical connections. Student worksheets contain a blank concept map with linking phrases and a list of terms to be used by the student to complete the map.

TECHNOLOGY RESOURCES

One-Stop Planner CD-ROM
Finding the right resources is easy with the One-Stop Planner CD-ROM. You can view and print any resource with just the click of a mouse. Customize the suggested lesson plans to match your daily or weekly calendar and your district's requirements. Powerful test generator software allows you to create customized assessments using a databank of items.

The One-Stop Planner for each level includes the following:

- All materials from the Teaching Resources
- Bellringer Transparency Masters
- Block Scheduling Tools
- Standards Correlations
- Lab Inventory Checklist
- Safety Information
- Science Fair Guide
- Parent Involvement Tools
- Spanish Audio Scripts
- Spanish Glossary
- Assessment Item Listing
- Assessment Checklists and Rubrics
- Test Generator

***sci*LINKS**
*sci*LINKS numbers throughout the text take you and your students to some of the best on-line resources available. Sites are constantly reviewed and updated by the National Science Teachers Association. Special "teacher only" sites are available to you once you register with the service.

go.hrw.com
To access Holt, Rinehart and Winston Web resources, use the home page codes for each level found on page 1 of the Pupil's Editions. The codes shown on the Chapter Organizers for each chapter in the Annotated Teacher's Edition take you to chapter-specific resources.

Smithsonian Institution
Find lesson plans, activities, interviews, virtual exhibits, and just general information on a wide variety of topics relevant to middle school science.

CNNfyi.com
Find the latest in late-breaking science news for students. Featured news stories are supported with lesson plans and activities.

CNN Presents Science in the News Video Library
Bring relevant science news stories into the classroom. Each video comes with a Teacher's Guide and set of Critical Thinking Worksheets that develop listening and media analysis skills. Tapes in the series include:

- Eye on the Environment
- Multicultural Connections
- Scientists in Action
- Science, Technology & Society

Guided Reading Audio CD Program
Students can listen to a direct read of each chapter and follow along in the text. Use the program as a content bridge for struggling readers and students for whom English is not their native language.

Interactive Explorations CD-ROM
Turn a computer into a virtual laboratory. Students act as lab assistants helping Dr. Crystal Labcoat solve real-world problems. Activities develop students' inquiry, analysis, and decision-making skills.

Interactive Science Encyclopedia CD-ROM
Give your students access to more than 3,000 cross-referenced scientific definitions, in-depth articles, science fair project ideas, activities, and more.

ADDITIONAL COMPONENTS

Holt Anthology of Science Fiction
Science Fiction features in the Pupil's Edition preview the stories found in the anthology. Each story begins with a Reading Prep guide and closes with Think About It questions.

Professional Reference for Teachers
Articles written by leading educators help you learn more about the National Science Education Standards, block scheduling, classroom management techniques, and more. A bibliography of professional references is included.

Holt Science Posters
Seven wall posters highlight interesting topics, such as the Physics of Sports, or useful reference material, such as the Scientific Method.

Holt Science Skills Workshop: Reading in the Content Area
Use a variety of in-depth skills exercises to help students learn to read science materials strategically.

Key

These materials are blackline masters.

All titles shown in green are found in the *Teaching Resources* booklets for each course.

Science & Math Skills Worksheets

The *Holt Science and Technology* program helps you meet the needs of a wide variety of students, regardless of their skill level. The following pages provide examples of the worksheets available to improve your students' science and math skills, whether they already have a strong science and math background or are weak in these areas. Samples of assessment checklists and rubrics are also provided.

In addition to the skills worksheets represented here, *Holt Science and Technology* provides a variety of worksheets that are correlated directly with each chapter of the program. Representations of these worksheets are found at the beginning of each chapter in this Annotated Teacher's Edition. Specific worksheets related to each chapter are listed in the Chapter Organizer. Worksheets and transparencies are found in the softcover *Teaching Resources* for each course.

Many worksheets are also available on the HRW Web site. The address is **go.hrw.com.**

Science Skills Worksheets: **Thinking Skills**

BEING FLEXIBLE

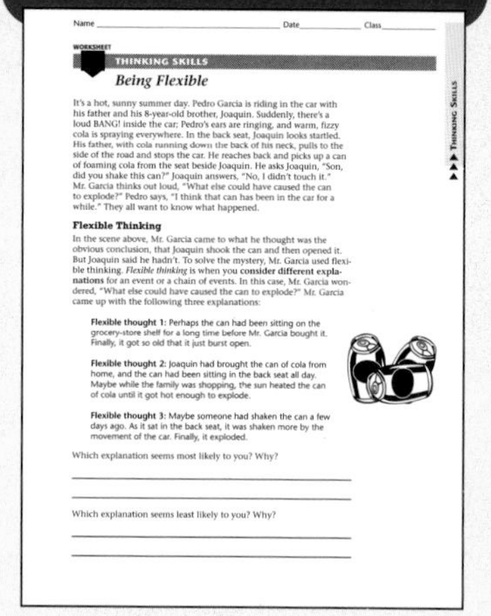

USING YOUR SENSES

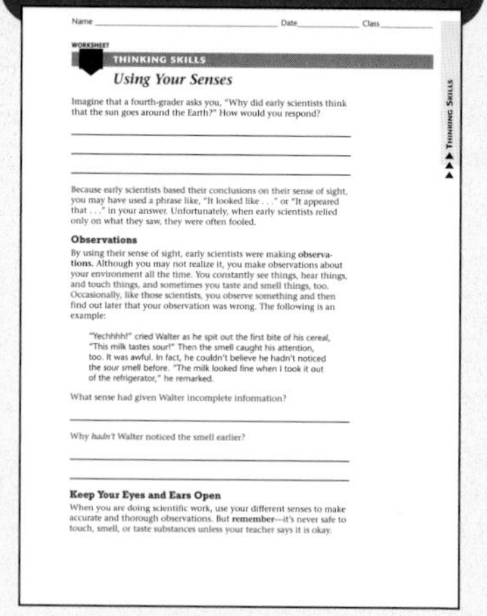

THINKING OBJECTIVELY

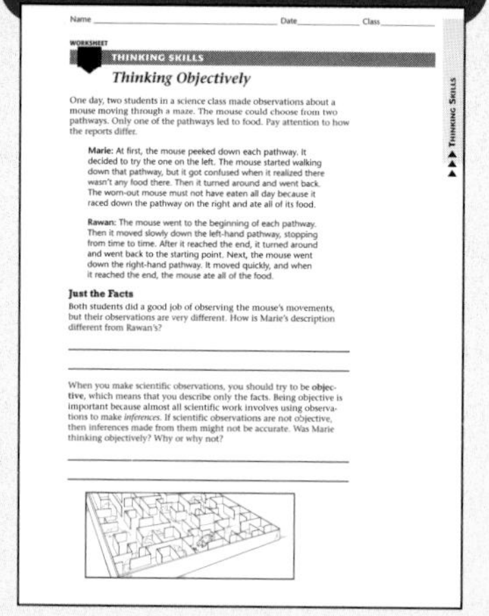

UNDERSTANDING BIAS

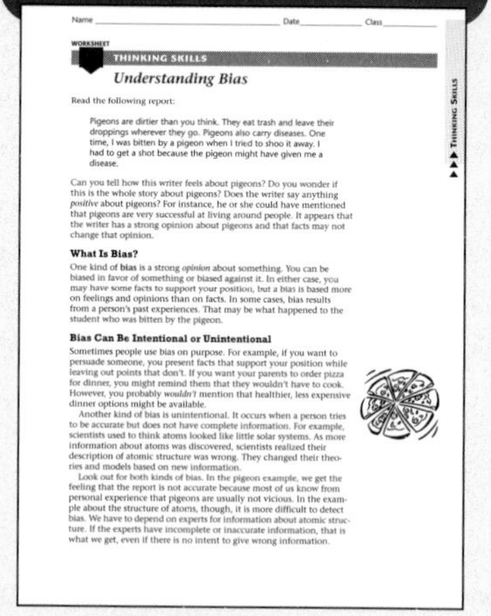

USING LOGIC

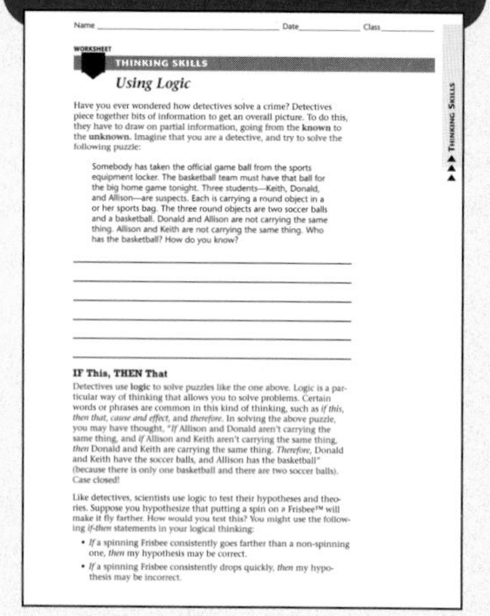

BOOSTING YOUR MEMORY

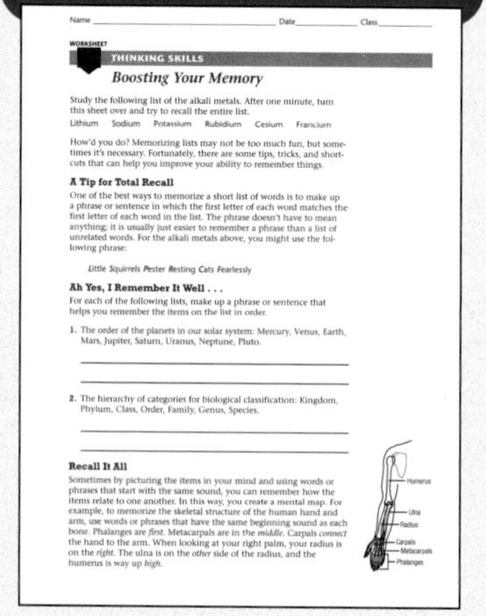

IMPROVING YOUR STUDY HABITS

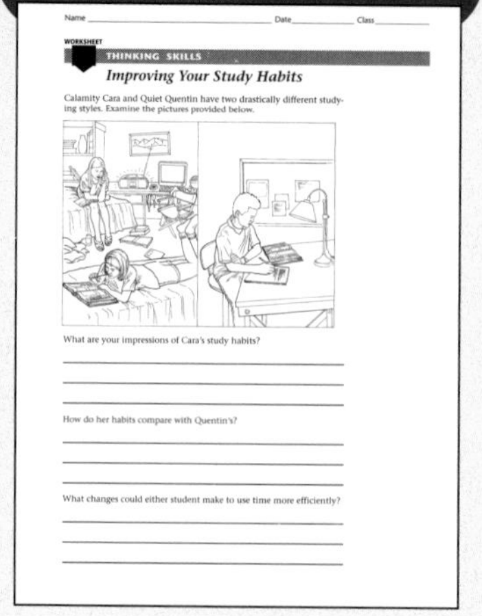

READING A SCIENCE TEXTBOOK

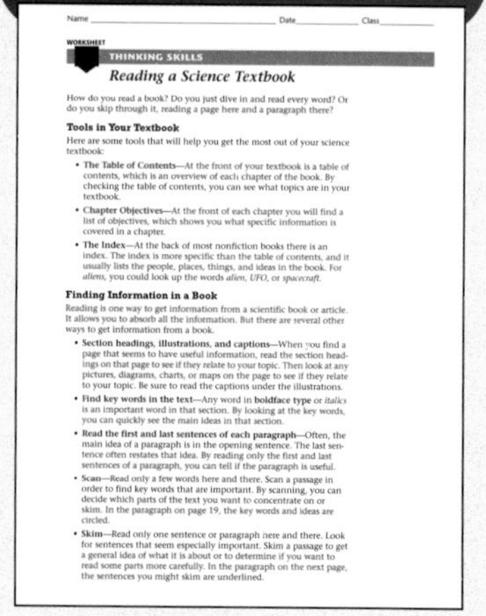

Science Skills Worksheets: Experimenting Skills

SAFETY RULES!

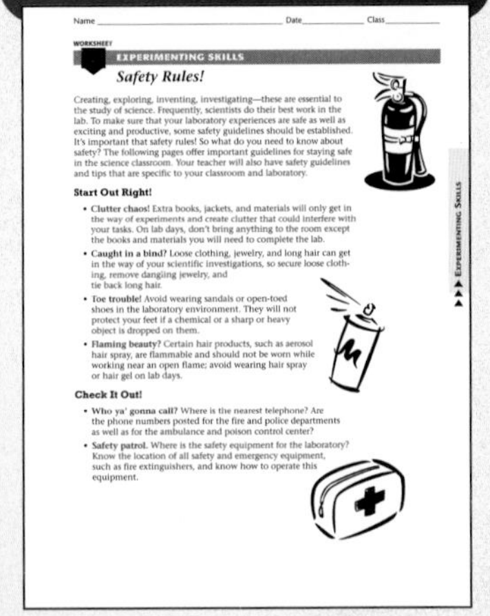

DOING A LAB WRITE-UP

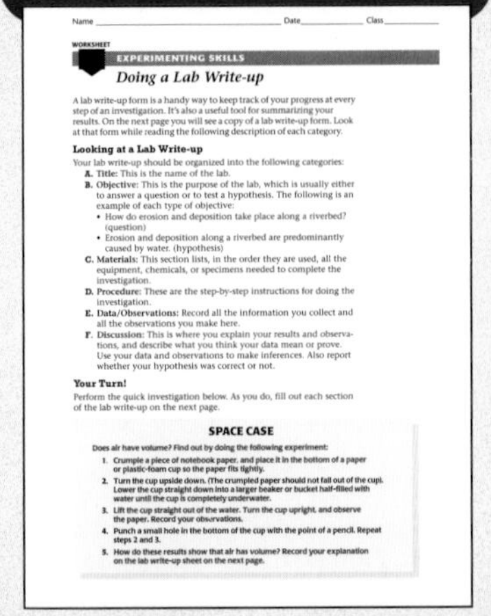

UNDERSTANDING VARIABLES

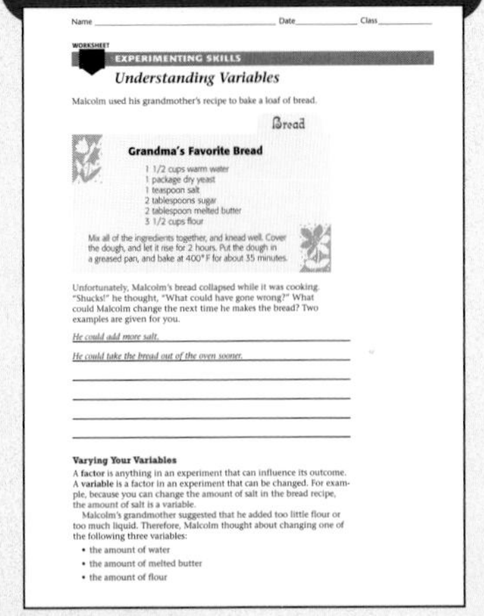

WORKING WITH HYPOTHESES

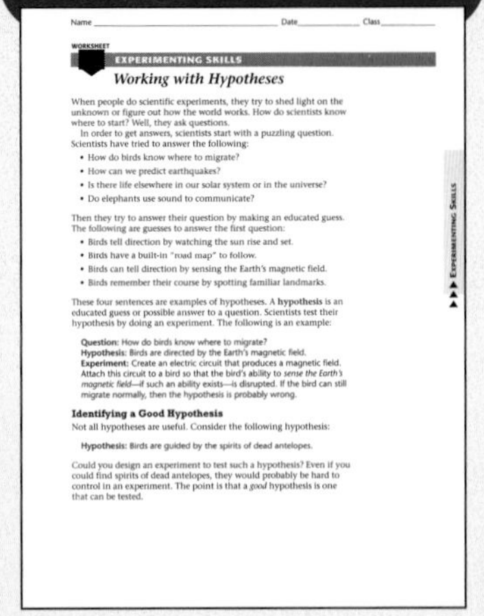

DESIGNING AN EXPERIMENT

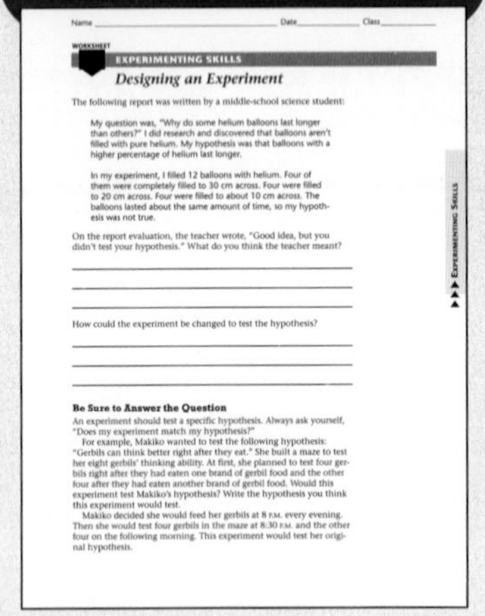

USING THE INTERNATIONAL SYSTEM OF UNITS (SI)

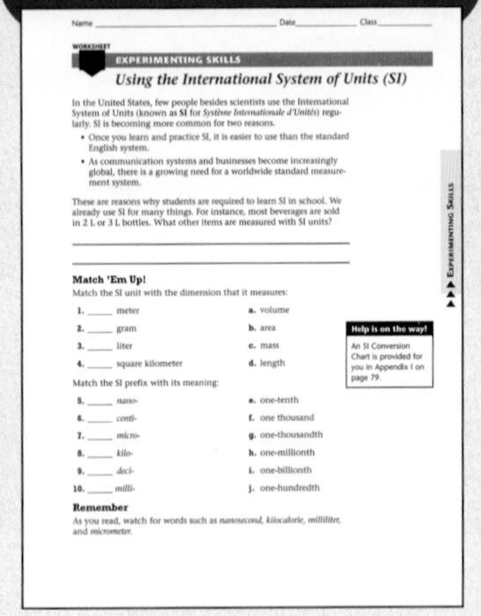

MEASURING

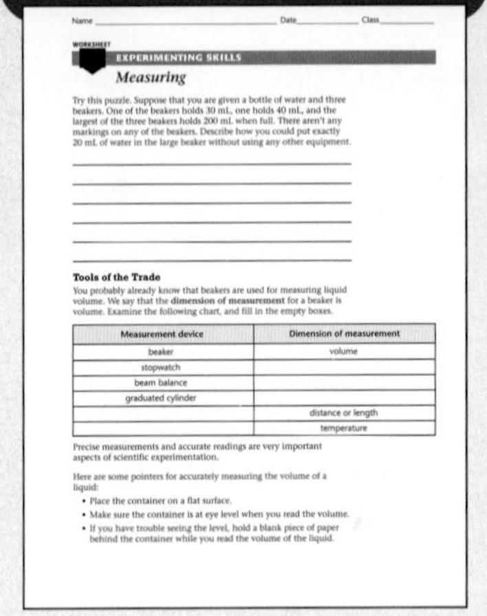

Science Skills Worksheets: Researching Skills

CHOOSING YOUR TOPIC

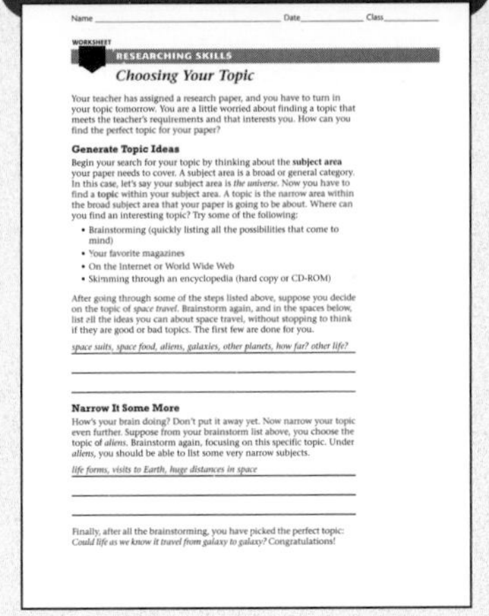

ORGANIZING YOUR RESEARCH

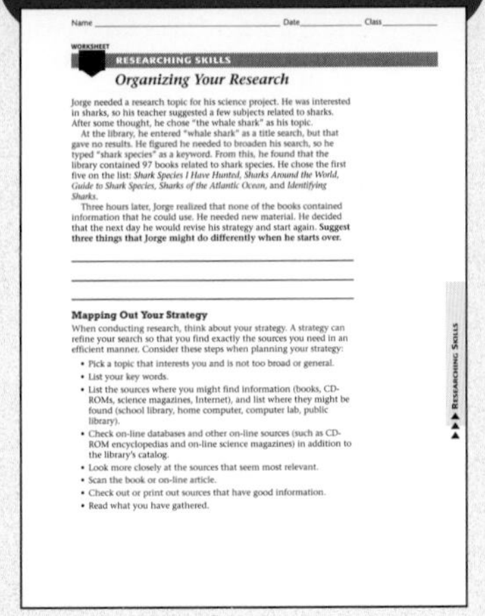

FINDING USEFUL SOURCES

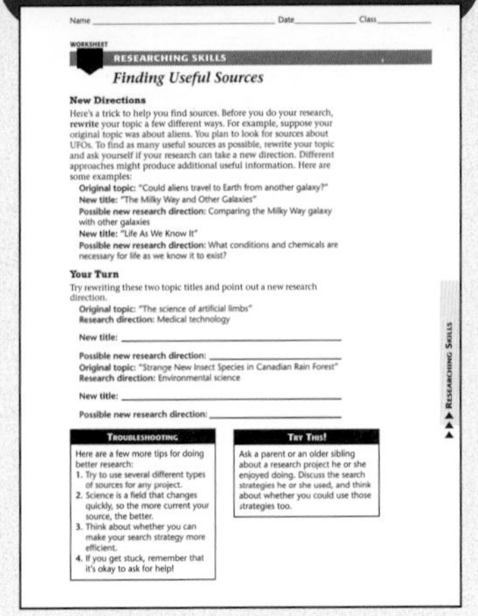

RESEARCHING ON THE WEB

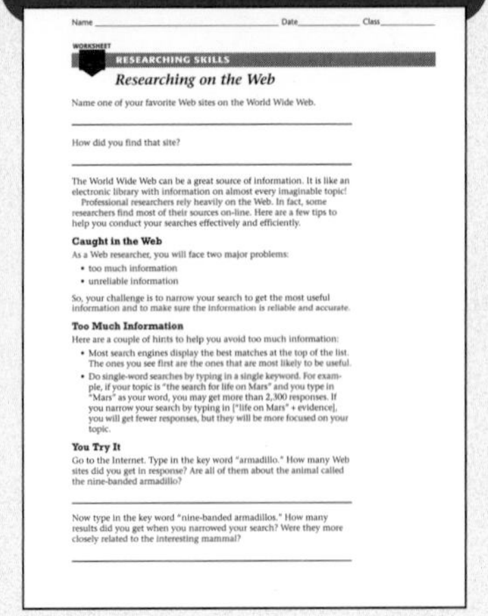

Science & Math Skills Worksheets (continued)

Science Skills Worksheets: Researching Skills (continued)

IDENTIFYING BIAS

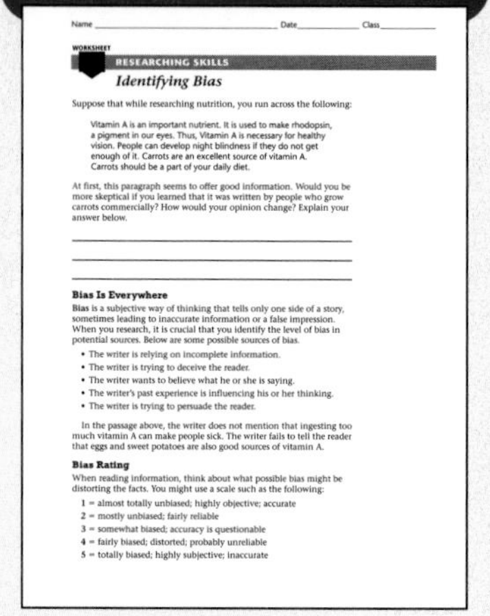

TAKING NOTES

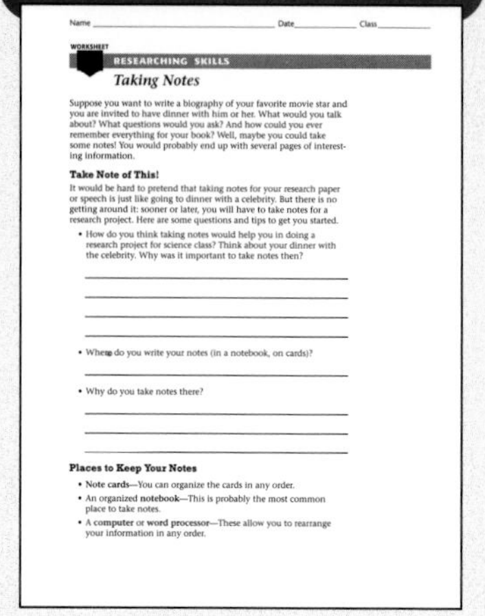

SCIENCE WRITING

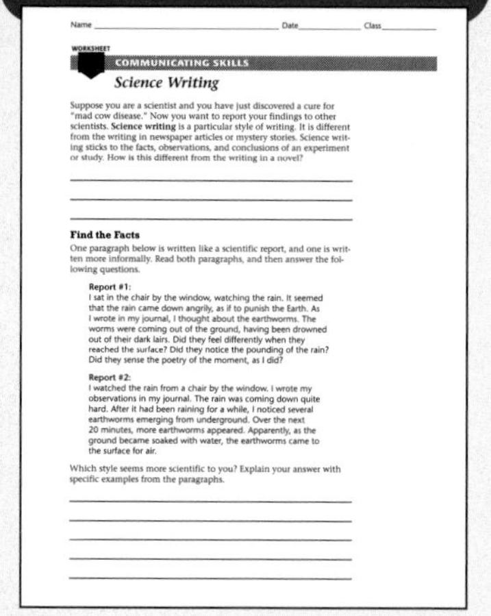

Science Skills Worksheets: Communicating Skills

SCIENCE DRAWING

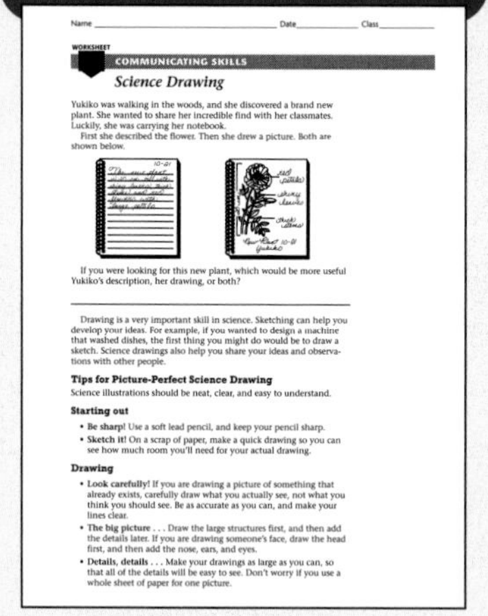

USING MODELS TO COMMUNICATE

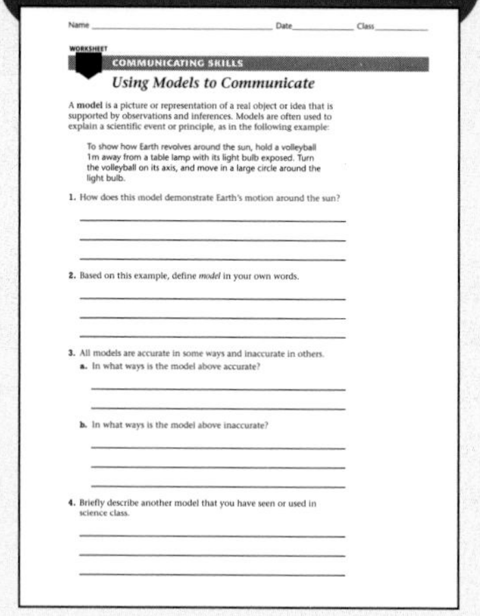

INTRODUCTION TO GRAPHS

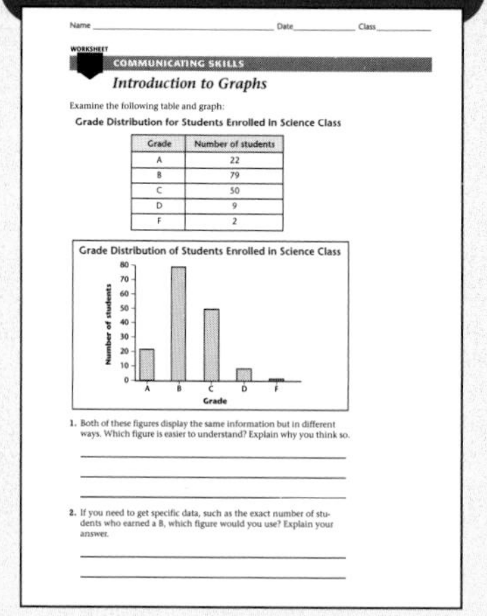

GRASPING GRAPHING

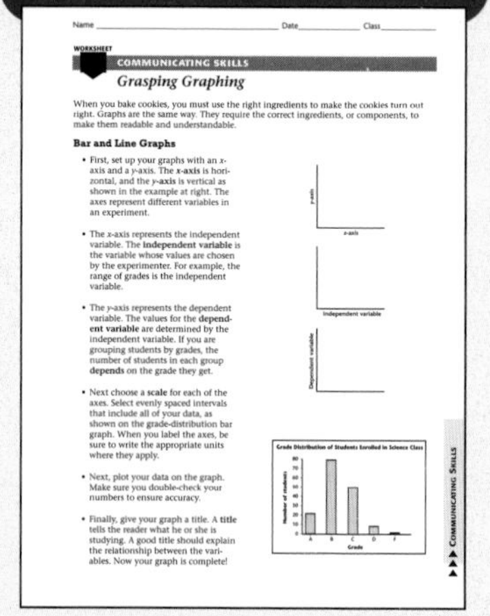

INTERPRETING YOUR DATA

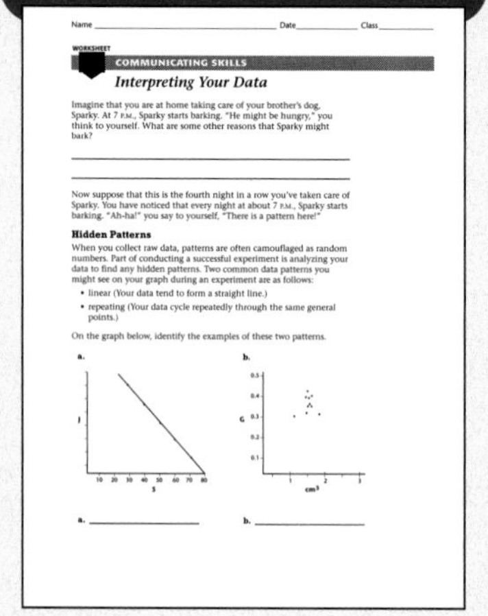

RECOGNIZING BIAS IN GRAPHS

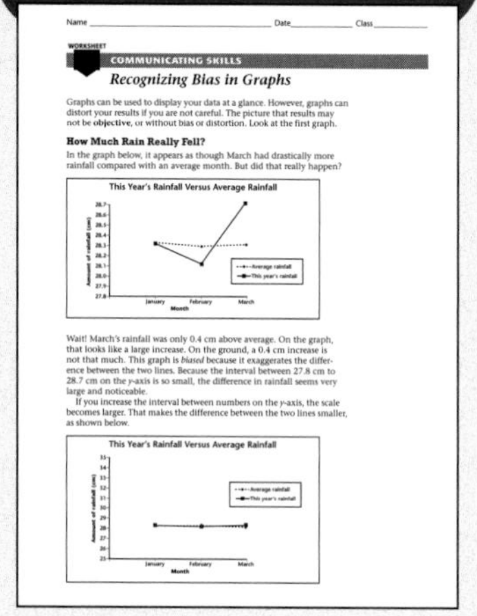

MAKING DATA MEANINGFUL

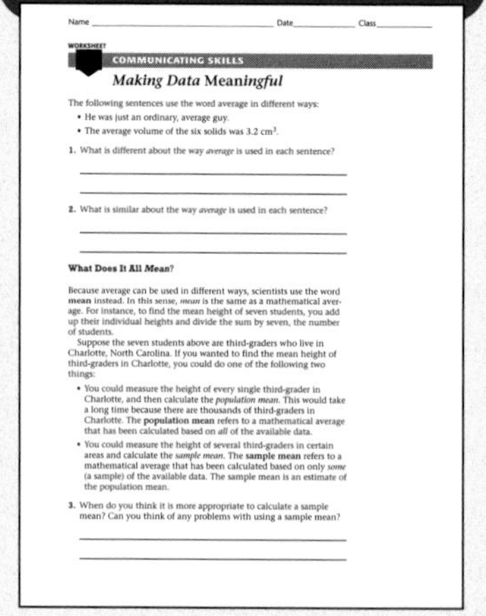

HINTS FOR ORAL PRESENTATIONS

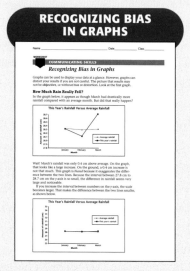

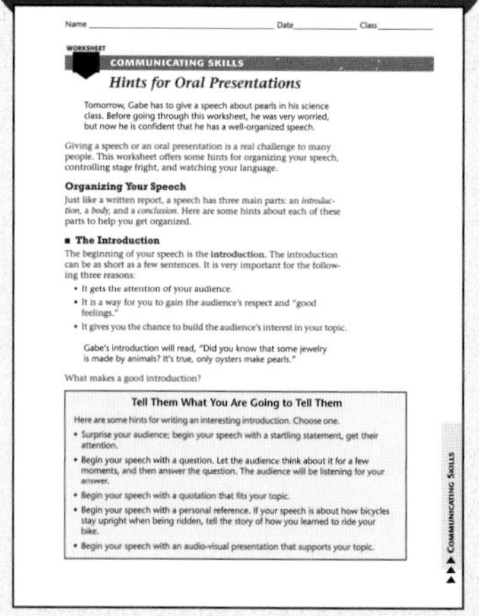

Math Skills for Science

ADDITION AND SUBTRACTION

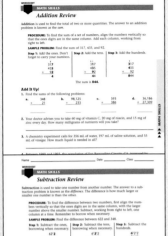

Addition Review

Addition is used to find the total of two or more quantities. The answer to an addition problem is known as the *sum*.

PROCEDURE: To find the sum of a set of numbers, align the numbers vertically so that the ones digits are in the same column. Add each column, working from right to left.

SAMPLE PROBLEM: Find the sum of 317, 435, and 92.

Step 1: Add the ones. Don't forget to carry your number.

Step 2: Add the tens.

Step 3: Add the hundreds.

The sum is **844**.

Add It Up!
1. Find the sums of the following problems:
   a. 348 + 21   b. 98,125 + 233   c. 593 + 386   d. 36,186 + 27,309

2. Your doctor advises you to take 60 mg of vitamin C, 20 mg of niacin, and 15 mg of zinc every day. How many milligrams of nutrients will you take?

3. A chemistry experiment calls for 356 mL of water, 197 mL of saline solution, and 55 mL of vinegar. How much liquid is needed in all?

Subtraction Review

Subtraction is used to take one number from another number. The answer to a subtraction problem is known as the *difference*. The difference is how much larger one number is than the other.

PROCEDURE: To find the difference between two numbers, first align the numbers vertically so that the ones digit are in the same column, with the larger number above the smaller number. Subtract, working from right to left, one column at a time. Remember to borrow when necessary.

SAMPLE PROBLEM: Find the difference between 622 and 348.

The difference of the numbers is **274**.

Take It Away!
1. Find the difference in the following problems:
   a. 88 − 36   b. 1695 − 352   c. 47,220 − 36,195   d. 6048 − 3724

2. 571 − 338 =   3. 8317 − 211 =

4. Mars has a diameter of 6790 km. The diameter of Jupiter is 142,984 km. How much larger is the diameter of Jupiter than the diameter of Mars?

5. A horse is born with a mass of 36 kg. It is expected to have a mass of 495 kg when fully grown. How much mass will it gain?

6. Traveling with the wind, a plane reaches a speed of 212 m/s. On the return trip, the same plane flies into the wind and achieves a speed of only 179 m/s. How much faster does the plane fly with the wind?

MULTIPLICATION

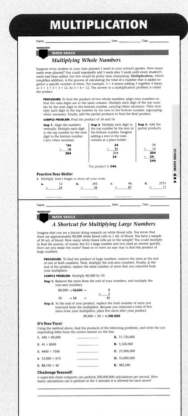

Multiplying Whole Numbers

Suppose every student in your class planted 5 seeds in your school's garden. How many seeds were planted? You could repeatedly add 5 seeds plus 5 seeds until every student's seeds had been added, but this would be pretty time consuming. **Multiplication**, which simplifies addition, is the process of calculating the total of a number that is added together a specific number of times. For example, 3 × 4 means adding 3 together 4 times, or 3 + 3 + 3 + 3 = 12. So 3 × 4 = 12. The answer to a multiplication problem is called the *product*.

SAMPLE PROBLEM: Find the product of 34 and 16.

Step 1: Align the numbers vertically. Multiply each digit in the top number by the ones digit in the bottom number. Carry when necessary.

Step 2: Multiply each digit in the top number by the tens in the bottom number. Imagine adding a zero in the ones column as a place holder.

Step 3: Add the partial products.

The product is **544**.

Practice Your Skills!
a. 12 × 24   b. 245 × 36   c. 46 × 87   d. 2751 × 11

A Shortcut for Multiplying Large Numbers

Imagine that you are a doctor doing research on white blood cells. You know that there are approximately 80,000 white blood cells in 1 mL of blood. You have a sample of 50 mL of blood. How many white blood cells are in the sample? You could multiply to find the answer, of course, but it's a large number and you need an answer quickly. How can you make this easier? Read on to learn an easy way to find the product of large numbers.

PROCEDURE: To find the product of large numbers, remove the zeros at the end of one or both numbers. Next, multiply the non-zero numbers. Finally, at the end of the product, replace the same number of zeros that you removed from your multipliers.

SAMPLE PROBLEM: Multiply 80,000 by 50.

Step 1: Remove the zeros from the end of your numbers, and multiply the non-zero numbers.

Step 2: At the end of your product, replace the total number of zeros you removed from the multipliers. Because you removed a total of five zeros from your multipliers, place five zeros after your product.

80,000 × 50 = 4,000,000

It's Your Turn!
Using the method above, find the products of the following problems, and write the corresponding letter from the correct answer on the line.

1. 300 × 90,000   A. 31,720,000
2. 45 × 8500   B. 3,524,000
3. 4400 × 7500   C. 27,000,000
4. 52,000 × 610   D. 33,000,000
5. 88,100 × 40   E. 382,500

Challenge Yourself!
A super-fast chess computer can perform 200,000,000 calculations per second. How many calculations can it perform in the 3 minutes it is allowed for each move?

DIVISION

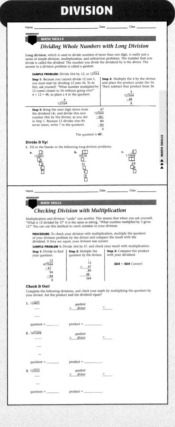

Dividing Whole Numbers with Long Division

Long division, which is used to divide numbers of more than one digit, is really just a series of simple division, multiplication, and subtraction problems. The number that you divide is called the *dividend*. The number you divide the dividend by is the *divisor*. The answer to a division problem is called a *quotient*.

SAMPLE PROBLEM: Divide 564 by 12, or 12)564.

Step 1: Because you cannot divide 12 into 5, you must start by dividing 12 into 56. To do this, ask yourself, "What number multiplied by 12 comes closest to 56 without going over?" 4 × 12 = 48, so place 4 in the quotient.

Step 2: Bring the next digit down from the dividend (4), and divide this new number (84) by the divisor, as you did in Step 1. Because 12 divides into 84 seven times, write 7 in the quotient.

Step 3: Multiply the 4 by the divisor and place the product under the 56. Then subtract that product from 56.

The quotient is **47**.

Divide It Up!
1. Fill in the blanks in the following long-division problems:

Checking Division with Multiplication

Multiplication and division "undo" one another. This means that when you ask yourself, "What is 12 divided by 3?" it is the same as asking, "What number multiplied by 3 gives 12?" You can use this method to catch mistakes in your division.

PROCEDURE: To check your division with multiplication, multiply the quotient of division problems by the divisor and compare the result with the dividend. If they are equal, your division was correct.

Step 1: Divide to find your quotient.

Step 2: Multiply the quotient by the divisor.

Step 3: Compare the product with your dividend.

564 = 564 Correct!

Check It Out!
Complete the following divisions, and check your math by multiplying the quotient by your divisor. Are the product and the dividend equal?

1. 15)405
2. 14)694
3. 12)252

AVERAGES

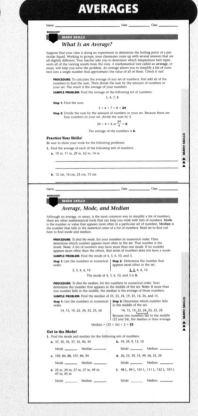

What Is an Average?

Suppose that your class is doing an experiment to determine the boiling point of a particular liquid. Working in groups, your classmates come up with several answers that are all slightly different. Your teacher asks you to determine which temperature best represents all of the varying results from the class. A mathematical tool called an *average*, or *mean*, will help you solve the problem. An average allows you to simplify a list of numbers into a single number that *approximates* the value of all of them. Check it out!

PROCEDURE: To calculate the average of any set of numbers, first add all of the numbers to find the sum. Then divide the sum by the amount of numbers in your set. The result is the average of your numbers.

SAMPLE PROBLEM: Find the average of the following set of numbers.

3, 4, 7, 8

Step 1: Find the sum.

3 + 4 + 7 + 8 = 24

Step 2: Divide the sum by the amount of numbers in your set. Because there are four numbers in your set, divide the sum by 4.

24 ÷ 4 = 6

The average of the numbers is **6**.

Practice Your Skills!
Be sure to show your work for the following problems.
1. Find the average of each of the following sets of numbers.
   a. 19 m, 11 m, 29 m, 62 m, 14 m
   b. 12 cm, 16 cm, 25 cm, 15 cm

Average, Mode, and Median

Although an average, or mean, is the most common way to simplify a list of numbers, there are other mathematical tools that can help you work with lists of numbers. **Mode** is the number or value that appears most often in a particular set of numbers. **Median** is the number that falls in the *numerical center* of a list of numbers. Read on to find out how to find mode and median.

PROCEDURE: To find the *mode*, list your numbers in numerical order. Then determine which number appears most often in the set. That number is the mode. Note: If more than one number appears the most, each number is a mode. If no number appears more often than the others, that series of numbers does not have a mode.

SAMPLE PROBLEM: Find the mode of 4, 3, 6, 10, and 3.

Step 1: List the numbers in numerical order.

3, 3, 4, 6, 10

Step 2: Determine the number that appears most often in the set.

3, 3, 4, 6, 10

The mode of 3, 3, 4, 6, 10, and 3 is **3**.

PROCEDURE: To find the *median*, list the numbers in numerical order. Next determine the number that appears in the middle of the set. Note: If more than one number falls in the middle, the median is the average of these numbers.

SAMPLE PROBLEM: Find the median of 25, 22, 24, 19, 25, 14, 26, and 15.

Step 1: List the numbers in numerical order.

14, 15, 19, 22, 24, 25, 25, 26

Step 2: Determine which number falls in the middle of the set.

Because two numbers fall in the middle (22 and 24), the median is their average.

Median = (22 + 24) ÷ 2 = **23**

Get in the Mode!
1. Find the mode and median for the following sets of numbers.
   a. 17, 10, 33, 17, 32, 40, 34   b. 19, 29, 9, 12, 10
   Mode _____ Median _____   Mode _____ Median _____
   c. 109, 84, 88, 107, 84, 94   d. 26, 53, 39, 53, 49, 56, 53, 26
   Mode _____ Median _____   Mode _____ Median _____
   e. 25 m, 24 m, 27 m, 27 m, 49 m, 47 m, 45 m   f. 98 L, 99 L, 101 L, 111 L, 132 L, 103 L
   Mode _____ Median _____   Mode _____ Median _____

POSITIVE AND NEGATIVE NUMBERS

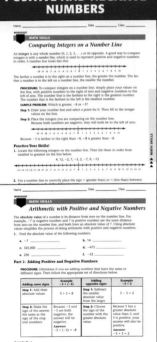

Comparing Integers on a Number Line

An **integer** is any whole number (0, 1, 2, 3, . . .) or its opposite. A good way to compare integers is with a *number line*, which is used to represent positive and negative numbers in order. A number line looks like this:

The farther a number is to the right on a number line, the greater the number. The farther a number is to the left on a number line, the smaller the number.

PROCEDURE: To compare integers on a number line, simply place your values on the line, with positive numbers to the right of zero and negative numbers to the left of zero. The number that is the farthest to the right is the greatest number. The number that is the farthest to the left is the smallest number.

SAMPLE PROBLEM: Which is greater, −8 or −3?

Step 1: Draw your number line and select a point for 0. Then fill in the integer values on the line.

Step 2: Place the integers you are comparing on the number line. Because both numbers are negative, they will both be to the left of zero.

Because −3 is farther to the right than −8, −3 is greater than −8.

Practice Your Skills!
1. Locate the following integers on the number line. Then list them in order from smallest to greatest on the line below.

4, 12, −2, 7, −5, 2, −7, 9, −13

2. Use a number line to correctly place the sign > (greater than) or < (less than) between

Arithmetic with Positive and Negative Numbers

The **absolute value** is the number's distance from zero on the number line. For example, −7 (a negative number) and 7 (a positive number) are the same distance from zero on the number line, and both have an absolute value of 7. Using absolute values simplifies the process of doing arithmetic with positive and negative numbers.

1. Find the absolute value of the following numbers.
   a. −6 _____   c. 6 _____
   b. 325,000 _____   d. −475 _____
                        e. −52 _____

Part 1: Adding Positive and Negative Numbers

PROCEDURE: Determine if you are adding numbers that have the same or different signs. Then follow the appropriate set of directions below.

	Example −3 + (−5)	Adding opposite signs	Example −5 + 5
Step 1: Add their absolute values.	3 + 5 = 8	**Step 1:** Subtract the smaller absolute value from the larger.	5 − 3 = 2
Step 2: Make the sign of the answer the same as the sign of the original numbers.	Because −3 and −5 are both negative, the answer will be negative. **Answer:** −3 + (−5) = −8	**Step 2:** Choose the sign of the number with the greater absolute value.	Because 5 has a greater absolute value than 3, and 5 is positive, your answer will also be positive. **Answer:** −3 + 5 = 2

Add It Up!
2. Complete the following equations. When finished, go back and check your signs.
   a. 14 + (−17) = _____   d. −9 + (−23) = _____
   c. −16 + 21 = _____   e. −12 + 13 = _____
   e. 15 + (−6) = _____   f. −7 + (−7) = _____

FRACTIONS

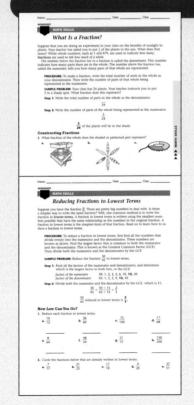

What Is a Fraction?

Suppose that you are doing an experiment in your class on the benefits of sunlight to plants. Your teacher has asked you to put 1/3 of the plants in the sun. What does that mean? While whole numbers, such as 1 and 879, are used to indicate *how many*, **fractions** are used to tell *how much of a whole*.

The number below the fraction bar in a fraction is called the **denominator**. This number indicates how many parts there are in the whole. The number above the fraction bar, called the **numerator**, tells you how many parts of that whole are represented.

PROCEDURE: To make a fraction, write the total number of units in the whole as your denominator. Then write the number of parts of that whole being represented as the numerator.

SAMPLE PROBLEM: Your class has 24 plants. Your teacher instructs you to put 5 in a shady spot. What fraction of the plants will be in the shade?

Step 1: Write the total number of parts in the whole as the denominator.

Step 2: Write the number of parts of the whole being represented as the numerator.

5/24 of the plants will be in the shade.

Constructing Fractions
1. What fraction of the whole does the shaded or patterned part represent?

2. Write True or False next to each equation.
   a. 3 1/3 = 9/3   b. 21/4 = 5 1/4

Reducing Fractions to Lowest Terms

Suppose you have the fraction 20/30. Those are pretty big numbers to deal with. Is there a simpler way to write the same fraction? Well, one common method is to write the fraction in *lowest terms*. A fraction in lowest terms is written using the smallest numbers possible that have the same relationship as the numbers in the original fraction. A fraction in lowest terms is the simplest form of that fraction. Read on to learn how to reduce a fraction to lowest terms.

PROCEDURE: To reduce a fraction to lowest terms, first find all the numbers that divide evenly into the numerator and the denominator. These numbers are known as factors. Find the largest factor that is common to both the numerator and the denominator. This is known as the Greatest Common Factor (GCF). Then divide both the numerator and the denominator by the GCF.

SAMPLE PROBLEM: Reduce 30/45 to lowest terms.

Step 1: Find all the factors of the numerator and denominator, and determine which is the largest factor to both, i.e. the GCF.

factors of the numerator   30: 1, 2, 3, 5, 6, 10, **15**, 30
factors of the denominator 45: 1, 3, 5, 9, **15**, 45

Step 2: Divide both the numerator and the denominator by the GCF, which is 15.

30/45 = 30 ÷ 15 / 45 ÷ 15 = 2/3

30/45 reduced to lowest terms is **2/3**.

How Low Can You Go?
1. Reduce each fraction to lowest terms.
   a. 10/12   b. 36/60   c. 75/100   d. 17/68
   e. 8/54   f. 48/54   g. 11/200   h. 150/200

2. Circle the fractions below that are already written in lowest terms.
   a. 7/77   b. 21/23   c. 17/19   d. 9/20   e. 37/51

Improper Fractions and Mixed Numbers

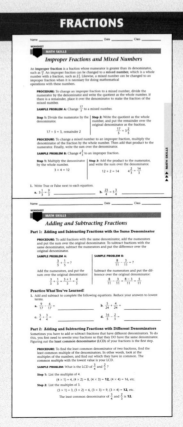

An **improper fraction** is a fraction whose numerator is greater than its denominator. An improper fraction can be changed to a **mixed number**, which is a whole number with a fraction, such as 2 1/2. Likewise, a mixed number can be changed to an improper fraction when it is necessary for doing mathematical operations with these numbers.

PROCEDURE: To change an improper fraction to a mixed number, divide the numerator by the denominator and write the quotient as the whole number. If there is a remainder, place it over the denominator to make the fraction of the mixed number.

SAMPLE PROBLEM: a. Change 17/3 to a mixed number.

Step 1: Divide the numerator by the denominator.

17 ÷ 3 = 5, remainder 2

Step 2: Write the quotient as the whole number, and put the remainder over the original denominator as the fraction.

12/3 = 5 2/3

PROCEDURE: To change a mixed number to an improper fraction, multiply the denominator of the fraction by the whole number. Then add that product to the numerator. Finally, write the sum over the denominator.

SAMPLE PROBLEM: Change 4 2/3 to an improper fraction.

Step 1: Multiply the denominator by the whole number.

3 × 4 = 12

Step 2: Add the product to the numerator, and write the sum over the denominator.

12 + 2 = 14   4 2/3 = 14/3

Adding and Subtracting Fractions

Part 1: Adding and Subtracting Fractions with the Same Denominator

PROCEDURE: To add fractions with the same denominator, add the numerators and put the sum over the same denominator. To subtract fractions with the same denominator, subtract the numerators and put the difference over the original denominator.

SAMPLE PROBLEM A:
1/3 + 1/3 = ?

Add the numerators, and put the sum over the same denominator:
1/3 + 1/3 = 1 + 1 / 3 = 2/3

SAMPLE PROBLEM B:
8/11 − 3/11 = ?

Subtract the numerators and put the difference over the original denominator:
8/11 − 3/11 = 8 − 3 / 11 = 5/11

Practice What You've Learned!
1. Add and subtract to complete the following equations. Reduce your answers to lowest terms.
   a. 4/17 + 5/17 =   b. 4/24 + 4/24 =
   c. 1/4 + 1/4 =   d. 16/7 − 2/7 =

Part 2: Adding and Subtracting Fractions with Different Denominators
Sometimes you need to add or subtract fractions that have different denominators. To do this, you first need to rewrite your fractions so that they DO have the same denominator. Figuring out the least common denominator (LCD) of your fractions is the first step.

PROCEDURE: To find the least common denominator of two fractions, find the common multiples of the denominators. In other words, look at the multiples of the numbers, and find out which they have in common. The common multiple with the lowest value is your LCD.

SAMPLE PROBLEM: What is the LCD of 3/4 and 2/3?

Step 1: List the multiples of 4.
(4 × 1) = 4, (4 × 2) = 8, (4 × 3) = **12**, (4 × 4) = 16, etc.

Step 2: List the multiples of 3.
(3 × 1) = 3, (3 × 2) = 6, (3 × 3) = 9, (3 × 4) = **12**, etc.

The least common denominator of 3/4 and 2/3 is **12**.

Multiplying and Dividing Fractions

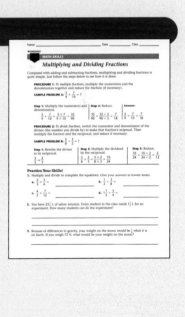

Compared with adding and subtracting fractions, multiplying and dividing fractions is quite simple. Just follow the steps below to see how it is done.

PROCEDURE: To multiply fractions, multiply the numerators and the denominators together and reduce the fraction (if necessary).

SAMPLE PROBLEM A: 5/9 × 7/10 = ?

Step 1: Multiply the numerators and denominators.

Step 2: Reduce.

Answer:

5/9 × 7/10 = 5 × 7 / 9 × 10 = 35/90   35/90 = 35 ÷ 5 / 90 ÷ 5 = 7/18   7/18

PROCEDURE: To divide fractions, switch the numerator and denominator of the divisor (the number you divide by) to make that fraction's reciprocal. Then multiply the fraction and the reciprocal, and reduce if necessary.

SAMPLE PROBLEM B: 3/4 ÷ 2/3 = ?

Step 1: Rewrite the divisor as its reciprocal.

Step 2: Multiply the dividend by the reciprocal.

Step 3: Reduce.

3/4 ÷ 2/3   3/4 × 3/2 = 9/8   10/24 = 10 ÷ 2 / 24 ÷ 2 = 5/12

Practice Your Skills!
1. Multiply and divide to complete the equations. Give your answers in lowest terms.
   a. 2/5 × 1/6 =   b. 1/2 ÷ 1/8 =
   c. 4/5 × 7/12 =   d. 1/2 ÷ 1/4 =

2. You have 23 1/2 L of saline solution. Every student in your class needs 1 1/4 L for an experiment. How many students can do the experiment?

3. Because of differences in gravity, your weight on the moon would be 1/6 what it is on Earth. If you weigh 72 N, what would be your weight on the moon?

Science & Math Skills Worksheets (continued)

Math Skills for Science (continued)

RATIOS AND PROPORTIONS

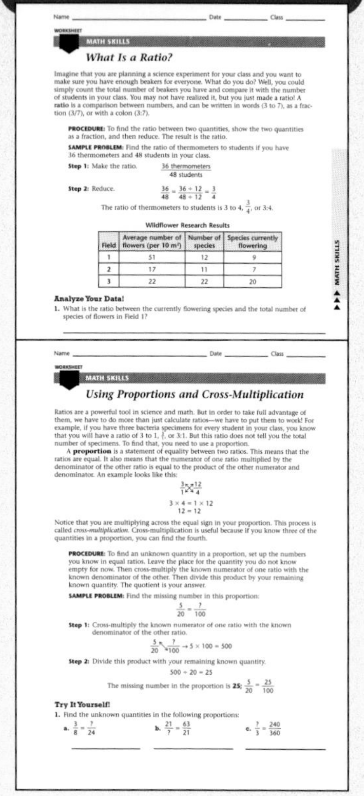
MATH SKILLS

What Is a Ratio?

MATH SKILLS

Using Proportions and Cross-Multiplication

DECIMALS

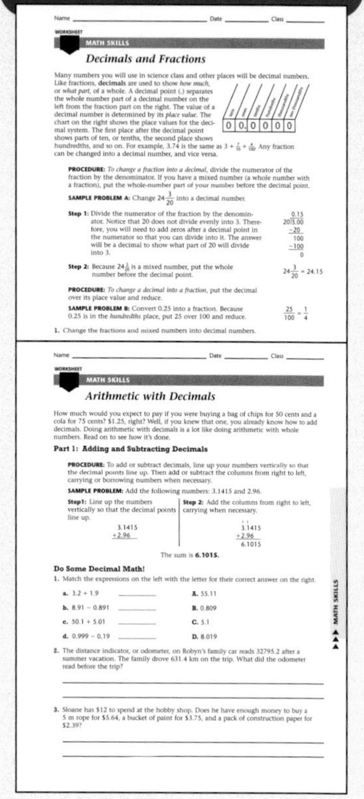
MATH SKILLS

Decimals and Fractions

MATH SKILLS

Arithmetic with Decimals

PERCENTAGES

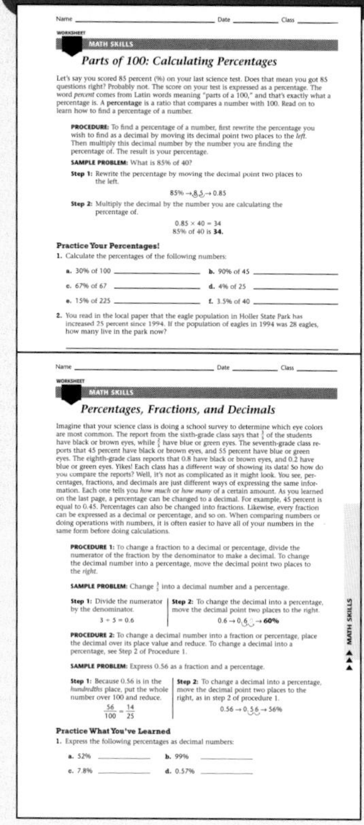
MATH SKILLS

Parts of 100: Calculating Percentages

MATH SKILLS

Percentages, Fractions, and Decimals

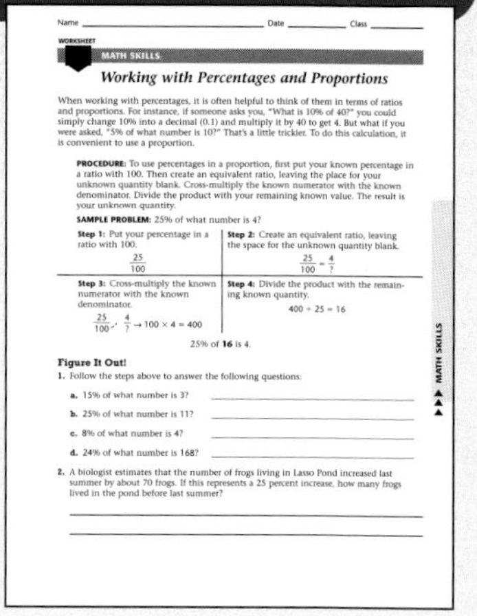
MATH SKILLS

Working with Percentages and Proportions

POWERS OF 10

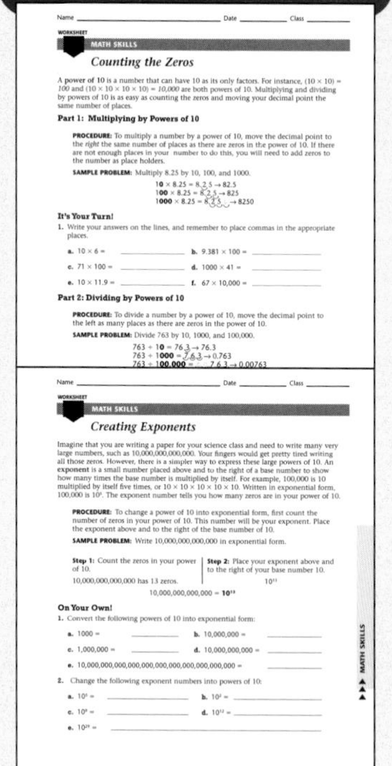
MATH SKILLS

Counting the Zeros

MATH SKILLS

Creating Exponents

SCIENTIFIC NOTATION

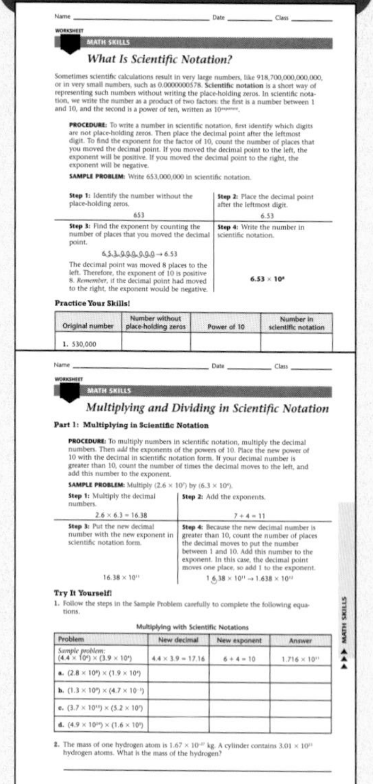
MATH SKILLS

What Is Scientific Notation?

MATH SKILLS

Multiplying and Dividing in Scientific Notation

SI MEASUREMENT AND CONVERSION

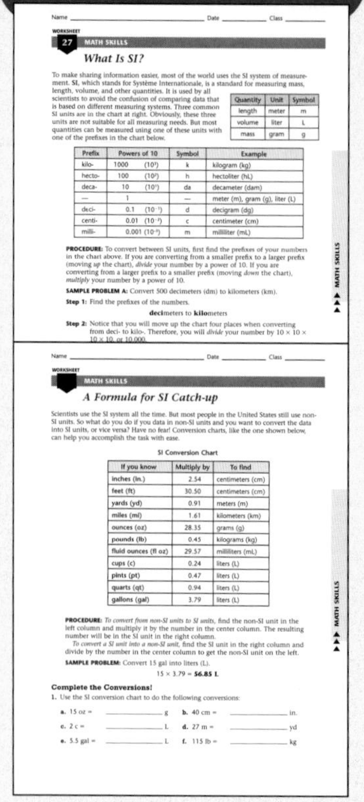
MATH SKILLS

What Is SI?

MATH SKILLS

A Formula for SI Catch-up

Math Skills for Science (continued)

GEOMETRY

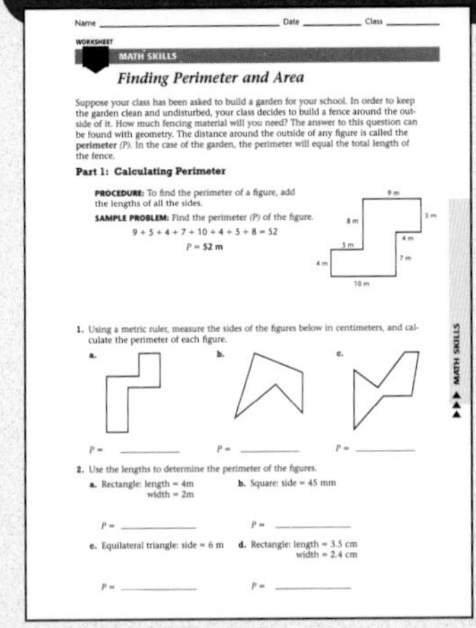

WORKSHEET — MATH SKILLS

Finding Perimeter and Area

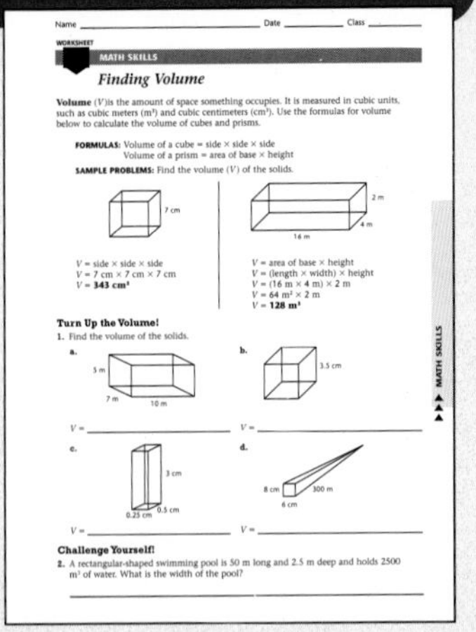

Suppose your class has been asked to build a garden for your school. In order to keep the garden clean and undisturbed, your class decides to build a fence around the outside of it. How much fencing material will you need? The answer to this question can be found with geometry. The distance around the outside of any figure is called the perimeter (*P*). In the case of the garden, the perimeter will equal the total length of the fence.

Part 1: Calculating Perimeter

PROCEDURE: To find the perimeter of a figure, add the lengths of all the sides.

SAMPLE PROBLEM: Find the perimeter (*P*) of the figure.

$9 + 5 + 4 + 7 + 10 + 4 + 5 + 8 = 52$

$P = 52$ m

1. Using a metric ruler, measure the sides of the figures below in centimeters, and calculate the perimeter of each figure.

P = ___   P = ___   P = ___

2. Use the lengths to determine the perimeter of the figures.
   a. Rectangle: length = 4m width = 2m   b. Square: side = 45 mm
   c. Equilateral triangle: side = 6 m   d. Rectangle: length = 3.5 cm width = 2.4 cm

WORKSHEET — MATH SKILLS

Finding Volume

Volume (*V*) is the amount of space something occupies. It is measured in cubic units, such as cubic meters (m³) and cubic centimeters (cm³). Use the formulas for volume below to calculate the volume of cubes and prisms.

FORMULAS: Volume of a cube = side × side × side
Volume of a prism = area of base × height

SAMPLE PROBLEMS: Find the volume (*V*) of the solids.

$V = \text{side} \times \text{side} \times \text{side}$
$V = 7 \text{ cm} \times 7 \text{ cm} \times 7 \text{ cm}$
$V = 343 \text{ cm}^3$

$V = \text{area of base} \times \text{height}$
$V = (\text{length} \times \text{width}) \times \text{height}$
$V = (16 \text{ m} \times 4 \text{ m}) \times 2 \text{ m}$
$V = 64 \text{ m}^2 \times 2 \text{ m}$
$V = 128 \text{ m}^3$

Turn Up the Volume!

1. Find the volume of the solids.

V = ___   V = ___
V = ___   V = ___

Challenge Yourself!

2. A rectangular-shaped swimming pool is 50 m long and 2.5 m deep and holds 2500 m³ of water. What is the width of the pool?

THE UNIT FACTOR AND DIMENSIONAL ANALYSIS

WORKSHEET — MATH SKILLS

The Unit Factor and Dimensional Analysis

The measurements you take in science class, whether for time, mass, weight, or distance, are more than just numbers—they are also units. To make comparisons between measurements, it is convenient to have your measurements in the same units. A mathematical tool called a **unit factor** is used to convert back and forth between different kinds of units. A unit factor is a ratio that is equal to 1. Because it is equal to 1, multiplying a measurement by a unit factor changes the measurement's units but does not change its value. The skill of converting with a unit factor is known as **dimensional analysis**. Read on to see how it works.

Part 1: Converting with a Unit Factor

PROCEDURE: To convert units with a unit factor, determine the conversion factor between the units you have and the units you want to convert to. Then create the unit factor by making a ratio, or a fraction, between the units you want to convert to in the numerator and the units you already have in the denominator. Finally, multiply your measurement by this unit factor to convert to the new units.

SAMPLE PROBLEM A: Convert 3.5 km to millimeters.

Step 1: Determine the conversion factor between kilometers and millimeters.
1 km = 1,000,000 mm

Step 2: Create the unit factor. Put the units you want to convert to in the numerator and the units you already have in the denominator.
$$\frac{1,000,000 \text{ mm}}{1 \text{ km}} = 1$$

Step 3: Multiply the unit factor by the measurement. Notice that the original unit of the measurement cancels out with the unit in the denominator of the unit factor, leaving the units you are converting to.
$$3.5 \text{ km} \times \frac{1,000,000 \text{ mm}}{1 \text{ km}} = 3,500,000 \text{ mm}$$

On Your Own!

1. Convert the following measurements using a unit factor:

Conversion	Unit factor	Answer
a. 2.34 cm = ? mm		
b. 54.6 mL = ? L		
c. 12 kg = ? g		

MATH IN SCIENCE: INTEGRATED SCIENCE

WORKSHEET — MATH IN SCIENCE: INTEGRATED SCIENCE

Math Skills Used: Multiplication, Division, Decimals

Density

Calculate density, and identify substances using a density chart.

Density is a measure of the amount of mass in a certain volume. This physical property is often used to identify and classify substances. It is usually measured in grams per cubic centimeters, or g/cm³. The chart on the right lists the density of some common materials.

FORMULA: $\text{density} = \frac{\text{mass}}{\text{volume}}$

$D = \frac{m}{V}$

SAMPLE PROBLEM: What is the density of a billiard ball that has a volume of 100 cm³ and a mass of 250 g?

$D = \frac{250 \text{ g}}{100 \text{ cm}^3}$
$D = 2.5 \text{ g/cm}^3$

Densities of Substances

Substance	Density (g/cm³)
Gold	19.3
Mercury	13.5
Lead	11.4
Iron	7.87
Aluminum	2.7
Bone	1.7–2.0
Gasoline	0.66–0.69
Air (dry)	0.00119

Your Turn:

1. A loaf of bread has a volume of 2270 cm³ and a mass of 454 g. What is the density of the bread?

2. A liter of water has a mass of 1000 g. What is the density of water? (Hint: 1 mL = 1 cm³)

3. A block of wood has a density of 0.6 g/cm³ and a volume of 1.2 cm³. What is the mass of the block of wood? Be careful!

4. Use the data below to calculate the density of each unknown substance. Then use the density chart above to determine the identity of each substance.

Mass (g)	Volume (cm³)	Density (g/cm³)	Substance
Example: 4725	350	4725 ÷ 350 = 13.5	mercury
a. 171	15		
b. 148	40		
c. 475	250		
d. 680	1000		

WORKSHEET — MATH IN SCIENCE: INTEGRATED SCIENCE

Math Skills Used: Multiplication, Division, Decimals, Percentages, Geometry

The Pressure Is On!

Use math to learn about force and pressure.

You are under pressure! Even though you may not be aware of it, the air above you presses down on every square centimeter of your body with the weight of a 1.03 kg mass! Because water is so much denser than air, pressure in water is many times greater than this. Pressure is defined as the force exerted on a particular area. The unit for pressure is the pascal (Pa), which is the force (one newton (N)) exerted on one square meter (m²).

FORMULA: $\text{Pressure (Pa)} = \frac{\text{Force (N)}}{\text{Area (m}^2\text{)}}$ $\quad Pa = \frac{N}{m^2}$

Apply Some Pressure!

Use the formula for pressure to answer the following questions:

1. An elephant that weighs 40,000 N stands on one leg during a circus performance. The area on the bottom of the elephant's foot is 0.4 m². How much pressure is exerted on the elephant's foot?

2. A carpenter hammers a nail with a force of 45 N with every stroke. The head of the nail has a surface area of 0.002 m². How much pressure is exerted on the nailhead with each stroke?

3. A brick falls from the third floor of a construction site. The brick hits the ground on its end, which measures 0.15 m by 0.25 m, with a force of 30 N. How much pressure is exerted by the brick on the ground? (Hint: Area of a rectangle = width × length)

Pressure in the Atmosphere

The air pressure we live under is about 101,000 Pa at sea level. Use this value to complete the following problems. Show all your work.

4. A mountain climber climbs to the top of Mt. Everest, which at 8848 m is the highest point on Earth. Because most of the air in the atmosphere is below this altitude, air pressure is about 50% less at the peak than at sea level. What is the air pressure exerted on the mountain climber?

5. A meteorologist reports that air pressure is reduced to 8,585 Pa by an approaching hurricane. What percentage change from normal air pressure does this represent?

WORKSHEET — MATH IN SCIENCE: INTEGRATED SCIENCE

Math Skills Used: Multiplication, Division, Decimals, Percentages, Decimals

Sound Reasoning

Use your math skills to understand dolphin echolocation.

Dolphins use echolocation to find their way through murky waters. They do this by emitting a clicking sound and listening for an echo. The direction and delay of the echo give the dolphins information about what objects are nearby and where the objects are located.

1. Sound travels about 1530 m/s in sea water. How many times faster does sound travel in sea water than in air? (The speed of sound in air at 25°C is about 345 m/s.)

2. A dolphin emits a click that is reflected off an object. If it takes 0.2 seconds for the sound to be sent and to come back, how far away is the object?

3. How long would it take the sound to be sent and returned from the same object in air?

4. Assume that the speed of sound decreases by 6 m/s for every 10°C decrease in water temperature. If a dolphin swam to the Arctic Ocean, where the water is about 5°C, how would the dolphin's ability to estimate the distance to an object be affected?

WORKSHEET — MATH IN SCIENCE: INTEGRATED SCIENCE

Math Skills Used: Addition, Multiplication, Fractions, Decimals, Scientific Notation, SI Measurement and Conversion

Using Temperature Scales

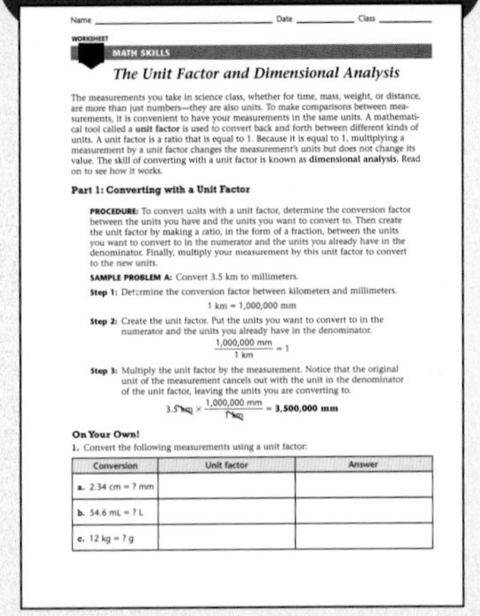

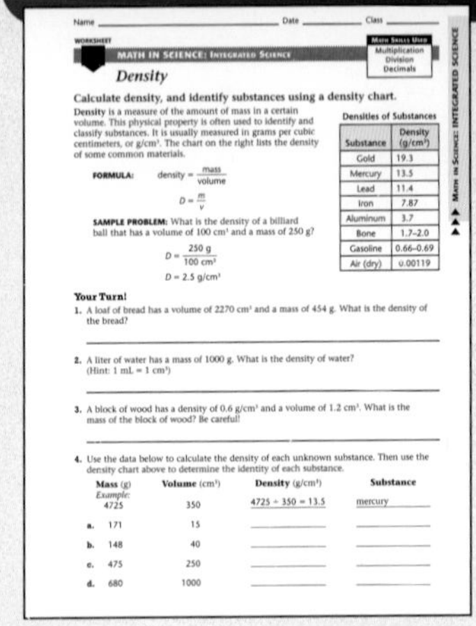

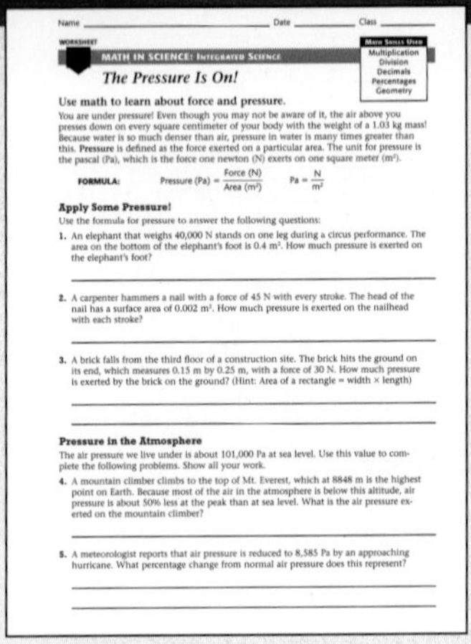

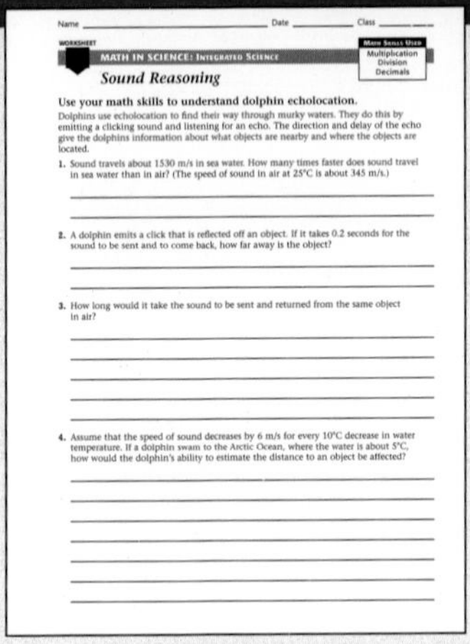

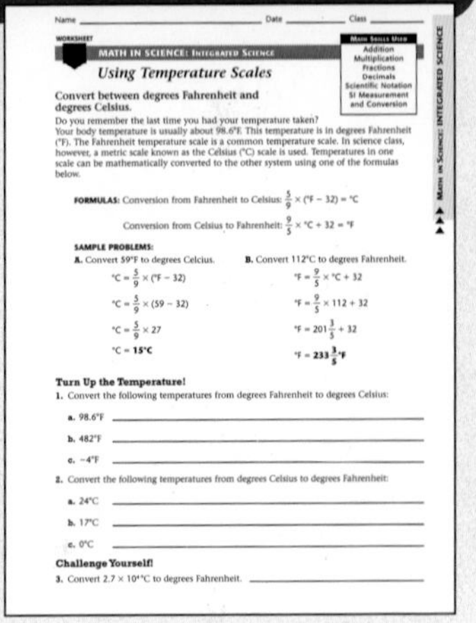

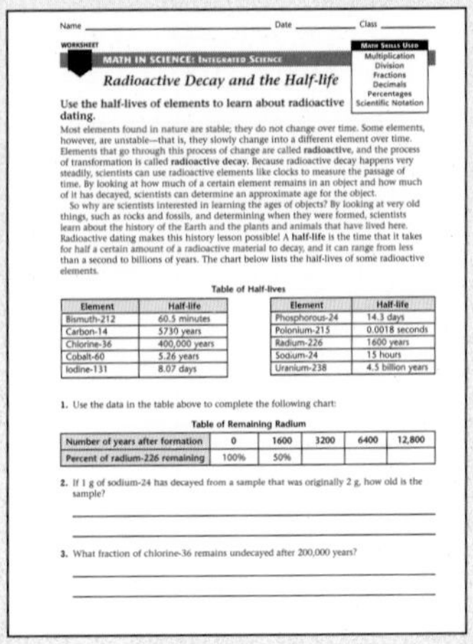

Convert between degrees Fahrenheit and degrees Celsius.

Do you remember the last time you had your temperature taken? Your body temperature is usually about 98.6°F. This temperature is in degrees Fahrenheit (°F). The Fahrenheit temperature scale is a common temperature scale. In science class, however, a metric scale known as the Celsius (°C) scale is used. Temperatures in one scale can be mathematically converted to the other system using one of the formulas below.

FORMULAS: Conversion from Fahrenheit to Celsius: $\frac{5}{9} \times (°F - 32) = °C$

Conversion from Celsius to Fahrenheit: $\frac{9}{5} \times °C + 32 = °F$

SAMPLE PROBLEMS:

A. Convert 59°F to degrees Celsius.
$°C = \frac{5}{9} \times (°F - 32)$
$°C = \frac{5}{9} \times (59 - 32)$
$°C = \frac{5}{9} \times 27$
$°C = 15°C$

B. Convert 112°C to degrees Fahrenheit.
$°F = \frac{9}{5} \times °C + 32$
$°F = \frac{9}{5} \times 112 + 32$
$°F = 201\frac{3}{5} + 32$
$°F = 233\frac{3}{5}°F$

Turn Up the Temperature!

1. Convert the following temperatures from degrees Fahrenheit to degrees Celsius:
   a. 98.6°F
   b. 482°F
   c. −4°F

2. Convert the following temperatures from degrees Celsius to degrees Fahrenheit:
   a. 24°C
   b. 17°C
   c. 0°C

Challenge Yourself!

3. Convert 2.7 × 10⁶°C to degrees Fahrenheit.

WORKSHEET — MATH IN SCIENCE: INTEGRATED SCIENCE

Math Skills Used: Multiplication, Division, Decimals, Percentages, Scientific Notation

Radioactive Decay and the Half-life

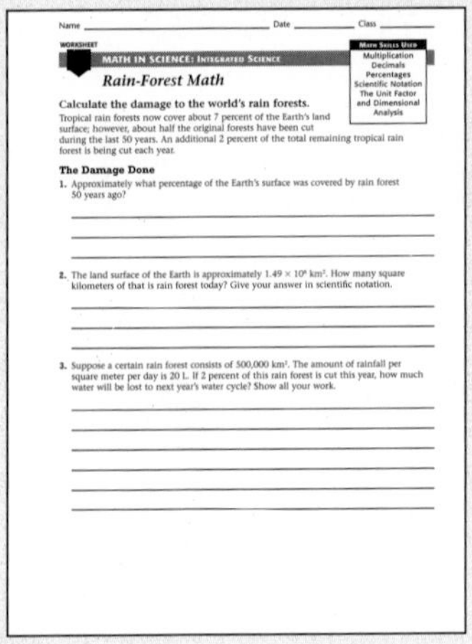

Use the half-lives of elements to learn about radioactive dating.

Most elements found in nature are stable; they do not change over time. Some elements, however, are unstable—that is, they slowly change into a different element over time. Elements that go through this process of change are called **radioactive**, and the process of transformation is called **radioactive decay**. Because radioactive decay happens very steadily, scientists can use radioactive elements like clocks to measure the passage of time. By looking at how much of a certain element remains in an object and how much of it has decayed, scientists can determine an approximate age for the object.

So why are scientists interested in learning the ages of objects? By looking at very old things, such as rocks and fossils, and determining when they were formed, scientists learn about the history of the Earth and the plants and animals that have lived here. Radioactive dating makes this history lesson possible! A **half-life** is the time that it takes for half a certain amount of a radioactive material to decay, and it can range from less than a second to billions of years. The chart below lists the half-lives of some radioactive elements.

Table of Half-lives

Element	Half-life	Element	Half-life
Bismuth-212	60.5 minutes	Phosphorous-24	14.3 days
Carbon-14	5730 years	Polonium-215	0.0018 seconds
Chlorine-36	400,000 years	Radium-226	1600 years
Cobalt-60	5.26 years	Sodium-24	15 hours
Iodine-131	8.07 days	Uranium-238	4.5 billion years

1. Use the data in the table above to complete the following chart:

Table of Remaining Radium

Number of years after formation	0	1600	3200	6400	12,800
Percent of radium-226 remaining	100%	50%			

2. If 1 g of sodium-24 has decayed from a sample that was originally 2 g, how old is the sample?

3. What fraction of chlorine-36 remains undecayed after 200,000 years?

WORKSHEET — MATH IN SCIENCE: INTEGRATED SCIENCE

Math Skills Used: Multiplication, Decimals, Fractions, Percentages, Scientific Notation, The Unit Factor and Dimensional Analysis

Rain-Forest Math

Calculate the damage to the world's rain forests.

Tropical rain forests now cover about 7 percent of the Earth's land surface; however, about half the original forests have been cut during the last 50 years. An additional 2 percent of the total remaining tropical rain forest is being cut each year.

The Damage Done

1. Approximately what percentage of the Earth's surface was covered by rain forest 50 years ago?

2. The land surface of the Earth is approximately 1.49 × 10⁸ km². How many square kilometers of that is rain forest today? Give your answer in scientific notation.

3. Suppose a certain rain forest consists of 500,000 km². The amount of rainfall per square meter per day is 20 L. If 2 percent of this rain forest is cut this year, how much water will be lost to next year's water cycle? Show all your work.

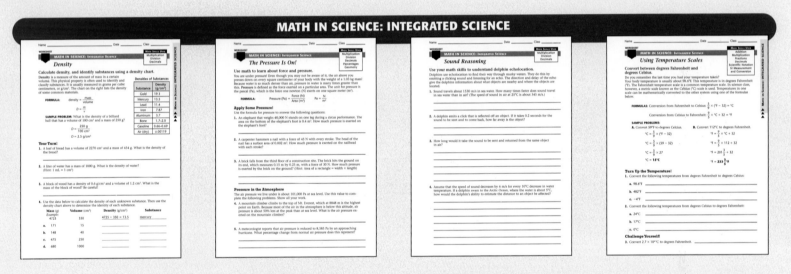

Science & Math Skills Worksheets (continued)

Math Skills for Science (continued)

MATH IN SCIENCE: EARTH SCIENCE

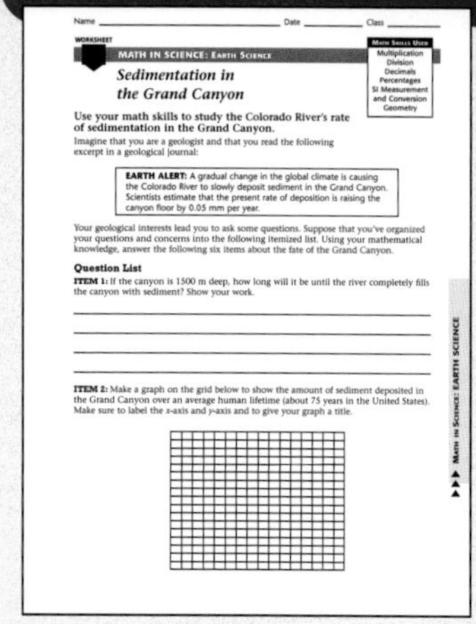

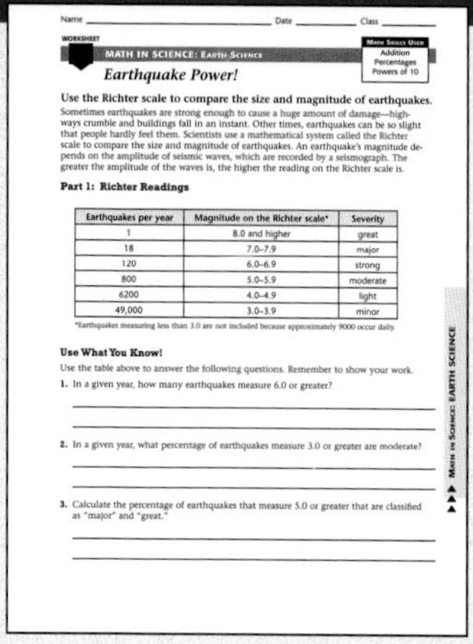

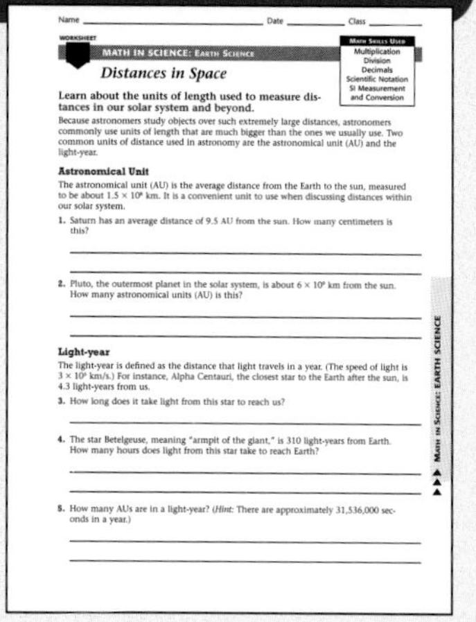

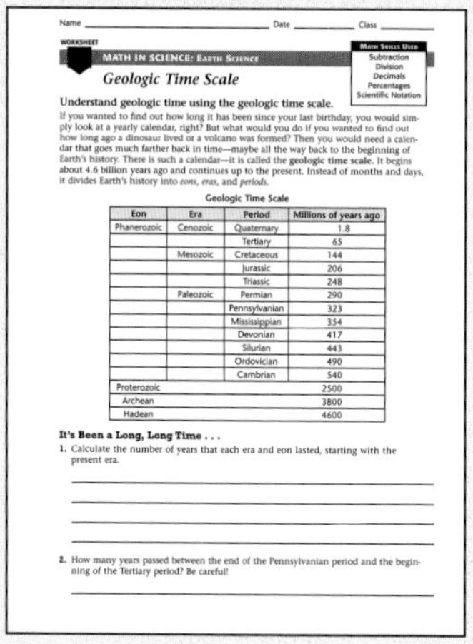

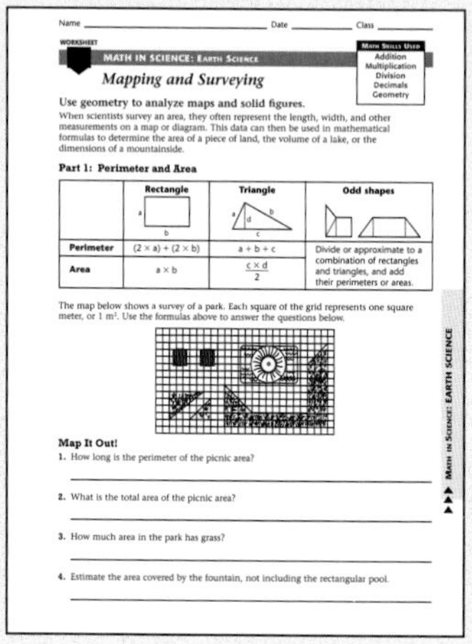

Assessment Checklist & Rubrics

The following is just a sample of over 50 checklists and rubrics contained in this booklet.

RUBRICS FOR WRITTEN WORK

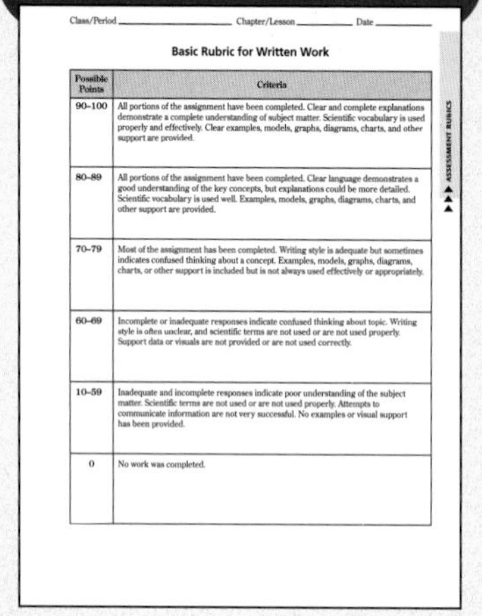

RUBRIC FOR EXPERIMENTS

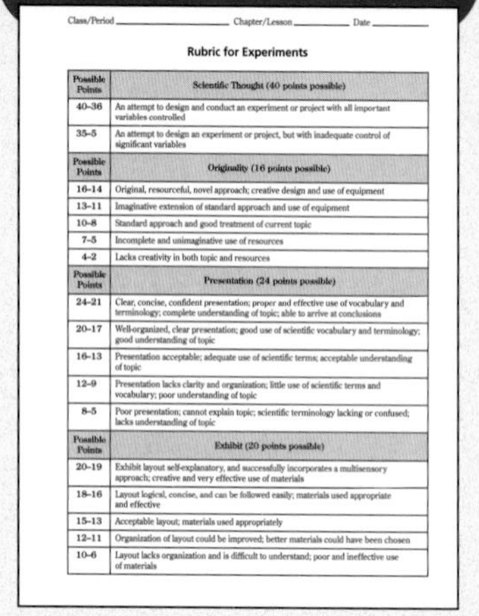

TEACHER EVALUATION OF COOPERATIVE LEARNING

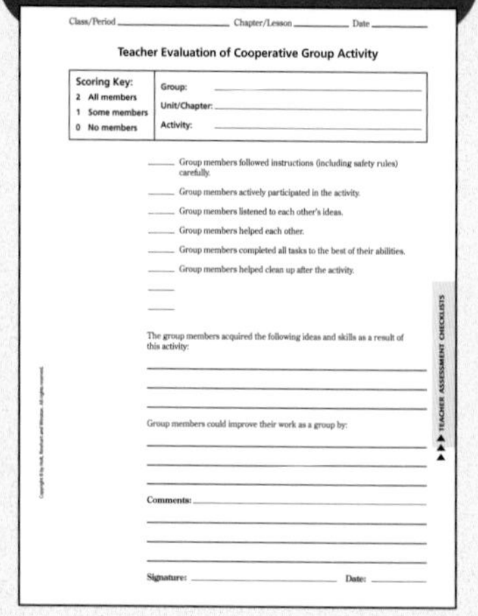

TEACHER EVALUATION OF STUDENT PROGRESS

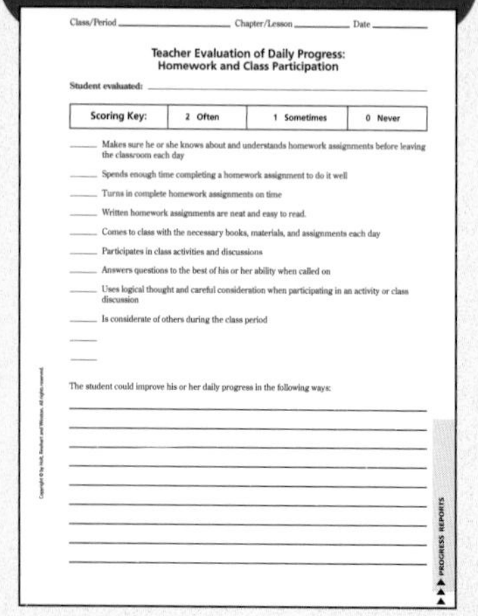

HOLT SCIENCE & TECHNOLOGY

EARTH SCIENCE NATIONAL SCIENCE EDUCATION STANDARDS CORRELATIONS

The following lists show the chapter correlation of ***Holt Science and Technology: Astronomy*** with the *National Science Education Standards* (grades 5-8)

UNIFYING CONCEPTS AND PROCESSES

Standard	Chapter Correlation
Systems, order, and organization Code: UCP 1	**Chapter 2** 2.1 **Chapter 3** 3.1, 3.2, 3.3 **Chapter 4** 4.1, 4.2, 4.3, 4.4
Evidence, models, and explanation Code: UCP 2	**Chapter 1** 1.1, 1.2 **Chapter 2** 2.1, 2.3 **Chapter 3** 3.2 **Chapter 4** 4.1, 4.2, 4.4 **Chapter 5** 5.1, 5.4
Change, constancy, and measurement Code: UCP 3	**Chapter 1** 1.2 **Chapter 3** 3.1, 3.2 **Chapter 4** 4.1, 4.2, 4.4 **Chapter 5** 5.1, 5.4
Evolution and equilibrium Code: UCP 4	**Chapter 2** 2.1, 2.3 **Chapter 5** 5.1, 5.2, 5.3, 5.4
Form and function Code: UCP 5	**Chapter 4** 4.2, 4.3, 4.4 **Chapter 5** 5.1, 5.3, 5.4

HISTORY AND NATURE OF SCIENCE

Standard	Chapter Correlation
Science as a human endeavor Code: HNS 1	**Chapter 1** 1.1, 1.2, 1.3 **Chapter 2** 2.1, 2.2 **Chapter 3** 3.1, 3.2 **Chapter 4** 4.1, 4.3 **Chapter 5** 5.1, 5.2, 5.3, 5.4
Nature of science Code: HNS 2	**Chapter 1** 1.1 **Chapter 2** 2.1, 2.2 **Chapter 4** 4.1, 4.3
History of science Code: HNS 3	**Chapter 1** 1.1, 1.3 **Chapter 2** 2.1, 2.2 **Chapter 3** 3.1, 3.2 **Chapter 4** 4.1, 4.2, 4.3, 4.4

SCIENCE IN PERSONAL AND SOCIAL PERSPECTIVES

Standard	Chapter Correlation
Personal health Code: SPSP 1	**Chapter 2** 2.1
Risks and benefits Code: SPSP 4	**Chapter 1** 1.3 **Chapter 2** 2.1
Science and technology in society Code: SPSP 5	**Chapter 1** 1.1, 1.2, 1.3 **Chapter 2** 2.1, 2.2 **Chapter 3** 3.1 **Chapter 4** 4.1, 4.3 **Chapter 5** 5.1, 5.2, 5.3, 5.4

SCIENCE AND TECHNOLOGY

Standard	Chapter Correlation
Abilities of technological design Code: ST 1	**Chapter 1** 1.1, 1.3 **Chapter 3** 3.1, 3.2 **Chapter 4** 4.3 **Chapter 5** 5.1, 5.4
Understandings about science and technology Code: ST 2	**Chapter 1** 1.1, 1.2, 1.3 **Chapter 2** 2.1, 2.2 **Chapter 3** 3.1 **Chapter 4** 4.3 **Chapter 5** 5.1, 5.2, 5.3, 5.4

SCIENCE AS INQUIRY

Standard	Chapter Correlation
Abilities necessary to do scientific inquiry Code: SAI 1	**Chapter 1** 1.1, 1.2, 1.3 **Chapter 2** 2.1, 2.2, 2.3 **Chapter 3** 3.1, 3.2, 3.3 **Chapter 4** 4.1, 4.2, 4.3, 4.4 **Chapter 5** 5.1, 5.2, 5.4

EARTH SCIENCE NATIONAL SCIENCE EDUCATION CONTENT STANDARDS

STRUCTURE OF THE EARTH SYSTEM

Standard	Chapter Correlation
Land forms are the result of a combination of constructive and destructive forces. Constructive forces include crustal deformation, volcanic eruption, and deposition of sediment, while destructive forces include weathering and erosion. Code: ES 1c	**Chapter 3** 3.1

EARTH'S HISTORY

Standard	Chapter Correlation
The earth processes we see today, including erosion, movement of lithospheric plates, and changes in atmospheric composition, are similar to those that occurred in the past. Earth history is also influenced by occasional catastrophes, such as the impact of an asteroid or comet. Code: ES 2a	**Chapter 3** 3.3
Fossils provide important evidence of how life and environmental conditions have changed. Code: ES 2b	**Chapter 2** 2.3

EARTH IN THE SOLAR SYSTEM

Standard	Chapter Correlation
The earth is the third planet from the sun in a system that includes the moon, the sun, eight other planets and their moons, and smaller objects, such as asteroids and comets. The sun, an average star, is the central and largest body in the solar system. Code: ES 3a.	**Chapter 2** 2.1, 2.2 **Chapter 3** 3.1, 3.2, 3.3
Most objects in the solar system are in regular and predictable motion. Those motions explain such phenomena as the day, the year, phases of the moon, and eclipses. Code: ES 3b	**Chapter 1** 1.1, 1.2 **Chapter 2** 2.1 **Chapter 3** 3.1, 3.2, 3.3
Gravity is the force that keeps planets in orbit around the sun and governs the rest of the motion in the solar system. Gravity alone holds us to the earth's surface and explains the phenomenon of the tides. Code: ES 3c	**Chapter 1** 1.1 **Chapter 2** 2.1 **Chapter 3** 3.2
The sun is the major source of energy for phenomenon on the earth's surface, such as growth of plants, winds, ocean currents, and the water cycle. Seasons result from variations in the amount of the sun's energy hitting the surface, due to the tilt of the earth's rotation on its axis and the length of the day. Code: ES 3d	**Chapter 1** 1.2

Master Materials List

For added convenience, Science Kit® provides materials-ordering software on CD-ROM designed specifically for *Holt Science and Technology*. Using this software, you can order complete kits or individual items, quickly and efficiently.

CONSUMABLE MATERIALS	AMOUNT	PAGE
Aluminum foil, approx. 5 x 5 cm	1	54
Balloon	1	127
Battery, D-cell	2	118
Battery, D-cell, weak	1	118
Bottle, 2 L, with cap	1	168
Box, cardboard, large	1	148, 160
Card, index, 3 x 5 in.	1	54
Card, index, 3 x 5 in.	12	160
Cardboard toilet-paper tube	1	162
Cardboard wrapping-paper tube	1	162
Clay, modeling	1 stick	88, 162, 168
Flashlight bulb	1	118
Foam board	1 sheet	168
Marker, permanent, black	1	24
Oil, cooking	50 mL	49
Paper, construction	1 sheet	162
Paper, heavy white	1 sheet	78
Paper brad	2	148
Paper clip	1	3
Paper clip, jumbo	2	148
Pencil, assorted, colored	1 box	24
Pencil, colored (red, blue, green)	3	164
Poster board	1 sheet	24, 54
Poster board, square, 16 x 16 cm	1	166
Stakes with flags	10	63
Straw, straight plastic	1	3, 127
String	30 cm	3, 40, 127, 166
Tape, duct	1 roll	168
Tape, electrical, 20–30 cm	1	118
Tape, masking	1 roll	54, 127, 160, 162
Tape, transparent	1 roll	166
Wire, uninsulated	50 cm	148

NONCONSUMABLE EQUIPMENT	AMOUNT	PAGE
Ball, inflated, large	1	160
Ball, styrene, 3–4 cm diam.	1	148
Ball, styrene, 7–8 cm diam.	1	89
Beaker, 150 mL	1	49
Bucket, 5 gal	1	168
Calculator, scientific	1	24, 166
Compass, drawing	1	164
Convex lens, 3 cm diam. (different focal lengths)	2	162
Flashlight	1	88
Globe, world	1	89
Hole punch	1	148
Lamp, goose-neck	1	78, 89, 162
Measuring tape, metric	1	166
Meterstick	1	54, 166
Protractor	1	3, 166
Rocket launcher	1	168
Ruler, metric	1	24, 54, 88, 148, 162, 164, 166
Scissors	1	54, 148, 162, 166, 168
Stopwatch	1	168
Thumbtack	1	54
Thumbtack	2	40
Wire, insulated copper, with ends stripped, approx. 20 cm	2	118

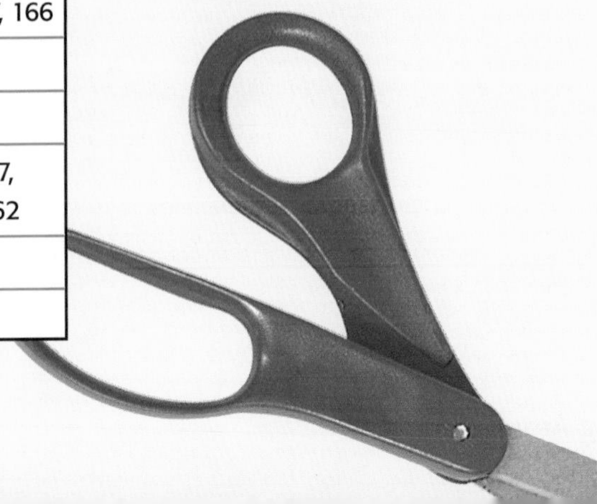

Answers to Concept Mapping Questions

The following pages contain sample answers to all of the concept mapping questions that appear in the Chapter Reviews. Because there is more than one way to do a concept map, your students' answers may vary.

CHAPTER 1 Observing the Sky

18.

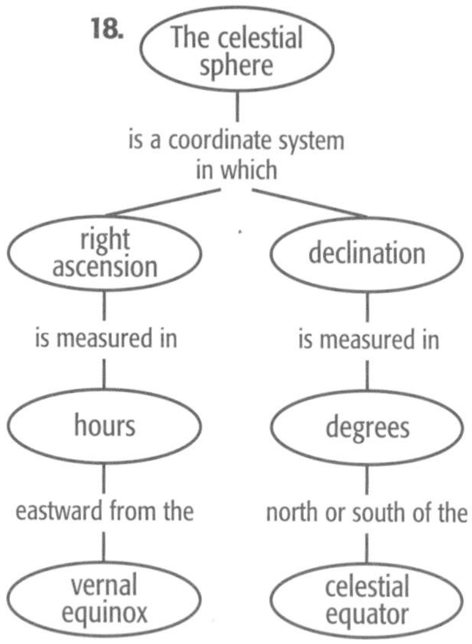

CHAPTER 2 Formation of the Solar System

21.

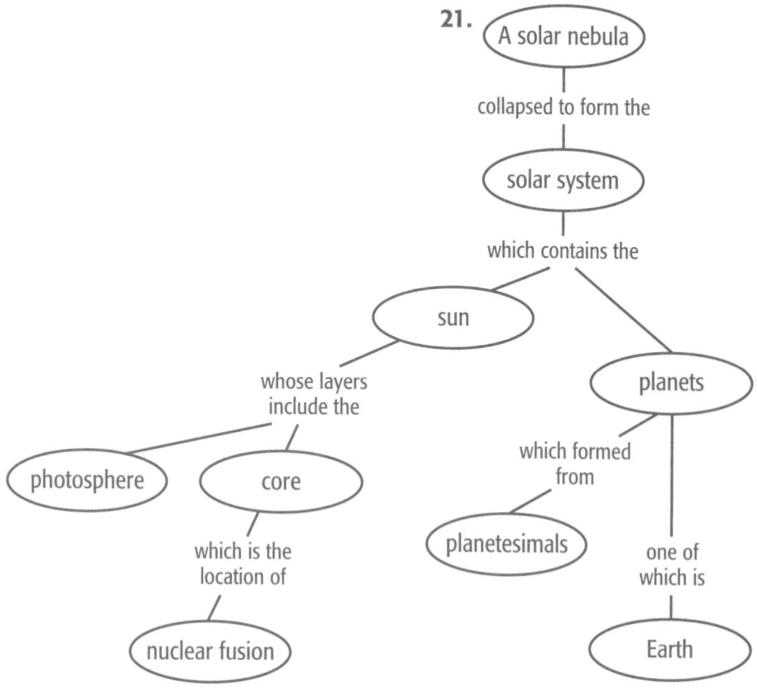

CHAPTER 3 A Family of Planets

22.

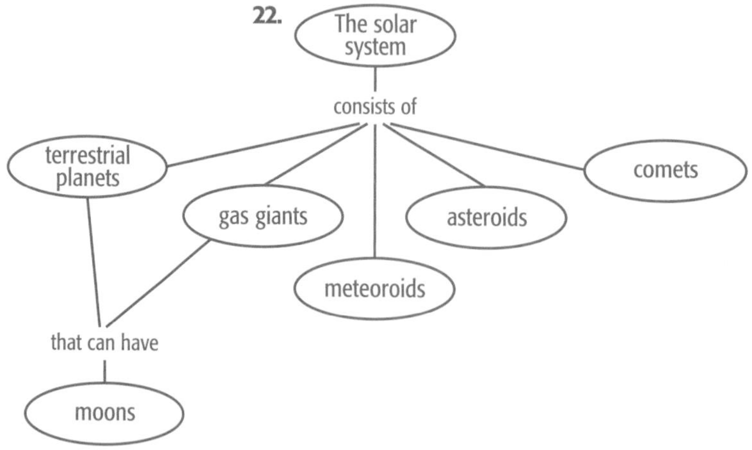

CHAPTER 4 The Universe Beyond

18.

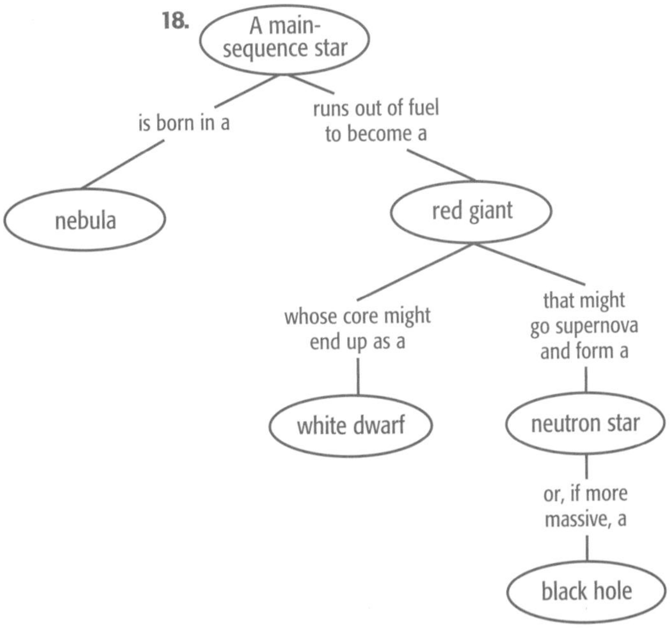

CHAPTER 5 Exploring Space

20.

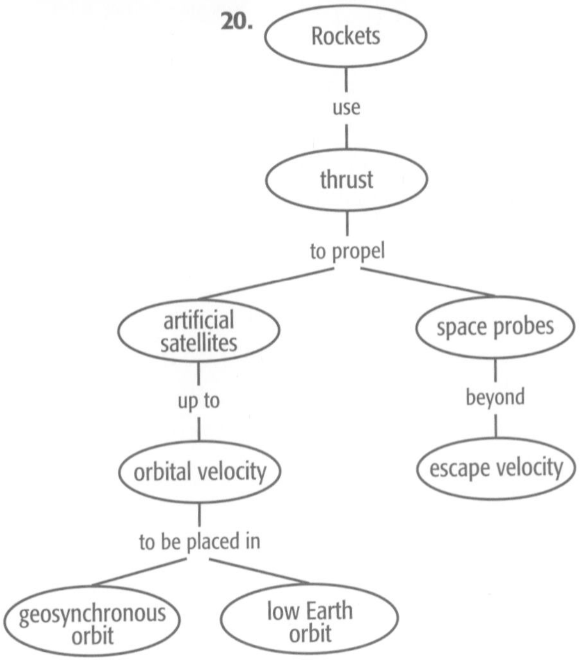

To the Student

This book was created to make your science experience interesting, exciting, and fun!

Go for It!

Science is a process of discovery, a trek into the unknown. The skills you develop using *Holt Science & Technology*—such as observing, experimenting, and explaining observations and ideas—are the skills you will need for the future. There is a universe of exploration and discovery awaiting those who accept the challenges of science.

Science & Technology

You see the interaction between science and technology every day. Science makes technology possible. On the other hand, some of the products of technology, such as computers, are used to make further scientific discoveries. In fact, much of the scientific work that is done today has become so technically complicated and expensive that no one person can do it entirely alone. But make no mistake, the creative ideas for even the most highly technical and expensive scientific work still come from individuals.

Activities and Labs

The activities and labs in this book will allow you to make some basic but important scientific discoveries on your own. You can even do some exploring on your own at home! Here's your chance to use your imagination and curiosity as you investigate your world.

Keep a ScienceLog

In this book, you will be asked to keep a type of journal called a ScienceLog to record your thoughts, observations, experiments, and conclusions. As you develop your ScienceLog, you will see your own ideas taking shape over time. You'll have a written record of how your ideas have changed as you learn about and explore interesting topics in science.

Know "What You'll Do"

The "What You'll Do" list at the beginning of each section is your built-in guide to what you need to learn in each chapter. When you can answer the questions in the Section Review and Chapter Review, you know you are ready for a test.

Check Out the Internet

You will see this sciLINKS NSTA logo throughout the book. You'll be using *sci*LINKS as your gateway to the Internet. Once you log on to *sci*LINKS using your computer's Internet link, type in the *sci*LINKS address. When asked for the keyword code, type in the keyword for that topic. A wealth of resources is now at your disposal to help you learn more about that topic.

In addition to *sci*LINKS you can log on to some other great resources to go with your text. The addresses shown below will take you to the home page of each site.

internetconnect

This textbook contains the following on-line resources to help you make the most of your science experience.

go.hrw.com	sciLINKS NSTA	Smithsonian Institution® Internet Connections	CNNfyi.com
Visit **go.hrw.com** for extra help and study aids matched to your textbook. Just type in the keyword HST HOME.	Visit **www.scilinks.org** to find resources specific to topics in your textbook. Keywords appear throughout your book to take you further.	Visit **www.si.edu/hrw** for specifically chosen on-line materials from one of our nation's premier science museums.	Visit **www.cnnfyi.com** for late-breaking news and current events stories selected just for you.

Chapter Organizer

CHAPTER ORGANIZATION	TIME MINUTES	OBJECTIVES	LABS, INVESTIGATIONS, AND DEMONSTRATIONS
Chapter Opener **pp. 2–3**	45	National Standards: UCP 3, SAI 1, ST 1, 2, SPSP 5	**Start-Up Activity,** Indoor Stargazing, p. 3
Section 1 **Astronomy– The Original Science**	45	▶ Identify the units of a calendar. ▶ Evaluate calendars from different ancient civilizations. ▶ Explain how our modern calendar developed. ▶ Summarize how astronomy began in ancient cultures and developed into a modern science. UCP 2, SAI 2, ST 2, SPSP 5, HNS 1–3, ES 3b, 3c; Labs SAI 1, ST 1, ES 3b	**Design Your Own,** Create a Calendar, p. 24 **Datasheets for LabBook,** Create a Calendar
Section 2 **Mapping the Stars**	90	▶ Describe constellations, and explain how astronomers use them. ▶ Explain how to measure altitude. ▶ Explain right ascension and declination. ▶ Evaluate the scale of the universe. UCP 3, SAI 1, ST 2, SPSP 5, HNS 1, ES 3d; Labs UCP 2, SAI 1, HNS 1, ES 3b	**QuickLab,** Using a Sky Map, p. 12 **Skill Builder,** The Sun's Yearly Trip Through the Zodiac, p. 160 **Datasheets for LabBook,** The Sun's Yearly Trip Through the Zodiac **Inquiry Labs,** Constellation Prize
Section 3 **Telescopes– Then and Now**	90	▶ Compare and contrast refracting telescopes with reflecting telescopes. ▶ Explain why the atmosphere is an obstacle to astronomers and how they overcome the obstacle. ▶ List the types of electromagnetic radiation, other than visible light, that astronomers use to study space. SAI 1, ST 2, SPSP 4, 5, HNS 1, 3; Labs SAI 1, ST 1	**Demonstration,** Mystery of the Floating Penny, p. 19 in ATE **Demonstration,** p. 20 in ATE **Skill Builder,** Through the Looking Glass, p. 162 **Datasheets for LabBook,** Through the Looking Glass **Whiz-Bang Demonstrations,** Refraction Action **Long-Term Projects and Research Ideas,** Celestial Inspiration

See page **T23** *for a complete correlation of this book with the*

NATIONAL SCIENCE EDUCATION STANDARDS.

TECHNOLOGY RESOURCES

Guided Reading Audio CD
English or Spanish, Chapter 1

One-Stop Planner CD-ROM with Test Generator

CNN. **Science, Technology & Society,** Taking Earth's Pulse, Segment 21

Scientists in Action, Discovering a New Planet, Segment 24

Chapter 1 • Observing the Sky

CLASSROOM WORKSHEETS, TRANSPARENCIES, AND RESOURCES	SCIENCE INTEGRATION AND CONNECTIONS	REVIEW AND ASSESSMENT
Directed Reading Worksheet **Science Puzzlers, Twisters & Teasers**		
Directed Reading Worksheet, Section 1 **Reinforcement Worksheet,** Stella Star, Ace Reporter	**Cross-Disciplinary Focus,** p. 4 in ATE **Multicultural Connection,** pp. 5, 6, 7 in ATE **Real-World Connection,** p. 9 in ATE	**Homework,** p. 6 in ATE **Homework,** p. 8 in ATE **Self-Check,** p. 9 **Section Review,** p. 10 **Quiz,** p. 10 in ATE **Alternative Assessment,** p. 10 in ATE
Directed Reading Worksheet, Section 2 **Transparency 180,** Spring Constellations in the Northern Hemisphere **Transparency 181,** Finding Stars in the Night Sky **Transparency 182,** Ascension and Declination Lines **Transparency 183,** Considering Scale in the Universe	**Cross-Disciplinary Focus,** p. 11 in ATE **Real-World Connection,** p. 13 in ATE **Multicultural Connection,** p. 13 in ATE **Physics Connection,** p. 15 **MathBreak,** Understanding Scale, p. 16 **Math and More,** p. 16 in ATE **Cross-Disciplinary Focus,** p. 16 in ATE **Science, Technology, and Society:** Planet or Star? p. 30	**Self-Check,** p. 12 **Homework,** p. 14 in ATE **Section Review,** p. 17 **Quiz,** p. 17 in ATE **Alternative Assessment,** p. 17 in ATE
Directed Reading Worksheet, Section 3 **Transparency 299,** How Your Eyes Work **Transparency 184,** Refracting Telescope **Transparency 184,** Reflecting Telescope **Critical Thinking Worksheet,** Through the Eyes of a Telescope **Transparency 185,** The Electromagnetic Spectrum	**Connect to Physical Science,** p. 18 in ATE **Math and More,** p. 20 in ATE **Connect to Life Science,** p. 21 in ATE **Eye on the Environment:** Eyes in the Sky, p. 31	**Homework,** p. 19 in ATE **Homework,** p. 22 in ATE **Section Review,** p. 23 **Quiz,** p. 23 in ATE **Alternative Assessment,** p. 23 in ATE

internetconnect

go.hrw.com **Holt, Rinehart and Winston On-line Resources**

go.hrw.com

For worksheets and other teaching aids related to this chapter, visit the HRW Web site and type in the keyword: **HSTOBS**

sciLINKS NSTA **National Science Teachers Association**

www.scilinks.org

Encourage students to use the *sci*LINKS numbers listed in the internet connect boxes to access information and resources on the **NSTA** Web site.

END-OF-CHAPTER REVIEW AND ASSESSMENT

Chapter Review in Study Guide
Vocabulary and Notes in Study Guide
Chapter Tests with Performance-Based Assessment, Chapter 1 Test
Chapter Tests with Performance-Based Assessment, Performance-Based Assessment 1
Concept Mapping Transparency 18

Chapter Resources & Worksheets

Visual Resources

TEACHING TRANSPARENCIES

#180

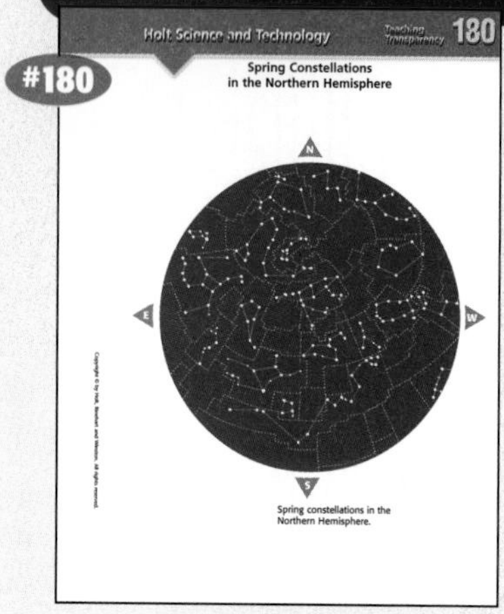

#181

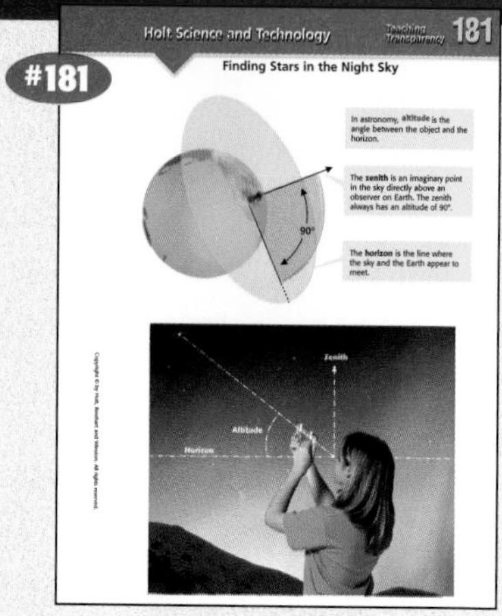

#182

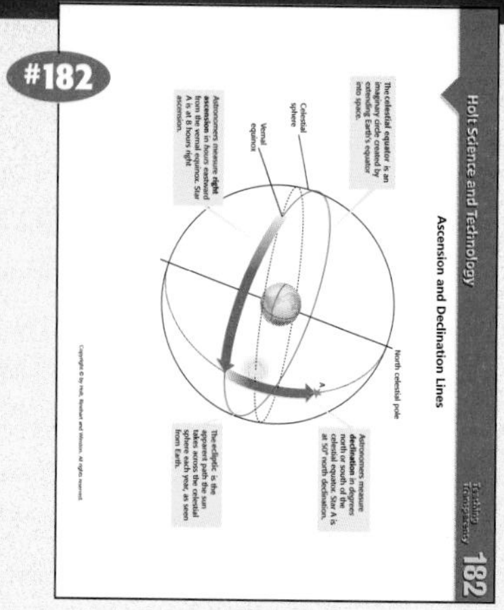

#183

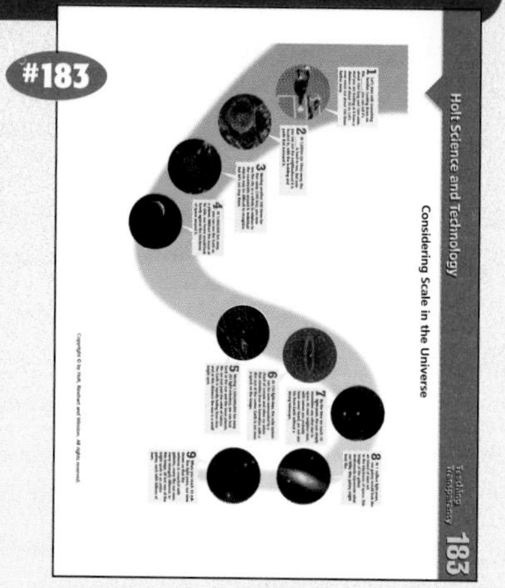

TEACHING TRANSPARENCIES

#184

#185

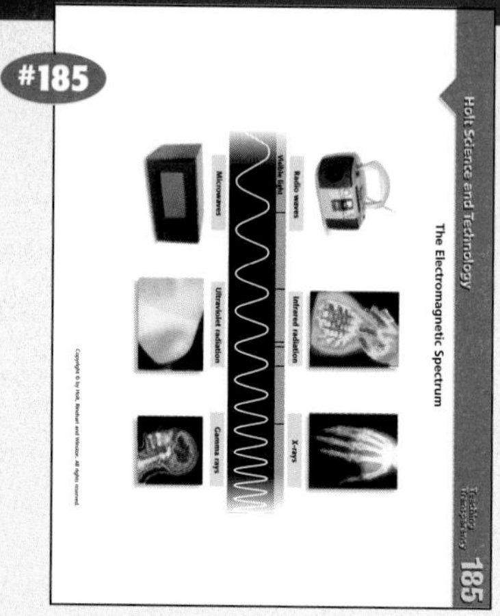

#299

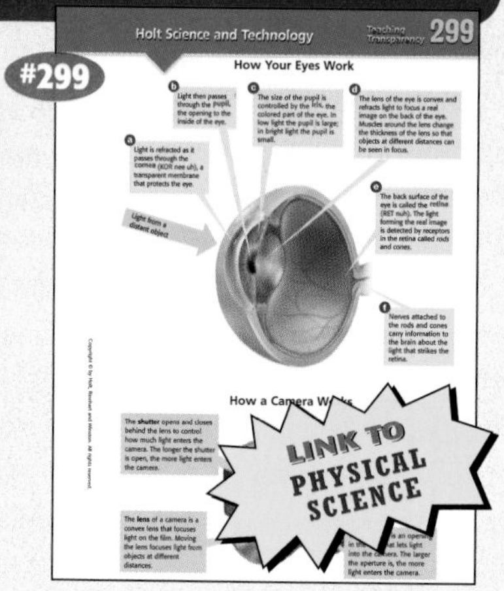

CONCEPT MAPPING TRANSPARENCY

#18

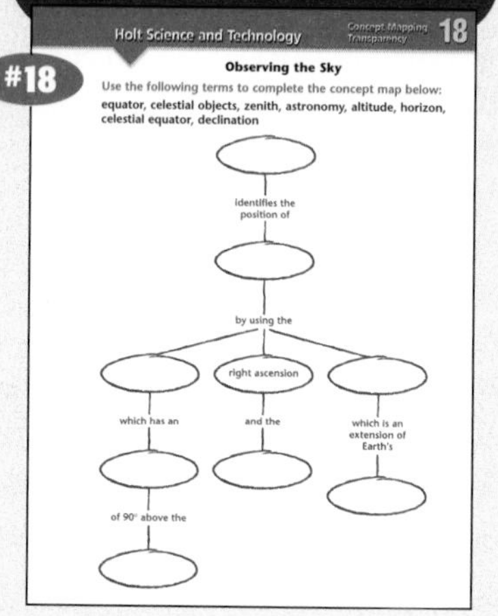

Meeting Individual Needs

DIRECTED READING

#1

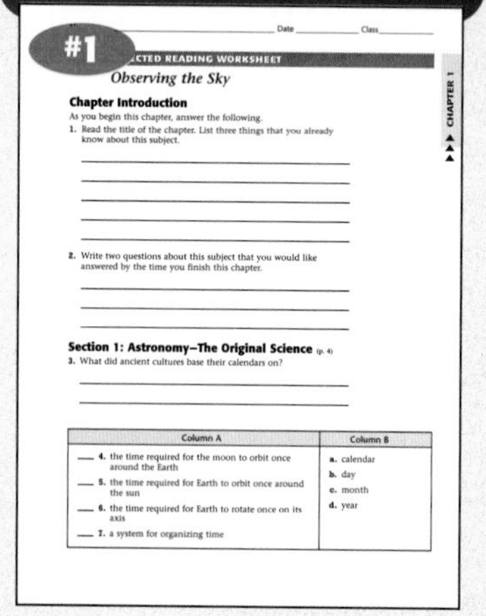

REINFORCEMENT & VOCABULARY REVIEW

#1

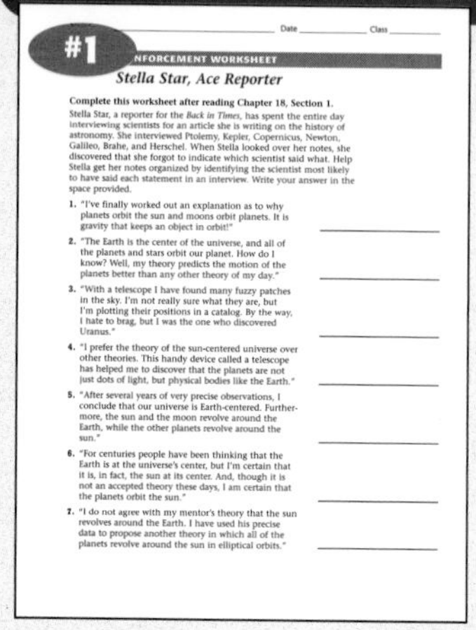

#1

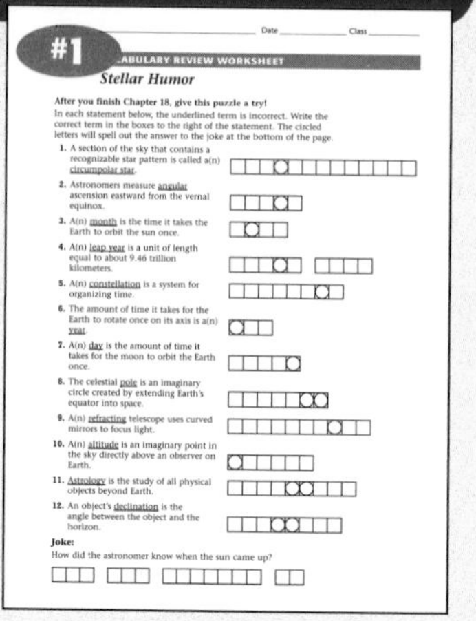

SCIENCE PUZZLERS, TWISTERS & TEASERS

#1

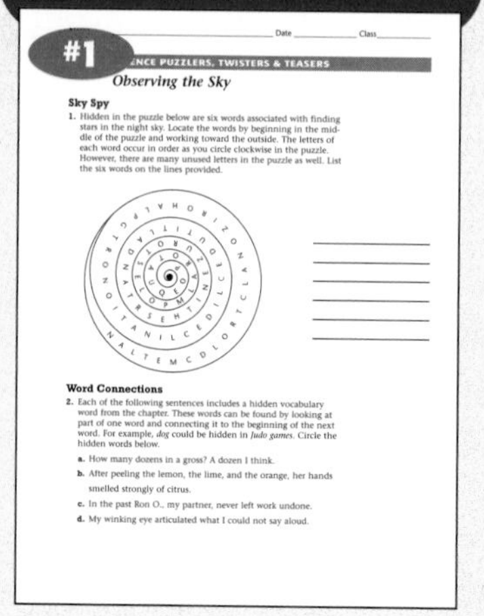

Chapter 1 • Observing the Sky

Review & Assessment

STUDY GUIDE

#1 Vocabulary & Notes Worksheet — *Observing the Sky*

#1 Chapter Review Worksheet — *Observing the Sky*

CHAPTER TESTS WITH PERFORMANCE-BASED ASSESSMENT

#1 *Chapter 1 Test*

#1 *Chapter 1 Performance-Based Assessment* (Making Models)

Lab Worksheets

INQUIRY LABS

#1 Student Worksheet — *Constellation Prize* (Design Your Own)

WHIZ-BANG DEMONSTRATIONS

#1 Teacher-Led Demonstration — *Refraction Action* (Discovery Lab)

LONG-TERM PROJECTS & RESEARCH IDEAS

#1 Student Worksheet — *Celestial Inspiration* (Design Your Own)

DATASHEETS FOR LABBOOK

#1 Create a Calendar

#1 The Sun's Yearly Trip Through the Zodiac

#1 Through the Looking Glass

Applications & Extensions

CRITICAL THINKING & PROBLEM SOLVING

#1 Critical Thinking Worksheet — *Through the Eyes of a Telescope*

SCIENCE TECHNOLOGY

#21 *Science in the News:* Critical Thinking Worksheets — Segment 21 — Taking Earth's Pulse

SCIENTISTS IN ACTION

#24 *Science in the News:* Critical Thinking Worksheets — Segment 24 — Discovering a New Planet

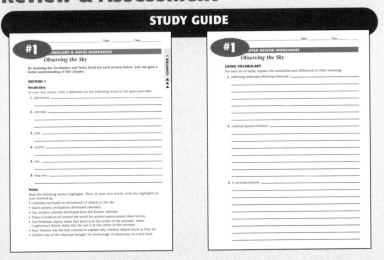

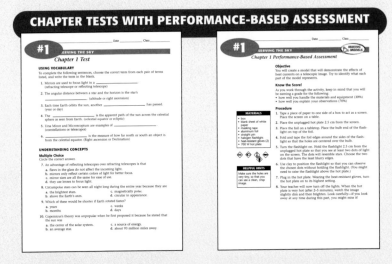

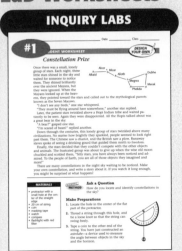

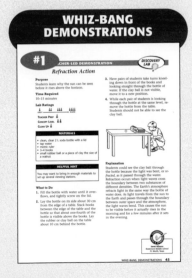

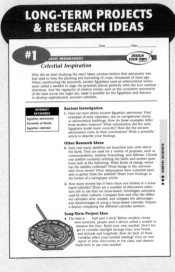

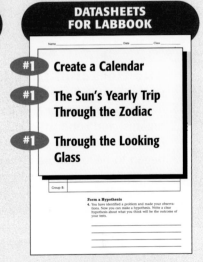

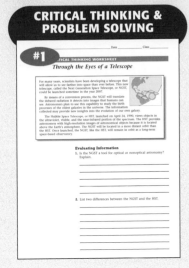

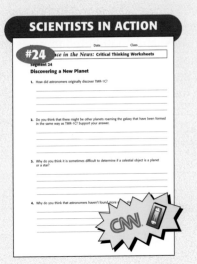

Chapter Background

SECTION 1

Astronomy—The Original Science

▶ **Maya Calendars**

The Maya of Central America used two calendars, a ceremonial calendar of 260 days and an astronomical calendar of 365 days, divided into 18 months of 20 days each. The Maya created an additional 5-day month for religious ceremony. These interlocking calendars enabled the Maya to predict when eclipses would occur and when Venus would rise.

▶ **The Herschel Family**

By the time William Herschel was 36, he seemed destined for a career as a musician. He was a gifted organist and conducted an orchestra in Bath, England. But Herschel had a great interest in stargazing, and he began to devote more of his time to astronomy. Finding the available telescopes to be inadequate, he set up his own forge and mirror-grinding shop to make large-mirror telescopes. His telescopes were of extremely high quality and power, surpassing even those used at the Royal Observatory, at Greenwich, at that time.

- Herschel was joined by his sister Caroline, and soon the two were conducting systematic telescopic surveys of the skies. In addition to discovering Uranus, Herschel developed new observational techniques; made important discoveries concerning nebulae, star clusters, and double stars; and contributed immeasurably to the cataloging of stars. Herschel's son John continued his father's study of double-star systems and cataloged stars in the Southern Hemisphere.

A model of Galileo's telescope

IS THAT A FACT!

- Caroline Herschel made many significant discoveries and is considered to be the first modern female astronomer. She discovered eight comets and three nebulae. In 1828, Britain's Astronomical Society awarded her a gold medal for her collaborations with her brother.

SECTION 2

Mapping the Stars

▶ **Sky Maps**

Some star maps show what the night sky looks like during a particular season in the Northern or Southern Hemisphere. These star maps are circular, and their edges represent the horizon. They are labeled with cardinal directions, and a + represents the zenith. Stars are represented by dots—the larger the dot is, the brighter the star is. To use the map, a stargazer should hold the map overhead and orient it according to the cardinal directions.

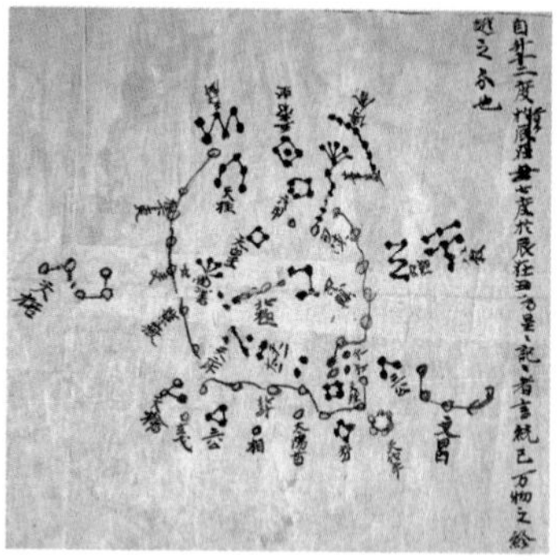

▶ **The Messier Catalog**

The Messier Catalog (1784) is one of the most well-known astronomical catalogs. It was compiled by French astronomer Charles Messier, whom King Louis XV dubbed the "comet ferret." Through the small telescopes available to Messier, comets looked like indistinct blotches. Many of Messier's blurred blotches weren't comets, however, but star clusters, nebulae, and galaxies. After he realized his mistake, Messier began to compile a catalog of these "noncomets" to spare other comet seekers the frustration he experienced.

IS THAT A FACT!

- Messier's catalog of more than 100 star clusters, nebulae, and galaxies is widely used today by amateur astronomers with small telescopes. The catalog numbers are still used by professional astronomers. The objects on his list, such as the Crab nebula and the Pleiades, retain their Messier designations, M1 and M45, respectively.

SECTION 3

Telescopes—Then and Now

▶ Linking Radio Telescopes

To improve image resolution and detect very faint emissions, international teams of astronomers sometimes link telescopes from opposite sides of the world. Recently, scientists have taken this technique a step further with the Very Long Baseline Interferometry (VLBI) Space Observatory Program. In this program, astronomers from around the world link their ground-based radio telescopes with a radio telescope that is orbiting the Earth. Each time the two telescopes link, they function as a single telescope with a width two and one-half times the diameter of the Earth! The VLBI technique has produced images of objects that are billions of light years away.

▶ X-ray Telescopes

X-ray telescopes, such as the one aboard the *Einstein Observatory* satellite (launched in 1978), have discovered double-star systems in which one of the stars has collapsed, becoming a neutron star or a black hole. The *Chandra X-ray Observatory* (launched in 1999) has made more detailed observations than any other X-ray telescope.

▶ Charge Coupled Devices

Modern professional astronomers who use optical telescopes rarely look through their telescopes. Instead, they view images on computer monitors. This is possible because most modern optical telescopes are equipped with a semiconductor device known as a charge coupled device (CCD), which converts the individual light particles (photons) from celestial objects into electrons. The electrons are detected, counted, and rendered as an image on a computer screen.

▶ Gamma-ray Telescopes

Gamma-ray telescopes are designed to detect gamma rays, which behave more like "bullets of energy" than waves. To detect this type of radiation, a gamma-ray telescope is equipped with a particle detector that collects data resulting from the collision of a gamma-ray photon with an atom. The data can be used to determine both the energy of the ray and the direction of the ray's source. The gamma-ray telescope aboard the *Compton Gamma-ray Observatory* satellite (launched in 1991) has detected objects known as gamma-ray bursters—brilliant, brief flashes of tremendous energy that last no more than a few minutes and then disappear.

IS THAT A FACT!

- The Hubble Space Telescope's resolution and sensitivity are so acute that it could detect the light from a firefly 16,000 km away!

For background information about teaching strategies and issues, refer to the *Professional Reference for Teachers.*

CHAPTER 1

Observing the Sky

Pre-Reading Questions

Students may not know the answers to these questions before reading the chapter, so accept any reasonable response.

Suggested Answers

1. Constellations are sections of the sky that contain recognizable star patterns.
2. Some objects in the universe emit invisible radiation. Astronomers use non-optical telescopes, such as X-ray telescopes and radio telescopes, to observe objects they cannot see.

CHAPTER 1

Observing the Sky

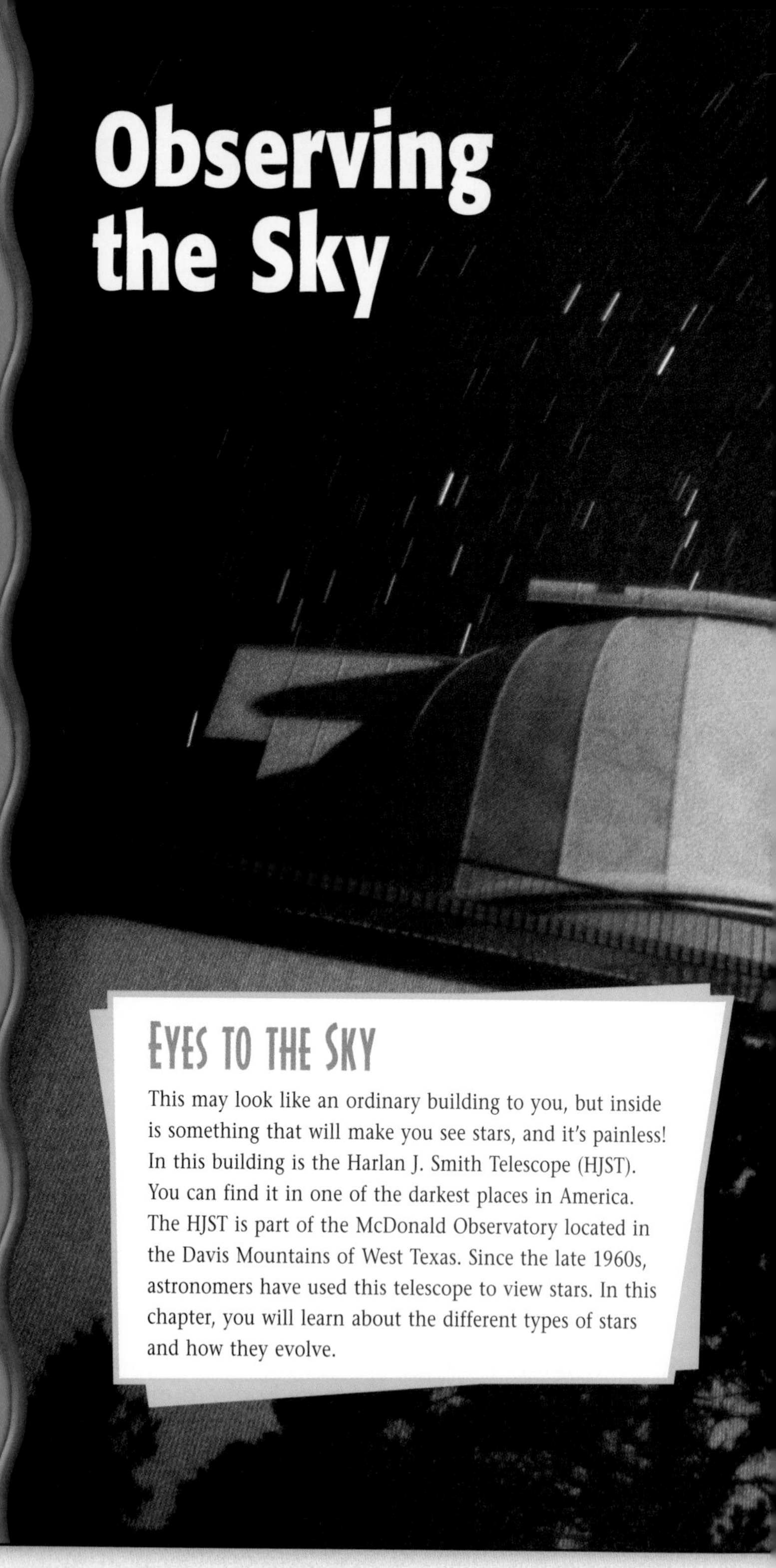

Sections

EYES TO THE SKY

This may look like an ordinary building to you, but inside is something that will make you see stars, and it's painless! In this building is the Harlan J. Smith Telescope (HJST). You can find it in one of the darkest places in America. The HJST is part of the McDonald Observatory located in the Davis Mountains of West Texas. Since the late 1960s, astronomers have used this telescope to view stars. In this chapter, you will learn about the different types of stars and how they evolve.

Pre-Reading Questions

1. What are constellations?
2. How do astronomers observe objects they cannot see?

internetconnect

HRW On-line Resources

go.hrw.com

For worksheets and other teaching aids, visit the HRW Web site and type in the keyword: **HSTOBS**

*sci*LINKS NSTA

www.scilinks.com

Use the *sci*LINKS numbers at the end of each chapter for additional resources on the **NSTA** Web site.

Smithsonian Institution

www.si.edu/hrw

Visit the Smithsonian Institution Web site for related on-line resources.

CNNfyi.com

www.cnnfyi.com

Visit the CNN Web site for current events coverage and classroom resources.

START-UP Activity

INDOOR STARGAZING

In this activity, you will measure an object's altitude using a simple instrument called an astrolabe (AS troh LAYB).

Procedure

1. Attach one end of a 12 cm long **piece of string** to the center of the straight edge of a **protractor** with tape. Attach a **paper clip** to the other end of the string.
2. Tape a **soda straw** lengthwise along the straight edge of the protractor. Your astrolabe is complete!
3. Hold the astrolabe in front of your face so you can look along the straw with one eye. The curve of the astrolabe should be pointed toward the floor.
4. Looking along the straw, use your astrolabe to sight one corner of the ceiling.
5. Pinch the string between your thumb and the protractor. Count the number of degrees between the string and the 90° marker on the protractor. This angle is the altitude of the corner. Record this measurement in your ScienceLog.

Analysis

6. How does this activity relate to observing objects in the sky? Explain how you would find the altitude of a star.

TRY at HOME

3

START-UP Activity

INDOOR STARGAZING

MATERIALS
For Each Group:
• piece of string (12 cm long)
• protractor
• tape
• paper clip
• soda straw

Teacher's Notes

Have students take more measurements of the corner of the room from different locations. Why did their measurements differ? (The altitude depends on the location of the observer.)

The angle between the string and the 90° marker should fall between 20° and 50°.

Answer to START-UP Activity

6. Answers will vary. Students should note that the astrolabe is an instrument that can also be used to locate objects in the sky, such as stars. Students should also note that it is possible to measure the angle between the horizon and an object in the sky. Students could use the astrolabe they made to measure the altitude of a star.

SECTION 1

Focus

Astronomy—The Original Science

In this section, students will learn that the units of a calendar are based on the movements of the sun and moon. Students will learn how different cultures based their calendars on different interpretations of astronomical observations. The section then follows the historical development of the calendar we use today. Students will explore the changing science of astronomy from 7,000 years ago through the European Renaissance and up to present times.

Bellringer

Have students suppose that they need to explain the concepts of a *year,* a *month,* and a *day* to a small child. For each concept, have students illustrate the motion of the Earth, moon, and sun. Students should write a caption describing each illustration. Sheltered English

1) Motivate

ACTIVITY

Many ancient astronomers attempted to predict and explain eclipses. Even though the ancient Greeks explained how they occur, eclipses were still considered bad portents until the nineteenth century. To help students understand how our relatively small moon can eclipse the sun, have them form small groups and give them a marble and a basketball. The basketball represents the sun and the marble represents the moon. Challenge them to simulate a solar eclipse using the two spheres.

SECTION 1 READING WARM-UP

Terms to Learn

astronomy	month
calendar	day
year	leap year

What You'll Do

- Identify the units of a calendar.
- Evaluate calendars from different ancient civilizations.
- Explain how our modern calendar developed.
- Summarize how astronomy began in ancient cultures and developed into a modern science.

Astronomy—The Original Science

Astronomy is the study of all physical objects beyond Earth. Before astronomy became a science, people in ancient cultures used the seasonal cycles of celestial objects to make calendars and organize their lives. Over time, some people began to observe the sky for less practical reasons—mainly to understand Earth's place in the universe. Today, astronomers all over the world are using new technologies to better understand the universe.

The Stars and Keeping Time

Most ancient cultures probably did not fully understand how celestial objects in our solar system move in relation to each other. However, they did learn the seasonal movements of these objects as they appeared in the Earth's sky and based their calendars on these cycles. People in ancient cultures gradually learned to depend on calendars to keep track of time. For example, by observing the yearly cycle of the sun's movement among the stars, early farmers learned the best times of year to plant and harvest various foods.

After learning the seasonal cycles of celestial objects many civilizations made calendars. One such calendar is shown in **Figure 1.** A **calendar** is a system for organizing time. Most calendars organize time within a single unit called a year. A **year** is the time required for the Earth to orbit the sun once. Within a year are smaller units of time called months. A **month** is roughly the amount of time required for the moon to orbit the Earth once. Within a month are even smaller units of time called days. A **day** is the time required for the Earth to rotate once on its axis.

Ancient Calendars Ancient cultures based their calendars on different observations of the sky. Examine **Figure 2** at the top of the next page to see how different cultures around the world used objects in the sky differently to keep track of time.

Figure 1 *This stone is a calendar used by the Aztecs in pre-colonial America.*

4

CROSS-DISCIPLINARY FOCUS

Social Studies Although many societies base their calendars on the movements of the sun or the moon, a calendar's starting date is often linked to cultural or religious traditions. For example, both the Muslim and the Hebrew calendars are based on the phases of the moon, but they differ in a number of significant ways. Have interested students research a calendar used by another culture and find out the cultural significance of that calendar's starting date, the number of days per month, and the number of days per year. Have students give a class presentation about the calendar they studied.

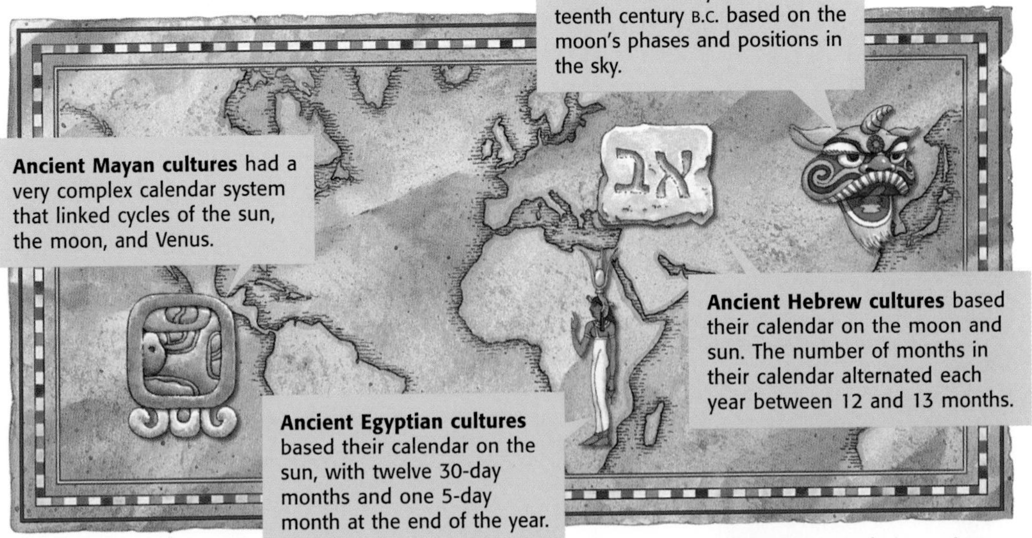
Ancient Chinese cultures made calendars as early as the fourteenth century B.C. based on the moon's phases and positions in the sky.
Ancient Mayan cultures had a very complex calendar system that linked cycles of the sun, the moon, and Venus.
Ancient Hebrew cultures based their calendar on the moon and sun. The number of months in their calendar alternated each year between 12 and 13 months.
Ancient Egyptian cultures based their calendar on the sun, with twelve 30-day months and one 5-day month at the end of the year.

Figure 2 *People in ancient cultures based their calendars on different kinds of celestial cycles.*

Toward a Modern Calendar The early Roman calendar had exactly 365 days in a year and 7 days in a week. The calendar worked well at first, but gradually the seasons shifted away from their original positions in the year.

It was then determined that there are actually about 365.25 days in a year. To correct this, Julius Caesar created the *Julian calendar.* He began by adding 90 days to the year 46 B.C., which put the seasons back to their original positions. He then added an extra day every 4 years to keep them from shifting again. A year in which an extra day is added to the calendar is called a **leap year.**

In the mid-1500s, people noticed that the Julian calendar was incorrect. Pope Gregory XIII presented this problem to a group of astronomers who determined that there are actually 365.242 days in a year. To solve the problem, a new calendar—the *Gregorian calendar*—was created. The Pope dropped 10 days from the year 1582 and restricted leap years to years that are divisible by 4 but not by 100 (except for years that are divisible by 400). This lowered the number of leap years that occur and made the average length of 1 year closer to 365.242 days. Today most countries use the Gregorian calendar, which scientists calculate will be accurate for another 3,000 years.

5

2 Teach

Multicultural CONNECTION

The lunar calendar of the Natchez peoples of the Mississippi River Valley reflected the seasonal rhythms of their culture. The names of the months in their calendar—strawberry month, peach month, maize month, turkey month, and chestnut month—reflect the hunter-gatherer nature of their society. Ask students if they can identify the time period that corresponds to each Natchez month.
Sheltered English

RESEARCH

The ancient Egyptians developed a calendar to help them predict when the Nile River would flood and when they could plant crops. The Egyptians structured their calendar around Sirius, the brightest star in the night sky. Based on the rising of Sirius at dawn, the Egyptians calculated that the year is 365 days long. Have interested students research stories about Sirius from Egyptian mythology and find out more about Egyptian astronomy.

Directed Reading Worksheet Section 1

IS THAT A FACT!

Even though the Gregorian calendar was adopted by many countries in 1582, England and its American colonies continued to recognize March 25 as the first day of the year until 1752. In other words, March 24, 1700, was followed by March 25, 1701!

2 Teach, continued

Meeting Individual Needs

Advanced Learners There are many theories about why Stonehenge was built. One theory proposes that the great circle of standing stones served as a calendar; another theory argues that it was an observatory for charting the movements of the sun and stars. Perhaps it served both purposes. Invite students to investigate some of the theories about the astronomical significance of Stonehenge. Suggest that students include a diagram in their report that shows how archaeologists think Stonehenge originally looked and how the sun's movement could be tracked by this structure.

Homework

PORTFOLIO

Making Models Ask students to research one of the ancient astronomical sites mentioned in this section and build a scale model of it. Additional sites of interest include the Big Horn Medicine Wheel in Wyoming, the Pyramid of Khufu in Giza, Egypt, or the Anasazi Sun Dagger in Chaco Canyon, New Mexico. Have students share their model with the class and explain the significance of the site. Students may wish to use a flashlight to demonstrate how the structures marked the path of the sun and moon. As an extension, students could create their own sundial or design their own structure to track the movements of the sun.

Figure 3 *Some stones are still standing at the site near Nabta, in the Sahara Desert.*

Early Observers—The Beginnings of Astronomy

Scientists have found evidence for ancient astronomical activities all over the world. Some records are more complete than others. However, they all show that early humans recognized the cycles of celestial objects in the sky.

Nabta The earliest record of astronomical observations is a 6,000 to 7,000-year-old group of stones near Nabta, in southern Egypt. Some of the stones are positioned such that they would have lined up with the sun during the summer solstice 6,000 years ago. The *summer solstice* occurs on the longest day of the year. Artifacts found at the site near Nabta suggest that it was created by African cattle herders. These people probably used the site for many purposes, including trade, social bonding, and ritual. **Figure 3** shows some of the stones at the site near Nabta.

Stonehenge Another ancient site that was probably used to make observations of the sky is Stonehenge, near Salisbury, England. Stonehenge, shown in **Figure 4,** is a group of stones arranged primarily in circles. Some of the stones are aligned with the sunrise during the summer and winter solstices. People have offered many explanations for the purpose of Stonehenge as well as for who built and used it. Careful studies of the site reveal that it was built over a period of about 1,500 years, from about 3000 B.C. to about 1500 B.C. Most likely, Stonehenge was used as a place for ceremony and ritual. But the complete truth about Stonehenge is still a mystery.

Figure 4 *Although its creators have long since gone, Stonehenge continues to indicate the summer and winter solstices each year.*

The Babylonians The ancient civilization of Babylon was the heart of a major empire located in present-day Iraq. From about 700 B.C. to about A.D. 50, the Babylonians precisely tracked the positions of planets and the moon. They became skilled at forecasting the movements of these celestial bodies, which enabled them to make an accurate calendar.

6

Multicultural Connection

One Chinese myth about solar eclipses describes hungry dragons that periodically raid the sky and take bites out of the sun! During solar eclipses, Chinese warriors would beat drums and gongs and shoot arrows into the sky to kill the dragons. The job of Chinese astronomers was to predict when the dragons would become hungry so that warriors could be prepared to save the sun from being completely devoured. Encourage student groups to find out about the mythology of solar eclipses in other cultures. Students may wish to perform these myths as skits for the class.

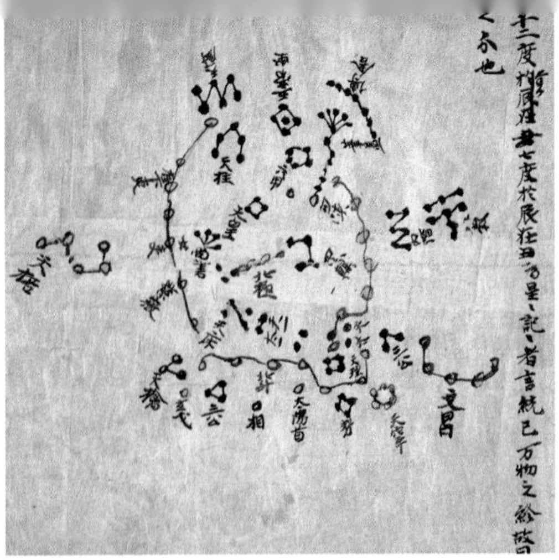

Figure 5 *This ancient Chinese manuscript is the world's oldest existing portable star map. It is more than 1,000 years old.*

Ancient Chinese Cultures As early as 1000 B.C., ancient Chinese cultures could predict eclipses. *Eclipses* occur when the sun, the moon, and the Earth line up in space. The Chinese had also named 800 stars by 350 B.C. The Chinese skillfully tracked and predicted the same motions in the sky as the civilizations that influenced Western astronomy. The Chinese continued to improve their knowledge of the sky at the same time as many other civilizations, as shown in **Figure 5.**

The Ancient Greeks Like many other civilizations, the ancient Greeks learned to observe the sky to keep track of time. But the Greeks also took a giant leap forward in making astronomy a science. Greek philosophers tried to understand the place of Earth and humans in the universe. Their tools were logic and mathematics, especially geometry. One of the most famous Greek philosophers, Aristotle (ER is TAHT'L), successfully explained the phases of the moon and eclipses. He also correctly argued that the Earth is a sphere—an idea that was not very popular in his time.

Native Americans Archaeological records show that many of the pre-colonial civilizations in the Americas were skilled in observing the sky. Perhaps the most highly-skilled observers were the Maya, who flourished in the present-day Yucatan about 1,000 years ago. The Maya had complex systems of mathematics and astronomy. Many Mayan buildings, such as the one in **Figure 6,** are aligned with celestial bodies during certain astronomical events.

The Ancient Arabs After Greek, Roman, and early Christian civilizations weakened, the ancient Arabs inherited much of the Greeks' knowledge of astronomy. The Arabs continued to develop astronomy as a science while Europe fell into the Dark Ages. Today many stars have Arabic names. The Arabs also invented the astrolabe, algebra, and the number system that we use today.

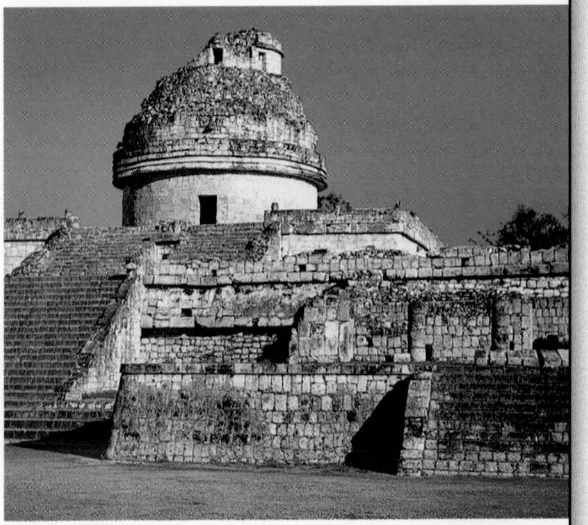

Figure 6 *This Mayan building is the Caracol at Chichén Itzá, in the Yucatán. Many parts of the building align with Venus and the sun on certain days.*

Multicultural CONNECTION

Modern astronomy had its beginnings in Arabic and Greek culture. Have students research the following star names and describe their origin:

Betelgeuse, Alnitak, Rigel, Aldebaran, Castor, and Pollux

Ask them to find out the origin and meaning of each star's name and the name's significance. Encourage students to record any other interesting information they find about the stars. (The name *Betelgeuse* is Arabic and means "the armpit of the giant." It refers to the fact that the star marks the general area of the constellation Orion's shoulder. *Alnitak* is Arabic for "belt" and is one of the stars in Orion's belt. *Rigel* is derived from the Arabic words for "left leg of the giant" and marks Orion's left leg or foot. *Aldebaran* means "follower" in Arabic. It appears to follow the star cluster Pleiades across the sky. The names *Castor* and *Pollux* come from Greek mythology; these twin stars form the heads of the twins in the constellation Gemini.)

internetconnect

SCILINKS. NSTA

TOPIC: Early Theories in Astronomy
GO TO: www.scilinks.org
***sci*LINKS NUMBER:** HSTE435

SCIENCE HUMOR

Q: Why doesn't the sun have long hair?

A: Eclipse it regularly.

2 Teach, *continued*

DISCUSSION

The Scientific Mind Johannes Kepler spent much of his life seeking an explanation for the orbits of the planets. A humble man, he often wrote about himself in the third person and was highly self-critical. He once wrote that "that man [Kepler] has in every way a doglike nature. In this man there are two opposite tendencies: always to regret any wasted time and always to waste it willingly." In his writings, Kepler also revealed his inquisitive nature: "He was constantly on the move, ferreting among the sciences, politics, and private affairs . . . he explored various fields of mathematics, as if he were the first man to do so, which later on he found to have already been discovered. He argued with men of every profession for the profit of his mind." Discuss with students what the quotations reveal about Kepler's personality and way of thinking. Have students consider how Kepler's persistence, self-criticism, and open-mindedness may have contributed to his discovery of the laws of planetary motion.

Homework

Research Have students find out why many people were reluctant to accept Copernicus's theory about a sun-centered universe. Have them summarize their findings in a one-page report.

The Who's Who of Early Astronomy

The science of astronomy has come a long way since the early days. The earliest astronomers had no history to learn from—almost everything they knew about the universe came from what they could discover with their own eyes and minds. Not surprisingly, most early astronomers thought that the universe consisted of the sun, moon, and planets, with all the stars occupying the edge of the universe. While they could not have known that our solar system is a very small part of a much larger universe, they had to start somewhere.

Figure 7 *According to the Ptolemaic theory, the Earth is at the center of the universe.*

Ptolemy In A.D. 140, a Greek astronomer named Claudius Ptolemy (KLAW dee uhs TAHL uh mee) wrote a book that combined all the ancient knowledge of astronomy that he could find. Ptolemy expanded Aristotle's theories with careful mathematical calculations in what was called the *Ptolemaic theory.* As shown in **Figure 7,** Ptolemy thought that the Earth is at the center of the universe—with the sun and the other planets revolving around the Earth.

Even though it was incorrect, the Ptolemaic theory predicted the motions of the planets better than any known method at that time. For more than 1,500 years in Europe, the Ptolemaic theory was the most popular theory for the structure of the universe.

Copernicus In 1543, a Polish astronomer named Nicolaus Copernicus (NIK uh LAY uhs koh PUHR ni kuhs) published a new theory that would eventually revolutionize astronomy. According to his theory, which is shown in **Figure 8,** the sun is at the center of the universe and the planets—including the Earth—orbit the sun. While Copernicus was correct about all the planets orbiting the sun, his theory did not immediately replace Ptolemy's theory.

Figure 8 *According to Copernicus's theory, the sun is at the center of the universe.*

8

SCIENCE HUMOR

Q: What did Copernicus say about Ptolemy's theory of an Earth-centered universe?

A: Ptolemy another one!

Tycho Brahe Danish astronomer Tycho Brahe (TIE koh BRAW uh) used several large tools, such as the one shown in **Figure 9,** to observe the sky. Tycho favored an Earth-centered theory that was different from Ptolemy's. Tycho believed that the other planets revolve around the sun but that the sun and the moon revolve around the Earth. While Tycho's theory was not correct, he did record very precise observations of the planets and stars for several years.

Johannes Kepler After Tycho died, his assistant, Johannes Kepler, continued Tycho's work. Kepler did not agree with Tycho's theory, but he recognized how precise and valuable Tycho's data were. In 1609, after analyzing the data, Kepler announced some new laws of planetary motion. Kepler stated that all the planets revolve around the sun in elliptical orbits and that the sun is not in the exact center of the orbits.

Figure 9 *Tycho used the mural quadrant, which is a large quarter-circle on a wall, to measure the positions of stars and planets.*

Galileo Galilei In 1609, Galileo became the first person to use a telescope to observe celestial bodies. His telescope is shown in **Figure 10.** Galileo discovered four moons orbiting Jupiter, craters and mountains on the moon, sunspots on the sun, and phases of Venus. These discoveries showed that the planets are not just dots of light—they are physical bodies like the Earth. Galileo favored Copernicus's theory over Ptolemy's.

Figure 10 *Galileo's telescope is much simpler than those used by astronomers today.*

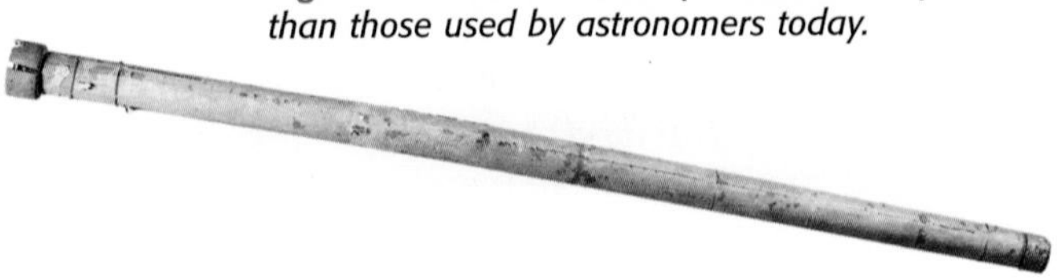

Isaac Newton Finally, in 1687 a scientist named Sir Isaac Newton explained *why* planets orbit the sun and why moons orbit planets. Newton explained that the force that keeps all of these objects in their orbit is the same one that holds us on the Earth—gravity. Newton's laws of motion and gravitation completed the work of Copernicus, Tycho, Kepler, and Galileo.

Self-Check

Name two astronomers who favored an Earth-centered universe and two astronomers who favored a sun-centered universe. *(See page 200 to check your answer.)*

3 Extend

DEBATE

The Structure of the Universe
Have teams role-play a debate between Ptolemy, Copernicus, Brahe, Kepler, and Newton. Suggest that students prepare for the debate by researching how each scientist formed his theories. For example, Copernicus used mathematics to analyze the observations made by earlier astronomers—he made few personal observations. Ptolemy, on the other hand, was a keen observer, but he could only reconcile his theory with his observations by developing a complex, but inaccurate system to explain the apparent motion of the planets. Encourage students to research the lives of these scientists and base their positions on the scientists' ideas. When students are role-playing, remind them that each scientist based his theories on his own observations and the theories of scientists who came before him.

REAL-WORLD CONNECTION

Galileo was the first person to use a telescope to make observations of celestial bodies. The power of the telescope Galileo used to discover Jupiter's moons was equivalent to that of most modern binoculars. Have students determine when Jupiter is visible from where they live and use a sky chart to locate it in the night sky. If Jupiter is not visible, encourage students to observe Saturn with binoculars and try to find its rings. Sheltered English

SCIENTISTS AT ODDS

Tycho Brahe was eccentric and contrary. As a young man, he insulted a fellow student and was challenged to a duel. During the duel, part of his nose was sliced off, and for the rest of his life he wore a metal nose prosthesis. Brahe was also a notoriously bad landlord who cheated and abused the peasants who worked for him. Given his bad temperament, it's not surprising that Brahe withheld vital information from his assistant Johannes Kepler. Kepler gained full access to Brahe's observations after Brahe's death and used them to prove that the planets revolve in elliptical orbits around the sun.

Answer to Self-Check

Ptolemy and Tycho Brahe thought the universe was Earth-centered. Copernicus and Galileo thought the universe was sun-centered.

4 Close

Quiz

1. What are most calendars based on? (They are based on the movements of the sun and the moon.)
2. What was Copernicus's theory about the structure of the universe? (He argued that the sun is at the center of the universe, and all the planets revolve around the sun.)
3. How did Newton's theories explain why planets orbit the sun and why moons orbit planets? (He explained that the force of gravity keeps the planets and moons in orbit.)

ALTERNATIVE ASSESSMENT

PORTFOLIO Have students make an illustrated timeline that describes three events important to the development of the modern calendar and that locates at least three ancient civilizations that contributed to the development of astronomy as a science. Students should also detail the evolution of modern astronomy to the present. Encourage students to use reference materials to create additional timeline entries about the history of astronomy. Students may even wish to speculate about the future of space observation and exploration. Sheltered English

Modern Astronomy

With Galileo's successful use of the telescope and Newton's discoveries about planetary motion, astronomy began to become the modern science that it is today. Gradually, people began to think of stars as more than dots of light at the edge of the universe.

From Fuzzy Patches to an Expanding Universe William Herschel, who discovered Uranus in 1781, used a telescope to study the stars in our galaxy. As he studied these stars, he found small, fuzzy patches in the sky. Herschel did not know what these patches were, but he did record their positions in a catalog.

The invention of photography in the 1800s allowed astronomers to make even better observations of the sky. In 1923, Edwin Hubble used photography to discover that some of the patches Herschel had found are actually other galaxies beyond our own. Before this discovery, scientists thought that the Milky Way galaxy was the entire universe! Hubble also discovered that the universe is expanding. In other words, distant objects in space are moving farther and farther away from each other.

Figure 11 *Today computers and telescopes are linked together. Computers not only control telescopes, but they also process the information gathered by the telescopes so that astronomers may better analyze it.*

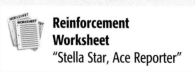

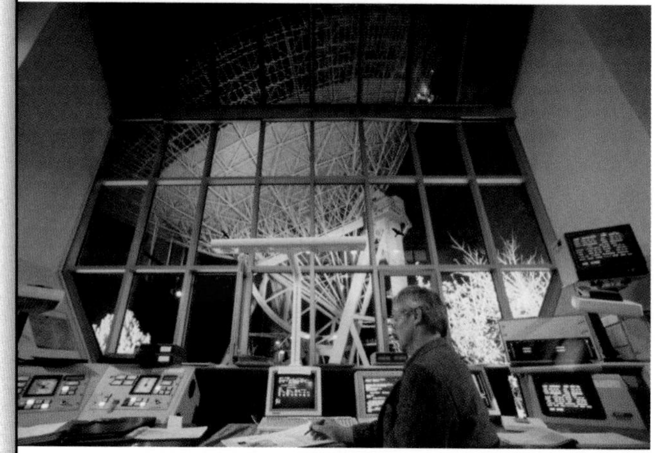

Larger and Better Telescopes Today astronomers still gaze at the sky, trying to assign order to the universe. Larger and better telescopes on Earth and in space, supercomputers, spacecraft, and new models of the universe allow us to study objects both near and far. Many questions about the universe have been answered, but our studies continue to bring new questions to investigate.

internetconnect

SCILINKS NSTA

TOPIC: The Stars and Keeping Time, Early Theories in Astronomy
GO TO: www.scilinks.org
***sci*LINKS NUMBER:** HSTE430, HSTE435

SECTION REVIEW

1. Which ancient civilization's calendar gave rise to our modern calendar?
2. What advantage did Galileo have over the astronomers that went before him, and how did it help him?
3. **Analyzing Relationships** Is Copernicus's theory completely correct? Why or why not? How does his theory relate to what we know today about the sun's position in our solar system and in the universe?

10

Answers to Section Review

1. The calendar we use today is based on the early Roman calendar, which had 365 days in a year and 7 days in a week.
2. Galileo used a telescope to study the night sky. The telescope enabled him to discover that planets and moons are physical bodies.
3. Copernicus's theory is not completely correct. We now know that the sun is the center of our solar system, but it is not the center of the universe. In Copernicus's time, people did not realize that the solar system is a small part of our galaxy.

internetconnect

SCILINKS NSTA

TOPIC: The Stars and Keeping Time
GO TO: www.scilinks.org
***sci*LINKS NUMBER:** HSTE430

Reinforcement Worksheet
"Stella Star, Ace Reporter"

SECTION 2

READING WARM-UP

Mapping the Stars

Terms to Learn

constellation
altitude
right ascension
declination
celestial equator
ecliptic
light-year

What You'll Do

- Describe constellations and explain how astronomers use them.
- Explain how to measure altitude.
- Explain right ascension and declination.
- Evaluate the scale of the universe.

Ancient cultures organized the sky by linking stars together in patterns. These patterns reflected the culture's beliefs and legends. Different civilizations often gave the stars names that indicated the stars' positions in their pattern. Today we can see the same star patterns that people in ancient cultures saw. Modern astronomers still use many of the names given to stars centuries ago.

Astronomers can now describe a star's location with precise numbers. These advances have led to a better understanding of just how far away stars are and how big the universe is.

Constellations

When people in ancient cultures linked stars in a section of the sky into a pattern, they named that section of the sky according to the pattern. **Constellations** are sections of the sky that contain recognizable star patterns. Many cultures organized the sky into constellations that honored their gods or reflected objects in their daily lives. Constellations helped people organize the sky and track the apparent motions of planets and stars.

In the Eye of the Beholder . . . Different civilizations had different names for the same constellations. For example, where the Greeks saw a hunter (Orion) in the northern sky, the Japanese saw a drum (*tsuzumi*), as shown in **Figure 12.** Today different cultures still interpret the sky differently.

Figure 12 *The drawing at left shows that the ancient Greeks saw Orion as a hunter. The drawing at right shows that the Japanese saw the same set of stars as a drum.*

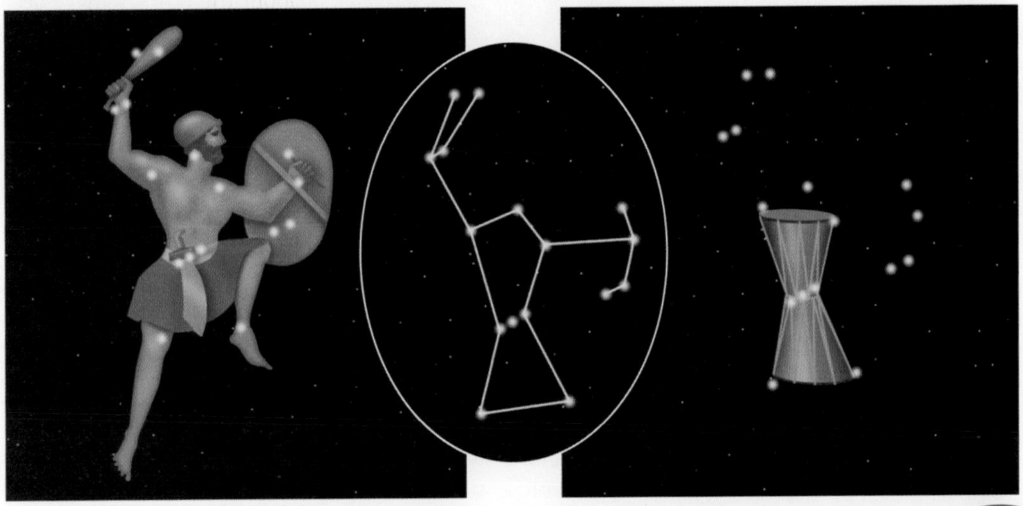

11

SECTION 2

Focus

Mapping the Stars

This section discusses constellations and their significance to ancient and modern astronomers. Students will learn how to use a sky map to find stars in the night sky. They will also learn how the rotation and revolution of the Earth determine which stars are visible at any given time. The section explores how astronomers use right ascension and declination to map the stars and describe their location. The section concludes with a discussion of the size and scale of the universe.

Bellringer

Ask students if it is possible to determine the direction of the North Pole by looking at the stars. Have students explain their answers in their ScienceLog.

1 Motivate

DISCUSSION

Ask students to think of other possible names for the constellation in **Figure 12.** Discuss why people such as farmers, poets, and astronomers have been inspired to name and identify constellations. As an extension, ask students to observe the night sky at home and name their own constellations. Students can share sketches of these constellations in class.

Directed Reading Worksheet Section 2

IS THAT A FACT!

The International Astronomical Union has standardized the boundaries of the 88 constellations so that the total area of the celestial sphere can be classified according to the constellations. Thus, the constellations fit together like a jigsaw puzzle that surrounds the Earth.

CROSS-DISCIPLINARY FOCUS

Language Arts Many of the names of constellations are derived from Greek and Roman mythology. Have student groups research the mythology of Cepheus, Cassiopeia, Perseus, Pegasus, Hercules, or the Hydra. Groups can write a skit to retell the myth for the class. Then have groups use a star chart to locate their constellation.

2 Teach

Answer to Self-Check

No, the object is within the boundaries of the constellation.

Group Activity

Classroom Planetarium

Divide the class into groups of four. Assign each group a different season, and have the groups locate a sky map for that time of year. Have students copy the map with tracing paper, marking the stars that form constellations and any other celestial objects. Then have groups place a sheet of aluminum foil over a piece of cardboard and tape the tracing paper on top. Have students use a pencil to carefully poke small holes through the tracing paper and aluminum. Students can create larger holes to show planets and other bright objects. After students remove the tracing paper, have them locate the constellations and prepare a guided tour of the night sky in their season. To begin the tour, place the aluminum-foil transparencies on an overhead projector in a darkened room. Be sure to cover the top of the projector completely. As groups give their tours, they can highlight individual constellations by using a piece of colored cellophane.

Safety Caution: Be sure to periodically check the projector for overheating.

Answer to QuickLab

4. The directions are reversed because sky maps are made to be looked at upside down.

Teaching Transparency 180
"Spring Constellations in the Northern Hemisphere"

Self-Check

If a celestial object is said to be "in the constellation of Ursa Minor," does it have to be a part of the stick figure that makes up that constellation? Explain. *(See page 200 to check your answer.)*

Regions of the Sky When you think of constellations, you probably think of the stick figures made by connecting bright stars with imaginary lines. To an astronomer, however, a constellation is something more. As you can see in **Figure 13** below, a constellation is an entire region of the sky. Each constellation shares a border with its neighboring constellations. For example, in the same way that the state of Texas is a region of the United States, Ursa Major is a region of the sky. Every star or galaxy in the sky is located within a constellation. Modern astronomers divide the sky into 88 constellations. Around the world, astronomers use the same names for these constellations to make communication easier.

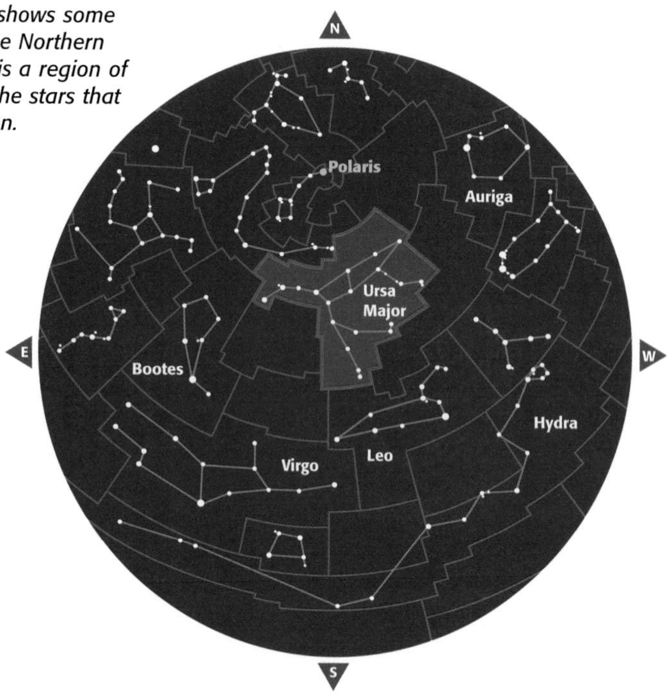

Figure 13 *This sky map shows some of the constellations in the Northern Hemisphere. Ursa Major is a region of the sky that includes all the stars that make up that constellation.*

QuickLab

Using a Sky Map

1. Hold your **textbook** over your head with the cover facing upward. Turn the book so that the direction at the bottom of the sky map is the same as the direction you are facing.
2. Notice the location of the constellations in relation to one another.
3. If you look up at the **sky** at night in the spring, you should see the stars positioned as they are on your map.
4. Why are *E* and *W* on sky maps the reverse of how they appear on land maps?

Seasonal Changes As we go around the sun each year, the constellations change from season to season. This is one reason that people in ancient cultures were able to keep track of the right time of year to plant and harvest their crops. Notice that the sky map in Figure 13 shows the night sky as seen from the Northern Hemisphere in the spring. This map would not be accurate for the other three seasons. Sky maps for summer, fall, and winter are in the Appendix of this book.

12

MISCONCEPTION ALERT

Students may think that the constellations have always looked the same from Earth. Point out that our solar system and the stars in our galaxy are moving at different speeds as they revolve around the Milky Way. In addition, because the stars are at varying distances from the Earth, they appear to move in the sky at different speeds, a phenomenon known as parallax. Thus, a hundred thousand years ago, the constellations looked much different than they do today.

Finding Stars in the Night Sky

You can use what you learned in the Investigate to make your own observations of the sky. Have you ever tried to show another person a star or planet by pointing to it—only to have them miss what you were seeing? With just a few new references, as shown in **Figure 14,** you can tell them exactly where it is.

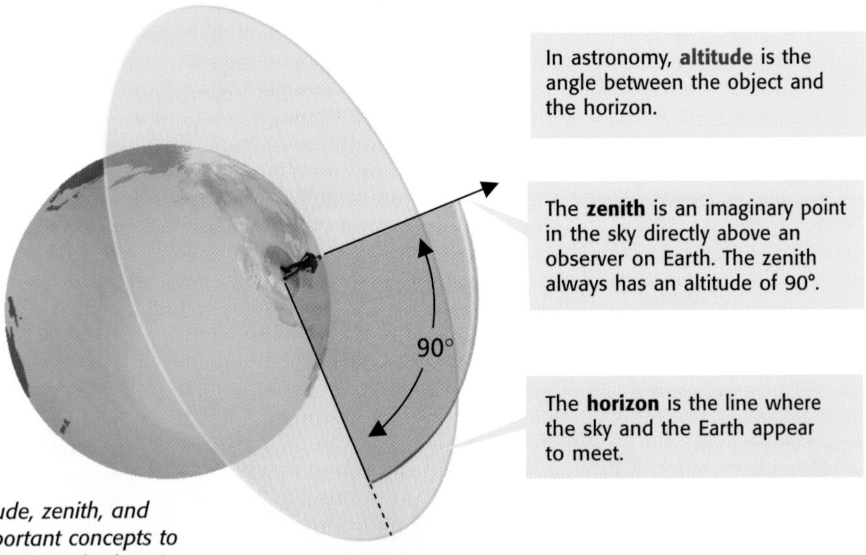

In astronomy, **altitude** is the angle between the object and the horizon.
The **zenith** is an imaginary point in the sky directly above an observer on Earth. The zenith always has an altitude of 90°.
90°
The **horizon** is the line where the sky and the Earth appear to meet.

Figure 14 *Altitude, zenith, and horizon are important concepts to know when describing the locations of celestial objects.*

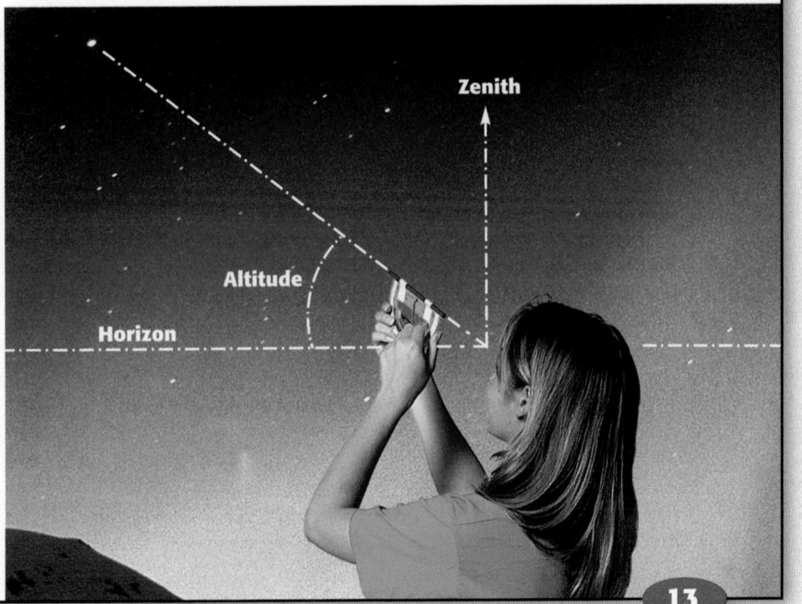

Figure 15 *With an astrolabe, you can measure the altitude of a star by measuring the angle between your horizon and the star. The altitude of any celestial object depends on where you are and when you look.*

ACTIVITY

Tell students that a watch with an hour hand can be used to tell direction during the daytime. Have students hold a watch horizontally with the hour hand pointing directly at the sun. If they halve the distance between the hour hand and the 12 with a toothpick, the toothpick will be pointing south. Ask students how they would adapt this method to work in the Southern hemisphere.

REAL-WORLD CONNECTION

Amateur astronomers can measure the sky with their hands. If you hold your arm extended and make a fist that begins at the horizon, you can gauge roughly 10°. If you open your hand and line up your little finger with the horizon, you have marked off 20°. Of course, the hands of middle-school students may be smaller. Sheltered English

MISCONCEPTION ALERT

Students may be confused by the term *altitude* when used in astronomy. Point out that altitude does not denote height or elevation, but rather the angle between an object, the horizon, and the observer. As the Earth rotates, the altitude of the stars changes. The altitude of an object is also affected by the location of the observer.

Multicultural CONNECTION

The astrolabe that students built at the beginning of this chapter is perhaps the first scientific instrument ever made. It was invented by the ancient Greeks to record the altitude of certain stars and constellations. Arabian astronomers adapted the instrument and made detailed tables of star positions for use in navigation. The exact position of the observer can be calculated by measuring the altitude and azimuth of a star and comparing those measurements to the star tables. Islamic astronomers and mathematicians worked together to create detailed reference tables for navigators and scientists.

Teaching Transparency 181
"Finding Stars in the Night Sky"

internetconnect

sciLINKS NSTA
TOPIC: Constellations
GO TO: www.scilinks.org
***sci*LINKS NUMBER:** HSTE440

2 Teach, *continued*

MISCONCEPTION ALERT

It is a common misconception that each star in a constellation is the same distance from Earth. In fact, most of the stars in a constellation are not near each other in space. They appear to be near each other because of our perspective from Earth. If Earth were in a different location, we would see the same stars in different patterns or we might see different stars altogether.

Homework

Locating Polaris The Big Dipper is an easily recognizable group of stars that can be seen from the mid-northern latitudes all year. If students are unfamiliar with the Big Dipper, draw it on the board or show them a picture of it. Ask students to use a star chart to locate the Big Dipper on a clear night. After students have located the Big Dipper, they can easily find Polaris (the North Star). The two stars that make up the front of the dipper bowl point directly toward Polaris. To find Polaris, students should estimate the distance between the two stars that make up the front of the bowl. Students can pinpoint the North Star by extending an imaginary line that is five times the length of that distance.

Teaching Transparency 182 "Ascension and Declination Lines"

Describing a Star's Position

Finding a star's altitude is one thing, but describing its position in a way that doesn't depend on where you are is another. To do this, astronomers have invented a reference system known as the *celestial sphere.* The celestial sphere surrounds the Earth and is what we look through when we observe the sky. Similar to the way we use latitude and longitude to plot positions on Earth, astronomers use right ascension (RA) and declination (dec) to plot positions in the sky. **Right ascension** is a measure of how far east an object is from the point at which the sun appears on the first day of spring. This point is called the *vernal equinox.* **Declination** is a measure of how far north or south an object is from the celestial equator.

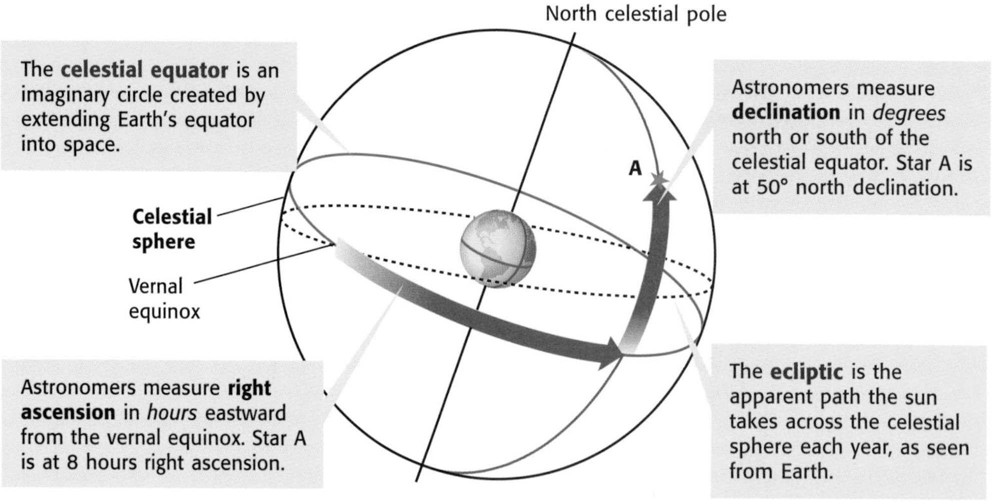

North celestial pole
The celestial equator is an imaginary circle created by extending Earth's equator into space.
Celestial sphere
Vernal equinox
A
Astronomers measure declination in degrees north or south of the celestial equator. Star A is at 50° north declination.
Astronomers measure right ascension in hours eastward from the vernal equinox. Star A is at 8 hours right ascension.
The ecliptic is the apparent path the sun takes across the celestial sphere each year, as seen from Earth.

Figure 16 *Time-lapse photography traces northern circumpolar stars, which never set below the horizon.*

Circumpolar Stars You see different stars in the sky depending on your location, the time of year, and the time of night. Why is this so? As **Figure 16** dramatically illustrates, the Earth rotates once on its axis each day. Because of this, most observers see some stars rise above and set below the horizon much like the sun does each day. Also, the combination of the Earth's motion around the sun and the tilt of Earth's axis causes different stars to be visible during different times of the year. Near the poles, however, stars are circumpolar. *Circumpolar stars* are stars that can be seen at all times of year and all times of night.

IS THAT A FACT!

Polaris has not always been the North Star. Nearly 5,000 years ago, a faint star named Thuban in the constellation Draco held that honor. Because the Earth wobbles on its axis, the location of the North celestial pole changes on a 25,780-year cycle. Some theories argue that the Great Pyramid of Giza was built so its main passageway aligned with Thuban, which—because it did not appear to move in the night sky—symbolized immortality. In 12,000 years, Polaris will be replaced by Vega as the pole star.

The Size and Scale of the Universe

Copernicus noticed that stars never shifted their relative position. If the stars were nearby, he reasoned, their position would appear to shift like the planets' positions do as the Earth travels around the sun. Based on this observation, Copernicus thought that the stars must be very far away from the planets.

Measuring Distance in Space Today we know that Copernicus was correct—the stars are very far away from Earth. In fact, stars are so distant that a new unit of length—the light-year—was created to measure their distance. A **light-year** is a unit of length equal to the distance that light travels through space in 1 year. One light-year is equal to about 9.46 trillion kilometers! **Figure 17** below illustrates how far away some stars that we see really are.

Even after astronomers figured out that stars were very distant, the nature of the universe was hard to understand. Some astronomers thought that our galaxy, the Milky Way, included every object in space. The other galaxies that astronomers found were thought by some to be fuzzy clouds within the Milky Way. In 1935, Edwin Hubble discovered that the Andromeda Galaxy, which is the closest major galaxy to our own, was past the edge of the Milky Way. This discovery confirmed the belief of many astronomers that the universe is much larger than was previously thought.

Physics CONNECTION

Have you ever noticed that when a driver in a passing car blows the horn, the horn's sound gets lower? This is called the *Doppler effect.* It works with both sound and light. As a light source moves away quickly, its light looks redder. This particular Doppler effect is called *red shift.* The farther apart two galaxies are moving, the faster the galaxies are moving apart. From the perspective of each galaxy, the other galaxy looks redder. Because all galaxies except our close neighbors are moving apart, the universe must be expanding.

Figure 17 *While the stars in the constellation Orion may appear to be near each other when seen from Earth, they are actually very far apart from one another.*

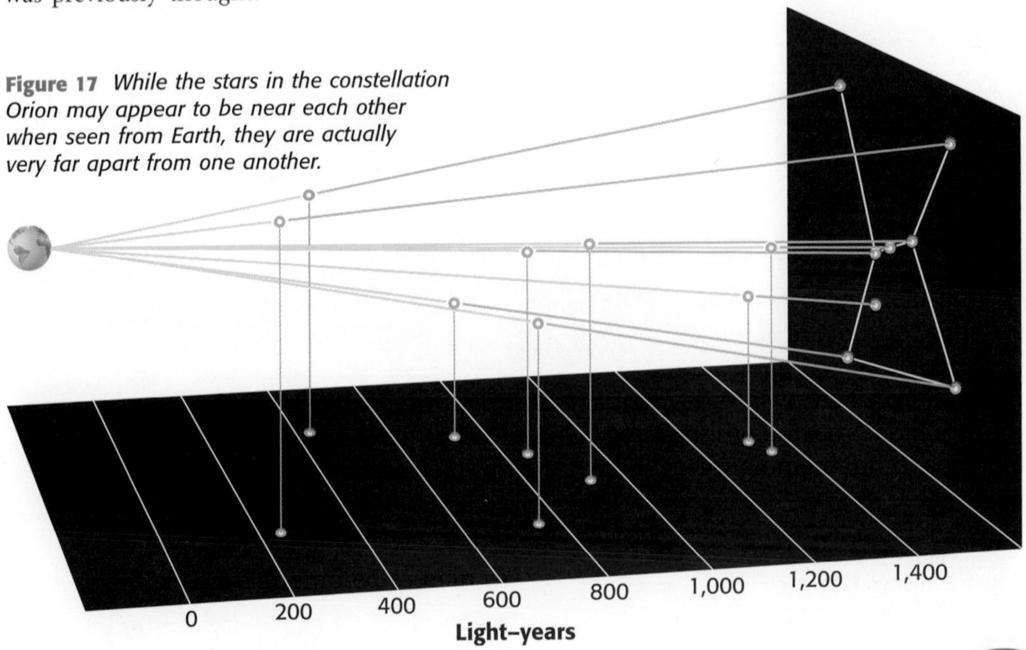

WEIRD SCIENCE

As scientists have attempted to map the universe and determine its size and scale, they've discovered that clusters of galaxies are not spread uniformly through the universe. Galaxy clusters seem to be aligned around vast spherical voids as if they were located on the film of a giant soap bubble. Some of the voids are 300 million light-years across. These discoveries have led astronomers to suggest that the universe looks something like a huge conglomeration of soap bubbles!

DISCUSSION

Students may assume that because the universe is expanding, every star they see is moving away from Earth. Point out that the only stars visible with the unaided eye are the ones in our galaxy. The Milky Way is not expanding for the same reason that our solar system is not expanding: because gravity holds moving bodies in orbit. Galaxies such as the Milky Way and the Andromeda galaxy are part of a galaxy cluster of 30 galaxies known as the Local Group. The galaxies that make up a galaxy cluster are held together by gravity. The expansion of the universe occurs as galaxy clusters move apart from one another.

If the expansion of the universe were compared to baking a chocolate chip cookie, the chocolate chips would represent galaxy clusters. As the cookie bakes, the dough expands, and the space between chocolate chips increases; the chocolate chips, however, do not change in size.

SCIENTISTS AT ODDS

The Greek astronomer Aristarchus of Samos came up with a method for calculating the distance of heavenly bodies more than 2,200 years ago. He calculated that the moon was much smaller than the sun and therefore much closer to Earth than previously thought. He also suggested that the known planets revolved around the sun and that the stars were very far away. Ironically, Aristarchus was ridiculed for his theory of a sun-centered universe, and his ideas were dismissed by other scientists of the time.

3 Extend

Using the Figure

After students have examined the images on these two pages, ask them to notice that the first four images in the series are photographs, the next three are illustrations, and the final two are photographs. Lead a discussion on why it is not possible to obtain photographs for every image in a series showing the actual solar system.

Going Further

Over a week or two, have students use a sky map to identify some of the brighter stars in the night sky. Even if they live in a city, students should be able to locate Betelgeuse, Rigel, and Sirius. In addition, they may be able to spot Venus, Mars, or Jupiter. Students should keep an observer's log in which they record the date; time; sky conditions; instruments used, if any (binoculars are an excellent aid, if available); descriptions and names of stars observed; and drawings of constellations. Students can supplement their logs with astronomical research on the stars they observe.

MATH and MORE

Have students convert the following numbers:

1,200 (1.2×10^3)
150,000 (1.5×10^5)
3.2×10^6 (3,200,000)
790,000,000 (7.9×10^8)
5.6×10^{12} (5,600,000,000,000)

Answers to MATHBREAK

Steps 3–4: 10,000 times farther
Steps 4–5: 1,500 times farther

Considering Scale in the Universe Today astronomers are studying the most distant objects yet detected in the universe. Every few months, newspapers announce new discoveries as astronomers probe deeper into space. Astronomers still argue about the size of the universe. The farthest objects we can observe are at least 10 billion light-years away.

When thinking about the universe and all the objects in it, it is important to think about scale. For example, stars appear to be very small in the night sky. But we know that most stars are a lot larger than the Earth. Examine the diagram on these two pages to better understand the scale of objects in the universe.

1 Let's start with something familiar, a baseball diamond. You are looking down on home plate from a distance of about 10 m.

2 At 1,000 m away, home plate is hard to see, but now you can see the baseball stadium and the neighborhood it is located in.

3 Moving another 100 times farther away (100 km), you now see the city as a whole in relation to the countryside around it.

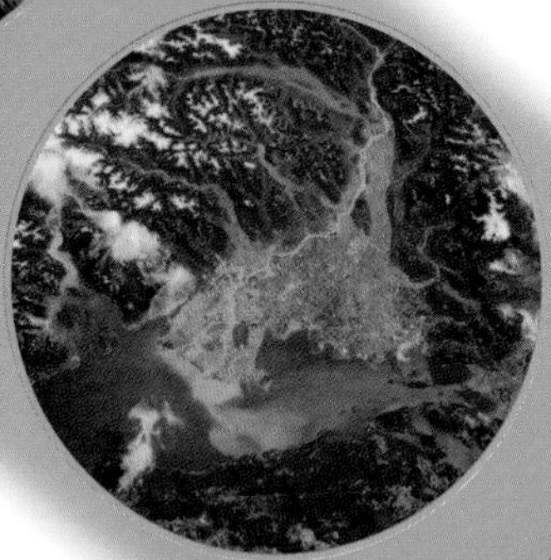

4 At 1,000,000 km away, you can see the Earth as a planet, with its companion, the moon.

MATH BREAK

Understanding Scale

From steps 1 to 2 and from steps 2 to 3 in the diagram at right, you increased your distance by a factor of 100. How many times farther away are you in step 4 than you were in step 3? How many times farther away in step 5 than you were in step 4?

16

Cross-Disciplinary Focus

Mathematics Calculating the position of objects in the universe involves complex mathematical concepts. Since the first observations of the stars were recorded, mathematics have been used to track their movements and calculate the length of days, months, and years. Math and astronomy evolved together. Today, computers are used to model the structure of the universe, but astronomical discoveries still challenge the ways math is used to describe space and time. General Relativity is just one example of this synthesis. Students may be interested in finding out how astronomy has influenced the development of mathematics, physics, or philosophy.

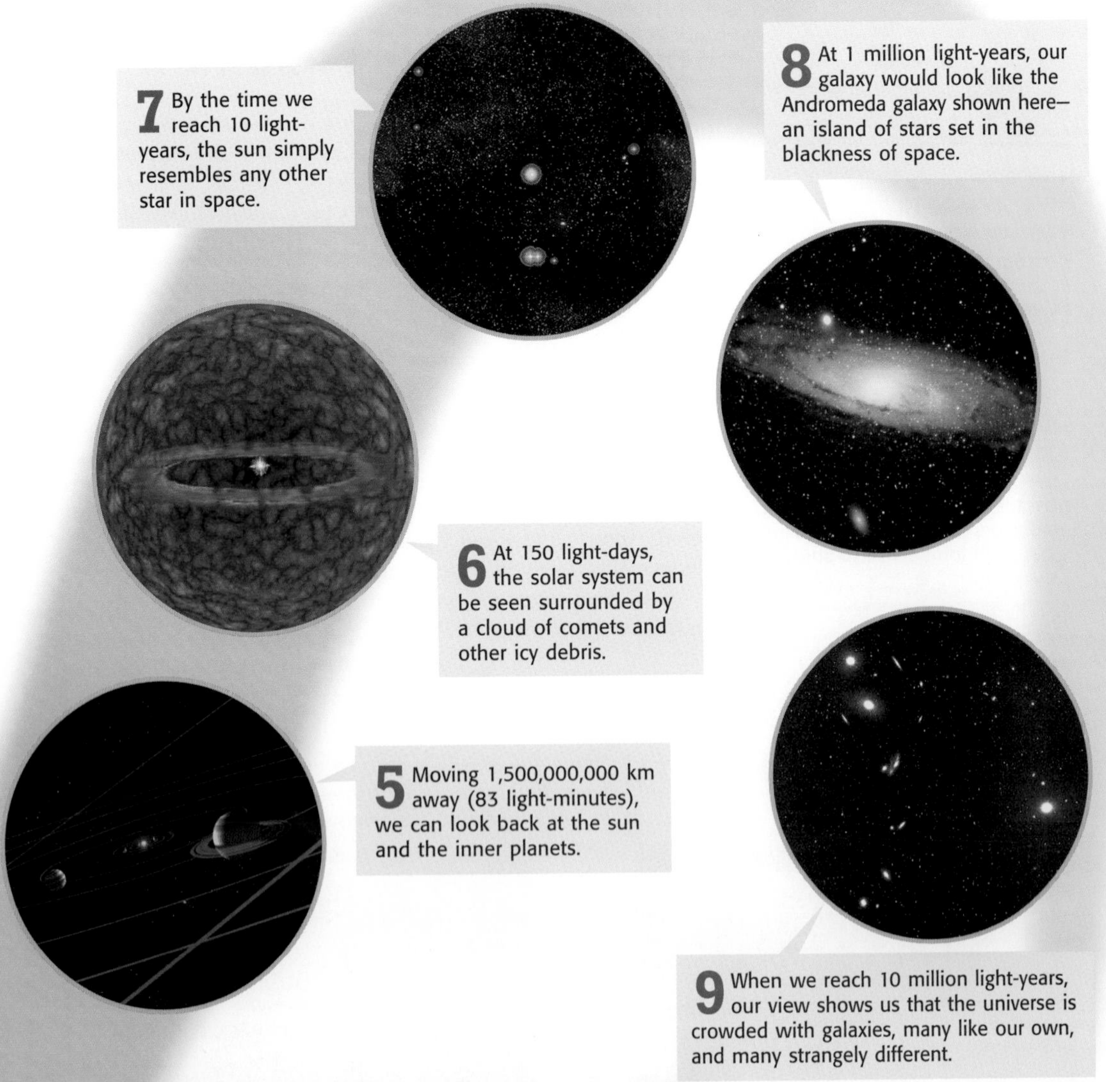

5 Moving 1,500,000,000 km away (83 light-minutes), we can look back at the sun and the inner planets.
6 At 150 light-days, the solar system can be seen surrounded by a cloud of comets and other icy debris.
7 By the time we reach 10 light-years, the sun simply resembles any other star in space.
8 At 1 million light-years, our galaxy would look like the Andromeda galaxy shown here—an island of stars set in the blackness of space.
9 When we reach 10 million light-years, our view shows us that the universe is crowded with galaxies, many like our own, and many strangely different.

SECTION REVIEW

1. How do constellations relate to patterns of stars? How are constellations like states?
2. How do astronomers plot a star's exact position?
3. **Analyzing Relationships** As shown in the diagram above, there are faraway objects that we can see only with telescopes. There are also objects in the universe that are too small for our unaided eyes to see. How do we detect these small objects?

internetconnect

sciLINKS. NSTA

TOPIC: Constellations
GO TO: www.scilinks.org
***sci*LINKS NUMBER:** HSTE440

Answers to Section Review

1. Constellations are sections of the sky that contain easily recognizable patterns of stars. Constellations are similar to states in that both are regions of a much larger area. Like states, constellations share borders with each other.
2. Astronomers measure right ascension and declination to plot a star's exact position.
3. Scientists use microscopes to study objects that are too small for the unaided eye to see.

4 Close

Quiz

1. What is the celestial equator? (an imaginary circle extending from Earth's equator into space)
2. What is a circumpolar star? (It is a star that can be seen all year and at all times of night from a given location.)
3. How did Edwin Hubble's discovery that the Andromeda galaxy was far away and outside of our own galaxy contribute to astronomers' knowledge about the size of the universe? (It confirmed many astronomers' theories that the universe was much larger than previously thought.)

Alternative Assessment

Celestial Guidebook Have students develop a guidebook for the novice stargazer that includes a glossary of astronomical terms. Encourage students to include diagrams, illustrations, and analogies to help clarify their entries.

Activity

Field Trip If there is an observatory or planetarium in your area, plan a field trip for the class. A cloudless night is best. Afterwards, have students record their thoughts and observations in their ScienceLog.

LabBook PG 160
The Sun's Yearly Trip Through the Zodiac

Teaching Transparency 183
"Considering Scale in the Universe"

SECTION 3

Focus

Telescopes—Then and Now

In this section, students will learn how reflecting and refracting telescopes work and compare their strengths and weaknesses. The section discusses the electromagnetic spectrum and how non-optical telescopes are used to detect radiation that cannot be seen. Students will learn about radio telescopes and other tools astronomers use to study the invisible radiation emitted by celestial objects.

Bellringer

Ask students: Have you ever bent or slowed down light? How? (Students may mention wearing glasses or looking through a microscope.)

1 Motivate

ACTIVITY

Making a Waterdrop Lens

Give pairs of students a 6 × 6 cm square of plastic wrap, and have them place it over some print on a newspaper. Put a drop of water on each piece of plastic. Have students note the shape of the drop and how it magnifies the newsprint. Tell students that the rounded, or convex, waterdrop is a very simple lens, similar in principle to the kinds of lenses used in some telescopes.

Directed Reading Worksheet Section 3

Teaching Transparency 299 "How Your Eyes Work"

LINK TO PHYSICAL SCIENCE

SECTION 3 READING WARM-UP

Terms to Learn

telescope
refracting telescope
reflecting telescope
electromagnetic spectrum

What You'll Do

- Compare and contrast refracting telescopes with reflecting telescopes.
- Explain why the atmosphere is an obstacle to astronomers and how they overcome the obstacle.
- List the types of electromagnetic radiation, other than visible light, that astronomers use to study space.

Telescopes—Then and Now

For professional astronomers and amateur stargazers, the telescope is the standard tool for observing the sky. A **telescope** is an instrument that collects *electromagnetic radiation* from the sky and concentrates it for better observation. You will learn more about electromagnetic radiation later in this section.

Optical Astronomy

An optical telescope collects visible light for closer observation. The simplest optical telescope is made with two lenses. One lens, called the *objective lens,* collects light and forms an image at the back of the telescope. The bigger the objective lens, the more light the telescope can gather. The second lens is located in the eyepiece of the telescope. This lens magnifies the image produced by the objective lens. Different eyepieces can be selected depending on the magnification desired.

Without a telescope, you can see about 6,000 stars in the night sky. With an optical telescope, you can see millions of stars and other objects. **Figure 18** shows how much more you can see with an optical telescope.

Figure 18 *The image at left shows a section of the sky as seen with the unaided eye. The image at right shows what the small clusters of stars in the left image look like when seen through a telescope.*

CONNECT TO PHYSICAL SCIENCE

The human retina contains receptors called *cones* and *rods* which perceive different wavelengths of light. Cones are found in the central part of the retina and perceive color. Rods, located at the outer part of the retina, perceive only black and white. When little light is present, rods perceive detail better than cones. For this reason, stargazers sometimes look at objects by using their peripheral vision rather than looking at an object straight on. This method takes advantage of the rods' ability to detect faint objects in the sky. Use Transparency 299 at left, to discuss the structure of the eye and encourage interested students to test this technique using a telescope, binoculars, or their unaided eyes.

Refracting Telescopes Telescopes that use a set of lenses to gather and focus light are called **refracting telescopes.** The curved objective lens in a refracting telescope bends light that passes through it and focuses the light to be magnified by the eyepiece. **Figure 19** shows how refracting telescopes work. A refracting telescope's size is limited by the objective lens. If the curved lens is too large, the glass sags under its own weight, distorting images. This is why most professional astronomers use *reflecting telescopes*.

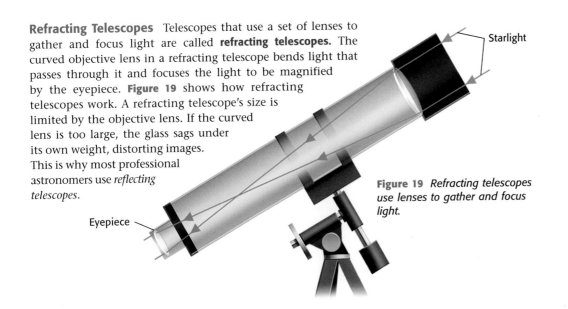

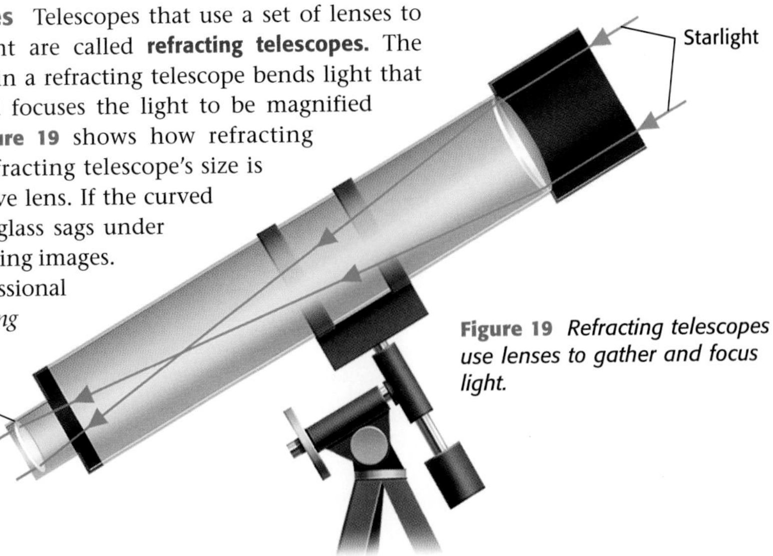

Figure 19 *Refracting telescopes use lenses to gather and focus light.*

Reflecting Telescopes Telescopes that use curved mirrors to gather and focus light are called **reflecting telescopes.** Light enters the telescope and is reflected from a large, curved mirror to a focal point above the mirror. As shown in **Figure 20,** reflecting telescopes use a second mirror in front of the focal point to reflect the light, in this case, through a hole in the side of the telescope. Here the light is collected for observation.

One advantage of reflecting telescopes over refracting telescopes is that mirrors can be made very large, which allows them to gather more light than lenses gather. Also, mirrors are polished on their curved side, preventing light from entering the glass. Therefore, any flaws in the glass do not affect the light. A third advantage is that mirrors reflect all colors of light to the same place, while lenses focus different colors of light at slightly different distances. Reflecting telescopes thus allow all colors of light from an object to be seen in focus at the same time.

LabBook

Want to make your own telescope? Turn to page 162 in the LabBook to find out how to build and use a telescope.

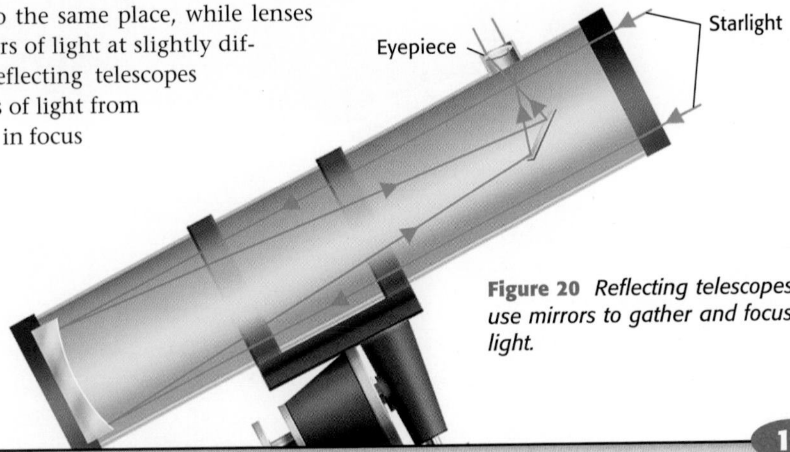

Figure 20 *Reflecting telescopes use mirrors to gather and focus light.*

2 Teach

READING STRATEGY

Prediction Guide Have students predict whether the following statements are true or false:

- Without a telescope, you can see about 6,000 stars. (true)
- Mirrors are used in some telescopes. (true)
- Telescopes are often located in humid areas because water vapor in the air enhances the visibility of stars. (false)

DEMONSTRATION

Mystery of the Floating Penny Tell students that you can make a penny float on water. Drop a penny in a small bowl. Ask a student to raise the bowl until the penny just disappears from sight. Now slowly pour water into the bowl until the penny "floats" into view. Repeat the demonstration with other students, and ask them if they can solve this mystery. (Students may deduce that light bends or refracts as it passes from air to water; this makes the penny appear to float.)

Explain that light travels at a speed of about 300,000 km/s through air but at only about 225,000 km/s through water and, as it slows down, it bends. Astronomers use the same trick to bend and focus light with curved pieces of glass called lenses.

Homework

Making Observations Binoculars are actually a pair of low-power refracting telescopes, and they can make it possible to see five times as many stars as could be viewed with the naked eye. Students with access to binoculars can make observations of the moon, stars, or planets. A pair of 7 × 35 or 7 × 50 binoculars is best for nighttime observation. The most difficult thing about using binoculars is keeping them steady: suggest that students sit in a comfortable lawn chair and rest their elbows on the armrests. Invite students to share their observations with the class.

LabBook PG 162
Through the Looking Glass

Teaching Transparency 184
"Refracting Telescope"
"Reflecting Telescope"

2 Teach, *continued*

DEMONSTRATION

Students may not understand how moisture in the atmosphere can distort the images seen through a telescope. Demonstrate the effect of moisture in the atmosphere with a water spray bottle and a projector. In a darkened room, turn on the projector and shine it on the wall. Spray a mist of water about halfway between the projector and the wall. Ask students to describe what they see. Point out that much of the water in the atmosphere is actually water vapor, which is a gas, but it can cause similar problems for powerful telescopes. Sheltered English

MATH and MORE

While astronomers usually refer to a telescope by the diameter of its objective lens or mirror, a telescope's ability to collect light is proportional to the *area* of its main mirror or lens. Have students use the formula for finding a circle's area ($A = \pi r^2$ [$\pi = 3.1416$]) to compare the light-collecting capabilities of a 1 m, 5 m, and 10 m mirror. (For the 1 m mirror: $3.1416 \times 0.25 m^2 = 0.79 m^2$; for the 5 m mirror: $3.1416 \times 6.25 m^2 = 19.64 m^2$; for the 10 m mirror: $3.1416 \times 25 m^2 = 78.54 m^2$. The 5 m mirror can collect 25 times more light than the 1 m mirror; the 10 m mirror can collect 100 times more light than the 1 m mirror and 4 times more than the 5 m mirror.)

Critical Thinking Worksheet
"Through the Eyes of a Telescope"

Figure 21 *The 36 hexagonal mirrors in each of the Keck Telescopes combine to form a light-reflecting surface that is 10 m across.*

Very Large Reflecting Telescopes In some very large reflecting telescopes, several mirrors work together to collect light and deliver it to the same focus. The Keck Telescopes, in Hawaii, shown in **Figure 21,** are twin telescopes that each have 36 hexagonal mirrors working together. Linking several mirrors allows more light to be collected and focused in one spot.

Optical Telescopes and the Atmosphere The light gathered by telescopes on Earth is affected by the atmosphere. Earth's atmosphere causes starlight to shimmer and blur. Also, light pollution from large cities can make the sky look bright, which limits an observer's ability to view faint objects. Astronomers often place telescopes in dry areas to avoid water vapor in the air. Mountaintops are also good places to use a telescope because the air is thinner at higher elevations. The fact that air pollution and light pollution are generally lower on mountaintops also increases the visibility of stars.

Optical Telescopes in Space! To avoid interference by the atmosphere altogether, scientists have put telescopes in space. Although the mirror in the Hubble Space Telescope, shown below in **Figure 22,** is only 2.4 m across, the optical telescope produces images that are as good or better than any images produced by optical telescopes on Earth.

Figure 22 *The Hubble Space Telescope has provided clearer images of objects in deep space than any ground-based optical telescope.*

20

Science Bloopers

When the Hubble Space Telescope was deployed in 1990, it became immediately apparent that the telescope was not operating correctly—images transmitted back to Earth were unfortunately blurred. It was discovered that there was a minute flaw in the telescope's main mirror. The mirror had been ground about 0.0002 cm (about $\frac{1}{50}$ the width of a human hair) flatter than it should have been. Although much of the image distortion was corrected with computer processing, the telescope was much less powerful than originally hoped. During a 1993 repair mission, space shuttle astronauts placed a number of corrective devices on the telescope that made it fully operational.

Non-Optical Astronomy

For thousands of years, humans have observed the universe with their eyes. But scientists eventually discovered that there are more forms of radiation than the kind we can see—*visible light.* In 1800, William Herschel discovered an invisible form of radiation called *infrared radiation.* We sense infrared radiation as heat.

In 1852, James Clerk Maxwell showed that visible light is a form of *electromagnetic radiation.* Each color of visible light represents a different wavelength of electromagnetic radiation. Visible light is just a small part of the electromagnetic spectrum, as shown in **Figure 23.** The **electromagnetic spectrum** is made of all of the wavelengths of electromagnetic radiation. Humans can see radiation only from blue light, which has a short wavelength, to red light, which has a longer wavelength. The rest of the electromagnetic spectrum is invisible to us!

Most electromagnetic radiation is blocked by the Earth's atmosphere. Think of the atmosphere as a screen that lets only certain wavelengths of radiation in. These wavelengths include infrared, visible light, some ultraviolet, and radio. All other wavelengths are blocked.

Activity

Artificial light at night is often needed for safety and security. But it also causes light pollution that interferes with stargazing. Do some research on this problem, and list some possible solutions. What compromises can be made so that people feel safe and stargazers can see objects in the night sky?

TRY at HOME

Figure 23 *Radio waves have the longest wavelengths and gamma rays have the shortest. Visible light is only a small band of the electromagnetic spectrum.*

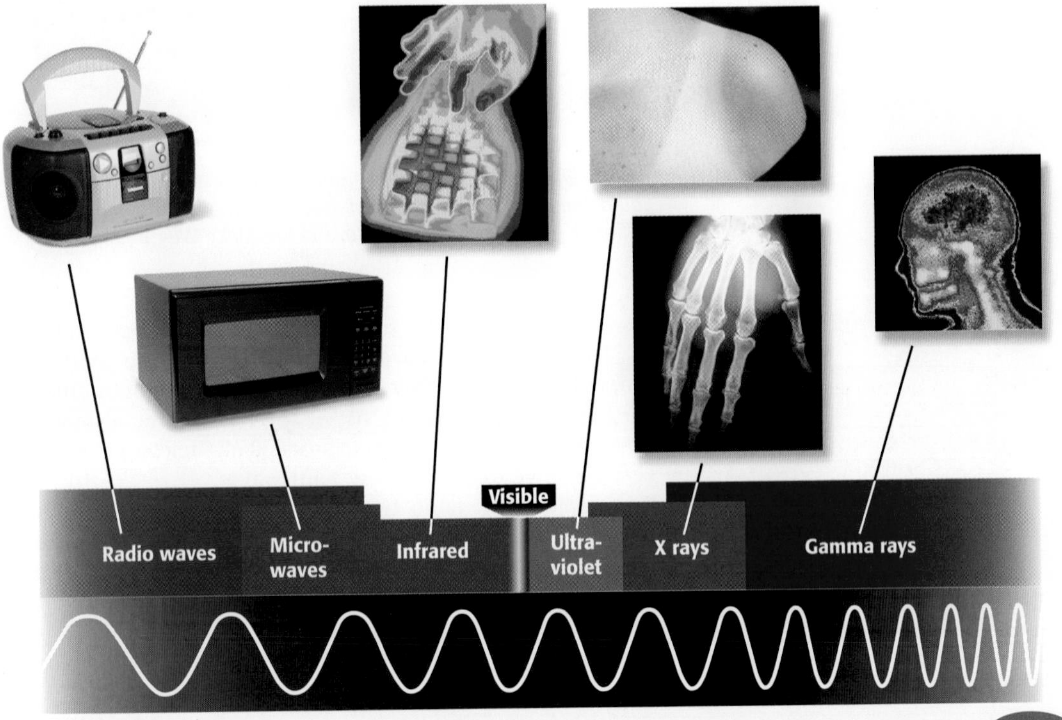

Answer to Activity

Placing special shields over outdoor lights is one simple way to reduce light pollution. The shields keep streets safely illuminated but reduce the amount of light radiated skyward. Invite students to look up the International Dark-Sky Association on the Internet.

RETEACHING

To help students comprehend how little of the electromagnetic spectrum is visible to the human eye, have them visualize a piano. Tell them the part of the electromagnetic spectrum that humans can see is comparable to one key on the piano. Sheltered English

CONNECT TO LIFE SCIENCE

Human eyes can detect only visible light, but some organisms have eyes more like non-optical telescopes. Insects such as bees, for example, can see ultraviolet radiation. Flowers, in turn, have ultraviolet patterns that direct bees to their center. Have interested students find out what it is like to look at the world through the eyes of a bee or a bioluminescent deep-sea fish. Encourage students to find out about experimental telescope designs that are modeled after the eyes of animals. One example is the Lobster Eye X-ray telescope.

IS THAT A FACT!

Although the sun appears to be yellowish in color, it is radiating energy across the electromagnetic spectrum. When observed with an X-ray telescope, the sun appears nearly black, but sunspots are brilliantly active with magnetic storms and solar flares that release X rays.

WEIRD SCIENCE

Some LEO satellites reflect sunlight off their bodies and dish antennas. These flashes can be many times brighter than any star in the sky and can damage telescope sensors. To find out when these flashes will occur and where they will be visible, look up "Iridium flash" on the Internet.

Teaching Transparency 185, "The Electromagnetic Spectrum"

internetconnect

SCLINKS. NSTA

TOPIC: Telescopes
GO TO: www.scilinks.org
***sci*LINKS NUMBER:** HSTE445

3 Extend

BRAIN FOOD

Some astronomers study the universe by heading deep into abandoned mines! These astronomers are looking for evidence of neutrinos (a type of subatomic particle emitted by stars and supernovae). Most neutrinos pass right through the Earth without colliding with any matter. Neutrino observatories are built several kilometers beneath the Earth's surface to shield them from all other types of radiation. The observatories are enormous tanks of extremely pure water or a solution similar to dry cleaning fluid. When a neutrino enters the tank and has a chance collision with an atomic nucleus, photoreceptors detect a faint flash of light and astronomers record a "hit."

Group Activity

Invite pairs of students to construct a simple Newtonian reflecting telescope. The activity works best on a clear night, when the moon is visible. Instruct students to turn off the lights and place a makeup mirror (a curved, focusing mirror) near a window so that the moon and some stars are reflected in it. One student should hold a hand mirror in front of the makeup mirror so that he or she can see a reflection of the makeup mirror in the hand mirror. Then the other student should use a magnifying glass to view the reflection in the hand mirror. Students should be able to see the craters and mountains of the moon.

The Night Sky Through Different Eyes Astronomers are interested in all forms of electromagnetic radiation because different objects radiate at different wavelengths. For each type of radiation, a different type of telescope or detector is needed. For example, infrared telescopes have polished mirrors similar to those of reflecting telescopes, but the detectors are more sensitive to infrared waves than to visible light waves. As you can see in **Figure 24,** the universe looks much different when observed at other wavelengths.

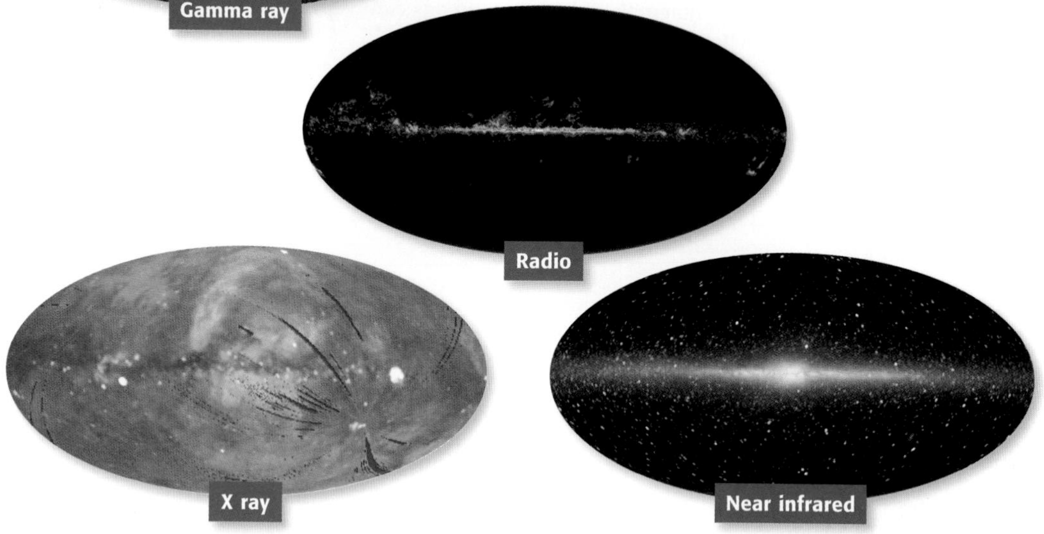

Figure 24 *Each image shows the night sky as it would appear if we could see other wavelengths of electromagnetic radiation. The "cloud" that goes across each picture is the Milky Way galaxy.*

Figure 25 *The Arecibo radio telescope is 305 m across. That is about the length of three football fields arranged end to end!*

Radio Telescopes Radio telescopes receive and focus radio waves. Radio telescopes have to be much larger than optical telescopes because radio wavelengths are about 1 million times longer than optical wavelengths. Also, very little radio radiation reaches Earth from objects in space. Radio telescopes must be very sensitive to detect these faint waves.

The surface of a radio telescope does not have to be as flawless as the lens of an optical telescope. In fact, the surface of a radio telescope does not even have to be completely solid. When it was first built, the Arecibo radio telescope, shown in **Figure 25,** was covered with chicken wire! To a radio wave, a surface made of chicken wire is solid because the wavelength is so much longer than the diameter of the holes.

22

Homework

Research Have students research a non-optical telescope and prepare a report or poster on it. Encourage students to diagram how the telescope works, research the history of the telescope, explain what the telescope was intended for, and report on the discoveries it has enabled. Students can share their research with the class.

WEIRD SCIENCE

Shortly after Marconi invented the radio in the 1890s, people became interested in listening for messages from intelligent life in the universe. In 1901, a reward of 100,000 francs was offered to the first person to communicate with aliens.

Linking Radio Telescopes Together Astronomers can get clearer images of radio waves by using two or more radio telescopes at the same time. When radio telescopes are linked together, they work like a single giant telescope. For example, the Very Large Array (VLA), shown in **Figure 26,** consists of 27 separate telescopes that can be spread out 30 km. When the dishes are spread out to the maximum distance, they work as a single telescope that is 30 km across! The larger the area that linked telescopes cover, the more detailed the collected data are.

Figure 26 *The radio telescopes of the Very Large Array near Socorro, New Mexico, work together as one giant telescope.*

X-ray Vision Most electromagnetic waves are blocked by the Earth's atmosphere. To detect these blocked waves, scientists have put special telescopes in space. These telescopes include ultraviolet telescopes, infrared telescopes, gamma-ray telescopes, and X-ray telescopes. Each type of telescope is made to receive one type of radiation. For example, **Figure 27** shows a telescope that is designed to detect X rays.

Figure 27 *Launched in 1999, the Chandra X-ray Observatory is the most powerful X-ray telescope ever built.*

SECTION REVIEW

1. Name one way in which refracting telescopes and reflecting telescopes are similar and one way they are different.
2. Name two ways the atmosphere limits what astronomers can detect. What single method do astronomers use to solve both problems?
3. **Summarizing Data** Make two lists—one for electromagnetic wavelengths that commonly penetrate Earth's atmosphere and one for other wavelengths. Which wavelengths can astronomers detect from Earth? How do they detect each wavelength?

internet**connect**

sciLINKS NSTA

TOPIC: Telescopes
GO TO: www.scilinks.org
***sci*LINKS NUMBER:** HSTE445

Answers to Section Review

1. They both collect light and focus it. Refracting telescopes use only lenses, but reflecting telescopes use mirrors in addition to lenses.
2. The atmosphere distorts radiation passing through it, and light pollution can limit an astronomer's ability to see faint objects. (Also, the atmosphere filters out most wavelengths of the electromagnetic spectrum.) Placing a telescope in space can solve these problems.
3. wavelengths that enter the atmosphere: visible light, infrared, some ultraviolet radiation, and radio waves; wavelengths that are blocked by the atmosphere: X rays, gamma rays, and some ultraviolet radiation. A specialized telescope is needed to detect each type of radiation that enters the atmosphere.

Group Activity

Planning an Observatory Ask students to find out about all of the environmental factors that influence the choice of an observatory site. These factors include light pollution, air pollution, elevation, and a reliable infrastructure. After students have learned about these factors, have them work together in groups to draft a proposal for building an observatory somewhere on Earth. Have groups present their proposal to the class and explain their choice of telescope and location.

4 Close

Quiz

1. What limits the size and magnification of a refracting telescope? (If the objective lens is too large, gravity will cause the glass to sag, distorting the image.)
2. What is the advantage of linking radio telescopes? (When radio telescopes are linked together, they act as a very large unit and are more powerful. This allows scientists to make observations of extremely distant objects.)

Alternative Assessment

PORTFOLIO

Have students imagine that they are trying to gather support for building the largest radio-telescope array ever. Have them write a persuasive letter in which they describe how radio telescopes differ from optical telescopes and how building such a large array could further our understanding of the universe. Students should include a diagram of how their array would collect signals from a wide area.

Create a Calendar
Teacher's Notes

Time Required
One 45-minute class period

Lab Ratings

EASY → HARD

- TEACHER PREP: 2
- STUDENT SET-UP: 1
- CONCEPT LEVEL: 3
- CLEAN UP: 1

MATERIALS

The materials listed on the student page are enough for a group of 2–3 students.

Preparation Notes
This activity will require math skills. You may need to review with students how to multiply fractions.

As an extension activity, students may research the rotation and revolution of other planets. Students can then create a calendar for one of the other planets.

Michael E. Kral
West Hardin Middle School
Cecilia, Kentucky

Design Your Own Lab

USING SCIENTIFIC METHODS

Create a Calendar

Imagine that you live in the first colony on Mars. You have been trying to follow the Earth calendar, but it just isn't working anymore. Mars takes almost two Earth years to revolve around the sun—almost 687 Earth days to be exact! That means that there are only two Martian seasons for every Earth calendar year. One year, you get winter and spring, but the next year, you get only summer and fall! And Martian days are longer than Earth days. Mars takes 24.6 Earth hours to rotate on its axis. Even though they are similar, Earth days and Martian days just don't match. This won't do!

MATERIALS

- poster board
- metric ruler
- colored pencils
- calculator (optional)
- marker

Ask a Question

1. How can I create a calendar based on the Martian cycles of rotation and revolution that includes months, weeks, and days?

Form a Hypothesis

2. In your ScienceLog, write a few sentences that answer the question above.

Test the Hypothesis

3. Use the following formulas to determine the number of Martian days in a Martian year:

$$\frac{\text{687 Earth days}}{\text{1 Martian year}} \times \frac{\text{24 Earth hours}}{\text{1 Earth day}} = \text{Earth hours per Martian year}$$

$$\text{Earth hours per Martian year} \times \frac{\text{1 Martian day}}{\text{24.6 Earth hours}} = \text{Martian days per Martian year}$$

4. Decide how to divide your calendar into a system of Martian months, weeks, and days. Will you have a leap day, a leap week, a leap month, or a leap year? How often will it occur?

5. Choose names for the months and days of your calendar. In your ScienceLog, explain why you chose each name. If you have time, explain how you would number the Martian years. For instance, would the first year correspond to a certain Earth year?

6. Follow your design to create your own calendar for Mars. Draw the calendar on your piece of poster board. Make sure it is brightly colored and easy to follow.

7. Present your calendar to the class. Explain how you chose your months, weeks, and days.

Analyze the Results

8. What advantages does your calendar design have? Are there any disadvantages to your design?

9. Which student or group created the most original calendar? Which design was the most useful? Explain.

10. What might you do to improve your calendar?

Draw Conclusions

11. Take a class vote to decide which design should be chosen as the new calendar for Mars. Why was this calendar chosen? How did it differ from other designs?

12. Why is it useful to have a calendar that matches the cycles of the planet on which you live?

25

Answers

8. Accept all reasonable responses.
9. Accept all reasonable responses.
10. Accept all reasonable responses. Students may suggest simplifying their design.
11. Accept all reasonable responses.
12. Accept all reasonable responses.

Datasheets for LabBook

Chapter Highlights

Vocabulary Definitions

Section 1

astronomy the study of all physical objects beyond Earth

calendar a system for organizing time; most calendars organize time within a single unit called a year

year the time required for the Earth to orbit the sun once

month roughly the amount of time required for the moon to orbit the Earth once

day the time required for the Earth to rotate once on its axis

leap year a year in which an extra day is added to the calendar

Section 2

constellation a section of the sky that contains a recognizable star pattern

altitude the angle between an object in the sky and the horizon

right ascension a measure of how far east an object is from the point at which the sun appears on the first day of spring

declination a measure of how far north or south an object is from the celestial equator

celestial equator imaginary circle created by extending Earth's equator into space

ecliptic the apparent path the sun takes across the celestial sphere each year

light-year a unit of length equal to the distance that light travels through space in 1 year

Chapter Highlights

Section 1

Vocabulary

astronomy *(p. 4)*
calendar *(p. 4)*
year *(p. 4)*
month *(p. 4)*
day *(p. 4)*
leap year *(p. 5)*

Section Notes

- Calendars are based on movements of objects in the sky.
- Many ancient civilizations developed calendars.
- Our modern calendar developed from the Roman calendar.
- There is evidence all around the world for ancient astronomical observations.
- The Ptolemaic theory states that Earth is at the center of the universe, while Copernicus's theory states that the sun is at the center of the universe.
- Isaac Newton was the first scientist to explain why celestial objects move as they do.
- Galileo's use of the telescope brought the technology of astronomy to a new level.

Section 2

Vocabulary

constellation *(p. 11)*
altitude *(p. 13)*
right ascension *(p. 14)*
declination *(p. 14)*
celestial equator *(p. 14)*
ecliptic *(p. 14)*
light-year *(p. 15)*

Section Notes

- Astronomers divide the sky into 88 sections called *constellations.*
- Different constellations are visible from different locations, at different times of the year, and at different times of night.
- Star patterns appear as they do because of Earth's position in space. Most stars that appear close together are actually very far apart.

☑ Skills Check

Math Concepts

KEEPING IT SIMPLE Scientific notation is a way that scientists and others can use large numbers more easily. By using exponents, many place-holding zeros can be eliminated.

For example:
1,000 can be written as 1×10^3, and
1,000,000 can be written as 1×10^6.

Notice that the exponent represents the number of zeros in each number. For more practice with scientific notation, turn to page 183 in the Appendix.

Visual Understanding

OPTICAL ILLUSION Constellations look like they do only because we see them from our location on Earth in patterns we recognize. Look back at Figure 17 on page 15. The constellation Orion would be unrecognizable if seen from the side.

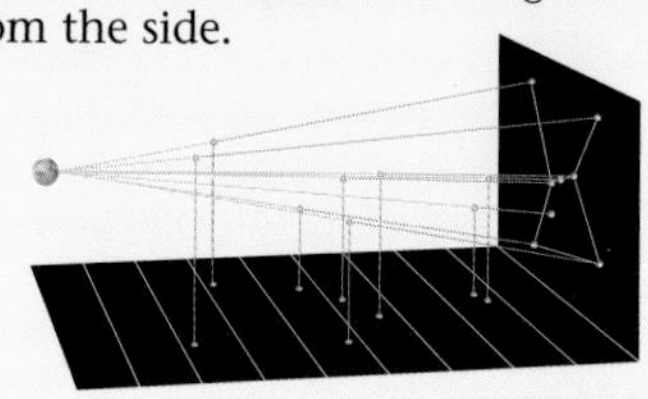

26

Lab and Activity Highlights

Create a Calendar PG 24

The Sun's Yearly Trip Through the Zodiac PG 160

Through the Looking Glass PG 162

Datasheets for LabBook (blackline masters for these labs)

SECTION 2

- The north celestial pole, the celestial equator, the zenith, and the horizon are imaginary markers used to locate objects in the sky.
- Right ascension and declination, which are similar to latitude and longitude, give coordinates of objects in the sky.
- Astronomers measure the distance to most objects in the universe in light-years.
- The size and distance of celestial objects detected in the universe can be difficult to determine. Scale must always be considered.

Labs

The Sun's Yearly Trip Through the Zodiac *(p. 160)*

SECTION 3

Vocabulary

telescope *(p. 18)*
refracting telescope *(p. 19)*
reflecting telescope *(p. 19)*
electromagnetic spectrum *(p. 21)*

Section Notes

- Telescopes collect and focus electromagnetic radiation.
- Humans can see only visible light. To detect other wavelengths of radiation, astronomers use special telescopes or detectors.
- Types of telescopes include optical, radio, ultraviolet, infrared, X-ray, and gamma-ray.
- Some telescopes are launched into space to avoid the blurring effects of Earth's atmosphere or to collect radiation that can't penetrate Earth's atmosphere.
- Telescopes are often linked together to function as one giant telescope.

Labs

Through the Looking Glass *(p. 162)*

internetconnect

GO TO: go.hrw.com

Visit the HRW web site for a variety of learning tools related to this chapter. Just type in the keyword:

KEYWORD: HSTOBS

sciLINKS NSTA

GO TO: www.scilinks.org

Visit the **National Science Teachers Association** on-line Web site for Internet resources related to this chapter. Just type in the *sci*LINKS number for more information about the topic:

TOPIC: Images from Space	***sci*LINKS NUMBER:** HSTE425
TOPIC: The Stars and Keeping Time	***sci*LINKS NUMBER:** HSTE430
TOPIC: Early Theories in Astronomy	***sci*LINKS NUMBER:** HSTE435
TOPIC: Constellations	***sci*LINKS NUMBER:** HSTE440
TOPIC: Telescopes	***sci*LINKS NUMBER:** HSTE445

27

VOCABULARY DEFINITIONS, *continued*

SECTION 3

telescope an instrument that collects electromagnetic radiation from the sky and concentrates it for better observation

refracting telescope a telescope that uses a set of lenses to gather and focus light

reflecting telescope a telescope that uses curved mirrors to gather and focus light

electromagnetic spectrum all the wavelengths of electromagnetic radiation

Blackline masters of these Chapter Highlights can be found in the **Study Guide.**

Lab and Activity Highlights

LabBank

Inquiry Labs
Constellation Prize

Whiz-Bang Demonstrations
Refraction Action

Long-Term Projects & Research Ideas,
Celestial Inspiration

Chapter Review Answers

Using Vocabulary

1. Both reflecting and refracting telescopes are used to study objects in space. Refracting telescopes use lenses to magnify and focus an image. Reflecting telescopes use curved mirrors.
2. Both the celestial equator and the horizon are imaginary lines that help an observer locate objects in space. The celestial equator extends from Earth's equator into space and is always in the same place. The horizon is the line where the Earth and the sky appear to meet; it is determined by the observer's location.
3. Both X rays and microwaves are forms of electromagnetic radiation that the human eye cannot detect. X rays have much shorter wavelengths than microwaves.
4. Both right ascension and declination measure the location of celestial objects. Right ascension refers to how far east along the celestial equator an object is from the point at which vernal equinox occurs. Declination is a measure of how far north or south an object is from the celestial equator.
5. A leap year and a light-year both use the revolution of the Earth around the sun as a reference point. A leap year is a year in which an extra day has been added to the calendar. A light-year is a unit of distance. It refers to the distance that light travels in space during the course of one year.

Chapter Review

USING VOCABULARY

For each set of terms, explain the similarities and differences in their meanings.

1. reflecting telescope/refracting telescope
2. celestial equator/horizon
3. X rays/microwaves
4. right ascension/declination
5. leap year/light-year

UNDERSTANDING CONCEPTS

Multiple Choice

6. The length of a day is based on
   a. the Earth orbiting the sun.
   b. the rotation of the Earth on its axis.
   c. the moon orbiting the Earth.
   d. the rotation of the moon on its axis.

7. Which of the following civilizations directly affected the development of our modern calendar?
   a. The Chinese
   b. The Maya
   c. The Romans
   d. The Polynesians

8. According to __?__, the Earth is at the center of the universe.
   a. the Ptolemaic theory
   b. Copernicus's theory
   c. Galileo's theory
   d. none of the above

9. The first scientist to successfully use a telescope to observe the night sky was
   a. Tycho.
   b. Galileo.
   c. Herschel.
   d. Kepler.

10. Astronomers divide the sky into
    a. galaxies.
    b. constellations.
    c. zeniths.
    d. phases.

11. The stars that you see in the sky depend on
    a. your latitude.
    b. the time of year.
    c. the time of night.
    d. All of the above

12. The altitude of an object in the sky is its angular distance
    a. above the horizon.
    b. from the north celestial pole.
    c. from the zenith.
    d. from the prime meridian.

13. Right ascension is a measure of how far east an object in the sky is from
    a. the observer.
    b. the vernal equinox.
    c. the moon.
    d. Venus.

14. Telescopes that work grounded on the Earth include all of the following except
    a. radio telescopes.
    b. refracting telescopes.
    c. X-ray telescopes.
    d. reflecting telescopes.

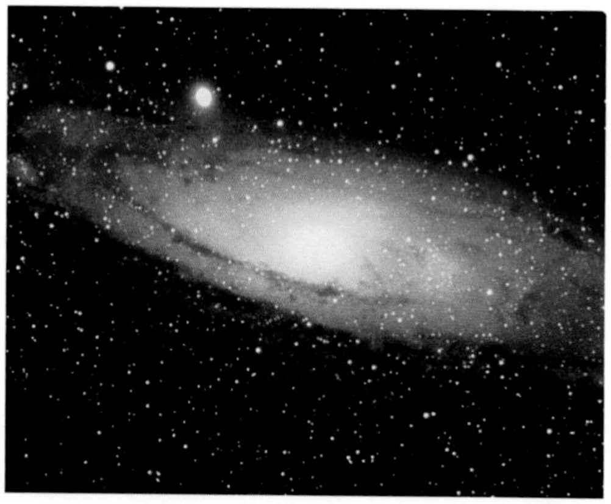

28

Understanding Concepts

Multiple Choice

6. b
7. c
8. a
9. b
10. b
11. d
12. a
13. b
14. c
15. d

15. Which of the following is true about X-ray and radio radiation from objects in space?
   a. Both types of radiation can be observed with the same telescope.
   b. Separate telescopes are needed to observe each type of radiation, and both telescopes can be on Earth.
   c. Separate telescopes are needed to observe each type of radiation, and both telescopes must be in space.
   d. Separate telescopes are needed to observe each type of radiation, but only one of the telescopes must be in space.

Short Answer

Write one or two sentences to answer the following questions:

16. Explain how right ascension and declination are similar to latitude and longitude.

17. How does a reflecting telescope work?

Concept Mapping

18. Use the following terms to create a concept map: right ascension, declination, celestial sphere, degrees, hours, celestial equator, vernal equinox.

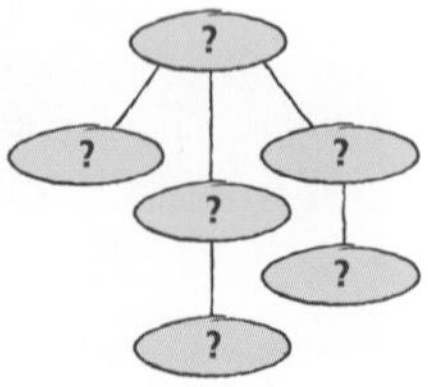

CRITICAL THINKING AND PROBLEM SOLVING

19. Why was it easier for people in ancient cultures to see celestial objects in the sky than it is for most people today?

20. Many forms of radiation do not penetrate Earth's atmosphere. While this limits astronomer's activities, how does it benefit humans in general?

MATH IN SCIENCE

21. How many kilometers away is an object whose distance is 8 light-years?

INTERPRETING GRAPHICS

Examine the sky map below, and answer the questions that follow. (Hint: The star Aldebaran is located at about 4 hours, 30 minutes right ascension, 16 degrees declination.)

Celestial Coordinates

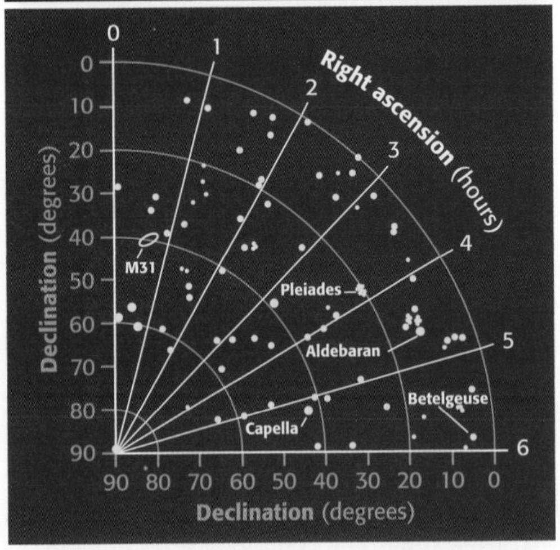

22. What object is located at 5 hr, 55 min right ascension and 7 degrees declination?

23. What are the celestial coordinates for the Andromeda galaxy (M31)? (Round off right ascension to the nearest half-hour.)

Reading Check-up

Take a minute to review your answers to the Pre-Reading Questions found at the bottom of page 2. Have your answers changed? If necessary, revise your answers based on what you have learned since you began this chapter.

29

Short Answer

16. Lines of latitude and longitude divide the Earth into a system of coordinates that can be used to describe a location. Similarly, right ascension and declination allow astronomers to locate objects using coordinates. Both systems are based on spherical objects.
17. Reflecting telescopes use a large mirror to gather and focus light. A second mirror, located in front of the focal point, directs light toward an eyepiece for observation.

Concept Mapping

18. An answer to this exercise can be found at the front of this book.

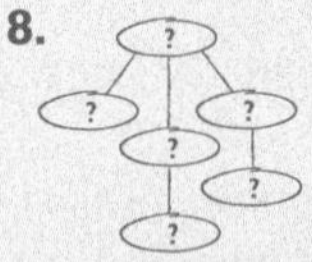

Critical Thinking and Problem Solving

19. Before the invention of electric lights, there was much less light pollution and atmospheric pollution; therefore, celestial objects were much easier to observe.
20. The Earth's atmosphere absorbs many forms of radiation that are dangerous to humans, including X rays and ultraviolet radiation.

Math in Science

21. $(9.46 \times 10^{12}) \times 8 = 7.57 \times 10^{13}$, or 75.7 trillion kilometers away

Interpreting Graphics

22. Betelgeuse
23. 0 hours, 30 minutes right ascension, 40° declination

Concept Mapping Transparency 18

Blackline masters of this Chapter Review can be found in the **Study Guide.**

Science, Technology, and Society

Planet or Star?

Background

Dozens of possible planets have been detected outside our solar system. Because these objects are too distant to be observed directly, astronomers gather evidence indirectly. The most common method is to observe slight variations in the light emitted by a star. As a planet orbits a star, its gravity tugs on the star. This causes the star's velocity to change (the "wobble" described in the student page). This wobble is detectable because the star's spectrum changes due to the Doppler effect.

Because most stars are moving away from Earth, the light they emit is shifted towards the red end of the spectrum. When a star's velocity decreases, the red shift decreases; when its velocity increases, the red shift increases. A periodic variation in a star's red shift indicates that it is being pulled by an unseen object. The gravitational attraction of a planet as massive as Jupiter could cause an observable variation in a star's red shift.

Science, Technology, and Society

Planet or Star?

Humans have long wondered if there are inhabited planets in our galaxy or in far-off galaxies. For the first time, NASA's powerful Hubble Space Telescope has photographed what some astronomers believe is a young planet within our own galaxy. This gaseous object, called TMR-1C, is nearly 450 light-years from Earth. Is it really a planet, or is it a star?

Discovering Planets

Scientists have had trouble finding planets beyond our solar system because distant planets are often masked by the light of brighter stars. *Protoplanets,* planets in the process of forming, may be difficult to see because they are often surrounded by clouds of cosmic dust. As a planet revolves around a star, its gravity tugs on the star. This causes the star to move back and forth slightly. If the planet is massive enough, astronomers can see this movement as a "wobble" in the star's motion. Scientists use state-of-the-art technology to detect these minute changes in the star's velocity relative to Earth.

The picture of TMR-1C could be the first photographic evidence that planets exist outside our solar system. Astronomers discovered TMR-1C racing through space at 32,000 km/h in the constellation of Taurus. Scientists believe that TMR-1C was hurled into space by two stars that acted like a giant slingshot. The Hubble Space Telescope's camera used sensitive infrared light to penetrate through the cosmic clouds surrounding TMR-1C. Because TMR-1C is still hot from forming, it emits light, which is picked up by the telescope's camera.

The Birth of a Planet

Scientists believe that it takes millions of years for planets to form. Photographs of TMR-1C, however, have led some researchers to speculate that this process may be much quicker than was previously thought. The stars that ejected TMR-1C are only a few hundred thousand years old. Researchers have not determined for certain whether TMR-1C is a planet. If TMR-1C turns out to be older than these stars, it could not have been ejected from them. If that is the case, TMR-1C may prove to be a *brown dwarf* rather than a planet. Meanwhile, the research continues until scientists know for certain.

▲ *TMR-1C is 209 billion km from possible parent stars.*

Think About It!

▶ So far, only a few of the many recently discovered planets may be habitable. One such planet, near the star 70 Virginis, is just the right distance from its star for the planet's water to be liquid rather than solid or gaseous. What other features would be necessary for this planet to sustain life as we know it on Earth?

30

Answer to Think About It

Accept all reasonable answers. Have students consider why the other planets in our solar system are not habitable. In addition to liquid water, elements such as carbon are necessary for life. Carbon is essential in forming organic compounds. Organic compounds also require nitrogen and phosphorus.

Students should also consider a planet's orbit. If a planet has an extremely elliptical orbit, it may venture far enough away from its star to cause extreme temperature changes.

Students might also consider a planet's atmospheric composition. The Earth's atmosphere protects organisms from ultraviolet radiation and regulates heat. Our atmosphere is primarily nitrogen, carbon dioxide, and oxygen. These gases can be lethal to humans, however, if they are not in proper proportions.

EYE ON THE ENVIRONMENT

Eyes in the Sky

Have you ever gazed up at the sky on a crystal-clear night? What did you see? You probably noticed the moon and countless twinkling stars. It may surprise you to learn that some of those points of light are not stars at all. A few of them may be phonies.

Phony Stars Exposed

Some of the objects that we think are stars are really satellites circling Earth in low Earth orbit (LEO). The satellites in LEO specialize in observation. You might say that when we watch the sky, satellites are watching us as well. LEO is ideal for observation because of its proximity to Earth's surface.

In order to stay in orbit, satellites in LEO must travel very fast. Traveling at approximately 27,358 km/h, one of these satellites can circle the Earth in only 90 minutes! During these revolutions, some satellites gather weather information, while others might transmit phone calls or observe remote terrain. These "eyes in the sky" can even observe you taking a walk.

Space Junk Explosion

Like many things, satellites do not last forever. They eventually break down and may even explode into hundreds of pieces. Most of the time, these pieces continue to travel in LEO for many years. Some of these pieces are large enough to be catalogued by the United States Space Command. As of January 1, 2000, about 2,647 human-made satellites were recorded orbiting, along with 6,022 pieces of debris, or space junk. This debris poses no immediate threat to astronauts or space shuttles that travel through LEO, but there is the potential that one little piece of space junk could smash into an unwary space traveler with explosive results!

The Satellites Just Keep on Coming

We are dependent on satellites for many everyday tasks. Our ever-increasing quest for knowledge drives us to launch more satellites every year. In the booming satellite industry, there is fierce competition for a position in LEO. Many companies are willing to pay top dollar to ensure their position in space. With LEO quickly becoming a satellite highway, it may soon face a traffic jam.

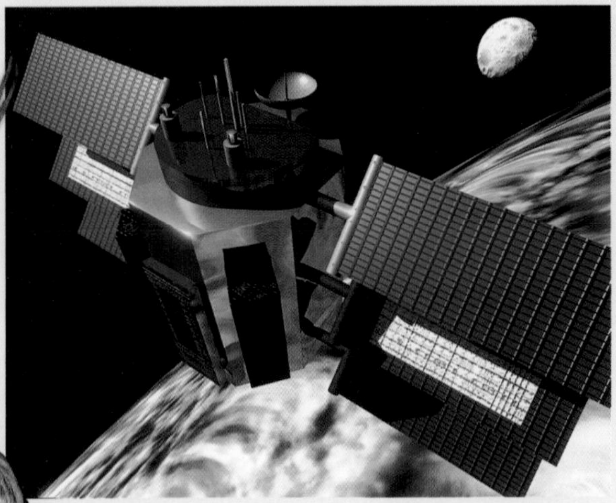

Satellite Search

► Unlike stars, satellites in LEO move noticeably across the sky. Research different types of satellites that orbit Earth. Look at the night sky, and try to spot some satellites. What kinds of satellites did you find? Present your observations to the class.

31

EYE ON THE ENVIRONMENT

Eyes in the Sky

Teaching Strategy

Encourage students to find out more about the problem of space debris. Suggest that they work in groups to come up with ideas to address this problem.

Answers to Satellite Search

The best time to see satellites is from May through August, in the early evening and around dawn. A satellite looks like a star or airplane, but it moves across the sky in a straight line, fast enough to see. It will fade out of sight before it reaches the horizon. Satellites can be seen moving from west to east or from pole to pole. Some people report seeing a zigzag pattern of light moving across the sky; this is an optical illusion caused by slight muscle movements of the eyes. The slower the light moves, the higher the satellite is in orbit. This can help students determine what kind of satellite they have spotted. TV broadcasting satellites do not appear to move at all and, therefore, can rarely be detected by human eyes. These satellites travel in geosynchronous Earth orbits at a speed that matches the Earth's rotation.

Chapter Organizer

CHAPTER ORGANIZATION	TIME MINUTES	OBJECTIVES	LABS, INVESTIGATIONS, AND DEMONSTRATIONS
Chapter Opener **pp. 32–33**	45	National Standards: SAI 1, HNS 1, 3, ES 3c	**Start-Up Activity,** Strange Gravity, p. 33
Section 1 **A Solar System Is Born**	90	▶ Explain the basic process of planet formation. ▶ Compare the inner planets with the outer planets. ▶ Describe the difference between rotation and revolution. ▶ Describe the shape of the orbits of the planets, and explain what keeps them in their orbits. UCP 1, 2, 4, SAI 1, ST 2, HNS 1–3, SPSP 1, 4, 5, ES 3a–3c	**QuickLab,** Staying in Focus, p. 40 **Whiz-Bang Demonstrations,** Can You Vote on Venus?
Section 2 **The Sun: Our Very Own Star**	90	▶ Describe the basic structure and composition of the sun. ▶ Explain how the sun produces energy. ▶ Describe the surface activity of the sun, and name some of its effects on Earth. ST 2, SPSP 5, HNS 1–3, ES 3a; Labs SAI 1	**Demonstration,** Observing Sunspots, p. 43 in ATE **Discovery Lab,** How Far Is the Sun? p. 54 **Datasheets for LabBook,** How Far Is the Sun?
Section 3 **The Earth Takes Shape**	90	▶ Describe the shape and structure of the Earth. ▶ Explain how the Earth got its layered structure and how this process affects the appearance of Earth's surface. ▶ Explain the development of Earth's atmosphere and the influence of early life on the atmosphere. ▶ Describe how the Earth's oceans and continents were formed. UCP 2, 4, SAI 1, ES 2b	**Demonstration,** p. 48 in ATE **QuickLab,** Mixing It Up, p. 49 **Long-Term Projects & Research Ideas,** A Two-Sun Solar System

See page ***T23*** *for a complete correlation of this book with the*

NATIONAL SCIENCE EDUCATION STANDARDS.

TECHNOLOGY RESOURCES

Guided Reading Audio CD
English or Spanish, Chapter 2

One-Stop Planner CD-ROM with Test Generator

CNN. Science, Technology & Society,
Solar Storms, Segment 22

Science Discovery Videodiscs
Image and Activity Bank with Lesson Plans: Sunspots

Chapter 2 • Formation of the Solar System

CLASSROOM WORKSHEETS, TRANSPARENCIES, AND RESOURCES	SCIENCE INTEGRATION AND CONNECTIONS	REVIEW AND ASSESSMENT
Directed Reading Worksheet **Science Puzzlers, Twisters & Teasers**		
Directed Reading Worksheet, Section 1 **Math Skills for Science Worksheet,** Density **Transparency 186,** Earth's Rotation and Revolution **Transparency 187,** Ellipse **Transparency 188,** Gravity and the Motion of the Moon **Critical Thinking Worksheet,** A Balooney Universe	**Multicultural Connection,** p. 34 in ATE **Biology Connection,** p. 36 **Math and More,** p. 37 in ATE **Cross-Disciplinary Focus,** p. 37 in ATE **MathBreak,** Kepler's Formula, p. 40 **Math and More,** p. 40 in ATE **Apply,** p. 41 **Cross-Disciplinary Focus,** p. 41 in ATE **Scientific Debate:** Mirrors in Space, p. 61	**Self-Check,** p. 35 **Homework,** pp. 35, 36, 41 in ATE **Self-Check,** p. 37 **Section Review,** p. 38 **Section Review,** p. 42 **Quiz,** p. 42 in ATE **Alternative Assessment,** p. 42 in ATE
Transparency 189, Structure of the Sun and Its Atmosphere **Directed Reading Worksheet,** Section 2 **Transparency 248,** The Periodic Table of the Elements **Transparency 190,** Fusion of Hydrogen in the Sun **Reinforcement Worksheet,** Stay on the Sunny Side	**Math and More,** p. 44 in ATE **Multicultural Connection,** p. 44 in ATE **Biology Connection,** p. 45 **Connect to Physical Science,** p. 45 in ATE **Cross-Disciplinary Focus,** p. 46 in ATE **Science, Technology, and Society:** Don't Look at the Sun! p. 60	**Homework,** p. 46 in ATE **Section Review,** p. 47 **Quiz,** p. 47 in ATE **Alternative Assessment,** p. 47 in ATE
Teaching Transparency 122, The Composition of the Earth **Directed Reading Worksheet,** Section 3 **Math Skills for Science Worksheet,** Reducing Fractions to Lowest Terms **Reinforcement Worksheet,** Third Rock from the Sun	**Connect to Geology,** p. 49 in ATE **Chemistry Connection,** p. 50 **Math and More,** p. 50 in ATE **Environment Connection,** p. 51 **Connect to Life Science,** p. 51 in ATE	**Self-Check,** p. 48 **Section Review,** p. 53 **Quiz,** p. 53 in ATE **Alternative Assessment,** p. 53 in ATE

internetconnect

go.hrw.com — **Holt, Rinehart and Winston On-line Resources**

go.hrw.com

For worksheets and other teaching aids related to this chapter, visit the HRW Web site and type in the keyword: **HSTSOL**

sciLINKS NSTA — **National Science Teachers Association**

www.scilinks.org

Encourage students to use the *sci*LINKS numbers listed in the internet connect boxes to access information and resources on the **NSTA** Web site.

END-OF-CHAPTER REVIEW AND ASSESSMENT

Chapter Review in Study Guide
Vocabulary and Notes in Study Guide
Chapter Tests with Performance-Based Assessment, Chapter 2 Test
Chapter Tests with Performance-Based Assessment, Performance-Based Assessment 2
Concept Mapping Transparency 19

Chapter Resources & Worksheets

Visual Resources

TEACHING TRANSPARENCIES

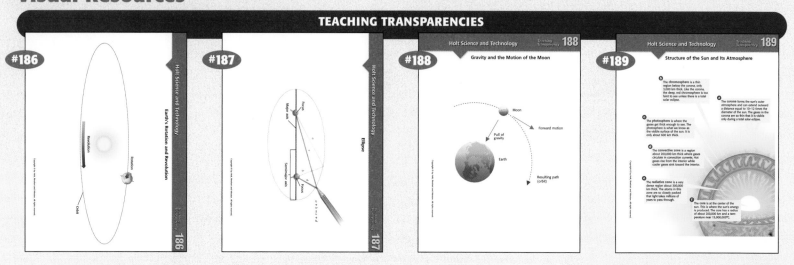

#186

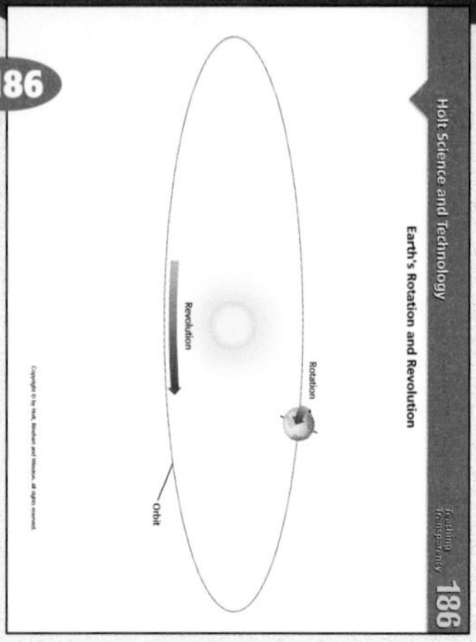

#187

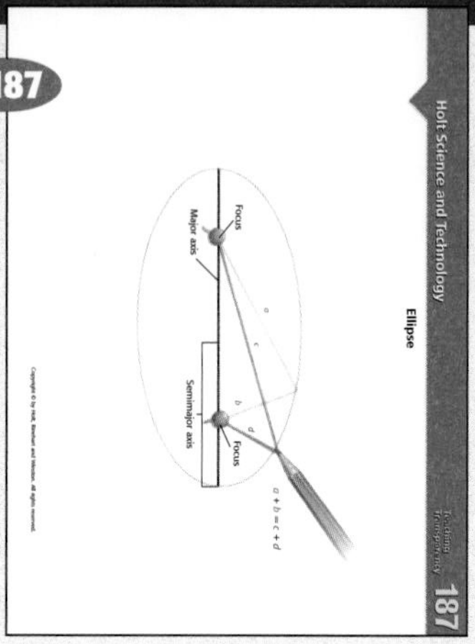

#188

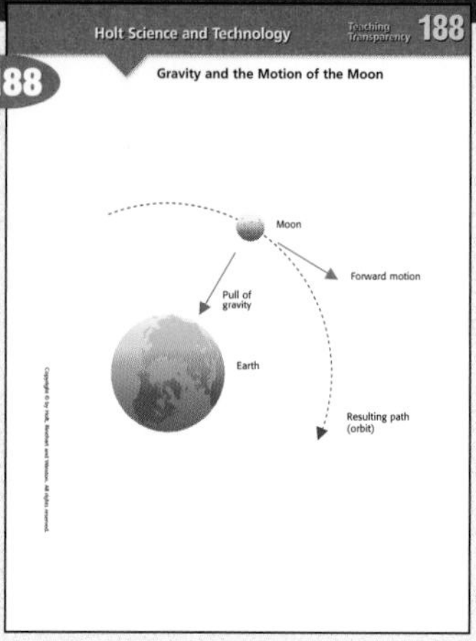

#189

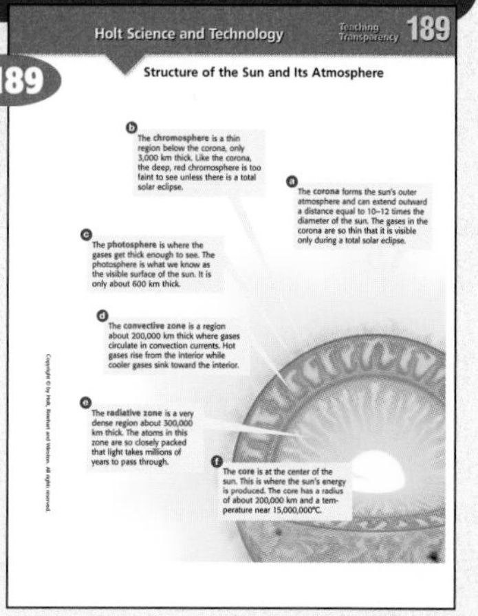

TEACHING TRANSPARENCIES

#190

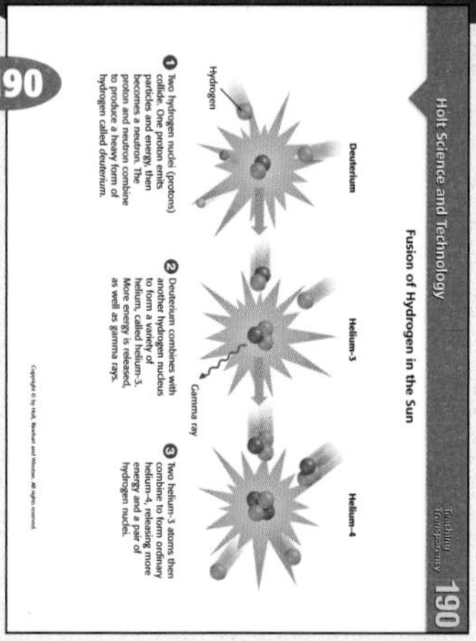

#122

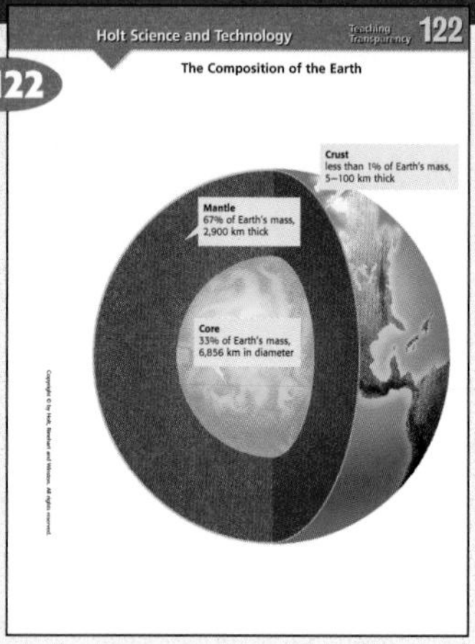

#248

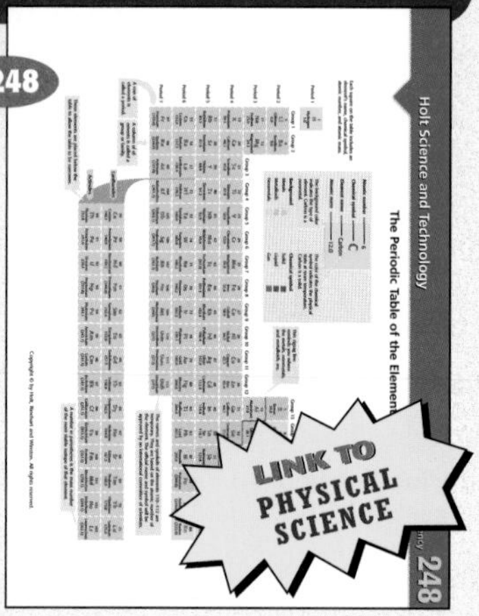

CONCEPT MAPPING TRANSPARENCY

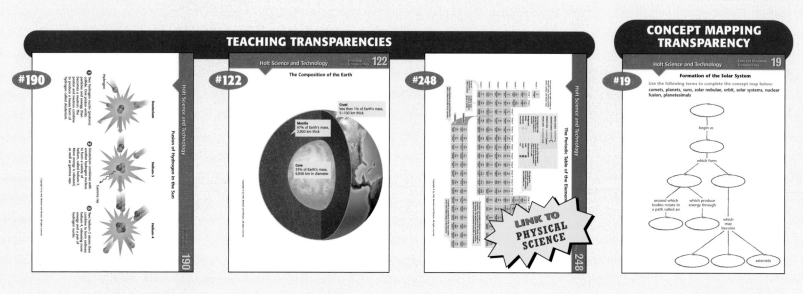

#19

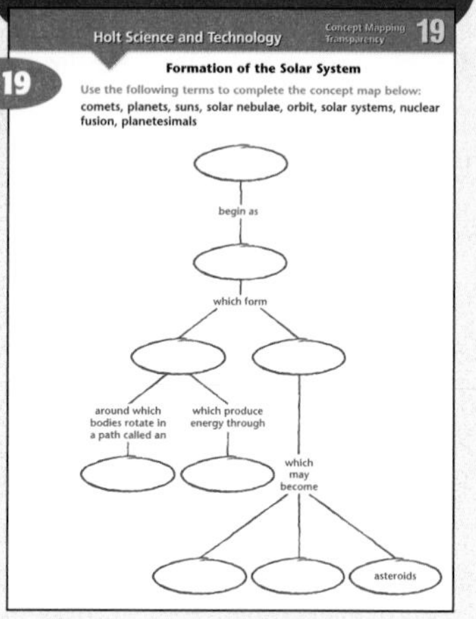

Meeting Individual Needs

DIRECTED READING

#2

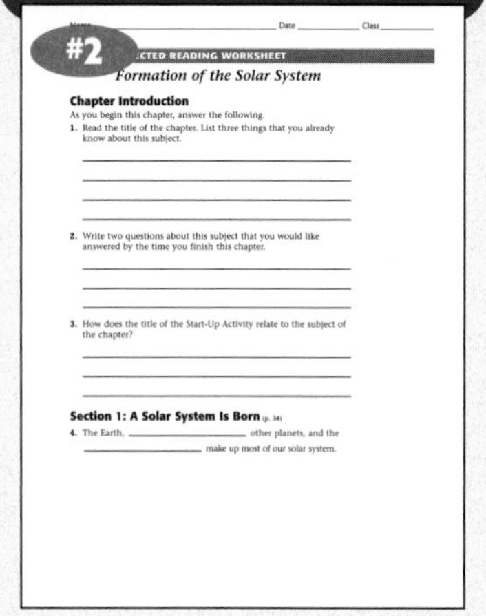

REINFORCEMENT & VOCABULARY REVIEW

#2

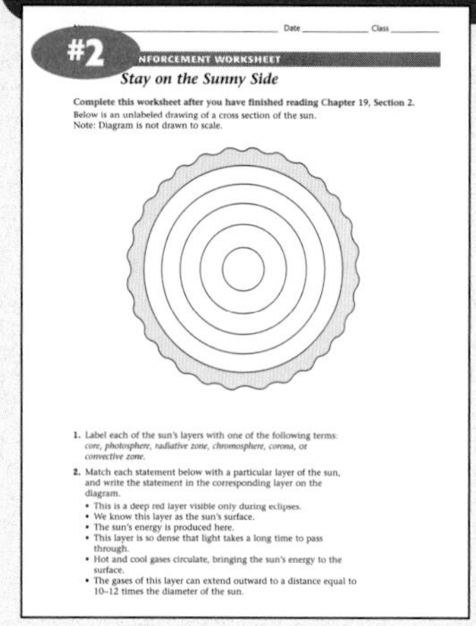

#2

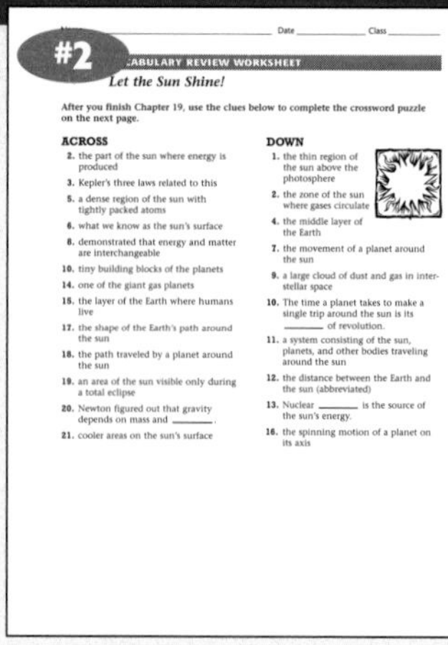

SCIENCE PUZZLERS, TWISTERS & TEASERS

#2

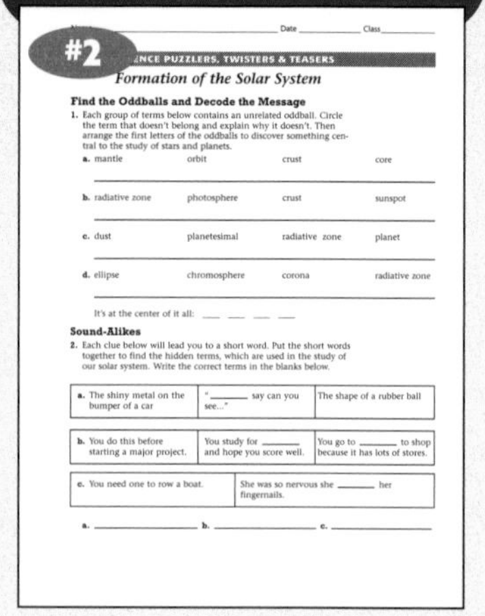

Chapter 2 • Formation of the Solar System

Review & Assessment

STUDY GUIDE

#2 Vocabulary & Notes Worksheet
Formation of the Solar System

#2 Chapter Review Worksheet
Formation of the Solar System

CHAPTER TESTS WITH PERFORMANCE-BASED ASSESSMENT

#2 Formation of the Solar System
Chapter 2 Test

#2 Formation of the Solar System
Chapter 2 Performance-Based Assessment

Lab Worksheets

WHIZ-BANG DEMONSTRATIONS

#2 Teacher-Led Demonstration
Can You Vote on Venus?

LONG-TERM PROJECTS & RESEARCH IDEAS

#2 Student Worksheet
A Two-Sun Solar System?

DATASHEETS FOR LABBOOK

#2 How Far Is the Sun?

Applications & Extensions

CRITICAL THINKING & PROBLEM SOLVING

#2 Critical Thinking Worksheet
A Balooney Universe

SCIENCE TECHNOLOGY

#22 Science in the News: Critical Thinking Worksheets
Segment 22
Solar Storms

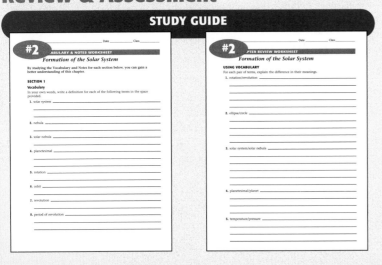

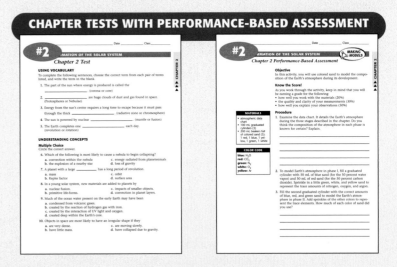

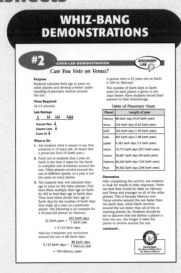

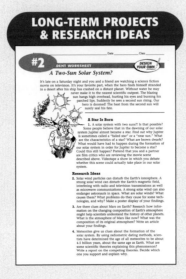

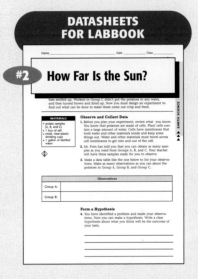

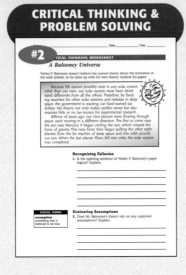

Chapter Background

SECTION 1

A Solar System Is Born

▶ A Computer Model of Planet Building

The Planetary Science Institute, in Tucson, Arizona, produced a computer program in the late 1970s to test hypotheses about the formation of planetesimals and planets. The program has given credence to the theory that particle collisions within a swirling, collapsing nebula could have led to the creation of our solar system. The program simulates the motion of particles at various distances from the sun and tracks the results of collisions based on actual physical and mechanical properties, such as gas drag and particle speed. Run with various starting conditions, the program shows small particles aggregating into numbers of larger bodies and the eventual production of a system of planets.

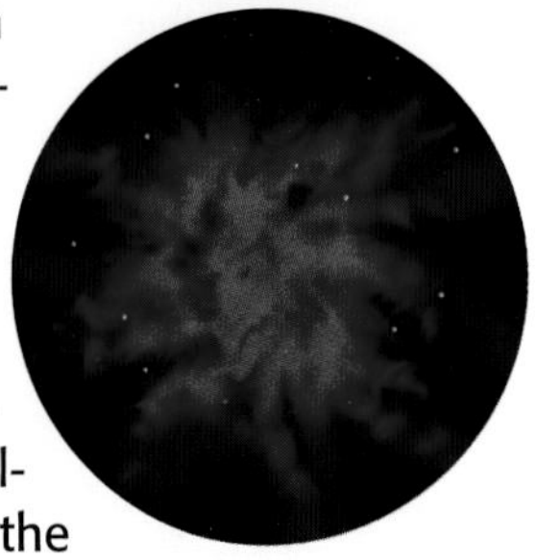

▶ The Orbit of Comets

Orbits represent the entire closed path of an orbiting body. A planet or asteroid orbit has an elliptical shape. Scientists observe that near the sun comets seem to have a parabolic orbit (shaped like an open-ended ellipse). This could indicate that comets come from the outer reaches of the solar system. Scientists theorize that some comets originate in an enormous spherical cloud surrounding the solar system. This region, named the Oort cloud, may contain 100 billion of these icy bodies. The gravitational pull of another object can knock a comet out of the Oort cloud, after which it is "captured" by the gravity of our sun.

IS THAT A FACT!

- A star begins life when fusion reactions start (at about 10 million degrees Celsius). It can burn steadily for billions of years, converting hydrogen to helium in its core. As the hydrogen runs out, the core collapses and heats up. The star's atmosphere expands and cools, and the star becomes a red giant.

▶ High-Mass Stars: "Live Fast and Die Young"

Stars with mass similar to that of our sun have a life cycle of 10 to 11 billion years. High-mass stars, with a mass at least 10 times that of our sun, actually burn up much quicker—in 50 million to 100 million years—and burn much brighter. When a high-mass star runs out of fuel, its core collapses, and the star becomes a supernova. A supernova explosion is one of the most violent events in the universe.

SECTION 2

The Sun: Our Very Own Star

▶ Movement of Energy Within the Sun

Because the matter in the sun's core is so dense, energy has difficulty escaping. Photons released by nuclear fusion in the sun's core cannot travel more than 1 cm before colliding with another particle. Each time this happens, a photon's energy is scattered in a random direction.

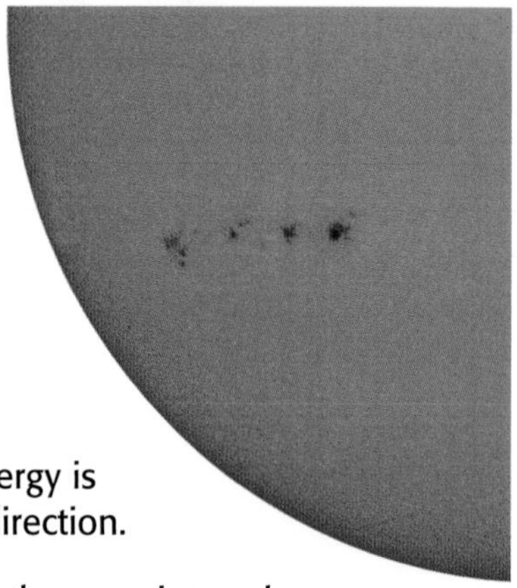

- When energy escapes the core, it travels more rapidly through the convection zone. The energy finally passes into space as visible light, X rays, ultraviolet, infrared, and other types of radiation.

IS THAT A FACT!

- It can take millions of years for the energy of a photon to travel from the sun's core to its surface!

▶ The Sunspot Cycle

The increasing and decreasing number of sunspots in an 11-year cycle appears to be driven by the magnetic field in the sun's surface layers. The field seems to "wind up" much as a rubber band does (perhaps because of the difference in rate of rotation between the sun's poles and its equator). This process intensifies the magnetic field; therefore, more sunspots appear, and the sun becomes much more active. Where the sun is most active, giant explosions called solar flares occur.

- Solar flares spew out electrically charged particles that affect human technology on Earth. Despite the great distance between the sun and Earth, solar flares can disrupt TV programs, open electronically controlled garage doors, damage satellites, and even cause power blackouts.

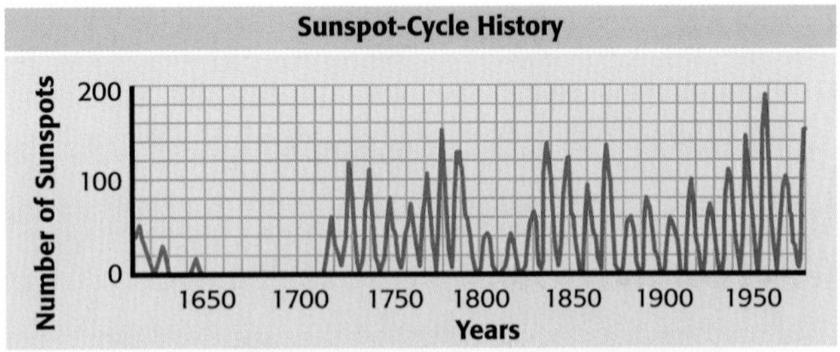

SECTION 3

The Earth Takes Shape

▶ Evidence of Earth's Origins

Many different sciences have contributed to our understanding of Earth's origin. Much remains to be discovered through computer models and the study of other planets. The following evidence has shaped the current scientific theories about the formation of Earth and its atmosphere:

- The oldest rocks on Earth are nearly 4 billion years old.
- Some of the oldest rocks are sedimentary in origin, so we know that oceans must have existed early in the history of Earth.

- The sun was cooler when the Earth was forming. We know this from the study of how hydrogen fusion reactions work.
- The Earth must have had a dense atmosphere with greenhouse gases early in its life, or it would have been too cold to have liquid oceans.
- The oldest fossils of primitive life are stromatolites, blue-green algae colonies that originated between 3.7 billion and 3.4 billion years ago. Simple life-forms probably appeared on Earth before this time (between 4.6 billion and 3.9 billion years ago).
- Blue-green algae use photosynthesis to get energy from sunlight to produce oxygen. Evidence from the oxidation of minerals in the rock record indicates that oxygen started to appear in significant concentrations in Earth's atmosphere between 2.5 billion and 2.0 billion years ago.

- Water that formed the oceans came from the early Earth's interior and was released by outgassing during the differentiation process. As the Earth heated and differentiated, water that was chemically bound in minerals was carried to the surface of the planet along with magma. Water vapor was then released to form the early atmosphere. Even at current rates of volcanism, the water vapor released from lava flows would be more than enough to fill the Earth's oceans in 500 million years.

For background information about teaching strategies and issues, refer to the *Professional Reference for Teachers.*

CHAPTER 2

Formation of the Solar System

Pre-Reading Questions

Students may not know the answers to these questions before reading the chapter, so accept any reasonable response.

Suggested Answers

1. The gravitational attraction of the sun keeps planets in their orbits.
2. The sun shines because nuclear fusion in its core produces energy.
3. The Earth is round because it became large enough for internal pressure to crush the materials inside it.

CHAPTER 2

Formation of the Solar System

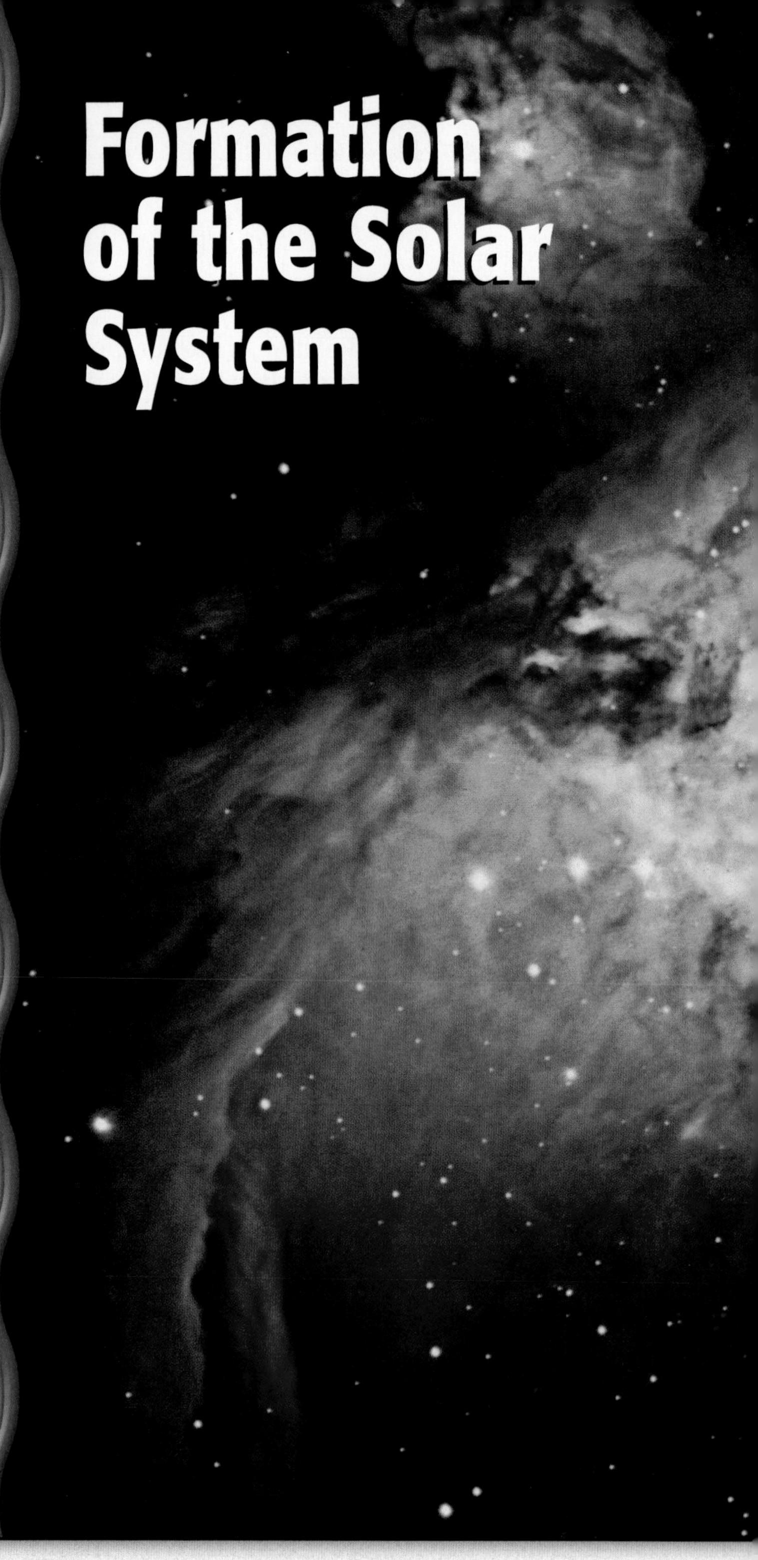

Sections

Pre-Reading Questions

1. What keeps the planets in their orbits?
2. Why does the sun shine?
3. Why is the Earth round?

32

internet connect

HRW On-line Resources

go.hrw.com

For worksheets and other teaching aids, visit the HRW Web site and type in the keyword: **HSTSOL**

sciLINKS NSTA

www.scilinks.com

Use the *sci*LINKS numbers at the end of each chapter for additional resources on the **NSTA** Web site.

Smithsonian Institution

www.si.edu/hrw

Visit the Smithsonian Institution Web site for related on-line resources.

CNNfyi.com

www.cnnfyi.com

Visit the CNN Web site for current events coverage and classroom resources.

A STAR FACTORY

The Orion Nebula, a vast cloud of dust and gas 35 trillion miles across, is part of the familiar Orion constellation (*below*). Here, swirling clouds of dust and gas give birth to systems like our own solar system. In this chapter, you will learn about the formation of our sun and the planets that race around it.

START-UP Activity

STRANGE GRAVITY

If you drop a heavy object, will it fall faster than a lighter one? According to the law of gravity, the answer is no. In 1971, *Apollo 15* astronaut David Scott stood on the moon and dropped a feather and a hammer. Television audiences were amazed to see both objects strike the moon's surface at the same time. Now you can perform a version of this classic experiment in the classroom.

Procedure

1. Select **two pieces of identical notebook paper.** Crumple one piece of paper into a ball.
2. Place the flat piece of paper on top of a **book** and the paper ball on top of the flat piece of paper.
3. Hold the book waist high, and then drop it to the floor.

Analysis

4. Which piece of paper reached the bottom first? Did either piece of paper fall slower than the book? Explain your observations in your ScienceLog.
5. Now hold the crumpled paper in one hand and the flat piece of paper in the other. Drop both pieces of paper at the same time. What else affected the speed of the falling paper besides gravity? Record your observations in your ScienceLog, and share your ideas with your classmates.

TRY at HOME

START-UP Activity

STRANGE GRAVITY

MATERIALS
For Each Student:
• 2 pieces of notebook paper
• book

Teacher's Notes

You might point out to students that when David Scott performed this experiment on the moon's surface, he paid homage to Galileo. While Galileo did predict that the mass of an object does not affect the rate at which the object falls, it is uncertain whether he proved this theory by dropping cannonballs of different masses from the Leaning Tower of Pisa, as legend tells.

Answers to START-UP Activity

4. Both pieces of paper should reach the bottom at the same time. They should have fallen at the same rate as the book. Gravity causes all objects to fall at the same rate, regardless of their mass.
5. The crumpled piece of paper should reach the floor first. While gravity pulled both pieces toward the floor, the crumpled piece of paper hit the ground first because it fell with less air resistance.

SECTION 1

Focus

A Solar System Is Born

This section describes the solar system and explains how it formed from a collapsing nebula. The nebula first formed planetesimals, then planets formed in the outer regions, and finally a star (the sun) formed at the nebula's center. Students will learn why the planets that formed close to the sun are rocky, while those far from the sun are large and gaseous. The section concludes with a discussion of planetary orbits and rotation.

Bellringer

Display this question on the board or an overhead projector:

Could astronauts land on a star in the same way that they landed on the moon? Why or why not? (No; stars are composed of gas, not solid rock like the moon. Stars are also a lot hotter!)

1) Motivate

COOPERATIVE LEARNING

Display a poster of the solar system or a selection of photographs of the planets and the sun. Form student groups, and have each group brainstorm to come up with a list of facts they know about the solar system and some questions they want to answer. Then ask each group to study the display and to note the following:

- what a planet's orbit looks like
- how planets close to the sun differ from those far away

Discuss students' observations and hypotheses about why these conditions exist.
Sheltered English

SECTION 1 READING WARM-UP

Terms to Learn

solar system	orbit
nebula	revolution
solar nebula	period of revolution
planetesimal	ellipse
rotation	astronomical unit

What You'll Do

- Explain the basic process of planet formation.
- Compare the inner planets with the outer planets.
- Describe the difference between rotation and revolution.
- Describe the shape of the orbits of the planets, and explain what keeps them in their orbits.

A Solar System Is Born

You probably know that Earth is not the only planet orbiting the sun. In fact, it has eight fellow travelers in its cosmic neighborhood. Together these nine planets and the sun are part of the solar system. The **solar system** is composed of the sun (a star) and the planets and other bodies that travel around the sun. But how did our solar system come to be?

The Solar Nebula

All the ingredients for building planets are found in the vast, seemingly empty regions between the stars. But these regions are not really empty—they contain a mixture of gas and dust. The gas is mostly hydrogen and helium, while the dust is made up of tiny grains of elements such as carbon and iron. The dust and gas clump together in huge interstellar clouds called **nebulas** (or *nebulae*), which are so big that light takes many years to cross them! Nebulas, like the one shown in **Figure 1,** are cold and dark. Over time, light from nearby stars interacts with the dust and gas, forming many new chemicals. Eventually, complex molecules similar to those necessary for life form deep within the nebulas. These clouds are the first ingredients of a new planetary system.

Gravity Pulls Matter Together Because these clouds of dust and gas consist of matter, they have mass. *Mass,* which is a measure of the amount of matter in an object, is affected by the force of gravity. But because the matter in a nebula is so spread out, the attraction between the dust and gas particles is very small. If a nebula's density were great enough, then the attraction between the particles might be strong enough to pull everything together into the center of the cloud. But even large clouds don't necessarily collapse toward the center because there is another effect, or force, that pushes in the opposite direction of gravity. You'll soon find out what that force is.

Figure 1 *The Horsehead nebula is a cold, dark cloud of gas and dust as well as a possible site for future star formation.*

34

Multicultural CONNECTION

Many cultures have myths that describe the creation of the sun. An Australian aboriginal myth explains that people and animals lived in total darkness before the sun appeared. One day an emu egg was thrown into the sky and collided with a pile of dry wood. The wood burst into flame, and a fire burned in the sky. The Great Spirit replenishes the firewood to keep the sun burning. Have interested students find other solar creation myths and make illustrated storyboards of the myths they discover.

Pressure Pushes Matter Apart *Temperature* is a measure of how fast the particles in an object move around. If the gas molecules in a nebula move very slowly, the temperature is very low and the cloud is cold. If they move fast, the temperature is high and the cloud is warm. Because the cloud has a temperature that is above absolute zero, the gas molecules are moving. There is no particular structure in the cloud, and individual gas molecules can move in any direction. Sometimes they crash into each other. As shown in **Figure 2,** these collisions create a push, or *pressure,* away from the other gas particles. This pressure is what finally balances the gravity and keeps the cloud from collapsing.

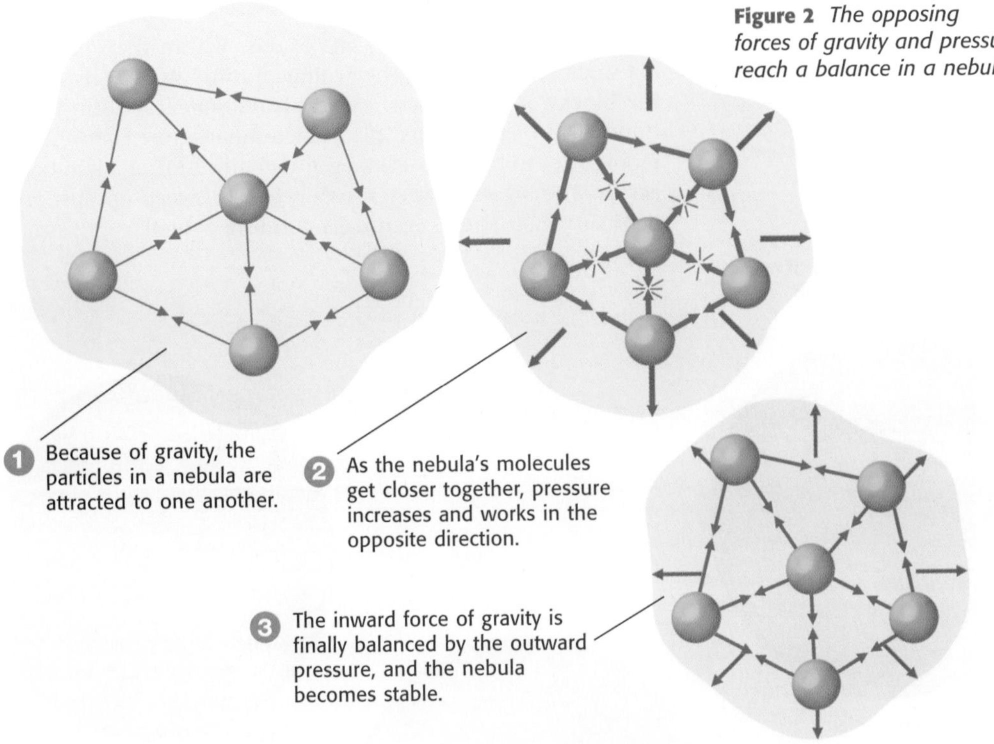

1 Because of gravity, the particles in a nebula are attracted to one another.
2 As the nebula's molecules get closer together, pressure increases and works in the opposite direction.
3 The inward force of gravity is finally balanced by the outward pressure, and the nebula becomes stable.

Figure 2 *The opposing forces of gravity and pressure reach a balance in a nebula.*

The Solar Nebula Forms Sometimes something happens to upset this balance. Two nebulas can crash into each other, for example, or a nearby star can explode, causing material from the star to crash into the cloud. These events compress small regions of the cloud so that gravity overcomes the pressure. Gravity then causes the cloud to collapse inward. At this point, the stage is set for the formation of a star and, as in the case of our sun, its planets. The **solar nebula** is the name of the nebula that formed into our own solar system.

Self-Check

What keeps a nebula from collapsing? *(See page 200 to check your answer.)*

35

2 Teach

Using the Figure

Have students refer to the three steps in **Figure 2** as they explain the force that pulls particles together (gravity) and the force that pushes them apart (pressure due to the collision of particles).

Be sure that students understand the role of temperature in this system. (As temperature increases, particles speed up, collisions increase, and pressure increases.)

Discussion

Have student volunteers describe in their own words an example of a system that is in equilibrium because opposing forces of gravity (pulling) and pressure (pushing) balance one another. (One example is a person sitting in a chair; gravity pulls down with a force equal to the force with which the chair pushes up.)

Homework

Research In October 1995, astronomers discovered the first planet orbiting a star outside of our solar system. The planet is in orbit around the star 51 Pegasi. Astronomers did not directly observe the planet. Instead they observed and measured the wobble in the star's velocity, apparently caused by the gravitational pull of the planet. Since then, astronomers have discovered more planets around other stars. Have students find out how many planets have been discovered and write a brief report comparing what we know about the planets, including our own.

MISCONCEPTION ALERT

Make sure students understand that temperature is a measure of random molecular motion, or vibration, of the particles in a material. This is not the same as the bulk motion of a material. For example, a cold gas or liquid can flow at a fast speed, but this motion does not affect its temperature.

Answers to Self-Check

The balance between gravity and pressure keeps a nebula from collapsing.

Directed Reading Worksheet Section 1

2 Teach, continued

BRAIN FOOD

On Earth a cubic meter of air at sea level has a mass of about 1 kg. Each molecule of air is separated by only one-billionth of a meter (a nanometer). The best artificial vacuums that can be created in laboratories can reduce the number of air molecules in a given volume by a factor of 1 billion. This means that the molecules are one-millionth of a meter apart (a micrometer). How much space is in outer space? In young stellar nurseries, the amount of matter in a cubic meter is smaller by another factor of 1 billion and gas molecules are 1 mm apart! But this is still 10 billion times more dense than interstellar space!

ACTIVITY

Modeling Planetesimal Formation Have students work in pairs. Each pair will need a couple of sheets of wax paper and a small spray bottle with some water tinted by food coloring. Have students spray a little water on a sheet of wax paper. As students observe the wax paper after each spray, they will see large drops form. Discuss whether this is an accurate model of planetesimal formation, and note how gravity, rather than surface tension, causes planetesimals to form.

Biology CONNECTION

Some of the complex molecules created in the cold, dark clouds that eventually form stars and planets contain amino acids. Amino acids are the building blocks of proteins and life. Scientists wonder if some of this material survives in the planetesimals that formed far from the sun—the comets. Could comets have brought life-forming molecules to Earth?

From Planetesimals to Planets

Once the solar nebula started to collapse, things happened quickly, at least on a cosmic time scale. As the dark cloud collapsed, matter in the cloud got closer and closer together. This made the attraction between particles even stronger. The stronger attraction pulled the cloud together, and the gas and dust particles moved at a faster rate, increasing the temperature at the center of the cloud.

As things began to get crowded near the center of the solar nebula, particles of dust and gas in the cloud began to bump into other particles more often. Eventually much of the dust and gas began slowly rotating about the center of the cloud. The rotating solar nebula eventually flattened into a disk.

Planetesimals Sometimes bits of dust within the solar nebula stuck together when they collided, forming the tiny building blocks of the planets, called **planetesimals.** Within a few hundred thousand years, the planetesimals grew from microscopic sizes to boulder-sized, eventually measuring a kilometer across. The biggest planetesimals began to sweep up dust and debris in their paths, eventually forming planets.

Figure 3 The Process of Solar System Formation

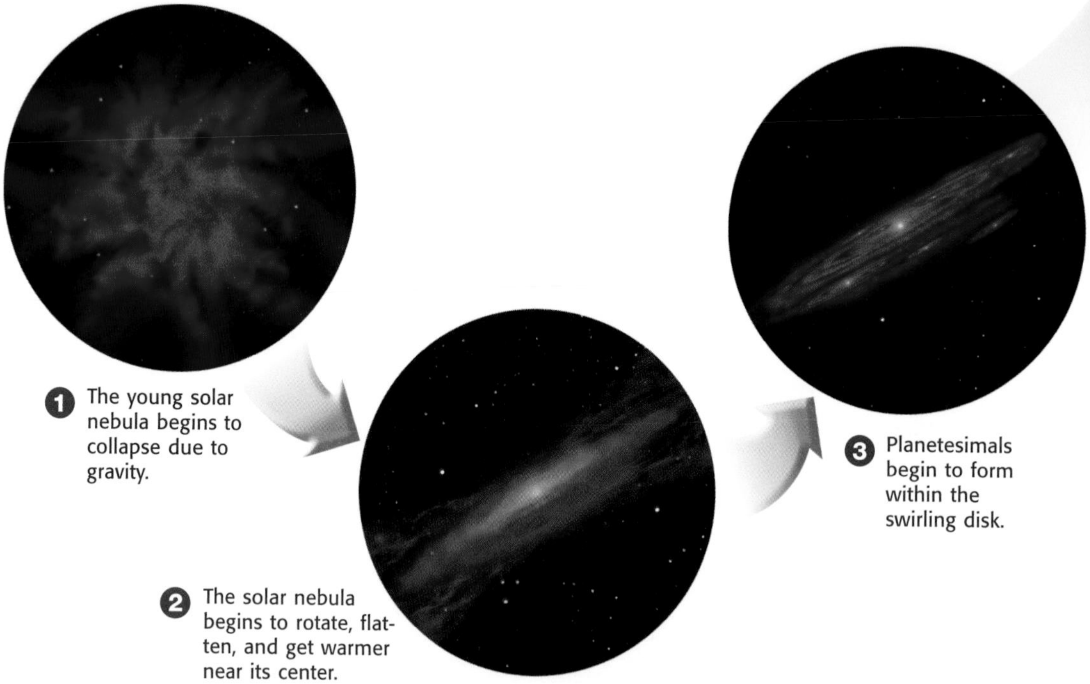

1 The young solar nebula begins to collapse due to gravity.
2 The solar nebula begins to rotate, flatten, and get warmer near its center.
3 Planetesimals begin to form within the swirling disk.

Homework

Prepare a Presentation Have students find information about the asteroid belt, the Kuiper belt, the Oort cloud, and comets. Ask them to explain one or more of these phenomena using the steps shown in **Figure 3.** Encourage students to find a creative way to present their findings.

IS THAT A FACT!

Scientists think that all Earth-like planetesimals have a thin atmosphere during formation. During the accretion process, this atmosphere is stripped away. If a subsequent atmosphere develops, it comes primarily from gases released during the differentiation of the planet's mantle.

4 Because of their greater gravitational attraction, the largest planetesimals begin to collect more and more of the dust and gas of the solar nebula.

5 Smaller planetesimals collide with the larger ones, and planets begin to grow.

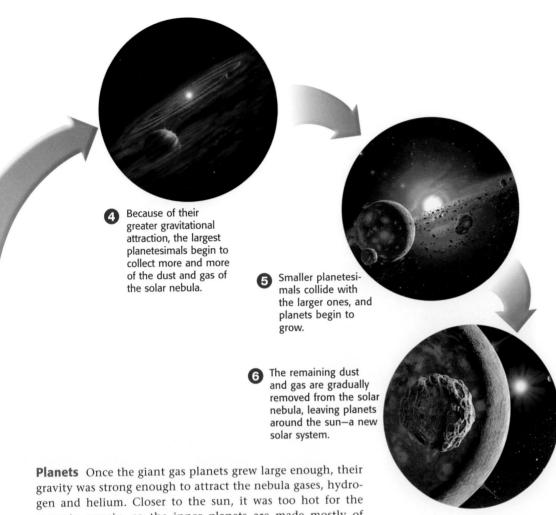

6 The remaining dust and gas are gradually removed from the solar nebula, leaving planets around the sun—a new solar system.

Planets Once the giant gas planets grew large enough, their gravity was strong enough to attract the nebula gases, hydrogen and helium. Closer to the sun, it was too hot for the gases to remain, so the inner planets are made mostly of rocky material.

Craters and Comets Collisions with smaller planetesimals became more violent as pieces of debris became larger, leaving many craters on the surface of the rocky planets. We see evidence of this today particularly on Mercury, Mars, and our moon.

In the final steps of planet formation, the remaining planetesimals crashed down on the planets or got thrown to the outer edge of the solar nebula by the gravity of the larger planets. Occasionally something, perhaps a passing star, sends them journeying toward the sun. If the planetesimal is icy, we see this visitor as a *comet.*

Self-Check

Why are the giant gas planets so large? *(See page 200 to check your answer.)*

Meeting Individual Needs

Learners Having Difficulty

Have students list characteristics of the inner and the outer planets. (inner planets: rocky, small, thin atmosphere, few or no moons, Earth and Mars have a molten core, dense; outer planets: mostly gas, huge, thick atmosphere, many moons, rocky core, not dense)

Using a diagram of the solar system with the orbits of the planets drawn to scale, guide students to explain what caused these differences. (Being close to the sun caused gases to burn away and allows only high-temperature solids, such as rock, to condense.)

Sheltered English

MATH and MORE

Density is a measure of the amount of matter in a specific unit of space. Have students answer the questions below, and have them create a bar graph comparing the densities of different planets.

- How many times denser than Jupiter is Mercury? ($\frac{5.43}{1.32} = 4.11$)
- How many times denser than Saturn is Earth? ($\frac{5.52}{0.69} = 8.00$)

Planet	Mean Density (g/cm^3)
Mercury	5.43
Venus	5.20
Earth	5.52
Mars	3.93
Jupiter	1.32
Saturn	0.69
Uranus	1.32
Neptune	1.64
Pluto	2.05

Math Skills Worksheet "Density"

Cross-Disciplinary Focus

History Gerard Peter Kuiper (rhymes with "viper") lived from 1902 to 1973 and is often called the father of modern planetary science. Kuiper made discoveries about Saturn and its largest moon, Titan, as well as about Mars, Uranus, Neptune, Pluto, and Jupiter. Have students find out more about his discoveries.

Answers to Self-Check

The giant gas planets were massive enough for their gravity to attract hydrogen and helium.

2 Teach, *continued*

Guided Practice

Writing Discuss how Boyle's and Charles's laws help us understand the formation of the solar system.

- Boyle's law: at a constant temperature, the volume of a gas is inversely proportional to the pressure.
- Charles's law: at constant pressure, the volume of a gas is directly proportional to the temperature.

Review with students the difference between inverse and direct relationships, and have them give examples. Ask students to explain, in writing, why the temperature of a nebula increases as it becomes denser.

Reteaching

Draw four large squares on the board, and label them as follows:

1. The Solar Nebula
2. The Nebula Collapsing
3. The Planetesimals Form
4. The Sun and Planets Form

Have volunteers help you sketch each stage of solar-system formation in the appropriate square. Use arrows and phrases to indicate changes in temperature and the balance between gravity and pressure. Sheltered English

Independent Practice

Concept Mapping Have students construct a concept map that explains the formation of the solar system. Make sure that students correctly identify the physical processes involved at each stage.

Birth of a Star But what was happening at the middle of the solar nebula? The central part of the solar nebula contained so much mass and had become so hot that hydrogen fusion began. This created so much pressure at the center of the solar nebula that outward pressure balanced the inward force of gravity. At this point, the gas stopped collapsing. As the sun was born, the remaining gas and dust of the nebula were blown into deep space by a strong solar wind, and the new solar system was complete.

From the time the nebula first started to collapse, it took nearly 10 million years for the solar system to form. So how do we know that our ideas of star and planet formation are correct when nobody was around to watch it? Powerful telescopes, such as the Hubble Space Telescope, are now able to show us some of the fine details inside distant nebulas. One such nebula is shown in **Figure 4.** For the first time, scientists can see disks of dust around stars that are in the process of forming.

Figure 4 *The Orion nebula contains several "star nurseries"—disks of gas and dust where new stars form. The insets show newly-formed stars within some of these disks.*

internet**connect**

sciLINKS. NSTA

TOPIC: The Planets
GO TO: www.scilinks.org
***sci*LINKS NUMBER:** HSTE455

SECTION REVIEW

1. What two forces balance each other to keep a nebula of dust and gas from collapsing or flying apart?
2. Why does the composition of the giant gas planets differ from that of the rocky inner planets?
3. Explain why there is only one planet in each orbit around the sun.
4. **Making Inferences** Why do all the planets go around the sun in the same direction, and why do the planets all lie in a flat plane?

Answers to Section Review

1. gravity and pressure
2. Giant gas planets were far enough from the sun to collect lighter gases. Close to the sun, it was hot enough that only rocky material and dust were present.
3. The largest planetesimal in an orbit collected all of the material in its path and became a planet.
4. The planets formed from the flattened disk of the nebula, which rotated in one direction. The dust and gas that formed the planets moved in the same direction that the nebula was spinning.

Planetary Motion

The solar system, which is now 4.6 billion years old, is not simply a collection of stationary planets and other bodies around the sun. Each one moves according to strict physical laws. The ways in which the Earth moves, for example, cause seasons and even day and night.

Rotation and Revolution How does the motion of the Earth cause day and night? The answer has to do with the Earth's spinning on its axis, or **rotation.** As the Earth rotates, only one-half of the Earth faces the sun at any given time. The half facing the sun is light (day), and the half facing away from the sun is dark (night).

In addition to rotating on its axis, the Earth also travels around the sun in a path called an **orbit.** This motion around the sun along its orbit is called **revolution.** The other planets in our solar system also revolve around the sun. The amount of time it takes for a single trip around the sun is called a **period of revolution.** The period for the Earth to revolve around the sun is 365 days. Mercury orbits the sun in 88 days.

BRAIN FOOD

All planets *revolve* around the sun in the same direction. If you could look down on the solar system from above the sun's north pole, you would see all the planets revolving in a counterclockwise direction. Not all planets *rotate* in the same direction, however. Venus, Uranus, and Pluto rotate backward compared with the rest of the planets.

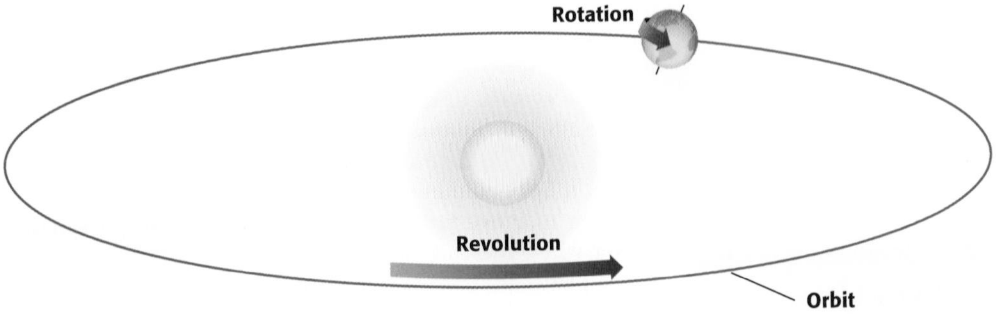

Figure 5 *A planet rotates on its own axis and revolves around the sun in a path called an orbit.*

Planetary Orbits But why do the planets continue to revolve around the sun? Does something hold them in their orbit? Why doesn't gravity pull the planets toward the sun? Or why don't they fly off into space? To answer these questions, we need to go back in time to look at the discoveries made by the scientists of the 1500s and 1600s.

Danish astronomer Tycho Brahe (TIE koh BRAW uh) carefully observed the positions of the planets for over a quarter of a century. When he died in 1601, his young assistant, Johannes Kepler, inherited all of his records. Kepler set out to understand the motions of the planets and to make a simple description of the solar system.

READING STRATEGY

Mnemonics Encourage students to create a mnemonic device to help them differentiate between planet rotation and revolution. For example, they might link the long *a* in *rotation* with the fact that Earth makes one rotation in a *day*. The following rhyme may also help them remember:

As we rotate, we spin about
our axis and live a day.
A revolution is a voyage
around the sun and a year
will pass away.

Sheltered English

BRAIN FOOD

The rings of ice and rock that circle the gas giants (Jupiter, Saturn, Uranus, and Neptune) may have formed when asteroids collided with the moons of these planets. Earth is also developing a system of rings. These rings are not moon debris, however, but debris from satellites and space missions. Have interested students research the problem of orbiting space trash and the proposed solutions to clean it up. Students can also design their own solution to address the problem of orbiting debris.

Teaching Transparency 186
"Earth's Rotation and Revolution"

MISCONCEPTION ALERT

Students may believe that the Earth's elliptical orbit brings it closer to the sun in the summer, warming the planet. The shape of Earth's orbit has nothing to do with the seasons; the seasons are caused by the tilt of Earth on its axis. In the summer, the Northern Hemisphere is tilted toward the sun. In the winter, the Northern Hemisphere is tilted away from the sun. Earth is actually closest to the sun during the Northern Hemisphere's winter.

2 Teach, *continued*

QuickLab

MATERIALS

- string, about 12 cm long
- unlined paper
- 2 thumbtacks
- pencil

Safety Caution: Students should use care with thumbtacks to avoid injuring themselves or damaging the surface on which they work. Have them put a piece of cardboard under their sheet of paper.

Answer to QuickLab

4. The closer together the foci are, the more circular the ellipse is.

MATH and MORE

Have students use a ruler to measure segments *a, b, c,* and *d* in **Figure 6** and then test Kepler's first law of motion. Point out that the illustration shows the string at two distinct points in its description of an ellipse.

Teaching Transparency 187
"Ellipse"

internetconnect

SCILINKS NSTA

TOPIC: The Planets
GO TO: www.scilinks.org
***sci*LINKS NUMBER:** HSTE455

TOPIC: Kepler's Laws
GO TO: www.scilinks.org
***sci*LINKS NUMBER:** HSTE460

QuickLab

Staying in Focus

1. Take a short piece of **string,** and pin both ends to a **piece of paper** with two **thumbtacks.**
2. Keeping the string stretched tight at all times, use a **pencil** to trace out the path of an ellipse.
3. Change the distance between the thumbtacks to change the shape of the ellipse.
4. How does the position of the thumbtacks (foci) affect the ellipse?

TRY at HOME

Kepler's First Law of Motion Kepler's first discovery, or *first law of motion,* came from his careful study of the movement of the planet Mars. He discovered that the planet did not move in a circle around the sun, but in an elongated circle called an *ellipse.* An **ellipse** is a closed curve in which the sum of the distances from the edge of the curve to two points (called *foci*) inside the ellipse is always the same, as shown in **Figure 6.**

Figure 6 Parts of an Ellipse

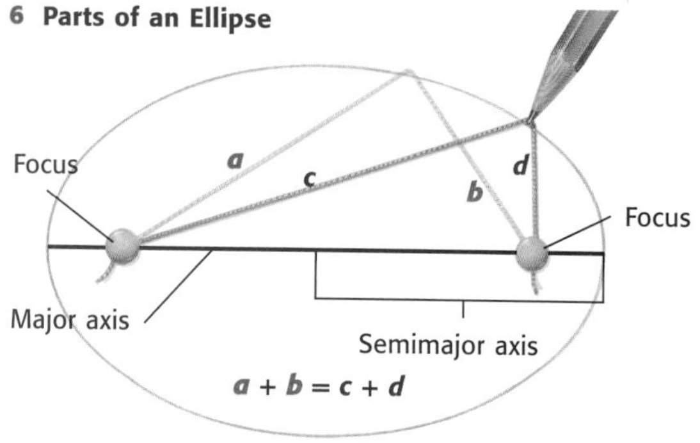

The maximum length of an ellipse is called its *major axis,* and half of this distance is the *semimajor axis,* which is usually used to give the size of an ellipse. The semimajor axis of Earth's orbit, for example, is 150 million kilometers. It represents the average distance between the Earth and the sun and is called one **astronomical unit,** or one AU.

Kepler's Second Law Kepler also discovered that the planets seem to move faster when they are close to the sun and slower when they are farther away. To illustrate this, imagine that a planet is attached to the sun by a string. The string will sweep out the same area in equal amounts of time. To keep the area of *A,* for example, equal to the area of *B,* the planet must move farther around its orbit in the same amount of time. This is Kepler's *second law of motion.*

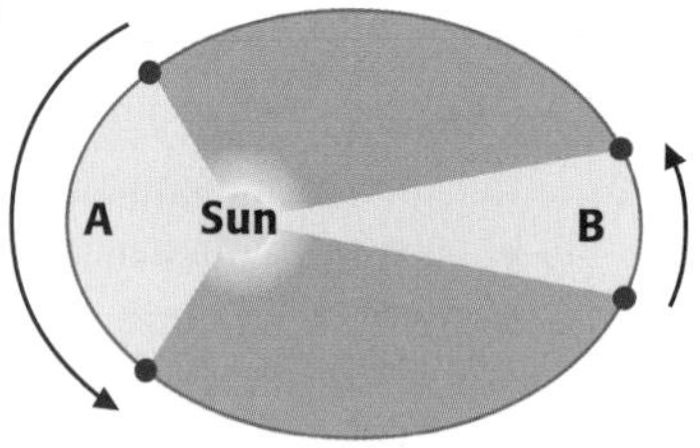

Kepler's Third Law Kepler's *third law of motion* compares the period of a planet's revolution with its semimajor axis. By doing some mathematical calculations, Kepler was able to demonstrate that by knowing a planet's period of revolution, the planet's distance from the sun can be calculated.

MATH BREAK

Kepler's Formula

Kepler's third law can be expressed with the formula

$$P^2 = a^3$$

where P is the period of revolution and a is the semimajor axis of an orbiting body. For example, Mars's period is 1.88 years, and its semimajor axis is 1.523 AU. Therefore, $1.88^2 = 1.523^3 = 3.53$. If astronomers know either the period or the distance, they can figure the other one out.

Science Bloopers

Johannes Kepler was obsessed with trying to describe the geometric harmony of the universe. He believed that there were five perfect geometric solids that fit precisely between the six known planets and that this pattern contained the divine meaning of the solar system. Although Kepler was wrong, his efforts to prove this idea enabled him to discover the elliptical orbit of the planets.

Newton's Law of Universal Gravitation

Kepler wondered what caused the planets closest to the sun to move faster than the planets farther away, but he never got an answer. It was Sir Isaac Newton who finally put the puzzle together. He did this with his ideas about *gravity.* Newton didn't understand *why* gravity worked or what caused it. Even today, modern scientists do not fully understand gravity. But Newton was able to combine the work of earlier scientists to explain *how* the force of attraction between matter works.

An Apple One Day Newton reasoned that small objects fall toward the Earth because the Earth and the objects are attracted to each other by the force of gravity. But because the Earth has so much more mass than a small object, say an apple, only the object appears to move.

Newton thus developed his *law of universal gravitation,* which states that the force of gravity depends on the product of the masses of the objects divided by the square of the distance between them. In other words, if two objects are moved twice as far apart, the gravitational attraction between them will decrease by a factor of $2 \times 2 = 4$, as shown in **Figure 7.** If the objects are moved 10 times as far apart, the gravitational attraction will decrease by a factor of $10 \times 10 = 100$.

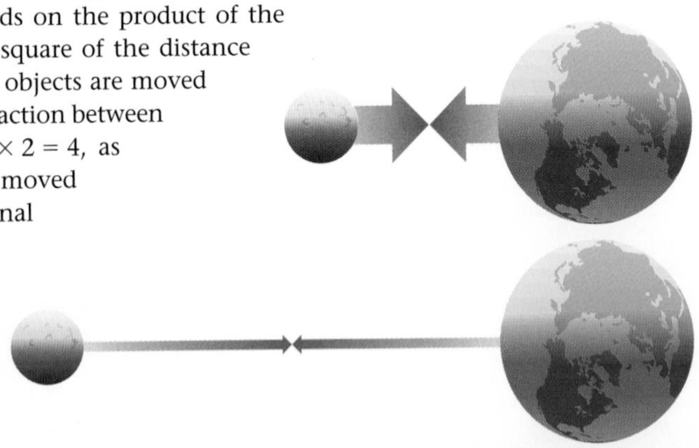

Figure 7 *If two objects are moved twice as far apart, the gravitational attraction between them will be four times less.*

APPLY

Newton's Law and Satellites

Space engineers that plan the paths of orbiting satellites must be able to calculate the height of the most appropriate orbit and the location of the satellite at each moment. To do this, they must take into account both Kepler's laws of motion and Newton's law of universal gravitation. Try this exercise: If the mass of the Earth were twice its actual mass, by how much would the gravity increase on a satellite in orbit around Earth? If the satellite were suddenly moved three times farther away, would Earth's gravitational pull on the satellite increase or decrease? By how much?

41

3 Extend

Cross-Disciplinary Focus

Writing **Language Arts** While Kepler described the orbits of planets, Sir Isaac Newton (1642–1727) showed *why* they orbit. His law of universal gravitation explains why planets do not fly off into space:

- Every object in the universe attracts every other object in the universe with a force dependent on its mass and the square of the distance between them.

Newton's law of inertia explains why planets do not fall into the sun:

- An object remains in a state of rest or motion unless acted upon by an outside force.

Have students use these ideas to compose a letter to Kepler explaining why the planets stay in orbit.

Homework

PORTFOLIO The Dutch astronomer and mathematician Christiaan Huygens (1629–1695) discovered Saturn's largest moon, Titan, in 1655. He knew that Saturn and Titan take 30 Earth years to orbit the sun and observed that the Titanians' lives "must be very different from ours, having such tedious winters." Have students write a short story describing life on another planet and provide information on the planet's climate and the length of its days and years.

Answers to APPLY

If Earth's mass were doubled, the effect of gravity on a satellite would be doubled. If the satellite were moved three times farther away, gravity would decrease by nine times ($3 \times 3 = 9$).

WEIRD SCIENCE

When you consider the motion of the Earth's rotation, the Earth's revolution around the sun, and the sun's movement around the Milky Way galaxy, you are actually traveling more than 900,000 km/h just standing still.

4 Close

Quiz

1. Explain the imbalance that creates a solar nebula. (In a nebula, gravity and gas pressure are balanced. If an outside force, such as an explosion, causes the particles to move closer together, gravity may then trigger the collapse of the cloud.)
2. Why does the center of a collapsing nebula form a star? (Pressure is so intense among the crowded particles that atoms fuse, giving off enormous amounts of energy.)
3. How do planets form? (Particles swirling in a cloud of dust and gas stick together, forming planetesimals, which accumulate more matter and finally form planets.)

ALTERNATIVE ASSESSMENT

Writing Have students write a story in their ScienceLog that would explain to a seventeenth-century astronomer how the sun and the planets of our solar system formed. A seventeenth-century astronomer would not know, by name, nebulas or planetesimals. Students should share their stories with the class.

Teaching Transparency 188
"Gravity and the Motion of the Moon"

Critical Thinking Worksheet
"A Balooney Universe"

Activity

When the space shuttle is in orbit, we see the astronauts floating around as they work. Many people talk about this as a "zero-g" environment, meaning no gravity. Is this correct? Are shuttle astronauts affected by gravity? Do research to find out what happens when objects are in orbit around Earth.

TRY at HOME

Falling Down and Around How did Newton explain the orbit of the moon around the Earth? After all, according to gravity, the moon should come crashing into the Earth. And this is what the moon would do if it were not moving at a high velocity. In fact, if it were not for gravity, the moon would simply shoot off away from the Earth.

To understand this better, imagine twirling a ball on the end of a string. As long as you hold the string, the ball will orbit your hand. As soon as you let go of the string, the ball will fly off in a straight path. This same principle applies to the moon. But instead of a hand holding a string, gravity is keeping the moon from flying off in a straight path. **Figure 8** shows how this works. This same principle holds true for all bodies in orbit, including the Earth and other planets in our solar system.

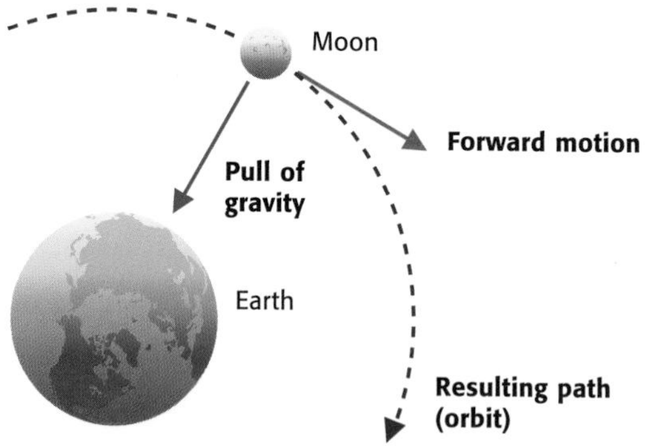

Figure 8 *Gravity is actually causing the moon to fall toward the Earth, changing what would be a straight-line path. The resulting path is a curved orbit.*

SECTION REVIEW

1. On what properties does the force of gravity between two objects depend?
2. Will a planet or comet be moving faster in its orbit when it is farther from or closer to the sun? Explain.
3. How does gravity keep a planet moving in an orbit around the sun?
4. **Applying Concepts** Suppose a certain planet had two moons, one of which was twice as far from the planet as the other. Which moon would complete one revolution of the planet first? Explain.

internet connect
sciLINKS NSTA
TOPIC: Kepler's Laws
GO TO: www.scilinks.org
***sci*LINKS NUMBER:** HSTE460

42

Answers to Section Review

1. mass and distance
2. According to Kepler's second law, a planet sweeps out equal areas in equal amounts of time. When the planet is close to the sun, it must travel a longer distance along its orbit to sweep out the same amount of area. Because speed is distance traveled per unit of time, the planet will travel faster when it is close to the sun.
3. The motion of a planet is balanced between falling toward the sun and moving in a straight line past the sun. The resultant path is a curved orbit around the sun.
4. The closer moon would finish first. Kepler's third law states that period of revolution is related to the distance of an orbiting body from the object it orbits (its semimajor axis).

SECTION 2

READING WARM-UP

The Sun: Our Very Own Star

Terms to Learn

corona
chromosphere
photosphere
convective zone
radiative zone
core
nuclear fusion
sunspot

What You'll Do

- Describe the basic structure and composition of the sun.
- Explain how the sun produces energy.
- Describe the surface activity of the sun, and name some of its effects on Earth.

There is nothing special about our sun, other than the fact that it is close enough to the Earth to give us light and warmth. Otherwise, the sun is similar to most of the other stars in our galaxy. It is basically a large ball of gas made mostly of hydrogen and helium held together by gravity. But let's take a closer look.

The Structure of the Sun

Although it may look like the sun has a solid surface, it does not. When we see a picture of the sun, we are really seeing through the sun's outer atmosphere, down to the point where the gas becomes so thick we cannot see through it anymore. As shown in **Figure 9,** the sun is composed of several layers.

Figure 9 **Structure of the Sun and Its Atmosphere**

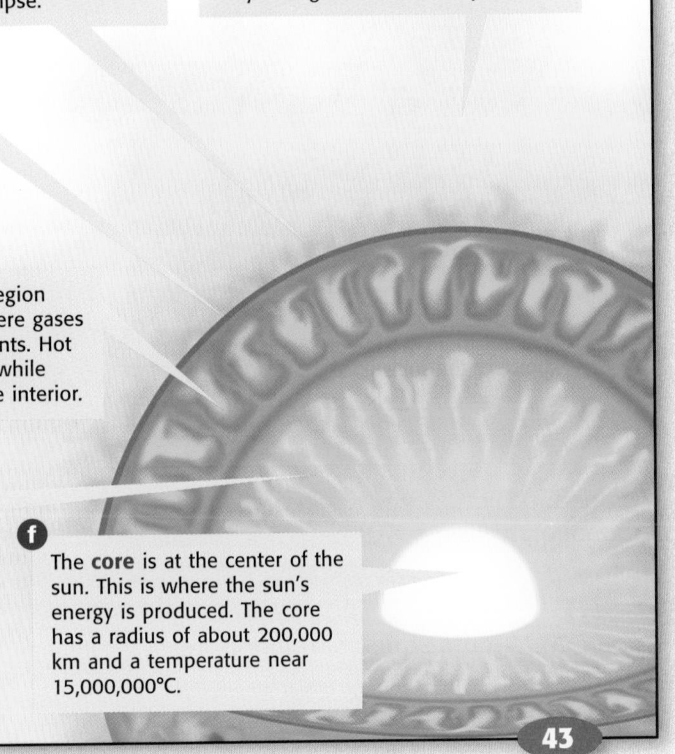

a The corona forms the sun's outer atmosphere and can extend outward a distance equal to 10–12 times the diameter of the sun. The gases in the corona are so thin that it is visible only during a total solar eclipse.
b The chromosphere is a thin region below the corona, only 3,000 km thick. Like the corona, the deep, red chromosphere is too faint to see unless there is a total solar eclipse.
c The photosphere is where the gases get thick enough to see. The photosphere is what we know as the visible surface of the sun. It is only about 600 km thick.
d The convective zone is a region about 200,000 km thick where gases circulate in convection currents. Hot gases rise from the interior while cooler gases sink toward the interior.
e The radiative zone is a very dense region about 300,000 km thick. The atoms in this zone are so closely packed that light can take millions of years to pass through.
f The core is at the center of the sun. This is where the sun's energy is produced. The core has a radius of about 200,000 km and a temperature near 15,000,000°C.

43

SECTION 2

Focus

The Sun: Our Very Own Star

This section describes the structure of the sun. Students will learn early theories about the source of the sun's energy and why nuclear fusion is the accepted model today. Finally, students will learn how the sun's surface activity affects the Earth.

Bellringer

Have students write about the following quotation by Henry Thoreau:

The sun is but a morning star.

1 Motivate

DEMONSTRATION

Observing Sunspots Clamp a pair of binoculars in a ring stand and cut a hole in a piece of cardboard that fits around the eyepiece of one binocular lens. Darken the classroom and orient the binoculars toward the sun. Hold a mirror in the shadow of the cardboard and project an image of the sun onto a wall. Focus the image and have students identify sunspots and other features of the sun.

Safety Caution: Do not look at the sun through the binoculars.

IS THAT A FACT!

During an eclipse in 1868, a French astronomer named Pierre Janssen detected a new element in the chromosphere of the sun that was unknown on Earth. The new element, called helium (named after the Greek word for the sun, *helios*) was not discovered on Earth until 1895.

WEIRD SCIENCE

Even though the temperature of the corona can reach 2 million degrees Celsius, particles in the corona are so far apart that they don't transfer much thermal energy. A spaceship could enter the sun's corona and not burn up, despite the high temperature.

Teaching Transparency 189 "Structure of the Sun and Its Atmosphere"

Directed Reading Worksheet Section 2

2 Teach

USING THE FIGURE

Refer students to **Figure 9** on the previous page. Have students find dictionary definitions for the name of each of the sun's layers and write an additional caption that explains why that name is appropriate for that particular layer. Sheltered English

READING STRATEGY

Prediction Guide Before students read the section on energy production in the sun, ask them what they think the major source of the sun's energy is.

a. It burns fuel, releasing energy.

b. Gravity is causing it to collapse, releasing energy.

c. Intense pressure is fusing atoms, releasing energy.

d. all of the above

(c)

MATH and MORE

Have students create a line graph showing the differences in the temperature of the sun's layers from the core to the corona.

core: 15,000,000°C

radiative zone: 8,000,000°C

convective zone: 500,000°C

photosphere: 6,000°C

chromosphere: 4,000°–50,000°C

corona: 2,000,000°C

BRAIN FOOD

Despite the large size of Jupiter and Saturn, the sun itself contains over 99 percent of all the matter in the solar system.

Energy Production in the Sun

The sun has been shining on the Earth for about 4.6 billion years. How can it stay hot for so long? And what makes it shine? Over the years, several theories have been proposed to answer these questions. Because the sun is so bright and hot, many people thought that it was burning fuel to create the energy. But the amount of energy that is released during burning would not be enough to power the sun. If the sun were simply burning, it would last for only 10,000 years.

Burning or Shrinking? It eventually became clear that burning wouldn't last long enough to keep the sun shining. Scientists began to think that the sun was slowly shrinking due to gravity and that perhaps this would release enough energy to heat the sun. While the release of gravitational energy is more powerful than burning, it is still not enough to power the sun. If all of the sun's gravitational energy were released, the sun would last for only 45 million years. We know that dinosaurs roamed the Earth more than 65 million years ago, so this couldn't be the explanation. Something even more powerful was needed.

Figure 10 *Ideas about the source of the sun's energy have changed over time.*

Some type of burning fuel was first thought to be the source of the sun's energy.

A shrinking sun was another explanation for solar energy.

44

Multicultural CONNECTION

Ancient cultures imagined the sun as a glorious god. The Greeks called their sun god *Helios* and depicted him driving a flaming chariot across the sky. For the Egyptians, *Ra* was a sun god and the creator and controller of the universe. The Japanese considered their emperor to be a descendant of their sun goddess, *Amaterasu*.

Nuclear Fusion At the beginning of the twentieth century, Albert Einstein demonstrated that matter and energy are interchangeable. Matter can be converted to energy according to his famous formula: $E = mc^2$, where E is energy, m is mass, and c is the speed of light. Because the speed of light is so large, even a small amount of matter can produce a large amount of energy. This idea paved the way for an understanding of a very powerful source of energy. **Nuclear fusion** is the process by which two or more nuclei with small masses (such as hydrogen) join together, or fuse, to form a larger, more massive nucleus (such as helium). During the process, energy is produced—a lot of it!

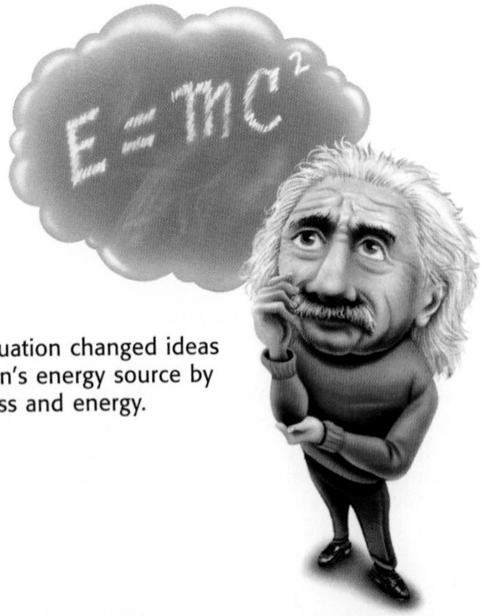

Einstein's equation changed ideas about the sun's energy source by equating mass and energy.

Biology CONNECTION

At the time Darwin introduced his theory of evolution, scientists thought that the sun was a few million years old at most. Some scientists argued that evolution—which takes place over billions of years—was therefore impossible because the sun could not have been shining that long. The nuclear fusion that fuels the sun, however, gives it a lifespan of at least 10 billion years!

Atomic Review

Let's do a little review. *Atoms* are the smallest particles of matter that keep their chemical identity. An atom consists of a *nucleus* surrounded by one or more *electrons,* which have a negative charge. A nucleus is made up of two types of particles—*protons,* with a positive charge, and *neutrons,* with no charge. The positively charged protons in the nucleus are balanced by an equal number of negatively charged electrons. The number of protons and electrons gives the atom its chemical identity. A helium atom, for example, has two protons and two electrons.

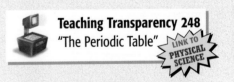

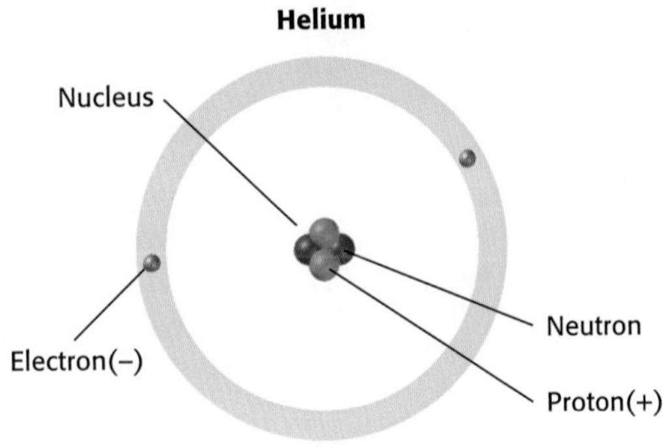

45

COOPERATIVE LEARNING

Escape from the Sun Have groups create a board game to model the movement of energy in the sun. Students should begin by making a game board out of poster board. The board should accurately illustrate the structure of the sun from the core to the corona. Then have students create a series of index cards with questions and answers about the sun. A player begins the game as a proton and attempts to "collide" with another proton in the sun's core. A player "collides" when he or she correctly answers a question. Players will continue through each step of the fusion process by correctly answering more questions. They will then leave the core as energy and continue traveling to the convective and radiative zones by correctly answering more questions. The object of the game is to reach the Earth's surface as infrared, UV, or visible light energy.

CONNECT TO PHYSICAL SCIENCE

As generations of stars are born, grow old, and re-form, heavy elements have become more abundant in the universe. Our solar system formed late in the history of the universe and has thus incorporated more heavy elements in its structure. Use Transparency 248 to discuss the origin of the elements in the periodic table.

Teaching Transparency 248
"The Periodic Table" LINK TO PHYSICAL SCIENCE

BRAIN FOOD

Stars are the crucibles in which the heavy elements of the universe are forged. The calcium in our bones and the iron in our blood originated in stars—we are made of "star stuff." The big bang produced mainly helium and hydrogen, the fuel that powers stars. All other elements in the universe are produced during the life cycle of stars. Our sun is massive enough to create elements as heavy as oxygen, and red giants can produce elements as heavy as sodium. Elements heavier than iron are synthesized only when extremely massive supergiants become supernovae.

internet connect

SCLINKS NSTA
TOPIC: The Sun
GO TO: www.scilinks.org
***sci*LINKS NUMBER:** HSTE465

3 Extend

DEBATE

Nuclear Fusion: Feasible Energy Source for Earth?
Nuclear fusion is a reaction that produces tremendous amounts of energy. If that energy could be harnessed, nuclear fusion would provide a practically unlimited energy source. Nuclear fusion, however, requires such high temperatures and pressures that it has not been a feasible source of energy on Earth. Scientists have attempted to duplicate solar fusion using magnetic fields and lasers, but the research is very expensive. Do its potential benefits outweigh the burden of this expense? Why or why not? Who should fund the research? Why? Ask students to research the most recent fusion studies and to debate these questions.

GOING FURTHER

Writing The magnetic cycle of the sun produces sunspots, prominences, solar flares, and solar wind. Have students read further and prepare a report on what causes these phenomena and how they affect Earth's atmosphere. Students may also wish to investigate the links between sunspot cycles and climate change on Earth.

Homework

Concept Mapping Have students create a concept map that explains the process of solar nuclear fusion.

Teaching Transparency 190
"Fusion of Hydrogen in the Sun"

Figure 11 *Like charges repel, just like similar poles on a pair of magnets.*

Fusion in the Sun Under normal conditions, the nuclei of hydrogen atoms never get close enough to combine. This is because they are positively charged, and like charges repel each other, as shown in **Figure 11.** In the center of the sun, however, the temperature and pressure are very high because of the huge amount of matter within the core. This gives the hydrogen nuclei enough energy to overcome the repulsive force, allowing the conversion of hydrogen to helium, as shown in **Figure 12.**

Figure 12 Fusion of Hydrogen in the Sun

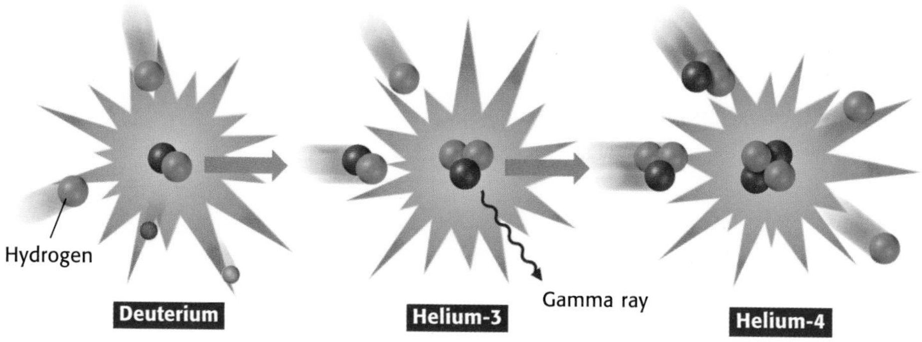

1. Two hydrogen nuclei (protons) collide. One proton emits particles and energy, then becomes a neutron. The proton and neutron combine to produce a heavy form of hydrogen called *deuterium.*
2. Deuterium combines with another hydrogen nucleus to form a variety of helium called helium-3. More energy is released, as well as gamma rays.
3. Two helium-3 atoms then combine to form ordinary helium-4, releasing more energy and a pair of hydrogen nuclei.

BRAIN FOOD

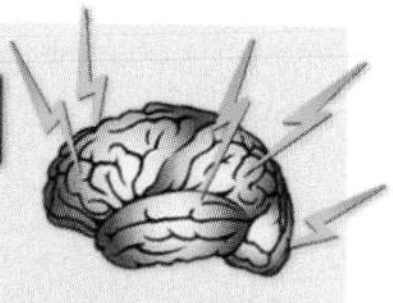

The energy released during the nuclear fusion of 1 g of hydrogen is equal to about 100 tons of TNT! Each second, the sun converts about 5 million tons of matter into pure energy.

The energy produced in the core of the sun takes millions of years to reach the sun's surface. In the radiative zone, the matter is so crowded that the light and energy keep getting blocked and sent off in different directions. Eventually the energy reaches the convective zone, where hot gases carry it up to the photosphere relatively quickly. From there the energy leaves the sun as light, taking only 8.3 minutes to reach Earth.

Activity on the Sun's Surface

The photosphere, or the visible surface of the sun, is a very dynamic place. As energy from the sun's interior reaches the surface, it causes the gas to boil and churn, a result of the rising and sinking of gases in the convective zone below.

46

CROSS-DISCIPLINARY FOCUS

Health Explain that atoms of the same element with varying numbers of neutrons are called *isotopes*. Isotopes that are unstable are called *radioactive*. Radioactive isotopes are useful in treating some cancers. Have students talk with a local oncologist or the local American Cancer Society chapter to find out more about such treatments.

IS THAT A FACT!

We have learned from observing sunspots that the sun rotates. Because the sun is made of gases, it rotates faster at its equator than at its poles. Sunspots at the equator take about 25 days to go around, while sun spots near the poles take about 35 days.

Sunspots The circulation of the gases within the sun, in addition to the sun's own rotation, produces magnetic fields that reach out into space. But these magnetic fields also tend to slow down the activity in the convective zone. This causes areas on the photosphere above to be slightly cooler than surrounding areas. These areas show up as sunspots. **Sunspots** are cooler, dark spots on the sun, as shown in **Figure 13.**

The number of sunspots and their location on the sun change in a regular cycle. Records of the number of sunspots have been kept ever since the invention of the telescope. In **Figure 14,** the sunspot cycle is shown, with the exception of the years 1645–1715, when sunspots were not observed.

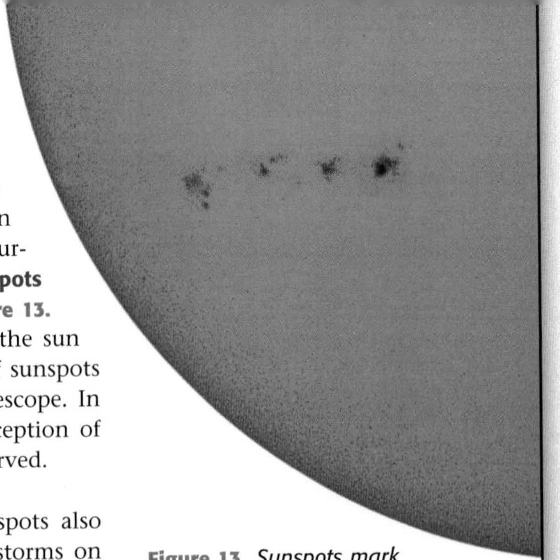

Figure 13 *Sunspots mark cooler areas on the sun's surface. They are related to changes in the magnetic properties of the sun.*

Solar Flares The magnetic fields that cause sunspots also cause disturbances in the solar atmosphere. Giant storms on the surface of the sun, called *solar flares,* have temperatures of up to 5 million degrees Celsius. Solar flares send out huge streams of particles from the sun. These particles interact with the Earth's upper atmosphere, causing spectacular light shows called *auroras*. Solar flares can interrupt radio communications on Earth. They can also affect satellites in orbit. Scientists are trying to find ways to predict solar activity and give advanced warning of such events.

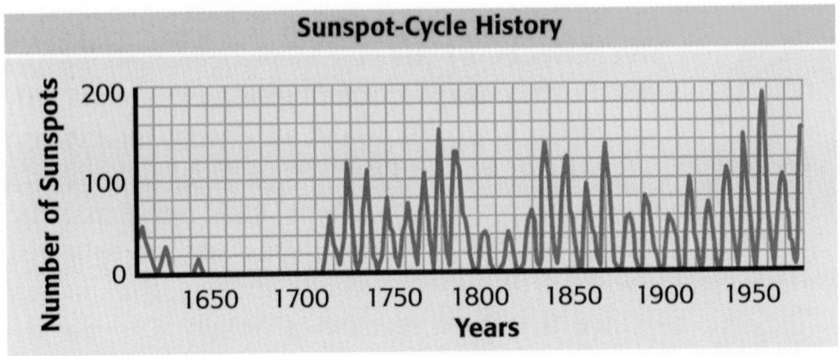

Figure 14 *This graph shows the number of sunspots that have occurred each year since Galileo's first observations, in 1610.*

SECTION REVIEW

1. According to modern understanding, what is the source of the sun's energy?
2. If nuclear fusion in the sun's core suddenly stopped today, would the sky be dark in the daytime tomorrow? Why?
3. **Interpreting Illustrations** In Figure 12, the nuclear fusion process ends up with one helium-4 nucleus and two free protons. What might happen to the two protons next?

internetconnect

SCILINKS NSTA

TOPIC: The Sun
GO TO: www.scilinks.org
***sci*LINKS NUMBER:** HSTE465

47

4 Close

Quiz

1. How do you know that gravity does not produce the sun's energy? (If all of the sun's gravitational energy were released, the sun would last only 45 million years; the solar system is at least 4.6 billion years old.)
2. What happens during nuclear fusion? (Hydrogen nuclei fuse, forming helium atoms and releasing huge amounts of energy.)
3. How does energy produced by nuclear fusion move from the sun's core to space? (It moves very slowly through the radiative zone, circulates through the convective zone, and passes through the photosphere and into the chromosphere and corona.)

ALTERNATIVE ASSESSMENT

Have students explain, orally or in writing, how energy released from the collision of two protons in the sun's core warms a car seat on Earth. Students should account for the following:

- nuclear fusion
- the movement of energy through the radiative and convective zones
- Earth's atmosphere
- the amount of time this process takes

Answers to Section Review

1. nuclear (hydrogen) fusion
2. No; it would take millions of years for the last energy made in the core to reach the surface of the sun.
3. The two free protons (hydrogen nuclei) might collide, starting the process again.

Reinforcement Worksheet
"Stay on the Sunny Side"

Section 3

Focus

The Earth Takes Shape

This section explores the formation of Earth and explains how gravity and rising temperatures caused the planet to become spherical and separate into layers of different density. Students will learn about the stages in the development of Earth's atmosphere and how our atmosphere sustains life today. The section concludes with a discussion of how oceans and continents formed.

Bellringer

Tell students that the Earth is approximately 4.6 billion years old. The first fossil evidence of life on Earth has been dated to nearly 3.5 billion years ago.

Have them write a paragraph in their ScienceLog describing what Earth might have been like during the first billion years of its existence.

1 Motivate

Demonstration

Heat water in a beaker until it boils, and ask students to describe what is happening. (Water vapor is released from the heated liquid.)

Explain that gases released from Earth's molten surface helped create its first atmosphere. Explain that the gases in our atmosphere are held by gravity, and ask students to speculate why there is very little hydrogen or helium in our atmosphere if these are the most abundant elements in the universe. (These gases are so light that Earth's gravity cannot trap them.) Sheltered English

Section 3 — Reading Warm-Up

Terms to Learn

crust
mantle
core

What You'll Do

- Describe the shape and structure of the Earth.
- Explain how the Earth got its layered structure and how this process affects the appearance of Earth's surface.
- Explain the development of Earth's atmosphere and the influence of early life on the atmosphere.
- Describe how the Earth's oceans and continents were formed.

The Earth Takes Shape

Investigating the early history of the Earth is not easy because no one was there to study it directly. Scientists develop ideas about what happened based on their knowledge of chemistry, biology, physics, geology, and other sciences. Astronomers are also gathering evidence from other stars where planets are forming to better understand how our own solar system formed.

The Solid Earth Takes Form

As scientists now understand it, the Earth formed from the accumulation of planetesimals. This would have taken place within the first 10 million years of the collapse of the solar nebula—the blink of an eye on the cosmic time scale!

The Effects of Gravity When a young planet is still small, it can have an irregular shape, like a potato. As more matter builds up on the young planet, the force of gravity increases and the material pushing toward the center of the planet gets heavier. When a rocky planet, such as Earth, reaches a diameter of about 350 km, pressure from all this material becomes greater than the strength of the rock. At this point, the planet starts to become spherical in shape as the rock in the center is crushed by gravity.

Figure 15 *The Earth has not always looked as inviting as it does today.*

The Effects of Heat As planetesimals fell to Earth, the energy of their motion made the Earth warmer. A second source of energy for heating the Earth was radioactive material, which was present in the solar nebula. Radioactive material radiates energy, and as this energy collected within the Earth, it also heated the planet. Once the Earth reached a certain size, the interior could not cool off as fast as its temperature rose, and the rocky material inside began to melt. As you will see on the next page, the effects of heat and gravity contributed to the formation of the Earth's layers.

Self-Check

Why is the Earth spherical in shape, while most asteroids and comets are not? ***(See page 200 to check your answer.)***

48

Answer to Self-Check

Earth has enough mass that gravitational pressure crushed and melted rocks during its formation. The force of gravity pulled this material toward the center, forming a sphere. Asteroids are not massive enough for their interiors to be crushed or melted.

The Earth and Its Layers Have you ever dropped pebbles into water or tried mixing oil and vinegar together for a salad? What happens? The heavier material (either solid or liquid) sinks, and the lighter material floats to the top. This is because of gravity. The material with a higher density is more strongly attracted and falls to the bottom. The same thing happened in the young Earth. As its rocks melted, the heavy elements, such as nickel and iron, sank to the center of the Earth, forming what we call the *core.* Lighter materials floated to the surface. This process is illustrated in **Figure 16.**

Figure 16 Earth's Materials Separate into Layers

All materials in the early Earth are randomly mixed.
Rocks melt, and dense materials separate and sink.
Less-dense materials rise, and layers are formed.

The Earth's Interior The Earth is divided into three distinct layers according to the composition of its materials. These layers are shown in **Figure 17.** Geologists map the interior of the Earth by measuring how sound waves pass through the planet during earthquakes and underground explosions.

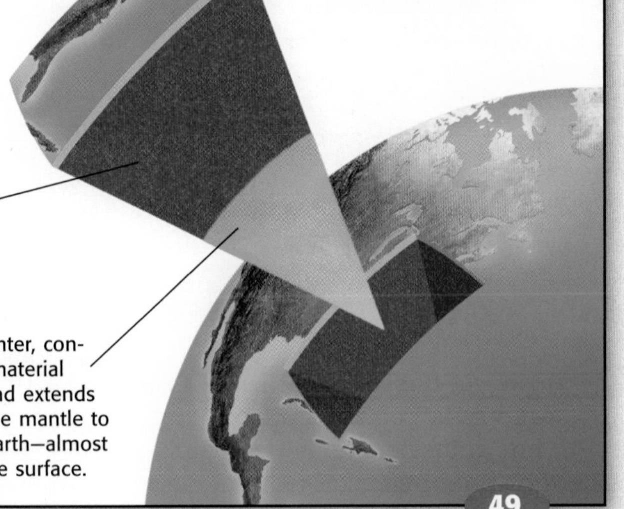

1 The **crust** is the outermost layer of the Earth. It forms a thin skin over the entire planet, ranging from 5 km to 100 km thick.
2 The **mantle** lies below the crust, extending from about 100 km to about 2,900 km below the surface. The mantle contains denser rocks than the crust.
3 The **core,** at the center, contains the heaviest material (nickel and iron) and extends from the base of the mantle to the center of the Earth—almost 6,400 km below the surface.

Figure 17 *The interior of the Earth consists of three layers.*

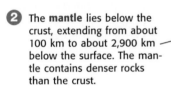

QuickLab

Mixing It Up

Have you ever mixed oil and water and watched what happened? Try this.

1. Pour 50 mL of **water** into a 150 mL **beaker.**
2. Add 50 mL of **cooking oil** to the water. Stir vigorously.
3. Let the mixture stand undisturbed for a few minutes.
4. What happens to the oil and water?
5. How does this relate to the interior of the early Earth?

2 Teach

QuickLab

MATERIALS

For Each Group:
- 50 mL water
- 150 mL beaker
- 50 mL cooking oil

Answers to QuickLab

4. The oil floats on top of the water.
5. The water, which is denser than oil, sinks to the bottom in the same way that iron and nickel sank to the center of the Earth.

CONNECT TO GEOLOGY

Have students use the transparency listed below to compare Mars with the core of Earth in terms of diameter and mass. The Earth's core is 33 percent of Earth's mass. Although Mars has approximately the same volume as Earth's core, its mass is only 11 percent of Earth's mass. Ask students to compare the density of Mars with the density of the Earth's core and to explain the differences they note. (Mars is less dense than the core of the Earth. This is because Earth's core formed as a result of differentiation, and denser elements sank to the core.) Sheltered English

Teaching Transparency 122 "The Composition of the Earth"

Directed Reading Worksheet Section 3

Science Bloopers

Impact craters have left scars on planets and moons throughout the solar system. In 1826, an eccentric Bavarian astronomer named Franz von Paula Gruithuisen was one of the first to suggest that lunar craters were caused by meteorite impacts. However, he also asserted that other lunar features were built by a race of moon creatures called Selenites, and his theory of crater formation was not taken seriously. Students will enjoy reading and reporting on other imaginative descriptions of the moon by authors such as Jules Verne. Even astronomer Johannes Kepler wrote about creatures living on the moon.

2 Teach, *continued*

INDEPENDENT PRACTICE

Poster Project Have students create a series of drawings and captions showing how Earth's atmosphere first formed and how it changed over time. Encourage students to use creative approaches, such as comic-strip frames, to communicate the concepts. Sheltered English

MATH and MORE

Remind students that ratios are a means of comparing two values using division. Have students calculate the ratio of oxygen to nitrogen in Earth's present atmosphere. (They can round percentages to the nearest tenth.)

21:78 rounds to 20:80

20:80 = 2:8 or 1:4

The ratio is one part oxygen to four parts nitrogen.

Math Skills Worksheet "Reducing Fractions to Lowest Terms"

internetconnect

SciLINKS NSTA

TOPIC: The Layers of the Earth
GO TO: www.scilinks.org
***sci*LINKS NUMBER:** HSTE470

TOPIC: The Oceans
GO TO: www.scilinks.org
***sci*LINKS NUMBER:** HSTE475

Chemistry CONNECTION

The Cassini Mission to Saturn (launched in October 1997) will study the chemistry of Saturn's moon Titan. Titan's atmosphere, like Earth's, is composed mostly of nitrogen, but it also contains many hydrogen-rich compounds. Scientists want to study how molecules essential to life may form in this atmosphere.

The Atmosphere Evolves

Other than the presence of life, one of the biggest differences between the Earth of today and the Earth of 4.6 billion years ago is the character of its atmosphere. Earth's atmosphere today is composed of 21 percent oxygen, 78 percent nitrogen, and about 1 percent argon (with tiny amounts of many other gases). But it has not always been this way. Read on to discover how the Earth's atmosphere has changed through time.

Earth's First Atmosphere Earth's early atmosphere was very different from the atmosphere of today. In the 1950s, laboratory experiments on the origins of life were based on the hypothesis that Earth's early atmosphere was largely made up of methane, ammonia, and water. And because the solar nebula was rich in hydrogen, many scientists thought that Earth's first atmosphere also contained a lot of hydrogen compounds.

Figure 18 *This is an artist's view of what Earth's surface may have looked like shortly after Earth's formation.*

New Evidence New evidence is changing the way we think about Earth's first atmosphere. For one thing, 85 percent of the Earth's matter probably came from material similar to *meteoroids*—planetesimals made of rock. The other 15 percent probably came from the outer solar system in the form of *comets*—planetesimals made of ice.

Volcanic Gases During the final stages of formation, the Earth was hit many times by planetesimals, and the surface was very hot, even molten in places, as illustrated in **Figure 18.** The ground would have been venting large amounts of gas released from the heated minerals. The composition of meteorites tells us that much of that gas would have been water vapor and carbon dioxide. These two gases are also commonly released during volcanic eruptions. Earth's first atmosphere was probably a steamy atmosphere made of water vapor and carbon dioxide.

50

SCIENCE HUMOR

Q: Have you heard about the new restaurant on the moon?

A: great food, lousy atmosphere

The Role of Impacts Planetesimal impacts may have helped release gases from the Earth. In addition, they may have also helped to knock some of those gases back into space. Because planetesimals travel very fast, their impacts can speed up gas molecules in the atmosphere enough for them to overcome gravity and escape into space.

Heavier elements, such as iron, that were on the surface of the Earth also reacted chemically with water, giving off hydrogen—the lightest element. And because the early Earth was very warm, this hydrogen also had enough energy to escape.

Comets brought in a range of elements, such as carbon, hydrogen, oxygen, and nitrogen. They may also have brought water that eventually helped form the oceans, as shown in **Figure 19.**

Figure 19 *Comets may have brought some of the water that formed Earth's early oceans.*

Earth's Second Atmosphere After the Earth cooled off and the core formed, it became possible for the Earth's second atmosphere to take shape. This atmosphere formed from gases contributed by both volcanoes and comets. Volcanoes, like the one in **Figure 20,** produced large amounts of water vapor, along with chlorine, nitrogen, sulfur, and large amounts of carbon dioxide. This carbon dioxide kept the planet much warmer than it is today.

Figure 20 *As this volcano in Hawaii shows, a large amount of gas is released during an eruption.*

Environment Connection

Because carbon dioxide is a very good *greenhouse gas*—one that traps thermal energy—scientists have tried to estimate how much carbon dioxide the Earth must have had in its second atmosphere in order to keep it as warm as it was. For example, if all of the carbon dioxide that is now tied up in the rocks and minerals of the ocean floor were released, it would make an atmosphere of carbon dioxide 60 times as thick as our present atmosphere.

Independent Practice

Writing Ask students to choose one step in the development of Earth's atmosphere and eliminate it. Then ask them to describe what the composition of Earth's atmosphere would be like if this step had not occurred.

Connect to Life Science

If the early Earth had contained a lot of oxygen in its atmosphere, the chemical processes that gave rise to life probably would not have occurred! Oxygen is very reactive, combining with other elements readily. High levels of oxygen would have prevented organic molecules from combining, thus stopping the development of early forms of life.

Misconception Alert

Movies and films have popularized the notion that large meteors threaten Earth and could cause colossal destruction. Although several tons of meteoroid material enters Earth's atmosphere each day, most pieces have a mass of only a few milligrams. Only the largest meteors reach Earth's surface and become meteorites. Meteor showers that are detectable only by radio telescopes occur regularly.

Is That a Fact!

Earth is growing heavier by thousands of metric tons every year. Microscopic dust constantly filters through the atmosphere from space and lands on our planet.

3 Extend

READING STRATEGY

Activity Before students read this page, ask them to write down what they know about ultraviolet rays from the sun. (Students may note that UV rays help the body form vitamin D but that they also cause sunburn, snow blindness, cataracts, and skin cancer.)

Have students share their facts and discuss the ways people protect themselves from UV radiation.

Ask students what effect they think UV rays would have if Earth had no atmosphere to absorb them. Have students assess their ideas after they have finished reading this section.
Sheltered English

DEBATE

Life on Earth: Could It Happen Again? Ask students to imagine that life on Earth is completely destroyed. Encourage students to debate whether life could evolve again with our current atmosphere. Students should consider conditions on primitive Earth as well as the requirements for life as we know it.

Earth's Current Atmosphere How did this early atmosphere change to become the atmosphere we know today? It happened with the help of solar ultraviolet (UV) radiation, the very thing that we worry about now for its cancer-causing ability. Solar UV light is dangerous because it has a lot of energy and can break molecules apart in the air or in your skin. Today we are shielded from most of the sun's ultraviolet rays by Earth's protective ozone layer. But Earth's early atmosphere had no ozone, and many molecules were broken apart in the atmosphere. The pieces were later washed out into shallow seas and tide pools by rain. Eventually a rich supply of these pieces of molecules collected in protected areas, forming a rich organic solution that is sometimes called a "primordial soup."

The Source of Oxygen Although there was no ozone, water offered protection from the effects of ultraviolet radiation. In these sheltered pools of water, complex molecules may have been able to form. Then, sometime between 4.6 and 3.9 billion years ago, life began on Earth. By 3.7 to 3.4 billion years ago, living organisms had evolved that were able to photosynthesize energy from sunlight and produce oxygen as a byproduct. These early life-forms are still around today, as shown in **Figure 21.**

Figure 21 *Fossilized algae (left) are among the earliest signs of life discovered. Today's stromatolites (right) are mats of microorganisms thought to be similar to the first life on Earth.*

Eventually, between 2.5 and 2.0 billion years ago, the amount of oxygen started to increase rapidly—reaching about 20 percent of the amount we have in the atmosphere today. As plants began to cover the land, oxygen levels increased because plants produce oxygen during photosynthesis. Therefore, it was the emergence of life that completely changed our atmosphere into the one we have today.

MISCONCEPTION ALERT

Primordial means "original," coming from the Latin for "first order." Students may think that the early oceans were the primordial "soup" from which life arose. Recent work suggests that life may have actually begun in a hydrothermal vent system where organisms evolved that could derive energy from chemosynthesis.

WEIRD SCIENCE

Could life exist on Jupiter? Portions of its atmosphere have water, moderate temperatures, and gases that could sustain life. Carl Sagan and Edwin E. Salpeter have postulated the existence of floating organisms that synthesize food from Jupiter's atmosphere, providing food for other organisms.

Oceans and Continents

It is hard to say exactly when the first oceans appeared on Earth, but they probably formed early, as soon as the Earth was cool enough for rain to fall and remain on the surface. We know that Earth's second atmosphere had plenty of water vapor. After millions of years of rainfall, water began to cover the Earth, and by 4 billion years ago, a giant global ocean covered the planet. For the first few hundred million years of the Earth's history, there were no continents.

So how and when did the continents appear? Continental crust material is very light compared with material in the mantle. The composition of the granite and other rocks making up the continents tells geologists that the rocks of the crust have melted and cooled many times in the past. Each time the rocks melted, the heavier elements sank, leaving the lighter ones to rise to the surface. This process is illustrated in **Figure 22.**

internet**connect**

sciLINKS. NSTA

TOPIC: The Layers of the Earth, The Oceans
GO TO: www.scilinks.org
***sci*LINKS NUMBER:** HSTE470, HSTE475

The Growth of Continents After a while, some of the rocks were light enough that they no longer sank, and they began to pile up on the surface. This was the beginning of the earliest continents. After gradually thickening, the continents slowly rose above the surface of the ocean. These scattered young continents didn't stay in the same place, however, because the slow convection in the mantle pushed them around. By around 2.5 billion years ago, continents really started to grow. By 1.5 billion years ago, the upper mantle had cooled and become denser and heavier, so it was easier for the colder parts of it to sink. Then the real continental action, or *plate tectonics,* began.

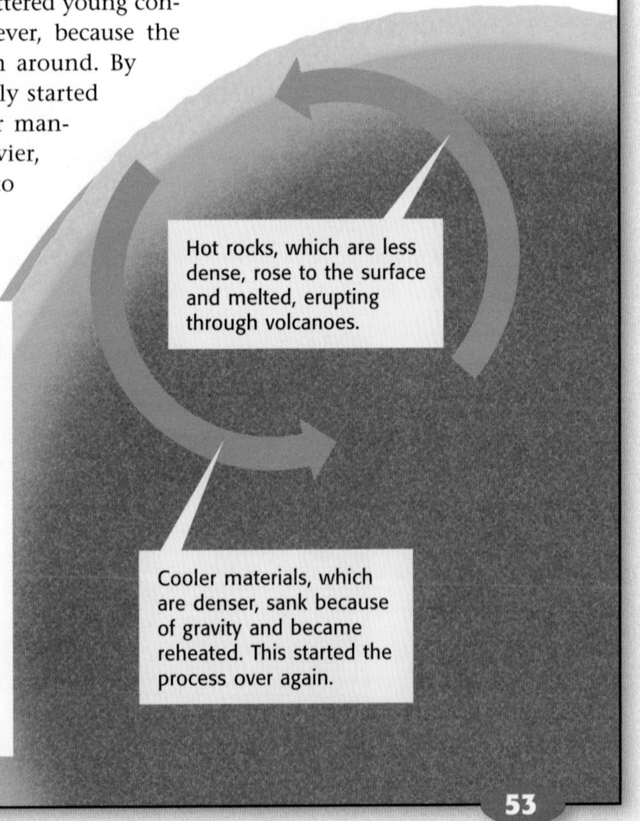

Hot rocks, which are less dense, rose to the surface and melted, erupting through volcanoes.
Cooler materials, which are denser, sank because of gravity and became reheated. This started the process over again.

Figure 22 *The slow convective motion in the Earth's mantle was the engine that caused mantle rock to rise and sink, forming the continents.*

SECTION REVIEW

1. Why did the Earth separate into distinct layers?
2. How did the Earth's atmosphere change composition to become today's nitrogen and oxygen atmosphere?
3. Which are older, oceans or continents? Explain.
4. **Drawing Conclusions** If the Earth were not hot inside, would we have moving continents (plate tectonics)? Explain.

53

4 Close

Quiz

1. Why was there a large amount of water vapor in Earth's second atmosphere? (Volcanic eruptions produced large amounts of water vapor. Comets crashing into the forming Earth also brought water.)
2. How and when did oxygen become abundant in Earth's atmosphere? (Sometime between 3.7 and 3.4 million years ago, life-forms evolved that could produce oxygen through photosynthesis; over millions of years, oxygen levels increased.)
3. How has the relationship between ozone and life on Earth changed since the time of Earth's early atmosphere? (The absence of ozone in Earth's early atmosphere allowed molecules to be broken apart by UV radiation. These broken-down molecules combined to form the complex molecules that gave rise to life. Currently, the ozone layer protects life on Earth from the harmful effects of UV radiation.)

Alternative Assessment

Have students review this section and write facts about each stage of Earth's development on 3 × 5 in. cards. Mix the cards as a deck. Students should form teams and play a quiz game. Teams will earn points by assigning the correct fact to the correct stage of the Earth's development.

Answers to Section Review

1. Melting inside the Earth allowed heavy material to sink to the center and lighter materials to rise to the surface.
2. The Earth's first atmosphere contained methane, ammonia, and water. Later, volcanoes added carbon dioxide, chlorine, nitrogen, and sulfur. Comets brought carbon, hydrogen, nitrogen, and oxygen. Solar energy created new chemicals that led to the formation of living organisms. These organisms greatly changed the composition of the atmosphere by adding oxygen.
3. Oceans are older because they formed as soon as the Earth was cool enough to allow rain to collect. Continents formed later as lighter materials separated from the Earth's mantle and rose above sea level.
4. No; convection in the mantle causes crustal movement and plate tectonics.

Reinforcement Worksheet
"Third Rock from the Sun"

Discovery Lab

How Far Is the Sun?
Teacher's Notes

Time Required
One 45-minute class period

Lab Ratings
EASY → HARD

Teacher Prep 2
Student Set-Up 1
Concept Level 4
Clean Up 1

MATERIALS

The materials listed on the student page are enough for a group of 2–3 students.

Safety Caution
Remind students to review all safety cautions and icons before beginning this lab activity. Also caution students never to look directly at the sun.

Preparation Notes
Conduct this activity on a sunny day. This lab works best in the late afternoon because the sun is lower in the sky. The sunlight should come through the window at an angle as close to perpendicular as possible. It may help to lower the blinds so that the sunlight will pass through a narrow opening.

Sample data is provided in the table below.

Diameter of image	Distance from hole to image
2 cm	214 cm

Discovery Lab
USING SCIENTIFIC METHODS

How Far Is the Sun?

It doesn't slice, it doesn't dice, but it can give you an idea of how big our universe is! You can build your very own stellar-distance measuring device from household items. Amaze your friends by figuring out how many metersticks can be placed between Earth and the sun.

MATERIALS

- poster board
- scissors
- square of aluminum foil
- thumbtack
- masking tape
- index card
- meterstick
- metric ruler

Ask a Question

1. How many metersticks could I place between the Earth and the sun?

Conduct an Experiment

2. Measure and cut a 434 cm square from the middle of the poster board. Tape the foil square over the hole in the center of the poster board.
3. Carefully prick the foil with a thumbtack to form a tiny hole in the center. Congratulations—you have just constructed your very own stellar-distance measuring device!
4. Tape the device to a window facing the sun so that sunlight shines directly through the pinhole. **Caution:** Do not look directly into the sun.
5. Place one end of the meterstick against the window and beneath the foil square. Steady the meterstick with one hand.

54

Daniel Bugenhagen
Yutan Jr.–Sr. High School
Yutan, Nebraska

6 With the other hand, hold the index card close to the pinhole. You should be able to see a circular image on the card. This image is the sun.

7 Move the card back until the image is large enough to measure. Be sure to keep the image on the card sharply focused. Reposition the meterstick so that it touches the bottom of the card.

8 Ask your partner to measure the diameter of the image on the card with the metric ruler. Record the diameter of the image in your ScienceLog.

9 Record the distance between the window and the index card by reading the point at which the card rests on the meterstick.

10 Calculate the distance between Earth and the sun using the following formula:

$$\text{Distance between the sun and Earth} = \text{Sun's diameter} \times \frac{\text{Distance to the image}}{\text{Image's diameter}}$$

Hint: The sun's diameter is 1,392,000,000 m.

1 cm	=	10 mm
1 m	=	100 cm
1 km	=	1,000 m

Analyze the Results

11 According to your calculations, how far is the sun from the Earth? Don't forget to convert your measurements to meters.

Draw Conclusions

12 You could put 150 billion metersticks between Earth and the sun. Compare this information with your result in step 11. Do you think that this activity was a good way to measure the Earth's distance from the sun? Support your answer.

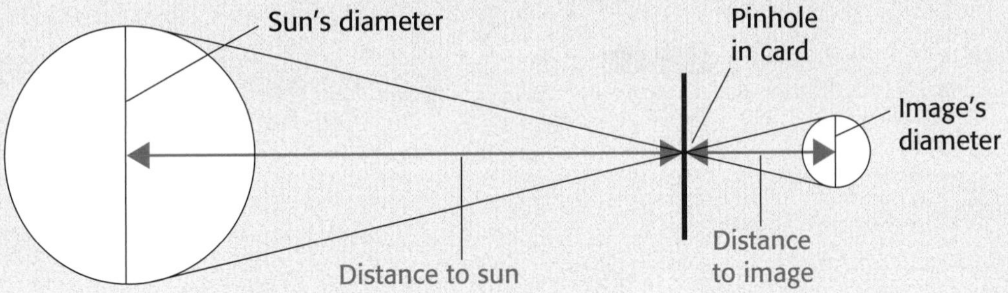

Discovery Lab

Background

On the board, draw the diagram at the bottom of the page and explain that this activity uses triangles and proportions to find the distance to the sun. Because the sun forms the image on the paper, there must be a proportionate relationship between the triangles in the diagram. The hole divides the proportions, so the distance between the image and the hole is related to the distance between the sun and the hole.

Answers

11. Answers will vary, but based on the sample data and the formula provided, the sun is 148,944,000,000 m from Earth. The sun is actually 149,600,000,000 m away.
12. Answers will vary. Accept all well-supported answers. According to the sample data, the calculated value was within 0.5 percent of the actual value. So it is generally a good way to measure the distance from the Earth to the sun.

Datasheets for LabBook

Math Skills Worksheet "Using Proportions and Cross-Multiplication"

Chapter Highlights

VOCABULARY DEFINITIONS

SECTION 1

solar system the system composed of the sun (a star) and the planets and other bodies that travel around the sun

nebula a large cloud of dust and gas in interstellar space; the location of star formation

solar nebula the nebula that formed into the solar system

planetesimal the tiny building blocks of the planets that formed as dust particles stuck together and grew in size

rotation the spinning motion of a body on its axis

orbit the elliptical path a body takes as it travels around another body in space; the motion itself

revolution the elliptical motion of a body as it orbits another body in space

period of revolution the time it takes for one body to make one complete orbit, or *revolution,* around another body in space

ellipse a closed curve in which the sum of the distances from the edge of the curve to two points inside the ellipse is always the same

astronomical unit (AU) the average distance between the Earth and the sun, or approximately 150,000,000 km

Chapter Highlights

SECTION 1

Vocabulary

solar system *(p. 34)*
nebula *(p. 34)*
solar nebula *(p. 35)*
planetesimal *(p. 36)*
rotation *(p. 39)*
orbit *(p. 39)*
revolution *(p. 39)*
period of revolution *(p. 39)*
ellipse *(p. 40)*
astronomical unit *(p. 40)*

Section Notes

- The solar system formed out of a vast cloud of cold gas and dust called a nebula.
- Gravity and pressure were balanced, keeping the cloud unchanging until something upset the balance. Then the nebula began to collapse.
- Collapse of the solar nebula caused heating in the center. As material crowded closer together, planetesimals began to form.
- The central mass of the nebula became the sun. Planets formed from the surrounding disk of material.
- It took about 10 million years for the solar system to form, and it is now 4.6 billion years old.
- The orbit of one body around another has the shape of an ellipse.
- Planets move faster in their orbits when they are closer to the sun.
- The square of the period of revolution of the planet is equal to the cube of its semimajor axis.
- Gravity depends on the masses of the interacting objects and the square of the distance between them.

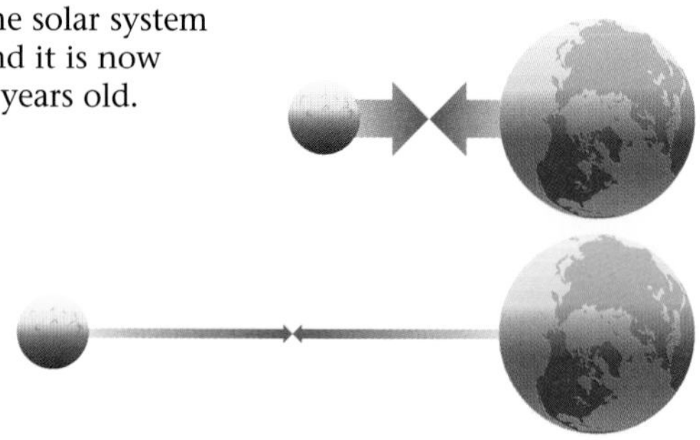

☑ Skills Check

Math Concepts

SQUARES AND CUBES Let's take another look at Kepler's third law of motion. Expanding the formula $P^2 = a^3$ to $P \times P = a \times a \times a$ may be an easier way to consider the calculation. The period of Venus, for example, is 0.61 years, and its semimajor axis is 0.72 AU. Thus,

$$P^2 = a^3$$
$$P \times P = a \times a \times a$$
$$0.61 \times 0.61 = 0.72 \times 0.72 \times 0.72$$
$$0.37 = 0.37$$

Visual Understanding

LIKE AN ONION The sun is formed of six different layers of gas. From the inside out, the layers are the core, radiative zone, convective zone, photosphere, chromosphere, and corona. Look back at Figure 9 on page 43 to review the characteristics of each layer.

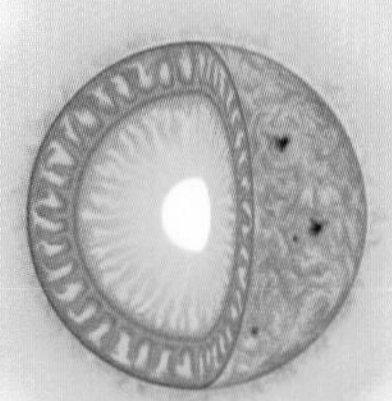

56

Lab and Activity Highlights

How Far Is the Sun? PG 54

Datasheets for LabBook
(blackline masters for this lab)

SECTION 2

Vocabulary

corona *(p. 43)*
chromosphere *(p. 43)*
photosphere *(p. 43)*
convective zone *(p. 43)*
radiative zone *(p. 43)*
core *(p. 43)*
nuclear fusion *(p. 45)*
sunspot *(p. 47)*

Section Notes

- The sun is a gaseous sphere made primarily of hydrogen and helium.
- The sun produces energy in its core by a process called nuclear fusion.
- Magnetic changes within the sun cause sunspots and solar flares.

SECTION 3

Vocabulary

crust *(p. 49)*
mantle *(p. 49)*
core *(p. 49)*

Section Notes

- The Earth is divided into three main layers—crust, mantle, and core.
- Materials with different densities separated because of melting inside Earth. Heavy elements sank to the center because of Earth's gravity.
- Earth's original atmosphere formed from the release of gases brought to Earth by meteorites and comets.
- Earth's second atmosphere arose from volcanic eruptions and impacts by comets. The composition was largely water and carbon dioxide.
- The presence of life dramatically changed Earth's atmosphere, adding free oxygen.
- Earth's oceans formed shortly after the Earth did, when it had cooled off enough for rain to fall.
- Continents formed when lighter materials gathered on the surface and rose above sea level.

internetconnect

go.hrw.com **GO TO:** go.hrw.com

Visit the **HRW** Web site for a variety of learning tools related to this chapter. Just type in the keyword:

KEYWORD: HSTSOL

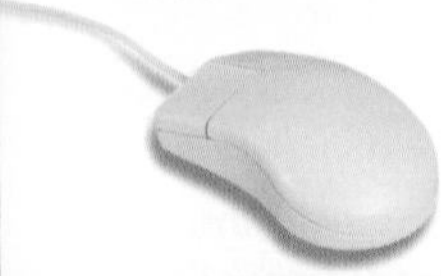

sciLINKS NSTA **GO TO:** www.scilinks.org

Visit the **National Science Teachers Association** on-line Web site for Internet resources related to this chapter. Just type in the *sci*LINKS number for more information about the topic:

TOPIC: The Planets	***sci*LINKS NUMBER:** HSTE455
TOPIC: Kepler's Laws	***sci*LINKS NUMBER:** HSTE460
TOPIC: The Sun	***sci*LINKS NUMBER:** HSTE465
TOPIC: The Layers of the Earth	***sci*LINKS NUMBER:** HSTE470
TOPIC: The Oceans	***sci*LINKS NUMBER:** HSTE475

Vocabulary Definitions, *continued*

Section 2

corona the sun's outer atmosphere, which can extend outward a distance equal to 10–12 times the diameter of the sun

chromosphere a thin region of the sun's atmosphere between the corona and the photosphere; too faint to see unless there is a total solar eclipse

photosphere the layer of the sun at which point the gases get thick enough to see; the surface of the sun

convective zone a region of the sun where gases circulate in convection currents, bringing the sun's energy to the surface

radiative zone a very dense region of the sun in which the atoms are so closely packed that light can take millions of years to pass through

core the center of the sun where the sun's energy is produced

nuclear fusion the process by which two or more nuclei with small masses join together, or fuse, to form a larger, more massive nucleus, along with the production of energy

sunspot an area on the photosphere of the sun that is cooler than surrounding areas, showing up as a dark spot

Section 3

crust the thin, outermost layer of the Earth, or the uppermost part of the lithosphere

mantle the layer of the Earth between the crust and the core

core the central, spherical part of the Earth below the mantle

Lab and Activity Highlights

LabBank

Whiz-Bang Demonstrations, Can You Vote on Venus?

Long-Term Projects & Research Ideas, A Two-Sun Solar System

Vocabulary Review Worksheet

Blackline masters of these Chapter Highlights can be found in the **Study Guide.**

Chapter Review Answers

Using Vocabulary

1. Rotation is the spinning of a body on its axis. Revolution is the movement of a smaller body around a larger body.
2. An ellipse is a closed curve in which the sum of the distances from the edge of the curve to two points inside the ellipse is always the same. A circle is an ellipse with only one focus.
3. The solar system is composed of the sun, its planets, and other bodies in orbit around the sun. The solar nebula was an interstellar cloud of gas and dust that eventually became the solar system.
4. A planetesimal is a tiny building block of a planet. A planet is a large object made of planetesimals.
5. Temperature is a measure of the average kinetic energy of randomly moving particles in an object. Pressure is a force or push.
6. The photosphere is the layer of the sun that we can see, or the surface of the sun. The corona is the sun's outer atmosphere that can be seen only during a solar eclipse.
7. radiative zone
8. Rotation
9. plate tectonics

Understanding Concepts

Multiple Choice

10. d
11. a
12. a
13. c
14. b
15. c
16. a
17. a

Chapter Review

USING VOCABULARY

For each pair of terms, explain the difference in their meanings.

1. rotation/revolution
2. ellipse/circle
3. solar system/solar nebula
4. planetesimal/planet
5. temperature/pressure
6. photosphere/corona

To complete the following sentences, choose the correct term from each pair of terms below.

7. It takes millions of years for light energy to travel through the sun's __?__. *(radiative zone* or *convective zone)*
8. __?__ of the Earth causes night and day. *(Rotation* or *Revolution)*
9. Convection in Earth's mantle causes __?__. *(plate tectonics* or *nuclear fusion)*

UNDERSTANDING CONCEPTS

Multiple Choice

10. Impacts in the early solar system
    a. brought new materials to the planets.
    b. released energy.
    c. dug craters.
    d. All of the above

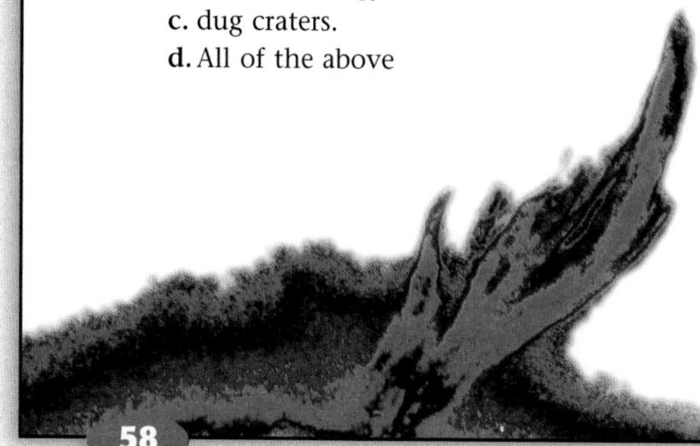

11. Which type of planet will have a higher overall density?
    a. one that forms close to the sun
    b. one that forms far from the sun
12. Which process releases the most energy?
    a. nuclear fusion
    b. burning
    c. shrinking due to gravity
13. Which of the following planets has the shortest period of revolution?
    a. Pluto c. Mercury
    b. Earth d. Jupiter
14. Which gas in Earth's atmosphere tells us that there is life on Earth?
    a. hydrogen c. carbon dioxide
    b. oxygen d. nitrogen
15. Which layer of the Earth has the lowest density?
    a. the core
    b. the mantle
    c. the crust
16. What is the term for the speed of gas molecules?
    a. temperature c. gravity
    b. pressure d. force
17. Which of the following objects is least likely to have a spherical shape?
    a. a comet c. the sun
    b. Venus d. Jupiter

58

Concept Mapping Transparency 19

Blackline masters of this Chapter Review can be found in the **Study Guide.**

Short Answer

18. An external force, perhaps from a collision with another nebula or from a nearby exploding star, pushed inward on the nebula. This force was strong enough to overcome the pressure of the nebula and trigger its collapse.
19. The square of the period of revolution is equal to the cube of the semimajor axis: $P \times P = a \times a \times a$. (Students' drawings should resemble Figure 6.)

Short Answer

18. Why did the solar nebula begin to collapse to form the sun and planets if the forces of pressure and gravity were balanced?

19. How is the period of revolution related to the semimajor axis of an orbit? Draw an ellipse and label the semimajor axis.

20. How did our understanding of the sun's energy change over time?

Concept Mapping

21. Use the following terms to create a concept map: solar nebula, solar system, planetesimals, sun, photosphere, core, nuclear fusion, planets, Earth.

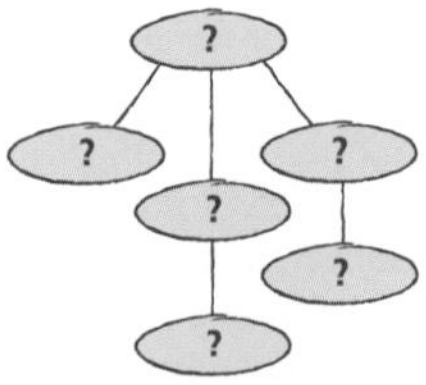

CRITICAL THINKING AND PROBLEM SOLVING

Write one or two sentences to answer the following questions:

22. Explain why nuclear fusion works inside the sun but not inside Jupiter, which is also made mostly of hydrogen and helium.

23. Why is it less expensive to launch an interplanetary spacecraft from the international space station in Earth's orbit than from Earth itself?

24. Soon after the formation of the universe, there was only hydrogen and helium. Heavier elements, such as carbon, oxygen, silicon, and all the matter that makes up the heavier minerals and rocks in the solar system, were made inside an earlier generation of stars. Do you think the first generation of stars had any planets like Earth, Venus, Mercury, and Mars? Explain.

MATH IN SCIENCE

25. Suppose astronomers discover a new planet orbiting our sun. The orbit has a semimajor axis of 2.52 AU. What is the planet's period of revolution?

26. If the planet in the previous question is twice as massive as the Earth but is the same size, how much would a person who weighs 100 lb on Earth weigh on this planet?

INTERPRETING GRAPHICS

Examine the illustration below, and answer the questions that follow.

27. Do you think this is a rocky, inner planet or a gas giant?

28. Did this planet form close to the sun or far from the sun? Explain.

29. Does this planet have an atmosphere? Why or why not?

Reading Check-up

Take a minute to review your answers to the Pre-Reading Questions found at the bottom of page 32. Have your answers changed? If necessary, revise your answers based on what you have learned since you began this chapter.

59

20. At first, people thought the sun was burning fuel. Later, scientists thought that the sun releases energy because it is shrinking. Finally, nuclear fusion was identified as the source of the sun's energy.

Concept Mapping

21. 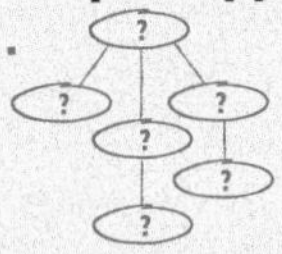

An answer to this exercise can be found at the front of this book.

Critical Thinking and Problem Solving

22. The mass of Jupiter is too small. The pressure in Jupiter's core is not high enough to reach the temperatures needed to initiate nuclear fusion. Fusion requires temperatures of 10 million degrees and masses about 75 times that of Jupiter.
23. The space station is farther from Earth's center, so the effect of gravity is less. It will take less fuel to escape Earth's gravity if you start at the station rather than at Earth's surface.
24. No; Earth, Venus, Mercury, and Mars formed mostly from rocky material. The only type of planet that could have orbited the first generation of stars is a gas giant.

Math in Science

25. Using Kepler's third law of motion, $P \times P = a \times a \times a$, where a = 2.52 AU gives a value of 16 for one side of the equation. Since 4 × 4 = 16 AU, the period of revolution must be 4 years.
26. Because the planet is twice as massive as Earth, the person would weigh twice as much, or 200 lb.

Interpreting Graphics

27. It is a rocky inner planet.
28. It probably formed close to the sun. The planet is rocky, with a relatively thin atmosphere, and the sun is visible as a disk in the sky rather than as a pinpoint of light.
29. Yes; there are clouds in the sky, and the surface of the planet has been weathered.

Science, Technology, and Society

Don't Look at the Sun!

Background

The McMath-Pierce solar telescope has a 91.5 m focal length. Such a long focal length allows us to see a lot of details on a sunspot. The facility that houses the telescope looks like an upside-down *V*. The vertical side of this *V* is 30 m tall and contains the heliostat. The sun strikes the heliostat, which is a large, flat, rotating mirror. After sunlight strikes the heliostat, it travels 50 m underground to another mirror, which reflects it back to the observation room. In the observation room, the light is broken down into its different wavelengths by a spectrograph. The spectrograph also photographs the image that results from this process.

The McMath-Pierce telescope is also used to study the spectra of planets, comets, and other stars. Spectrography gives us important information about these objects, such as the location of magnetic fields and the temperature, pressure, and density of the gases surrounding the object.

Science, Technology, and Society

Don't Look at the Sun!

You know you are not supposed to look at the sun, right? But how can we learn anything about the sun if we can't look at it? By using a solar telescope, of course! Where would you find one of these, you ask? Well, if you travel about 70 km southwest of Tucson, Arizona, you will arrive at Kitt Peak National Observatory, where you will find three of them. One telescope in particular has gone to great lengths to give astronomers extraordinary views of the sun!

Top Selection

In 1958, Kitt Peak was chosen from more than 150 mountain ranges to be the site for a national observatory. Located in the Sonoran Desert, Kitt Peak is a part of lands belonging to the Tohono O'odham nation. The McMath-Pierce Facility houses the three largest solar telescopes in the world. Astronomers come from around the globe to use these telescopes. The largest of the three, called the McMath-Pierce telescope, creates an image of the sun that is almost 1 m wide!

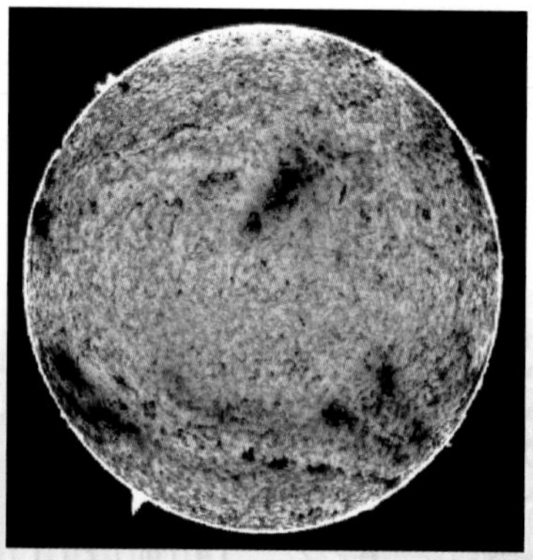

▲ *This is an image of the sun as viewed through the McMath-Pierce solar telescope.*

Too Hot to Handle

Have you ever caught a piece of paper on fire using only a magnifying glass and the rays from the sun? Sunlight that has been focused can produce a great amount of thermal energy—enough to start a fire. Now imagine a magnifying glass 1.6 m in diameter focusing the sun's rays. The resulting heat could melt metal. This is what would happen to a conventional telescope if it were pointed directly at the sun.

To avoid a meltdown, the McMath-Pierce solar telescope uses a mirror that produces a large image of the sun. This mirror directs the sun's rays down a diagonal shaft to another mirror 50 m underground. This mirror is adjustable to focus the sunlight. The sunlight is then directed to a third mirror, which directs the light to an observing room and instrument shaft.

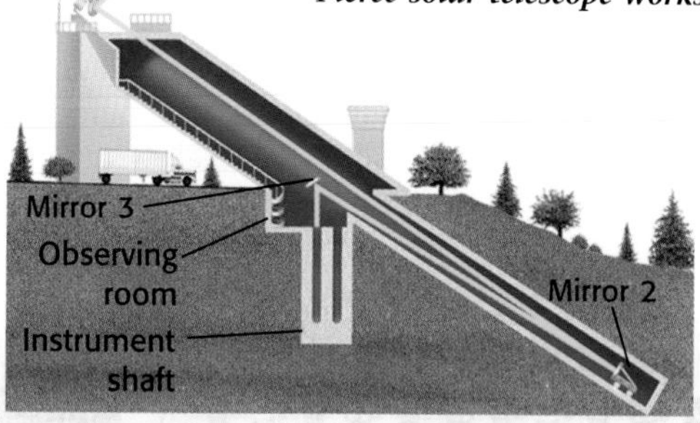

▼ *This cutaway drawing shows how the McMath-Pierce solar telescope works.*

Scope It Out

► Kitt Peak Observatory also has optical telescopes, which differ from solar telescopes. Do some research to find out how optical telescopes work and what the ones at Kitt Peak are used for.

60

Answer to Scope It Out

There are two types of optical telescopes—reflecting and refracting. A reflecting telescope uses a mirror to collect and reflect the light. This mirror is at the back of a tube. A secondary mirror brings the light into focus. A refracting telescope uses glass lenses to magnify and focus an image. Although the large telescopes built today are reflectors, earlier telescopes were refractors. The telescope Galileo built was a refracting telescope, while the one Newton built was a reflecting telescope. Students should visit the official Kitt Peak Web site to discover what objects its optical telescopes are currently being used to study.

SCIENTIFICDEBATE

Mirrors in Space

People who live in areas that do not get much sunshine are more prone to health problems such as depression and alcoholism. The people of Siberia, Russia, experience a shortage of sunshine during the winter, when the sun shines only 6 hours on certain days. Could there be a solution to this problem?

A Mirror From *Mir*

In February 1999, the crew of the space station *Mir* was scheduled to insert a large, umbrellalike mirror into orbit. The mirror was designed to reflect sunlight to Siberia. Once placed into orbit, however, problems arose and the crew was unable to unfold the mirror. Had things gone as planned, the beam of reflected sunlight was expected to be 5 to 10 times brighter than the light from the moon. If the first mirror had worked, this would have opened the door for Russia to build many more mirrors that are larger in diameter. These larger mirrors would have been launched into space to lengthen winter days, provide additional heat, and even reduce the amount of electricity used for lighting. The idea of placing mirrors in space, however, caused some serious concerns about the effects it could have.

▲ *The end of a winter day in Siberia*

Overcrowding

The first mirror was about 30 m in diameter. Because it was put in Low Earth Orbit (LEO), the light beam would have been obstructed by the Earth's horizon as the mirror made its orbit. As a result, it would have reflected light on a single area for only about 30 seconds. In order to shine light on Siberia on a large scale, hundreds of larger mirrors would have to be used. But using this many mirrors could result in collisions with satellites that share LEO.

Damage to Ecosystems

It is very difficult to determine what effects extra daylight would have on Siberian ecosystems. Many plants and animals have cycles for various biological functions, such as feeding, sleeping, moving, and reproducing. Extra light and increased temperatures could adversely affect these cycles. Birds might migrate so late that they wouldn't survive the trip across the colder climates because food would be scarce. Plants might sprout too soon and freeze. Arctic ice might melt and cause flooding.

Light Pollution

Astronomers may also be affected by orbiting mirrors. Already astronomers must plan their viewing times to avoid the passing of bright planets and satellites. More sunlight directed toward the Earth would increase light pollution and could make seeing into space more difficult. A string of several hundred mirrors shining light toward the Earth would likely cause additional light pollution in certain locations as the mirrors passed overhead.

What's the Current Status?

► Find out more about the Russian project and where it stands now. If you had to decide whether to pursue this project, what would you decide? Why?

Scientific Debate
Mirrors in Space

Background

Another application of the technology used in the space mirror is the "solar sail." A solar sail is simply a flat, reflective membrane that catches energy particles in the solar wind. Perhaps in the future spaceships will use solar sails to propel them through the solar system.

Answer to What's the Current Status?

The group responsible for the space-mirror project is a company based in Russia called the Space Regatta Consortium. Unfortunately, this company is having economic trouble, so the ultimate goal of the project may never be realized. Students' responses will vary. Accept all reasonable answers.

Chapter Organizer

CHAPTER ORGANIZATION	TIME MINUTES	OBJECTIVES	LABS, INVESTIGATIONS, AND DEMONSTRATIONS
Chapter Opener **pp. 62–63**	45	National Standards: SAI 1, HNS 1, 3, ES 3a	**Start-Up Activity,** Measuring Space, p. 63
Section 1 **The Nine Planets**	90	▶ List the names of the planets in the order they orbit the sun. ▶ Describe three ways in which the inner and outer planets are different from each other. UCP 1, 3, SAI 1, ST 2, SPSP 5, HNS 1, 3, ES 1c, 3a, 3b; Labs UCP 2, SAI 1, ST 1	**Demonstration,** p. 66 in ATE **Making Models,** Why Do They Wander? p. 164 **Datasheets for LabBook,** Why Do They Wander?
Section 2 **Moons**	135	▶ Describe the current theory for the origin of Earth's moon. ▶ Describe what causes the phases of Earth's moon. ▶ Explain the difference between a solar eclipse and a lunar eclipse. UCP 1–3, SAI 1, HNS 1, 3, ES 3a–3c; Labs UCP 2, SAI 1, ST 1, ES 3b	**QuickLab,** Clever Insight, p. 78 **Interactive Explorations CD-ROM,** Space Case *A* ***Worksheet*** *is also available in the* ***Interactive Explorations Teacher's Edition.*** **Making Models,** Eclipses, p. 88 **Datasheets for LabBook,** Eclipses **Discovery Lab,** Phases of the Moon, p. 89 **Datasheets for LabBook,** Phases of the Moon
Section 3 **Small Bodies in the Solar System**	90	▶ Explain why comets, asteroids, and meteoroids are important to the study of the formation of the solar system. ▶ Compare the different types of asteroids with the different types of meteoroids. ▶ Describe the risks to life on Earth from cosmic impacts. UCP 1, ES 2a, 3a, 3b	**Demonstration,** p. 83 in ATE **Labs You Can Eat,** Meteorite Delight **Whiz-Bang Demonstrations,** Crater Creator **Whiz-Bang Demonstrations,** Space Snowballs **Long-Term Projects & Research Ideas,** What Did You See, Mr. Messier?

See page **T23** *for a complete correlation of this book with the*

NATIONAL SCIENCE EDUCATION STANDARDS.

TECHNOLOGY RESOURCES

Guided Reading Audio CD
English or Spanish, Chapter 3

One-Stop Planner CD-ROM with Test Generator

CNN **Scientists in Action,** Future Mars Astronauts, Segment 25

Interactive Explorations CD-ROM
CD 2, Exploration 7, Space Case

Chapter 3 • A Family of Planets

CLASSROOM WORKSHEETS, TRANSPARENCIES, AND RESOURCES	SCIENCE INTEGRATION AND CONNECTIONS	REVIEW AND ASSESSMENT
Directed Reading Worksheet **Science Puzzlers, Twisters & Teasers**		
Transparency 191, The Inner Planets **Directed Reading Worksheet,** Section 1 **Math Skills for Science Worksheet,** A Shortcut for Multiplying Large Numbers **Science Skills Worksheet,** Grasping Graphing **Transparency 191,** The Outer Planets **Critical Thinking Worksheet,** Martian Holiday	**Math and More,** p. 65 in ATE **Connect to Environmental Science,** p. 66 in ATE **Math and More,** p. 68 in ATE **Physics Connection,** p. 69 **Cross-Disciplinary Focus,** p. 69 in ATE **Cross-Disciplinary Focus,** p. 70 in ATE **Connect to Meteorology,** p. 70 in ATE **Apply,** p. 73 **Connect to Environmental Science,** p. 73 in ATE	**Homework,** p. 66 in ATE **Section Review,** p. 69 **Section Review,** p. 74 **Quiz,** p. 74 in ATE **Alternative Assessment,** p. 74 in ATE
Directed Reading Worksheet, Section 2 **Transparency 223,** Two Motions Combine to Form Projectile Motion **Transparency 192,** Formation of the Moon **Transparency 193,** Phases of the Moon **Transparency 194,** Solar Eclipse and Lunar Eclipse **Reinforcement Worksheet,** The Planets of Our Solar System **Reinforcement Worksheet,** Lunar and Solar Eclipses	**Physics Connection,** p. 76 **Math and More,** pp. 76, 78 in ATE **MathBreak,** Orbits Within Orbits, p. 79 **Cross-Disciplinary Focus,** p. 79 in ATE **Connect to Life Science,** p. 80 in ATE **Holt Anthology of Science Fiction,** *The Mad Moon,* p. 95	**Homework,** pp. 76, 78, 80 in ATE **Section Review,** p. 79 **Self-Check,** p. 81 **Section Review,** p. 82 **Quiz,** p. 82 in ATE **Alternative Assessment,** p. 82 in ATE
Directed Reading Worksheet, Section 3	**Cross-Disciplinary Focus,** p. 87 in ATE **Scientific Debate:** Is Pluto Really a Planet? p. 94	**Section Review,** p. 87 **Quiz,** p. 87 in ATE **Alternative Assessment,** p. 87 in ATE

END-OF-CHAPTER REVIEW AND ASSESSMENT

Chapter Review in Study Guide
Vocabulary and Notes in Study Guide
Chapter Tests with Performance-Based Assessment, Chapter 3 Test
Chapter Tests with Performance-Based Assessment, Performance-Based Assessment 3
Concept Mapping Transparency 20

internet**connect**

go.hrw.com **Holt, Rinehart and Winston On-line Resources**

go.hrw.com

For worksheets and other teaching aids related to this chapter, visit the HRW Web site and type in the keyword: **HSTFAM**

sciLINKS NSTA **National Science Teachers Association**

www.scilinks.org

Encourage students to use the *sci*LINKS numbers listed in the internet connect boxes to access information and resources on the **NSTA** Web Site.

Chapter Resources & Worksheets

Visual Resources

TEACHING TRANSPARENCIES

#191

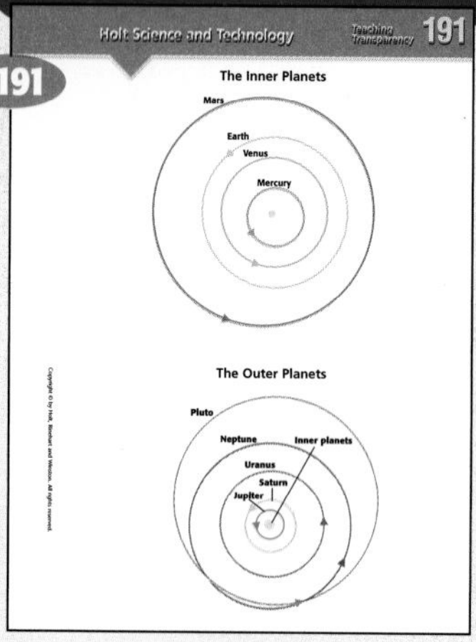

#192

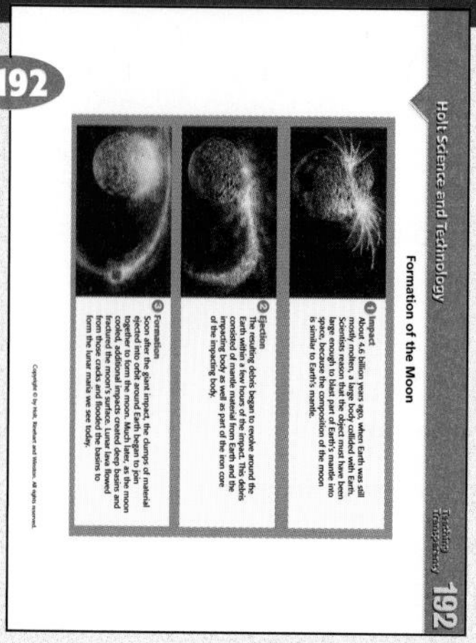

#193

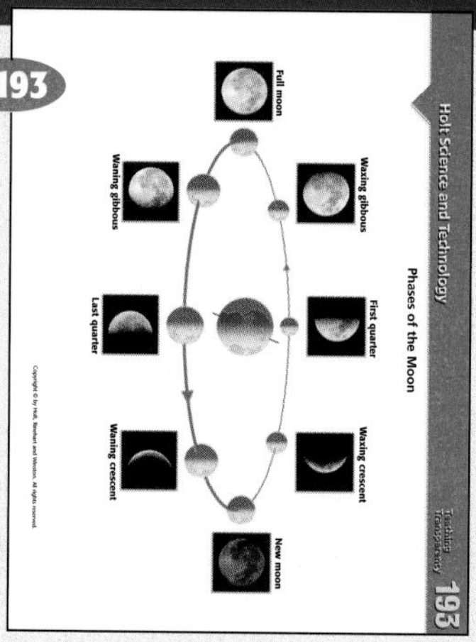

#194

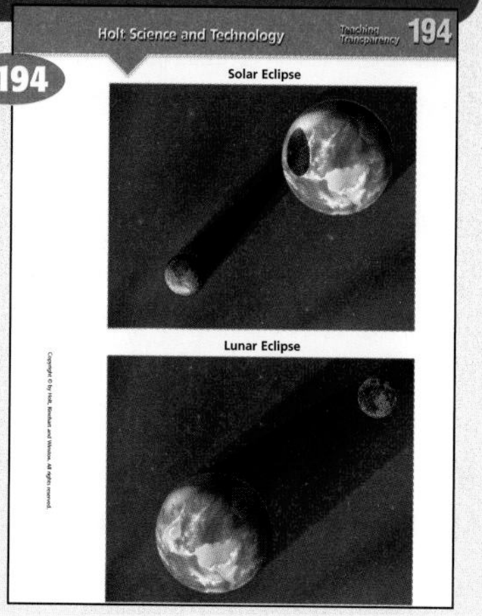

TEACHING TRANSPARENCIES

#223

LINK TO PHYSICAL SCIENCE

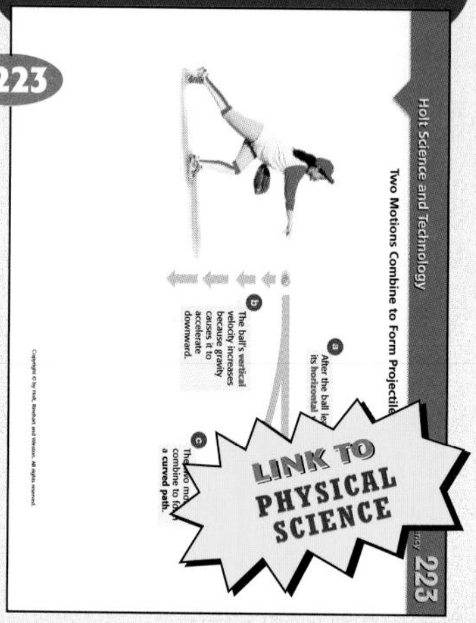

CONCEPT MAPPING TRANSPARENCY

#20

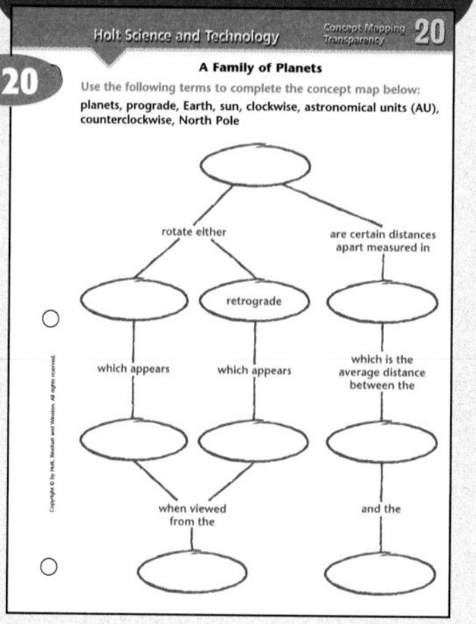

Meeting Individual Needs

DIRECTED READING

#3

Date ______ Class ______

DIRECTED READING WORKSHEET

A Family of Planets

Chapter Introduction

As you begin this chapter, answer the following.

1. Read the title of the chapter. List three things that you already know about this subject.
2. Write two questions about this subject that you would like answered by the time you finish this chapter.
3. How does the title of the Start-Up Activity relate to the subject of the chapter?

Section 1: The Nine Planets (p. 64)

4. In 1957, the former Soviet Union launched Sputnik. What was Sputnik?

Measuring Interplanetary Distances (p. 64)

5. The amount of time it takes light to travel around the Earth seven and a half times is ______.
6. How many light-minutes are there in one astronomical unit?
7. Distances within the solar system must be measured in light-years. True or False? (Circle one.)

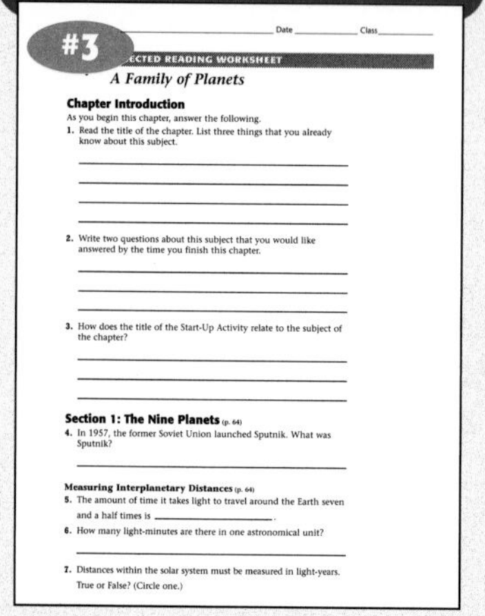

REINFORCEMENT & VOCABULARY REVIEW

#3

Date ______ Class ______

REINFORCEMENT WORKSHEET

The Planets of Our Solar System

Complete this worksheet after you have finished reading Chapter 20, Section 2.

Read the directions below, and write your answers in the spaces provided on the next page.

1. Write the name of each planet on the line next to the planet on the diagram.
2. Draw a red circle around the group of terrestrial planets.
3. Draw a green circle around the group of gas giants.
4. Using a brown-colored pencil, draw the asteroid belt in its proper place.
5. Draw the Kuiper belt in blue.
6. Write the number of moons each planet has in the box next to each planet.
7. The following is a list of some of the moons in our solar system. In the space provided, write the name of the moon next to the planet it orbits.

   Charon Triton Deimos Ganymede Phobos
   Miranda Europa Luna Titan

8. Match each of the following characteristics to the appropriate planet, and write the corresponding letter in the space provided. Each planet has two of the characteristics.

   A. It is the smallest planet.
   B. It has a density of less than one.
   C. A year is only 88 Earth days long.
   D. An inner planet that has retrograde rotation.
   E. It has sulfuric acid clouds.
   F. It can support life.
   G. It has the brightest ring system.
   H. It has the Great Red Spot.
   I. It is the gas giant farthest from the sun.
   J. It has Olympus Mons, the largest mountain in the solar system.
   K. It has a moon more than half its size.
   L. It is tilted on its side.
   M. It is about 13 light-minutes from the sun.
   N. Its day is more than half as long as its year.
   O. Its day is 16 hours and 7 minutes.
   P. Temperatures range from −13°C to 37°C.
   Q. It is 2.7 light-hours from the sun.
   R. Its surface temperature is −153°C.

#3

Date ______ Class ______

REINFORCEMENT WORKSHEET

Lunar and Solar Eclipses

Complete this worksheet after you have finished reading Chapter 20, Section 2.

A lunar or solar eclipse happens when the Earth, sun, and moon line up in such a way that an unusual phenomenon occurs.

1. Imagine you are at a place on Earth that is experiencing a total solar eclipse. Is it daytime or nighttime? Describe the event that you are observing.
2. Draw a sketch showing the relative positions of the Earth, moon, and sun during a solar eclipse.
3. Imagine you are at a place on Earth that is experiencing a total lunar eclipse. Is it daytime or nighttime? Describe the event that you are observing.
4. Draw a sketch showing the relative positions of the Earth, moon, and sun during a lunar eclipse.

SCIENCE PUZZLERS, TWISTERS & TEASERS

#3

Date ______ Class ______

SCIENCE PUZZLERS, TWISTERS & TEASERS

A Family of Planets

Planetary Omission Puzzles

1. When combined and rearranged, the missing letters from the alphabets below will spell a word from the chapter. What are the words?

   BCFGHJKLMNPQUVWXYZ

   a. ______

   ABDFGHIJKLNPQRSUVWXYZ

   b. ______

Dr. Emma Nint

BRAIN BUSTER!

2. Dr. Emma Nint has a dream of renaming the planets of our solar system with a more rational, scientific system. She has devised a numerical system for naming the planets, but has not given you a complete list *or* an explanation of her naming system. Figure out what each set of numbers represents and complete her list. (You'll probably need to refer to your book for help.)

   The three listed planets are:

   1/39.53/2320/p

   8/30.06/49528/n

   21/19.19/51118/u

   Write the names of the other planets in the solar system using the doctor's system.

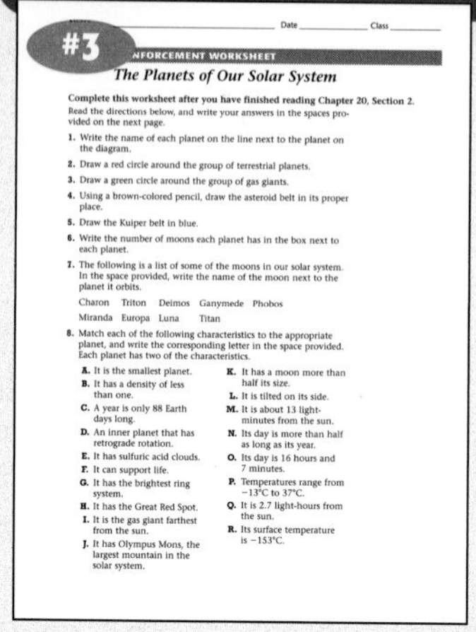

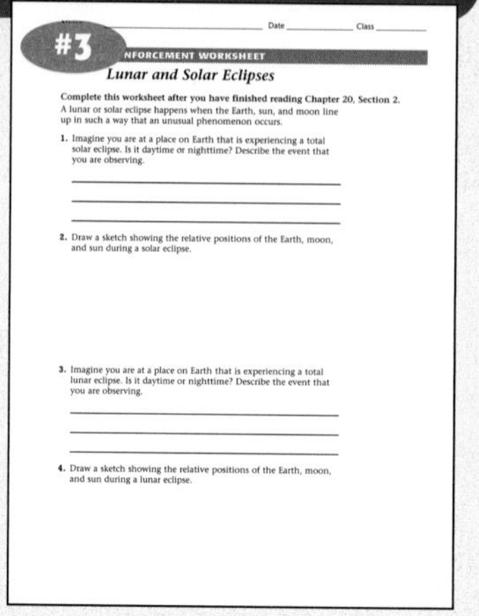

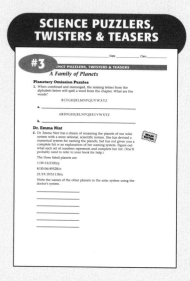

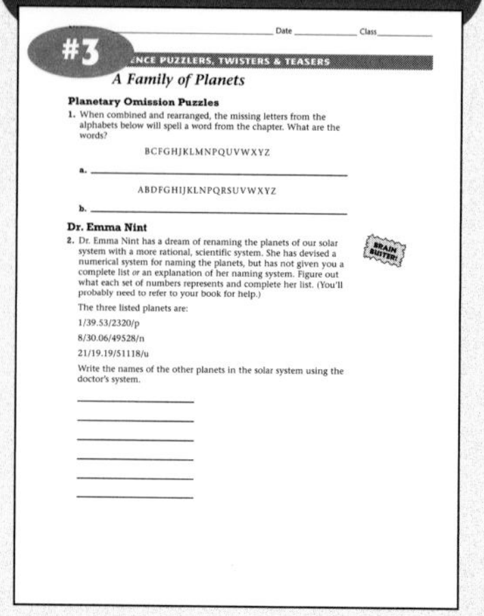

Review & Assessment

STUDY GUIDE

#3 VOCABULARY & NOTES WORKSHEET

A Family of Planets

By studying the Vocabulary and Notes listed for each section below, you can gain a better understanding of this chapter.

SECTION 1

Vocabulary
In your own words, write a definition for each of the following terms in the space provided.

1. astronomical unit (AU)

2. terrestrial planets

3. prograde rotation

4. retrograde rotation

5. gas giants

Notes
Read the following section highlights. Then, in your own words, write the highlights in your ScienceLog.
• The solar system has nine planets.
• Distances within the solar system can be expressed in astronomical units (AU) or in light-minutes.

#3 CHAPTER REVIEW WORKSHEET

A Family of Planets

USING VOCABULARY
For each pair of terms, explain the difference in their meanings.

1. terrestrial planet/gas giant

2. asteroid/comet

3. meteor/meteorite

4. satellite/moon

5. Kuiper belt/Oort cloud

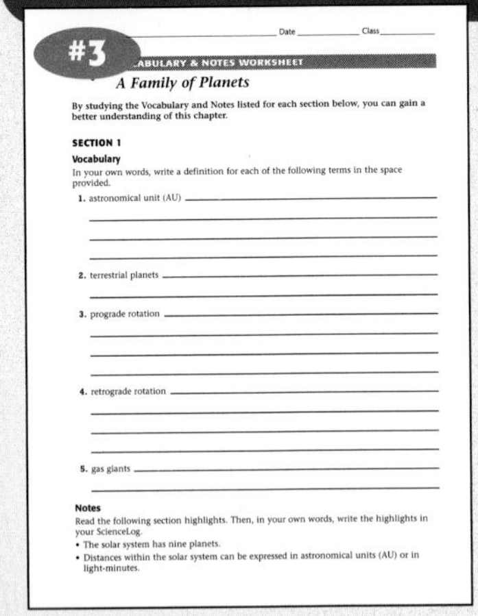

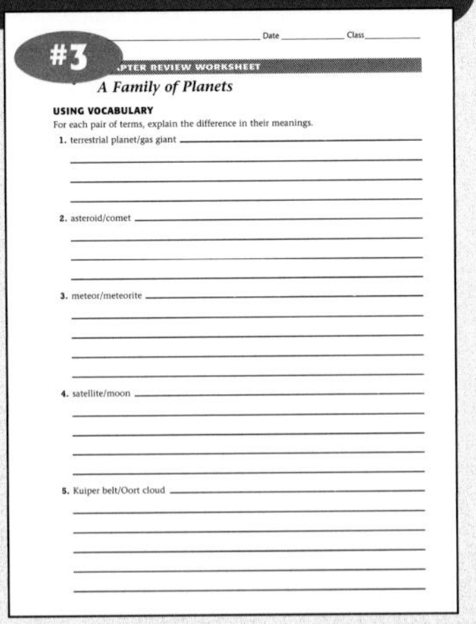

CHAPTER TESTS WITH PERFORMANCE-BASED ASSESSMENT

#3 FAMILY OF PLANETS

Chapter 3 Test

USING VOCABULARY
To complete the following sentences, choose the correct term from each pair of terms listed, and write the term in the blank.

1. Unlike most planets, Venus has _____ rotation, which means that it spins in a clockwise direction. (prograde or retrograde)

2. A meteoroid is called a _____ only after it has struck the ground on Earth. (meteorite or meteor)

3. _____ are natural or artificial bodies that orbit larger celestial bodies, such as planets. (Satellites or Eclipses)

4. The inner planets of our solar system are called _____. (gas giants or terrestrial planets)

5. _____ are also referred to as "dirty snowballs." (Comets or Asteroids)

UNDERSTANDING CONCEPTS

Multiple Choice
Circle the correct answer.

6. Which of the following celestial bodies is most likely to have many craters?
   a. a giant gaseous planet
   b. a white dwarf star
   c. a terrestrial planet with no atmosphere
   d. a terrestrial planet with a thick atmosphere

7. Annular solar eclipses occur because
   a. the moon reflects more sunlight than the Earth does.
   b. the Earth's shadow is too small to completely cover the moon.
   c. the moon is too far away from Earth to completely hide the sun.
   d. All of the above

8. An astronomical unit (AU) is the average distance
   a. between Mercury and the sun.   c. light travels in 1 minute.
   b. between Mercury and Pluto.   d. between Earth and the sun.

9. Which of these is the best clue that Pluto is not a gaseous planet?
   a. the size of its orbit   c. its distance from the sun
   b. its density   d. its proximity to the Oort cloud

10. Which of the following gases traps the most heat in the atmosphere of Venus?
    a. carbon dioxide   c. nitrogen
    b. oxygen   d. argon

#3 FAMILY OF PLANETS **SKILL BUILDER**

Chapter 3 Performance-Based Assessment

Objective
Certain properties of a planet determine its surface gravity. In this activity, you will work with a formula that allows you to predict the surface gravity of an imaginary planet.

Know the Score!
As you work through the activity, keep in mind that you will be earning a grade for the following:
• the quality of your work with the data (50%)
• the quality of your analysis and explanation of your findings (50%)

MATERIALS
• Planetary Data Table
• pencil
• scratch paper
• calculator

Procedure
1. Imagine that a new planet has been discovered beyond Pluto. You have been chosen to join a group of scientists who will explore this planet, but first you must estimate this planet's surface gravity. For any given planet, when diameter and density are multiplied together and then divided by the surface gravity, the result is a constant—a number that is the same for all planets.

(diameter) × (density) ÷ (surface gravity) = constant

2. Begin by using your Planetary Data Table to solve the equation above for Earth. Calculate the constant, and round it to the nearest whole number.

3. Calculate the constant for Mercury.

4. Calculate the constant for Venus.

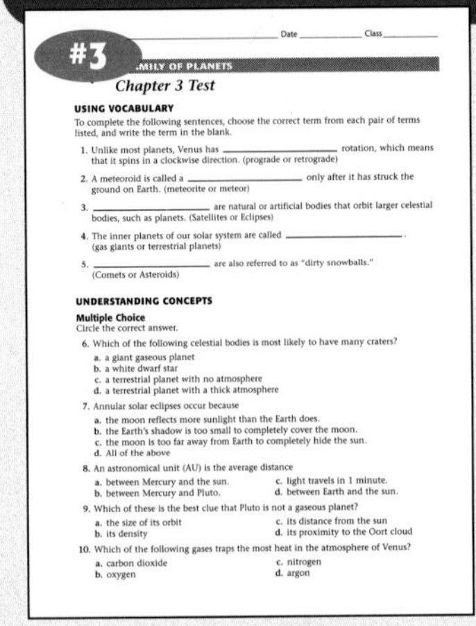

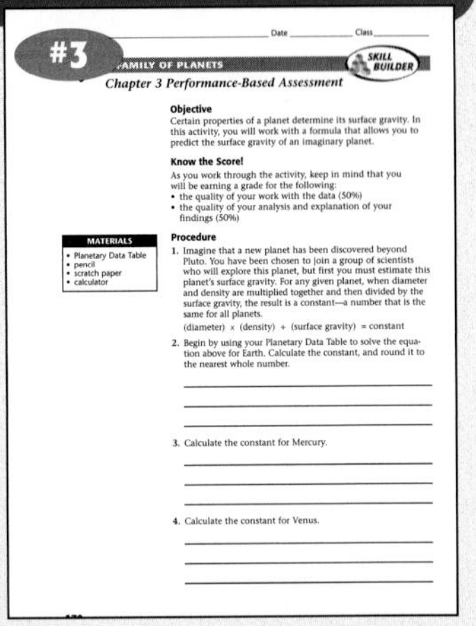

Lab Worksheets

LABS YOU CAN EAT

#3 STUDENT WORKSHEET **DISCOVERY LAB**

Meteorite Delight

Chunks of rock and metal race through space. What happens when they enter the Earth's atmosphere? Most burn up as they plummet, but some land on the ground. These objects are called meteorites. Meteorites come in two major forms: stony, which look similar to Earth rocks, and iron, which appear shiny and metallic.

There are two ways to discover meteorites. A meteorite *fall* occurs when someone sees the meteorite, traces its path to Earth, and recovers it. A meteorite *find* occurs when someone discovers a stony meteorite at shoulder height directly above the ground without having seen it fall.

In this activity, you will work in groups of two or more students to simulate the impact of stony and iron meteorites on the ground. Rice-cereal balls will serve as meteorites to help you better understand meteorite finds and falls.

MATERIALS
• large baking pan or cookie sheet
• box of plain puffed rice cereal
• 12 plain rice-cereal balls
• 2 cocoa-flavored rice cereal balls

SCIENTIFIC METHOD
Ask a Question
How do meteorite finds differ from meteorite falls?

Conduct an Experiment
1. Fill the baking pan with puffed rice cereal. Smooth the top of the cereal so that it is level with the top of the pan. Then place 10 of the rice-cereal balls without cocoa across the top of the pan.

2. Place the pan at one end of the classroom. Decide who will drop the cereal balls and who will make observations. The rice-cereal balls should stand next to the pan while the observer stands across the room.

3. To conduct the first trial, hold a plain rice-cereal ball (representing a stony meteorite) at shoulder height directly above the pan. While the observer is watching, drop the ball.

4. The observer should then examine the pan and identify which ball was just dropped. Record in the "Observed" column of the Meteorite Observation Chart, on page 83, whether the meteorite was correctly identified.

5. Repeat steps 3–4 with another plain rice-cereal ball and with two cocoa-flavored rice balls (representing iron meteorites), dropping the balls one at a time.

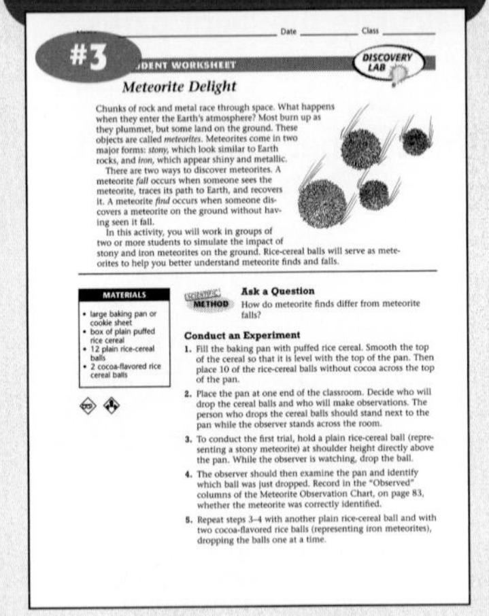

WHIZ-BANG DEMONSTRATIONS

#3 TEACHER-LED DEMONSTRATION **MAKING MODELS**

Crater Creator

...about impact craters and factors that contribute to their...

Time Required
15–20 minutes

Lab Ratings
TEACHER PREP
CONCEPT LEVEL
CLEAN UP

MATERIALS
• several sheets of newspaper
• cardboard box or plastic pan at least 10 cm deep
• all-purpose flour
• piece of cardboard, about 10 × 20 cm
• sifter or sieve
• tempera paint powder or chocolate-drink-mix powder
• small, medium, and large marbles or ball bearings
• metric measuring tape

USEFUL TERMS

ejecta blanket
a layer of ejecta (or debris) that lies like a blanket close to the impact crater

raised rim
a ring of debris deposited around the crater's edge

rays
material ejected away from the craters, seen as long lines

What to Do
1. Spread the newspapers on the floor. This can get messy. Place the box or pan on the floor in the center of the newspapers, and add enough flour to fill the container so that the flour is 6–8 cm deep. Smooth the surface with a piece of cardboard. Use the sieve or sifter to dust the surface of the flour with a light coating of tempera paint powder or chocolate-drink-mix powder.

2. Tell students that you will be simulating impact craters on lunar or planetary surfaces. The marbles will represent meteors or asteroids, and the flour simulates the surface.

3. After each impact, ask students to observe the flour's surface for the features of impact craters: ejecta, raised rim, and rays. Ejecta surrounds a crater; it is a layer of debris that spreads on impact. The raised rim is the edge of the crater itself. This is the circle of debris that marks the perimeter of the impact. Rays are formed as material is ejected from the surface and radiates away from the impact.

4. Drop a small marble or ball bearing onto the flour from a height of 50 cm, 100 cm, and 150 cm. Then throw the marble from a height of 100 cm. Finally, throw the marble into the flour from a different angle.

continued...

continued...

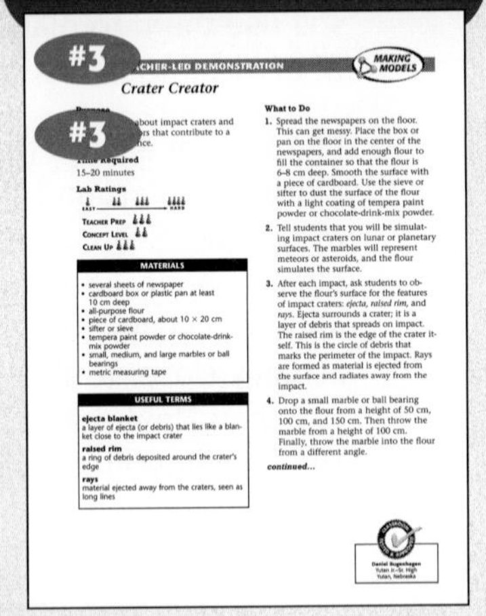

LONG-TERM PROJECTS & RESEARCH IDEAS

#3 STUDENT WORKSHEET **DESIGN YOUR OWN**

What Did You See, Mr. Messier?

Imagine that you are outside on a clear night observing the sky through a telescope. Suddenly, you notice a bright, fuzzy object that appears to have a tail of light coming from one side. Are your eyes playing tricks on you, or have you just found a comet? How can you tell? Well, you might start by checking the Messier Catalogue. The Messier Catalogue is a list of 109 celestial bodies compiled by Charles Messier, an eighteenth-century astronomer and comet chaser. Messier compiled this catalogue of objects that could be mistaken for comets in order to make comet hunting easier.

INTERNET KEYWORDS
Messier Catalogue
comets
Charles Messier

Look Up!
1. Find out more about Charles Messier and the Messier Catalogue in the library and on the Internet. What types of celestial bodies are included in the Messier Catalogue? Why are these celestial bodies likely to be confused with comets? Visit an area at night that does not have light interference, and identify as many Messier objects as you can. Create a guide to help others find and identify these objects.

Another Research Idea
2. Many Near Earth Objects (NEOs) have crashed into Earth. What clues did these objects leave behind? Investigate the physical and environmental impact of NEOs. Explain how scientists use crater information to determine the size, mass, and speed of the NEO that made the crater. Describe your results in a scientific article.

Long-Term Project Ideas
3. Have you ever really looked at the moon? Observe the moon every night for at least 2 months, and keep a moon journal. Try to make your observations from the same place and at the same time each night. Use binoculars to make observations. Sketch the moon, and describe its color, shape, position in the sky, and phase. Present your observations on a poster. Be sure to include illustrations.

HELPFUL HINT
The eight phases of the moon are the following: new moon, waxing crescent moon, first quarter moon, waxing gibbous moon, full moon, waning gibbous moon, third quarter moon, and waning crescent moon.

4. Many meteor showers and comet appearances are predictable. For example, Halley's comet passes by the Earth every 76 to 77 years. Find out the date of the next meteor shower or appearance of a comet. Observe the event, and record your observations. Why do comets pass by the Earth periodically? Investigate the sightings of Halley's comet over the last 2,000 years. How did ancient astronomers predict the occurrence of this comet? Write a magazine article about your observations and research.

EARTH SCIENCE

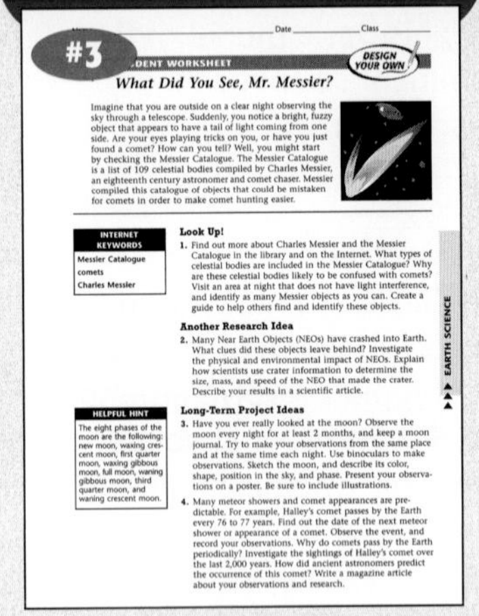

DATASHEETS FOR LABBOOK

#3 **Why Do They Wander?**

#3 **Eclipses**

#3 **Phases of the Moon**

3. Make a data table like the one below to list your observations. Make as many observations as you can about the potatoes in Group A, Group B, and Group C.

Observations
Group A:
Group B:

Form a Hypothesis
4. You have identified a problem and made your observations. Now you can make a hypothesis. Write a clear hypothesis about what you think will be the outcome of your tests.

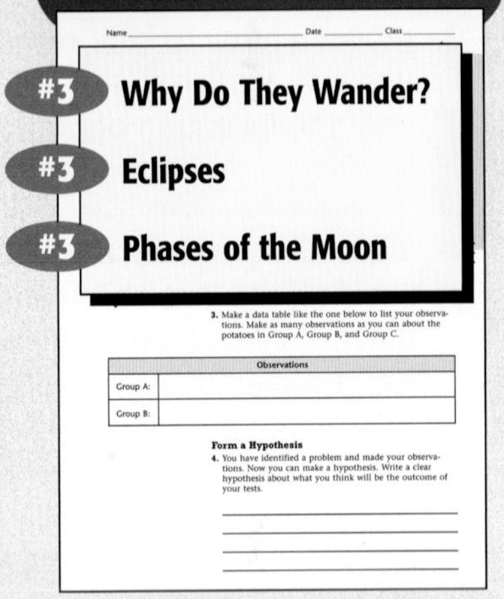

Applications & Extensions

CRITICAL THINKING & PROBLEM SOLVING

#3 CRITICAL THINKING WORKSHEET

Martian Holiday

MILKY WAY TRAVEL AGENCY

Package 1: Mars—Red, Hot, and Fantastic!
Are you ready for the trip of a lifetime? Then pack your favorite bathing suit and get ready for the solar system's most exotic resort planet. You may not have known it, but Mars has plenty of water! Enjoy water-skiing, surfing, and sailing all day long! If you think Hawaii's Mauna Loa is nice, you'll be blown away by Olympus Mons, the biggest mountain in the solar system! If you're lucky, you might even see this magnificent extinct shield volcano erupting! What a sight!

TRAVEL THE RIGHT WAY—THE MILKY WAY

Evaluating Sources
1. Would you describe the above passage as an advertisement or a scientific article? Explain how you can tell.

2. The brochure indicates that Mars has plenty of water and is a great place for water-skiing, surfing, and sailing. Is this accurate? Explain.

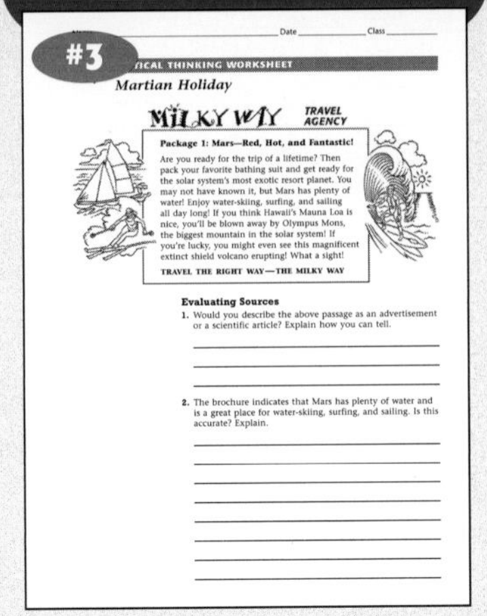

SCIENTISTS IN ACTION

#25 Science in the News: Critical Thinking Worksheets

Segment 25
Future Mars Astronauts

1. Why do you think NASA wants to send a manned mission to Mars?

2. Why is NASA concerned about what astronauts will eat on Mars?

3. Do you think that students' ideas could one day help NASA plan a manned mission to Mars? Why or why not?

4. Would you like to go to Mars? Why or why not?

CNN

INTERACTIVE EXPLORATIONS

#2–7 **Exploration 7 Worksheet**

Space Case

1. You've been asked to help Estelle de la Luna. What is your mission?

2. Describe the different parts of the equipment on the front table in the lab.

3. What happens when you click on the equipment? Describe the setup now.

4. What do you think the numbered squares represent?

DISC 2

CD-ROM

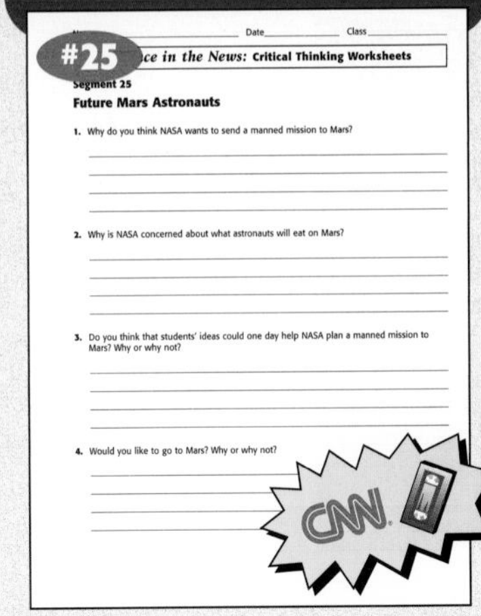

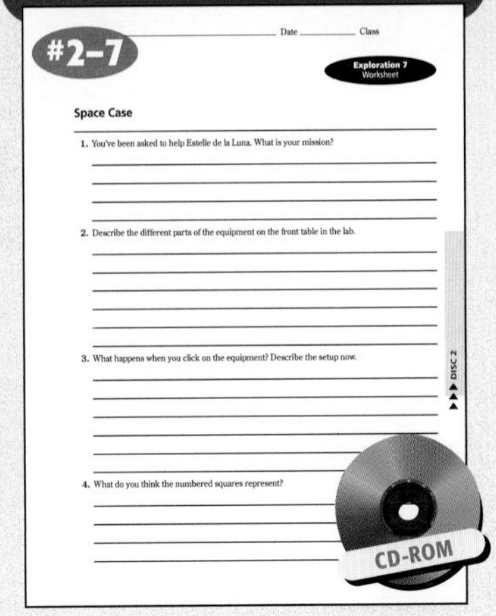

Chapter Background

Section 1

The Nine Planets

▶ Ptolemy

In the second century A.D., the astronomer Claudius Ptolemy formulated the first scientific theory that the Earth was the center of the universe. He argued that everything in the universe revolves around or falls toward Earth's center. In Ptolemy's model, the stars moved in a rotating sphere, and the motion of planets, moons, and comets was explained by a series of large and small circles turning inside one another. Although Ptolemy's theories about the mechanism of planetary movement were later rejected, his basic model of the universe remained the predominant scientific theory until the invention of the telescope in 1609.

▶ The Copernican Revolution

Some of the first observations Galileo made with the newly invented telescope were of Jupiter and its moons. He observed that the moons of Jupiter revolve around Jupiter and not Earth. He also discovered that Venus has phases, like our moon has. This evidence helped Galileo argue that Ptolemy's model of the solar system must be wrong and that Copernicus's heliocentric theory was correct. The Copernican revolution had a profound social impact and provided impetus for the Age of Enlightenment.

▶ A Day on Mercury

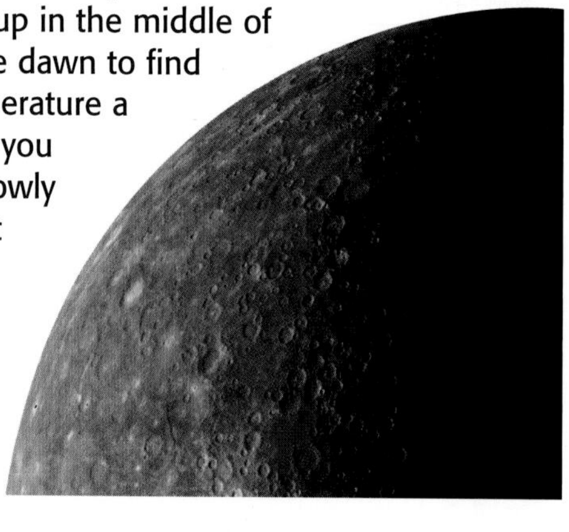

Imagine waking up in the middle of winter just before dawn to find the outside temperature a frigid −173°C! As you watch the sun slowly rise over the next several days, you notice that it appears three times as big as it does from Earth. You also notice that the sky is black. This is because Mercury has an extremely thin atmosphere, so it doesn't scatter blue light, like Earth's atmosphere does. Forty-four Earth days later, it would be noon on Mercury and the middle of summer as well. The temperature would be a toasty 427°C. The range of Mercury's surface temperatures is the most extreme of any planet in the solar system.

IS THAT A FACT!

- The planet Mercury has been known and studied for more than 2,000 years. Its wanderings may have been noted by Hypatia (415–370 B.C.), an Egyptian mathematician and philosopher and the first known female astronomer. Hypatia was also a student of Plato.
- Although Kepler's laws of motion were formulated almost 400 years ago, space scientists and engineers still use them to plan and calculate the flight paths of artificial satellites orbiting the Earth.
- Pluto is not always the farthest planet from the sun. Pluto's orbit around the sun takes 248 Earth years to complete. Because of its highly elliptical orbit, for about 20 years it is actually closer to the sun than Neptune is. The last time Pluto was closer to the sun than Neptune was from 1979 to 1999. The next time will be in the twenty-third century.

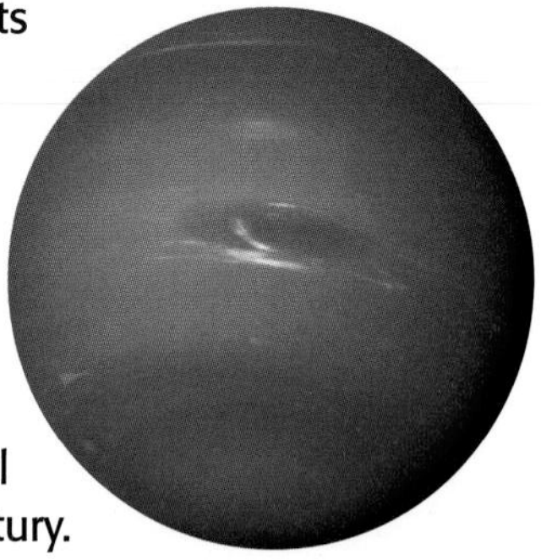

Section 2

Moons

▶ The Origin of the Moon

At a conference on satellites in 1974, William Hartmann and Donald Davis first presented the leading modern hypothesis of how the moon formed. This theory, called the impact model, stated the following:

- A smaller planetary body forming at about the same time as Earth collided with Earth late in Earth's formation. The collision blew rocky debris into orbit around Earth. That debris aggregated to form the moon.

Support for the Impact Model

The impact model has held up for the following reasons:

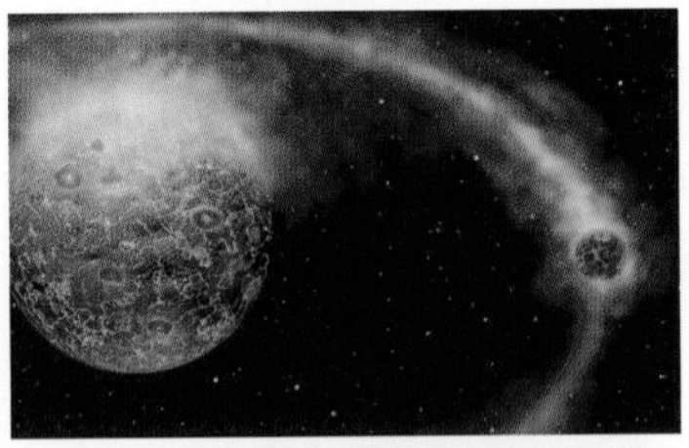

- **Composition** The terrestrial planets in our solar system, such as the Earth, all formed from the solar nebula and therefore tend to have similar ratios of common elements, such as iron. The moon, however, is relatively iron deficient. This means that the differentiation of Earth into distinct layers must have been happening *before* the formation of the moon. Because the iron-deficient composition of the moon closely matches that of the Earth's mantle, the internal differentiation of the Earth is a plausible mechanism for the present composition of the moon. Also, the oxygen-isotope composition of the moon is the same as Earth's. Other solar-system bodies have different oxygen-isotope compositions.
- **Orbital Properties** Computer simulations show that it is nearly impossible for an object with the mass of Earth to capture an object with as much mass as the moon. Instead they show that, although it would be a rare event, it is possible that a glancing blow from a Mars-sized object could throw enough Earth material into orbit to form the moon. The present size, distance, and orbital speed of the moon can all be accounted for by the impact theory.

Earth Tides

As the moon revolves around the Earth, it causes tides—even on land! The distance from the center of Earth to its surface increases by a few centimeters as the moon passes overhead. This change is not as noticeable as ocean tides, but it can be detected by very sensitive instruments.

IS THAT A FACT!

- Four moons in the solar system are larger than Earth's moon: Jupiter's Ganymede, Callisto, and Io, and Saturn's Titan. Earth's moon is special because it is very large relative to the planet it orbits. Pluto's moon, Charon, however, is more that half the size of Pluto.

SECTION 3

Small Bodies in the Solar System

The Oort Cloud

To explain the origin of comets, a Dutch astronomer named Jan Oort suggested in the 1950s that a spherical cloud of comets surrounds the solar system. He estimated that the cloud is 40,000–100,000 AU from the sun and that trillions of icy bodies may be contained within it.

The Kuiper Belt

The Dutch-American astronomer Gerard Kuiper proposed in 1949 that a belt of icy bodies must lie beyond the orbits of Pluto and Neptune to explain the source of short-period comets (comets with a relatively short orbit). Kuiper argued that comets were icy planetesimals that formed during the condensation of our solar nebula. Because the icy bodies are so far from any large planet's gravitational field (30–100 AU), they can remain on the fringe of the solar system. Some theorists speculate that the large moons Triton and Charon were once members of the Kuiper belt before being captured by Neptune and Pluto. These moons and short-period comets have similar physical and chemical properties.

For background information about teaching strategies and issues, refer to the *Professional Reference for Teachers.*

CHAPTER 3

A Family of Planets

Pre-Reading Questions

Students may not know the answers to these questions before reading the chapter, so accept any reasonable response.

Suggested Answers

1. Planets and moons are large and spherical. Comets, asteroids, and meteoroids are smaller and generally have irregular shapes. Planets can be large or small and gaseous or rocky. Most comets are icy bodies within the Oort cloud and the Kuiper belt. Asteroids are rocky bodies, most of which are within the asteroid belt. Meteoroids are thought to be the debris left over from asteroid collisions.
2. The number of impact craters on a planet's surface tells us how old the surface is. A planet with few craters has a young surface, indicating that its rocks are recycled. Flowing water leaves characteristic marks, such as stream channels, on a planet's surface.

CHAPTER 3

Sections

A Family of Planets

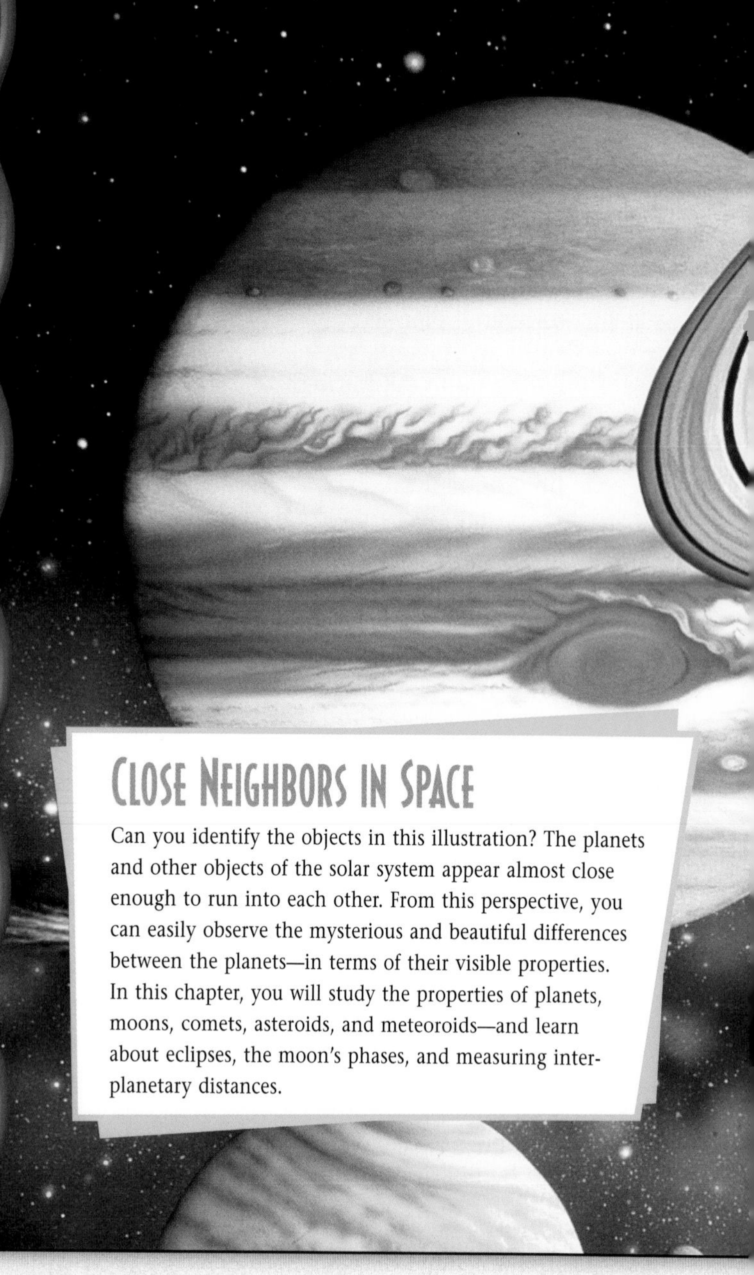

Close Neighbors in Space

Can you identify the objects in this illustration? The planets and other objects of the solar system appear almost close enough to run into each other. From this perspective, you can easily observe the mysterious and beautiful differences between the planets—in terms of their visible properties. In this chapter, you will study the properties of planets, moons, comets, asteroids, and meteoroids—and learn about eclipses, the moon's phases, and measuring interplanetary distances.

Pre-Reading Questions

1. What are the differences between planets, moons, asteroids, comets, and meteoroids?
2. How can surface features tell us about a planet's history?

62

internet**connect**

HRW On-line Resources

go.hrw.com

For worksheets and other teaching aids, visit the HRW Web site and type in the keyword: **HSTFAM**

sciLINKS NSTA

www.scilinks.com

Use the *sci*LINKS numbers at the end of each chapter for additional resources on the **NSTA** Web site.

Smithsonian Institution

www.si.edu/hrw

Visit the Smithsonian Institution Web site for related on-line resources.

CNNfyi.com

www.cnnfyi.com

Visit the CNN Web site for current events coverage and classroom resources.

START-UP Activity

MEASURING SPACE

Earth's distance from the sun is about 150 million kilometers, or 1 AU. *AU* stands for astronomical unit, which is the average distance between Earth and the sun. Do the following exercise to get a better idea of your solar neighborhood.

Procedure

1. Plant a **stake with a flag attached** at the goal line of a **football field**. This stake represents the sun. Then use the table to plant **9 more stakes with flags** representing the position of each planet.

Analysis

2. After you have positioned all the "planets," what do you notice about how the planets are spaced?

Interplanetary Distances

Planet	Distance from sun in AU	Scaled distance in yards
Mercury	0.39	1.0
Venus	0.72	1.8
Earth	1.00	2.5
Mars	1.52	3.9
Jupiter	5.20	13.3
Saturn	9.58	24.4
Uranus	19.20	48.9
Neptune	30.05	76.6
Pluto	39.24	100

63

START-UP Activity

MEASURING SPACE

MATERIALS

For Each Group:
- 10 stakes
- 10 flags

Teacher's Notes

The planetary data presented in this chapter are the most current available at the time of publication. Because of the vast size of the solar system, instrument limitations, and differences in methods of gathering data, the values given have varying margins of error. As measuring precision increases, these values are updated. Therefore, other sources may show different values for the same statistics.

Answer to START-UP Activity

2. The inner four planets are close together compared with the outer planets.

Section 1

Focus

The Nine Planets

This section begins with an explanation of the units used to measure astronomical distances. Then the section discusses each planet in our solar system.

Bellringer

Ask students to write about the following scenario:

Suppose that you were in charge of gathering the materials and supplies needed to live on Mars for a month. What materials would you need? What would you eat? How would you breathe? Where would you live?

1) Motivate

ACTIVITY

Remind students that the gravitational force between objects depends on their masses and the square of the distance between the objects. Weight, measured in *newtons,* is the measurement of the gravitational force acting on a mass. Have students make a chart showing what their weight would be on the different planets. Remind students that their mass will not change. Have them start by calculating their weight on Mercury. As they read about the surface gravity on each planet, have them add to their chart.

Teaching Transparency 191
"The Inner Planets"

Directed Reading Worksheet Section 1

Section 1 Reading Warm-Up

The Nine Planets

Terms to Learn

astronomical unit (AU)
terrestrial planets
prograde rotation
retrograde rotation
gas giants

What You'll Do

- List the names of the planets in the order they orbit the sun.
- Describe three ways in which the inner and outer planets are different from each other.

Ancient people knew about the existence of planets and could predict their motions. But it wasn't until the seventeenth century, when Galileo used the telescope to study planets and stars, that we began our first exploration of these alien worlds. Since the former Soviet Union launched *Sputnik 1*—the first artificial satellite—in 1957, over 150 successful missions have been launched to moons, planets, comets, and asteroids. **Figure 1** shows how far we have come since Galileo's time.

Galileo Galilei

Figure 1 *Galileo Galilei (left) discovered Jupiter's four largest moons using the newly invented telescope in 1610. The* Galileo *spacecraft (right) arrived at Jupiter on December 7, 1995.*

Measuring Interplanetary Distances

As you have seen, one way scientists measure distances in space is by using the astronomical unit. The **astronomical unit (AU)** is the average distance between the Earth and the sun. Another way to measure distances in space is by the distance light travels in a given amount of time. Light travels at about 300,000 km per second in space. This means that in 1 second, light travels a distance of 300,000 km—or about the distance you would cover if you traveled around Earth 7.5 times.

In 1 minute, light travels nearly 18,000,000 km! This distance is also called 1 *light-minute.* For example, it takes light from the sun 8.3 minutes to reach Earth, so the distance from the Earth to the sun is 8.3 light-minutes. Distances within the solar system can be measured in light-minutes and light-hours, but the distances between stars are measured in light-years!

Figure 2 *One astronomical unit equals about 8.3 light-minutes.*

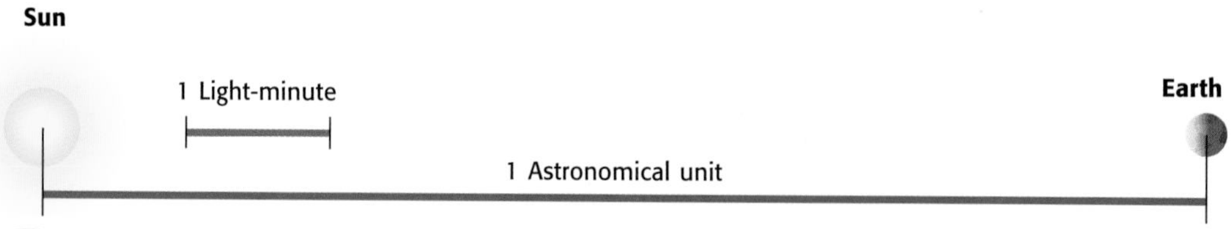

MISCONCEPTION ALERT

Tell students that the diameters of the Earth and the sun are not to scale in **Figure 2.** If they were, the sun would be a little less than 2 mm across and the Earth would be too small to see. The lengths of the light-minute and the AU, however, are to scale. Ask students why the AU is the *average* distance between the Earth and sun. (The Earth's orbit is elliptical, therefore the distance between the Earth and the sun is continually changing.)

The Inner Planets

The solar system is divided into two groups of planets—the inner planets and the outer planets. As you learned from the Investigate, the inner planets are more closely spaced than the outer planets. Other differences between the inner and outer planets are their sizes and the materials of which they are made. The inner planets are called **terrestrial planets** because they are like Earth—small, dense, and rocky. The outer planets, except for icy Pluto, are much larger and are made mostly of gases.

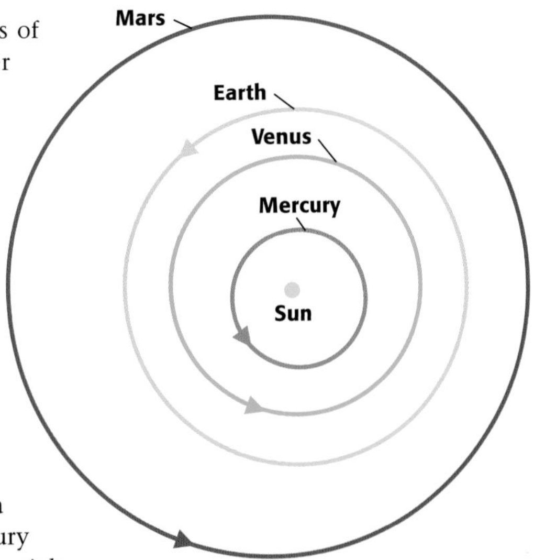

Figure 3 *The lines show orbits of the inner planets. The arrows indicate the direction of motion and the location of each planet on January 1, 2005.*

Mercury—Closest to the Sun If you were to visit the planet Mercury, you would find a very strange world. For one thing, on Mercury you would weigh only 38 percent of what you weigh on Earth. The weight you experience on Earth is due to *surface gravity,* which is less on less massive planets. Also, a day on Mercury is almost 59 Earth days long! This is because Mercury spins on its axis much more slowly than Earth does. The spin of an object in space is called *rotation.* The amount of time it takes for an object to rotate once is called its *period of rotation.*

Another curious thing about Mercury is that its year is only 88 Earth days long. As you know, a year is the time it takes for a planet to go around the sun once. The motion of a body as it *orbits* another body in space is called *revolution.* The time it takes for an object to revolve around the sun once is called its *period of revolution.* Every 88 Earth days, or 1.5 Mercurian days, Mercury completes one revolution around the sun.

Figure 4 *This image of Mercury was taken by the* Mariner 10 *spacecraft on March 24, 1974, from a distance of 5,380,000 km.*

Mercury Statistics	
Distance from sun	**3.2** light-minutes
Period of rotation	**58** days, **16** hours
Period of revolution	**88** days
Diameter	**4,879** km
Density	**5.43** g/cm^3
Surface temperature	**−173** to **427**°C
Surface gravity	**38%** of Earth's

65

2) Teach

READING STRATEGY

Mnemonics Have students create a mnemonic device to help them remember the order of the planets:

Mercury, **V**enus, **E**arth, **M**ars, **J**upiter, **S**aturn, **U**ranus, **N**eptune, and **P**luto

MISCONCEPTION ALERT

Tell students that planets, asteroids, comets, and moons shine because sunlight is reflected off their surfaces. Most photographs shown in astronomy books are false-color images. Chances are, if the caption does not state that the image is true-color, it probably is not what your eye would see. False-color images serve a valuable function—they bring out details of the object that the human eye would not ordinarily be able to see.

MATH and MORE

If light travels 18,000,000 km in 1 minute, how far away is Earth from the sun if it takes sunlight 8.3 minutes to reach Earth?

(18,000,000 km/minute × 8.3 minutes = 149,400,000 km)

How far is Mercury from the sun if it takes sunlight 3.2 minutes to reach its surface? (57,600,000 km)

Remind students that these numbers are rounded and are therefore imprecise.

Math Skills Worksheet
"A Shortcut for Multiplying Large Numbers"

BRAIN FOOD

Inform students that the density value given in statistics boxes is the bulk density for each planet. Different layers of planets have different densities. The cores are denser than the surface layers, for example. Although Mercury is about 29 percent smaller than Mars, its surface gravity is about the same. What does this tell us about the two planets? Because the force of gravity depends on how massive an object is and because Mercury is smaller than Mars, Mercury must have a higher density than Mars. Astronomers speculate that Mercury has more iron, a relatively dense element, in its core than Mars does.

2 Teach, continued

DEMONSTRATION

As you discuss the inner planets and Jupiter with students, keep a stopwatch on your desk. Tell them to imagine that they will be traveling at the speed of light to each planet they are learning about. For example, 3 minutes into your discussion of Mercury, tell students that light from the sun has reached this planet. It will take 43 minutes, or an entire class period, to reach Jupiter. When students leave class, they can set their watches to mark their planetary journey throughout the rest of the day.

CONNECT TO ENVIRONMENTAL SCIENCE

The greenhouse effect caused by the concentration of carbon dioxide in Venus's atmosphere creates surface temperatures hot enough to melt lead. Could an increased greenhouse effect cause Earth's atmosphere to become more like Venus's? Earth's current atmosphere is primarily nitrogen and oxygen. Deforestation and fossil fuel use have caused CO_2 levels in our atmosphere to rise steadily since the industrial revolution. Scientists have already noticed a possible global warming trend, and they are concerned that it could have far-reaching effects on Earth's biological systems. Have students write a short story describing how Earth's atmosphere could become more like the atmosphere of Venus. How would life change? What would happen if Earth's atmosphere was more like the atmosphere of Mars?

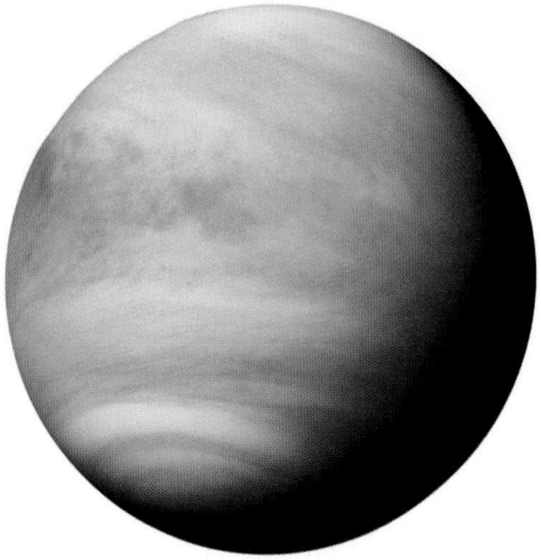

Figure 5 *This image of Venus was taken by* Mariner 10 *on February 5, 1974. The uppermost layer of clouds consists of sulfuric acid.*

Venus Statistics	
Distance from sun	**6.0** light-minutes
Period of rotation	**243** days, (R)*
Period of revolution	**224** days, **17** hours
Diameter	**12,104** km
Density	**5.24** g/cm³
Surface temperature	**464°C**
Surface gravity	**91%** of Earth's

*R = retrograde rotation

Venus—Earth's Twin? In many ways Venus is more similar to Earth than is any other planet—they have about the same size, mass, and density. But in other ways Venus is very different from Earth. Unlike on Earth, on Venus the sun rises in the west and sets in the east. This is because Venus rotates in the opposite direction that Earth rotates. Earth is said to have **prograde rotation,** because when viewed from above its north pole, Earth appears to spin in a *counterclockwise* direction. If a planet spins in a *clockwise* direction, it is said to have **retrograde rotation.**

The Atmosphere of Venus At 90 times the pressure of Earth's atmosphere, the atmosphere of Venus is the densest of the terrestrial planets. It consists mostly of carbon dioxide, but it also contains some of the most corrosive acids known. The carbon dioxide in the atmosphere traps thermal energy from sunlight in a process known as the *greenhouse effect.* This is why the surface temperature is so high. With an average temperature of 464°C, Venus has the hottest surface of any planet in the solar system.

Figure 6 *This false-color image of a volcano on the surface of Venus was made with radar data gathered by the* Magellan *spacecraft. Bright areas indicate massive lava flows.*

Mapping Venus's Surface Between 1990 and 1992, the *Magellan* spacecraft mapped the surface of Venus by using radar waves. The radar waves traveled through the clouds and bounced off the planet's surface. The radar image in **Figure 6** shows that, like Earth, Venus has an active surface.

66

Homework

Using Maps Interestingly, most of the features of Venus are named after female scientists, historical figures, and goddesses. Many of Mercury's craters are named after artists and musicians, and most craters of the moon are named after famous scientists. Have students use maps of the inner planets to learn more about their features and the origin of their names.

IS THAT A FACT!

Venus is the second-brightest object in the night sky, after the moon. Venus is often called the morning star or the evening star because it always rises and sets with the sun. Also, the planet rotates much more slowly than Earth. A day on Venus is longer than a year on Earth!

Earth—An Oasis in Space As viewed from space, Earth is like a sparkling blue oasis suspended in a black sea. Constantly changing weather patterns create the swirls of clouds that blanket the blue and brown sphere we call home. Why did Earth have such good fortune while its two nearest neighbors, Venus and Mars, are unsuitable for life as we know it?

Water on Earth Earth is fortunate enough to have formed at just the right distance from the sun. The temperatures are warm enough to prevent most of its water from freezing but cool enough to keep it from boiling away. Liquid water was the key to the development of life on Earth. Water provides a means for much of the chemistry that living things depend on for survival.

The Earth from Space You might think the only goal of space exploration is to make discoveries beyond Earth. But NASA has a program to study Earth using satellites—just as we study other planets. The goal of this project, called the Earth Science Enterprise, is to study the Earth as a system and to determine the effects humans have in changing the global environment. By studying Earth from space, we hope to understand how different parts of the global system—such as weather, climate, and pollution—interact.

Figure 7 *Earth is the only planet we know of that supports life.*

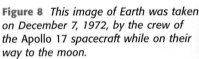

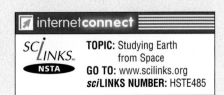

Figure 8 *This image of Earth was taken on December 7, 1972, by the crew of the* Apollo 17 *spacecraft while on their way to the moon.*

Earth Statistics	
Distance from sun	**8.3** light-minutes
Period of rotation	**23** hours, **56** minutes
Period of revolution	**365** days, **6** hours
Diameter	**12,756** km
Density	**5.52** g/cm^3
Surface temperature	**−13** to **37**°C
Surface gravity	**100%** of Earth's

RETEACHING

Discuss with students why Earth is referred to in their text as an oasis. Ask students what an oasis is. (An oasis is a hospitable place in an otherwise inhospitable area.)

Then ask them how Earth qualifies as an oasis in space. Tell them to focus on the importance of Earth's distance from the sun and the presence of large amounts of liquid water on Earth's surface. Earth's mass also plays an important role because it allows the planet to "hold" the gases around it that constitute Earth's life-sustaining atmosphere.

MEETING INDIVIDUAL NEEDS

Writing Have students research the Mars Arctic Research Station, the first fully simulated Mars base. The project will allow scientists to test technology that might be used during a manned expedition to Mars. A large impact crater on Devon Island, in the Arctic Circle, was selected for the research station because a polar desert on Earth closely matches the Martian environment. Have students compile their findings in a short report.

MISCONCEPTION ALERT

Earth is not a perfect sphere. The diameter of Earth as measured from the North Pole to the South Pole is 44 km less than the diameter as measured at the equator. None of the other planets or stars are perfectly spherical either. Therefore, all of the planetary diameters given in this chapter are equatorial diameters.

WEIRD SCIENCE

The Earth and its moon revolve around the sun like a "double planet." They can be thought of as the unequal ends of a weighted barbell. The center of gravity for the Earth-moon system, called the *barycenter,* is actually 1,700 km below the Earth's surface. This barycenter is what follows the curved line of Earth's orbit. Around this center of gravity, the moon and Earth wobble as they circle the sun.

internetconnect

SCILINKS NSTA

TOPIC: Studying Earth from Space

GO TO: www.scilinks.org

***sci*LINKS NUMBER:** HSTE485

2 Teach, *continued*

MATH and MORE

Have students use the planetary statistics tables to make a comparative bar graph of each planet's distance to the sun and its *average* surface temperature. Challenge students to draw conclusions about the relationship between the two statistics. Is there a linear relationship between the two? (no)

Why is Mercury colder than Venus even though it is 3 light-minutes closer to the sun? (Mercury does not have an atmosphere dense enough to trap solar radiation.)

Science Skills Worksheet
"Grasping Graphing"

USING THE FIGURE

The southern icecap of Mars is just visible in the lower right part of the image in **Figure 9.** Have students describe the differences between Mercury, Venus, Mars, and Earth. Ask them to refer to **Figure 10** to answer the following question:

What evidence suggests that there was once water on Mars?

MISCONCEPTION ALERT

Students may believe that the planets always have the same brightness. Actually, planets appear brighter when they are closer to Earth. For example, as Mars and Earth orbit the sun, the distance between the two planets varies from about 75 million kilometers to about 375 million kilometers. This change causes the apparent brightness of Mars to vary by a factor of 25.

Figure 9 *This* Viking *orbiter image shows the eastern hemisphere of Mars. The large circular feature in the center is the impact crater Schiaparelli, with a diameter of 450 km.*

Mars Statistics	
Distance from sun	**12.7** light-minutes
Period of rotation	**24** hours, **37** minutes
Period of revolution	**1** year, **322** days
Diameter	**6,794** km
Density	**3.93** g/cm^3
Surface temperature	**−123** to **37**°C
Surface gravity	**38%** of Earth's

Mars—The Red Planet Other than Earth, Mars is perhaps the most studied planet in the solar system. Much of our knowledge of Mars has come from information gathered by the *Viking 1* and *Viking 2* spacecraft that landed on Mars in 1976 and from the *Pathfinder* spacecraft that landed on Mars in 1997.

The Atmosphere of Mars Because of its thin atmosphere and its great distance from the sun, Mars is a cold planet. Mid-summer temperatures recorded by the *Pathfinder* lander ranged from –13°C to –77°C. The atmosphere of Mars is so thin that the air pressure at the planet's surface is roughly equal to the pressure 30 km above Earth's surface—about three times higher than most planes fly. The pressure is so low that any liquid water would quickly boil away. The only water you'll find on Mars is in the form of ice.

Water on Mars Even though liquid water cannot exist on Mars's surface today, there is strong evidence that it did exist there in the past! **Figure 10** shows a region on Mars with features that look like dry river beds on Earth. This means that in the past Mars might have been a warmer place with a thicker atmosphere. Where is the water now?

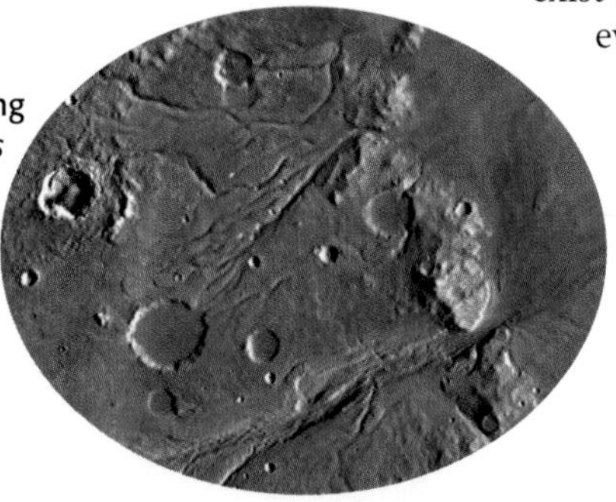

Figure 10 *This* Viking *orbiter image shows a drainage system on Mars formed by running water.*

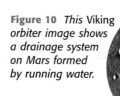

68

Science Bloopers

In the late 1800s, Giovanni Schiaparelli (1835–1910), an Italian astronomer, was studying Mars. He thought that he saw straight lines crisscrossing the surface of the red planet. He called these lines *canali.* In Italian this means "channels," but the word was erroneously translated to English as "canals." Partly because of this misconception, for nearly 100 years, many people believed that Mars had supported intelligent beings at some time in its past—beings that had built canals. This belief was disproved in the 1960s, when a spacecraft sent to Mars found no canals.

Mars has two polar icecaps that contain both frozen water and frozen carbon dioxide, but this cannot account for all the water. Looking closely at the walls of some Martian craters, scientists have found that the debris surrounding the craters looks as if it were made by a mud flow rather than by the movement of dry material. Where does this suggest some of the "lost" Martian water went? Many scientists think it is frozen beneath the Martian soil.

Martian Volcanoes Mars has a rich volcanic history. Unlike on Earth, where volcanoes occur in many places, Mars has only two large volcanic systems. The largest, the Tharsis region, stretches 8,000 km across the planet. The largest mountain in the solar system, Olympus Mons, is an extinct shield volcano similar to Mauna Kea, on the island of Hawaii. Mars is not only smaller and cooler than Earth, but it also has a slightly different chemical composition. Those factors may have prevented the Martian crust from moving around as Earth's crust has, so the volcanoes kept building up in the same spots. Images and data sent back by probes like the *Sojourner* rover, shown in **Figure 11**, are helping to explain Mars's mysterious past.

Physics CONNECTION

At sea level on Earth's surface, water boils at 100°C, but if you try to boil water on top of a high mountain, you will find that the boiling point is lower than 100°C. This is because the atmospheric pressure is less at high altitude. The atmospheric pressure on the surface of Mars is so low that liquid water can't exist at all!

Figure 11 *The* Sojourner *rover, part of the Mars Pathfinder mission, is shown here creeping up to a rock named Yogi to measure its composition. The dark panel on top of the rover collected the solar energy used to power its motor.*

SECTION REVIEW

1. What three characteristics do the inner planets have in common?
2. List three differences and three similarities between Venus and Earth.
3. **Analyzing Relationships** Mercury is closest to the sun, yet Venus has a higher surface temperature. Explain why this is so.

69

Answers to Section Review

1. Answers will vary. Sample answer: The inner planets are small and dense, and they are made of rocky material.
2. Similarities include size, density, mass, surface gravity, and bulk composition.

   Some differences are that Venus has retrograde rotation, Venus's surface temperature is much hotter, and Venus's atmosphere is much denser. (Also, Venus's atmosphere has a much more acidic composition, and the conditions on Venus are unsuitable for life.)
3. Unlike Mercury, Venus has a thick atmosphere that traps energy from the sun.

LabBook PG 164

Why Do They Wander?

MISCONCEPTION ALERT

As Mars moves eastward through Earth's night sky, it appears to gradually slow to a stop and then reverse its direction for several weeks. Then it resumes its normal west-to-east motion through the sky. This curious looped path puzzled astronomers in the past. Today we know that Earth passes Mars as the two planets orbit the sun, and thus Mars seems to move backward for a time. This is called *retrograde motion,* not to be confused with *retrograde rotation.*

CROSS-DISCIPLINARY FOCUS

Literature Percival Lowell (1855–1916), an American astronomer, wrote several books on the existence of an advanced civilization on Mars. Unfortunately, what Lowell observed were optical illusions caused by Earth's atmosphere and by dust storms and natural features on the surface of Mars. Lowell's books had a profound effect on the writings of H. G. Wells (1866–1946) and Edgar Rice Burroughs (1875–1950). Have interested students read and report on *War of the Worlds*, by Wells, or *A Princess of Mars*, by Burroughs.

internetconnect

SCLINKS NSTA

TOPIC: The Nine Planets
GO TO: www.scilinks.org
***sci*LINKS NUMBER:** HSTE480

2 Teach, continued

BRAIN FOOD

Some astronomers think of Jupiter as a small star that never reached maturity. In fact, the Galileo probe mentioned in the text found that the relative amounts of hydrogen and helium in Jupiter's atmosphere are very similar to those in the sun. Jupiter's 30,000°C core temperature is not high enough to initiate the fusion reactions that occur in the sun's core however. Had Jupiter been about 75 times more massive, it would have been hot enough to initiate nuclear reactions and become a second star in our solar system.

CROSS-DISCIPLINARY FOCUS

Writing **Language Arts** In 1980, Carl Sagan wrote in *Cosmos,* "The Earth is a place. It is by no means the only place. It is not even a typical place. No planet or star or galaxy can be typical, because the Cosmos is mostly empty. The only typical place is within the vast, cold, universal vacuum, the everlasting night of intergalactic space, a place so strange and desolate that, by comparison, planets and stars and galaxies seem achingly rare and lovely." Ask students to think about Sagan's quote and write a paragraph or poem about the emptiness of space.

Teaching Transparency 191
"The Outer Planets"

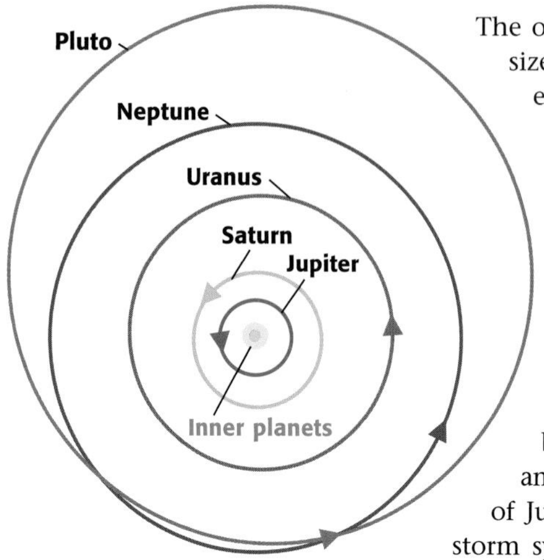

Figure 12 *This view of the solar system shows the orbits and positions of the outer planets on January 1, 2005.*

The Outer Planets

The outer planets differ significantly in composition and size from the inner planets. All of the outer planets, except for Pluto, are gas giants. **Gas giants** are very large planets that don't have any known solid surfaces—their atmospheres blend smoothly into the denser layers of their interiors, very deep beneath the outer layers.

Jupiter—A Giant Among Giants Like the sun, Jupiter is made primarily of hydrogen and helium. The outer part of Jupiter's atmosphere is made of layered clouds of water, methane, and ammonia. The beautiful colors in **Figure 13** are probably due to trace amounts of organic compounds. Another striking feature of Jupiter is the Great Red Spot, which is a long-lasting storm system that has a diameter of about one and a half times that of Earth! At a depth of about 10,000 km, the pressure is high enough to change hydrogen gas into a liquid. Deeper still, the pressure changes the liquid hydrogen into a metallic liquid state. Unlike most planets, Jupiter radiates much more energy into space than it receives from the sun. This is because energy is continuously transported from Jupiter's interior to its outer atmospheric layers, where it is radiated into space.

NASA Missions to Jupiter There have been five NASA missions to Jupiter—two Pioneer missions, two Voyager missions, and the recent Galileo mission. The *Voyager 1* and *Voyager 2* spacecraft sent back images that revealed a thin faint ring around the planet, as well as the first detailed images of its moons. The *Galileo* spacecraft reached Jupiter in 1995 and released a probe that plunged into Jupiter's atmosphere. The probe sent back data on the atmosphere's composition, temperature, and pressure.

Figure 13 *This* Voyager 2 *image of Jupiter was taken at a distance of 28.4 million kilometers. Io, one of Jupiter's 28 known moons, can also be seen in this image.*

Jupiter Statistics	
Distance from sun	**43.3** light-minutes
Period of rotation	**9** hours, **56** minutes
Period of revolution	**11** years, **313** days
Diameter	**142,984** km
Density	**1.33** g/cm^3
Temperature	**−153**°C
Gravity	**236**% of Earth's

70

CONNECT TO METEOROLOGY

All planets with atmospheres have weather. Jupiter's Great Red Spot appears to be very similar to a hurricane system on Earth, but it has lasted for centuries, driven by the planet's internal energy. Have students write a humorous but accurate weather forecast for one of the planets with an atmosphere.

IS THAT A FACT!

The solar system has two main bodies—the sun and Jupiter. In terms of mass, the rest of the solar system is insignificant! Jupiter has one-thousandth the mass of the sun but is roughly 317 times more massive than Earth, and Jupiter's volume is 1,321 times that of Earth.

Saturn Statistics	
Distance from sun	**1.3** light-hours
Period of rotation	**10** hours, **39** minutes
Period of revolution	**29** years, **155** days
Diameter	**120,536** km
Density	**0.69** g/cm^3
Temperature	**−185**°C
Gravity	**92%** of Earth's

Figure 14 *This* Voyager 2 *image of Saturn was taken from 21 million kilometers away. The dot you see below the rings is the shadow of Tethys, one of Saturn's moons.*

Saturn—Still Forming Saturn, the second largest planet in the solar system, has roughly 764 times the volume of Earth and is 95 times more massive. Its overall composition, like Jupiter's, is mostly hydrogen and helium, with methane, ammonia, and ethane in the upper atmosphere. Saturn's interior is probably very similar to that of Jupiter. Like Jupiter, Saturn gives off a lot more energy than it receives from the sun. Scientists believe that, in Saturn's case, the extra energy is caused by helium raining out of the atmosphere and sinking to the core. In essence, Saturn is still forming!

The Rings of Saturn Although all of the gas giants have rings, Saturn's rings are the largest. Saturn's rings start near the top of Saturn's atmosphere and extend out 136,000 km, yet they are only a few hundred meters thick. The rings consist of icy particles that range in size from a few centimeters to several meters across. **Figure 15** shows a close-up view of Saturn's rings.

NASA Goes to Saturn Launched in 1997, the *Cassini* spacecraft is designed to study Saturn's rings, its moons, and its atmosphere. It will return more than 300,000 color images, beginning in 2004.

Figure 15 *The different colors in this* Voyager 2 *image of Saturn's rings show differences in the chemical composition.*

USING THE TABLE

Have students compare the density of Saturn with the densities of other planets, including Earth. Then have them compare the density of Saturn with the density of water. What conclusions can they draw from this information? (If Saturn were put in an ocean large enough, Saturn would float.)

USING THE FIGURE

Ask students to measure the circumference of Saturn in **Figure 14** and ask them to hypothesize why Saturn appears to bulge around its equator. Tell students that there are two clues in the Saturn Statistics table. Point out that Saturn's low density (0.69 g/cm^3) and its fast period of rotation (10 hours and 30 minutes) cause the gaseous planet to bulge along its equator.

BRAIN FOOD

When Galileo saw Saturn's rings through a telescope in 1610, he supposedly exclaimed, "Saturn has ears!" Point out to students that *Voyager 2* counted more than 100,000 ringlets in Saturn's ring system. The ring particles range from the size of a dust speck to the size of a house. Ask students to find out more about the Cassini mission to Saturn, including what kind of information the Cassini color images will provide.

IS THAT A FACT!

Saturn has the most violent winds of any planet in our solar system. At Saturn's equator, the wind blows at nearly 1,700 km/h—not exactly good weather for playing outside.

WEIRD SCIENCE

Although Saturn has a similar composition to Jupiter, it appears less colorful. This is because its colder atmosphere causes thick, white ammonia clouds to condense, blocking our view.

2 Teach, *continued*

READING STRATEGY

Prediction Guide Before students read this page, ask them if they agree with the following statements. Students will learn the answers as they continue to explore Section 1.

- Uranus was discovered in the eighteenth century. (true)
- The orbits of the moons of Uranus are almost perpendicular to the planet's orbit around the sun. (true)

USING THE FIGURE

Using **Figure 17,** point out that because Uranus has an 82.1° tilt, its poles point toward the sun during part of its year. In contrast, Venus's 2.7° tilt means that, as with most planets, its poles never point directly toward the sun. Students can simulate these axial tilts using a globe and an object to represent the sun. As students revolve around the sun, have them tilt the globe to represent the axial tilts of Venus, Earth (23.5°), and Uranus. Point out the times that Uranus's poles point toward the sun. For consistency, the "axial tilts" of the planets are often described as angles less than 90°. In contrast, *obliquity* values for planets, which also measure the tilt of a planet's axis, are greater than 90° for planets with retrograde rotation. These planets are thought to have tipped over after colliding with other massive bodies shortly after they formed. In essence, their "rotational north poles" now point "south" in space. This is why the obliquity values for Venus, Uranus, and Pluto are 177.3°, 97.9°, and 122.5°, respectively.

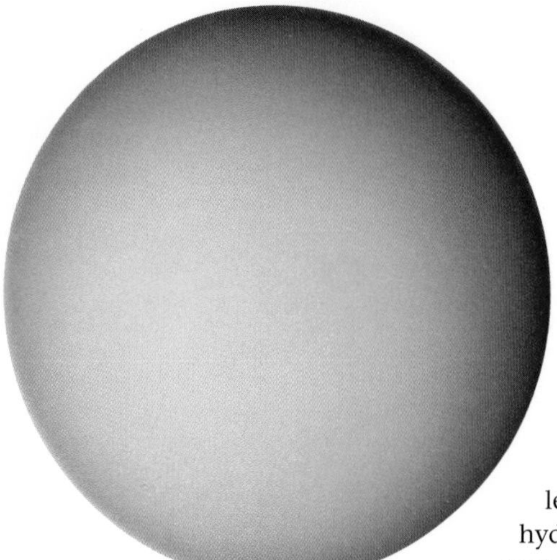

Figure 16 *This image of Uranus was taken by* Voyager 2 *at a distance of 9.1 million kilometers.*

Uranus Statistics	
Distance from sun	**2.7** light-hours
Period of rotation	**17** hours, **14** minutes (R)*
Period of revolution	**83** years, **274** days
Diameter	**51,118** km
Density	**1.27** g/cm^3
Temperature	**–214°C**
Gravity	**89%** of Earth's

*R = retrograde rotation

Uranus—A Small Giant Uranus (YOOR uh nuhs) was discovered by the English amateur astronomer William Herschel in 1781. Viewed through a telescope, Uranus looks like a featureless blue-green disk. The atmosphere is mainly hydrogen and methane gas, which absorbs the red part of sunlight very strongly. Uranus and Neptune are much smaller than Jupiter and Saturn, and yet they have similar densities. This suggests that they have lower percentages of light elements and more water in their interiors.

A Tilted Planet Uranus has about 63 times the volume of Earth and is nearly 15 times as massive. One especially unusual quality of Uranus is that it is tipped over on its side—the axis of rotation is tilted by almost 90° and lies almost in the plane of its orbit. **Figure 17** shows how far Uranus's axis is inclined. For part of a Uranus year, one pole points toward the sun while the other pole is in darkness. At the other end of Uranus's orbit the poles are reversed. Scientists suggest that early in its history, Uranus got hit by a massive object that tipped the planet over.

Figure 17 *Uranus's axis of rotation is tilted so that it is nearly parallel to the plane of Uranus's orbit. In contrast, the axes of most other planets are closer to being perpendicular to the plane of their orbits.*

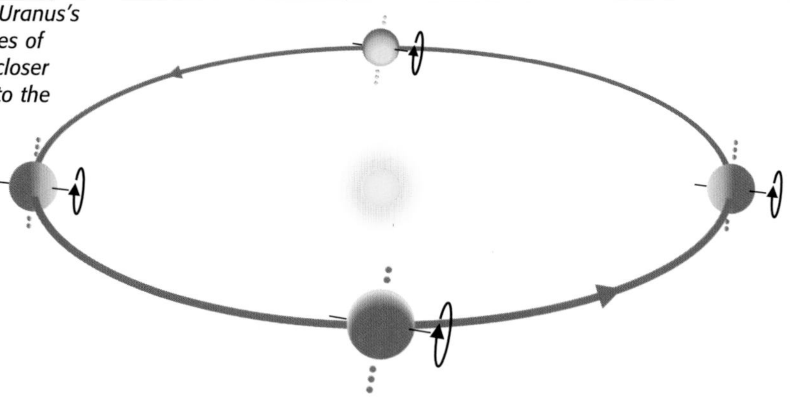

72

Science Bloopers

Uranus was discovered in 1781 by an English music teacher named William Herschel. Herschel originally named the planet *Georgium Sidus,* Latin for George's Star, after England's King George III. No one outside of England liked the name.

A few years later, an astronomer named J. E. Bode suggested the name Uranus because it would continue the tradition of naming the planets after Greek or Roman gods.

APPLY

Surviving Space

Imagine that it is the year 2120 and you are the pilot of an interplanetary spacecraft on your way to explore Pluto. In the middle of your journey, your navigation system malfunctions, giving you only one chance to land safely. You will not be able to make it to your original destination or back to Earth, so you must choose one of the other planets to land on. Your equipment includes two years' supply of food, water, and air. You will be stranded on the planet you choose until a rescue mission can be launched from Earth. Which planet will you choose to land on? How would your choice of this planet increase your chances of survival? Explain why you did not choose each of the other planets.

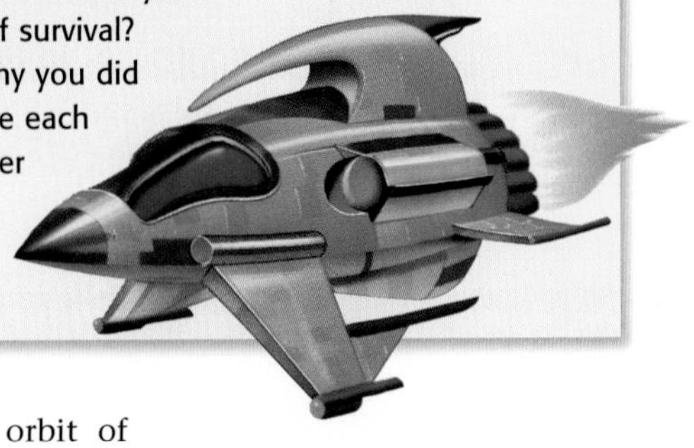

Neptune—The Blue World Irregularities in the orbit of Uranus suggested to early astronomers that there must be another planet beyond Uranus whose gravitational force causes Uranus to move off its predicted path. By using the predictions of the new planet's orbit, astronomers discovered the planet Neptune in 1846.

The Atmosphere of Neptune The *Voyager 2* spacecraft sent back images that gave us much new information about the nature of Neptune's atmosphere. Although the composition of Neptune's atmosphere is nearly the same as that of Uranus's atmosphere, Neptune's atmosphere contains belts of clouds that are much more visible. At the time of *Voyager 2*'s visit, Neptune had a Great Dark Spot, similar to the Great Red Spot on Jupiter. And like the interiors of Jupiter and Saturn, Neptune's interior releases energy to its outer layers. This helps the warm gases rise and the cool gases sink, setting up the wind patterns in the atmosphere that create the belts of clouds. *Voyager 2* images also revealed that Neptune has a set of very narrow rings.

Figure 18 *This* Voyager 2 *image of Neptune, taken at a distance of more than 7 million kilometers, shows the Great Dark Spot as well as some bright cloud bands.*

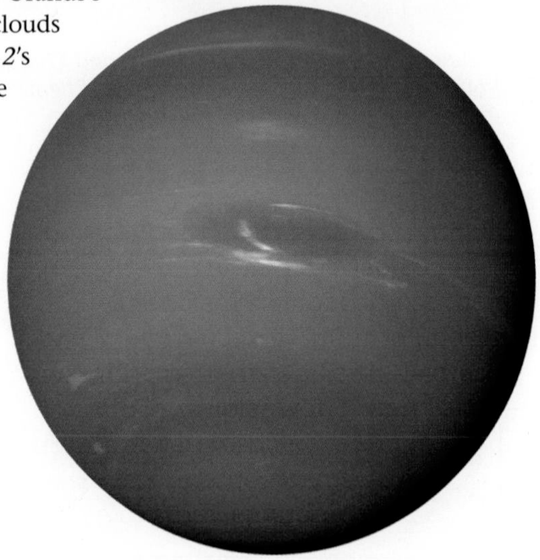

Neptune Statistics	
Distance from sun	**4.2** light-hours
Period of rotation	**16** hours, **7** minutes
Period of revolution	**163** years, **265** days
Diameter	**49,528** km
Density	**1.64** g/cm^3
Temperature	**−225**°C
Gravity	**112%** of Earth's

3 Extend

Answers to APPLY

Answers will vary. No matter which planet students choose, they should have a logical explanation for their choice.

BRAIN FOOD

Point out that Neptune was discovered in 1846 by the British astronomer John Adams and the French astronomer Joseph Leverrier. The discovery of Neptune was a triumph for modern physics. Using Newton's laws of motion and gravity, the astronomers accurately predicted Neptune's position. They found discrepancies in Uranus's motion that could not be explained by its gravitational interactions with the sun and the other known planets. Have students look up Newton's laws of motion and gravity. Then ask them to explain, in their own words, how deviations in one planet's orbit could indicate the presence of an unknown planet.

Group Activity

Packing for Space Have students make a list of the resources they would need to live in space. Remind them that it is very expensive to bring items from Earth because it takes a tremendous amount of energy to reach the velocity needed to escape the Earth's gravity. If an item could not be brought from Earth, have students suggest another planet where they could find that resource.

CONNECT TO ENVIRONMENTAL SCIENCE

Since the *Voyager* spacecraft passed Neptune's moon Triton in 1989, scientists have noticed an interesting trend in Triton's atmosphere. Images from the Hubble Space Telescope taken in 1998 indicate that Triton is going through a rapid period of global warming. As Triton warms, frozen nitrogen on its surface melts and contributes nitrogen gas to its thin atmosphere. This process has happened so rapidly that the atmospheric pressure of Triton has doubled in less than 10 years! Scientists hope to use the global warming trends on Triton to understand warming patterns on Earth. Because Triton is a much simpler world than Earth—with a thinner atmosphere, a surface of frozen nitrogen, and no oceans—it is a good place to study environmental change.

4 Close

Quiz

1. Which planets have retrograde rotation? (Venus, Uranus, and Pluto)
2. Which planet has the lowest density? (Saturn)
3. Which planet has the greatest number of moons? (Saturn)
4. Which planet has the shortest period of rotation? (Jupiter)
5. Which planet has the largest known volcano? (Mars)

Alternative Assessment

PORTFOLIO

Ask students to create a mobile of the planets. The mobile should have the planets in order, and their sizes should be in correct proportion to one another.

BRAIN FOOD

In question 4 of the Section Review, students are asked why the gas giants do not have statistics for surface temperature or surface gravity. Temperature, diameter, and gravity measurements will vary depending on where the surface is measured. The surfaces of the gas giants are sometimes defined as the level of the atmosphere at which the pressure is 1 bar (~1 atm). The values listed in this book are for the 1 bar level.

Critical Thinking Worksheet
"Martian Holiday"

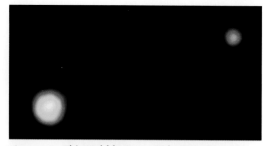

Figure 19 *This Hubble Space Telescope image is one of the clearest ever taken of Pluto (left) and its moon, Charon.*

Pluto Statistics	
Distance from sun	**5.5** light-hours
Period of rotation	**6** days, **9** hours (R)*
Period of revolution	**248** years
Diameter	**2,390** km
Density	**2.05** g/cm³
Surface temperature	**−236**°C
Surface gravity	**6**% of Earth's

*R = retrograde rotation

Figure 20 *An artist's view of the sun and Charon from Pluto shows just how little light and heat Pluto receives from the sun.*

Pluto—A Double Planet? Pluto is the farthest planet from the sun. It is also the smallest planet—less than half the size of Mercury. Another reason Pluto is unusual is that its moon, Charon (KER uhn), is more than half its size! In fact, Charon is the largest satellite relative to its planet in the solar system. **Figure 19** shows Pluto and Charon together.

From Earth, it is hard to separate the images of Pluto and Charon because they are so far away. **Figure 20** shows just how far away from the sun Pluto and Charon really are—from the surface of Pluto the sun appears to be only a very distant, bright star.

From calculations of Pluto's density, we know that it must be made of rock and ice. A very thin atmosphere of methane has been detected. While Pluto is covered by nitrogen ice, Charon is covered by water ice. Pluto is the only planet that has not been visited by a NASA mission, but plans are underway to finally visit this world and its moon in 2010.

internetconnect

SCILINKS NSTA

TOPIC: The Nine Planets
GO TO: www.scilinks.org
***sci*LINKS NUMBER:** HSTE480

SECTION REVIEW

1. How are the gas giants different from the terrestrial planets?
2. What is so unusual about Uranus's axis of rotation?
3. What conclusion can you draw about a planet's properties just by knowing how far it is from the sun?
4. **Applying Concepts** Why is the word *surface* not included in the statistics for the gas giants?

74

Answers to Section Review

1. Gas giants are much larger and more massive, they occupy the outer solar system, and they are much more widely spaced than the terrestrial planets.
2. Uranus's axis of rotation is tilted so that each pole points toward the sun for part of Uranus's year.
3. A variety of answers are acceptable: Planets farther from the sun tend to have lower surface temperatures; they are spaced farther apart; their period of revolution is much longer than that of the inner planets; and with the exception of Pluto, they are more likely to be large, gaseous planets with a large number of moons. (This is not necessarily the case for other solar systems.)
4. Gas giants have no definite surface. Their atmosphere blends smoothly into the denser layers of their interior.

SECTION 2
READING WARM-UP

Terms to Learn

satellite
phases
eclipse

What You'll Do

- Describe the current theory for the origin of Earth's moon.
- Describe what causes the phases of Earth's moon.
- Explain the difference between a solar eclipse and a lunar eclipse.

Figure 21 Apollo 17 *astronaut Harrison Schmidt—the first geologist to walk on the moon—samples the lunar soil.*

Moons

Satellites are natural or artificial bodies that revolve around larger bodies like planets. Except for Mercury and Venus, all of the planets have natural satellites called *moons.*

Luna: The Moon of Earth

We know that Earth's moon—also called *Luna*—has a different overall composition from the Earth because its density is much less than Earth's. This tells us that the moon has a lower percentage of heavy elements than the Earth has. The composition of lunar rocks brought back by Apollo astronauts suggests that the composition of the moon is similar to that of the Earth's mantle.

The Surface of the Moon The explorations of the moon's surface by the Apollo astronauts have given us insights about other planets and moons of the solar system. For example, the lunar rocks brought back during the Apollo missions were found to be about 4.6 billion years old. Because these rocks have hardly changed since they formed, we know the solar system itself is about 4.6 billion years old.

In addition, we know that the surfaces of bodies that have no atmospheres preserve a record of almost all the impacts they have had with other objects. As shown in **Figure 22,** the moon's history is written on its face! Because we now know the age of the moon, we can count the number of impact craters on the moon and use that number to calculate the rate of cratering that has occurred since the birth of our solar system. By knowing the rate of cratering, scientists are able to use the number of craters on the surface of any body to estimate how old its surface is—without having to bring back rock samples!

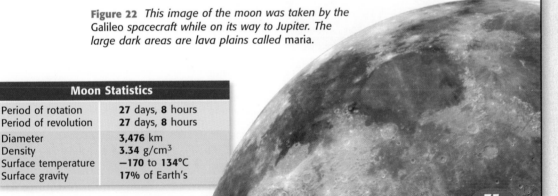

Figure 22 *This image of the moon was taken by the* Galileo *spacecraft while on its way to Jupiter. The large dark areas are lava plains called* maria.

Moon Statistics	
Period of rotation	**27** days, **8** hours
Period of revolution	**27** days, **8** hours
Diameter	**3,476** km
Density	**3.34** g/cm^3
Surface temperature	**−170** to **134**°C
Surface gravity	**17**% of Earth's

WEIRD SCIENCE

The first astronauts to land on the moon were quarantined after their mission. NASA wanted to make sure that the astronauts didn't bring back any disease-causing organisms from the moon.

Directed Reading Worksheet Section 2

internet**connect**

SCI LINKS NSTA

TOPIC: The Earth's Moon
GO TO: www.scilinks.org
***sci*LINKS NUMBER:** HSTE490

SECTION 2

Focus

Moons

In this section, students learn about Earth's moon—its origins, phases, and eclipses. Then they are introduced to some of the moons of the other planets in our solar system.

Bellringer

Discuss the following quote from Shakespeare's *Romeo and Juliet.* When Romeo swears by the moon, Juliet responds:

"O, Swear not by the moon, the inconstant moon,
That monthly changes in her circled orb,
Lest that thy love prove likewise variable."

1 Motivate

DISCUSSION

The term *maria,* used in **Figure 22,** comes from the Latin word for "sea." Early astronomers, including Galileo, thought that these dark lava plains were oceans of water. The 1998 Lunar Prospector mission indicates that there could be water on our moon—an essential resource for lunar pioneers. The shadowed craters near the poles may contain as much as 300 million metric tons of water ice! The water probably arrived on the moon from impacts with icy bodies. It can exist only in the permanently shadowed regions of the moon's poles; elsewhere, daytime temperatures can reach 134°C. Have students illustrate a lunar base, including a description of how pioneers could obtain liquid water.

2 Teach

READING STRATEGY

Prediction Guide Before students read this page, ask them: Where did the moon come from? What evidence is there to support this theory? As students read the rest of this section, have them construct a chart that describes some of the major moons in our solar system and their possible origin.

MATH and MORE

Every second, the moon travels 1 km in its orbit, but during that second, it also falls about 14 mm toward the Earth. Because of the moon's velocity and the pull of gravity, it travels along a path that follows the curved surface of the Earth. This condition, known as free fall, keeps the moon in orbit around the Earth. Explain to students that the condition of free fall, or weightlessness, does not mean that there is no gravity. The Earth's gravity acts on the moon in the same way it acts on an apple that falls out of a tree. The difference is that the moon, unlike the apple, is moving forward much, much faster than it is falling. Use the transparency listed below to discuss the moon's orbit.

Teaching Transparency 223
"Two Motions Combine to Form Projectile Motion"
LINK TO PHYSICAL SCIENCE

Teaching Transparency 192
"Formation of the Moon"

Physics CONNECTION

Did you know that the moon is falling? It's true. Because of gravity, every object in orbit around Earth is falling toward the planet. But the moon is also moving forward at the same time. The combination of the moon's forward motion and its falling motion results in the moon's curved orbit around Earth.

Lunar Origins Before rock samples from the Apollo missions confirmed the composition of the moon, there were three popular explanations for the formation of the moon: (1) it was a separate body captured by Earth's gravity, (2) it formed at the same time and from the same materials as the Earth, and (3) the newly formed Earth was spinning so fast that a piece flew off and became the moon. Each idea had problems. If the moon were captured by Earth's gravity, it would have a completely different composition from that of Earth, which is not the case. On the other hand, if the moon formed at the same time as the Earth or as a spin off of the Earth, the moon would have exactly the same composition as Earth, which it doesn't.

The current theory is that a large, Mars-sized object collided with Earth while the Earth was still forming. The collision was so violent that part of the Earth's mantle was blasted into orbit around Earth to form the moon. This theory is consistent with the composition of the lunar rocks brought back by the Apollo missions.

Formation of the Moon

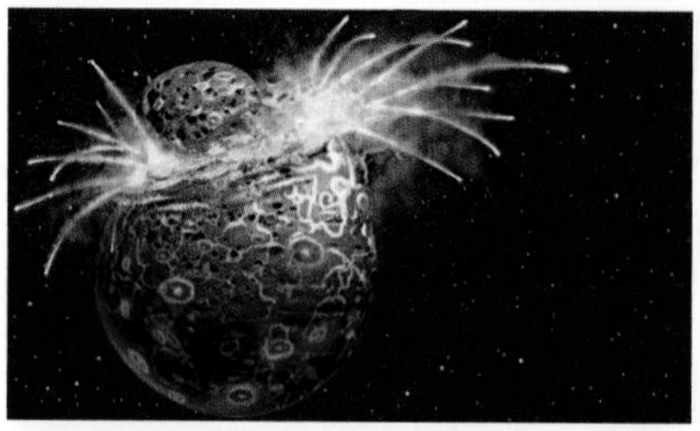

1 Impact
About 4.6 billion years ago, when Earth was still mostly molten, a large body collided with Earth. Scientists reason that the object must have been large enough to blast part of Earth's mantle into space, because the composition of the moon is similar to Earth's mantle.

2 Ejection
The resulting debris began to revolve around the Earth within a few hours of the impact. This debris consisted of mantle material from Earth and the impacting body as well as part of the iron core of the impacting body.

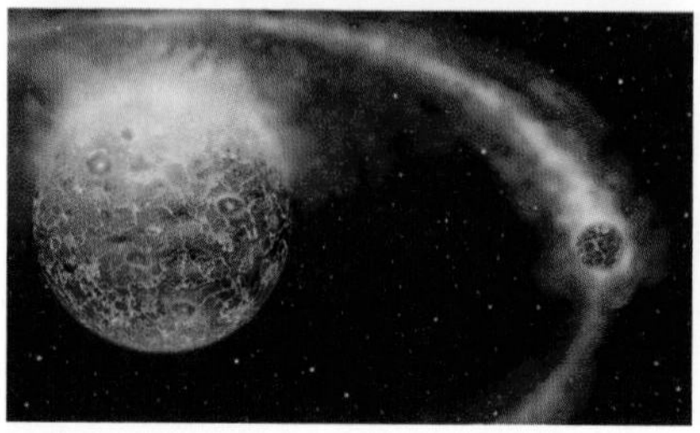

3 Formation
Soon after the giant impact, the clumps of material ejected into orbit around Earth began to join together to form the moon. Much later, as the moon cooled, additional impacts created deep basins and fractured the moon's surface. Lunar lava flowed from those cracks and flooded the basins to form the lunar maria we see today.

Homework

PORTFOLIO

Moon Journal Have students keep a record of the moon for 2 weeks. Have them make drawings of what they see, label the phase, and record the time of day and the position of the moon when they observed it. Emphasize that students should observe the moon from the same place and time each night and use the same landmark for observation. Students could use newspapers or a calendar to determine the current phase of the moon and the time the moon rises and sets during that phase. If you live near a body of water with tides, have students compare the times of high tides with the times that the moon rises.

Phases of the Moon From Earth, one of the most noticeable aspects of the moon is its continually changing appearance. Within a month, its Earthward face changes from a fully lit circle to a thin crescent and then back to a circle. These different appearances of the moon result from its changing position with respect to the Earth and the sun. As the moon revolves around the Earth, the amount of sunlight on the side of the moon that faces the Earth changes. The different appearances of the moon due to its changing position are called **phases.** The phases of the moon are shown in **Figure 23.**

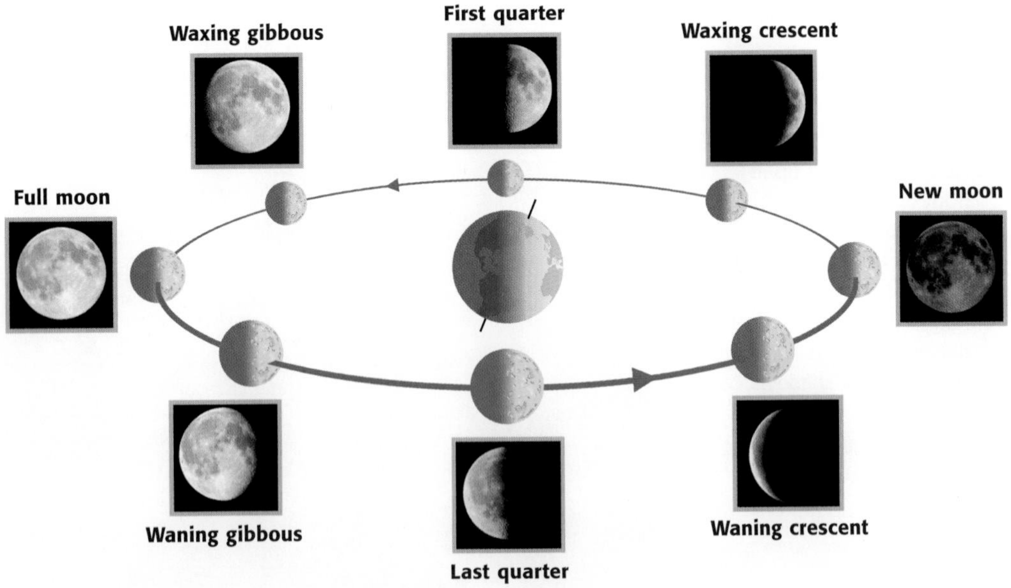

Figure 23 *The relative positions of the moon, sun, and Earth determine which phase the moon is in. The photo insets show how the moon looks from Earth at each phase.*

Waxing and Waning When the moon is *waxing,* it means that the sunlit fraction we can see from Earth is getting larger. When it is *waning,* the sunlit fraction is getting smaller. Notice in Figure 23 that even as the phases of the moon change, the total amount of sunlight the moon gets remains the same. Half the moon is always in sunlight, just as half the Earth is always in sunlight. But because the period of rotation for the moon is the same as its period of revolution, on Earth we always see the same side of the moon. If you lived on the far side of the moon, you would see the sun for half of each lunar day, but you would never see the Earth!

ACTIVITY

Modeling the Earth and Moon Pick three volunteers. One will be the moon, another will be Earth, and the last will be the sun. Have the sun stand 5 m from the Earth and hold a bright flashlight. Instruct the moon to stand 1 m away from Earth. Tell the moon to slowly orbit the Earth, keeping his or her face turned toward Earth. Have the sun turn on the flashlight and point the light toward Earth and the moon. Darken the room. Ask students:

How much of the moon is lit by the flashlight? (half)

When the moon is between Earth and the sun, what phase is the moon in? (new)

As the moon moves around Earth, ask the students which phase is being demonstrated by the moon's motion and the pattern of light on the moon.

Sheltered English

MEETING INDIVIDUAL NEEDS

Learners Having Difficulty Students may have a difficult time remembering the terms *waxing* and *waning*. To help students perform this simple activity, ask them to cup their right hand. When the moon's crescent is this shape, it is waxing, or growing larger. Then ask students to cup their *left* hand. Tell students that when the moon is this shape, it is waning. Tell them a waning moon shows what's *left*.

IS THAT A FACT!

Waxing means "growing," while *waning* means "shrinking." In the first quarter of a lunar phase, the moon is one quarter of the way through its cycle of phases. At this point, sunlight is shining on the right half of the moon. During the last quarter, sunlight is shining on the left half of the moon.

Teaching Transparency 193
"Phases of the Moon"

2 Teach, *continued*

QuickLab

MATERIALS

- heavy white paper
- 2 spherical objects
- objects with other shapes
- lamp

Safety Caution: Strongly caution students against looking directly at the sun (especially through binoculars or a telescope). Explain that doing so can result in permanent damage to their eyes or even blindness.

Answer to QuickLab

5. Spherical objects always cast a curved shadow.

MATH and MORE

To better understand the uniqueness of a solar eclipse on Earth, have students calculate the following: What is the ratio of the moon's diameter (3,476 km) to the sun's diameter (1,392,000 km)? (1:400)

What is the ratio of their distances from Earth if the moon is about 384,000 km from Earth and the sun is about 150,000,000 km from Earth? (1:390)

Help students understand that because the Earth is nearly 400 times closer to the moon than to the sun and because the sun is 400 times larger than the moon, the moon and sun appear to be the same size in the sky.

QuickLab

Clever Insight

Pythagoras (540–510 B.C.) and Aristotle (384–322 B.C.) used observations of lunar eclipses and a little logic to figure out that Earth is a sphere. Can you?

1. Cut out a circle of **heavy white paper.** This will represent Earth.
2. Find **two spherical objects** and several other **objects** with different shapes.
3. Hold each object up in front of a **lamp** (representing the sun) so that its shadow falls on the white paper circle.
4. Rotate your objects in all directions, and record the shapes of the shadows they make.
5. Which objects always cast a curved shadow?

Eclipses An **eclipse** occurs when the shadow of one celestial body falls on another. A *lunar eclipse* happens when the Earth comes between the sun and the moon, and the shadow of the Earth falls on the moon. A *solar eclipse* happens when the moon comes between the Earth and the sun, and the shadow of the moon falls on part of Earth.

Solar Eclipses By a remarkable coincidence, the moon in the sky appears to be nearly the same size as the sun. So during a solar eclipse, the disk of the moon almost always covers the disk of the sun. However, because the moon's orbit is not completely circular, sometimes the moon is farther away from the Earth, and a thin ring of sunlight shows around the outer edge of the moon. This type of solar eclipse is called an *annular eclipse*. **Figure 24** illustrates the position of the Earth and the moon during a solar eclipse.

Figure 24 *Because the shadow of the moon on Earth is small, a solar eclipse can be viewed from only a few locations.*

NEVER look directly at the sun! You can permanently damage your eyes.

Figure 25 *This is an image of the sun's corona during the February 26, 1998, eclipse in the Caribbean. The solar corona is visible only when the entire disk of the sun is blocked by the moon.*

78

Teaching Transparency 194
"Solar Eclipse"
"Lunar Eclipse"

Homework

Naming the Full Moon Students may be surprised to learn that every full moon has a name. The most familiar moon is the harvest moon, which occurs in the fall. Have students find out about other full moons, such as the hunter's moon or the sap moon, and report on the origins of the names.

Lunar Eclipses As you can see in **Figure 26,** the view during a lunar eclipse is also spectacular. Earth's atmosphere acts like a lens and bends some of the sunlight into the Earth's shadow, and the interaction of the sunlight with the molecules in the atmosphere filters out the blue light. With the blue part of the light removed, most of the remaining light that illuminates the moon is red.

Figure 26 *Because of atmospheric effects on Earth, the moon can have a reddish color during a lunar eclipse.*

Figure 27 *During a lunar eclipse, the moon passes within the Earth's shadow.*

The Moon's Orbit Is Tilted! From our discussion of the moon's phases, you might now be asking the question, "Why don't we see solar and lunar eclipses every month?" The answer is that the moon's orbit around the Earth is tilted—by about 5°—with respect to the orbit of the Earth around the sun. This tilt is enough to place the moon out of Earth's shadow for most full moons and the Earth out of the moon's shadow for most new moons.

MATH BREAK

Orbits Within Orbits

The average distance between the Earth and the moon is about 384,400 km. As you have read, the average distance between the Earth and the sun is 1 AU, or about 150,000,000 km. Assume that the orbit of the Earth around the sun and the orbit of the moon around the Earth are perfectly circular. Using the distances given above, calculate the maximum and minimum distances between the moon and the sun.

SECTION REVIEW

1. What evidence suggests that Earth's moon formed from a giant impact?
2. Why do we always see the same side of the moon?
3. How are lunar eclipses different from solar eclipses?
4. **Analyzing Methods** How does knowing the age of a lunar rock help astronomers estimate the age of the surface of a planet with no atmosphere?

Answers to Section Review

1. The composition of the moon is similar to that of the Earth's mantle. A large impact could have ejected part of Earth's mantle into orbit.
2. The moon's period of revolution around the Earth is the same as its period of rotation.
3. During a lunar eclipse, the Earth comes between the sun and the moon and Earth's shadow falls on the moon. During a solar eclipse, the moon comes between the Earth and the sun and the moon's shadow falls on the Earth.
4. Lunar rocks collected from the moon and dated indicate that the moon is 4.6 billion years old. Thus, the moon's surface shows the results of 4.6 billion years of cosmic impacts. A planet with no atmosphere and a similar crater density will be about as old as the moon.

Reteaching

Have students describe the location of the moon in relation to Earth and the sun during solar and lunar eclipses. Encourage them to demonstrate the positions using paper cutouts to represent the sun, the moon, and Earth. Sheltered English

BRAIN FOOD

Galileo wrote, "The sun, with all those planets revolving around it and depending upon it, can still ripen a bunch of grapes as if it had nothing else in the universe to do." Ask students to write a short story about what would happen if the sun released more or less energy than it does now.

Cross-Disciplinary Focus

Writing **History** Thales of Miletus, a Greek astronomer of the sixth century B.C., was famous for correctly predicting eclipses. Historians think he predicted the eclipse of May 28, 585 B.C. On that day, the Lydian Alyattes and the Median Cyaxeres were engaged in battle. When a mysterious darkness occurred (the eclipse), it frightened the warriors and interrupted the battle. Have interested students research how eclipses were interpreted by ancient civilizations. Suggest that they compile their findings in a short report.

Answers to MATHBREAK

maximum: 150,000,000 km + 384,400 km = 150,384,400 km
minimum: 150,000,000 km − 384,400 km = 149,615,600 km

2 Teach, *continued*

CONNECT TO LIFE SCIENCE

One of the most debated questions among scientists is whether there is life on other planets. Life as we know it requires liquid water. If liquid water exists on other planets or their moons, it is possible that there are also living organisms there. Scientists have been studying a group of organisms called extremophiles for clues about what extraterrestrial life might be like. Extremophiles are organisms that live in extreme environments, such as deep-ocean volcanic vents, hot springs, or highly acidic or basic environments. Scientists hope that by studying these organisms, they will have a better idea about where to look for life elsewhere in the solar system. Some of the most likely places to search for evidence of life are Mars and some of the moons of Jupiter. Have interested students find out about the status of NASA projects that are searching for extraterrestrial life and about organisms classified as extremophiles.

USING SCIENCE FICTION

Students will enjoy reading Stanley Weinbaum's "The Mad Moon" in the *Holt Anthology of Science Fiction*. Discuss the author's description of Jupiter's moon Io. How does the author's description compare with what we now know about Io? Have students use the story as inspiration to write their own description of a human colony on one of Jupiter's moons.

The Moons of Other Planets

The moons of the other planets range in size from very small to as large as terrestrial planets. All of the gas giants have multiple moons, and scientists are still discovering new moons. Some moons have very elongated, or elliptical, orbits, and some even revolve around their planet backward! Many of the very small moons may be captured asteroids. As we are learning from recent space missions, moons can be some of the most bizarre and interesting places in the solar system!

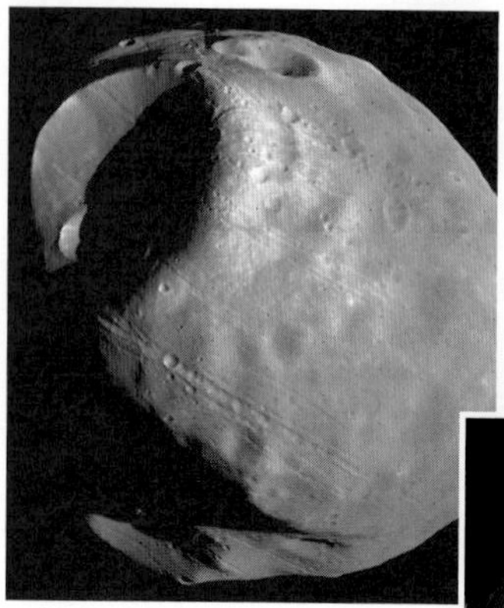

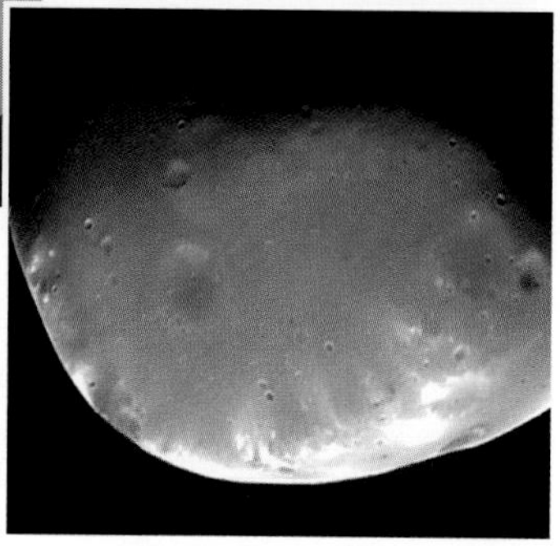

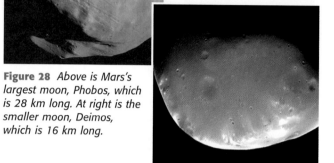

Figure 28 *Above is Mars's largest moon, Phobos, which is 28 km long. At right is the smaller moon, Deimos, which is 16 km long.*

The Moons of Mars Mars's two moons, Phobos and Deimos, are both small satellites that have irregular shapes. The two moons have very dark surfaces that reflect even less light than asphalt does. The surface materials are very similar to those found in asteroids, and scientists speculate that these two moons are probably captured asteroids.

The Moons of Jupiter Jupiter has a total of 28 known moons. The four largest—Ganymede, Callisto, Io, and Europa—were discovered in 1610 by Galileo and are known as the Galilean satellites. The largest moon, Ganymede, is even larger than the planet Mercury! Many of the smaller satellites are probably captured asteroids.

Moving outward from Jupiter, the first Galilean satellite is Io (IE oh), a truly bizarre world. Io is caught in a gravitational tug-of-war between Jupiter and Io's nearest neighbor, the moon Europa. This constant tugging stretches Io a little, causing it to heat up. Because of this, Io is the most volcanically active body in the solar system!

Recent pictures of the moon Europa support the idea that liquid water may lie beneath the moon's icy surface. This has many scientists wondering if life could have evolved in the subterranean oceans of Europa.

Figure 29 *At left is a* Galileo *image of Jupiter's innermost moon, Io. At right is a* Galileo *image of Jupiter's fourth largest moon, Europa.*

80

Homework

Writing | Have students research the moons of a planet other than Earth and write a short paper about them. Suggest that they compare the moons with each other and with Earth's moon and then research the possible reasons for the differences they find.

MISCONCEPTION ALERT

Students may think the moon is larger when it is close to the horizon. The moon appears larger because the observer's reference point is the skyline. The same phenomenon makes the sun appear larger. Challenge students to devise a way to verify this for themselves. Remind them not to look directly at the sun.

The Moons of Saturn Saturn has a total of 30 known moons. Most of these moons are small bodies made mostly of water ice with some rocky material. The largest satellite, Titan, was discovered in 1655 by Christiaan Huygens. In 1980, the *Voyager 1* spacecraft flew past Titan and discovered a hazy orange atmosphere, as shown in **Figure 30.** Titan's atmosphere is similar to what Earth's atmosphere may have been like before life began to evolve. In 1997, NASA launched the *Cassini* spacecraft to study Saturn and its moons, including Titan. By studying Titan, scientists hope to answer some of the questions about how life began on Earth.

Figure 30 *Titan is one of only two moons that have a thick atmosphere. Titan's hazy orange atmosphere is made of nitrogen plus several other gases, such as methane.*

Self-Check

What is one major difference between Titan and the early Earth that would suggest that there probably isn't life on Titan? *(See page 200 to check your answer.)*

The Moons of Uranus Uranus has 21 moons, three of which were just discovered by ground-based telescopes during the summer of 1999. Like the moons of Saturn, the four largest moons are made of ice and rock and are heavily cratered. The little moon Miranda, shown in **Figure 31,** has some of the most unusual features in the solar system. Miranda's surface includes smooth, cratered plains as well as regions with grooves and cliffs up to 20 km high. Current ideas suggest that Miranda may have been hit and broken apart in the past but was able to come together again, leaving a patchwork surface.

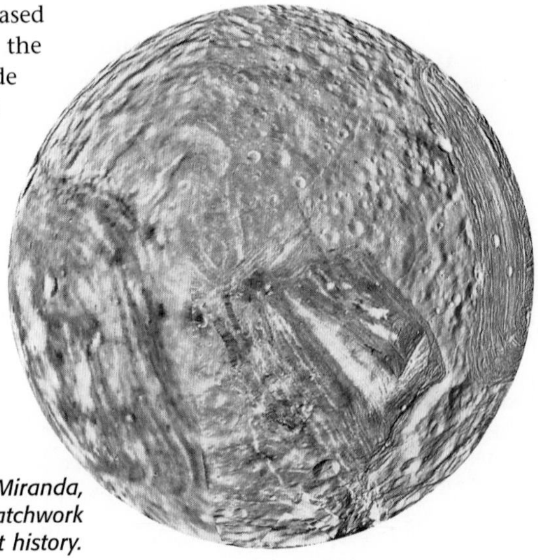

Figure 31 *This* Voyager 2 *image shows Miranda, the most unusual moon of Uranus. Its patchwork terrain indicates that it has had a violent history.*

3 Extend

BRAIN FOOD

Like planets, most moons are spherical in shape. Ask the class why this is the case. Why aren't some moons square, tube shaped, or pyramidal? Tell them that the force of gravity and the origin of celestial bodies have something to do with the answer. Lead them to the conclusion that as the mass of an object increases, the gravitational force that it exerts also increases. When a rocky object reaches a diameter of about 350 km, the gravitational force becomes greater than the strength of the material and the moon starts to become spherical.

Answer to Self-Check

The surface of Titan is much colder than the surface of the Earth. (In fact, the temperature is close to −178°C!)

RESEARCH

NASA is planning several missions to explore the moons of different planets. Have students select one of NASA's projects and find out the details of what was discovered or what NASA hopes to find. Have students imagine that they are scientists working on the project, and have them write a press release with the details of the project.

IS THAT A FACT!

Io, one of Jupiter's moons, is well known for the volcanoes on its surface. These volcanoes, which are the hottest in the solar system, regularly erupt yellow and red clouds of sulfur up to 300 km above the surface!

internet connect

SCILINKS NSTA

TOPIC: The Moons of Other Planets
GO TO: www.scilinks.org
***sci*LINKS NUMBER:** HSTE495

4 Close

Quiz

Have students complete the following sentences:

1. A naturally formed planetary satellite is a ________. (moon)
2. As Earth's moon waxes, the sunlit fraction we see from Earth becomes ________. (larger)
3. When the moon is waning, the sunlit fraction is becoming ________. (smaller)
4. If you lived on the far side of the moon, you would never see ________. (Earth)
5. The two moons of Mars are believed to be captured ________. (asteroids)
6. The four largest moons of Jupiter were discovered by ________. (Galileo)
7. Two moons with atmospheres are ________ (Triton) and ________. (Titan)

Alternative Assessment

PORTFOLIO

Provide students with construction paper, glue, scissors, and markers. Have them use these materials to make models of the nine planets and their moons.

Reinforcement Worksheet "The Planets of Our Solar System"

Reinforcement Worksheet "Lunar and Solar Eclipses"

Interactive Explorations CD-ROM "Space Case"

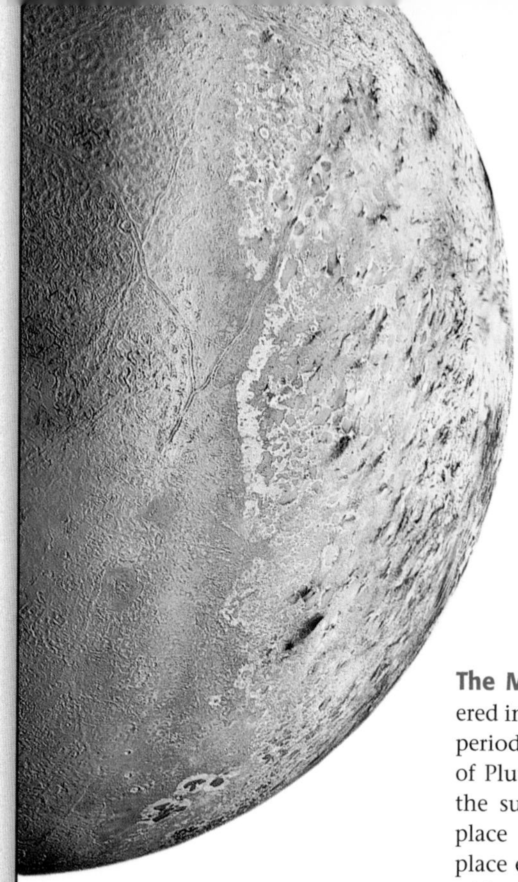

The Moons of Neptune Neptune has eight moons, only one of which is large. This moon, Triton, revolves around the planet in a *retrograde,* or "backward," orbit, suggesting that it may have been captured by Neptune's gravity. Triton has a very thin atmosphere made mostly of nitrogen gas. The surface of Triton consists mainly of frozen nitrogen and methane. *Voyager 2* images revealed that it is geologically active. "Ice volcanoes," or geysers, were seen ejecting nitrogen gas high into the atmosphere. The other seven moons of Neptune are small, rocky worlds much like the smaller moons of Saturn and Jupiter.

Figure 32 *This* Voyager 2 *image shows Neptune's largest moon, Triton. The polar icecap currently facing the sun may have a slowly evaporating layer of nitrogen ice, adding to Triton's thin atmosphere.*

The Moon of Pluto Pluto's only moon, Charon, was discovered in 1978. Charon's period of revolution is the same as Pluto's period of rotation—about 6.4 days. This means that one side of Pluto always faces Charon. In other words, if you stood on the surface of Pluto, Charon would always occupy the same place in the sky. Imagine Earth's moon staying in the same place every night! Because Charon's orbit around Pluto is tilted with respect to Pluto's orbit around the sun, as seen from Earth, Pluto is sometimes eclipsed by Charon. But don't hold your breath; this happens only once every 120 years!

internetconnect

SCI LINKS. NSTA

TOPIC: The Moons of Other Planets
GO TO: www.scilinks.org
***sci*LINKS NUMBER:** HSTE495

SECTION REVIEW

1. What makes Io the most volcanically active body in the solar system?
2. Why is Saturn's moon Titan of so much interest to scientists studying the origins of life on Earth?
3. What two properties of Neptune's moon Triton make it unusual?
4. **Identifying Relationships** Charon always stays in the same place in Pluto's sky, but the moon always moves across Earth's sky. What causes this difference?

82

Answers to Section Review

1. Io is caught in the middle of a gravitational "tug of war" between Jupiter and its other large moons.
2. Titan has a thick atmosphere of nitrogen, which scientists think is very similar to that of the early Earth.
3. Triton has a thin atmosphere of nitrogen, and it has a retrograde orbit around Neptune. Most moons have a prograde orbit and no atmosphere.
4. Pluto's period of rotation is the same as Charon's period of revolution. The Earth's period of rotation is much shorter than the moon's period of revolution.

SECTION 3 READING WARM-UP

Terms to Learn

comet	meteoroid
asteroid	meteorite
asteroid belt	meteor

What You'll Do

- Explain why comets, asteroids, and meteoroids are important to the study of the formation of the solar system.
- Compare the different types of asteroids with the different types of meteoroids.
- Describe the risks to life on Earth from cosmic impacts.

Small Bodies in the Solar System

In addition to planets and moons, the solar system contains many other types of objects, including comets, asteroids, and meteoroids. As you will see, these objects play an important role in the study of the origins of the solar system.

Comets

A **comet** is a small body of ice, rock, and cosmic dust loosely packed together. Because of their composition, some scientists refer to comets as "dirty snowballs." Comets originate from the cold, outer solar system. Nothing much has happened to them since the birth of the solar system some 4.6 billion years ago. Because comets are probably the leftovers from the process of planet formation, each comet is a sample of the early solar system. Scientists want to learn more about comets in order to piece together the chemical and physical history of the solar system.

Figure 33 *Comet Hale-Bopp appeared in North American skies in the spring of 1997.*

Comet Tails When a comet passes close enough to the sun, solar radiation heats the water ice so that the comet gives off gas and dust in the form of a long tail, as shown in **Figure 33.** Sometimes a comet has two tails—an *ion tail* and a *dust tail.* The ion tail consists of electrically charged particles called *ions.* The solid center of a comet is called its *nucleus.* Comet nuclei can range in size from less than half a kilometer to more than 100 km in diameter. **Figure 34** shows the different features of a comet when it passes close to the sun.

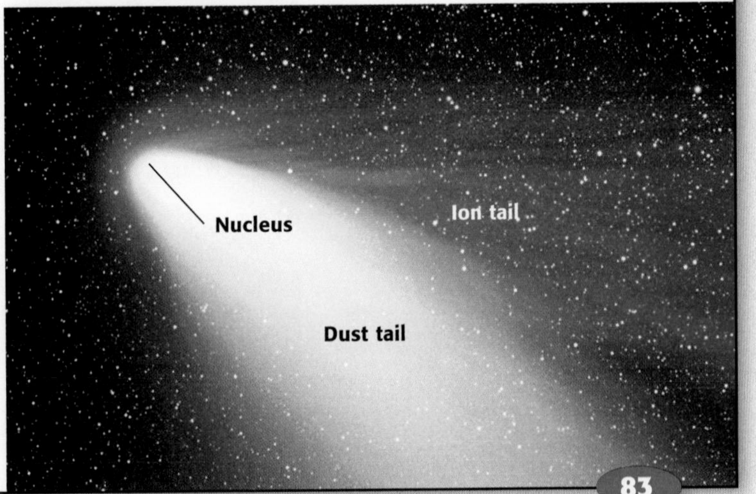

Figure 34 *This image shows the physical features of a comet when it is close to the sun. The nucleus of a comet is hidden by brightly lit gases and dust.*

83

SECTION 3

Focus

Small Bodies in the Solar System

This section explores the minor bodies of the solar system—comets, asteroids, and meteoroids. Students will learn what happens when these bodies collide with moons and planets.

Bellringer

Tell students that some early European cultures considered comets to be omens of bad fortune. In 1066, when Halley's comet appeared while Normans conquered England, many English people believed this superstition was proven true. Ask students to write in their ScienceLog about why the English were mistaken.

1 Motivate

DEMONSTRATION

Mix 2 cups of water, 2 tbsp of dirt, 1 tsp of ammonia (optional), and a few pebbles in a container. Then crush 2 cups of dry ice in a plastic bag while wearing protective gloves. Slowly pour the liquid mixture into the bag, mixing constantly. Mold this mixture to produce a model comet. After spreading plastic over your work area, carefully place the comet on top of an inverted foam cup, and use a hair dryer to simulate the solar wind that produces a comet's tail when it approaches the sun. Allow students to observe the comet. Tell students that comets are made of water ice, carbon dioxide ice, rock, organic material, and trace amounts of ammonia. Most comets are discovered by amateur astronomers using powerful binoculars.

IS THAT A FACT!

When the comet Shoemaker-Levy 9 broke apart and fell into Jupiter, some of the fragments generated explosions that produced fireballs larger than Earth.

Directed Reading Worksheet Section 3

2 Teach

BRAIN FOOD

In the past, the primary distinction between a comet and an asteroid was that comets have ices and asteroids do not. The development of sophisticated telescopes and remote-sensing instruments has challenged this distinction. There is evidence that some asteroids may contain ices and that some asteroids develop comet tails. Also, some comets have stopped producing tails and are beginning to look more like asteroids! In general, comets contain enough ice to become "active" and develop a tail, and asteroids do not. Asteroids range in size from a few kilometers to about 1,000 km across, while comet nuclei are rarely larger than 100 km.

Using the Figure

As you discuss **Figure 36,** point out to students that the Kuiper belt is like the asteroid belt—it is circular and relatively flat, lying close to the plane of the planets' orbits. The Oort cloud, on the other hand, is spherical and surrounds the entire solar system. The average period of revolution for a comet is about 10 million years. Comets that originate in the Oort cloud do not necessarily orbit the sun in the plane of the planets' orbits—most of them have inclined orbits. They can also have either retrograde or prograde orbits.

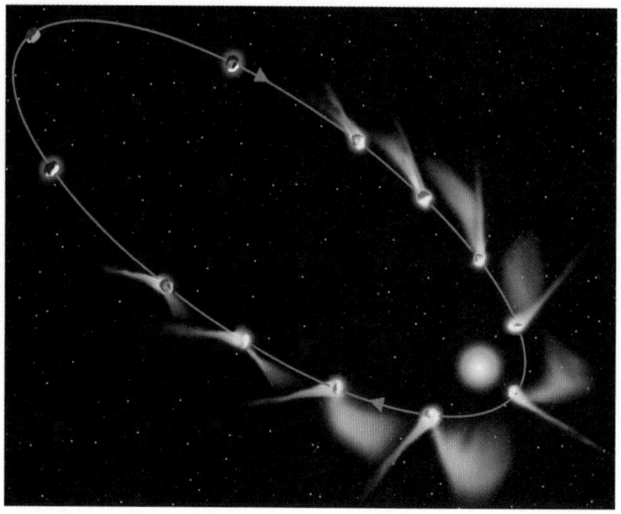

Figure 35 *When a comet's highly elliptical orbit carries it close to the sun, it can develop one or two tails. As shown here, the ion tail is blue and the dust tail is yellow.*

Comet Orbits All orbits are *ellipses*—circles that are somewhat stretched out of shape. Whereas the orbits of most planets are nearly circular, comet orbits are highly elliptical—they are very elongated.

Notice in **Figure 35** that a comet's ion tail always points directly away from the sun. This is because the ion tail is blown away from the sun by the solar wind, which also consists of ions. The dust tail tends to follow the comet's orbit around the sun and does not always point away from the sun. When a comet is close to the sun its tail can extend millions of kilometers through space!

Comet Origins Where do comets come from? Many scientists think they may come from a spherical region, called the *Oort* (ohrt) *cloud,* that surrounds the solar system. When the gravity of a passing planet or star disturbs part of this cloud, comets can be pulled in toward the sun. Another recently discovered region where comets exist is called the *Kuiper* (KIE per) *belt,* which is the region outside the orbit of Neptune. These two regions where comets orbit are shown in **Figure 36.**

Figure 36 *The Kuiper belt is a disk-shaped region that extends outward from the orbit of Neptune. The Oort cloud is a spherical region far beyond the orbit of Pluto.*

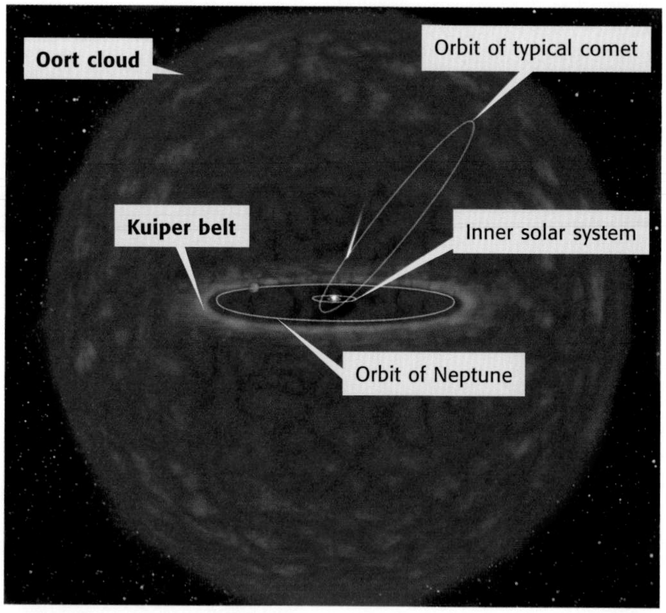

84

MISCONCEPTION ALERT

Students may be surprised to learn that comets don't have a tail during most of their orbit. It is only when they near the sun that they warm up and release a tail made of gas and dust. The comet nucleus has an irregular shape. Sometimes gas leaves the comet's surface unevenly in "jets." This can have an effect similar to that of a miniature rocket engine, pushing a comet slightly off course and making it difficult to find during its next orbit.

Asteroids

Asteroids are small, rocky bodies in orbit around the sun. They range in size from a few meters to more than 900 km in diameter. Asteroids have irregular shapes, although some of the larger ones are spherical. Most asteroids orbit the sun in a wide region between the orbits of Mars and Jupiter, called the **asteroid belt.** Like comets, asteroids are thought to be material left over from the formation of the solar system.

Types of Asteroids Asteroids can have a variety of compositions, depending on where they are located within the asteroid belt. In the outermost region of the asteroid belt, asteroids have dark reddish brown to black surfaces, which may indicate that they are rich in organic material. A little closer to the sun, asteroids have dark gray surfaces, indicating that they are rich in carbon. In the innermost part of the asteroid belt are light gray asteroids that have either a stony or metallic composition. **Figure 38** shows some examples of what some of the asteroids may look like.

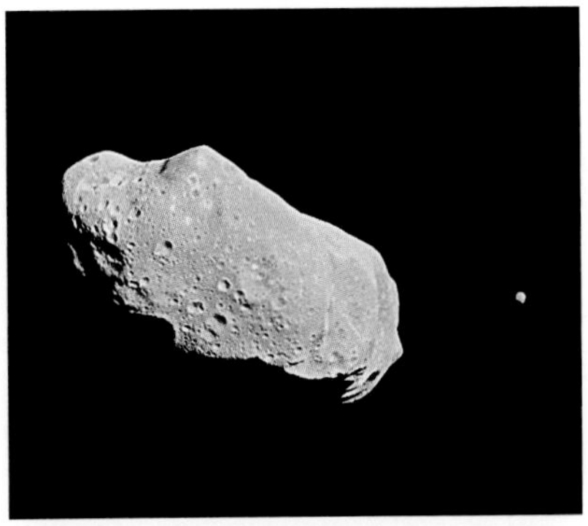

Figure 37 *The asteroid Ida has a small companion asteroid that orbits it called Dactyl. Ida is about 52 km long.*

Figure 38 *The asteroid belt is a disk-shaped region located between the orbits of Mars and Jupiter.*

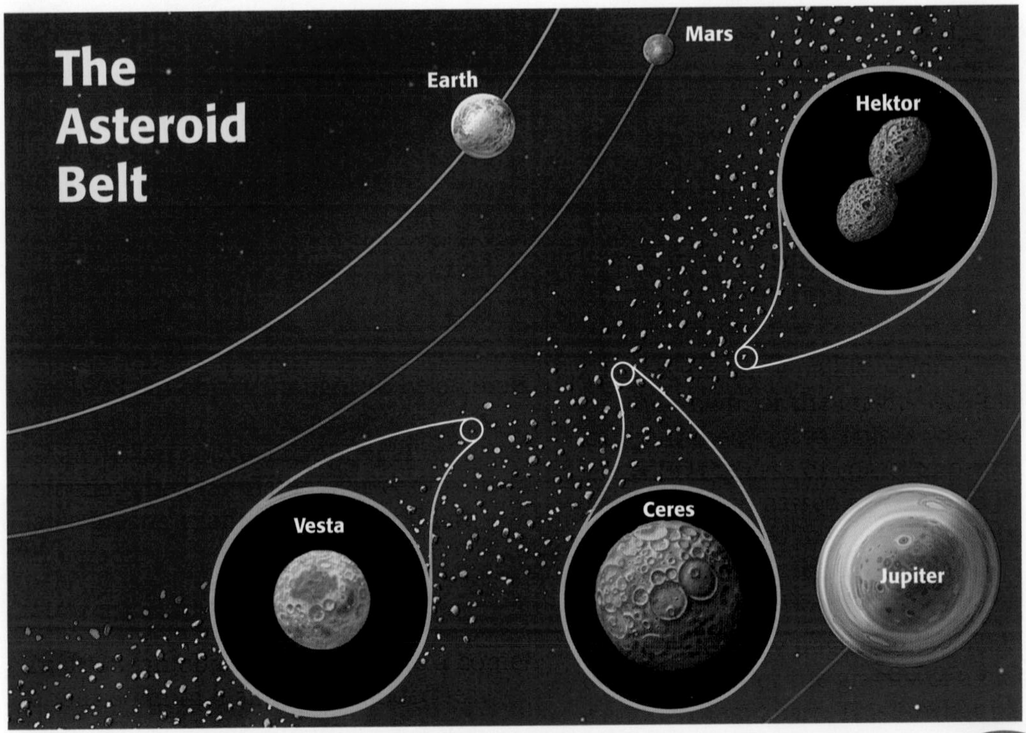

RETEACHING

Draw a diagram of a comet on the board. Ask volunteers to label the parts and to describe the composition of each part. Sheltered English

BRAIN FOOD

The orbits of some asteroids cross Earth's orbit. Every few million years, one of these asteroids hits the Earth. If an asteroid is larger than 10 km across, its impact can have catastrophic global effects. In the first few seconds of an impact event, both the impactor and part of the target become liquid and an impact crater forms. Shock waves spread out from the site, and debris is ejected high into the atmosphere. About 65 million years ago, a large asteroid struck the Earth on the Yucatan Peninsula. This event may have led to the mass extinction of the dinosaurs. In 1994, the world watched with awe as parts of the comet Shoemaker-Levy 9 collided with Jupiter, causing enormous explosions. This event has led NASA to devote more of its resources to finding and tracking asteroids whose orbits cross Earth's. Have students find out more about NASA's asteroid-tracking program.

WEIRD SCIENCE

In 1908, an object thought to be a comet about 60 m in diameter exploded less than 10 km above a remote part of Siberia. The blast flattened trees in an area greater than 2,000 km^2 and left no crater.

IS THAT A FACT!

Comets are fairly fragile; some break apart on their own, or the gravity of a planet can pull them apart. This is what happened in the case of comet Shoemaker-Levy 9, which passed too close to Jupiter. When it returned in 1994, fragments of the comet crashed into Jupiter's atmosphere.

INDEPENDENT PRACTICE

Concept Mapping Have students create a concept map using at least six vocabulary words in this chapter. Tell them that their map should illustrate logical connections between the terms they choose.

3 Extend

MEETING INDIVIDUAL NEEDS

Learners Having Difficulty
List the terms *meteoroid, meteor,* and *meteorite* on the board. For each of the terms, have students define the word, use it in a sentence, and draw an illustration. (A meteoroid is a small rocky body orbiting the sun. A meteor is the bright streak of light we see when a meteoroid enters our atmosphere. A meteorite is a meteoroid that does not burn completely and lands on the Earth's surface.) Sheltered English

ACTIVITY

Collecting Micrometeorites
Earth's atmosphere is constantly bombarded with microscopic meteorites that are too small to burn up. These micrometeorites float in the atmosphere and eventually settle to the ground. The best time to collect micrometeorites is after a meteor shower. Clean a small glass dish, and place it outside to collect rainwater. If you live in an area with little rain, fill the dish with distilled water and place it outside for several days. Place a small, strong magnet in a small plastic bag, and sweep the covered magnet slowly through the water, along the bottom and sides of the dish. Place the covered magnet in a second pan of distilled water, and remove the magnet, shaking the bag in the water to dislodge any particles. Evaporate the water over a hot plate, and drag a magnetized needle across the sides and bottom of the dish. Tap the needle onto a microscope slide, and examine the sediment with a microscope—any rounded and pitted metallic particles are probably micrometeorites.

BRAIN FOOD

The total mass of meteorites that fall to Earth each year is between 10,000 and 1 million metric tons!

Meteoroids

A **meteoroid** is a small, rocky body orbiting the sun. Meteoroids are similar to asteroids, but they are much smaller. In fact, most meteoroids probably come from asteroids. If a meteoroid enters Earth's atmosphere and strikes the ground, it is then called a **meteorite.** When a meteoroid falls into Earth's atmosphere, it is usually traveling at such a high speed that its surface heats up and melts. As it burns up, the meteoroid glows red hot and gives off an enormous amount of light. From the ground, we see a spectacular streak of light, or a shooting star. The bright streak of light caused by a meteoroid or comet dust burning up in the atmosphere is called a **meteor.**

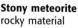

Figure 39 *Meteors are the streaks of light caused by meteoroids as they burn up in Earth's atmosphere.*

Meteor Showers Many of the meteors that we see come from very small (dust-sized to pebble-sized) rocks and can be seen on almost any night if you are far enough away from the city to avoid the glare of its lights. At certain times of the year, you can see large numbers of meteors, as shown in **Figure 39.** These events are called *meteor showers.* Meteor showers occur when Earth passes through the dusty debris left behind in the orbit of a comet.

Types of Meteorites Like their relatives the asteroids, meteorites have a variety of compositions. The three major types of meteorites—stony, metallic, and stony-iron—are shown in **Figure 40.** Many of the stony meteorites probably come from carbon-rich asteroids and may contain organic materials and water. Scientists use meteorites to study the early solar system. Like comets and asteroids, meteoroids are some of the building blocks of planets.

Figure 40 *There are three major types of meteorites.*

Stony meteorite
rocky material

Metallic meteorite
iron and nickel

Stony-iron meteorite
rocky material, iron, and nickel

SCIENTISTS AT ODDS

As late as the 1800s, scientists were skeptical that meteorites originate in space—despite records from the Chinese, Romans, and Greeks describing stones falling from the sky. In 1803, meteorites fell in France. A physicist documented the event, finally convincing scientists that meteorites fall from the sky.

WEIRD SCIENCE

In 1954, Mrs. E. Hulitt Hodge, of Alabama, was struck by a meteorite as she was taking her afternoon nap. Bruised, but not badly injured, she is one of only two people known to have been struck by a meteorite.

The Role of Impacts in the Solar System

Planets and moons that have no atmosphere have many more impact craters than those that do have atmospheres. Look at **Figure 41.** The Earth's moon has many more impact craters than the Earth because it has no atmosphere or tectonic activity. Fewer objects land on Earth because Earth's atmosphere acts like a shield. Smaller bodies burn up before they ever reach the surface. On the moon, there is nothing to stop them! Also, most craters left on Earth have been erased due to weathering, erosion, and tectonic activity.

Figure 41 *The surface of the moon preserves a record of billions of years of cosmic impacts.*

Impacts on Earth Objects smaller than about 10 m across usually burn up in the atmosphere, causing a meteor. Larger objects are more likely to strike Earth's surface. In order to estimate the risk of cosmic impacts, we need to consider how often large impacts occur.

The number of large objects that could collide with Earth is relatively small. Scientists estimate that impacts powerful enough to cause a natural disaster might occur once every few thousand years. An impact large enough to cause a global catastrophe—such as the extinction of the dinosaurs—is estimated to occur once every 30 million to 50 million years on average.

SECTION REVIEW

1. Why is the study of comets, asteroids, and meteoroids important in understanding the formation of the solar system?
2. Why do a comet's two tails often point in different directions?
3. Describe one reason asteroids may become a natural resource in the future.
4. **Analyzing Viewpoints** Do you think the government should spend money on programs to search for asteroids and comets with Earth-crossing orbits? Discuss why.

internet**connect**

SCILINKS NSTA

TOPIC: Comets, Asteroids, and Meteoroids
GO TO: www.scilinks.org
***sci*LINKS NUMBER:** HSTE500

Answers to Section Review

1. Comets, asteroids, and meteoroids represent the leftover building blocks of the solar system. Knowing the compositions of these bodies will help scientists piece together the history of the solar system.
2. A comet's ion tail is blown away from the sun by the solar wind, while its dust tail is not.
3. Answers will vary. Sample answer: Many asteroids are made of metals that could be used for industrial purposes.
4. Answers will vary.

4 Close

Quiz

Have students complete the following sentences:

1. ________ are small bodies of ice and cosmic dust. (Comets)
2. Most asteroids in our solar system are found between ________ and ________. (Mars, Jupiter)
3. Which asteroid has a small companion? (Ida)
4. ________ are meteoroids that fall to Earth. (Meteorites)

Alternative Assessment

PORTFOLIO

Have students create an illustrated field guide to small bodies in our solar system. The guide should incorporate all of the vocabulary used in this section as well as drawings, diagrams, and explanations for each object they include. Sheltered English

Cross-Disciplinary Focus

Geography The easiest place in the world to find meteorites is in Antarctica. Contrary to what most people believe, there is very little snowfall in Antarctica, and the snow never completely melts. In addition, glacial movement causes meteorites to collect in specific areas. Because of this, any rocks that are found on top of the snow are almost certainly meteorites—so all you have to do to find them is walk out on the glaciers and pick up rocks!

internet**connect**

SCILINKS NSTA

TOPIC: Comets, Asteroids, and Meteoroids
GO TO: www.scilinks.org
***sci*LINKS NUMBER:** HSTE500

Eclipses
Teacher's Notes

Time Required

One 45-minute class period

Lab Ratings

EASY → HARD

- Teacher Prep
- Student Set-Up
- Concept Level
- Clean Up

MATERIALS

The materials listed on the student page are enough for each student or for students working in groups of 2–3.

Answers

6. The flashlight represents the sun.
7. As viewed from Earth, step 4 modeled a lunar eclipse and step 5 modeled a solar eclipse.
8. As viewed from the moon, step 4 modeled a solar eclipse and step 5 modeled an eclipse of Earth.
9. There would be a lunar eclipse and a solar eclipse each month. This is because the model shows Earth and the moon orbiting in exactly the same plane around the sun. However, one plane is usually above or below the shadow of the other, so an eclipse does not always occur.

Making Models Lab

Eclipses

As Earth and the moon revolve around the sun, the Earth and the moon both cast shadows into space. An eclipse happens when one planetary body passes through the shadow of another. You can demonstrate how an eclipse happens by using clay models of planetary bodies.

MATERIALS

- modeling clay
- metric ruler
- sheet of notebook paper
- small flashlight

Procedure

1. Make two balls out of the modeling clay. One ball should have a diameter of about 4 cm and will represent the Earth. The other should have a diameter of about 1 cm and will represent the moon.
2. Place the two balls about 15 cm apart on the sheet of paper.
3. Hold the flashlight approximately 15 cm away from the larger ball. The flashlight and the two balls should be in a straight line. Keep the flashlight at about the same level as the clay. When the whole class is ready, your teacher will turn off the lights.
4. Turn on your flashlight. Shine the light on the closer ball, and sketch your model in your ScienceLog. Include the beam of light in your drawing.
5. Move the flashlight to the opposite side of the paper. The flashlight should now be about 15 cm away from the smaller clay ball. Repeat step 4.

Analysis

6. What does the flashlight in your model represent?
7. As viewed from Earth, what event did your model represent in step 4? in step 5?
8. As viewed from the moon, what event did your model represent in step 4? in step 5?
9. According to your model, how often would solar and lunar eclipses happen? Is this accurate? Explain.

88

Datasheets for LabBook

Joseph W. Price
H. M. Browne Junior High
Washington, D.C.

Discovery Lab

Phases of the Moon

When the moon is full, it's easy to see. But you may have wondered exactly what happens when the moon appears as a crescent or when you cannot see the moon at all. Does the Earth cast its shadow on the moon? In this activity, you will discover how and why the moon appears as it does in each phase.

MATERIALS

- globe
- light source
- plastic-foam ball

Procedure

1. Place your globe near the light source. Be sure that the North Pole is tilted toward the light. Rotate the globe so that the state of Texas faces the light.
2. Using the ball as your model of the moon, move the moon between the Earth (the globe) and the sun (the light). The side of the moon that faces the Earth will be in darkness. Write your observations of this new-moon phase in your ScienceLog.
3. Continue to move the moon in its orbit around the Earth. When part of the moon is illuminated by the light, as viewed from Earth, the moon is in the crescent phase. Add your observations to your ScienceLog.
4. If you have time, you may draw your own moon-phase diagram.

Analysis

5. About two weeks after the new moon, the entire moon is visible in the sky. Move the ball to show this event.
6. What other phases can you add to your diagram? For example, when do the quarter moons appear?
7. Explain why the moon sometimes appears as a crescent to viewers on Earth.

Joseph W. Price
H. M. Browne Junior High
Washington, D.C.

Phases of the Moon
Teacher's Notes

Time Required

One 45-minute class period

Lab Ratings

EASY → HARD

- TEACHER PREP: 2
- STUDENT SET-UP: 2
- CONCEPT LEVEL: 1
- CLEAN UP: 1

MATERIALS

The materials listed on the student page are enough for a group of 3–4 students. You can use a lamp or a flashlight as the light source.

Answers

5. At full moon, Earth is between the sun and the moon. To represent this phase, students should move the plastic-foam ball to the side of the globe opposite from the light source.
6. Students should demonstrate their understanding of the phases and the events that create them. The first-quarter moon occurs halfway between the new moon and the full moon phases, and the last-quarter moon occurs between the full moon and the new moon. In the model, students should move the plastic-foam ball one-quarter of the way around the globe and three-quarters of the way around the globe. These positions represent the first-quarter phase and last-quarter phase.
7. When the moon is in a direct line between Earth and the sun, the side of the moon facing Earth is dark. This is the new moon phase. During this phase, no illuminated area of the moon is visible from Earth. As the moon continues to move in its orbit around Earth, part of its illuminated half becomes visible. When a sliver of the moon is visible from Earth, the moon enters a crescent phase.

Datasheets for LabBook

Chapter Highlights

Vocabulary Definitions

Section 1

astronomical unit (AU) the average distance between the Earth and the sun, or approximately 150,000,000 km

terrestrial planets the small, dense, rocky planets of the inner solar system

prograde rotation the counterclockwise spin of a planet or moon as seen from above the planet's north pole

retrograde rotation the clockwise spin of a planet or moon as seen from above the planet's north pole

gas giants the large, gaseous planets of the outer solar system

Section 2

satellite a natural or artificial body that revolves around a planet

phases the different appearances of the moon due to varying amounts of sunlight on the side of the moon that faces the Earth; results from the changing relative positions of the moon, Earth, and the sun

eclipse an event in which the shadow of one celestial body falls on another

Chapter Highlights

Section 1

Vocabulary

astronomical unit (AU) *(p. 64)*
terrestrial planets *(p. 65)*
prograde rotation *(p. 66)*
retrograde rotation *(p. 66)*
gas giants *(p. 70)*

Section Notes

- The solar system has nine planets.
- Distances within the solar system can be expressed in astronomical units (AU) or in light-minutes.
- The inner four planets, called the terrestrial planets, are small and rocky.
- The outer planets, with the exception of Pluto, are gas giants.
- By learning about the properties of the planets, we get a better understanding of global processes on Earth.

Labs

Why Do They Wander? *(p. 164)*

Section 2

Vocabulary

satellite *(p. 75)*
phases *(p. 77)*
eclipse *(p. 78)*

Section Notes

- Earth's moon probably formed from a giant impact on Earth.
- The moon's phases are caused by the moon's orbit around the Earth. At different times of the month, we view different amounts of sunlight on the moon because of the moon's position relative to the sun and the Earth.
- Lunar eclipses occur when the Earth's shadow falls on the moon.

☑ Skills Check

Math Concepts

INTERPLANETARY DISTANCES The distances between planets are so vast that scientists have invented new units of measurement to describe them. One of these units is the astronomical unit (AU). One AU is equal to the average distance between the Earth and the sun—about 150 million kilometers. If you wanted to get to the sun from the Earth in 10 hours, you would have to travel at a rate of 15,000,000 km/h!

$$\frac{\text{150 million kilometers}}{\text{15 million kilometers/hour}} = \text{10 hours}$$

Visual Understanding

AXIAL TILT A planet's axis of rotation is an imaginary line that runs through the center of the planet and comes out its north and south poles. The tilt of a planet's axis is the angle between the planet's axis and the plane of the planet's orbit around the sun.

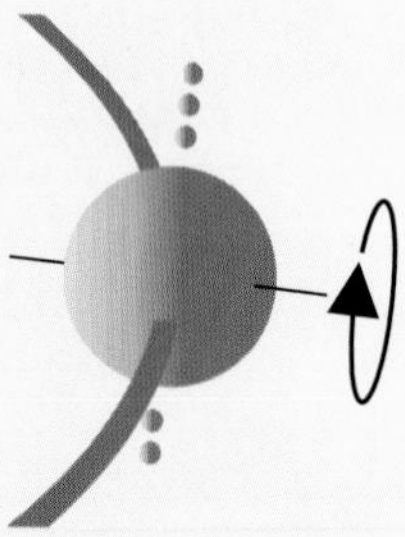

90

Lab and Activity Highlights

Eclipses PG 88

Phases of the Moon PG 89

Why Do They Wander? PG 164

Datasheets for LabBook
(blackline masters for these labs)

SECTION 2

- Solar eclipses occur when the moon is between the sun and the Earth, causing the moon's shadow to fall on the Earth.
- The plane of the moon's orbit around the Earth is tilted by 5° relative to the plane of the Earth's orbit around the sun.

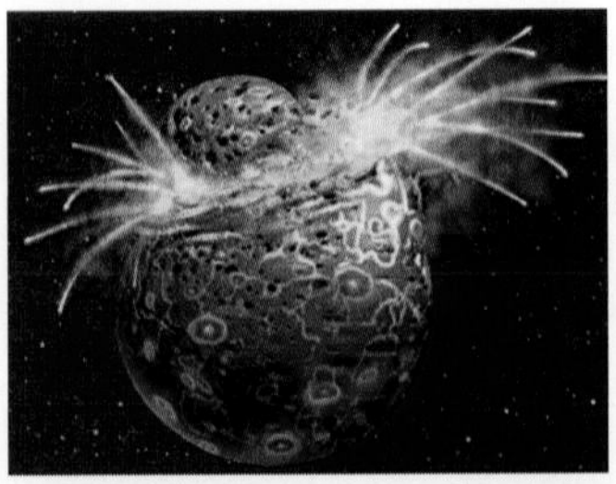

SECTION 3

Vocabulary

comet *(p. 83)*
asteroid *(p. 85)*
asteroid belt *(p. 85)*
meteoroid *(p. 86)*
meteorite *(p. 86)*
meteor *(p. 86)*

Section Notes

- Comets are small bodies of water ice and cosmic dust left over from the formation of the solar system.
- When a comet is heated by the sun, the ices convert to gases that leave the nucleus and form an ion tail. Dust also comes off a comet to form a second kind of tail called a dust tail.
- All orbits are ellipses—circles that have been stretched out.
- Asteroids are small, rocky bodies that orbit the sun between the orbits of Mars and Jupiter.
- Meteoroids are small, rocky bodies that probably come from asteroids.
- Meteor showers occur when Earth passes through the dusty debris along a comet's orbit.
- Impacts that cause natural disasters occur once every few thousand years, but impacts large enough to cause global extinctions occur once every 30 million to 50 million years.

internetconnect

go.hrw.com **GO TO:** go.hrw.com

Visit the **HRW** Web site for a variety of learning tools related to this chapter. Just type in the keyword:

KEYWORD: HSTFAM

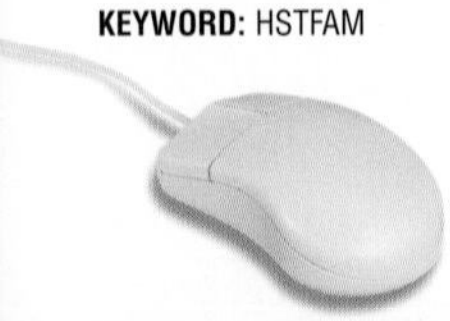

sciLINKS NSTA **GO TO:** www.scilinks.org

Visit the **National Science Teachers Association** on-line Web site for Internet resources related to this chapter. Just type in the ***sci*LINKS** number for more information about the topic:

TOPIC: The Nine Planets	***sci*LINKS NUMBER:** HSTE480
TOPIC: Studying Earth from Space	***sci*LINKS NUMBER:** HSTE485
TOPIC: The Earth's Moon	***sci*LINKS NUMBER:** HSTE490
TOPIC: The Moons of Other Planets	***sci*LINKS NUMBER:** HSTE495
TOPIC: Comets, Asteroids, and Meteoroids	***sci*LINKS NUMBER:** HSTE500

91

VOCABULARY DEFINITIONS, *continued*

SECTION 3

comet a small body of ice, rock, and cosmic dust loosely packed together that gives off gas and dust in the form of a tail as it passes close to the sun

asteroid a small, rocky body that revolves around the sun

asteroid belt the region of the solar system most asteroids occupy; roughly between the orbits of Mars and Jupiter

meteoroid a very small, rocky body that revolves around the sun

meteorite a meteoroid that reaches the Earth's surface without burning up completely

meteor a streak of light caused when a meteoroid or comet dust burns up in the Earth's atmosphere before it reaches the ground

Vocabulary Review Worksheet

Blackline masters of these Chapter Highlights can be found in the **Study Guide.**

Lab and Activity Highlights

LabBank

Labs You Can Eat, Meteorite Delight

Whiz-Bang Demonstrations
- Crater Creator
- Space Snowballs

Long-Term Projects & Research Ideas, What Did You See, Mr. Messier?

Interactive Explorations CD-ROM

CD 2, Exploration 7, "Space Case"

Chapter Review Answers

Using Vocabulary

1. The terrestrial planets are the small, rocky planets of the inner solar system. The gas giants are the large, gaseous planets of the outer solar system.
2. Asteroids are small bodies made of rocky material, while comets are small bodies made of ices and cosmic dust.
3. A meteor is a streak of light caused by a meteoroid burning up in the atmosphere. A meteorite is a meteoroid that has passed through the atmosphere and struck the ground.
4. A satellite is any object that revolves around another object, including artificial satellites, while a moon is a naturally formed satellite.
5. Both the Kuiper belt and the Oort cloud are regions where comets exist, but the Oort cloud is a spherical region outside the orbit of Pluto, while the Kuiper belt is a disk-shaped region beyond the orbit of Neptune.
6. AU
7. meteoroid
8. revolve
9. impacts

Understanding Concepts

Multiple Choice

10. d	**13.** a	**16.** d
11. d	**14.** a	**17.** a
12. c	**15.** d	**18.** b

Short Answer

19. Solar eclipses occur during the new moon. During the new moon, the side of the moon that faces the Earth is in darkness because the moon is between the sun and the Earth. This is the same arrangement that causes a solar eclipse.
20. We see evidence of them in meteors and meteorites.
21. Venus, Uranus, and Pluto

Chapter Review

USING VOCABULARY

For each pair of terms, explain the difference in their meaning.

1. terrestrial planet/gas giant
2. asteroid/comet
3. meteor/meteorite
4. satellite/moon
5. Kuiper belt/Oort cloud

To complete the following sentences, choose the correct term from each pair of terms listed below:

6. The average distance between the sun and the Earth is 1 __?__. *(light-minute,* or *AU)*
7. A small rock in space is called a __?__. *(meteor* or *meteoroid)*
8. The time it takes for the Earth to __?__ around the sun is one year. *(rotate* or *revolve)*
9. Most lunar craters are the result of __?__. *(volcanoes* or *impacts)*

UNDERSTANDING CONCEPTS

Multiple Choice

10. When do annular eclipses occur?
    - **a.** every solar eclipse
    - **b.** when the moon is closest to the Earth
    - **c.** only during full moon
    - **d.** when the moon is farthest from the Earth

11. Of the following, which is the largest body?
    - **a.** the moon
    - **b.** Pluto
    - **c.** Mercury
    - **d.** Ganymede
12. Which is not true about impacts?
    - **a.** They are very destructive.
    - **b.** They can bring water to dry worlds.
    - **c.** They only occurred as the solar system formed.
    - **d.** They can help us do remote geology.
13. Which of these planets does not have any moons?
    - **a.** Mercury
    - **b.** Mars
    - **c.** Uranus
    - **d.** none of the above
14. What is the most current theory for the formation of Earth's moon?
    - **a.** The moon formed from a collision between another body and the Earth.
    - **b.** The moon was captured by the Earth.
    - **c.** The moon formed at the same time as the Earth.
    - **d.** The moon formed by spinning off from the Earth early in its history.
15. Liquid water cannot exist on the surface of Mars because
    - **a.** the temperature is too hot.
    - **b.** liquid water once existed there.
    - **c.** the gravity of Mars is too weak.
    - **d.** the atmospheric pressure is too low.
16. Which of the following planets is not a terrestrial planet?
    - **a.** Mercury
    - **b.** Mars
    - **c.** Earth
    - **d.** Pluto
17. All of the gas giants have ring systems.
    - **a.** true
    - **b.** false
18. A comet's ion tail consists of
    - **a.** dust.
    - **b.** electrically charged particles of gas.
    - **c.** light rays.
    - **d.** comet nuclei.

92

Concept Mapping

22. 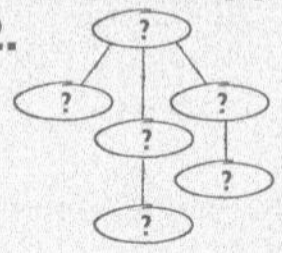

An answer to this exercise can be found at the front of this book.

Concept Mapping Transparency 20

Short Answer

19. Do solar eclipses occur at the full moon or at the new moon? Explain why.

20. How do we know there are small meteoroids and dust in space?

21. Which planets have retrograde rotation?

Concept Mapping

22. Use the following terms to create a concept map: solar system, terrestrial planets, gas giants, moons, comets, asteroids, meteoroids.

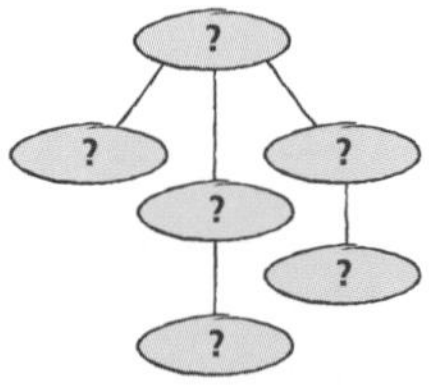

CRITICAL THINKING AND PROBLEM SOLVING

23. Even though we haven't yet retrieved any rock samples from Mercury's surface for radiometric dating, we know that the surface of Mercury is much older than that of Earth. How do we know this?

24. Where in the solar system might we search for life, and why?

25. Is the far side of the moon always dark? Explain your answer.

26. If we could somehow bring Europa as close to the sun as the Earth is, 1 AU, what do you think would happen?

MATH IN SCIENCE

27. Suppose you have an object that weighs 200 N (45 lbs.) on Earth. How much would that same object weigh on each of the other terrestrial planets?

INTERPRETING GRAPHICS

The graph below shows density versus mass for Earth, Uranus, and Neptune. Mass is given in Earth masses—the mass of Earth equals one. The relative volumes for the planets are shown by the size of each circle.

Density vs. Mass for Earth, Uranus, and Neptune

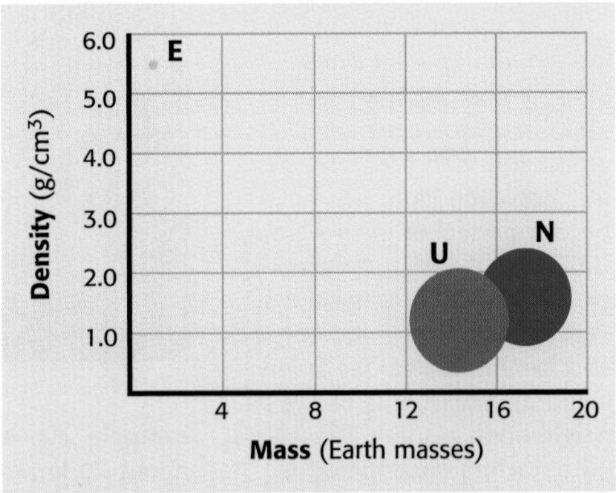

28. Which planet is denser, Uranus or Neptune? How can you tell?

29. You can see that although Earth has the smallest mass, it has the highest density. How can Earth be the densest of the three when Uranus and Neptune have so much more mass?

Reading Check-up

Take a minute to review your answers to the Pre-Reading Questions found at the bottom of page 62. Have your answers changed? If necessary, revise your answers based on what you have learned since you began this chapter.

Critical Thinking and Problem Solving

23. Mercury's surface is covered with impact craters that record the planet's history. The Earth's surface has only a few craters, indicating that the rocks on Earth's surface are continually recycled. (The two planets are approximately the same age.)
24. The search for life should include areas where liquid water is present because all life we know of depends on liquid water for survival.
25. No; the far side of the moon gets just as much sunlight as the near side. As the moon revolves around the Earth, it also rotates, which gives it night and day.
26. Answers will vary. If Europa was closer to the sun, it would heat up considerably. Europa is made mostly of ice, so much of its surface would probably melt to form oceans and an atmosphere.

Math in Science

27. Students will have to refer back to the tables in the chapter as well as understand which planets are terrestrial.
    Mercury $0.38 \times 200\ N = 76\ N$
    Venus $0.91 \times 200\ N = 182\ N$
    Mars $0.38 \times 200\ N = 76\ N$

Interpreting Graphics

28. Neptune is denser. It has a higher density value on the chart. (Also, Neptune has both a smaller volume and more mass, giving it a greater density than Uranus.)
29. The masses of Neptune and Uranus occupy a much larger volume than the mass of the Earth. (Density is the amount of mass that exists within a given volume of space.)

Blackline masters of this Chapter Review can be found in the **Study Guide.**

Scientific Debate
Is Pluto Really a Planet?

Background

Classifying Pluto can be problematic. Pluto simply does not fit in with the inner terrestrial planets or the outer gas giants. It seems that Pluto is a planet in a class all its own. There is much speculation about the origin of Pluto. Pluto's orbit is so inclined that it is doubtful that it formed from the primordial disk-shaped solar nebula that spawned the other planets. Pluto in many ways resembles Neptune's moon Triton. Pluto and Triton are similar in size, and both rotate in a direction counter to the other planets.

Some scientists believe that there was a collision between Pluto and Triton and that the force of the collision ejected Pluto from the Neptune system.

Another theory proposes that Pluto formed from the accretion of cometlike bodies at the beginning of the solar system, similar to the way the terrestrial planets originated from rocky planetesimals.

SCIENTIFICDEBATE

Is Pluto Really a Planet?

We have all learned that Pluto is the planet farthest from the sun in our solar system. Since it was discovered in 1930, astronomers have grouped it with the outer planets. However, Pluto has not been a perfect fit in this group. Unlike the other outer planets, which are large and gaseous, Pluto is small and made of rock and ice. Pluto also has a very elliptical orbit that is unlike its neighboring planets. These and other factors once fueled a debate as to whether Pluto should be classified as a planet.

A composite drawing of Pluto, Charon, Triton, and Halley's comet

Kuiper Belt

In the early 1990s, astronomers discovered a belt of comets outside the orbit of Neptune. The belt was named the Kuiper Belt in honor of Gerard Kuiper, a Dutch-born American astronomer. So what does this belt have to do with Pluto? Given its proximity to Pluto, some astronomers thought Pluto might actually be a large comet that escaped the Kuiper Belt.

Comet?

Comets are basically dirty snowballs made of ice and cosmic dust. Pluto is about 30 percent ice and 70 percent rock. This is much more rock than is in a normal comet. Also, at 2,390 km in diameter, Pluto is much larger than a comet. For example, Halley's comet is only about 20 km in diameter. Even so, Pluto's orbit is very similar to that of a comet. Both have orbits that are very elliptical.

Escaped Moon?

Pluto and its moon, Charon, have much in common with Neptune's moon, Triton. All three have atmospheres made of nitrogen and methane, which suggests that they share a similar origin. And because Triton has a "backward" orbit compared with Neptune's other moons, it may have been captured by Neptune's gravity. Some astronomers thought Pluto might also have been captured by Neptune but broke free by some cataclysmic event.

New Category of Planet?

Some astronomers suggested that perhaps we should create a new subclass of planets, such as the ice planets, to add to the gas-giant and terrestrial classification we currently use. Pluto would be the only planet in this class, but scientists think we are likely to find others.

As there are more new discoveries, astronomers will likely continue to debate these issues. To date, however, Pluto is still officially considered a planet. This decision is firmly grounded by the fact that Pluto has been called a planet since its discovery.

You Decide

▶ Do some additional research about Pluto, the Kuiper Belt, and comets. What do you think Pluto should be called?

Answer to You Decide

Answers will vary. Students should be able to support their views with the information gathered from additional research.

"The Mad Moon"

by Stanley Weinbaum

The third largest satellite of Jupiter, called Io, can be a hard place to live. Although living comfortably is possible in the small cities at the polar regions, most of the moon is hot, humid, and jungle-like. There is also *blancha,* a kind of tropical fever that causes hallucinations, weakness, and vicious headaches. Without proper medication a person with *blancha* can go mad or even die.

Just 2 years ago, Grant Calthorpe was a wealthy hunter and famous sportsman. Then the gold market crashed, and he lost his entire fortune. What better way for an experienced hunter and explorer to get a fresh start than to set out for a little space travel? The opportunity to rekindle his fortune by gathering ferva leaves so that they can be converted into useful human medications lures Calthorpe to Io.

There he meets the loonies—creatures with balloon heads and silly grins atop *really* long necks. The three-legged parcat Oliver quickly becomes Calthorpe's pet and helps him cope with the loneliness and the slinkers. The slinkers, well, they would just as soon *not* have Calthorpe around at all, but they are pretty good at making even this famous outdoorsman wonder why he ever took this job.

In "The Mad Moon," you'll discover a dozen adventures with Grant Calthorpe as he struggles to stay alive—and sane. Read Stanley Weinbaum's story "The Mad Moon" in the *Holt Anthology of Science Fiction.* Enjoy your trip!

95

Further Reading You can check out some of Stanley Weinbaum's best-known short stories in the following reprinted collections:

The Best of Stanley G. Weinbaum, Ballantine Books, Inc., 1978

The Black Flame, Tachyon Publications, 1995

SCIENCE FICTION

"The Mad Moon"
by Stanley Weinbaum

Even the bravest of human adventurers may not be prepared to deal with the madness on Jupiter's third habitable moon . . .

Teaching Strategy

Reading Level This story can be enjoyed by students of all levels, but it is one of the more challenging stories in the *Holt Anthology of Science Fiction.*

Background

About the Author In 1934, Stanley Weinbaum published his first science fiction story, "A Martian Odyssey." Many people read the story about alien life on Mars and enjoyed its author's lighthearted style. Weinbaum quickly wrote several other works that audiences adored. His writing demonstrated his fascination with alien life-forms and with unusual human characters.

Before becoming a writer, Weinbaum studied chemical engineering. During the Great Depression, writers sold stories for just a few pennies; yet Weinbaum gave up his science career to be a writer. Sadly, he died of cancer in 1935, less than 2 years after his first story was published. Although his list of works is short, many believe he is one of the best science fiction writers of all time.

Chapter Organizer

CHAPTER ORGANIZATION	TIME MINUTES	OBJECTIVES	LABS, INVESTIGATIONS, AND DEMONSTRATIONS
Chapter Opener **pp. 96–97**	45	National Standards: SAI 1, ST 2, SPSP 5, HNS 1	**Start-Up Activity,** Exploring Galaxies in the Universe, p. 97
Section 1 **Stars**	135	▶ Describe how color indicates temperature. ▶ Compare absolute magnitude with apparent magnitude, and discuss how each measures brightness. ▶ Describe the difference between the apparent motion of stars and the real motion of stars. UCP 1, 3, SAI 1, SPSP 5; Labs UCP 2, 3, SAI 1	**Demonstration,** Light Pollution, p. 98 in ATE **Demonstration,** p. 99 in ATE **QuickLab,** Not All Thumbs! p. 103 **Skill Builder,** Red Hot, or Not? p. 118 **Skill Builder,** I See the Light! p. 166 **Datasheets for LabBook** **Whiz-Bang Demonstrations,** Where Do the Stars Go?
Section 2 **The Life Cycle of Stars**	90	▶ Describe the quantities that are plotted in the H-R diagram. ▶ Explain how stars at different stages in their life cycle appear on different parts of the H-R diagram. UCP 1–3, 5, SAI 1, HNS 1, 2	**QuickLab,** Plotting Pairs, p. 105
Section 3 **Galaxies**	90	▶ Identify the various types of galaxies from pictures. ▶ Describe the contents of galaxies. ▶ Explain why looking at distant galaxies reveals what early galaxies looked like. UCP 1, 5, SAI 1, ST 1, 2, HNS 1, 2, SPSP 5	
Section 4 **Formation of the Universe**	90	▶ Describe the big bang theory. ▶ Explain evidence used to show support for the big bang theory. ▶ Explain how the expansion of the universe is explained by the big bang theory. UCP 1–3, 5, SAI 1	**Long-Term Projects & Research Ideas,** Contacting the Aliens

See page **T23** *for a complete correlation of this book with the*

NATIONAL SCIENCE EDUCATION STANDARDS.

TECHNOLOGY RESOURCES

Guided Reading Audio CD
English or Spanish, Chapter 4

One-Stop Planner CD-ROM with Test Generator

CNN **Scientists in Action,** Neutrino Breakthrough, Segment 4
Deep Space Photographers, Segment 26

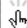

Chapter 4 • The Universe Beyond

CLASSROOM WORKSHEETS, TRANSPARENCIES, AND RESOURCES	SCIENCE INTEGRATION AND CONNECTIONS	REVIEW AND ASSESSMENT
Directed Reading Worksheet **Science Puzzlers, Twisters & Teasers**		
Directed Reading Worksheet, Section 1 **Transparency 291,** The Electromagnetic Spectrum **Math Skills for Science Worksheet,** Arithmetic with Positive and Negative Numbers **Math Skills for Science Worksheet,** Distances in Space **Transparency 195,** Finding the Distance to Stars with Parallax	**Physics Connection,** p. 99 **Biology Connection,** p. 100 **MathBreak,** Starlight, Star Bright, p. 101 **Cross-Disciplinary Focus,** p. 101 in ATE **Environment Connection,** p. 102 **Multicultural Connection,** p. 102 in ATE **Math and More,** p. 102 in ATE **Math and More,** p. 103 in ATE	**Homework,** p. 98 in ATE **Self-Check,** p. 102 **Section Review,** p. 104 **Quiz,** p. 104 in ATE **Alternative Assessment,** p. 104 in ATE
Directed Reading Worksheet, Section 2 **Transparency 196,** The H-R Diagram: A **Transparency 197,** The H-R Diagram: B **Reinforcement Worksheet,** Diagramming the Stars	**Cross-Disciplinary Focus,** p. 107 in ATE **Cross-Disciplinary Focus,** p. 108 in ATE **Weird Science:** Holes Where Stars Once Were, p. 124	**Section Review,** p. 109 **Quiz,** p. 109 in ATE **Alternative Assessment,** p. 109 in ATE
Directed Reading Worksheet, Section 3	**Cross-Disciplinary Focus,** p. 110 in ATE **Multicultural Connection,** p. 111 in ATE **Careers:** Astrophysicist–Jocelyn Bell-Burnell, p. 125	**Section Review,** p. 113 **Quiz,** p. 113 in ATE **Alternative Assessment,** p. 113 in ATE
Directed Reading Worksheet, Section 4 **Transparency 198,** The Big Bang Theory **Critical Thinking Worksheet,** Fleabert and the Amazing Watermelon Seed	**Multicultural Connection,** p. 115 in ATE **Apply,** p. 116	**Homework,** p. 116 in ATE **Section Review,** p. 117 **Quiz,** p. 117 in ATE **Alternative Assessment,** p. 117 in ATE

internet connect

go.hrw.com **Holt, Rinehart and Winston On-line Resources**

go.hrw.com

For worksheets and other teaching aids related to this chapter, visit the HRW Web site and type in the keyword: **HSTUNV**

sciLINKS NSTA **National Science Teachers Association**

www.scilinks.org

Encourage students to use the *sci*LINKS numbers listed in the internet connect boxes to access information and resources on the **NSTA** Web site.

END-OF-CHAPTER REVIEW AND ASSESSMENT

Chapter Review in Study Guide
Vocabulary and Notes in Study Guide
Chapter Tests with Performance-Based Assessment, Chapter 4 Test
Chapter Tests with Performance-Based Assessment, Performance-Based Assessment 4
Concept Mapping Transparency 21

Chapter Resources & Worksheets

Visual Resources

TEACHING TRANSPARENCIES

#195

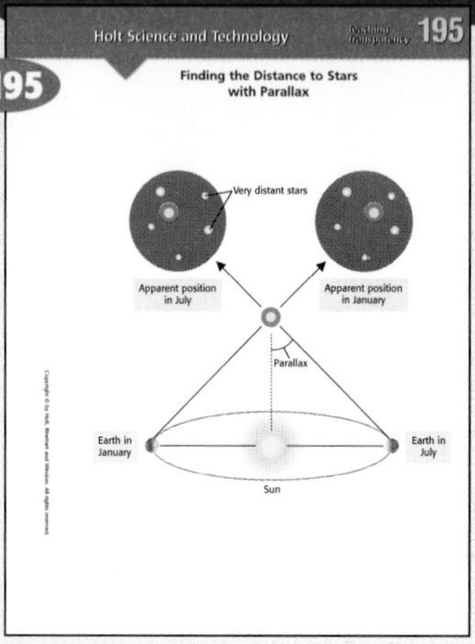

#196

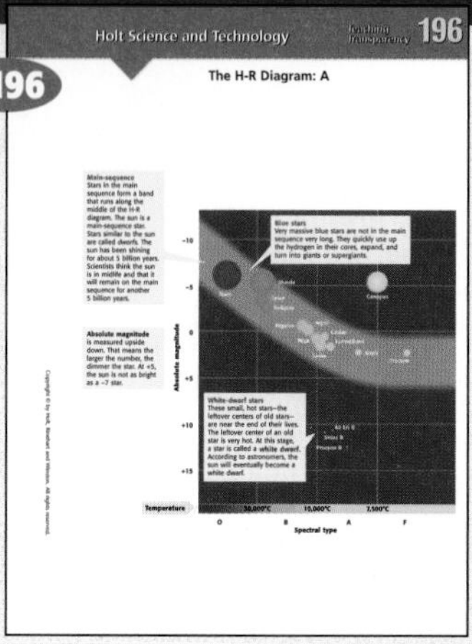

#197

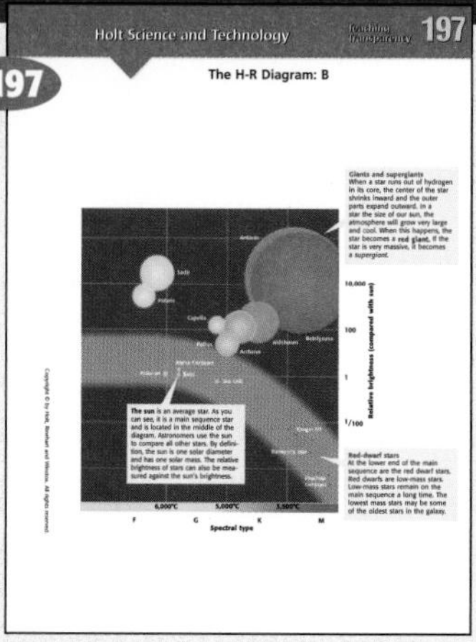

#198

TEACHING TRANSPARENCIES

#291

CONCEPT MAPPING TRANSPARENCY

#21

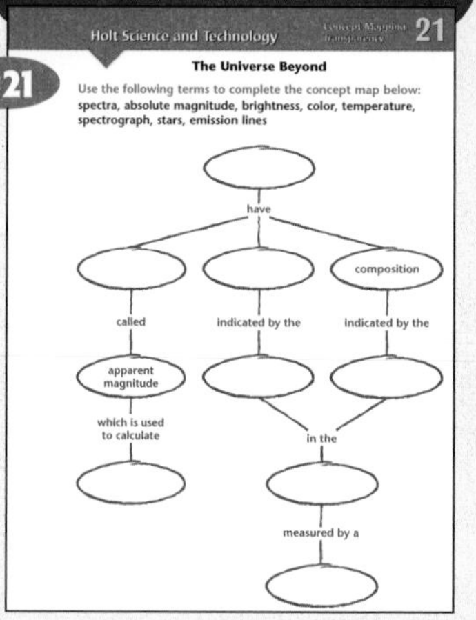

Meeting Individual Needs

DIRECTED READING

#4

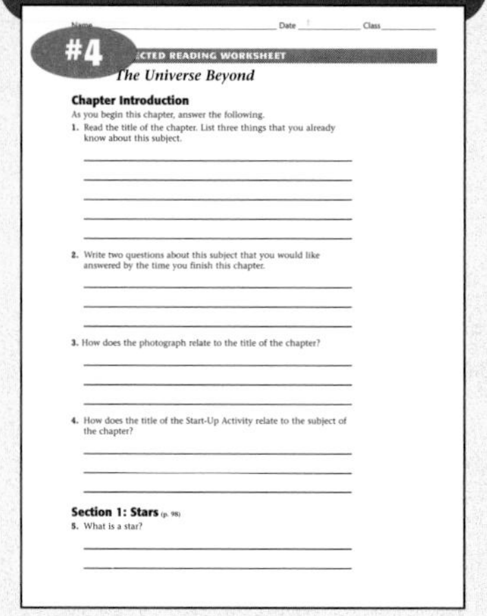

REINFORCEMENT & VOCABULARY REVIEW

#4

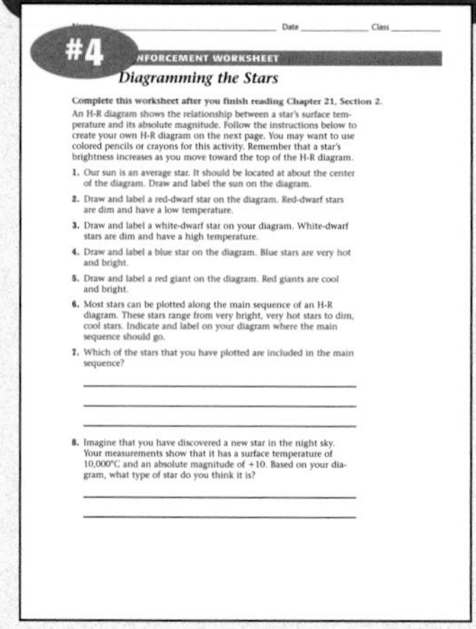

#4

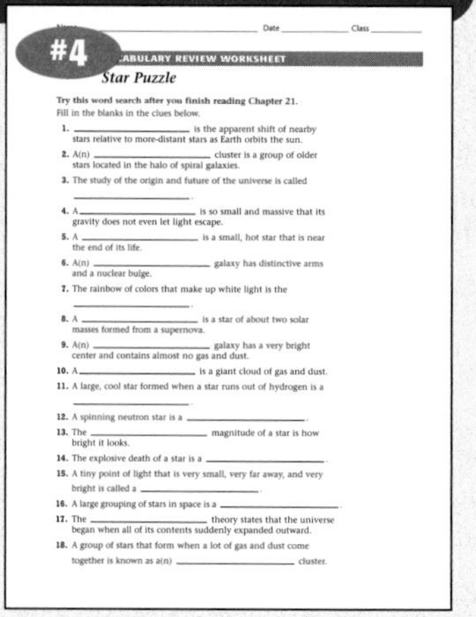

SCIENCE PUZZLERS, TWISTERS & TEASERS

#4

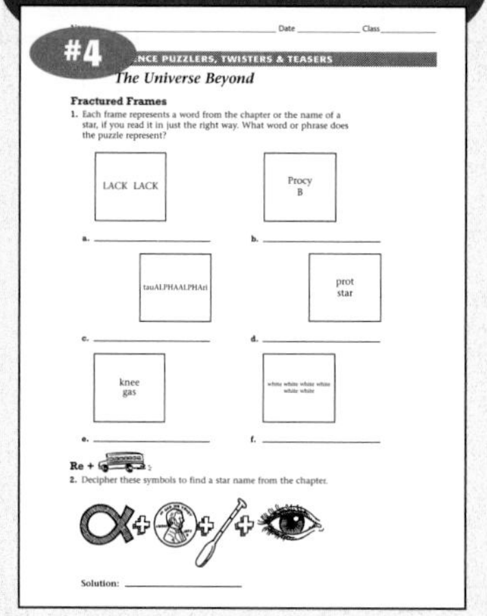

Chapter 4 • The Universe Beyond

Review & Assessment

STUDY GUIDE

#4 Vocabulary & Notes Worksheet — *The Universe Beyond*

#4 Chapter Review Worksheet — *The Universe Beyond*

CHAPTER TESTS WITH PERFORMANCE-BASED ASSESSMENT

#4 The Universe Beyond — *Chapter 4 Test*

#4 The Universe Beyond — *Chapter 4 Performance-Based Assessment*

Lab Worksheets

WHIZ-BANG DEMONSTRATIONS

#4 Teacher-Led Demonstration — *Where Do the Stars Go?*

LONG-TERM PROJECTS & RESEARCH IDEAS

#4 Student Worksheet — *Contacting the Aliens*

DATASHEETS FOR LABBOOK

#4 Red Hot, or Not?

#4 I See The Light!

Applications & Extensions

CRITICAL THINKING & PROBLEM SOLVING

#4 Critical Thinking Worksheet — *Fleabert & the Amazing Watermelon Seed*

SCIENTISTS IN ACTION

#4 *Science in the News:* Critical Thinking Worksheets — Segment 4 — Neutrino Breakthrough

#26

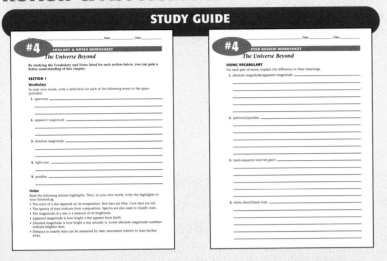

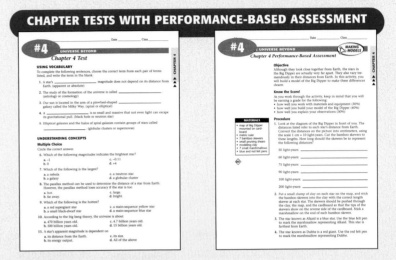

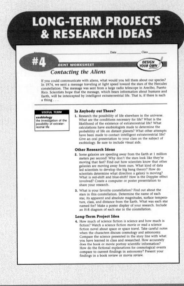

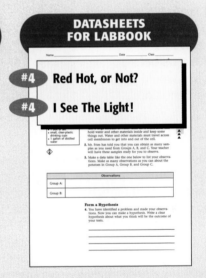

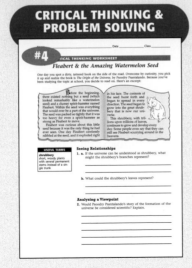

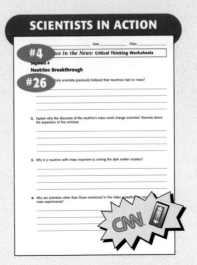

Chapter Background

Section 1

Stars

Space Distances

After the sun, the star closest to Earth is Proxima Centauri, located more than 4 light-years away. To travel an equivalent distance, a person would have to walk around the Earth more than 944 million times!

- Four space probes—*Voyagers 1* and *2* and *Pioneers 10* and *11*—are currently en route to interstellar space, traveling at a rate of approximately 40,000 km/h (25,000 mph). Even at this astounding speed, it would take 150,000 years before the probes would reach Proxima Centauri.

IS THAT A FACT!

- Although stars appear to twinkle in the sky, they actually shine with a steady light. They appear to twinkle because their light is distorted when it passes through the Earth's atmosphere. If you were standing on the moon, where there is no atmosphere, the stars would appear to shine steadily.

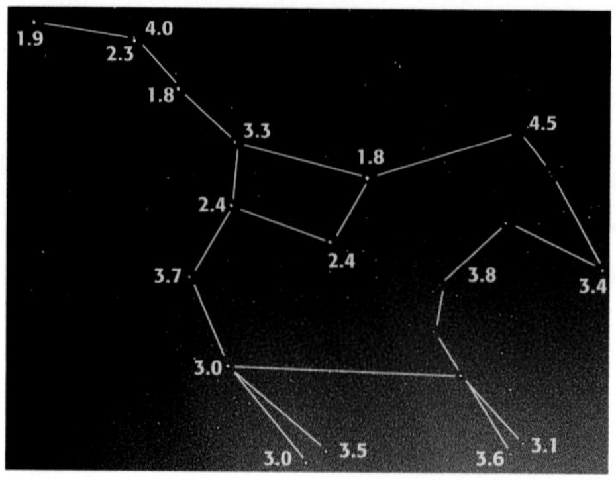

- The Big Dipper is not a constellation; it is an *asterism,* a familiar pattern of stars that may or may not be part of one of the 88 constellations. The Big Dipper is part of the constellation known as Ursa Major, or Big Bear.

- More than half of the stars in the universe exist in multiple systems. Of these, three-fifths are binary systems, three-tenths are triplets, and one-tenth are groups of four or more.

Section 2

The Life Cycle of Stars

The Birth of a Star

Like humans, stars undergo a life cycle that consists of birth, infancy, maturity, old age, and death. In space, clouds of gas and dust abound; drawn together by gravity, they eventually form a *protostar*. This fledgling star gives off no visible light and must undergo many changes before it is recognizable as a star. In a process that takes millions of years, the protostar contracts. This shrinkage causes an enormous buildup of pressure and heat. When its temperature reaches 10 million degrees Celsius, the protostar stops contracting, and the process of nuclear fusion begins. Once this hydrogen-fusing process is initiated, the star is born!

IS THAT A FACT!

- From the time our sun emerged as a protostar, it took about 10 million years to become a main-sequence star. A star with one-tenth the mass of the sun would mature in 100 million years, and a star with three times the mass of the sun would mature in 1 million years. Stars with greater mass are hotter and take less time to mature.

Section 3

Galaxies

▶ Observing Spiral Galaxies

Most spiral galaxies appear very thin when seen edge-on. The thickness of the spiral disk is only about one-fifth to one-twentieth the width of the disk. When seen edge-on, spiral galaxies resemble straight lines with a bulge in the middle. The relative size and shape of the bulge is an important clue to determining the type of galaxy.

▶ How Many Stars Are in a Galaxy?

To estimate the number of stars in a galaxy, astronomers consider the sun as one unit of mass. Large spiral galaxies, for example, have a mass of 1 billion to 1 trillion solar masses. If the average star is one solar mass—or each star is like the sun—this means these galaxies have more than 1 billion stars. Dwarf elliptical galaxies have only a few million solar masses, about one-thousandth the mass of a spiral galaxy. Giant elliptical galaxies have more mass than large spiral galaxies.

IS THAT A FACT!

- The word *galaxy* comes from the Greek word *gala,* meaning "milk." This is because, when seen from afar, galaxies have a milky-white appearance.

Section 4

Formation of the Universe

▶ Top-Down or Bottom-Up?

No one is certain how large-scale structures in the universe emerged. Some scientists support the top-down theory. This theory explains that areas of the universe with large-scale objects (the size of clusters and superclusters) were the first to collapse into gaseous, pancake-like shapes. Galaxies condensed from these structures.

- Other scientists support the *bottom-up theory.* This theory argues that areas of the universe with small-scale objects (the size of galaxies or smaller) were the first to form. Due to the gravitational forces, these areas aggregated into clusters and superclusters.

▶ Life on Other Planets?

Many scientists believe that in our galaxy alone there are hundreds of millions of planets similar to Earth. These planets may be able to support carbon-based life. Thus far, scientists do not have the technology to explore this possibility.

IS THAT A FACT!

- The William Herschel telescope, on La Palma, in the Canary Islands, is one of the world's biggest telescopes. With its 4.2 m mirror, it could detect a single candle burning 160,000 km away.
- In 1998, astronomers detected a gamma-ray burst that for 2 seconds was as bright as the entire universe. The cause of this vast energy release is unknown.

For background information about teaching strategies and issues, refer to the *Professional Reference for Teachers.*

CHAPTER 4

The Universe Beyond

Pre-Reading Questions

Students may not know the answers to these questions before reading the chapter, so accept any reasonable response.

Suggested Answers

1. Stars shine because nuclear reactions in their core produce large amounts of energy. This energy leaves the stars as light.
2. A galaxy is a large collection of stars in space.
3. According to the big bang theory, the universe began when all the contents of the universe, which were gathered in a small location, began to expand in all directions. Answers will vary to the last parts of this item. Scientists are in disagreement on this subject. Students may have interesting points of view.

CHAPTER 4

The Universe Beyond

Sections

Galaxies Galore

If you had a telescope, what would you look for? In the 1920s, astronomer Edwin Hubble chose to look for galaxies much like the NGC 3031 galaxy shown here. Basically, a galaxy is a large group of stars. In 1995 the Hubble Space Telescope was used to develop the single image called the Hubble Deep Field shown below. The segment of sky in that image contains nearly 2,000 galaxies! In this chapter, you will learn about the different types of galaxies.

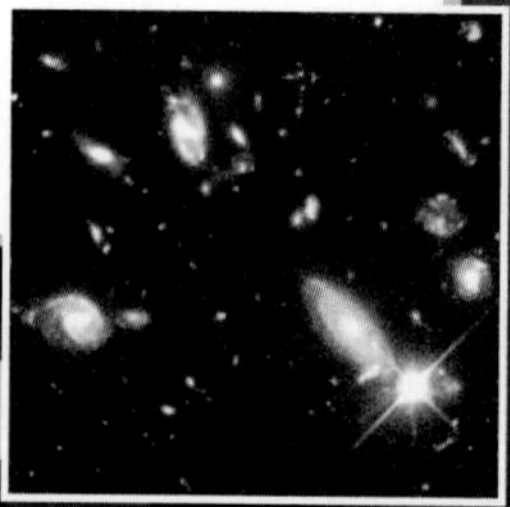

Hubble Deep Field image

Pre-Reading Questions

1. Why do stars shine?
2. What is a galaxy?
3. How did the universe begin, and how will it end? or will it?

internet connect

HRW On-line Resources

go.hrw.com

For worksheets and other teaching aids, visit the HRW Web site and type in the keyword: **HSTUNV**

sciLINKS NSTA

www.scilinks.com

Use the *sci*LINKS numbers at the end of each chapter for additional resources on the **NSTA** Web site.

Smithsonian Institution

www.si.edu/hrw

Visit the Smithsonian Institution Web site for related on-line resources.

CNNfyi.com

www.cnnfyi.com

Visit the CNN Web site for current events coverage and classroom resources.

START-UP Activity

EXPLORING GALAXIES IN THE UNIVERSE

Galaxies are large groupings of millions of stars. But not all galaxies are the same. In this activity, you will explore some of these differences.

Procedure

1. Look at the different galaxies in the Hubble Deep Field image on page 96. (The bright spot with spikes is a star that is much closer to Earth; you can ignore it.)
2. Can you find different types of galaxies? In your ScienceLog, make sketches of at least three different types. Make up a name that describes each type of galaxy.
3. In your ScienceLog, construct a chart to classify, compare, and describe the different characteristics you see in these galaxies.

Analysis

4. Why did you classify the galaxies the way you did?
5. Compare your types of galaxies with those of your classmates. Are there similarities?

97

START-UP Activity

EXPLORING GALAXIES IN THE UNIVERSE

Answers to START-UP Activity

4. Answers will vary.
5. There should be many similarities between the galaxies, but the galaxy names may not be similar.

Section 1

Focus

Stars

In this section, students learn that the color of a star indicates its temperature and that the star's spectrum indicates the elements in its atmosphere. They learn that stars are classified not only according to temperature but also by brightness. The section explores the difference between apparent magnitude and absolute magnitude and the difference between apparent motion and actual motion of stars.

Bellringer

On the board, write the following questions:

- What are stars made of?
- How do stars differ from one another?
- Do stars move?

Have students review their responses after completing this section.

1) Motivate

Demonstration

Light Pollution Demonstrate how ambient light affects the number of visible stars using a slide projector, a piece of aluminum foil, and a flashlight. Poke small holes in the foil, and in a dark room, project light through the foil. Tell students that they might see this number of stars on a dark night. Ask students to count the stars. Then shine the flashlight on the screen, and ask students to count the stars again. Discuss the natural and artificial sources of ambient light with students.
Sheltered English

Section 1 — Reading Warm-Up

Terms to Learn

spectrum
apparent magnitude
absolute magnitude
light-year
parallax

What You'll Do

- Describe how color indicates temperature.
- Compare absolute magnitude with apparent magnitude, and discuss how each measures brightness.
- Describe the difference between the apparent motion of stars and the real motion of stars.

Stars

Most stars look like faint dots of light in the night sky. But stars are actually huge, hot, brilliant balls of gas trillions of kilometers away from Earth. How do astronomers learn about stars when they are too far away to visit? They study starlight!

Color of Stars

Look closely at the flames on the candle and the Bunsen burner shown here. Which one has the hotter flame? How can you tell? Although artists may speak of *red* as a "hot" color, to a scientist, *red* is a "cool" color. The blue flame of the Bunsen burner is much hotter than the yellow flame of the candle. In the same way, the candle's yellow flame is hotter than the red glowing embers of a campfire.

If you look carefully at the night sky, you might notice the different colors of some familiar stars. Betelgeuse (BET uhl jooz), which is red, and Rigel (RIE juhl), which is blue, are the stars that form two corners of the constellation Orion, shown in **Figure 1.** This constellation is easy to see in the evenings during the winter months. Because these two stars are different colors, we can infer that they have different temperatures.

Figure 1 *Because Betelgeuse is red and Rigel is blue, astronomers know that Rigel is the hotter star.*

Composition of Stars

When you look at white light through a glass prism, you see a rainbow of colors called a **spectrum.** The spectrum consists of millions of colors, including the ones we recognize as red, orange, yellow, green, blue, indigo, and violet. A hot solid object, like the glowing wire inside a light bulb, gives off a *continuous spectrum*—one that shows all the colors. Astronomers use an instrument called a *spectrograph* to spread starlight out into its colors, just as you might use a prism to spread sunlight. Stars, however, don't have continuous spectra. Because they are not solid objects, stars give off spectra that are different from those of light bulbs.

98

Homework

PORTFOLIO

SpaceLog As students read this chapter, have them keep a SpaceLog at home. Encourage them to observe the night sky for 10 minutes every night and record their observations. Students can annotate their SpaceLog with photographs and articles from magazines or newspapers that relate to what they are learning in this chapter.

Hot, Dense Gas Stars are made of various gases that are so dense that they act like a hot solid. For this reason, the "surface" of a star, or the part that we see, gives off a continuous spectrum. But the light we see passes through the star's "atmosphere," which is made of cooler gases than the star itself. A star therefore produces a spectrum with various lines in it. To understand what these lines are, let's look at something you might be more familiar with than stars.

Making an ID Many restaurants use neon signs to attract customers. The gas in a neon sign glows orange-red when an electric current flows through it. If we were to look at the sign with an astronomer's spectrograph, we would not see a continuous spectrum. Instead we would see *emission lines*. Emission lines are bright lines that are made when certain wavelengths of light are given off, or emitted, by hot gases. Only some colors in the spectrum show up, while all of the other colors are missing. Every tube of neon gas, for example, emits light with the same emission lines. Each element has its own unique set of emission lines. Emission lines are like fingerprints for the elements. You can see some of these "fingerprints" in **Figure 2.**

Physics Connection

Police use spectrographs to "fingerprint" cars. Automobile manufacturers put trace elements in the paint of cars. Each make of car has its own special paint and therefore its own combination of trace elements. When a car is involved in a hit-and-run accident, the police can identify the make of the car by the paint that is left behind.

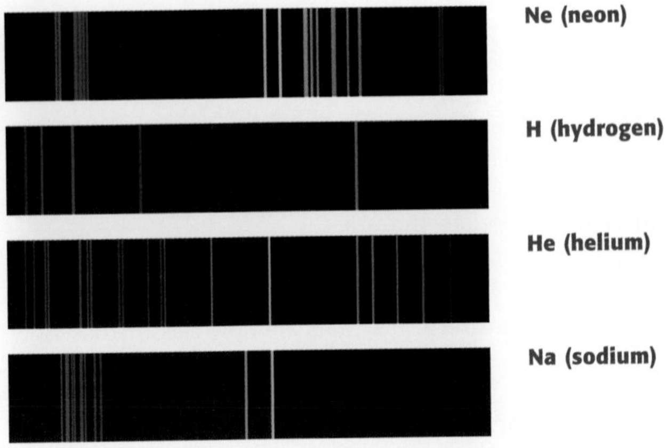

Figure 2 *Neon gas produces its own characteristic pattern of emission lines, as do hydrogen, helium, and sodium.*

Trapping the Light The spectrum produced by a star is not continuous, nor is it made of bright lines similar to those of the elements you saw above. Because a star's atmosphere is cooler than the star itself, the gases in its atmosphere absorb some of the star's light. The cooler gases in a star's atmosphere remove certain colors of light from the continuous spectrum of the hot star. In fact, the colors that the atmosphere absorbs are the same colors it would emit if heated.

99

2 Teach

Reading Strategy

Mnemonics Many people remember the colors of the spectrum by using the name **ROY G. BIV,** which stands for **R**ed, **O**range, **Y**ellow, **G**reen, **B**lue, **I**ndigo, and **V**iolet.
Sheltered English

Demonstration

MATERIALS

- 2 Bunsen burners
- 2 tripods
- 2 beakers
- water

Students may have trouble understanding how the color of a star indicates its temperature. Light two Bunsen burners, adjusting one so that it has a yellow flame and the other so that it has a bluish white flame. Place a beaker half-filled with water on a tripod over each flame, and have students time how long it takes for the water in each beaker to boil. Ask students to discuss other examples in which the color of an object indicates its temperature.

Directed Reading Worksheet Section 1

IS THAT A FACT!

Sometimes it is difficult to differentiate between stars and planets in the night sky. If it twinkles, it's probably a star. Planets, because of their proximity to Earth, appear as tiny disks shining with a steady light. Venus is an easy planet to spot; it can often be seen shining brightly in the west, immediately after the sun sets. Venus can also be seen in the morning, accompanying the rising sun. Venus is then called "the morning star."

2 Teach, *continued*

MEETING INDIVIDUAL NEEDS

Advanced Learners When electrons become excited or absorb energy, they are boosted to a higher energy level. When the electrons return to their normal energy level, they release energy at specific wavelengths. The specific wavelength emitted depends on the amount of energy the electron releases when it returns to its normal energy level. This wavelength is unique for each element. By studying the wavelength emitted, scientists can determine the elements that are present in a substance. Have students research which elements and compounds scientists have found by studying starlight, and have students reproduce some of the spectra in their ScienceLog.

USING THE FIGURE

As you discuss **Figures 2** and **3** with students, use Teaching Transparency 291 to show students what a continuous spectrum is. Have them compare this transparency with the emission spectra shown in the text. Students should find that the absorption spectrum in **Figure 3** matches the emission spectrum for hydrogen in **Figure 2.**

Teaching Transparency 291
"The Electromagnetic Spectrum"
LINK TO PHYSICAL SCIENCE

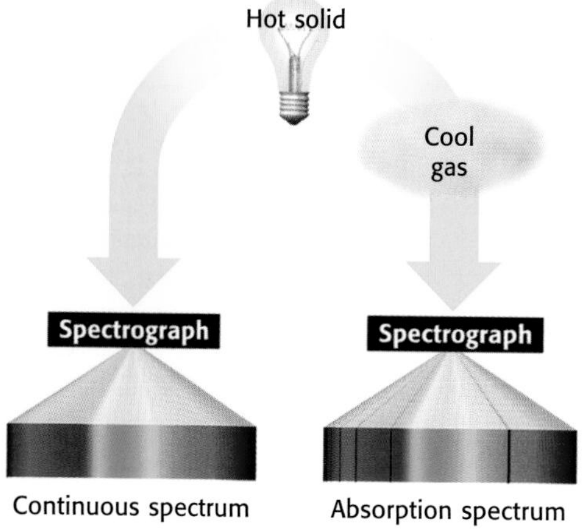

Figure 3 *An absorption spectrum (right) is produced when light passes through a cooler gas. Notice the dark lines in the spectrum.*

Cosmic Detective Work If light from a hot solid passes through a cooler gas, it produces an *absorption spectrum*—a continuous spectrum with dark lines where less light gets through. Take a look at **Figure 3.** Can you identify the element in the gas by comparing the position of the dark lines in its spectrum with the bright lines in Figure 2?

An astronomer's spectrum of a star shows an absorption spectrum. The pattern of lines shows some of the elements that are in the star's atmosphere. If a star were made of just one element, it would be simple to identify the element. But stars are a mixture of things, and all the different sets of lines for its elements appear together in a star's spectrum. Sorting out the patterns is often a puzzle.

Classifying Stars

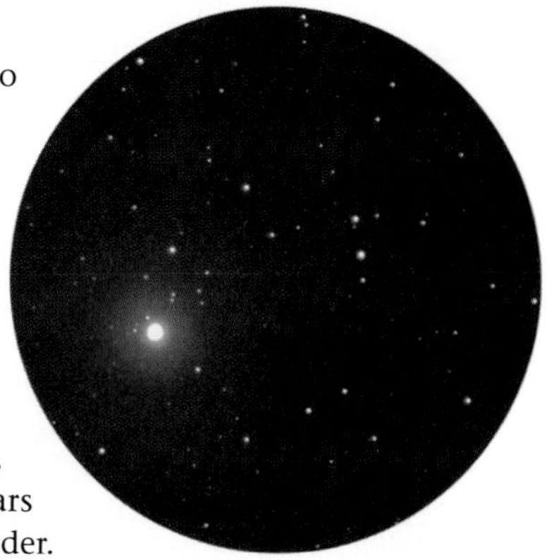

In the 1800s, people started to collect the spectra of lots of stars and tried to classify them. At first, letters were assigned to each type of spectra. Stars with spectra that had very noticeable hydrogen patterns were classified as A type stars. Other stars were classified as B, and so on. Later, scientists realized that the stars were classified in the wrong order.

Differences in Temperature Stars are now classified by how hot they are. We see the temperature differences as colors. The original class O stars are blue—they are very hot, the hottest of all stars. If you arrange the letters in order of temperature, they are no longer in alphabetical order. The resulting order of star classes—OBAFGKM—is shown in the table on the next page.

If you see a certain pattern of absorption lines in a star, you know that a certain element or molecule is in the star or its atmosphere. But the absence of a pattern doesn't mean the element isn't there; the temperature might not be high enough or low enough to produce absorption lines.

Biology CONNECTION

Our eyes are not sensitive to colors when light levels are low. There are two types of light-sensitive cells inside the eye: rods and cones. Rods are good at distinguishing shades of light and dark as well as shape and movement. Cones are good for distinguishing colors. Cones, however, do not work well in low light. This is why it is hard to distinguish between star colors.

Science Bloopers

The composition of the sun has been the subject of much speculation. In the nineteenth century, some scientists thought the sun was made of pure anthracite coal, because coal was one of the best heat-generating fuels of the time. But given the energy output of the sun, coal would have lasted only about 10,000 years. It took the discovery of radiation and nuclear energy for scientists to develop the current model of the sun's composition and structure.

Types of Stars				
Class	**Color**	**Surface temperature (°C)**	**Elements detected**	**Examples of stars**
O	blue	above 30,000	helium	10 Lacertae
B	blue-white	10,000–30,000	helium and hydrogen	Rigel, Spica
A	blue-white	7,500–10,000	hydrogen	Vega, Sirius
F	yellow-white	6,000–7,500	hydrogen and heavier elements	Canopus, Procyon
G	yellow	5,000–6,000	calcium and other metals	the sun, Capella
K	orange	3,500–5,000	calcium and molecules	Arcturus, Aldebaran
M	red	less than 3,500	molecules	Betelgeuse, Antares

Differences in Brightness With only their eyes to aid them, ancient astronomers also came up with a system to classify stars based on their brightness. They called the brightest stars in the sky *first magnitude* stars and the faintest stars *sixth magnitude* stars. But when they began to use telescopes, astronomers were able to see many stars that had previously been too faint to see. Rather than replace the old system of magnitudes, they added to it—positive numbers for dimmer stars and negative numbers for brighter stars. For example, with large telescopes, astronomers can see stars as dim as 29th magnitude. And the brightest star in the sky, Sirius, has a magnitude of –1.4.

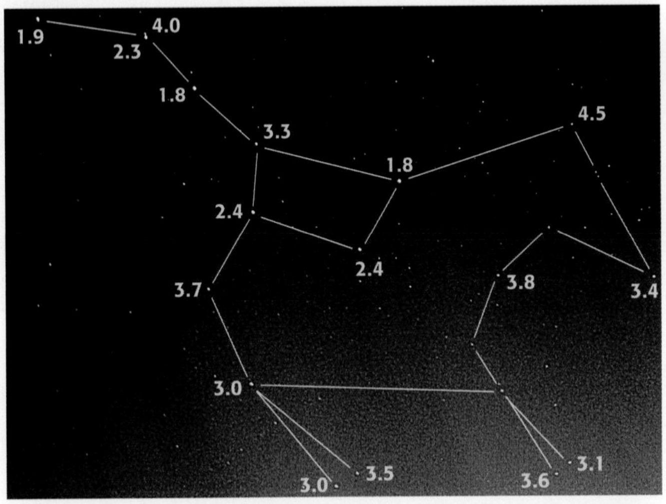

Figure 4 *The constellation Ursa Major, or the Great Bear, contains both bright and faint stars. Numbers indicate their relative brightness. What is the magnitude of the brightest star?*

MATH BREAK

Starlight, Star Bright

Magnitude is used to indicate how bright one object is compared with another. Five magnitudes equal a factor of 100 times in brightness. The brightest blue stars, for example, have an absolute magnitude of −10. The sun is about +5. How much brighter is a blue star than the sun? Since each five magnitudes is a factor of 100 and the blue star and the sun are 15 magnitudes different, the blue star must be $100 \times 100 \times 100$ times brighter than the sun. This is 1,000,000 (one million) times!

101

USING THE TABLE

Draw students' attention to the table of the types of stars. Have them explain how the stars are arranged (from the hottest to the coolest) and identify the hottest and the coolest stars. (10 Lacertae is the hottest; Betelgeuse and Antares are the coolest.)

Have them locate our sun on the table, describing its temperature relative to other stars. (The sun is a class G star with a surface temperature around 5,500°C.)

Be sure that students notice that the temperature of a star indicates the elements it contains.

CROSS-DISCIPLINARY FOCUS

History Hipparchus, a second-century Greek astronomer, developed the first system for star classification. His system divided the stars into six categories based on their apparent brightness. He called the stars that appeared brightest *first magnitude* and called the faintest stars *sixth magnitude*. When telescopes were invented, people learned that many stars were brighter than first-magnitude stars. By the eighteenth century, it was decided that a star of a specific magnitude would be about 2.5 times as bright as a star of the previous magnitude. The brightest stars were reclassified to have negative magnitudes.

RETEACHING

You may wish to draw a number line on the board to show students how the magnitude scale works. Explain how the visible stars were first classified on a scale of one to six and how the discovery of brighter and fainter stars expanded that scale.

IS THAT A FACT!

The brightness of astronomical objects other than stars is measured in star magnitudes as well. For example, Venus shines with an apparent magnitude of –4.6, while the full moon shines with an apparent magnitude of –12.5. With practice, the human eye can discern differences in brightness to one-tenth of a magnitude!

2 Teach, continued

Multicultural CONNECTION

Writing The constellation that includes the familiar Big Dipper or Big Bear is called Ursa Major. The ancient Greeks were probably the first to equate the constellation with a bear. Have students find out about the mythologies of other constellations. Students can also find their own constellation in the night sky, name it, and write a legend about it.

Answer to Self-Check

The two stars would have the same apparent magnitude.

MATH and MORE

Encourage students to compare the apparent magnitude of stars. Point out that a decrease in apparent magnitude by a factor of 1 indicates that a star is 2.5 times brighter than the star it is being compared with. Tell them that the star Rigel has an apparent magnitude of 0.18, while Pollux has an apparent magnitude of 1.16. Have them calculate how much brighter Rigel looks than Pollux.
($1.16 - 0.18 = 0.98$)

Students should find that Rigel appears about 2.5 times brighter than Pollux.

Math Skills Worksheet "Arithmetic with Positive and Negative Numbers"

internetconnect

SCILINKS NSTA
TOPIC: Stars
GO TO: www.scilinks.org
***sci*LINKS NUMBER:** HSTE510

How Bright Is That Star?

If you look at a row of street lights along a highway, like those shown in **Figure 5,** do they all look exactly the same? Does the light you are standing under look the same as a light several blocks away? Of course not! The nearest ones look bright, and the farthest ones look dim.

Figure 5 *You can estimate how far away each street light is by looking at its apparent brightness. Does this work with stars?*

Apparent Magnitude How bright a light looks, or appears, is called **apparent magnitude.** If you measure the brightness of a street light with a light meter, you will find that its brightness depends on the square of the distance between them. For example, a light that is 10 m away will appear four (2×2 or 2^2) times as bright as a light that is 20 m away. The same light will appear nine (3×3 or 3^2) times as bright as a light that is 30 m away.

Self-Check

If two identical stars are located the same distance away from Earth, what can you say about their apparent magnitudes? *(See page 200 to check your answer.)*

Environment CONNECTION

And speaking of street lights . . . Someone looking at the night sky in a city would not see as many stars as someone looking at the sky in the country. Light pollution is a big problem for astronomers and backyard stargazers alike. Certain types of lighting can help reduce glare, but there will continue to be a conflict between lighting buildings at night and seeing the stars.

But unlike street lights, some stars are brighter than others because of their size or energy output, not their distance from Earth. So how can you tell the difference?

Absolute Magnitude Astronomers use a star's apparent magnitude (how bright it seems to be) and its distance from Earth to calculate its absolute magnitude. **Absolute magnitude** is the actual brightness of a star. In other words, if all stars could be placed the same distance away, their absolute magnitudes would be the same as their apparent magnitudes and the brighter stars would look brighter. The sun, for example, has an absolute magnitude of +4.8—pretty ordinary for a star. But because the sun is so close to Earth, its apparent magnitude is −26.8, making it the brightest object in the sky.

102

MISCONCEPTION ALERT

Students may think that stars with negative absolute magnitude values are fainter than those with positive numbers. Point out that *decreasing* numbers indicate *increasing* brightness.

Distance to the Stars

Because they are so far away, astronomers use light-years to give the distances to the stars. A **light-year** is the distance that light travels in one year. Because the speed of light is about 300,000 km/s, it travels almost 9.5 trillion kilometers in one year. Obviously it would be easier to give the distance to the North Star as 431 light-years than 4,080,000,000,000,000 km. But how do astronomers measure a star's distance?

To get a clue, take a look at the QuickLab at right. Just as your thumb appeared to move, stars near the Earth seem to move compared with more-distant stars as Earth revolves around the sun, as shown in **Figure 6.** This apparent shift in position is called **parallax.** While this shift can be seen only through telescopes, using parallax and simple trigonometry (a type of math), astronomers can find the actual distance to stars that are close to Earth.

QuickLab

Not All Thumbs!

1. Hold your **thumb** in front of your face at arm's length.
2. Close one **eye** and focus on an **object** some distance behind your thumb.
3. Slowly move your **head** back and forth a small amount, and notice how your thumb seems to be moving compared with the background you are looking at.
4. Now move your thumb in close to your face and move your head the same amount. Notice how much more your thumb moves.

TRY at HOME

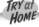

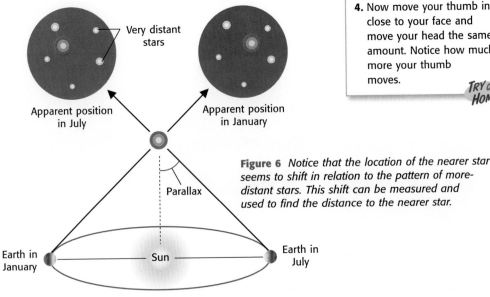

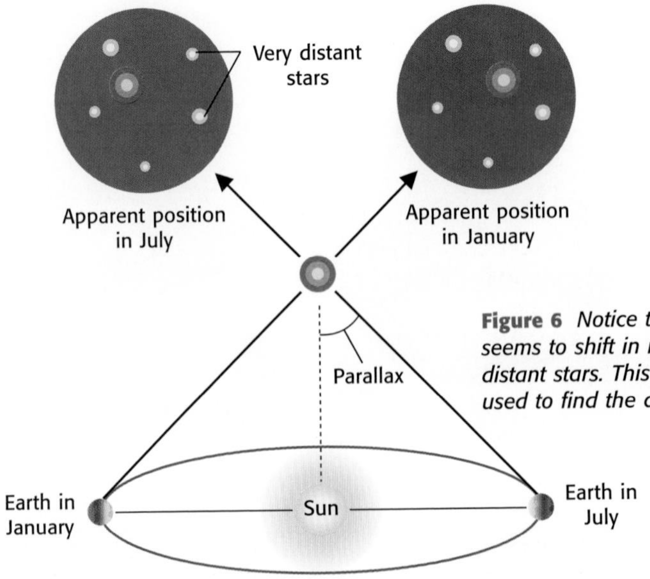

Figure 6 *Notice that the location of the nearer star seems to shift in relation to the pattern of more-distant stars. This shift can be measured and used to find the distance to the nearer star.*

Motions of Stars

As you know, the Earth rotates on its axis. As the Earth turns, different parts of its surface face the sun. This is why we have days and nights. The Earth also revolves around the sun. At different times of the year, you see different stars in the night sky. This is because the side of Earth that is away from the sun at night faces a different part of the universe.

LabBook

To learn more about parallax, turn to page 166 in the LabBook.

3 Extend

QuickLab

Teacher Notes: Explain the concept of parallax by asking students to imagine they are in a car traveling on a road lined with trees. Ask students to imagine looking out the window and to describe the apparent motion of the trees. (Students may answer that the trees closest to the car appear to move faster than those farther away.)

Tell students that they can determine the distance to a tree or a star if they can measure its apparent motion.

MATH and MORE

The textbook lists the distance light travels in a year as 9.5 trillion kilometers. Have students verify this by doing the calculation themselves. Ask students to calculate the distance light travels in 1 day. (approximately 26 million kilometers)

Math Skills Worksheet "Distances in Space"

LabBook PG 166
I See the Light!

IS THAT A FACT!

The trigonometric technique students used in the QuickLab is called triangulation. It is the same method used by ancient Egyptians and Greeks to measure distances. It also was used to map the city of Paris!

Teaching Transparency 195 "Finding the Distance to Stars with Parallax"

4 Close

Quiz

1. How does apparent magnitude differ from absolute magnitude? (Apparent magnitude is the measure of how bright a star appears from Earth, while absolute magnitude is a measure of the brightness of stars as if they were all the same distance away.)
2. What is parallax? (It is an apparent shift in position that occurs when stars nearest Earth seem to move relative to more-distant stars as Earth revolves around the sun.)
3. How is the distance from Earth to a star measured? (Scientists determine the distance to a star by using parallax and trigonometry.)
4. How is the apparent movement of the stars in the night sky different from the movement of the stars within a constellation? (The stars in the night sky rise and set as the Earth rotates. The stars in the constellation are all moving relative to one another. It takes thousands of years to observe their movement.)

Alternative Assessment

PORTFOLIO

Have students illustrate in their ScienceLog the way the distance to a star is measured. Students can explain their illustration to a partner.

Figure 7 *As Earth rotates on its axis, stars set in the western horizon.*

Apparent Motion Because of Earth's rotation, the sun appears to move across the sky. Likewise, if you look at the night sky long enough, the stars also appear to move. In fact, at night we can observe that the whole sky is rotating above us. As shown in **Figure 7,** the rest of the stars appear to rotate around Polaris, the North Star, which is directly above Earth's north pole. Because of Earth's rotation, all of the stars in the sky appear to make one complete circle around Polaris every 24 hours.

Actual Motion You now know that the apparent motion of the sun and stars in our sky is due to Earth's rotation. But each star is also really moving in space. Because stars are so distant, however, their real motion is hard to observe. If you could watch stars over thousands of years, their movement would be obvious. As shown in **Figure 8,** you would see that familiar star patterns slowly change their shapes.

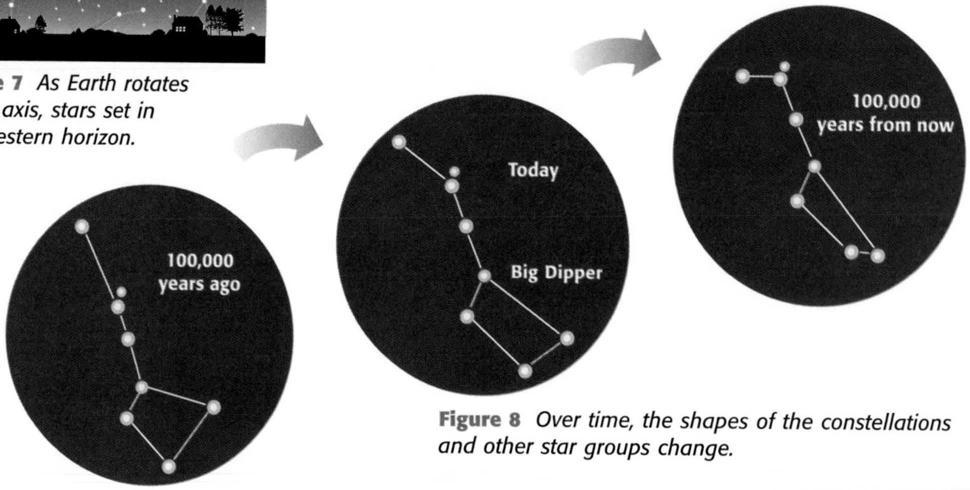

Figure 8 *Over time, the shapes of the constellations and other star groups change.*

internetconnect

sciLINKS NSTA

TOPIC: Stars
GO TO: www.scilinks.org
***sci*LINKS NUMBER:** HSTE510

SECTION REVIEW

1. Is a yellow star, such as the sun, hotter or cooler than an orange star? Explain.
2. Suppose you see two stars that have the same apparent magnitude. If one star is actually four times as far away as the other, how much brighter is the farther star?
3. **Interpreting Illustrations** Look back at Figure 7. How many hours passed between the first image and the second image? How can you tell?

104

Answers to Section Review

1. A yellow star is hotter than an orange star. Hotter temperatures are indicated by colors toward the blue end of the spectrum. Yellow is closer to blue than orange is.
2. The farther star would be 4^2, or 16, times brighter.
3. About 6 hours have passed. The stars would make a complete circle (360°) in 24 hours. In the illustrations, they have turned 90° in 6 hours.

SECTION 2 READING WARM-UP

The Life Cycle of Stars

Terms to Learn

H-R diagram
main sequence
white dwarf
red giant
supernova
neutron star
pulsar
black hole

What You'll Do

- Describe the quantities that are plotted in the H-R diagram.
- Explain how stars at different stages in their life cycle appear on different parts of the H-R diagram.

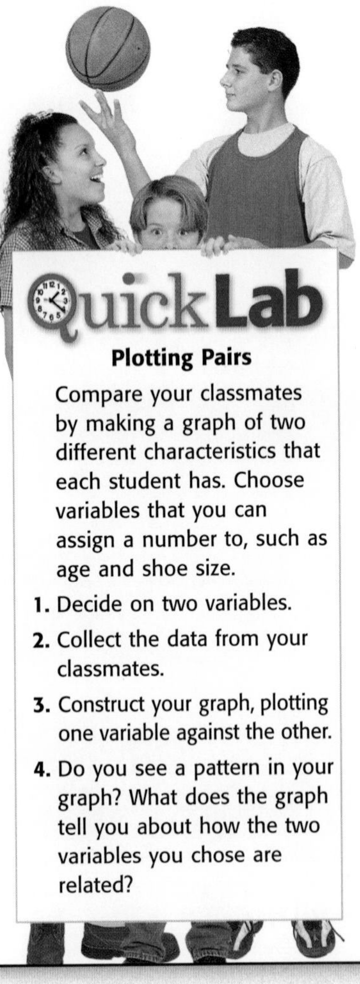

QuickLab

Plotting Pairs

Compare your classmates by making a graph of two different characteristics that each student has. Choose variables that you can assign a number to, such as age and shoe size.

1. Decide on two variables.
2. Collect the data from your classmates.
3. Construct your graph, plotting one variable against the other.
4. Do you see a pattern in your graph? What does the graph tell you about how the two variables you chose are related?

Just like people, stars are born, grow old, and eventually die. But unlike people, stars exist for billions of years. They are born when clouds of gas and dust come together and become very hot and dense. As stars get older, they lose some of their material. Usually this is a gradual change, but sometimes it happens in a big explosion. Either way, when a star dies, much of its material returns to space. There some of it combines with more gas and dust to form new stars. How do scientists know these things about stars? Read on to find out.

The Diagram That Did It!

In 1911, a Danish astronomer named Ejnar Hertzsprung (IE nahr HUHRTZ sprung) compared the temperature and brightness of stars on a graph. Two years later, American astronomer Henry Norris Russell made some similar graphs. Although they used different data, these astronomers had similar results. The combination of their ideas is now called the *Hertzsprung-Russell,* or *H-R, diagram.* The **H-R diagram** is a graph showing the relationship between a star's surface temperature and its absolute magnitude. Russell's original diagram is shown in **Figure 9.**

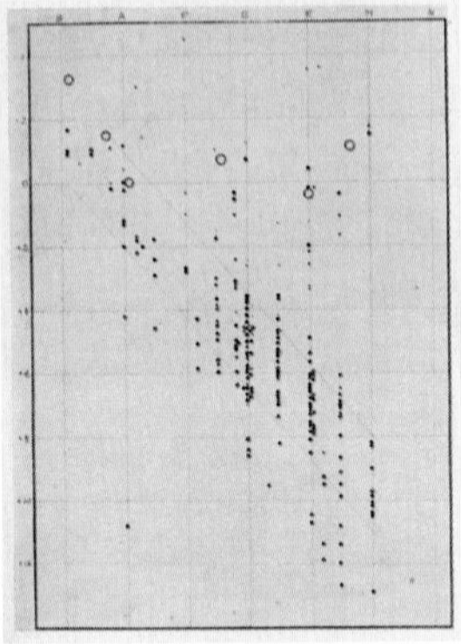

Figure 9 *Notice that a pattern begins to appear from the lower right to the upper left of the graph. Although it may not look like much, this graph began a revolution in astronomy.*

Over the years, the H-R diagram has become a tool for studying the nature of stars. It not only shows how stars are classified by temperature and brightness but also is a good way to illustrate how stars change over time. Turn the page to see a modern version of this diagram.

SECTION 2

Focus

The Life Cycle of Stars

This section explores how H-R diagrams plot the relationship between a star's surface temperature and its absolute magnitude. Students learn how the stars' positions on the diagram change as the stars move through their life cycle. Finally, students learn about stars that leave the main sequence and become supernovas, neutron stars, pulsars, or black holes.

Bellringer

Display photographs of Supernova 1987A and, if possible, a photograph of the Large Magellanic Cloud taken before the explosion. Explain that supernovas represent the "death" of stars that exceed a certain mass. In a few seconds, a supernova can release more energy than it previously did in its entire existence.

1 Motivate

DISCUSSION

Ask students to think about what they learned about stars in Section 1. Have them hypothesize how a star's magnitude, temperature, mass, density, and composition are interrelated. (Students might answer that the mass of a star affects its temperature and therefore its magnitude.)

Tell students that they will learn how a star's age determines its type. When its nuclear fuel begins to be used up, the star changes. Throughout their life cycles, stars vary in magnitude, temperature, mass, density, and composition.

IS THAT A FACT!

Most of the stars near our solar system are not as bright as the sun. How do we know this? When the 100 stars nearest Earth are arranged on the H-R diagram, we can see that almost all of them fall in the region of the red dwarfs. The sun is a brighter type G main-sequence star.

Directed Reading Worksheet Section 2

2 Teach

Group Activity

Divide the class into small groups, and provide each group with a piece of newsprint paper and markers. Direct each group to use these materials to create a flowchart describing the life of a star. Encourage them to refer to the H-R diagram as they work. Their chart should indicate that stars are formed when gas and dust are drawn together by gravity and nuclear fusion begins; that they enter the main sequence when they mature; and that they then may become a red giant, a supergiant, or eventually a white dwarf. Have students label their charts and write a descriptive caption for each stage.

Using the Figure

Remind students that the lower a star's magnitude is, the brighter the star is. By looking at the H-R diagram, students should be able to identify the sun as a main-sequence, yellowish dwarf star with medium brightness and a surface temperature of about 6,000°C. Have students describe other stars in the diagram in a similar manner.

The H-R Diagram

Look closely at the diagram on these two pages. Temperature is given along the bottom of the diagram. Absolute magnitude, or brightness, is given along the left side. Hot (blue) stars are located on the left, and cool (red) stars are on the right. Bright stars are at the top, and faint stars are at the bottom. The brightest stars are a million times brighter than the sun. The faintest are 1/10,000 as bright as the sun. As you can see, there seems to be a band of stars going from the top left to the bottom right corner. This diagonal pattern of stars is called the **main sequence.** A star spends most of its lifetime as a main-sequence star and then changes into one of the other types of stars shown here.

Main-sequence
Stars in the main sequence form a band that runs along the middle of the H-R diagram. The sun is a main-sequence star. Stars similar to the sun are called *dwarfs.* The sun has been shining for about 5 billion years. Scientists think the sun is in midlife and that it will remain on the main sequence for another 5 billion years.

Absolute magnitude
is measured upside down. That means the larger the number, the dimmer the star. At +5, the sun is not as bright as a −7 star.

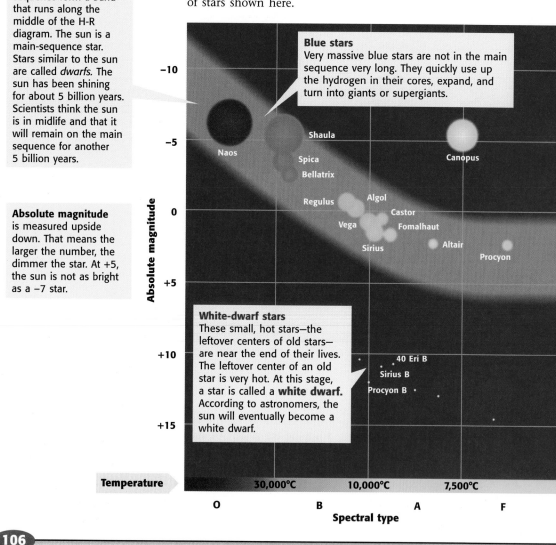

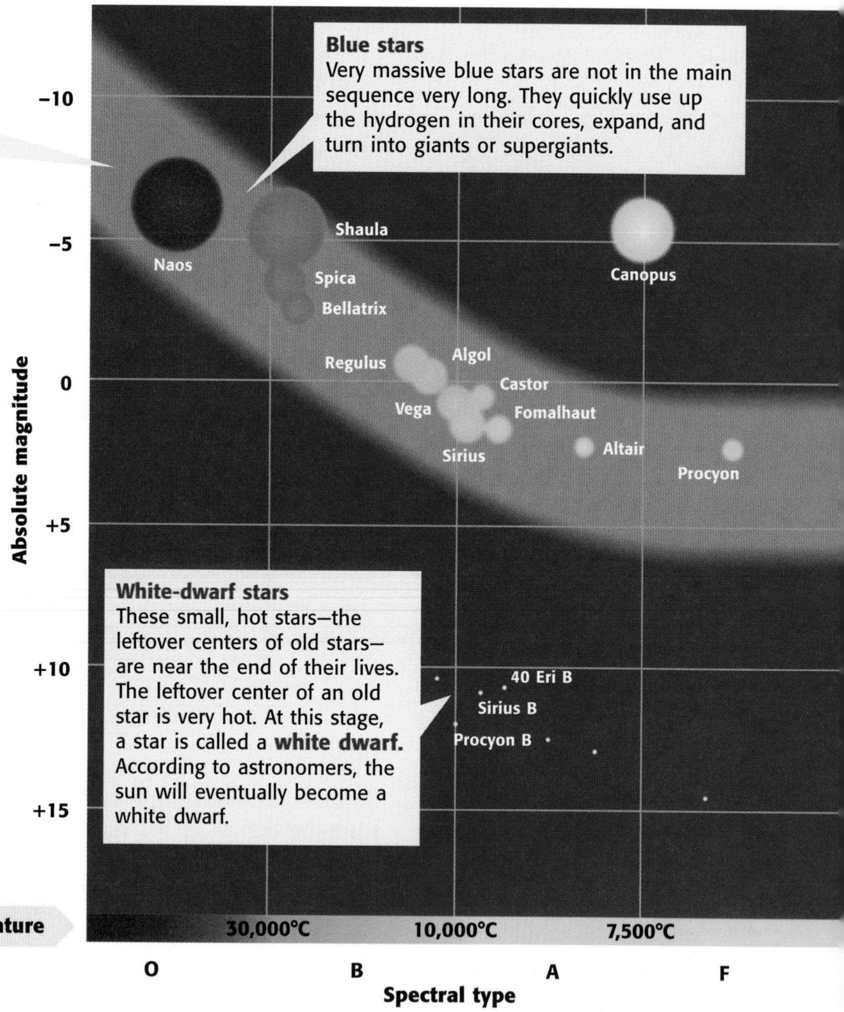
Blue stars
Very massive blue stars are not in the main sequence very long. They quickly use up the hydrogen in their cores, expand, and turn into giants or supergiants.
White-dwarf stars
These small, hot stars—the leftover centers of old stars—are near the end of their lives. The leftover center of an old star is very hot. At this stage, a star is called a **white dwarf.** According to astronomers, the sun will eventually become a white dwarf.
Absolute magnitude
−10
−5
0
+5
+10
+15
Naos
Shaula
Spica
Bellatrix
Canopus
Regulus
Algol
Castor
Vega
Fomalhaut
Sirius
Altair
Procyon
40 Eri B
Sirius B
Procyon B
Temperature
30,000°C
10,000°C
7,500°C
O
B
A
F
Spectral type

IS THAT A FACT!

Our sun probably took about 10 million years to enter the main sequence. It has been shining for about 5 billion years. In another 5 billion years, our sun will burn up all of its hydrogen and change from a yellow dwarf to a red giant. The sun's diameter will increase beyond the orbit of Venus and possibly even beyond the Earth's orbit. Current models suggest, however, that life on Earth will be long since extinct. In one billion years, the surface temperature of the sun will have increased by one percent. This change will probably make Earth an uninhabitable planet.

All stars begin as a ball of gas and dust in space as gravity pulls the gas and dust together into a sphere. As the sphere becomes denser, it gets hotter. When it is hot enough in the center, hydrogen turns into helium in a process called nuclear fusion and lots of energy is given off. A star is born!

Stars spend most of their lives on the main-sequence. Small-mass stars tend to be located at the lower right end of the main-sequence; more massive stars are found at the left end. As main-sequence stars age, they move up and to the right on the H-R diagram to become giants or supergiants. Such stars can then lose their atmospheres, leaving small cores behind, which end up in the lower left corner of the diagram as white dwarfs.

Giants and supergiants
When a star runs out of hydrogen in its core, the center of the star shrinks inward and the outer parts expand outward. In a star the size of our sun, the atmosphere will grow very large and cool. When this happens, the star becomes a **red giant.** If the star is very massive, it becomes a *supergiant.*

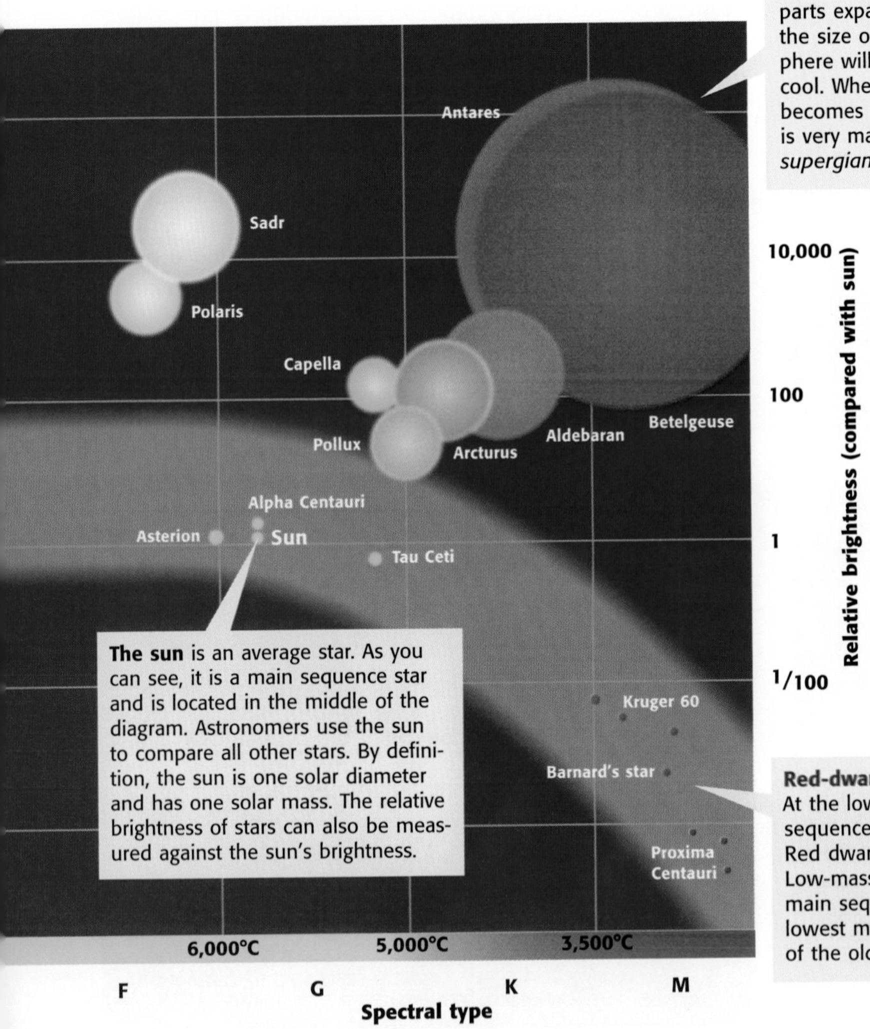

The sun is an average star. As you can see, it is a main sequence star and is located in the middle of the diagram. Astronomers use the sun to compare all other stars. By definition, the sun is one solar diameter and has one solar mass. The relative brightness of stars can also be measured against the sun's brightness.

Red-dwarf stars
At the lower end of the main sequence are the red dwarf stars. Red dwarfs are low-mass stars. Low-mass stars remain on the main sequence a long time. The lowest mass stars may be some of the oldest stars in the galaxy.

107

MEETING INDIVIDUAL NEEDS

Learners Having Difficulty
Have students locate where on the H-R diagram each of the following stars would be found:

	Magnitude	Temperature
Star A	+10	10,000°C
Star B	−2	5,000°C
Star C	+3	7,000°C
Star D	−9	3,500°C

Which star is a giant? (B)
Which star is a dwarf? (A)
Which star is a supergiant? (D)
Which star is most like the sun? (C)

CROSS-DISCIPLINARY FOCUS

Language Arts Divide the class into small groups, and challenge each group to create a crossword puzzle using the vocabulary and concepts from this section. Have them work together to write clues and to construct the puzzle. Then allow groups to exchange and solve the puzzles. Sheltered English

Teaching Transparency 196
"The H-R Diagram: A"

Teaching Transparency 197
"The H-R Diagram: B"

WEIRD SCIENCE

When a star the size of the sun becomes a white dwarf the size of Earth, the white dwarf is much denser than our planet. In fact, a teaspoon of the matter that makes up a white dwarf would weigh several metric tons on Earth!

3 Extend

CROSS-DISCIPLINARY FOCUS

History Encourage students to research the astral events of 1987, known as "the year of the supernova." Have them prepare a brief report and share their findings with the class. (In 1987, for the first time in almost 400 years, people on Earth witnessed the death of a star without using a telescope. The supernova was located in a satellite galaxy of the Milky Way called the Large Magellanic Cloud and was visible only from the Southern Hemisphere.)

MEETING INDIVIDUAL NEEDS

Advanced Learners Encourage students to research what happens as a red giant or supergiant ages. Direct them to focus on the physical changes that occur, preparing a brief report or poster describing the reactions that allow an old star to spend several million years alternately approaching and receding from the main sequence. (As a red giant or supergiant ages, its helium core contracts and grows hotter while its burning hydrogen mantle expands and cools. As a result, the star grows bigger and brighter. When the core reaches a temperature of 100 million degrees Celsius, its helium converts to carbon through nuclear fusion. Over the next several million years, the star alternately approaches and recedes from the main sequence.)

internetconnect

SCILINKS NSTA
TOPIC: Supernovas
GO TO: www.scilinks.org
***sci*LINKS NUMBER:** HSTE515

BRAIN FOOD

Many of the elements in your body were made during supernova explosions and then scattered into space. In other words, you are made of "starstuff"!

When Stars Get Old

While stars may stay on the main sequence for a long time, they don't stay there forever. Average stars, such as the sun, turn into red giants and then white dwarfs. But when massive stars get old, they may leave the main sequence in a more spectacular fashion. Stars much larger than the sun may explode with such violence that they turn into a variety of strange new objects. Let's take a look at some of these objects.

Supernovas Massive blue stars use up their hydrogen much faster than stars like the sun. This means they make a lot more energy, which makes them very hot and therefore blue! And compared with other stars, they don't last long. At the end of its life, a blue star may explode in a tremendous flash of light called a *supernova*. A **supernova** is basically the death of a large star by explosion. A supernova explosion is so powerful that it can be brighter than an entire galaxy for several days. Heavy elements, such as silver, gold, and lead, are formed by supernova explosions.

The ringed structure shown in **Figure 10** is the result of a supernova explosion that was first observed in February 1987. The star, located in a nearby galaxy, actually exploded before civilization began here on Earth, but it took 169,000 years for the light from the explosion to reach our planet!

Before (1984)

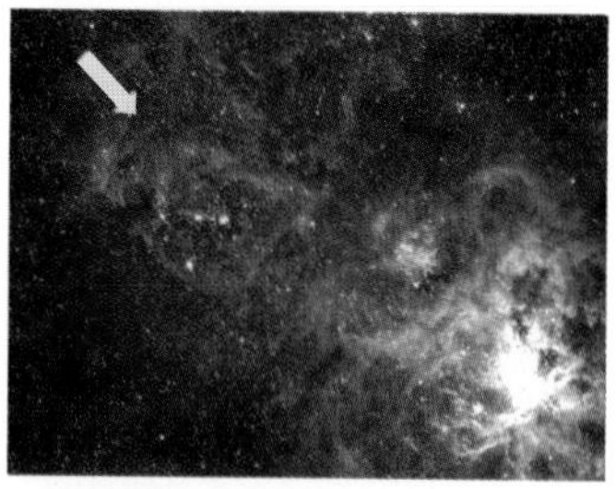

During (1987)

After (Hubble Space Telescope close-up, 1994)

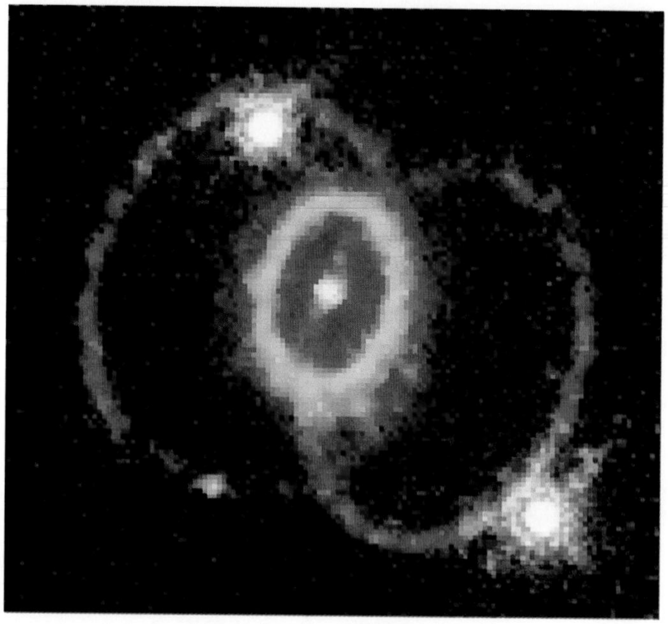

Figure 10 *Supernova 1987A was the first supernova visible to the unaided eye in 400 years. The first image shows what the original star must have looked like only a few hours before the explosion. Today its remains form a double ring of gas and dust, shown at right.*

108

IS THAT A FACT!

The Crab Nebula is an expanding cloud of gas created by a supernova explosion. It was first observed by Chinese astronomers in 1054; the nebula was so bright it could be seen during the day for several weeks.

SCIENCE HUMOR

When pulsars were first recorded, their regular pulses of energy were unlike anything else in the universe. Astronomers thought they might be signals transmitted by intelligent beings. Jokingly, pulsars were called LGM—an acronym for Little Green Men.

Neutron Stars So what happens to a star that becomes a supernova? The leftover materials in the center of a supernova are squeezed together to form a star of about two solar masses. But the star is only about 20 km in diameter. The particles inside the star become neutrons, so this star is called a **neutron star.** A neutron star is so dense that if you brought a teaspoon of it back to Earth, it would weigh nearly a billion metric tons!

Pulsars If a neutron star is spinning, it is called a **pulsar.** A pulsar sends out beams of radiation that also spin around very rapidly. These beams are much like the beams from a lighthouse. The beams are detected as rapid clicks or pulses by radio telescopes.

Black Holes Sometimes the leftovers of a supernova are so massive that they collapse to form a *black hole.* A **black hole** is an object with more than three solar masses squeezed into a ball only 10 km across—100 football fields long. A black hole's gravity is so strong that not even light can escape. That is why it is called a *black* hole. Contrary to some movie depictions, a black hole doesn't gobble up other stars. But if a star is nearby, some gas or dust from the star will spiral into the black hole, as shown in **Figure 11,** giving off X rays. It is by these X rays that astronomers can detect the existence of black holes.

Figure 11 *A black hole's gravity is so strong that it can pull in material from a nearby star, as shown in this artist's drawing.*

SECTION REVIEW

1. Are blue stars young or old? How can you tell?
2. In main-sequence stars, what is the relationship between brightness and temperature?
3. Arrange the following in order of their appearance in the life cycle of a star: white dwarf, red giant, main-sequence star. Explain your answer.
4. **Applying Concepts** Given that there are more low-mass stars than high-mass stars in the universe, do you think there are more white dwarfs or more black holes? Explain.

internet**connect**

sci*LINKS*. NSTA

TOPIC: Supernovas
GO TO: www.scilinks.org
***sci*LINKS NUMBER:** HSTE515

109

4 Close

Quiz

1. What information does the H-R diagram give us? (It tells us the relationship between a star's temperature and its brightness, which indicates its stage.)
2. What is a supernova? (the explosion of a massive star at the end of its life)
3. What is a neutron star? How does it differ from a pulsar? (A neutron star is the compressed core of a star that became a supernova. A pulsar is a spinning neutron star.)

ALTERNATIVE ASSESSMENT

Concept Mapping Have students create a concept map based on the vocabulary and concepts of this section.

Reinforcement Worksheet
"Diagramming the Stars"

Answers to Section Review

1. Blue stars are young. They use up their hydrogen quickly and become supernovas before they get very old.
2. In the main sequence, hotter stars are usually brighter.
3. The order would be main-sequence star, red giant, and white dwarf. As a main-sequence star runs out of fuel, its core shrinks and its atmosphere expands. It then becomes a red giant. Once the red giant loses its outer layers, its core remains as a white dwarf.
4. There would be more white dwarfs. White dwarfs are the remains of average-sized stars that grow old. Only giant stars become black holes.

SECTION 3

Focus

Galaxies

In this section students learn the differences between the three types of galaxies—spiral, elliptical, and irregular. Students also learn that galaxies have features known as nebulas, open clusters, and globular clusters. Finally, two different theories about the origin of galaxies are presented.

Bellringer

Show students a photograph of a spiral galaxy. Ask them to describe the evidence they see that indicates that the galaxy is rotating. Ask students, "What other objects have you seen that look similar? Do they rotate?"

Sheltered English

1) Motivate

DISCUSSION

Point out to students that galaxies can be thought of as star factories. Encourage them to identify the raw materials used by the "factory" to produce stars (clouds of gas and dust) and to describe how stars are assembled. (The gases and dust are drawn together by gravity, eventually forming stars.)

Tell students that the clouds of gases scattered throughout a galaxy often achieve a width of 200 light-years, and encourage them to speculate whether star formation is an ongoing process. (They should recognize that the process is ongoing because of the abundance of raw materials.)

Tell students that in this section they will learn about the different kinds of star factories, their contents, and theories about how they came to be.

SECTION 3 READING WARM-UP

Terms to Learn

galaxy	nebula
spiral galaxy	open cluster
elliptical galaxy	globular cluster
irregular galaxy	quasar

What You'll Do

- Identify the various types of galaxies from pictures.
- Describe the contents of galaxies.
- Explain why looking at distant galaxies reveals what early galaxies looked like.

Galaxies

Stars don't exist alone in space. They belong to larger groups that are held together by the attraction of gravity. The most common groupings are galaxies. **Galaxies** are large groupings of stars in space. Galaxies come in a variety of sizes and shapes. The largest galaxies contain more than a trillion stars. Some of the smaller ones have only a few million. Astronomers don't count the stars, of course; they estimate from the size and brightness of the galaxy how many sun-sized stars the galaxy might have.

Types of Galaxies

Edwin Hubble, the astronomer for whom the Hubble Space Telescope is named, began to classify galaxies in the 1920s, mostly by their shapes. We still use the galaxy names that Hubble originally assigned.

Figure 12 *The Milky Way galaxy is thought to be a spiral galaxy similar to the galaxy in Andromeda, shown here.*

Spiral Galaxies Spiral galaxies are what most people think of when you say *galaxy*. **Spiral galaxies** have a bulge at the center and very distinctive spiral arms. Hot blue stars in the spiral arms make the arms in spiral galaxies appear blue. The central region appears yellow because it contains cooler stars. **Figure 12** shows a spiral galaxy tilted, so you can see its pinwheel shape. Other spiral galaxies appear to be "edge-on." It is hard to tell what type of galaxy we are in because the gas, dust, and stars keep us from having a good view. It is like trying to figure out what pattern a marching band is making while you are in the band. Observing other galaxies and making measurements inside our galaxy lead astronomers to think that Earth is in a spiral galaxy.

CROSS-DISCIPLINARY FOCUS

Writing **History** Encourage students to research the work of an early twentieth century astronomer such as Sir Arthur Stanley Eddington (1882–1944). Eddington, an eminent British astronomer, was the first to propose that "spiral-structure nebulae" were actually separate galaxies, like the Milky Way. His ideas were published in 1914 in his book *Stellar Movements and the Structure of the Universe*. Ask them to prepare a brief report and be prepared to share their findings with the class.

Elliptical Galaxies About one-third of all galaxies are simply massive blobs of stars, as shown in **Figure 13.** Many look like spheres, while others are more elongated. Because we don't know how they are oriented, some of these galaxies could be cucumber shaped, with the round end facing us. These galaxies are called *elliptical galaxies*. **Elliptical galaxies** have very bright centers and very little dust and gas. Because there is so little gas, there are no new stars forming, and therefore elliptical galaxies contain only old stars. Some elliptical galaxies, like M87, at right, are huge and are therefore called *giant elliptical galaxies*. Others are much smaller and are called *dwarf elliptical galaxies*. There are probably lots of dwarf ellipticals, but because they are small and faint, they are very hard to detect.

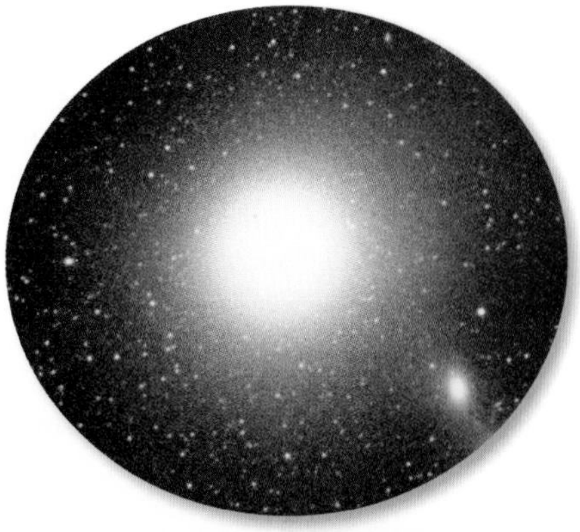

Figure 13 *Unlike the Milky Way, the galaxy known as M87 has no spiral arms.*

Irregular Galaxies When Hubble first classified galaxies, he had a group of leftovers. He named them "irregulars." **Irregular galaxies** are galaxies that don't fit into any other class. As their name suggests, their shape is irregular. Many of these galaxies, such as the Large Magellanic Cloud, shown in **Figure 14,** are close companions of large spiral galaxies, whose gravity may be distorting the shape of their smaller neighbors.

Figure 14 *The Large Magellanic Cloud, an irregular galaxy, is located within our own galactic neighborhood.*

Activity

Now that you know the names Edwin Hubble gave to different shapes of galaxies, look at the names you gave the galaxies in the Hubble Deep Field activity at the beginning of this chapter. Rename your types with the Hubble names. Look for examples of spirals, ellipticals, and irregular galaxies.

TRY at HOME

2 Teach

MEETING INDIVIDUAL NEEDS

Learners Having Difficulty

Help students differentiate between the types of galaxies by having them divide a large sheet of paper into thirds and draw a spiral, an ellipse, and an irregular shape. Have students list under each drawing other objects and one galaxy that have that shape.

Sheltered English

BRAIN FOOD

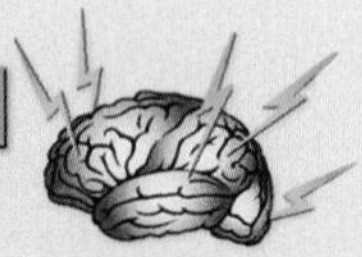

Challenge students to explain why the shape of galaxies indicates that stars are revolving around a center. (Students should recognize that galaxies would not have their characteristic shapes if they were not continuously rotating.)

What would happen if the stars stopped orbiting the center of a galaxy? (In the absence of movement, gravity would pull all of the stars and dust into a more spherical shape.)

Which galaxy shape is most similar to orbits in our solar system? (Spiral galaxies most resemble the orbital paths in our solar system.)

Multicultural CONNECTION

Many cultures have created legends about the Milky Way. The ancient Chinese believed that the Milky Way was a heavenly silver river, while early Scandinavians thought it was the path that souls took to reach heaven. American Indian legends say the stars of the Milky Way were campfires that guided souls to paradise.

IS THAT A FACT!

Earth is about $\frac{2}{3}$ of the distance from the center of the Milky Way to its edge. Our solar system revolves around the galaxy every 200 million years. The last time the solar system was in its current position was during the Triassic period, when dinosaurs first appeared on Earth!

Directed Reading Worksheet Section 3

3) Extend

BRAIN FOOD

Sometimes entire galaxies collide and form new galaxies. It is theorized that these collisions result in elliptical or irregular galaxies. The Milky Way and our closest neighboring spiral galaxy, Andromeda, are moving toward each other at 500,000 km per hour. Even at this speed, the galaxies will not collide for another 5 billion years.

DISCUSSION

Tell students that the material that exists between a galaxy's stars is called interstellar medium. Ask them to hypothesize about what makes up interstellar medium. (They should recognize that nebulae—giant clouds of gas and dust—make up interstellar medium.)

Challenge students to compare irregular, spiral, and elliptical galaxies and determine how much interstellar medium each has. (Irregular and spiral galaxies have more interstellar medium than elliptical galaxies have.)

internetconnect

SciLINKS NSTA
TOPIC: Galaxies
GO TO: www.scilinks.org
***sci*LINKS NUMBER:** HSTE520

Contents of Galaxies

Galaxies are composed of billions and billions of stars. But besides the stars and the planetary systems many of them probably have, there are larger features within galaxies that are made up of stars or the material of stars. Among these are gas clouds and star clusters.

Gas Clouds The Latin word for "cloud" is *nebula*. In space, **nebulas** (or *nebulae*) are giant clouds of gas and dust. Some types of nebulas glow by themselves, while others absorb light and hide stars. Still others reflect starlight, producing some amazing images. Some nebulas are regions where new stars form. **Figure 15** shows part of the Eagle nebula. Spiral galaxies generally contain nebulas, but elliptical galaxies don't.

Globular Clusters **Globular clusters** are groups of older stars. A globular cluster looks like a ball of stars, as shown in **Figure 16.** There may be 20,000 to 100,000 stars in an average globular cluster. Globular clusters are located in a spherical *halo* that surrounds spiral galaxies such as the Milky Way. Globular clusters are also common around giant elliptical galaxies.

Open Clusters **Open clusters** are groups of stars that are usually located along the spiral disk of a galaxy. Newly formed open clusters have many bright blue stars, as shown in **Figure 17.** There may be a few hundred to a few thousand stars in an open cluster.

Figure 15 *Part of a nebula in which stars are born is shown above. The finger-like shape to the left of the bright star is slightly wider than our solar system.*

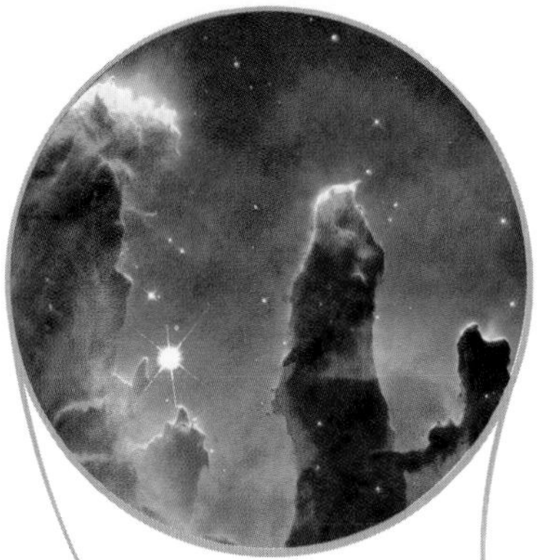

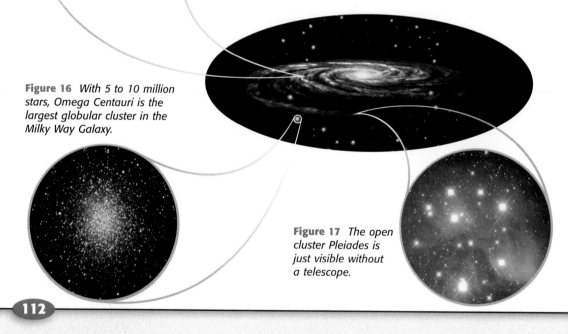

Figure 16 *With 5 to 10 million stars, Omega Centauri is the largest globular cluster in the Milky Way Galaxy.*

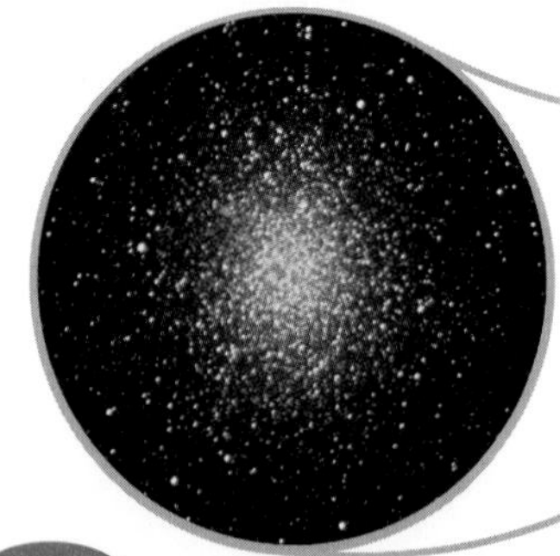

Figure 17 *The open cluster Pleiades is just visible without a telescope.*

112

SCIENTISTS AT ODDS

When the American astronomer Harlow Shapley mapped globular clusters in the universe, he found that they formed an enormous spherical system surrounding the Milky Way and, more importantly, that Earth was not at its center. This discovery led to a heated astronomical debate over whether other spiral nebulae in the distant universe are part of our galaxy or are separate "island universes." This led to the 1920 Shapley-Curtis debate at the National Academy of Sciences. The debate was resolved in 1924, when observations by Edwin Hubble showed that these "nebulae" were so far away that they must be distinct galaxies.

Origin of Galaxies

How did galaxies form in the first place? To answer this question, astronomers must travel back in time, exploring the early universe through telescopes. Scientists investigate the early universe by observing objects that are extremely far away in space. Because it takes time for light to travel through space, looking through a telescope is like looking back in time. The farther out one looks, the further back in time one travels.

Looking at distant galaxies reveals what early galaxies looked like. This helps give scientists an idea of how galaxies evolve through time and perhaps what caused them to form in the first place. Scientists have already found some very strange looking objects in the early universe.

Quasars Among the most distant objects are **quasars,** which look like tiny points of light. But because they are very far away, they must be extremely bright for their size. Quasars are among the most powerful energy sources in the universe. They may be young galaxies with massive black holes at their centers. Some scientists think that what we see as quasars are galaxies in the process of forming. In **Figure 18,** you can see a quasar that is 6 billion light-years away. You are seeing it as it was 6 billion years ago—long before the Earth even existed!

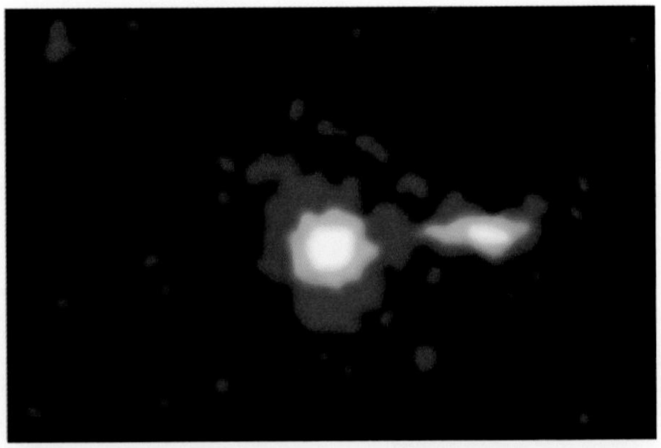

Figure 18 *The quasar known as PKS 0637-752 is as powerful as 10 trillion suns.*

SECTION REVIEW

1. Arrange these galaxies in order of decreasing size: spiral, giant elliptical, dwarf elliptical, irregular.
2. Describe the difference between an elliptical galaxy and a globular cluster.
3. **Analyzing Relationships** Suppose the quasar in Figure 18 suddenly underwent some dramatic change. How long would we have to wait to see this change? Explain.

internet**connect**

sciLINKS NSTA

TOPIC: Galaxies
GO TO: www.scilinks.org
***sci*LINKS NUMBER:** HSTE520

Meeting Individual Needs

Learners Having Difficulty
Help students differentiate between open and globular clusters by having them make two columns on a piece of paper. Have them label one column "Open" and the other "Globular." Have them reread the text, listing the characteristics of each kind of cluster in the appropriate column. Encourage students to focus on the differences between the two groups.
Sheltered English

4 Close

Quiz

1. What is a nebula? (It is an enormous cloud of gas and dust in space.)
2. What are open clusters? (They are groups of a few hundred to a few thousand stars that form when great amounts of gas and dust come together.)
3. Why is looking through a telescope at a distant galaxy like looking back in time? (The light from distant galaxies takes a very long time to travel through the vastness of space. The light that we see could have been emitted hundreds of millions or even billions of years ago.)

Alternative Assessment

PORTFOLIO Encourage students to work independently to write recipes for making different types of galaxies. Have them include ingredients as well as the procedure for making these groups of stars. Allow time for students to share their recipes with the class.

Answers to Section Review

1. giant elliptical, spiral, irregular, dwarf elliptical
2. Elliptical galaxies are much larger than globular clusters, and they may be accompanied by many globular clusters. Elliptical galaxies may have different shapes, but all globular clusters appear to be spherical.
3. The quasar is 6 billion light-years away, so it would take 6 billion years to observe any changes that occurred.

Section 4

Focus

Formation of the Universe

In this section, students learn that cosmology is the study of the origin and future of the universe. They learn about various interpretations of the big bang theory and about evidence supporting the theory. Finally, they learn about repeating patterns in the structure of the universe.

Bellringer

Discuss the four images in **Figure 19** with students. Have students describe the differences between each image. The first image represents the initial explosion, and the following images represent the expansion of the universe and the formation of the galaxies.

1 Motivate

Activity

The Expanding Universe Have students draw several dots on an uninflated balloon with a permanent marker and label them with letters. Ask them to measure the distances between the dots and record the information in their ScienceLog. Then have students blow up their balloon and tie the end. The students should then measure the distances between the dots again. Ask them to explain how this represents the expansion of the universe. (As the universe expands, the distance between every star and galaxy increases.) Can one dot represent the center of the universe? (no)

After students have finished this section, have them reevaluate this model and assess its accuracy.

Section 4 — Reading Warm-Up

Terms to Learn

cosmology
big bang theory
cosmic background radiation

What You'll Do

- Describe the big bang theory.
- Explain evidence used to show support for the big bang theory.
- Explain how the expansion of the universe is explained by the big bang theory.

Formation of the Universe

So far you've learned about the contents of the universe. But what about its history? How did the universe begin? How might it end? Questions like these are a special part of astronomy called *cosmology*. **Cosmology** is the study of the origin and future of the universe. Like other scientific theories, theories about the beginning and end of the universe must be tested by observations or experiments.

The Big Bang Theory

One of the most important theories in cosmology is the big bang theory. The **big bang theory** states that the universe began with a tremendous explosion. According to the theory, 12 to 15 billion years ago, all the contents of the universe were gathered together under extreme pressure, temperature, and density in a very tiny spot. Then, for some reason, it rapidly expanded. In the early moments of the universe, some of the expanding energy turned into matter that eventually became the galaxies, as shown in **Figure 19.**

A Big Crunch? As the galaxies move apart, they get older and eventually stop forming stars. What happens next depends on how much matter is contained in the universe. If there is enough matter, gravity will slow and eventually stop the expansion of the universe. The universe may even start collapsing to its original state, causing a "big crunch."

If there is not enough matter to stop the expansion, then as stars age and die, the universe will eventually become cold and dark. Recent observations suggest that there may not be enough matter to stop the universe from expanding forever, but the answer is still uncertain.

Figure 19 *The big bang caused the universe to expand in all directions.*

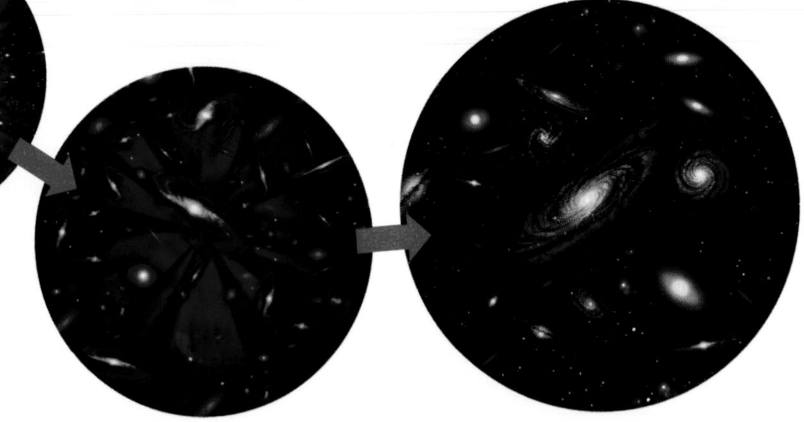

Teaching Transparency 198 "The Big Bang Theory"

Directed Reading Worksheet Section 4

Is That a Fact!

Scientists believe that the universe formed about 12–15 billion years ago. To count to 15 billion, a person would have to count one number every second, day, and night for 480 years!

Supporting the Theory So how do we know if the big bang really happened? In 1964, two scientists, using the antenna shown in **Figure 20,** accidentally found radiation coming from all directions in space. One explanation for this radiation is that it is **cosmic background radiation** left over from the big bang.

Think about what happens when an oven door is left open after the oven has been used. Thermal energy is transferred throughout the kitchen and the oven cools. Eventually the room and the oven are the same temperature. According to the big bang theory, thermal energy from the original explosion was distributed in every direction as the universe expanded. This cosmic background radiation—corresponding to a temperature of −270°C—now fills all of space.

Figure 20 *Robert Wilson (left) and Arno Penzias (right) discovered the cosmic background radiation, giving a big boost to the big bang theory.*

Universal Expansion

Today, the big bang theory is widely accepted by astronomers. But where did the idea of a big bang come from? The answer is found in deep space. No matter what direction we look, galaxies are moving away from us, as shown in **Figure 21.** This observation may make it seem like our galaxy is the center of the universe, with all other galaxies moving away from our own. But this is not the case. Careful measurements have shown that all distant galaxies are moving away from all other galaxies.

With the discovery that the universe is expanding, scientists began to wonder what it would be like to watch the universe evolve backwards through time. In reverse, the universe would appear to be contracting, not expanding. All matter would eventually come together to a single point. Thinking about what would happen if all of the matter in the universe were squeezed into such a small space led scientists to the big bang theory.

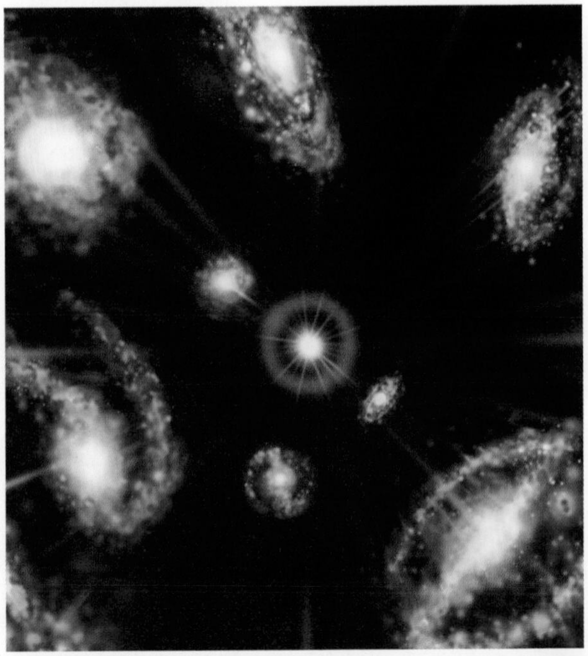

Figure 21 *The big bang theory explains the expansion of the universe we observe as galaxies move outward in all directions.*

2 Teach

READING STRATEGY

Prediction Guide Before students read this section, have them write a paragraph describing how they think the universe formed. Have them evaluate their responses after reading the section.

BRAIN FOOD

How do scientists know that galaxies are moving apart? They don't see the movement but rather see a shift toward the red end of the spectrum in the light from the stars making up the galaxies. This occurs because, as galaxies move away, the light waves that reach Earth are stretched out, making them appear to have longer wavelengths. This phenomenon is caused by the Doppler effect. For the same reason, the siren of an ambulance sounds higher in pitch when it is approaching than when it is receding.

Multicultural CONNECTION

The ancient Greeks believed that the universe began with Chaos (space), which produced Gaea (Earth). Gaea gave birth to Uranus (the starry heavens) as a cover for herself and then gave birth to the mountains, fields, seas, plants, and animals. Encourage students to learn how other cultures have explained the origin of the universe.

MISCONCEPTION ALERT

Make sure students realize that the big bang was not an explosion that happened "somewhere in space." Space and time did not exist before the big bang; they came into being with the big bang. Just before expansion, the universe was compressed in an infinitely dense ball. There was no "space" outside this ball. Thus, we are not receding away from the bang; rather, the explosion continues to expand. We aren't moving away from the point of the big bang because the big bang is happening everywhere.

3 Extend

Independent Practice

Writing Students can work independently to summarize, in writing, the big bang theory, including the evidence that supports it. Encourage students to investigate other theories of the origin of the universe. Direct them to select three such theories, summarizing their key points in a table.

Discussion

Remind students that one way to determine the age of the universe is to divide the distance to other galaxies by the speed at which they are moving away from us. Tell students that while scientists do not know the exact age of the universe, they believe it formed about 12–15 billion years ago.

Have students consider how many light-years away a celestial object would be if it existed during the formation of the universe. (It would have to be 12–15 billion light-years away.)

Homework

Universal Address Have students use reference materials to find out their universal address:

Name
Street address
City, State
Country
Continent
Planet
Solar system
Galaxy
Galaxy group
Galaxy cluster
Local supercluster
The universe

BRAIN FOOD

Objects in very distant space look "younger" than they really are. In fact, we cannot even be sure they still exist. If a distant galaxy disappeared, for example, people on Earth wouldn't know about it for billions of years.

A Raisin-Bread Model Imagine a loaf of raisin bread before it is baked. Inside the dough, each raisin is a certain distance from every other raisin. As the dough gets warm and rises, it expands and all of the raisins begin to move away from each other. No matter which raisin you observe, the other raisins are moving farther from it.

The universe itself is like the rising bread dough—it is expanding in all directions. And like the raisins, every distant galaxy is moving away from our galaxy as well as every other galaxy. In other words, there isn't any way to find the "center" of the universe.

How Old Is the Universe? One way scientists can measure the age of the universe is by measuring the distance to the farthest galaxies. Because light travels at a certain speed, the amount of time it takes light to travel this distance is a measure of the age of the universe. Another way to estimate the age of the universe is to calculate the ages of old, nearby stars. Because the universe must be at least as old as the oldest stars it contains, their ages provide a clue to the age of the universe. But according to these calculations, some stars are older than the universe itself! Astronomers continue to search for evidence that will solve this puzzle.

APPLY

Graphing Expansion

Suppose you decide to make some raisin bread. You would form a lump of dough, as shown in the top image. The lower image represents dough that has been rising for 2 hours. Look at raisin **B** in the top image. Measure how far it is from each of the other raisins—**A, C, D, E, F,** and **G**—in millimeters. Now measure how far each raisin has moved away from **B** in the lower image. Make a graph of speed (in units of mm/h) versus original distance (in mm). Remember that speed equals distance divided by time. For example, if raisin **E** was originally 15 mm from raisin **B** and is now 30 mm away, it moved 15 mm in 2 hours. Its speed is therefore 7.5 mm/h. Repeat the procedure, starting with raisin **D.** Plot your results on the same graph, and compare the two results. What can you conclude from the information you graphed?

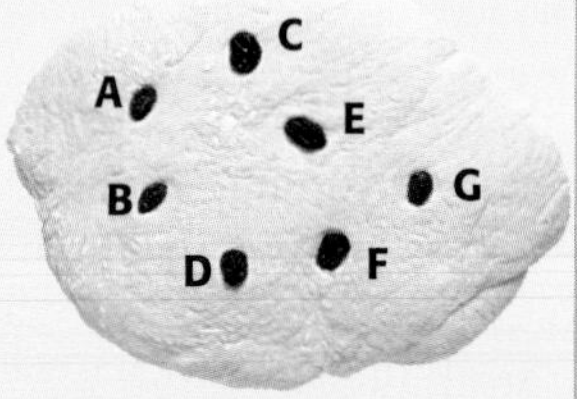

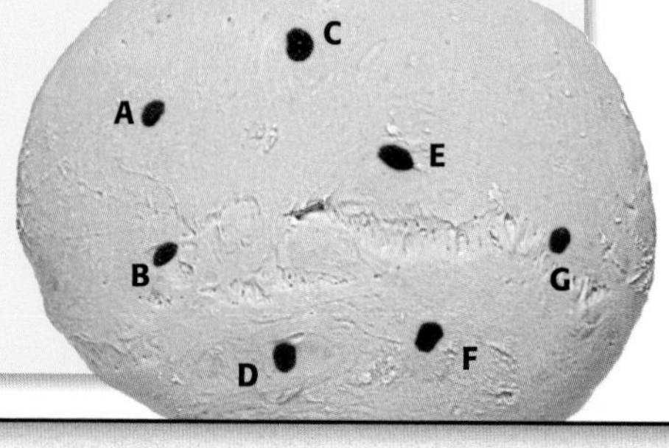

116

MISCONCEPTION ALERT

Students may have difficulty understanding that due to the great distances between the Earth and stars, the light they see actually was emitted from the star in the distant past. If a star is 100 light-years away, it takes 100 years for the light to travel that distance.

Answer to APPLY

The farther a raisin is from raisin **B** (or any other raisin), the faster it is moving away from that raisin. The same is true for galaxies in the expanding universe. **Note:** Student graphs should resemble the graph in the Chapter Review under Interpreting Graphics.

Structure of the Universe

The universe is an amazing place. From our home on planet Earth, it stretches out farther than we can see with our most sensitive instruments. It contains a variety of objects, some of which you have just learned about. But these objects are not simply scattered through the universe at random. The universe has a structure that is repeated over and over again.

A Cosmic Repetition You already know that the Earth is a planet. But planets are part of planetary systems. Our solar system is the one we are most familiar with, but recently planets have been detected in orbit around other stars. Scientists think that planetary systems are actually quite common in the universe. Stars are grouped in larger systems, ranging from star clusters to galaxies. Galaxies themselves are arranged in groups that are bound together by gravity. Even galaxy groups form galaxy clusters and superclusters, as shown in **Figure 22.**

Multiple Universes? Farther than the eye can see, the universe continues with this pattern, with great collections of galaxy clusters and vast empty regions of space in between. But is the universe itself alone? Some cosmologists think that our universe is only one of a great many other universes, perhaps similar to ours or perhaps not. At present, we cannot observe other universes. But someday, who knows? Maybe students in future classrooms will have much more to study!

Figure 22 *The Earth is only part of a vast system of matter.*

SECTION REVIEW

1. Name one observation that supports the big bang theory.
2. How does the big bang theory explain the observed expansion of the universe?
3. **Understanding Technology** Large telescopes gather more light than small telescopes gather. Why are large telescopes used to study very distant galaxies?

Answers to Section Review

1. The existence of cosmic background radiation supports the big bang theory. The observable expansion of the universe also supports the big bang theory.
2. According to the big bang theory, the expansion of the universe was the result of a massive explosion of all matter and energy.
3. Very distant galaxies are very faint. Only large telescopes can gather enough light to detect them.

4 Close

Quiz

1. What is cosmic background radiation? (It is the radiation that comes from all directions in space and is left over from the big bang.)
2. How is the structure of the universe repeated? (There are great collections of galaxy clusters—made up of similar components—with vast regions of empty space in between.)

Alternative Assessment

Board Game To reinforce chapter concepts, divide the class into small groups and challenge each group to create a board game. The game should lead players through the universe, encountering the features they have learned about in this chapter. Provide each group with a piece of poster board, plain index cards, and markers. Have them use the index cards to write clues directing players' movements through the "universe." For example, they might write, "If you can describe what a star is made of, move ahead to the nebula. If not, lose a turn." Have students create written rules and exchange their games.

Critical Thinking Worksheet
"Fleabert and the Amazing Watermelon Seed"

internetconnect

*sci*LINKS NSTA

TOPIC: Structure of the Universe
GO TO: www.scilinks.org
***sci*LINKS NUMBER:** HSTE525

Red Hot, or Not?
Teacher's Notes

Time Required

One 45-minute class period

Lab Ratings

EASY → HARD

TEACHER PREP: 2

STUDENT SET-UP: 2

CONCEPT LEVEL: 1

CLEAN UP: 1

MATERIALS

The materials listed on this page are enough for a group of 3–4 students.

Safety Caution

Remind students to review all safety cautions and icons before beginning this lab activity. Be sure the students disconnect the wires at each step. If they are left connected, they can get very hot.

Lab Notes

Students may find it difficult to hold the wires to the light bulb. In that case, you may use a light socket. Any miniature incandescent light bulb can be used as the flashlight bulb.

Kathy McKee
Hoyt Middle School
Des Moines, Iowa

Discovery Lab

USING SCIENTIFIC METHODS

Red Hot, or Not?

When you look at the night sky, some stars are brighter than others. Some are even different colors from what you might expect. For example, one star in the constellation Orion glows red. Sirius, the brightest star in the sky, glows a bluish white. Astronomers use these colors to estimate the temperature of the stars. In this activity, you will experiment with a light bulb and some batteries to discover what the color of a glowing object reveals about the temperature of the object.

MATERIALS

- electrical tape
- 2 conducting wires
- weak D cell
- flashlight bulb
- 2 fresh D cells

Ask a Question

1. How are the color and temperature of a star related?

Form a Hypothesis

2. In your ScienceLog, change the question above into a statement giving your best guess about what the relationship is between a star's color and temperature.

Test the Hypothesis

3. Tape one end of a conducting wire to the positive pole of the weak D cell. Tape one end of the second conducting wire to the negative pole.

4 Touch the free end of each wire to the light bulb. Hold one of the wires against the bottom tip of the light bulb. Hold the second wire against the side of the metal portion of the bulb. The bulb should light.

Make Observations

5 In your ScienceLog, record the color of the filament in the light bulb. Carefully touch your hand to the bulb. Observe the temperature of the bulb. Record your observations in your ScienceLog.

6 Repeat steps 3–5 with one fresh D cell.

7 Use the electrical tape to connect the two fresh D cells in a continuous circuit so that the positive pole of the first cell is connected to the negative pole of the second cell.

8 Repeat steps 3–5 using two fresh D cells.

Analyze Results

9 How did the color of the filament change in the three trials? How did the temperature change?

10 What information does the color of a star provide?

11 What color are stars with relatively high surface temperatures? What color are stars with relatively low surface temperatures?

Draw Conclusions

12 Arrange the following stars in order from highest to lowest surface temperature: Sirius is bluish white. Aldebaran is orange. Procyon is yellow-white. Capella is yellow. Betelgeuse is red.

Answers

9. With the weaker cell, the filament should burn with a dull red color. The filament burns bright red or orange with the stronger cell. With two fresh D cells, the filament becomes almost white. The temperature increases from one trial to the next.
10. Cooler objects emit red light. As an object becomes hotter, its color gradually changes from red to orange to white. Therefore, the color of the light emitted from the stars helps scientists determine the relative temperatures of stars.
11. Stars with relatively high surface temperatures are white or blue. Stars with relatively low surface temperatures are red or orange.
12. The order of the stars from highest to lowest surface temperature is as follows: Sirius, Procyon, Capella, Aldebaran, and Betelgeuse.

Datasheets for LabBook

Chapter Highlights

Vocabulary Definitions

Section 1

spectrum the rainbow of colors produced when white light passes through a prism or spectrograph

apparent magnitude how bright a light appears to an observer

absolute magnitude the actual brightness of a star

light-year a unit of length equal to the distance that light travels through space in 1 year

parallax an apparent shift in the position of an object when viewed from different locations

Section 2

H-R diagram Hertzsprung-Russell diagram; a graph that shows the relationship between a star's surface temperature and its absolute magnitude

main sequence a diagonal pattern of stars on the H-R diagram

white dwarf a small, hot star near the end of its life; the leftover center of an old star

red giant a star that expands and cools once it runs out of hydrogen fuel

supernova the death of a large star by explosion

neutron star a star in which all the particles have become neutrons; the collapsed remains of a supernova

pulsar a spinning neutron star that emits rapid pulses of light

black hole an object with more than three solar masses squeezed into a ball only 10 km across whose gravity is so strong that not even light can escape

Chapter Highlights

Section 1

Vocabulary

spectrum *(p. 98)*
apparent magnitude *(p. 102)*
absolute magnitude *(p. 102)*
light-year *(p. 103)*
parallax *(p. 103)*

Section Notes

- The color of a star depends on its temperature. Hot stars are blue. Cool stars are red.
- The spectra of stars indicate their composition. Spectra are also used to classify stars.
- The magnitude of a star is a measure of its brightness.
- Apparent magnitude is how bright a star appears from Earth.
- Absolute magnitude is how bright a star actually is. Lower absolute magnitude numbers indicate brighter stars.
- Distance to nearby stars can be measured by their movement relative to stars farther away.

Labs

I See the Light! *(p. 166)*

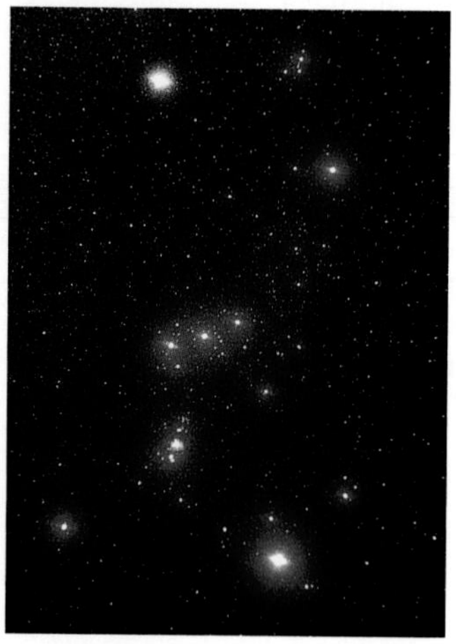

Section 2

Vocabulary

H-R diagram *(p. 105)*
main sequence *(p. 106)*
white dwarf *(p. 106)*
red giant *(p. 107)*
supernova *(p. 108)*
neutron star *(p. 109)*
pulsar *(p. 109)*
black hole *(p. 109)*

Section Notes

- New stars form from the material of old stars that have gone through their life cycles.
- The H-R diagram relates the temperature and brightness of a star. It also illustrates the life cycle of stars.
- Most stars are main-sequence stars. Red giants and white dwarfs are later stages in a star's life cycle.
- Massive stars become supernovas. Their cores turn into neutron stars or black holes.

☑ Skills Check

Math Concepts

SQUARING THE DIFFERENCE The difference in brightness (apparent magnitude) between a pair of similar stars depends on the difference in their distances from Earth. Compare a star that is 10 light-years away with a star that is 5 light-years away. One star is twice as close, so it is $2 \times 2 = 4$ times brighter than the other star. The star that is 5 light-years away is also 3^2, or 9, times brighter than one that is 15 light-years away.

Visual Understanding

READING BETWEEN THE LINES The composition of a star is determined by the absorption spectra it displays. Dark lines in the spectrum of a star indicate which elements are present. Look back at Figure 3 to review.

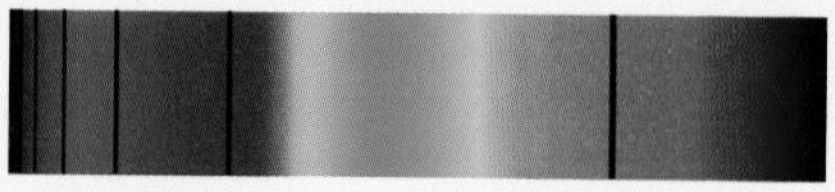

120

Lab and Activity Highlights

Red Hot, or Not? PG 118

I See the Light! PG 166

Datasheets for LabBook (blackline masters for these labs)

SECTION 3

Vocabulary

galaxy *(p. 110)*
spiral galaxy *(p. 110)*
elliptical galaxy *(p. 111)*
irregular galaxy *(p. 111)*
nebula *(p. 112)*
open cluster *(p. 112)*
globular cluster *(p. 112)*
quasar *(p. 113)*

Section Notes

- Edwin Hubble classified galaxies according to their shape. Major types include spiral, elliptical, and irregular galaxies.
- A nebula is a cloud of gas and dust. New stars are born in some nebulas.
- Open clusters are groups of stars located along the spiral disk of a galaxy. Globular star clusters are found in the halos of spiral galaxies and in elliptical galaxies.
- Because light travels at a certain speed, observing distant galaxies is like looking back in time. Scientists look at distant galaxies to learn what early galaxies looked like.

SECTION 4

Vocabulary

cosmology *(p. 114)*
big bang theory *(p. 114)*
cosmic background radiation *(p. 115)*

Section Notes

- The big bang theory states that the universe began with an explosion about 12 to 15 billion years ago.
- Cosmic background radiation fills the universe with radiation that is left over from the big bang. It is supporting evidence for the big bang theory.
- Observations show that the universe is expanding outward. There is no measurable center and no apparent edge.
- All matter in the universe is a part of larger systems, from planets to superclusters of galaxies.

internetconnect

GO TO: go.hrw.com

Visit the **HRW** Web site for a variety of learning tools related to this chapter. Just type in the keyword:

KEYWORD: HSTUNV

GO TO: www.scilinks.org

Visit the **National Science Teachers Association** on-line Web site for Internet resources related to this chapter. Just type in the ***sci*LINKS** number for more information about the topic:

TOPIC: The Hubble Space Telescope	***sci*LINKS NUMBER:** HSTE505
TOPIC: Stars	***sci*LINKS NUMBER:** HSTE510
TOPIC: Supernovas	***sci*LINKS NUMBER:** HSTE515
TOPIC: Galaxies	***sci*LINKS NUMBER:** HSTE520
TOPIC: Structure of the Universe	***sci*LINKS NUMBER:** HSTE525

121

VOCABULARY DEFINITIONS, *continued*

SECTION 3

galaxy a large grouping of stars in space

spiral galaxy a galaxy with a bulge in the center and very distinctive spiral arms

elliptical galaxy a spherical or elongated galaxy with a bright center and very little dust and gas

irregular galaxy a galaxy that does not fit into any other category; one with an irregular shape

nebula a large cloud of dust and gas in interstellar space; the location of star formation

open cluster a group of stars that are usually located along the spiral disk of a galaxy

globular cluster a group of older stars that looks like a ball of stars

quasar "quasi-stellar" object; a star-like source of light that is extremely far away; one of the most powerful sources of energy in the universe

SECTION 4

cosmology the study of the origin and future of the universe

big bang theory the theory that states the universe began with a tremendous explosion

cosmic background radiation radiation left over from the big bang that fills all of space

Vocabulary Review Worksheet

Blackline masters of these Chapter Highlights can be found in the **Study Guide.**

Lab and Activity Highlights

LabBank

Whiz-Bang Demonstrations, Where Do the Stars Go?

Long-Term Projects & Research Ideas, Contacting the Aliens

Chapter Review Answers

Using Vocabulary

1. Absolute magnitude is the actual brightness of a star, or how bright it would appear if all stars were the same distance from Earth. Apparent magnitude is how bright a star appears from Earth.
2. A spectrum is made when white light is broken into its colors by a prism or spectrograph. Parallax is a measure of the apparent shift in position of an object due to a difference in the location from which it is viewed.
3. A main-sequence star is a star that is stable and uses fusion to produce energy. A red giant became a giant star when its fusion stopped and its outer layers expanded.
4. A white dwarf is the leftover core of a small star at the end of its life. A black hole is the leftover core of a massive star at the end of its life.
5. An elliptical galaxy is composed mostly of older stars, and it contains very little dust or gas. It is shaped like a sphere or an elongated oval. A spiral galaxy has a bulge with cooler stars; spiral arms with hot blue stars, gas, and dust; and a halo of stars and globular clusters.
6. The big bang occurred when all the matter and energy of the universe suddenly expanded. The cosmic background radiation is the radiation coming from all directions in space. It may be evidence of the big bang.

Understanding Concepts

Multiple Choice

7. c
8. d
9. b
10. d
11. c
12. a
13. c

Chapter Review

USING VOCABULARY

For each pair of terms, explain the difference in their meanings.

1. absolute magnitude/apparent magnitude
2. spectrum/parallax
3. main-sequence star/red giant
4. white dwarf/black hole
5. elliptical galaxy/spiral galaxy
6. big bang/cosmic background radiation

UNDERSTANDING CONCEPTS

Multiple Choice

7. The majority of stars in our galaxy are
   a. blue.
   b. white dwarfs.
   c. main-sequence stars.
   d. red giants.

8. Which would be seen as the brightest star in the following group?
   a. Alcyone—apparent magnitude of 3
   b. Alpheratz—apparent magnitude of 2
   c. Deneb—apparent magnitude of 1
   d. Rigel—apparent magnitude of 0

9. A cluster of stars forms in a nebula. There are red stars, blue stars, yellow stars, and white stars. Which stars are most like the sun?
   a. red
   b. yellow
   c. blue
   d. white

10. Individual stars are moving in space. How long will it take to see a noticeable difference without using a telescope?
    a. 24 hours
    b. 1 year
    c. 100 years
    d. 100,000 years

11. You visited an observatory and looked through the telescope. You saw a ball of stars through the telescope. What type of object did you see?
    a. a spiral galaxy
    b. an open cluster
    c. a globular cluster
    d. an irregular galaxy

12. In which part of a spiral galaxy do you expect to find nebulas?
    a. the spiral arms
    b. the central region
    c. the halo
    d. all parts of the galaxy

13. Which statement about the big bang theory is accurate?
    a. The universe will never end.
    b. New matter is being continuously created in the universe.
    c. The universe is filled with radiation coming from all directions in space.
    d. We can locate the center of the universe.

122

Concept Mapping Transparency 21

Blackline masters of this Chapter Review can be found in the **Study Guide.**

Short Answer

14. Describe how the apparent magnitude of a star varies with its distance from Earth.

15. Name six types of astronomical objects in the universe. Arrange them by size.

16. Which contains more stars on average, a globular cluster or an open cluster?

17. What does the big bang theory have to say about how the universe will end?

Concept Mapping

18. Use the following terms to create a concept map: black hole, neutron star, main-sequence star, red giant, nebula, white dwarf.

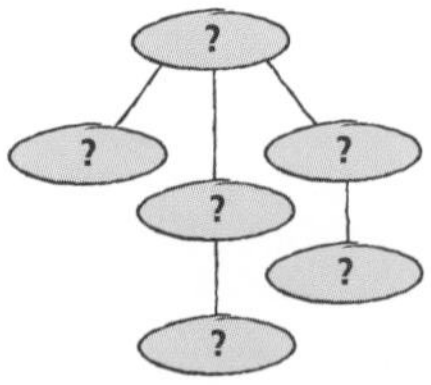

CRITICAL THINKING AND PROBLEM SOLVING

Write one or two sentences to answer the following questions:

19. If a certain star displayed a large parallax, what could you say about its distance from Earth?

20. Two M-type stars have the same apparent magnitude. Their spectra show that one is a red giant and the other is a red-dwarf star. Which one is farther from Earth? Explain your answer.

21. Look back at the H-R diagram in Section 2. Why do astronomers use absolute magnitudes to plot the stars? Why don't they use apparent magnitudes?

22. While looking at a galaxy through a nearby university's telescope, you notice that there are no blue stars present. What kind of galaxy is it most likely to be?

MATH IN SCIENCE

23. An astronomer observes two stars of about the same temperature and size. Alpha Centauri B is about 4 light-years away, and Sigma[2] Eridani A is about 16 light-years away. How much brighter does Alpha Centauri B appear?

INTERPRETING GRAPHICS

The following graph illustrates the Hubble law relating the distances of galaxies and their speed away from us.

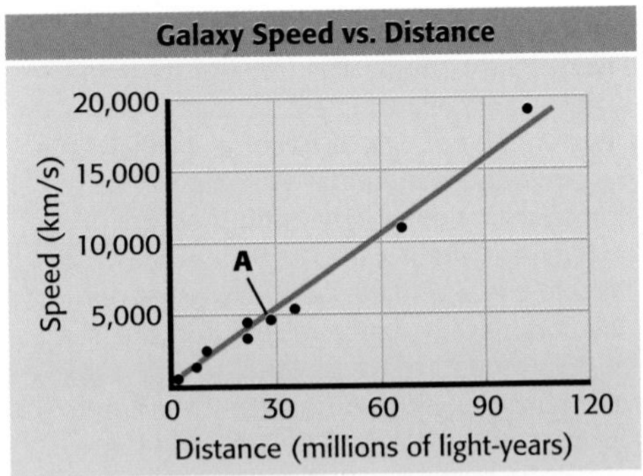

24. Look at the galaxy marked A in the graph. What is its speed and distance?

25. If a new galaxy with a speed of 15,000 km/s were found, at what distance would you expect it to be?

Take a minute to review your answers to the Pre-Reading Questions found at the bottom of page 96. Have your answers changed? If necessary, revise your answers based on what you have learned since you began this chapter.

Short Answers

14. The apparent magnitude decreases as distance increases.

15. Answers may vary. Possible answers include globular cluster, nebula, spiral arm, nuclear bulge, halo, spiral galaxy, elliptical galaxy, and galaxy cluster.

16. On average, globular clusters contain more stars.

17. If there is enough matter in the universe, gravity will slow or stop the expansion, perhaps even pulling everything back into a "big crunch." If there is not enough matter, everything will continue to expand outward, get older, cool down, and become dark.

Concept Mapping

18. 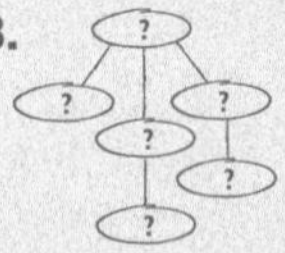 An answer to this exercise can be found at the front of this book.

CRITICAL THINKING AND PROBLEM SOLVING

19. The star would be relatively close to Earth.

20. The red giant is farther away. If it were the same distance as the red dwarf (or closer), it would be much brighter than the red dwarf.

21. Absolute magnitude is a physical property of the star. Apparent magnitude varies according to a star's distance and absolute magnitude.

22. The galaxy is most likely an elliptical galaxy because it lacks the gas and dust needed for star formation. Blue stars are young stars.

MATH IN SCIENCE

23. Alpha Centauri B is 16 times as bright because it is 4 times closer.

INTERPRETING GRAPHICS

24. Its speed is about 5,000 km/s, and its distance is about 30 million light-years.

25. almost 90 million light-years

Weird Science

Holes Where Stars Once Were

Background

Scientists theorize that two types of stars can turn into black holes. When an extremely large star (about 8 to 25 times as massive as the sun) runs out of fuel and dies, it usually explodes as a supernova. A star that is more than 25 times as massive as the sun may collapse without exploding. If the core of either type of star is at least three times more massive than the sun, the core will collapse under its own gravity and become a black hole.

Many scientists also think that black holes may have formed at the center of many galaxies in the early universe. As a galaxy forms, gases and stars rotate around its center in a swirling mass. Some of this matter may become so closely packed in the center of the forming galaxy that it eventually condenses into a single lump. The gravity of the resulting mass causes it to condense even further until it is so dense that it forms a black hole. These black holes typically are millions or even billions of times as massive as the sun.

WEIRD SCIENCE

HOLES WHERE STARS ONCE WERE

An invisible phantom lurks in outer space, ready to swallow up everything that comes near it. Once trapped in its grasp, matter is stretched, torn, and crushed into oblivion. Does this sound like a horror story? Guess again! Scientists call it a black hole.

Born of a Collapsing Star

As a star runs out of fuel, it cools and eventually collapses under the force of its own gravity. If the collapsing star is massive enough, it may shrink enough to become a black hole. The resulting gravitational attraction is so enormous that even light cannot escape!

Scientists predict that at the center of the black hole is a *singularity,* a tiny point of incredible density, temperature, and pressure. The area around the singularity is called the *event horizon.* The event horizon represents the boundary of the black hole. Anything that crosses the event horizon, including light, will eventually be pulled into the black hole. As matter comes near the event horizon, the matter begins to swirl in much the same way that water swirls down a drain.

▲ *The Hubble Space Telescope*

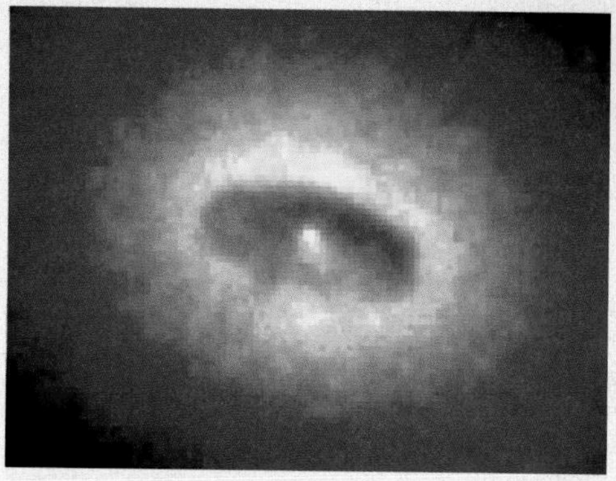

▲ *This photograph of M87 was taken by the Hubble Space Telescope.*

The Story of M87

For years, scientists had theorized about black holes but hadn't actually found one. Then in 1994, scientists found something strange at the core of a galaxy called M87. Scientists detected a disk-shaped cloud of gas with a diameter of 60 light-years, rotating at about 2 million kilometers per hour. When scientists realized that a mass more than 2 billion times that of the sun was crammed into a space no bigger than our solar system, they knew that something was pulling in the gases at the center of the galaxy.

Many astronomers think that black holes, such as the one in M87, lie at the heart of many galaxies. Some scientists suggest that there is a giant black hole at the center of our own Milky Way galaxy. But don't worry. The Earth is too far away to be caught.

Modeling a Black Hole

▶ Make a model to show how a black hole pulls in the matter surrounding it. Indicate the singularity and event horizon.

124

Answers to Modeling a Black Hole

Encourage students to use a variety of materials and to clearly mark the important parts of the black hole with toothpicks or flags.

CAREERS

ASTROPHYSICIST

Jocelyn Bell-Burnell became fascinated with astronomy at an early age. As a research student at Cambridge University, Bell-Burnell discovered pulsars, celestial objects that emit radio waves at short and regular intervals. Today Bell-Burnell is a leading expert in the field of astrophysics and the study of stars. She is currently head of the physics department at the Open University, in Milton Keynes, England.

At Cambridge University in 1967, Bell-Burnell and her adviser, Antony Hewish, completed work on a gigantic radio telescope designed to pick up signals from quasars. Bell-Burnell's job was to operate the telescope and analyze the "chart paper" recordings of the telescope on a graph. Each day, the telescope recorded 29.2 m of chart paper! After a month of operating the telescope, Bell-Burnell noticed a few "bits of scruff" that she could not explain—they were very short, pulsating radio signals. The signals were only 6.3 mm long, and they occurred only once every 4 days. What Bell-Burnell had accidentally found was a needle in a cosmic haystack!

LGM 1

Bell-Burnell and Hewish struggled to find the source of this mysterious new signal. They double-checked the equipment and began eliminating all of the possible sources of the signal, such as satellites, television, and radar. Because they could not rule out that the signal was coming from aliens, Bell-Burnell and Hewish called it LGM 1. Can you guess why? LGM stood for "Little Green Men"!

The Answer: Neutron Stars

Shortly after finding the first signal, Bell-Burnell discovered yet another strange, pulsing signal within the vast quantity of chart paper. This signal was similar to the first, except that it came from the other side of the sky. To Bell-Burnell, this second signal was exciting because it meant that her first signal was not of local origin and that she had stumbled on a new and unknown signal from space! By January 1968, Bell-Burnell had discovered two more pulsating signals. In March of that year, her findings were published, to the amazement of the scientific community. The scientific press coined the term *pulsars,* from pulsating radio stars. Bell-Burnell and other scientists reached the conclusion that her "bits of scruff" were caused by rapidly spinning neutron stars!

▲ *An artist's depiction of a pulsar*

Star Tracking

▶ Pick out a bright star in the sky, and keep a record of its position in relation to a reference point, such as a tree or building. Each night, record what time the star appears at this point in the sky. Do you notice a pattern?

CAREERS

Astrophysicist–Jocelyn Bell-Burnell

Background

One of the most fascinating properties of neutron stars is their incredible mass. Most neutron stars are only about 10 to 16 km in diameter, but their mass can be equal to the mass of our sun! The mass of a neutron star is so great that if you could stand on its surface and drop a coin, the coin would hit the ground at half the speed of light!

In 1991, two planets were discovered near a pulsar in the Virgo constellation. This discovery was remarkable because planets had not been detected beyond our solar system, and it suggested that there may be more planets in the universe than astronomers had previously imagined. It is extremely doubtful, however, that these two planets support life because the nearby neutron star bombards them with lethal radiation.

Answer to Star Tracking

This exercise helps students learn to make accurate astronomical observations over an extended period of time. Students should discover that the stars move in accordance with sidereal time, or "star time," in which a day lasts 23 hours and 56 minutes.

Chapter Organizer

CHAPTER ORGANIZATION	TIME MINUTES	OBJECTIVES	LABS, INVESTIGATIONS, AND DEMONSTRATIONS
Chapter Opener pp. 126–127	45	National Standards: UCP 2, SAI 1, ST 1, 2, SPSP 5, HNS 1, 3	**Start-Up Activity,** Rocket Fun, p. 127
Section 1 Rocket Science	45	▶ Outline the early development of rocket technology. ▶ Explain how a rocket works. ▶ Explain the difference between orbital velocity and escape velocity. UCP 2–5, SAI 1, ST 2, SPSP 5, HNS 1, 3; Labs SAI 1, ST 1	**Demonstration,** p. 128 in ATE **Design Your Own,** Water Rockets Save the Day! p. 168 **Datasheets for LabBook,** Water Rockets Save the Day! **Whiz-Bang Demonstrations,** Rocket Science
Section 2 Artificial Satellites	90	▶ Describe how the launch of the first satellite started the space race. ▶ Explain why some orbits are better than others for communications satellites. ▶ Describe how the satellite program has given us a better understanding of the Earth as a global system. UCP 3, 4, SAI 1, ST 2, SPSP 5, HNS 1, 3	**Inquiry Labs,** Crash Landing
Section 3 Space Probes	90	▶ Describe some of the discoveries made by space probes. ▶ Explain how space-probe missions help us better understand the Earth. ▶ Describe how future space-probe missions will differ from the original missions to the planets. UCP 4, 5, ST 2, SPSP 5, HNS 1, 3	**Long-Term Projects and Research Ideas,** Space Voyage
Section 4 Living and Working in Space	90	▶ Summarize the benefits of the manned space program. ▶ Explain how large projects such as the Apollo program and the *International Space Station* developed. ▶ Identify future possibilities for human exploration of space. UCP 4, 5, SAI 1, ST 2, SPSP 5, HNS 1, 3; Labs UCP 2, SAI 1, ST 1, 2	**Demonstration,** O-Ring Failure, p. 144 in ATE **Making Models,** Reach for the Stars, p. 148 **Datasheets for LabBook,** Reach for the Stars **Inquiry Labs,** Space Fitness **EcoLabs and Field Activities,** There's a Space for Us

See page **T23** *for a complete correlation of this book with the*

NATIONAL SCIENCE EDUCATION STANDARDS.

TECHNOLOGY RESOURCES

Guided Reading Audio CD
English or Spanish, Chapter 5

One-Stop Planner CD-ROM with Test Generator

CNN. **Science, Technology & Society,**
Mars Pathfinder, Segment 28
Surveying the Red Planet, Segment 29

Scientists in Action, Growing Plants in Space, Segment 16

Chapter 5 • Exploring Space

CLASSROOM WORKSHEETS, TRANSPARENCIES, AND RESOURCES	SCIENCE INTEGRATION AND CONNECTIONS	REVIEW AND ASSESSMENT
Directed Reading Worksheet **Science Puzzlers, Twisters & Teasers**		
Directed Reading Worksheet, Section 1 **Transparency 199,** How Rockets Work **Reinforcement Worksheet,** Ronnie Rocket	**Multicultural Connection,** p. 128 in ATE **Cross-Disciplinary Focus,** p. 129 in ATE **Connect to Physical Science,** p. 131 in ATE **MathBreak,** It's Just Rocket Science, p. 131	**Homework,** p. 130 in ATE **Section Review,** p. 131 **Quiz,** p. 131 in ATE **Alternative Assessment,** p. 131 in ATE
Directed Reading Worksheet, Section 2	**Multicultural Connection,** p. 133 in ATE **Real-World Connection,** p. 133 in ATE **Apply,** p. 133 **Environment Connection,** p. 134 **Connect to Physical Science,** p. 134 in ATE	**Self-Check,** p. 133 **Homework,** p. 135 in ATE **Section Review,** p. 135 **Quiz,** p. 135 in ATE **Alternative Assessment,** p. 135 in ATE
Directed Reading Worksheet, Section 3 **Transparency 200,** The Position of Space Probes **Transparency 251,** Forming Positive and Negative Ions **Critical Thinking Worksheet,** Spacecraft R' Us **Reinforcement Worksheet,** Probing Space	**Connect to Physical Science,** p. 138 in ATE **Cross-Disciplinary Focus,** p. 138 in ATE **Cross-Disciplinary Focus,** p. 139 in ATE **Connect to Physical Science,** p. 140 in ATE **Biology Connection,** p. 141 **Holt Anthology of Science Fiction:** *Why I Left Harry's All-Night Hamburgers*	**Homework,** p. 140 in ATE **Section Review,** p. 141 **Quiz,** p. 141 in ATE **Alternative Assessment,** p. 141 in ATE
Directed Reading Worksheet, Section 4	**Multicultural Connection,** p. 143 in ATE **Connect to Physical Science,** p. 143 in ATE **Connect to Life Science,** p. 143 in ATE **Biology Connection,** p. 144 **Math and More,** p. 144 in ATE **Cross-Disciplinary Focus,** p. 146 in ATE **Across the Sciences:** *International Space Station,* p. 154	**Homework,** pp. 143, 144 in ATE **Section Review,** p. 147 **Quiz,** p. 147 in ATE **Alternative Assessment,** p. 147 in ATE

END-OF-CHAPTER REVIEW AND ASSESSMENT

Chapter Review in Study Guide
Vocabulary and Notes in Study Guide
Chapter Tests with Performance-Based Assessment, Chapter 5 Test
Chapter Tests with Performance-Based Assessment, Performance-Based Assessment 5
Concept Mapping Transparency 22

internetconnect

go.hrw.com Holt, Rinehart and Winston On-line Resources

go.hrw.com

For worksheets and other teaching aids related to this chapter, visit the HRW Web site and type in the keyword: **HSTEXP**

sciLINKS NSTA National Science Teachers Association

www.scilinks.org

Encourage students to use the *sci*LINKS numbers listed in the internet connect boxes to access information and resources on the **NSTA** Web site.

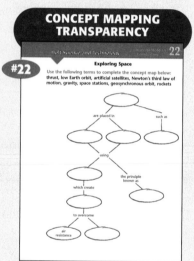

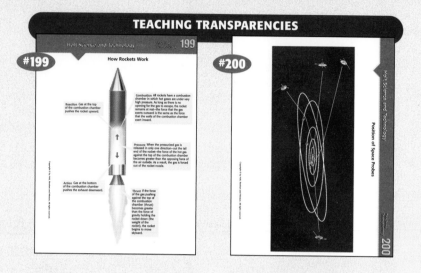

Chapter Resources & Worksheets

Visual Resources

TEACHING TRANSPARENCIES

#199

#200

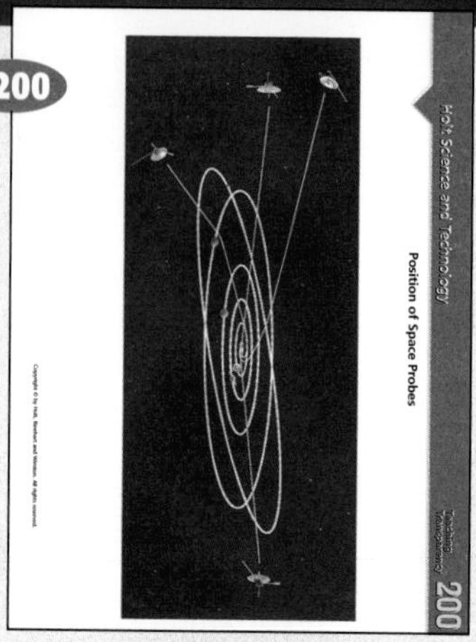

TEACHING TRANSPARENCIES

#251

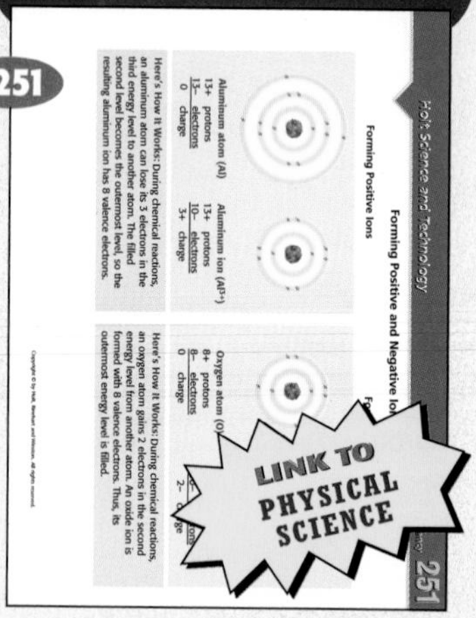

CONCEPT MAPPING TRANSPARENCY

#22

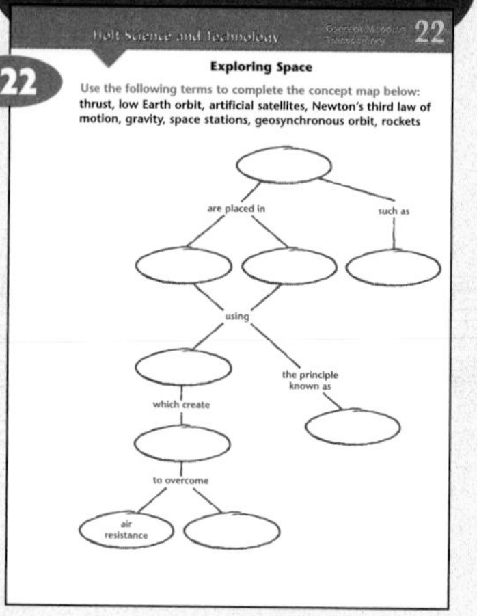

Meeting Individual Needs

DIRECTED READING

#5

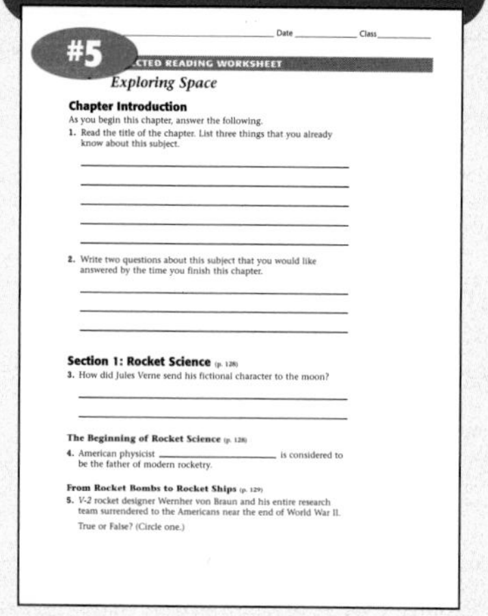

Date ______ Class ______

DIRECTED READING WORKSHEET

Exploring Space

Chapter Introduction

As you begin this chapter, answer the following.

1. Read the title of the chapter. List three things that you already know about this subject.

2. Write two questions about this subject that you would like answered by the time you finish this chapter.

Section 1: Rocket Science (p. 128)

3. How did Jules Verne send his fictional character to the moon?

The Beginning of Rocket Science (p. 128)

4. American physicist ______ is considered to be the father of modern rocketry.

From Rocket Bombs to Rocket Ships (p. 129)

5. *V-2* rocket designer Wernher von Braun and his entire research team surrendered to the Americans near the end of World War II.

True or False? (Circle one.)

REINFORCEMENT & VOCABULARY REVIEW

#5

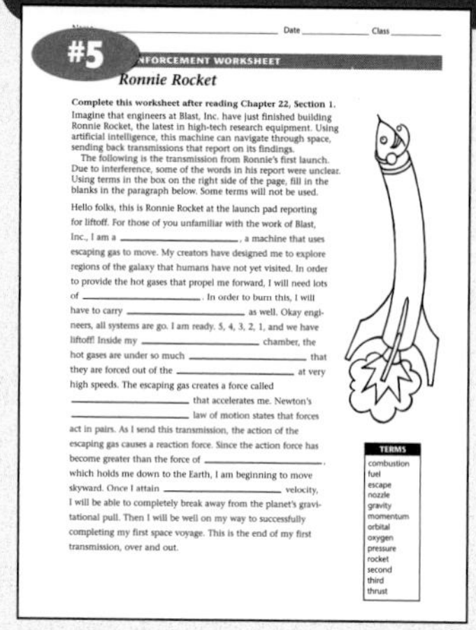

Date ______ Class ______

REINFORCEMENT WORKSHEET

Ronnie Rocket

Complete this worksheet after reading Chapter 22, Section 1.

Imagine that engineers at Blast, Inc. have just finished building Ronnie Rocket, the latest in high-tech research equipment. Using artificial intelligence, this machine can navigate through space, sending back transmissions that report on its findings.

The following is the transmission from Ronnie's first launch. Due to interference, some of the words in his report were unclear. Using terms in the box on the right side of the page, fill in the blanks in the paragraph below. Some terms will not be used.

Hello folks, this is Ronnie Rocket at the launch pad reporting for liftoff. For those of you unfamiliar with the work of Blast, Inc., I am a ______, a machine that uses escaping gas to move. My creators have designed me to explore regions of the galaxy that humans have not yet visited. In order to provide the hot gases that propel me forward, I will need lots of ______. In order to burn this, I will have to carry ______ as well. Okay engineers, all systems are go. I am ready. 5, 4, 3, 2, 1, and we have liftoff! Inside my ______ chamber, the hot gases are under so much ______ that they are forced out of the ______ at very high speeds. The escaping gas creates a force called ______ that accelerates me. Newton's ______ law of motion states that forces act in pairs. As I send this transmission, the action of the escaping gas causes a reaction force. Since the action force has become greater than the force of ______, which holds me down to the Earth, I am beginning to move skyward. Once I attain ______ velocity, I will be able to completely break away from the planet's gravitational pull. Then I will be well on my way to successfully completing my first space voyage. This is the end of my first transmission, over and out.

TERMS
combustion
fuel
escape
nozzle
gravity
momentum
orbital
oxygen
pressure
rocket
second
third
thrust

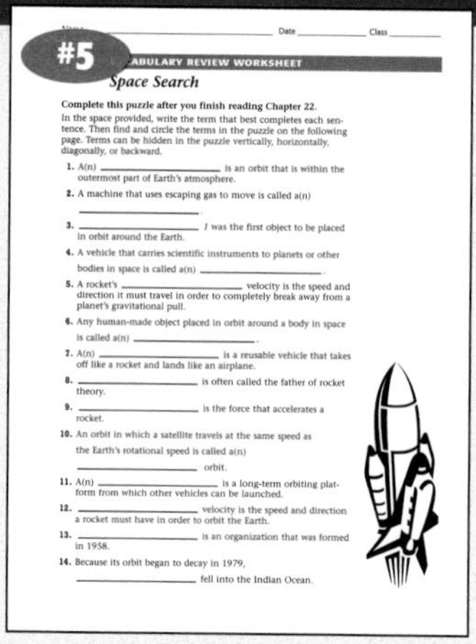

Date ______ Class ______

VOCABULARY REVIEW WORKSHEET

Space Search

Complete this puzzle after you finish reading Chapter 22.

In the space provided, write the term that best completes each sentence. Then find and circle the terms in the puzzle on the following page. Terms can be hidden in the puzzle vertically, horizontally, diagonally, or backward.

1. A(n) ______ is an orbit that is within the outermost part of Earth's atmosphere.
2. A machine that uses escaping gas to move is called a(n) ______.
3. ______ *I* was the first object to be placed in orbit around the Earth.
4. A vehicle that carries scientific instruments to planets or other bodies in space is called a(n) ______.
5. A rocket's ______ velocity is the speed and direction it must travel in order to completely break away from a planet's gravitational pull.
6. Any human-made object placed in orbit around a body in space is called a(n) ______.
7. A(n) ______ is a reusable vehicle that takes off like a rocket and lands like an airplane.
8. ______ is often called the father of rocket theory.
9. ______ is the force that accelerates a rocket.
10. An orbit in which a satellite travels at the same speed as the Earth's rotational speed is called a(n) ______ orbit.
11. A(n) ______ is a long-term orbiting platform from which other vehicles can be launched.
12. ______ velocity is the speed and direction a rocket must have in order to orbit the Earth.
13. ______ is an organization that was formed in 1958.
14. Because its orbit began to decay in 1979, ______ fell into the Indian Ocean.

SCIENCE PUZZLERS, TWISTERS & TEASERS

#5

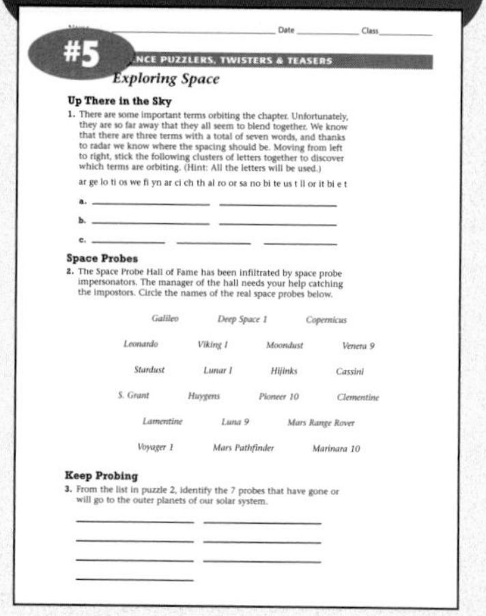

Date ______ Class ______

SCIENCE PUZZLERS, TWISTERS & TEASERS

Exploring Space

Up There in the Sky

1. There are some important terms orbiting the chapter. Unfortunately, they are so far away that they all seem to blend together. We know that there are three terms with a total of seven words, and thanks to radar we know where the spacing should be. Moving from left to right, stick the following clusters of letters together to discover which terms are orbiting. (Hint: All the letters will be used.)

ar ge lo ti os we fi yn ar ci ch th al ro or sa no bi te us t ll or it bi e t

a. ______ ______
b. ______ ______
c. ______ ______ ______

Space Probes

2. The Space Probe Hall of Fame has been infiltrated by space probe impersonators. The manager of the hall needs your help catching the impostors. Circle the names of the real space probes below.

Galileo *Deep Space 1* *Copernicus*
Leonardo *Viking I* *Moondust* *Venera 9*
Stardust *Lunar I* *Hijinks* *Cassini*
S. Grant *Huygens* *Pioneer 10* *Clementine*
Lamentine *Luna 9* *Mars Range Rover*
Voyager 1 *Mars Pathfinder* *Marinara 10*

Keep Probing

3. From the list in puzzle 2, identify the 7 probes that have gone or will go to the outer planets of our solar system.

Review & Assessment

STUDY GUIDE

#5 VOCABULARY & NOTES WORKSHEET

Exploring Space

By studying the Vocabulary and Notes listed for each section below, you can gain a better understanding of this chapter.

SECTION 1
Vocabulary
In your own words, write a definition for the following terms in the space provided.

1. rocket

2. NASA

3. thrust

4. orbital velocity

5. escape velocity

Notes
Read the following section highlights. Then, in your own words, write the highlights in your ScienceLog.
• Two pioneers of rocketry were Konstantin Tsiolkovsky and Robert Goddard.
• Rockets work according to Newton's third law of motion—for every action there is an equal and opposite reaction.
• NASA was formed in 1958, combining rocket research from several programs. It was originally formed to compete with the Soviet Union's rocket program.

SECTION 2
Vocabulary
In your own words, write a definition for the following terms in the space provided.

1. artificial satellite

#5 CHAPTER REVIEW WORKSHEET

Exploring Space

USING VOCABULARY
For each pair of terms, explain the difference in their meaning:

1. geosynchronous orbit/low Earth orbit

2. space probe/space shuttle

3. artificial satellite/moon

To complete the following sentences, choose the correct term from each pair of terms listed below:

4. The force that accelerates a rocket is called _____ (escape velocity or thrust)

5. Rockets need to have _____ in order to burn their fuel. (oxygen or nitrogen)

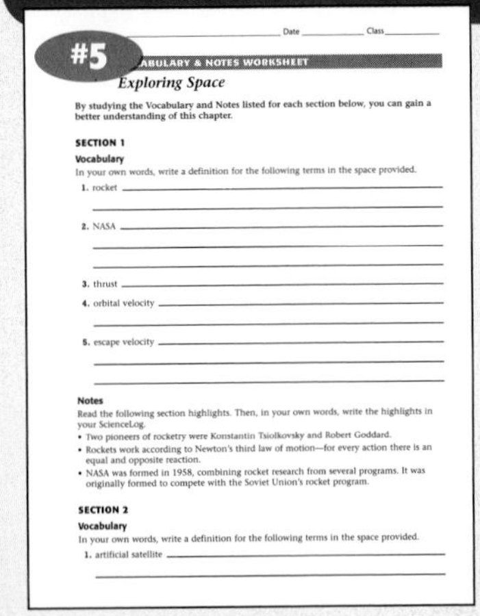

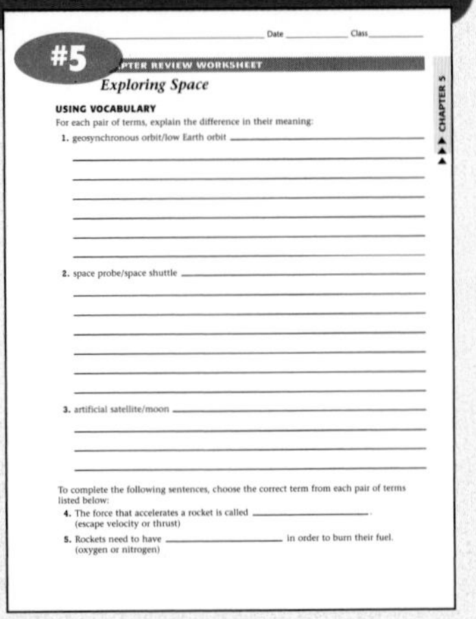

CHAPTER TESTS WITH PERFORMANCE-BASED ASSESSMENT

#5 EXPLORING SPACE

Chapter 5 Test

USING VOCABULARY
To complete the following sentences, choose the correct term from each pair of terms listed, and write the term in the blank.

1. A _____ is a reusable vehicle that lands like an airplane. (rocket or space shuttle)

2. The *Clementine* is a(n) _____ that discovered water at the south pole of the moon. (space probe or artificial satellite)

3. _____ is used for weather and communication satellites. (Low Earth orbit or Geosynchronous orbit)

4. *Skylab* was a(n) _____ that allowed scientists to conduct a wide variety of scientific studies. (space station or artificial satellite)

5. A _____ works by using hot gases under very high pressure. (low Earth orbit or rocket)

UNDERSTANDING CONCEPTS
Multiple Choice
Circle the correct answer.

6. _____ was the first person to build rockets.
a. Konstantin Tsiolkovsky   c. Wernher von Braun
b. Robert Goddard   d. Jules Verne

7. _____ transmitted the first images of the surface of Venus back to Earth.
a. *Venera 9*   c. *Viking 2*
b. *Magellan*   d. *Sojourner*

8. The first weather satellite to be placed in orbit around the Earth was the _____
a. *Sputnik 1*.   c. *Tiros 1*.
b. *Explorer 1*.   d. *Echo 1*.

9. _____ have allowed scientists to study the effect of humans on the global environment by remote sensing.
a. Satellites   c. Space stations
b. Space probes   d. Space shuttles

10. _____ was formed in response to the alarm the United States felt over possible Soviet superiority in space.
a. NASA   c. Geosynchronous orbit
b. Landsat   d. The International Space Station

#5 EXPLORING SPACE

Chapter 5 Performance-Based Assessment

Objective
You will make a model of the Earth and its geosynchronous orbit (GEO) to determine the least number of communications satellites needed to transmit a television program around the world.

Know the Score!
As you work through the activity, keep in mind that you will be earning a grade for the following:
• how well you follow the instructions to build the model (30%)
• how clearly and accurately you draw the communications paths on your model (30%)
• how well you complete your analysis (40%)

MATERIALS
• copy of diagram
• 10 × 10 cm piece of plastic foam
• cardboard tube
• ruler
• pushpins with colored heads (four of one color, three of different colors)

Procedure
1. Lay the diagram on the foam so that both circles rest on the foam. Set the end of the cardboard tube inside the smaller circle. Holding the tube in place, stick pins through the paper and foam at the points marked A, B, C, D, and S1.
   The curved surface of the cylinder represents the surface of the Earth. Points A, B, C, and D indicate different positions on Earth's surface. The outer circle of your model represents the geosynchronous orbit, or GEO. S1 represents a communications satellite in GEO directly over a television station at position A. On the diagram below left, label the GEO and the direction S1 is traveling.

2. On the same diagram, draw a line from position A to satellite S1. This represents the path that a television signal must travel before it is transmitted to other parts of the world.

3. Bend down so that your eye is level with the edge of the paper, and the pin at point C is directly in front of you. Why are you unable to see satellite S1?

4. Slowly rotate the model clockwise and stop when you see satellite S1. Stick a pin on the GEO at the point where S1 became visible. Label this new satellite S2.

5. Now rotate the model counterclockwise until satellite S1 reappears to the left of the roll. Insert a pin at this position on GEO, and label this satellite S3.

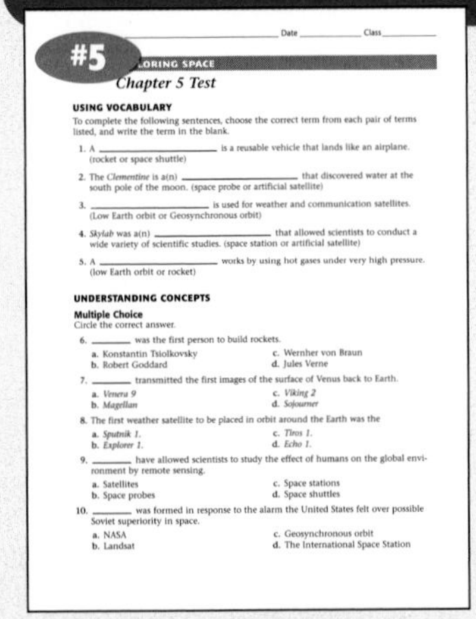

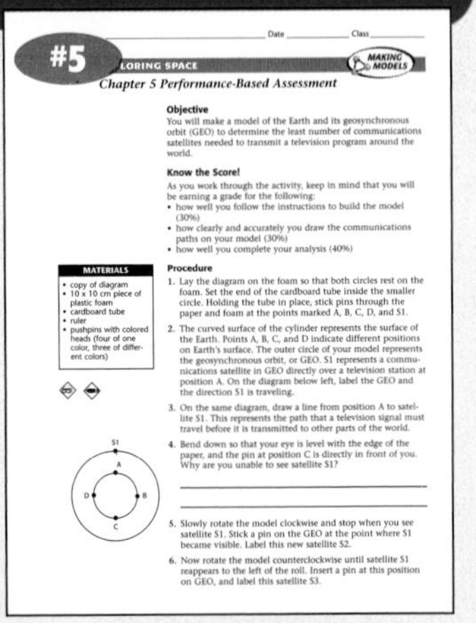

Lab Worksheets

INQUIRY LABS

#5 STUDENT WORKSHEET   **DESIGN YOUR OWN**

Crash Landing

Yuri Gagarin was the first person to travel in space. His mission was launched on April 12, 1961, and lasted 108 minutes.

He described the incredible view from his capsule as follows: "I could clearly see the outlines of continents, islands, and rivers. The horizon presents a very unusual beauty. A delicate blue halo surrounds the Earth, merging with the blackness of space in which the stars are bright and clear cut."

Gagarin almost didn't live to tell the tale of his historic flight. In the early days of the Soviet space program, the design and construction of the descent module were very experimental. In fact, the odds were 50:50 that Gagarin would survive his landing.

In this activity, you will evaluate the design and safety of early Soviet descent modules by building your own model.

USEFUL TERMS
cosmonaut
a Russian space traveler; literally, "universe sailor"
astronaut
an American space traveler; literally, "star sailor"
descent module
the vehicle used by space travelers to return to the Earth's surface
hatch
the door of the descent module

MATERIALS
• halved tennis ball
• 50 cm of masking tape
• 2 m of string
• scissors
• 2.5 × 2.5 cm cube of modeling clay
• 45 × 60 cm plastic garbage bag
• 2 small, raw eggs

SCIENTIFIC METHOD
Ask a Question
How do you design a model of a Soviet descent module that will land safely?

Procedure
1. Meet with your partner and share ideas about building your model. Consider the materials you have been given and think of the best way to use them to solve the problem. Keep in mind the following points:
• You will have one class period to design, build, and test the model and one class period to launch your model.
• Carefully consider your design before cutting any materials. No replacement building materials will be provided.
• For your launch to be successful, the hatch must face away from the ground and the egg must remain undamaged.

2. Design your model. With your partner, decide how to accomplish the objective using the materials provided.

3. Draw your design. Sketch your proposed design in your ScienceLog.

4. Build the model. Construct your model based on your drawing. Caution: Be extremely careful if you are poking holes in the tennis ball.

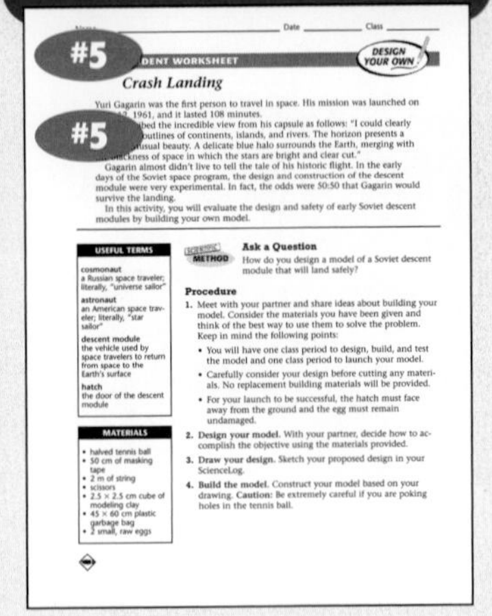

ECOLABS & FIELD ACTIVITIES

#5 STUDENT WORKSHEET   **DESIGN YOUR OWN**

There's a Space for Us

To: Dr. Ino Best, President of Arcotworm, Inc.
From: Dr. Noelle Deuitt, Director of Space Management
       International Union of Nations

Thanks to arcologically conscious companies like yours, we have made the most of the limited space on this planet. Unfortunately, the ever-increasing human population will exceed Earth's capacity in less than 15 years. We have no choice but to begin moving people to colonies beyond Earth. Mars is our first destination. Gather your best team of arcologists to design a colony. Except for the initial supplies, all materials must be from Mars. Consider the following as you design the colony: water supply, air supply, temperature control, source of energy, waste management, and food production. I trust that your arcologists can build an award-winning, life-sustaining colony.

LONG-TERM PROJECTS & RESEARCH IDEAS

#5 STUDENT WORKSHEET   **DESIGN YOUR OWN**

Space Voyage

Imagine that you are the lead scientist planning a space expedition to Proxima Centauri, the nearest star to the sun. You must do a lot of research on the current technology that is available to your crew. You've spent months working with engineers and space travel experts designing the equipment and plotting the course. But, before the crew can make such a huge trek, you must prepare them for it.

The Lead Scientist Speaks
1. Plan this trip using what is currently known about space and space travel. Where is Proxima Centauri? How long will the trip to Proxima Centauri take? (Don't forget that faster-than-light travel is impossible.) What kind of equipment will the crew need for a successful expedition? Prepare a lecture for the crew before they take off. What will they need to know about the trip? Videotape the lecture and share it with your class.

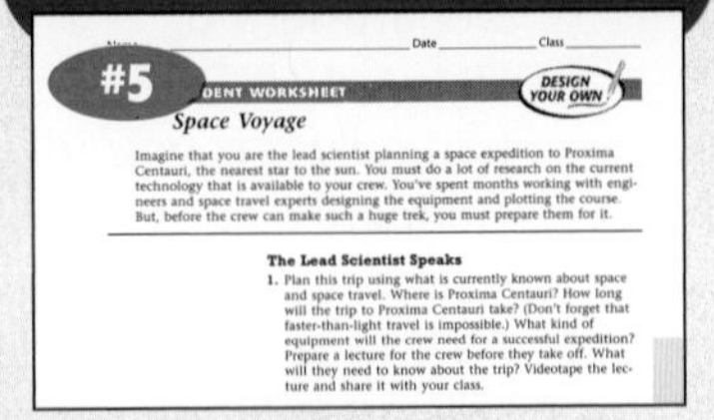

WHIZ-BANG DEMONSTRATIONS

#5 TEACHER-LED DEMONSTRATION   **MAKING MODELS**

Rocket Science

Purpose
Students learn about Newton's third law of motion and the basics of rocketry.

Time Required
20–25 minutes

Lab Ratings
TEACHER PREP
CONCEPT LEVEL
CLEAN UP

MATERIALS
• index card (3 × 8 in.)
• film canister with a lid that seals on the inside—do not use canisters with lids that close around the outside
• transparent tape
• small jar of construction paper
• scissors
• small jar of tap water
• seltzer tablet

What to Do
1. Tell students that in this demonstration you are going to prepare and launch a model rocket.
2. Roll the index card to form a tube 3 cm in diameter, and then slide the canister inside. Align the lid of the canister with one end of the index card, and securely tape the canister and the tube together. (The activity will not work as well if the paper and canisters come apart.)

3. Seal the tube by taping the seam where the edges of the card meet.

4. Cut two triangular paper fins from the construction paper. Attach them to the rocket just above its base and just below its midpoint. Explain to students that the fins act to stabilize the rocket in flight. Make a small cone of paper, and attach it to the top of the cylinder with tape to create the rocket's nose.

5. Take students outside to launch your rocket. If it is windy, place a quarter in the film canister to keep the rocket from blowing over.

6. Add enough water to fill approximately one-quarter of the canister.

7. Cut the seltzer tablet in half, and add one half to the water. QUICKLY snap the lid in place.

8. Set the rocket lid-side down on the ground. Step back, and prepare for liftoff! Rockets can shoot more than 5 m into the air.

Safety Information
The rocket may take 15–20 seconds to build up enough pressure to launch. Do not approach the rocket prematurely. Wear safety goggles when launching the rocket.

continued...

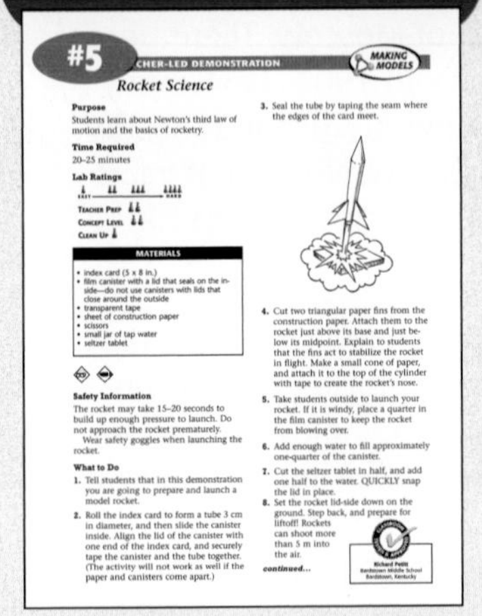

DATASHEETS FOR LABBOOK

Name _____ Date _____ Class _____

#5 Water Rockets Save the Day!

#5 Reach for the Stars

2. Mr. Fries has told you that you can obtain in many samples as you need from Groups A, B, and C. Your teacher will have these samples ready for you to observe.

3. Make a data table like the one below to list your observations. Make as many observations as you can about the potatoes in Group A, Group B, and Group C.

Observations	
Group A:	
Group B:	

Form a Hypothesis
4. You have identified a problem and made your observations. Now you can make a hypothesis. Write a clear hypothesis about what you think will be the outcome of your tests.

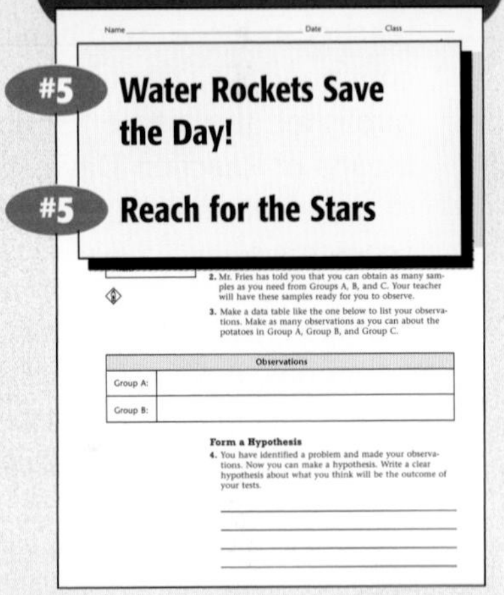

Applications & Extensions

CRITICAL THINKING & PROBLEM SOLVING

#5 CRITICAL THINKING WORKSHEET

Spacecraft R' Us

You receive the following memo from your boss.

Dear Spacecraft R' Us employee:

Spacecraft R' Us is having a spacecraft design contest!

Each employee must submit a design within 5 days. The company will build and launch the winning spacecraft! Your design should follow the contest rules below:

Contest Rules
The spacecraft must:
• benefit the lives of Earthlings
• serve a worthy purpose and provide valuable data

Your first step should be to decide whether your proposed spacecraft will be a probe, a satellite in LEO, or a satellite in GEO.

Good luck!
Emma Vous, President
Spacecraft R' Us

Compare and Contrast
1. a. What is the difference between a satellite and a probe regarding where they travel in space?

b. What is the difference between a satellite and a probe with regard to orbital velocity and escape velocity? Explain.

SCIENCE TECHNOLOGY

#28 Science in the News: Critical Thinking Worksheets

Segment 28
Mars Pathfinder

#29

1. Why do you think *Pathfinder* was able to provide more information than previous _____

2. Why do you think NASA wanted *Pathfinder* to land in rocky terrain instead of in a flatter, safer area?

3. Identify one design characteristic of the *Sojourner* rover that prepared it for the rocky terrain of Mars.

4. Do you think the high cost of space exploration brings? Explain your answer.

SCIENTISTS IN ACTION

#16 Science in the News: Critical Thinking Worksheets

Segment 16
Growing Plants in Space

1. List two types of stress a plant might experience.

2. Why do you think microgravity affects plants so adversely?

3. Why are plants an integral part of long-term space exploration?

4. How could the "reporter genes" discussed in the video be used here on Earth?

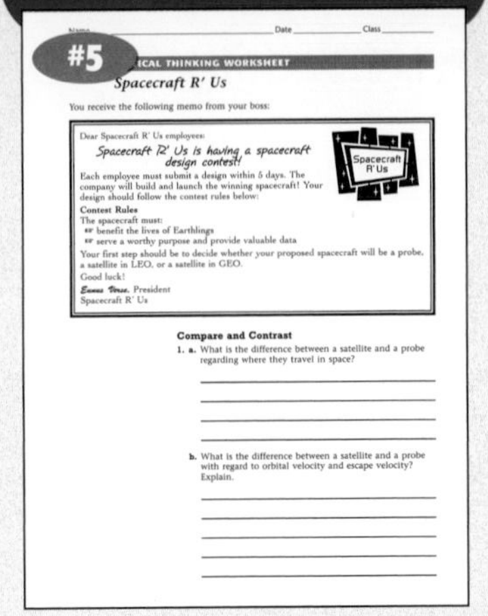

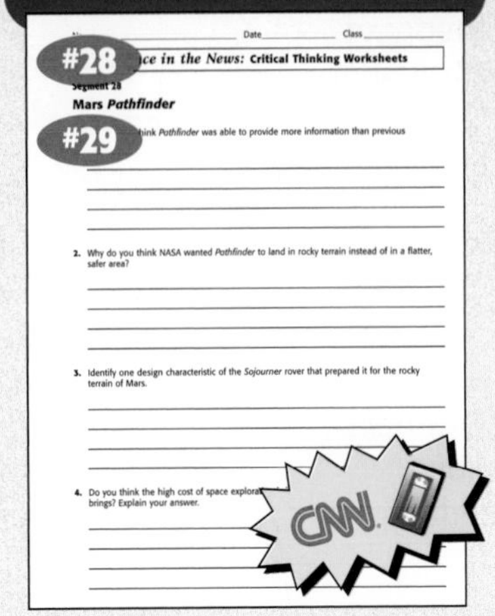

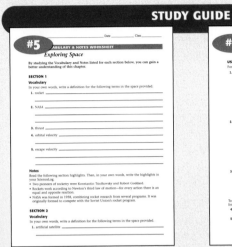

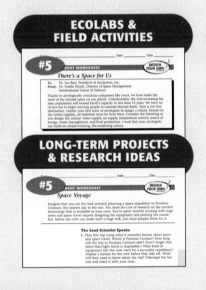

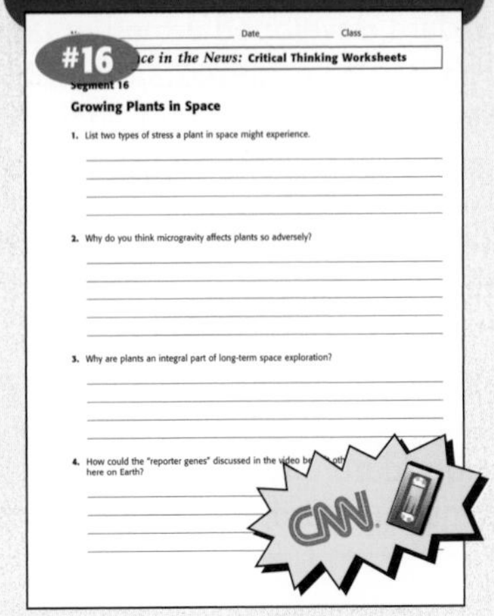

Chapter Background

SECTION 1

Rocket Science

▶ Konstantin Tsiolkovsky (1857–1935)

As a youth, Konstantin Tsiolkovsky, the father of rocket theory, demonstrated a keen interest in science and mathematics. At age 9, a bout of scarlet fever left him partially deaf, and he spent much of his time studying on his own. After studying chemistry, astronomy, mathematics, and mechanics in Moscow, Tsiolkovsky got a job in 1876 as a mathematics teacher in a community north of Moscow. There he continued his scientific pursuits. In 1903, Tsiolkovsky published the article "Exploration of Cosmic Space by Means of Reaction Devices," the culmination of years of theorization about the use of rocket engines for space travel.

- In later years, Tsiolkovsky elaborated on his earlier theories, developing a theory of rocket propulsion and anticipating a number of technologies used in contemporary space exploration, including multistage boosters and the use of chemical propellants to achieve enough thrust to overcome Earth's gravity.

▶ Robert Goddard (1882–1945)

In his youth, Robert Goddard was an enthusiastic reader of science fiction tales of space travel, and at an early age he wrote a paper titled "The Navigation of Space." In 1912, Goddard developed a mathematical theory of rocket propulsion. He achieved a major breakthrough in 1915 when he proved that rocket engines would work in a vacuum and thus could be used for space travel.

- In 1919, Goddard published his research in the landmark paper "A Method of Reaching Extreme Altitudes," in which he argued that rockets could be used to escape Earth's gravity. Some people found Goddard's theories ludicrous. The *New York Times,* for example, scoffed at Goddard and questioned his scientific qualifications. Goddard, undeterred, continued to design and experiment with rockets. In 1926, using a liquid fuel mixture of gasoline and oxygen, Goddard launched his first liquid-fueled rocket, which ascended to a height of nearly 13 m in 2.5 seconds.

- In 1929, Goddard launched his first rocket to carry scientific instruments. The rocket rose about 30 m and then crashed to Earth, where it caught fire. People living nearby called the state fire marshal, who banned Goddard from doing any further rocket tests in Massachusetts. With a Guggenheim grant of $50,000, Goddard set up a test site in an unpopulated area outside of Roswell, New Mexico. He launched increasingly complex rockets that featured innovations such as steering systems, fuel pumps, and cooling mechanisms.

IS THAT A FACT!

- At his death in 1945, Goddard's immense contributions to rocket technology were still relatively unknown. By 1960, however, the U.S. Department of Defense and NASA had fully recognized Goddard's achievements and paid his estate $1 million for the use of his 214 patented rocket-componentry designs. A year later, NASA named the Goddard Space Flight Center in Greenbelt, Maryland, in his honor.

SECTION 2

Artificial Satellites

▶ The Echo Satellites

The United States launched its first communications satellite, *Echo I,* into orbit on August 12, 1960. *Echo I* was surprisingly simple in its design, consisting of an aluminum-coated plastic balloon that inflated to a diameter of 30 m when it reached orbit. From a low

Earth orbit, *Echo I* reflected radio signals back to Earth until 1968. The United States placed a larger aluminized balloon satellite, *Echo II*, in orbit on January 25, 1964. *Echo II* remained functional until 1969.

IS THAT A FACT!

- The *Echo II* satellite was part of the first cooperative space effort between the United States and the Soviet Union, when a radio signal from an observatory in England reflected off *Echo II* and was received in the Soviet Union.

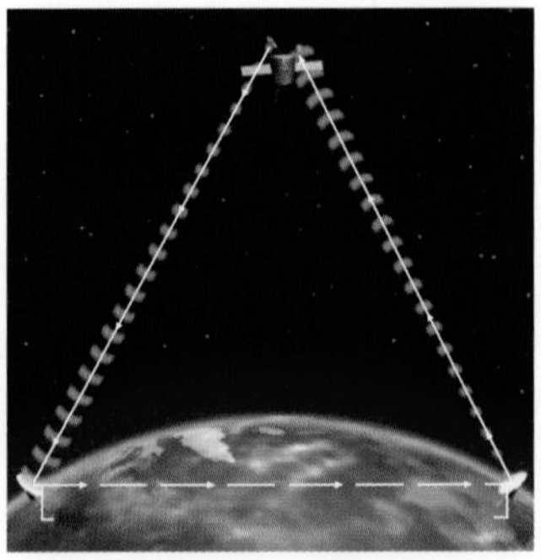

SECTION 3

Space Probes

▶ Soviet Lunar Probes

Although Soviet cosmonauts never landed on the moon, their *Luna* space probes gathered a remarkable amount of lunar data using robotics and remotely controlled devices. In 1966 the *Luna 9* became the first space probe to make a soft landing on the moon (previous probes crash-landed, and one shot past the moon into space). On impact, *Luna 9*'s egg-shaped instrument capsule rolled itself upright and automatically stabilized itself with four spring-loaded mechanisms. *Luna 9* sent the first television images of the lunar landscape back to Earth.

- Perhaps the most impressive of the Soviets' lunar space probes were *Luna 17* and *Luna 18,* which carried the eight-wheeled heavy-duty lunar rovers *Lunokhod 1* and *2.* From Earth, the vehicles were directed around treacherous craters to cover vast expanses of the moon's surface. The rovers took photos, collected soil samples, and carried out other tests. *Lunokhod 1* traveled over the moon's surface for 11 months and even recorded a solar eclipse, during which the temperature plunged 230°C.

SECTION 4

Living and Working in Space

▶ The Daily Routine Aboard Skylab

Measuring 36 m long and 6.4 m high, *Skylab* was luxuriously large in comparison with earlier spacecraft and had both working quarters and a living space. The living area included private sleeping quarters, a galley, a shower, and a suction toilet. Crew members carried out hundreds of astronomical and medical experiments.

- Astronauts were required to document everything they ate; measure the girth of their limbs, waists, and necks to check for muscle-tone loss; and wear electrodes while exercising so that their vital signs could be monitored. Astronauts did enjoy diversions such as "astrobatics"; in fact, *Skylab* astronaut Charles "Pete" Conrad commented, "We never went anywhere straight. We always did a somersault or a flip on the way."

IS THAT A FACT!

- By the time of the Skylab missions, the infamous spacebars and tubes of gooey "spacefood" had been replaced with much more recognizable and palatable frozen, canned, and dehydrated foods. With more than 80 food items to choose from, a crew might whip up a breakfast of scrambled eggs, sausage, strawberries, bread and jam, orange juice, and coffee and finish out the day with a dinner of filet mignon, potato salad, and ice cream.

For background information about teaching strategies and issues, refer to the *Professional Reference for Teachers.*

CHAPTER 5

Exploring Space

Pre-Reading Questions

Students may not know the answers to these questions before reading the chapter, so accept any reasonable response.

Suggested Answers

1. A satellite is any object in orbit around a planet or other body in the universe. A space probe is a human-made vehicle that carries scientific instruments to study objects in the universe.
2. Answers will vary. Students may note how technology developed for the space program has been adapted for life on Earth. They may also describe how scientific studies of planets and moons in our solar system have helped us understand the Earth's environment.
3. Answers will vary. Students may explain how the space stations such as *Skylab* and *Mir* have prepared astronauts to live and work in space. They may also note that the *International Space Station* is the next space station planned.

CHAPTER 5

Exploring Space

Sections

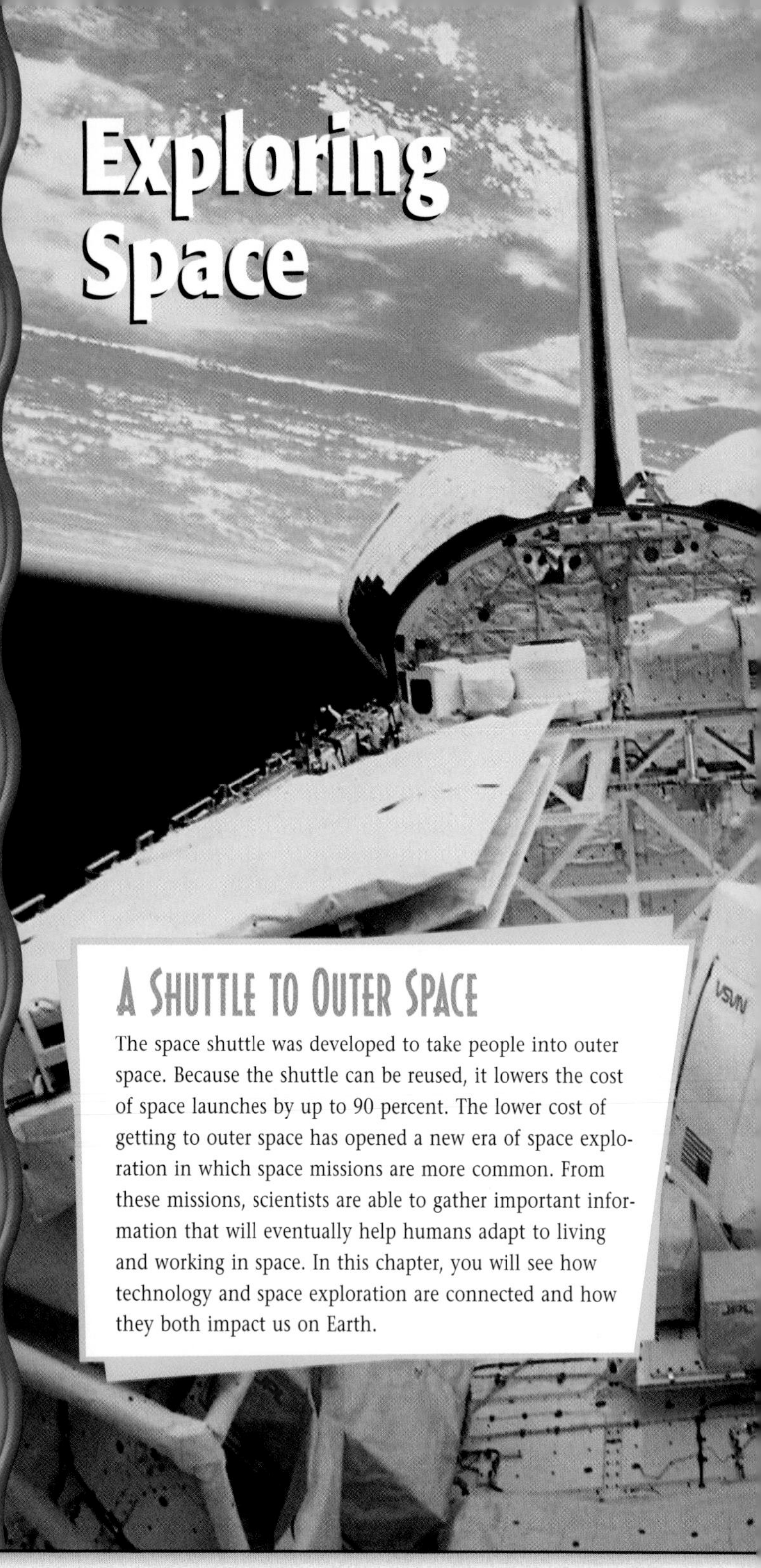

A Shuttle to Outer Space

The space shuttle was developed to take people into outer space. Because the shuttle can be reused, it lowers the cost of space launches by up to 90 percent. The lower cost of getting to outer space has opened a new era of space exploration in which space missions are more common. From these missions, scientists are able to gather important information that will eventually help humans adapt to living and working in space. In this chapter, you will see how technology and space exploration are connected and how they both impact us on Earth.

Pre-Reading Questions

1. What's the difference between a satellite and a space probe?
2. How has the space program benefited our daily lives?
3. How are humans preparing to live in space?

126

internetconnect

HRW On-line Resources
go.hrw.com
For worksheets and other teaching aids, visit the HRW Web site and type in the keyword: **HSTEXP**

sciLINKS NSTA
www.scilinks.com
Use the *sci*LINKS numbers at the end of each chapter for additional resources on the **NSTA** Web site.

Smithsonian Institution
www.si.edu/hrw
Visit the Smithsonian Institution Web site for related on-line resources.

CNNfyi.com
www.cnnfyi.com
Visit the CNN Web site for current events coverage and classroom resources.

START-UP Activity

ROCKET FUN

Rockets are used to send people into space. Rockets work by forcing hot gas out one end of a tube. As this gas escapes in one direction, the rocket moves in the opposite direction. While you may have let a full balloon loose many times before, here you will use a balloon to learn about the principles of rocket propulsion.

Procedure

1. Thread a **string** through a **drinking straw,** and tie the string between two things that won't move, such as chairs. Make sure that the string is tight.
2. Blow into a large **balloon** until it is the size of a grapefruit. Hold the neck of the balloon closed.
3. **Tape** the balloon to the straw so that the opening of the balloon points toward one end of the string.
4. Move the balloon and straw to one end of the string, and then release the neck of the balloon. Record what happens in your ScienceLog.
5. Fill the balloon until it is almost twice the size it was in step 2, and repeat steps 3 and 4. Again record your observations.

Analysis

6. What happened during the second test that was different from the first? Can you figure out why?

START-UP Activity

ROCKET FUN

MATERIALS
For Each Group:
• string
• drinking straw
• large balloon
• tape

Teacher's Notes

Discuss the limitations of using a balloon to model a launch vehicle. If the balloon were to "launch" something, what improvements should be made? (Students may suggest that the balloon would need to be more powerful and able to sustain thrust for a longer period of time. In addition, the balloon would need a steering or guidance device.)

Answer to START-UP Activity

6. Sample answer: The balloon went faster and farther because the air inside it was under greater pressure. In addition, the balloon had to expel more air in the second trial.

SECTION 1

Focus

Rocket Science

In this section, students learn about the contributions Konstantin Tsiolkovsky, Robert Goddard, and Wernher von Braun made to early rocket technology. Students also learn about the establishment of NASA and the development of rockets powerful enough to launch spacecraft into space. The section concludes with a discussion of the principles of rocket propulsion.

Bellringer

Ask students the question:

Why can't a commercial airplane be used for space exploration?

(Students may reason that commercial airplanes cannot carry enough fuel for space exploration, that their engines are not powerful enough to escape Earth's gravity, and that they cannot withstand the extreme cold of space or the heat of reentry into Earth's atmosphere. Point out that airplanes also require oxygen to burn fuel.) Sheltered English

1 Motivate

DEMONSTRATION

Attach a pre-stretched balloon over the mouth of a plastic bottle, and put the bottle in a bucket. Pour hot (but not boiling) water into the bucket. Explain that as the gases in the balloon become hot, they expand, causing the balloon to inflate. Explain that the expansion of hot gases is powerful enough to launch rockets into space. As rocket fuel burns, the heated gases inside the rocket expand. As the gases escape through the rocket nozzle, the rocket reacts by moving in the opposite direction—skyward.

SECTION 1 READING WARM-UP

Terms to Learn

rocket
NASA
thrust
orbital velocity
escape velocity

What You'll Do

- Outline the early development of rocket technology.
- Explain how a rocket works.
- Explain the difference between orbital velocity and escape velocity.

Rocket Science

How would you get to the moon? Before the invention of rockets, people could only dream of going into outer space. Science fiction writers, such as Jules Verne, were able to dress those dreams in scientific clothing by using what seemed like reasonable means of getting into space. For example, in a story he wrote in 1865, some of Verne's characters rode a capsule to the moon shot from a giant 900 ft long cannon.

But, as growing knowledge about the heavens was stimulating the imagination of writers and readers alike, an invention was slowly being developed that would become the key to exploring space. This was the rocket. A **rocket** is a machine that uses escaping gas to move.

The Beginning of Rocket Science

Around the year 1900, a Russian high school teacher named Konstantin Tsiolkovsky (KAHN stan teen TSEE uhl KAHV skee) began trying to understand the reasoning behind the motion of rockets. Tsiolkovsky's inspiration came from the fantastic, imaginative stories of Jules Verne. Tsiolkovsky believed that rockets were the key to space exploration. In his words, "The Earth is the cradle of mankind. But one does not have to live in the cradle forever." Tsiolkovsky is considered the father of rocket theory.

Although Tsiolkovsky explained how rockets work, he never built any rockets himself. That was left to American physicist Robert Goddard, who became known as the father of modern rocketry.

Figure 1 *Robert Goddard tests one of his early rockets.*

Modern Rocketry Gets a Boost Goddard, shown in **Figure 1**, conducted many rocket experiments in Massachusetts from 1915 to 1930. He then moved to New Mexico, where deserts provided enough room to conduct his tests safely. Between 1930 and 1941, Goddard tested more than 150 rocket engines, and by the time of World War II, his work was receiving much attention, most notably from the United States military.

128

Multicultural CONNECTION

Many nations have taken an active role in space exploration. China launched its first satellite in 1970, and by late 1980, it was launching Western communications satellites in its advanced booster rockets. Before achieving launch capability in 1980, India had a number of satellites launched by the United States and the Soviet Union. An Indian astronaut took part in a *Soyuz* visit to the *Salyut 7* space station in 1984. In 1993, Brazil launched its first satellite. The satellite measures air pollution and collects data from 500 sensors along the Amazon River basin. Encourage interested students to find out more about the space programs of other countries.

From Rocket Bombs to Rocket Ships

During World War II, Germany developed the V-2 rocket, shown in **Figure 2,** and used it to bomb England. The design for the V-2 rocket came from Wernher von Braun, a young Ph.D. student whose research was being supported by the German military. In 1945, near the end of the war, von Braun and his entire research team surrendered to the advancing Americans. The United States thus gained 127 of the best German rocket scientists, and rocket research in the United States boomed in the 1950s.

Figure 2 *The V-2 rocket is the direct ancestor of all modern space vehicles.*

The Birth of NASA The end of World War II marked the beginning of the Cold War—the arms race between the United States and the Soviet Union. The Soviet Union was made up of Russia and 15 other countries, forming a superpower that supported a military rivaling that of the United States.

On July 29, 1958, in response to the alarm Americans felt over a possible Soviet superiority in space, the National Aeronautics and Space Administration, or **NASA,** was formed. This organization combined all of the separate rocket-development teams in the United States. Their combined efforts led to the development of a series of rockets, including the Saturn V rocket and those used to launch the space shuttle, as shown in **Figure 3.**

Figure 3 *Some of the space vehicles developed by NASA during its first 40 years are shown here to scale.*

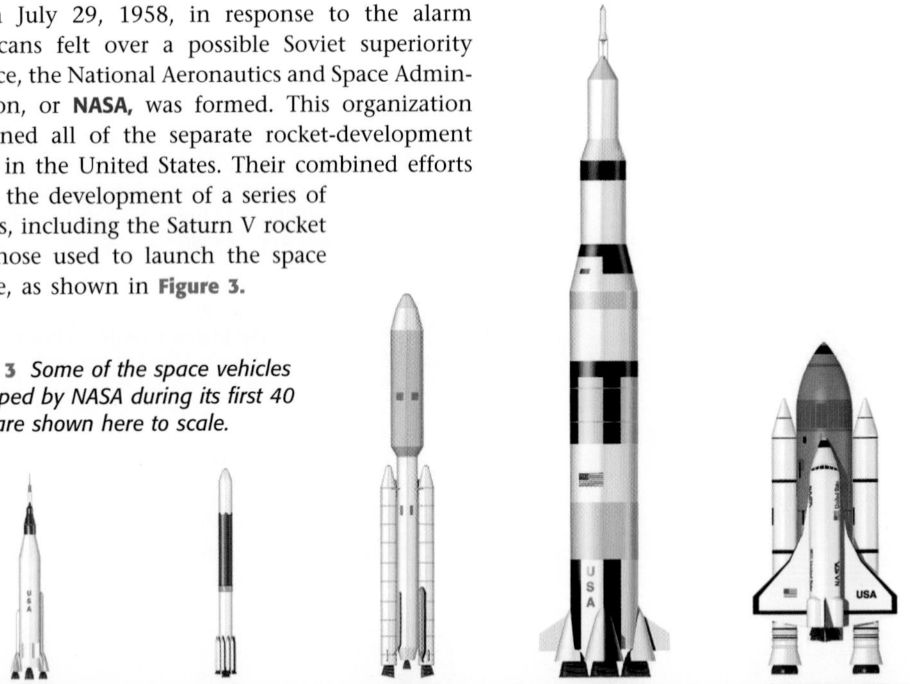

Mercury-Atlas	Delta	Titan IV	Saturn V	Space shuttle and boosters
1,400 kg payload	1,770 kg payload	18,000 kg payload	129,300 kg payload	29,500 kg payload
29 m tall	36 m tall	62 m tall	111 m tall	56 m tall

129

2 Teach

Cross-Disciplinary Focus

History Make sure students understand that the term *cold war* describes a period of tense or strained political relations without actual military aggression. You might explain to students that after World War II, the United States and its allies followed very different political and economic policies from the Soviet Union and its allies. The two powers viewed each other with suspicion and fear. Both countries responded by spending tremendous amounts of money to increase their military strength. An arms race led to the proliferation of nuclear weapons, which increased tensions further with the fear that nuclear war could destroy all of humanity. For both sides, space exploration became a yardstick of national superiority and played an important role in the development of military weapons.

Cross-Disciplinary Focus

PORTFOLIO

Language Arts The works of Jules Verne inspired both Goddard and Tsiolkovsky to develop rocket theory. Have interested students read sections from Jules Verne's *From the Earth to the Moon* or *Around the Moon.* Suggest that students compare Verne's descriptions of spaceships and how they were powered with what they are learning in this section. Ask them to consider how accurately Verne predicted the future of space travel. Have students summarize their thoughts in a written book report. Students may also wish to find out about the influence of H. G. Wells on the development of space science.

Science Humor

Robert Goddard experienced several spectacular failures while trying to develop the liquid-fuel rocket. Several rockets exploded on the launch pad before ever lifting off. After one failed test, Goddard dryly commented, "Well, there goes $10,000 up in smoke."

Directed Reading Worksheet Section 1

internet connect

*sci*LINKS NSTA

TOPIC: Rocket Technology
GO TO: www.scilinks.org
***sci*LINKS NUMBER:** HSTE530

3 Extend

LabBook PG 168
Water Rockets Save the Day!

MEETING INDIVIDUAL NEEDS

Learners Having Difficulty
Explain Newton's third law by asking students to imagine firefighters directing a hose at a fire. The reason why firefighters brace their bodies as they hold the hose is that the force of the water causes the nozzle to move backward in *reaction*.

But how can a gas move a heavy, solid rocket? Imagine a cannon shooting a cannon ball. You know the cannon ball goes far and fast in the direction it is shot. The cannon, which has a lot more mass than the ball, recoils backward at a much slower speed and in the opposite direction as the cannon ball travels. In the same manner, when a rocket is launched, the hot gases within the rocket rush out of the exhaust nozzle at high speeds. The rocket reacts by moving upward at a slower speed.

Homework

Poster Project Have students make a series of sketches that show the evolution of rocket design. Encourage them to use poster board so they can make scale models to compare the size of the spacecraft. Have students write a brief description of the function of each spacecraft. Alternately, have students write a report on the life of Konstantin Tsiolkovsky, Robert Goddard, or Wernher von Braun.

Teaching Transparency 199
"How Rockets Work"

How Rockets Work

Rockets work on a simple physical principle, known as *Newton's third law of motion*. This principle states that for every action there is an equal reaction in the opposite direction. For example, the air rushing backward from a balloon (the action) is paired with the forward motion of the balloon itself (the reaction).

In the case of rockets, however, the equality between the action and the reaction may not be obvious. This is because the mass of a rocket—which includes all of the fuel it carries—is much more than the mass of the hot gases as they come out of the exhaust nozzle. Because the hot gases are under extreme pressure, however, they exert a tremendous amount of force. The force that accelerates a rocket is called **thrust.** To learn more about how this works, look at **Figure 4.**

Figure 4 *Rockets work according to Newton's third law of motion.*

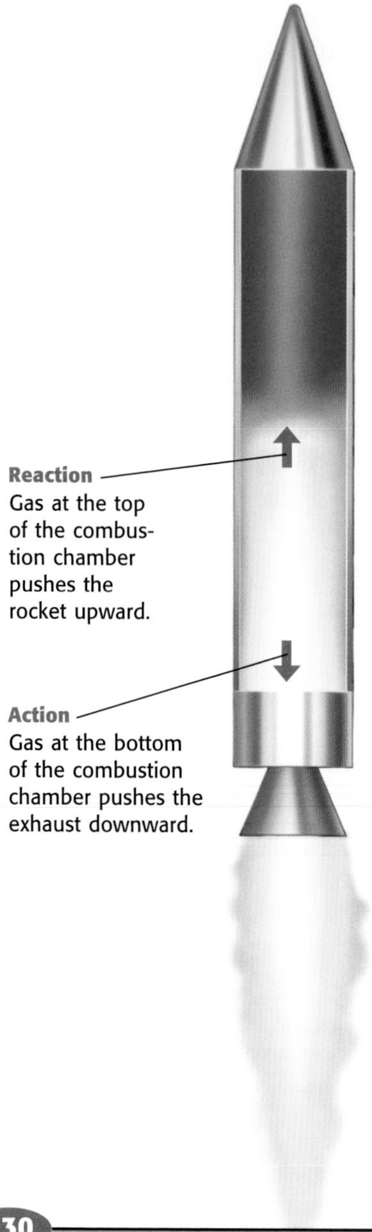

Combustion All rockets have a combustion chamber in which hot gases are under very high pressure. As long as there is no opening for the gas to escape, the rocket remains at rest. In this state, the force that the gas exerts outward is the same as the force that the walls of the combustion chamber exert inward.

Pressure When the pressurized gas is released in only one direction–out the tail end of the rocket–the force of the hot gas against the top of the combustion chamber becomes greater than the opposing force of the air outside. As a result, the gas is forced out of the rocket nozzle.

Thrust If the force of the gas pushing against the top of the combustion chamber (thrust) becomes greater than the force of gravity holding the rocket down (the weight of the rocket), the rocket begins to move skyward.

MISCONCEPTION ALERT

Rockets don't move by pushing against air in the atmosphere. The reaction to the force and direction of the exhaust causes a rocket to move. That is why rockets can accelerate in the vacuum of space, where there is nothing to push against. In fact, rockets accelerate more efficiently in space, where there is no friction to slow them down.

IS THAT A FACT!

As a rocket moves away from Earth, the gravitational pull and the air resistance exerted on the rocket decrease. In addition, the rocket's mass decreases as it burns fuel. Thus, rockets accelerate as they travel from Earth's surface. The space shuttle accelerates from zero to 27,000 km/h in a little over 8 minutes!

How Fast Is Fast Enough? It is not enough for a rocket to have sufficient thrust to just move upward. It must have enough thrust to achieve *orbital velocity.* **Orbital velocity** is the speed and direction a rocket must have in order to orbit the Earth. The lowest possible speed a rocket may go and still orbit the Earth is about 8 km/s.

For Earth, all speeds less than about 8 km/s are *suborbital.* If the rocket goes any slower, it will fall back to Earth. If a rocket travels fast enough, however, it can attain *escape velocity.* **Escape velocity** is the speed and direction a rocket must travel in order to completely break away from a planet's gravitational pull. As you can see in **Figure 5,** the speed a rocket must attain to escape the Earth is about 11 km/s.

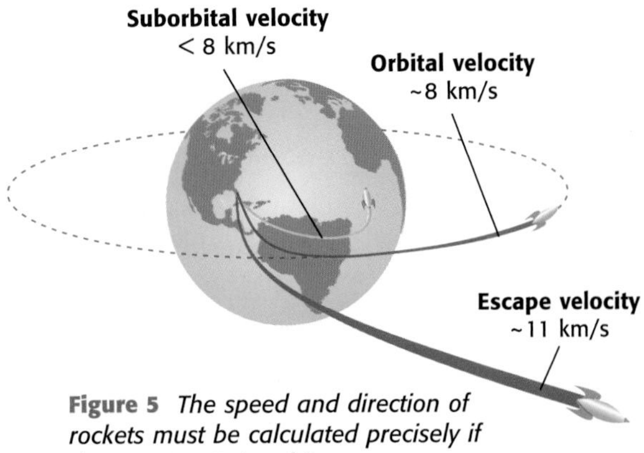

Figure 5 *The speed and direction of rockets must be calculated precisely if they are to attain orbit.*

You Need More Than Rocket Fuel . . . Rockets burn fuel to provide the thrust that propels them forward. But in order for something to burn, oxygen must be present. The earliest rocket fuel was gunpowder, which burns because oxygen is present in the atmosphere. Goddard was the first to use liquid fuel for rockets, which also burns in the presence of oxygen. But while oxygen is plentiful at the Earth's surface, in the upper atmosphere and in outer space, there is little or no oxygen. For this reason, rockets that go into outer space must carry enough oxygen with them to be able to burn their fuel. Otherwise the escaping gas would not create enough thrust to propel the rocket forward.

MATH BREAK

It's Just Rocket Science

As a burning gas (*g*) rushes out the back of a rocket (*r*), it provides thrust to move the rocket. The mass (*m*) and speed (*v*) of the gas and rocket are given by the following equation:

$$m_g \times v_g = m_r \times v_r$$

If the mass of a rocket is 100,000 kg, the speed of the gas leaving the rocket is 1,000 m/s, and the mass of the gas leaving the rocket is 1,000 kg, how fast will the rocket move?

SECTION REVIEW

1. What force must we overcome to reach outer space?
2. How does a rocket engine work?
3. What is the difference between orbital velocity and escape velocity?
4. **Making Inferences** How did World War II help us get into space exploration earlier than we otherwise would have?

internetconnect

sciLINKS NSTA

TOPIC: Rocket Technology
GO TO: www.scilinks.org
***sci*LINKS NUMBER:** HSTE530

Answers to Section Review

1. We must overcome the force of Earth's gravity.
2. Answers will vary. Rocket engines use the pressure of expanding gas to generate thrust. Newton's third law of motion explains why rockets move in a direction opposite to the direction of the escaping gas.
3. Orbital velocity is the speed and direction an object needs to travel to stay in orbit at a certain distance from a given body. Escape velocity is the speed and direction that an object needs to overcome the force of gravity.
4. Answers will vary. World War II led to an arms race between the United States and the Soviet Union. This encouraged competition between the two superpowers to achieve superiority in space.

CONNECT TO PHYSICAL SCIENCE

It is important that students understand the difference between velocity and speed. Speed is the rate at which an object moves. The speed of an object in a particular direction is its velocity. Think of velocity as the rate of change in an object's position. This distinction is very important in rocket science. For example, to save fuel, rockets are always launched in the direction that Earth rotates. Earth has a rotational velocity of nearly 0.5 km/s east. Standing still, a rocket travels 0.5 km/s east, so to reach orbital velocity, it only has to accelerate an additional 7.5 km/s.

Answer to MATHBREAK

10 m/s

4 Close

Quiz

1. How did the formation of NASA contribute to the development of the United States' rocket program? (NASA coordinated the efforts of many rocket research teams, resulting in the rapid development of a variety of rocket designs.)
2. How does Newton's third law of motion apply to rocket propulsion? (Newton's principle states that for every action there is an equal and opposite reaction. When hot gases rush out of the bottom of a rocket, the rocket moves in the opposite direction.)

ALTERNATIVE ASSESSMENT

Concept Mapping Have students create a concept map showing how a rocket accelerates.

SECTION 2

Focus

Artificial Satellites

In this section, students learn about the first artificial satellites. They will learn about different kinds of satellites, what they are used for, and which orbits they are placed in. Students also learn how remote sensing devices have helped us understand Earth as a global system. Finally, students will learn about current developments in satellite technology.

Bellringer

Ask students to list the ways they benefit from satellite technology. (Students might mention the Global Positioning System, satellite television, cellular phones, or accurate weather forecasts.)

Ask students to write two paragraphs describing the ways satellite technology affects their lives.

1 Motivate

ACTIVITY

Students may think that satellites and the Space Shuttle orbit far above Earth. Actually, satellites orbiting in LEO are only around 300 km above Earth. To give students an idea of how low this orbit really is, have students find two cities on a globe that are 300 km apart. For example, the distance from Boston to New York is about 300 km. Have students mark the distance on a piece of string and then turn the string perpendicular to the surface of the globe—LEO is only 4 percent of Earth's diameter. You may wish to contrast this altitude with a GEO orbit, which is 35,862 km high.

SECTION 2 READING WARM-UP

Terms to Learn

artificial satellite
low Earth orbit
geosynchronous orbit

What You'll Do

- Describe how the launch of the first satellite started the space race.
- Explain why some orbits are better than others for communications satellites.
- Describe how the satellite program has given us a better understanding of the Earth as a global system.

Artificial Satellites

In 1955, President Dwight D. Eisenhower announced that the United States would launch an artificial satellite as part of America's contribution to international space science. An **artificial satellite** is any human-made object placed in orbit around a body in space, such as Earth. The Soviets were also working on a satellite program—and launched their satellite first!

The Space Race Begins

On October 4, 1957, a Soviet satellite became the first object to be placed in orbit around the Earth. *Sputnik 1,* shown in **Figure 6,** carried instruments to measure the properties of Earth's upper atmosphere. Less than a month later, the Soviets launched *Sputnik 2.* This satellite carried a dog named Laika.

Two months later, the U.S. Navy attempted to launch its own satellite by using a Vanguard rocket, which was originally intended for launching weather instruments into the atmosphere. To the embarrassment of the United States, the rocket rose only 1 m into the air and exploded.

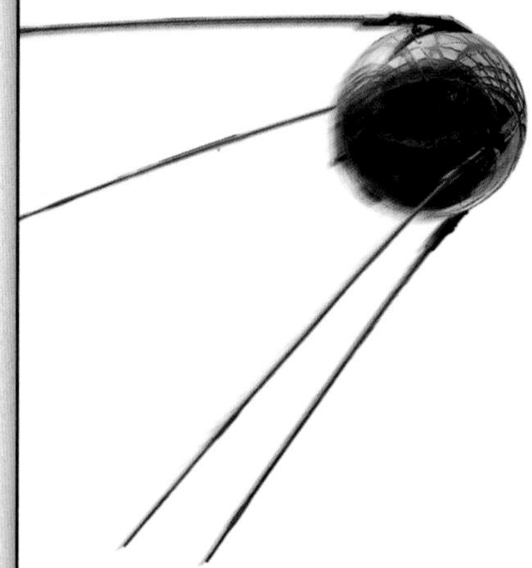

Figure 6 Sputnik 1 *was the first artificial satellite successfully placed in Earth orbit.*

The U.S. Takes a Close Second In the meantime, the U.S. Army was also busy modifying its military rockets to send a satellite into space, and on January 31, 1958, *Explorer 1,* the first United States satellite, was successfully launched. The space race was on!

Explorer 1, shown in **Figure 7,** carried scientific instruments to measure cosmic rays and small dust particles and to record temperatures of the upper atmosphere. *Explorer 1* discovered the Van Allen radiation belts around the Earth. These are regions in the Earth's magnetic field where charged particles from the sun have been trapped.

Figure 7 *From left to right, NASA scientists William Pickering, James Van Allen, and Wernher von Braun show off a model of the first successfully launched American artificial satellite,* Explorer 1.

132

Directed Reading Worksheet Section 2

internetconnect

SCILINKS NSTA
TOPIC: Artificial Satellites
GO TO: www.scilinks.org
***sci*LINKS NUMBER:** HSTE540

SCIENCE HUMOR

When the first American satellite exploded on the launch pad on December 6, 1957, the London *Daily Herald* poked fun at the embarrassing incident by printing the headline "Oh, What a Flopnik!" comparing it to the successful Soviet Sputnik missions.

Into the Information Age

The first United States weather satellite, *Tiros 1,* was launched in April 1960 and gave meteorologists their first look at the Earth and its clouds from above. Weather satellites have given us an understanding of how storms develop and change by helping us study wind patterns and ocean currents. You now can see weather satellite images on your television at almost any time of the day or night or download them from the Internet.

Just a few months after *Tiros 1* began returning signals to Earth, the United States launched its first communications satellite, *Echo 1*. This satellite bounced signals from the ground to other areas on Earth, as shown in **Figure 8.** Within 3 years, sophisticated communications-satellite networks were sending TV signals from continent to continent.

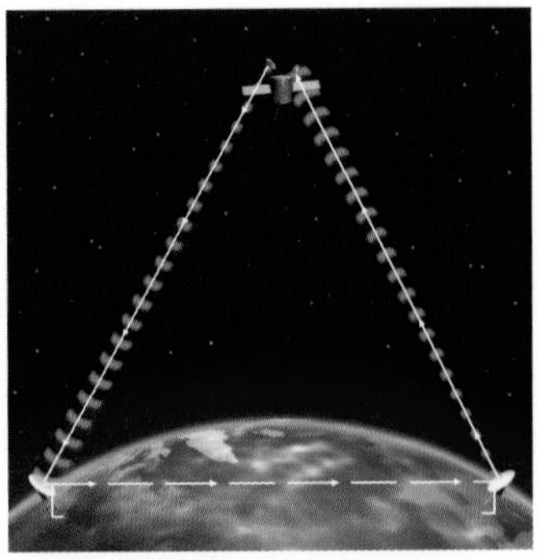

Figure 8 *Satellites can send signals beyond the curve of the Earth's surface, enabling communication around the world.*

Choose Your Orbit

All of the early satellites were placed in **low Earth orbit** (LEO), a few hundred kilometers above the Earth's surface. This location, while considered space, is still within the outermost part of Earth's atmosphere. A satellite in LEO travels around the Earth very quickly, which can place it out of contact much of the time.

Science fiction writer Arthur C. Clarke suggested a much higher orbit than LEO for weather and communications satellites. In this orbit, called a **geosynchronous orbit** (GEO), a satellite travels around the Earth at a speed that exactly matches the rotational speed of the Earth. This keeps the satellite positioned above the same spot on Earth at all times. Today there are many communications satellites in GEO. Ground stations are in continuous contact with these satellites, so your television program or phone call is not interrupted.

Self-Check

The space station being built by the United States and other countries is in LEO. What is one advantage of this location?

(See page 200 to check your answer.)

APPLY

Anything GOES

The height above the Earth's surface for a geosynchronous orbit is 35,862 km. Today, a network of Geostationary Operational Environment Satellites (GOES) provides us with an international network of weather satellites. What would happen if a GOES satellite were placed in LEO rather than in GEO? How would that adversely affect the information the satellite was able to collect?

2 Teach

REAL-WORLD CONNECTION

Write the following information on the board, and invite students to use a globe to pinpoint the location of the geosynchronous communications satellites that relay the signals of their favorite television shows.

- ABC uses *Telstar-402* at 89°W and *Telstar-5* at 97°W.
- CBS uses *Galaxy-6* at 99°W.
- NBC uses *Satcom-C1* at 137°W.
- Discovery Channel and ESPN use *Galaxy-5* at 125°W.
- The Weather Channel uses *Satcom-C3* at 131°W.

Answer to Self-Check

Answers will vary. Sample answer: It requires much less fuel to reach LEO.

Answers to APPLY

Answers will vary. In LEO, the satellite would not stay above the same point on the Earth's surface. Thus, it would not be able to provide continuous coverage of a single region of the world.

DISCUSSION

Tell students that the orbit of satellites is determined by three major variables: gravity, velocity, and distance. The force of gravity pulls satellites toward the Earth, so satellites must have a velocity great enough to remain in orbit. The closer a satellite is to Earth, the faster it must travel to remain in orbit. The result of these three variables is a curved path.

Multicultural CONNECTION

INTELSAT is an international not-for-profit communications satellite cooperative representing more than 140 nations. Decisions about the system's upkeep and future are reached by consensus among the member nations. INTELSAT satellites relay telephone calls, television broadcasts, and other telecommunications data. During the 1998 Winter Olympics, INTELSAT linked people from China, Germany, South Africa, the United States, Australia, and Japan to form an international 2,000-member chorus. Have groups of students work together to write a proposal to launch a satellite that would benefit the global community.

3 Extend

Going Further

Satellites such as those in the Landsat program are deployed in polar orbits; that is, they orbit Earth from pole to pole. Have students find out why polar orbits are best for mapping purposes. (One reason is that as the Landsat satellites orbit the Earth, the Earth rotates beneath them. In this way, the satellites can survey the entire planet without changing their orbit.)

Ask them to write a brief explanation of the advantages of polar orbits and to draw a diagram showing the path a satellite in a polar orbit would take. Students might also include depictions of satellites in other types of orbits.

Connect to Physical Science

What causes objects to heat up as they enter our atmosphere? People generally assume that friction from high-speed collisions with air molecules generates this thermal energy. Actually, friction plays a minor role compared with pressure. As an object such as a spacecraft enters our atmosphere, it compresses a layer of air about a meter deep beneath it. Imagine a snow plow pushing a mound of snow before it. As the layer of air beneath the spacecraft reaches tremendous pressures, it transfers thermal energy to the surface of the spacecraft by conduction, causing it to glow red-hot. If students have ever inflated a bike tire using a well-oiled pump, they have observed this effect: the repeated compression of air causes the pump to become hot. For this reason, LEO satellites orbit in the outer reaches of Earth's atmosphere at a point where air pressure is insignificant.

Environment Connection

After more than 40 years of space launches, the space near Earth is getting cluttered with "space junk." The United States Space Command—a new branch of the military—tracks nearly 10,000 pieces of debris larger than a few centimeters. Left uncontrolled, all this debris may become a problem for space vehicles in the future!

Results of the Satellite Programs

Satellites gather information by *remote sensing.* Remote sensing is the gathering of images and data from high above the Earth's surface. The images and data help us investigate the Earth's surface by measuring the light and other forms of energy that reflect off Earth. Some satellites use radar, which bounces high-frequency radio waves off the surface of objects and measures the returned signal.

Military Satellites The United States military, which has a keen interest in satellites for defense and spying purposes, recognized that LEO was a perfect location for placing powerful telescopes that could be turned toward the Earth to photograph activities on the ground anywhere in the world.

The period from the late 1940s to the late 1980s is known as the Cold War. During that time, the United States and the former Soviet Union built up their military forces in order to ensure that neither nation became more powerful than the other. Both countries monitored each other using spy satellites. **Figure 9** shows an image of part of the United States taken by a Soviet spy satellite during the Cold War.

The military also launches satellites into GEO to aid in navigation and to serve as early warning systems against missiles launched toward the United States. Even though the Cold War is over, spy satellites continue to play an important role in the United States's military defense.

Brain Food

Not all satellites look down on Earth. Among the most important satellites to astronomers, for example, are the Hubble Space Telescope and the Chandra X-ray Observatory, both of which look out toward the stars.

Figure 9 *This image was taken in 1989 by a Soviet spy satellite in LEO about 220 km above the city of San Francisco. Can you identify any objects on the ground?*

134

Weird Science

Geosynchronous satellites generally have a life span of 5–13 years. Because there are a limited number of locations around the equator in which geosynchronous satellites may orbit, "dead" satellites must be disposed of in some way. Currently, satellites use their remaining propellant to navigate into a higher "graveyard orbit." Once in a graveyard orbit, a dead satellite circles Earth every 2–5 days and does not interfere with operating satellites in geosynchronous orbits.

Eyes on the Environment

Satellites have given us a new vantage point for looking at the Earth. By getting above the Earth's atmosphere and looking down, we have been able to study the Earth in ways that were never before possible.

One of the most successful remote-sensing projects was the Landsat program, which began in 1972 and continues today. It has given us the longest continuous record of Earth's surface as seen from space. The newest Landsat satellite (number 7) was launched in 1999. It will gather images in several frequencies—from visible light that we can see to infrared. The Landsat program has produced millions of images that are being used to identify and track global and regional changes on Earth, as shown in **Figure 10.**

Remote sensing has allowed scientists to perform large-scale mapping, look at changes in patterns of vegetation growth, map the spread of urban development, help with mineral exploration, and study the effect of humans on the global environment.

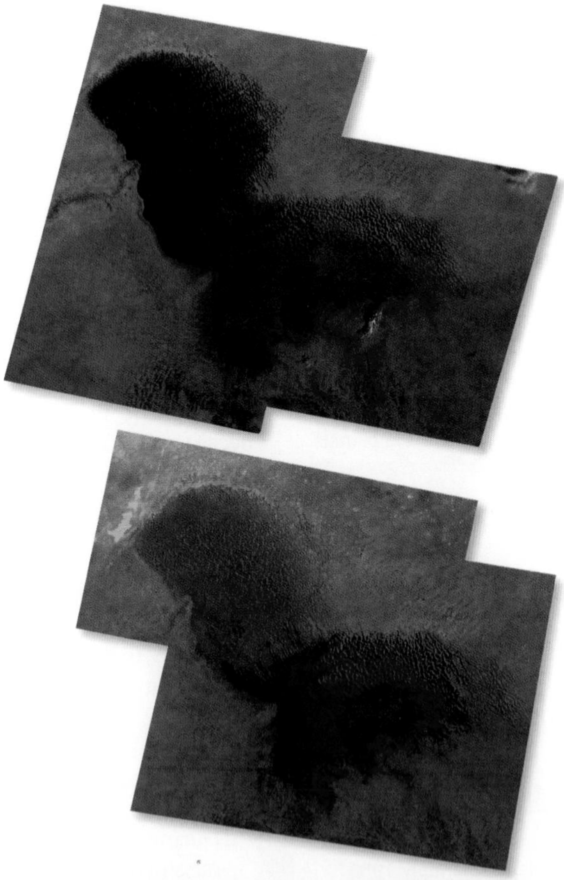

Figure 10 *These Landsat images of Lake Chad, Africa, show how environmental changes can be monitored from orbit. The top image was taken in 1973, and the bottom image was taken in 1987. Can you tell what changed?*

SECTION REVIEW

1. What types of satellites did the United States first place in orbit?
2. List two ways that satellites have benefited human society.
3. **Applying Concepts** The Hubble Space Telescope is located in LEO. Will the telescope move faster or slower around the Earth compared with a geosynchronous weather satellite? Explain.

internetconnect

sciLINKS. NSTA

TOPIC: Artificial Satellites
GO TO: www.scilinks.org
***sci*LINKS NUMBER:** HSTE540

135

Answers to Section Review

1. The first satellites launched by the United States carried scientific instruments to low Earth orbit.
2. Answers will vary. Satellites have improved communications and helped us study the Earth from space.
3. The Hubble Space telescope moves faster than a geosynchronous satellite. To maintain a LEO orbit, an object must travel very fast.

4 Close

Quiz

1. What is an artificial satellite? (any human-made object placed in orbit around a body in space)
2. What was the name of the first satellite to be placed in orbit, and what nation launched it? (The Soviet Union launched *Sputnik 1*.)
3. What is a geosynchronous orbit? (In a geosynchronous orbit, a satellite travels at a speed that matches the rotational speed of the Earth; it completes one orbit in the same length of time that Earth completes one rotation.)

ALTERNATIVE ASSESSMENT

Have students construct a timeline showing the development of artificial satellite technology from 1957 to the present.

Homework

Making Observations Have students go outside on a clear evening and look for satellites. Satellites do not produce their own light; they reflect sunlight and "Earthshine" off their surfaces. The best time to view satellites is about an hour after sunset or an hour before sunrise. Encourage students to lie on the ground or sit in a reclining chair and scan the skies for satellites. Students can use binoculars if they are available. A satellite will look like a star moving across the sky in a straight line. It will fade out of sight before it reaches the horizon. Satellites can be seen moving from west to east or from pole to pole. Geosynchronous satellites are difficult to detect because they do not appear to move at all.

SECTION 3

Focus

Space Probes

The section describes some of the discoveries made by the earliest space probes. Students will also learn about the data gathered by recent probes that have visited the inner and outer planets. The section discusses how space probe missions to other planets have helped us understand more about the Earth. Finally, students will learn about a new approach to space exploration—"faster, cheaper, and better."

Bellringer

Ask students to consider the following question:

Does exploring other planets benefit us here on Earth? Why or why not?

1 Motivate

ACTIVITY

Design Your Own Space Mission Have students imagine that they could send a space probe anywhere in the solar system. In their ScienceLogs, have students write a paragraph about where they would send their probe, what kind of instruments it would carry, what kind of data it would collect, and what its primary mission would be. Invite volunteers to read their paragraphs to the class and to elaborate on their choices.

Sheltered English

Directed Reading Worksheet Section 3

SECTION 3 READING WARM-UP

Terms to Learn

space probe

What You'll Do

- Describe some of the discoveries made by space probes.
- Explain how space-probe missions help us better understand the Earth.
- Describe how future space-probe missions will differ from the original missions to the planets.

Space Probes

The 1960s and early 1970s are known as the golden era of space exploration. The Soviets were the first to successfully launch a space probe. A **space probe** is a vehicle that carries scientific instruments to planets or other bodies in space. Unlike satellites, which stay in Earth orbit, space probes travel away from Earth. The early space probes gave us our first close encounters with the other planets and their moons.

Visits to Our Planetary Neighborhood

Because the Earth's moon and the inner planets of the solar system are so much closer to us than any other celestial bodies, they were the first to be targeted for exploration by the Soviet Union and the United States. Launched by the Soviets, *Luna 1* was the first space probe. In January of 1959, it flew past the moon. Two months later, an American space probe—*Pioneer 4*—accomplished the same feat. Follow along the next few pages to learn about space-probe missions since *Luna 1*.

The Moon

***Luna 9* (USSR)**
Launched: January 1966
Purpose: to land the first spacecraft on the moon

***Clementine* (US)**
Launched: January 1994
Purpose: to map the composition of the moon's surface

The Luna 9 and Clementine Missions *Luna 9,* a Soviet probe, made the first soft landing on the moon's surface. During the next 10 years, there were more than 30 lunar missions made by the Soviet Union and the United States. Thousands of images of the moon's surface were taken.

In 1994, the probe *Clementine* discovered possible evidence of water at the south pole of the moon. The image below was taken by the *Clementine* space probe and shows the area surrounding the south pole of the moon. You can see that some of the craters at the pole are permanently in shadow. Elsewhere on the moon, sunlight would cause any ice to vaporize. Ice may have been left by comet impacts. If this frozen water exists, it will be very valuable to humans seeking to colonize the moon.

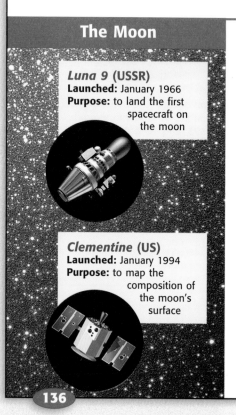

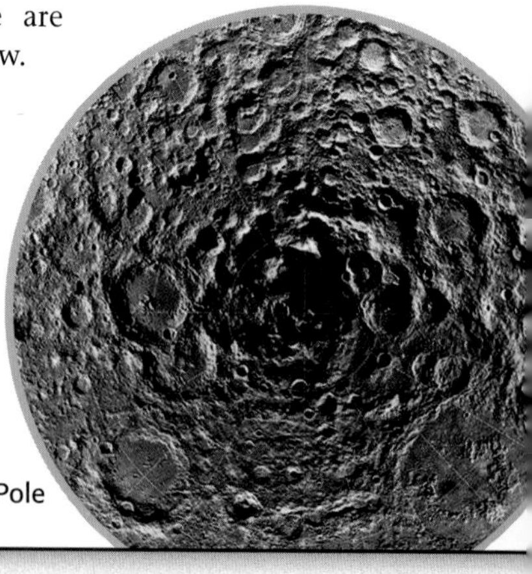

Lunar South Pole

IS THAT A FACT!

The level of navigational accuracy required to have a space probe reach another planet is comparable to throwing a baseball from Los Angeles so accurately that it would fly through a predetermined window in New York City's Empire State Building!

The Venera 9 Mission The Soviet Union landed the first probe on Venus. The probe, called *Venera 9,* parachuted into Venus's atmosphere and transmitted the first images of the surface. *Venera 9* found that surface temperature and atmospheric pressure on Venus are much higher than on Earth. It also found that the chemistry of the surface rocks is similar to that of rocks on Earth. Perhaps most importantly, *Venera 9* and earlier missions showed us a planet with a severe greenhouse effect. Scientists study Venus's atmosphere to learn about how greenhouse gases released into Earth's atmosphere trap thermal energy.

The Magellan Mission In 1989, the United States launched the *Magellan* probe, which used radar to map 98 percent of the surface of Venus. The Magellan mission showed that, in many ways, the geology of Venus is similar to that of Earth. Venus has features that suggest some type of plate tectonics occurs, as it does on Earth. Venus also has volcanoes, some of which may have been active recently. The diagram at below left shows the *Magellan* probe using radar to penetrate the thick cloud layer. The radar data were then transmitted back to Earth, where computers were able to use the data to generate three-dimensional maps like the one at below right.

Venus

***Venera 9* (USSR)**
Launched: June 1975
Purpose: to record the surface conditions of Venus

***Magellan* (US)**
Launched: May 1989
Purpose: to make a global map of the surface of Venus

2 Teach

USING THE FIGURE

Have students study the images of space probes in this section. Then have students design and draw their own version of a space probe. Have them outline their probe's mission and give the probe an appropriate name. Sheltered English

ACTIVITY

Designing a Mission Patch
Astronauts Gordon Cooper and Charles "Pete" Conrad, members of the 1965 *Gemini 5* mission, began a NASA tradition by designing a patch to be worn on their spacesuits that symbolized the purpose of their mission. As students read about the space-probe missions described in the section, have them choose one and then create a patch design that commemorates the purpose and accomplishments of that mission. Students might also include a motto on their patches. Patch designs are available on the NASA Web site.

USING SCIENCE FICTION

Have students read "Why I left Harry's All-Night Hamburgers" by Lawrence-Watt Evans in the *Holt Anthology of Science Fiction.*

Science Bloopers

For the first half of the twentieth century, a popular theory suggested that every planet had once supported life or would support it in the future. The theory was based on the idea that the sun has gradually cooled since its formation. Thus, Mars had once harbored life; it was currently Earth's turn, and Venus would be next. Some scientists thought that Venus might already be home to primitive life-forms equivalent to those of Earth's Cambrian period. However, the 1962 *Mariner 2* flyby showed that Venus was a constant 464°C. We also know now that the sun is becoming hotter, not cooler.

2 Teach, continued

Discussion

Ask students to discuss the advantages and disadvantages of using small space probes to explore the solar system and beyond. In what other types of situations do scientists use probes? Have students find out the amount of time it took for each probe to reach its destination. Remind students that if astronauts had been on these missions, the time would have to be doubled to allow for their return to Earth. Sheltered English

Connect to Physical Science

Voyagers 1 and *2*, *Galileo*, and *Ulysses*, have used a maneuver called a *gravity assist* to explore the solar system. In a gravity assist, spacecraft make use of a planet's gravitational pull to accelerate, slow down, or change direction. Accomplishing such maneuvers using gravity is a triumph of Newtonian physics, and it saves a tremendous amount of fuel. A slingshot analogy is sometimes used to describe gravity assists because of the way the spacecraft swings around the planet and is released, slingshotting out into space in a new flight path. *Voyagers 1* and *2* gained momentum with gravity assists from Jupiter, Saturn, Uranus, and Neptune. The *Ulysses* space probe obtained a gravity assist from Jupiter that sent it into a highly inclined trajectory, which eventually placed it in a polar orbit around the sun.

internetconnect

SciLINKS NSTA
TOPIC: Space Probes
GO TO: www.scilinks.org
***sci*LINKS NUMBER:** HSTE545

Mars

The Viking Missions In 1975, the United States sent a pair of probes—*Viking 1* and *Viking 2*—to Mars. Because the surface of Mars is more like the Earth's surface than that of any other planet, one of the main goals of the Viking missions was to look for signs of life. The probes contained instruments designed to collect soil samples and test them for evidence of life. However, no hard evidence was found. The Viking missions did find evidence that Mars was once much warmer and wetter than it is now. The probes sent back images of dry water channels on the planet's surface. This discovery led scientists to ask even more questions about Mars. Why and when did the Martian climate change?

***Viking 2* (US)**
Launched: September 1975
Purpose: to search for life on the surface of Mars

***Mars Pathfinder* (US)**
Launched: December 1996
Purpose: to use inexpensive technology to study the surface of Mars

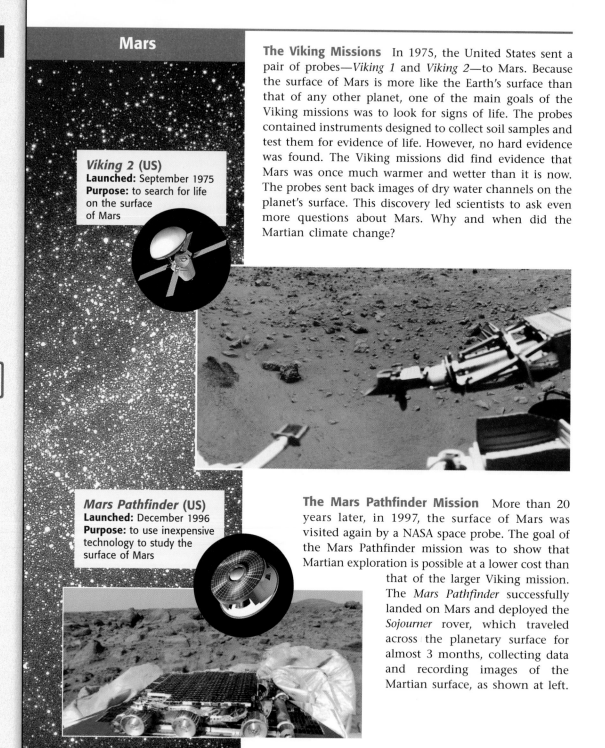

The Mars Pathfinder Mission More than 20 years later, in 1997, the surface of Mars was visited again by a NASA space probe. The goal of the Mars Pathfinder mission was to show that Martian exploration is possible at a lower cost than that of the larger Viking mission. The *Mars Pathfinder* successfully landed on Mars and deployed the *Sojourner* rover, which traveled across the planetary surface for almost 3 months, collecting data and recording images of the Martian surface, as shown at left.

138

Cross-Disciplinary Focus

Writing **History** On January 23, 1967, the United Nations Outer Space Treaty was signed. The treaty guarantees all nations the freedom to explore and use space. The treaty emphasizes a humanistic and pacifist philosophy, which governs the actions of countries as they explore outer space, the moon, and other celestial objects. Have students research this treaty and outline its major points.

The Pioneer and Voyager Missions The *Pioneer 10* and *Pioneer 11* space probes were the first to visit the outer planets. Among other things, these probes sampled the *solar wind*—the flow of particles coming from the sun. The Pioneer probes also found that the dark belts on Jupiter are warmer than the light belts and that these dark belts provide deeper views into Jupiter's atmosphere. In June of 1983, *Pioneer 10* became the first space probe to travel past the orbit of Pluto, the outermost planet.

The Voyager space probes were the first to detect Jupiter's faint rings, and *Voyager 2* was the first space probe to fly by the four gas giant planets—Jupiter, Saturn, Uranus, and Neptune. The paths of the Pioneer and Voyager space probes are shown below. Today they are all near the edge of the solar system and are still sending back information.

The Outer Solar System

Pioneer 10 **(US)**
Launched: March 1972
Purpose: to study Jupiter and the outer solar system

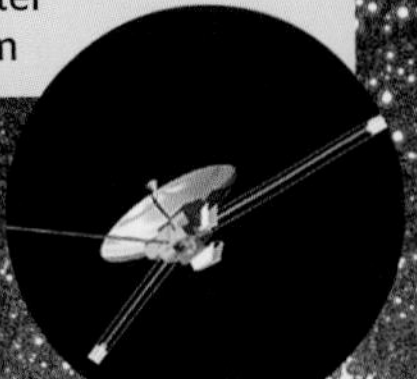

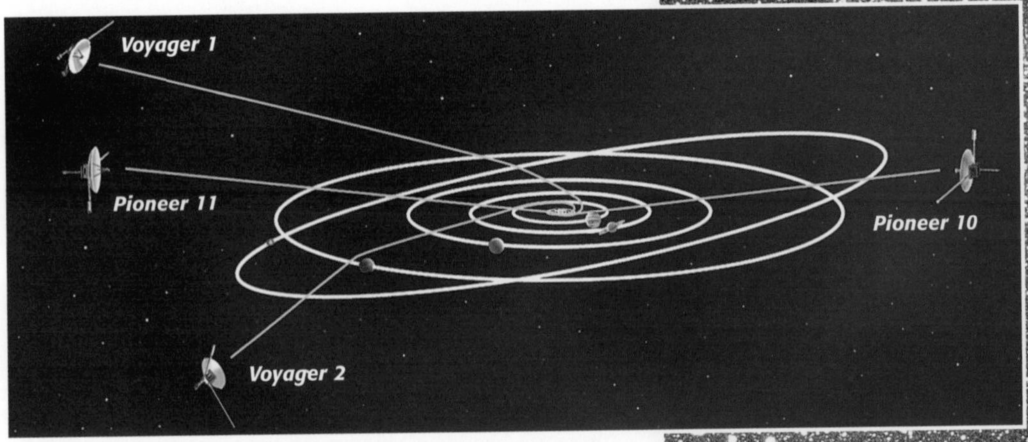

The Galileo Mission The *Galileo* space probe arrived at Jupiter in 1995. While *Galileo* itself began a long tour of Jupiter's moons, it sent a smaller probe into Jupiter's atmosphere to measure composition, density, temperature, and cloud structure. During its tour, *Galileo* gathered data that allowed scientists to study the geology of Jupiter's major moons and to examine Jupiter's magnetic properties more closely. The moons of Jupiter proved to be far more exciting than the earlier Pioneer and Voyager images had suggested. The *Galileo* probe discovered that two of Jupiter's moons have magnetic fields and that one of its moons, Europa, may have an ocean of liquid water lying under its icy surface.

Galileo **(US)**
Launched: October 1989
Purpose: to study Jupiter and its moons

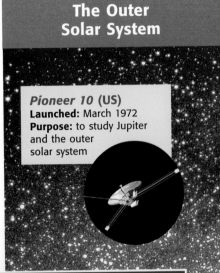

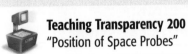

139

Cross-Disciplinary Focus

History When the *Voyager* space probes were launched in 1977, each carried two gold-plated phonograph records with a variety of sounds and music intended as a message for intelligent life in the universe. The probes also carried a variety of images and written messages. Share the following list with students and discuss the kinds of historical, scientific, and cultural information that the *Voyagers* carry:

- Greetings from Earth spoken in 55 different languages, ranging from ancient Sumerian to English
- Printed messages from U.S. President Jimmy Carter and U.N. Secretary General Kurt Waldheim
- The sound of surf, wind, thunder, birdcalls, cricket chirps, and a whale "song"
- Musical selections ranging from bagpipe music from Azerbaijan to "Johnny B. Goode" by Chuck Berry
- A diagram of the solar system; drawings of a man and a woman
- A variety of images, ranging from the Great Wall of China to rush-hour traffic in India to a house in New England

Have students suppose that the *Voyagers* are being launched today. Discuss how they might add to, revise, or update the information aboard the probes. Ask students:

What information would you consider most important? What important events or discoveries have occurred since 1977? What kinds of music or images would you want beings beyond our solar system to know about?

IS THAT A FACT!

In order to keep *Voyager 2's* cameras steady as the probe passed by the gas giants, NASA engineers had to keep the probe from spinning. In fact, they devised a way to reduce the probe's spin to a speed 30 times slower than that of an hour hand on a clock!

Teaching Transparency 200
"Position of Space Probes"

3 Extend

DEBATE

Faster, Cheaper, Better? Some scientists believe that the traditional space probe projects are obsolete. These projects are expensive and require considerable support staff to receive and interpret the data. Because future funding is uncertain, these projects could fold long before the probe reaches its destination. Other scientists feel that large, complex probes are the best way to explore the solar system. Larger probes can carry more equipment and gather more information than smaller, cheaper probes. Have students form two groups to research this debate. Student groups should present their findings as if they were NASA scientists going before Congress to secure funding for their projects.

Homework

Space Probe Profiles After reviewing the section, have students select one space probe they'd like to know more about. Have them create a profile of their probe that includes pictures of the probe and information about its mission and discoveries.

GOING FURTHER

Deep Space 1 carries 81 kg of xenon gas propellant, which is enough to operate the thruster at one-half throttle for over 20 months. Use Teaching Transparency 251 to show students how the xenon ions that propel the probe are formed.

Teaching Transparency 251
"Forming Positive and Negative Ions"
LINK TO PHYSICAL SCIENCE

Space Probes—A New Approach

NASA has a vision for missions that are "faster, cheaper, and better." The original space probes were very large, complex, and costly. Probes such as *Voyager 2* and *Galileo* took years to develop and carry out. One new program, called Discovery, seeks proposals for smaller science programs. The missions are supposed to bring faster results at much lower costs. The first six approved Discovery missions included sending small space probes to asteroids, another Mars landing, studies of the moon, the return of comet dust to Earth, collecting samples of the solar wind, and a tour of three comets.

Figure 11 Stardust *will visit a comet and collect samples of its dust tail.*

Stardust—Comet Detective

Launched in 1999, the *Stardust* space probe is a NASA Discovery mission and the first to focus only on a comet. As shown in **Figure 11,** it will arrive at the comet in 2004 and gather samples of the comet's dust tail, returning them to Earth in 2006. It will be the first time that material from beyond the orbit of the moon has been brought back to Earth. The comet dust should help scientists better understand the evolution of the sun and the planets.

***Deep Space 1*—The New Kid in Town** Another NASA project is the New Millennium program. Its purpose is to test new and risky technologies so that they can be used with confidence in the years to come. *Deep Space 1,* shown in **Figure 12,** undertook the first mission of this program. It is a space probe with an ion-propulsion system. Rather than burning chemical fuel, an ion rocket uses charged particles that exit the vehicle at high speed. An ion rocket still follows Newton's third law of motion, but it does so using a different source of propulsion.

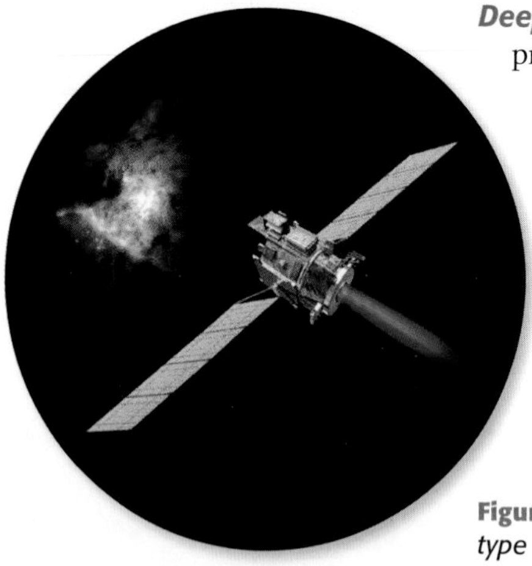

Figure 12 Deep Space 1 *uses a revolutionary type of propulsion—an ion drive.*

140

CONNECT TO PHYSICAL SCIENCE

NASA's *Deep Space 1* probe features a revolutionary ion-propulsion engine 10 times more efficient than chemical thrusters. Inside the probe, xenon gas is bombarded with electrons which ionize it. (Ions are electrically-charged atoms.) Positively-charged ions are drawn toward a high voltage grid at the open end of the engine and are expelled into space at a speed of 30 km/s. This may sound fast, but the thrust generated by *Deep Space 1* is 10,000 times weaker than that generated by a typical space probe. Although this thrust is equivalent to the weight of one sheet of paper on Earth, the probe will gradually accelerate to incredible speeds over many months. One engineer described this new method of propulsion as "acceleration with patience."

The Last of the Big Boys On October 15, 1997, the *Cassini* space probe was launched on a 7-year journey to Saturn. This is the last of the large old-style missions. The *Cassini* space probe will make a grand tour of Saturn's system of moons, much as *Galileo* toured Jupiter's system. As shown in **Figure 13,** a smaller probe, called the *Huygens probe,* will detach itself from *Cassini* and descend into the atmosphere of Saturn's moon Titan to study its chemistry.

Biology CONNECTION

The atmosphere of Titan, Saturn's largest moon, may be similar to Earth's early atmosphere. Scientists hope to study the chemistry of Titan's atmosphere for clues to how life developed on Earth.

Figure 13 *An artist's view of* Cassini *at Saturn, with* Huygens *falling toward Saturn's moon Titan.*

Future Missions Proposals for future missions include a first-ever space-probe visit to Pluto, an orbiter for Jupiter's moon Europa that will use radar to determine whether it has a liquid ocean, and a possible Mercury orbiter to survey the planet closest to the sun. These are just a few of the many exciting international missions planned for the future—opening up a new golden era of planetary exploration.

SECTION REVIEW

1. List three discoveries that have been made by space probes.
2. Which two planets best help us understand Earth's environment? Explain.
3. What are the advantages of the new Discovery program over the older space-probe missions?
4. **Inferring Conclusions** Why did we need space probes to discover water channels on Mars or ice on Europa?

internetconnect

sciLINKS NSTA

TOPIC: Space Probes
GO TO: www.scilinks.org
***sci*LINKS Number:** HSTE545

RESEARCH

The *Voyagers* are expected to continue gathering interplanetary and possibly interstellar data until about 2020, when their nuclear-powered energy supplies will run out. Have students research the *Voyagers'* latest discoveries and write an update on the spacecrafts' findings.

4 Close

Quiz

1. How is a space probe different from a satellite? (A space probe is a vehicle that carries scientific instruments to planets or other bodies in space. Unlike satellites, probes travel away from Earth rather than orbiting it. Students may also note that some probes become satellites of other planets.)
2. What was the main goal of the Viking missions? (to look for signs of life on Mars)
3. What new type of propulsion system is being tested with the *Deep Space 1* probe? (an ion-propulsion system)

ALTERNATIVE ASSESSMENT

PORTFOLIO

Have students find photographs of a space probe and construct a model of it. Encourage students to be creative in their choice of materials and to write a paragraph describing the probe, the function of its parts, and its mission.

Critical Thinking Worksheet
"Spacecraft R' Us"

Answers to Section Review

1. Sample answer: The *Viking* missions sent images of dry water channels on the surface of Mars. *Venera 9* recorded information about the surface and atmosphere of Venus. *Galileo* discovered that two of Jupiter's moons have magnetic fields.
2. Venus and Mars; both planets have surface features that are similar to Earth. In addition, the high levels of CO_2 in Venus's atmosphere produce a severe greenhouse effect. This may help us understand the greenhouse effect on Earth.
3. The Discovery program will produce results quickly and inexpensively.
4. Answers will vary. Students should note that the conditions on Mars or Europa are extreme, and that the danger and expense of sending humans is great.

SECTION 4

Focus

Living and Working in Space

This section explores how the political rivalry between the Soviet Union and the United States led to the Apollo program and the first crewed mission to the moon. The section discusses how reusable space shuttles have revolutionized space travel and research. Students also learn about space stations such as *Skylab* and *Mir* and future plans for the *International Space Station.*

Bellringer

Ask students to write a postcard from a space station orbiting Earth. They should describe the station, their mission, and their day-to-day lives.

1 Motivate

DISCUSSION

A "Walk" on the Moon Read students *Apollo 12* astronaut Alan Bean's description of his 1969 moon walk:

"Once on the Moon's surface you'll quickly discover that walking is pretty difficult, while running is easy. . . . You'll feel as light on your feet as you could possibly expect—lighter even. . . . After pushing off on one foot, there will be a long wait until you land on the other, exactly like running in slow motion. . . . As you run, you'll feel as if you're leaping long, impossible distances. And in fact you are."

Discuss some of the other ways that life on the moon would be different from life on Earth. Have students write a ScienceLog entry in the style of Bean's account.

SECTION 4 READING WARM-UP

Terms to Learn

space shuttle
space station

What You'll Do

- Summarize the benefits of the manned space program.
- Explain how large projects such as the Apollo program and the *International Space Station* developed.
- Identify future possibilities for human exploration of space.

Living and Working in Space

Although sending human explorers into space was an early goal of the space program, it had to come in small steps. The first steps were to test the control of spacecraft with rocket-powered airplanes. Test flights in high-speed aircraft through the upper atmosphere became the beginnings of the Mercury program. The goal of the Mercury program was to put a man in orbit and to test his ability to function in space. Test flights began in 1959, but the dates for manned flight kept getting delayed because of unreliable rockets.

Human Space Exploration

On April 12, 1961, a Soviet cosmonaut named Yuri Gagarin became the first human to orbit the Earth. The United States didn't achieve its first suborbital flight until May 5, 1961, when Alan Shepard reached space but not orbit. Because the Soviets were first once again, they appeared to be winning the Cold War. As a result, many Americans began to consider the military advantages of a strong presence in space. On May 25, 1961, an announcement was made that would set the tone for American space policy for the next 10 years.

Figure 14 *In 1962, John Glenn flew aboard* Friendship 7, *the first NASA spacecraft to orbit the Earth.*

> *"I believe that this nation should commit itself to achieving the goal, before this decade is out, of landing a man on the moon and returning him safely to the Earth. No single space project in this period will be more impressive to mankind, or more important for the long-range exploration of space; and none will be so difficult or expensive to accomplish."*
>
> *— John F. Kennedy, President of the United States*

Many people were expecting the simple announcement of an accelerated space program, but Kennedy's proclamation took everyone by surprise—especially the leaders at NASA. Go to the moon? The United States had not even achieved Earth orbit yet! But the American people took the challenge seriously, and by February 1962, a new spaceport site in Florida was purchased, a manned space-center site was bought, and John Glenn, shown in **Figure 14,** was successfully launched into orbit around the Earth.

142

SCIENCE HUMOR

As *Apollo 11* approached the moon, a special mechanism kept it rotating slowly. Had it not been rotating, the side of the spacecraft exposed to the sun would have quickly overheated. The *Apollo* astronauts comically referred to this rotisserie-like movement as the "barbecue mode."

After Neil Armstrong hopped off the ladder onto the moon's surface and made his historic speech, "Buzz" Aldrin followed. As the shorter astronaut stepped onto the moon, he joked, "That may have been a small step for Neil, but it was a pretty big one for me."

The Dream Comes True On July 20, 1969, the President's challenge was met. The *Apollo 11* landing module—the *Eagle,* shown in **Figure 15**—landed on the moon. Astronaut Neil Armstrong became the first human to set foot on a world other than Earth, forever changing the way we view ourselves and our planet.

Although the primary reason for the Apollo program was political (national pride), the Apollo missions also contributed to the advancement of science and technology. *Apollo 11* returned nearly 22 kg of moon rocks to Earth for study. Its crew also put devices on the moon to monitor moonquake activity and the solar wind. The results from these samples and studies completely changed our view of the solar system.

Figure 15 *Astronaut Neil Armstrong took this photo of Edwin "Buzz" Aldrin as he was about to become the second human being to step onto the moon.*

The Space Shuttle

The dream of human space flight and Kennedy's challenge were great for getting us into space, but they could not be the motivation for the continued political support of space exploration. The huge rockets required for launching spacecraft into orbit were just too expensive.

Early in the manned program, Wernher von Braun had suggested that a reusable space transportation system would be needed. Proposals for reusable launch vehicles were made in the 1950s and 1960s, but the Kennedy challenge overshadowed other efforts, and these ideas were not given serious attention. Finally in 1972, President Richard Nixon announced a space shuttle program to the American public, saying that this would be an economical way to get into space regularly. A **space shuttle** is a reusable vehicle that takes off like a rocket and lands like an airplane, as shown in **Figure 16.**

Figure 16 Columbia *was one of NASA's original shuttles.*

2 Teach

READING STRATEGY

Prediction Guide Have students predict whether the following statements are true or false:

- The space shuttle can be used only once. (false)
- Both the United States and the Soviet Union have launched space stations. (true)
- Many nations are collaborating on an international space station. (true)

Homework

Oral History Project Have students interview adults who remember the 1969 moon landing. Have students draft questions about the event and how the nation reacted to that historic moment. The National Geographic video *For All Mankind* will serve as an excellent introduction to this project. If possible, have students tape-record the interviews and then transcribe them. As an extension, student groups could compile and edit their interviews for a presentation or discussion about the cultural and scientific significance of the first crewed moon landing.

Multicultural CONNECTION

The first black person in space was a Cuban cosmonaut named Arnaldo Tamayo-Mendez. In 1980, he flew aboard *Soyuz 38* to the Soviet space station *Salyut 6.* Have interested students research the contributions that other ethnic groups have made to space programs.

CONNECT TO PHYSICAL SCIENCE

Make sure that students understand that rocket engines are powered by combustion. Combustion requires oxygen, so rockets must carry both fuel and an oxidizer into space. Because their volume as gases would be too great to be practical as rocket fuel, oxygen and hydrogen must be stored as liquids in pressurized fuel tanks.

CONNECT TO LIFE SCIENCE

During the second crewed mission to the moon (*Apollo 12,* November 14–24, 1969), astronauts retrieved some pieces of the space probe *Surveyor.* Amazingly, the pieces of *Surveyor* harbored bacteria from Earth that survived for two and a half years in the moon's dry, near-vacuum environment!

Directed Reading Worksheet Section 4

2 Teach, *continued*

Demonstration

O-Ring Failure The day of the *Challenger* disaster was unseasonably cold for Florida, with temperatures below freezing. The investigation that followed the tragedy traced the explosion to the failure of O-ring seals that were designed to prevent hot exhaust gases from leaking out of the spacecraft's rocket boosters. The rings had stiffened as a result of the cold temperatures and had failed to seal effectively. As a result, one of the rocket boosters leaked, leading to a catastrophic explosion 73 seconds after liftoff. To demonstrate how the cold weather contributed to the O-ring failure, place a rubber washer or gasket in a glass of ice water for a few minutes and then allow students to examine how inflexible it becomes.

Group Activity

Have students find out about the experiments conducted on *Skylab* or *Mir*. Groups should focus on biological, medical, space manufacturing, or astronomical experiments. Have groups share their findings in an oral presentation.

MATH and MORE

When fueled, the space shuttle has a mass of about 2 million kilograms. About 80 percent of this weight is propellant (fuel and oxidizer). Have students calculate the weight of the space shuttle's propellant.

(2,000,000 kg × 0.8 = 1,600,000 kg)

The first shuttle was launched on April 12, 1981, and was followed by two dozen successful missions until 1986, when tragedy struck. On January 28, 1986, the booster rocket on the space shuttle *Challenger* exploded just after takeoff, killing all seven of its astronauts. On board was Christa McAuliffe, who would have been the first teacher in space. All shuttle flights were suspended until this disaster could be explained. Finally in 1988, the space shuttle program resumed with the return of shuttle *Discovery* to space.

Figure 17 *Future space vehicles may provide inexpensive transportation not only between Earth and outer space but around the world.*

Commuter Shuttle? Currently efforts are underway to make space travel easier and cheaper. New space vehicles are being developed for more efficient space travel. The *X-33,* shown in **Figure 17,** was the first space plane that scientists attempted to develop. Although the *X-33* became too costly to complete, research continues on the next generation of space vehicles. Once in operation, space planes may lower the cost of getting material to LEO by 90 percent. New types of rockets and rocket fuels, as well as other means of sending vehicles into space, are being considered.

Biology CONNECTION

When a human body stays in space for long periods of time without having to work against gravity, the bones lose mass and muscles become weaker. Long space-station missions, which can last for months, are very important in order to study whether humans can survive voyages to Mars and other planets. These missions will last for several years.

Space Stations—People Working in Space

On April 19, 1971, the Soviets became the first to successfully place a manned space station in low Earth orbit. A **space station** is a long-term orbiting platform from which other vehicles can be launched or scientific research can be carried out. In June of the same year, a crew of three Soviet cosmonauts entered *Salyut 1* to conduct a 23-day mission. By 1982, the Soviets had put up a total of seven space stations. Because of this experience, the Soviet Union became the world leader in space-station development and in the study of the effects of weightlessness on humans. Their discoveries will be important for future manned flights to other planets—journeys that will take years to complete.

Homework

Many space technology innovations are made by private companies and individuals. Several awards are currently offered for the first private group to launch an inexpensive rocket into space. Ask students to find out more about the role of private companies in the future of space exploration and suggest that they learn about experimental projects such as the Roton rocket.

WEIRD SCIENCE

As astronaut William Pogue exercised on *Skylab*, he reported that his sweat "just sort of slithered around" instead of pooling on the floor beneath him. After exercising, he corralled the hovering sweat with a towel so that it wouldn't interfere with the spacecraft's equipment!

A Home Away from Home *Skylab,* the United States's first space station, was a science and engineering lab that orbited the Earth in LEO at a height of 435 km. The lab, shown in **Figure 18,** was used to conduct a wide variety of scientific studies, including astronomy, biological experiments, and experiments in space manufacturing. Three different crews spent a total of 171 days on board *Skylab*.

All objects in LEO, including *Skylab,* eventually spiral toward Earth. Even at several hundred kilometers above the Earth, there is still a very small amount of atmosphere. The atmosphere slows down any object in orbit unless something periodically pushes the object in the opposite direction. *Skylab*'s orbit began to decay in 1979. A space shuttle was supposed to return the lab to a higher orbit, but delays in the shuttle program prevented the rescue of *Skylab,* and it fell into the Indian Ocean.

Figure 18 Skylab, *in orbit above Earth, was lifted into space by a Saturn V rocket.*

From Russia with Peace In 1986, the Soviets began to launch the pieces for a much more ambitious space station called *Mir* (meaning "peace"). The Soviets, and later the Russians, used *Mir* to conduct astronomy experiments, provide biological and Earth orbital observations, and study manufacturing technologies in space. When completed, *Mir* had seven modules and measured 33 m long and 27 m wide.

Astronauts from the United States and other countries eventually became visitors to *Mir,* as shown in **Figure 19.** Almost continuously inhabited between 1987 and 1999, *Mir* became the inspiration to build the next generation of space station—the International Space Station.

Figure 19 Mir *provided an opportunity for American astronauts and Russian cosmonauts to live and work together in space.*

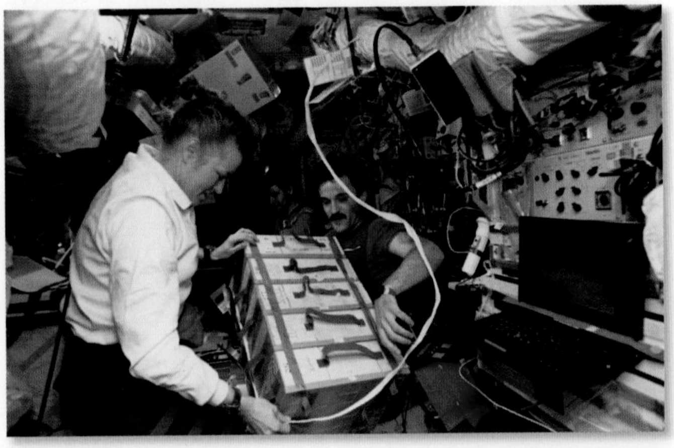

BRAIN FOOD

What happens to the trash that is generated on a space station? Even a small space station such as *Mir* generates trash. Transporting it back to Earth is a costly endeavor. Tossing the garbage out into orbit could be a hazard for other satellites or spacecraft. The *Mir* periodically filled a used cargo ship with trash and sent it in a rapidly decaying orbit into the Earth's atmosphere. When it entered the atmosphere it burned up. Ask students if they can think of other ways to safely dispose of, or recycle, space trash.

MISCONCEPTION ALERT

Students may presume that astronauts experience weightlessness because there is no gravity in space. Astronauts in a typical orbit 296 km above Earth are still affected by Earth's gravity; in fact, gravity is what keeps the spacecraft in orbit. The reason the astronauts have the sensation of weightlessness is that they are in a constant state of free fall as they orbit Earth. This apparent weightlessness is similar to what sky divers experience when they jump from airplanes.

SCIENCE HUMOR

The news that *Skylab* would re-enter the atmosphere and plummet to Earth generated mild panic among some people. Despite NASA's assurances that the debris would fall in oceans or unpopulated areas, a few quick profits were made from the sale of hard hats billed as "Skylab Survival Kits." Much of the debris fell into the Indian Ocean, but some charred fragments were found strewn across the Australian Outback, prompting Australian officials to present the United States with a $400 fine for littering!

internetconnect

SCILINKS NSTA

TOPIC: Space Exploration and Space Stations
GO TO: www.scilinks.org
***sci*LINKS NUMBER:** HSTE550

3 Extend

DEBATE

Space Exploration: Does Its Expense Outweigh Its Benefits? Encourage students to debate the costs of space exploration versus its potential benefits to humankind. Students should recognize that although space exploration is very expensive, it is difficult to measure or to predict how much could be gained by exploration. The space industry also employs many people, including scientists and laborers who build the rockets. On the other hand, there are many immediate problems on Earth, such as hunger, disease, homelessness, and illiteracy.

CROSS-DISCIPLINARY FOCUS

Social Studies Discuss how the political and economic changes of the mid- to late 1980s led to the collapse of the Soviet Union. Tell students that the 1975 Apollo-Soyuz Test Project was the result of a 1972 U.S.-Soviet agreement to conduct a joint venture in space. Remind them, however, that it took 20 years before such cooperation became commonplace. You might tell students that in 1995 the U.S. space shuttle *Atlantis* engaged in several dockings with *Mir* in preparation for future American-Russian collaborations on the *International Space Station.* Ask students if they think that such an event could have occurred if the political situation in Russia had not changed. Have students prepare a timeline of the important political, social, and scientific events of the age of space exploration.

Science CONNECTION

Working together to live in space? To learn more about the latest station in orbit, turn to page 154.

BRAIN FOOD

It will take more than 40 shuttle flights and 6 years to lift into space the 400 tons of materials needed for the construction of the *International Space Station.*

The International Space Station

In 1993, a design for a new space station was proposed that called for international involvement and a collaboration between the newly formed Russian Republic and the United States. The new space station is called the *International Space Station (ISS).* A drawing of the station when completed is shown in **Figure 20.**

The station is being assembled in LEO with materials brought up on the space shuttle or by Russian rockets. The United States is providing lab modules, the supporting truss, solar panels for power, living quarters, and a biomedical laboratory. The Russians are contributing a service module, docking modules, life support and research modules, and transportation to and from the station. Other components will come from Japan, Canada, and several European countries.

The *ISS* will provide many benefits—some of which we cannot even predict. What we do know is that it will be a good place to perform space-science experiments and perhaps to invent new technologies. Hopefully the *ISS* will also promote cooperation among countries and continue the pioneering spirit of the first astronauts and cosmonauts.

Figure 20 *This artist's view of the* International Space Station *shows what the station will look like once it is completed.*

IS THAT A FACT!

The *International Space Station* is the largest and most complex space project ever undertaken; it is more than four times larger than the *Mir* space station. The completed station will be nearly 110 m wide and 90 m long. It will have a mass of about 470,000 kg, and almost one acre of solar panels will power six scientific labs on the station.

The Moon, Mars, and Beyond

We may eventually need resources and living space beyond what Earth can provide. Space can provide abundant mineral resources. One interesting resource is a rare form of helium that can be found on the moon. Used as a fuel for nuclear reactors, it leaves no radioactive waste!

We have seen that there are also many scientific benefits to space exploration. For example, the far side of the moon can be 100 times darker than any observatory site on Earth. The moon also could be a wonderful place to locate factories that require a vacuum to process materials, as shown in **Figure 21.** A base in Earth orbit can produce materials that require low gravity. A colony or base on the moon or on Mars could be an important link to bringing space resources to Earth. The key will be to make these missions economically worthwhile.

Activity

Technological improvements intended for space exploration have often led to the invention of new products that improve our lives here on Earth. NASA has a special program that transfers these new ideas and technology to the public. Find out more about NASA's technology transfers on the Internet and about how many everyday technologies had their beginnings in the space program.

Figure 21 *Humans may eventually colonize the moon for scientific, economic, and perhaps even recreational reasons.*

SECTION REVIEW

1. How was the race to explore our solar system influenced by the Cold War?
2. How did missions to the moon benefit space science?
3. How will space stations help in the exploration of space?
4. **Making Inferences** Why did the United States quit sending people to the moon after the Apollo program ended?

internet connect

*sci*LINKS. NSTA

TOPIC: Space Exploration and Space Stations
GO TO: www.scilinks.org
***sci*LINKS NUMBER:** HSTE550

Answers to Section Review

1. Answers will vary. Students should note that Cold War tensions greatly accelerated the space programs of the United States and the Soviet Union.
2. Answers will vary. The Apollo missions helped us understand the geology of the moon and measure the solar wind.
3. Answers will vary. Space stations will serve as refueling, construction and research stations.
4. Answers will vary. Without a political reason to go to the moon, the United States government decided that the Apollo program was too expensive to continue.

Answers to Activity

Suggest that students use their findings to construct a "Space Age Spin-Offs" comic book that describes how a few items developed in the space program have made their way into our daily lives.

Going Further

Have a round-table discussion in which students impersonate the following people after having researched their lives and careers:

Robert Goddard, Konstantin Tsiolkovsky, Yuri Gagarin, John Glenn, Rita Mae Jemison, Valentina Tereshkova, Alexi Leonov, Edward White, Chuck Yeager, or Helen Sharman.

Have students discuss the history of the space program and then speculate on future innovations and developments.

4 Close

Quiz

1. What kind of vehicle has been proposed that would make space travel cheaper? (a space plane)
2. What is a space station? (It is a long-term orbiting platform from which other space vehicles can launch and where scientific research can be conducted.)
3. What resources might space someday provide? (minerals, living space, factory sites)

Alternative Assessment

PORTFOLIO

Make a Poster Have students make a poster that shows a day in the life of a space traveler. Events during the day might include making breakfast, exercising, conducting experiments, calling home, and relaxing.

Reach for the Stars
Teacher's Notes

Time Required

Two 45-minute class periods

Lab Ratings

EASY → HARD

- TEACHER PREP: 1
- STUDENT SET-UP: 3
- CONCEPT LEVEL: 2
- CLEAN UP: 2

MATERIALS

The materials listed in this lab are enough for 3–4 students.

Safety Caution

Remind students to review all safety cautions and icons before beginning this lab activity.

Alyson Mike
East Valley Middle School
East Helena, Montana

Making Models Lab

USING SCIENTIFIC METHODS

Reach for the Stars

Have you ever thought about living and working in space? Well, in order for you to do so, you would have to learn to deal with the new environment. Astronauts must adjust to the conditions of space. Meanwhile, they are also dealing with special tools used to repair and build space stations. In this activity, you will get the chance to model one tool that might help astronauts work in space.

MATERIALS

- cardboard box
- scissors
- metric ruler
- hole punch
- 2 brads
- metal wire
- 2 jumbo paper clips
- plastic-foam ball

Ask a Question

1. How can I build a piece of equipment that models how astronauts work in space?

Form a Hypothesis

2. Before you begin, write a hypothesis that answers the question in step 1. Explain your reasoning.

Test the Hypothesis

3. Cut three strips from the cardboard box. Each strip should be about 5 cm wide. The strips should be at least 20 cm long but not longer than 40 cm.
4. Punch holes near the center of each end of the three cardboard strips. The holes should be about 3 cm from the end of each strip.
5. Lay the strips end to end along your table. Slide the second strip toward the first strip so that a hole in the first strip lines up with a hole in the second strip. Slip a brad through the holes, and bend its ends out to attach the cardboard strips.

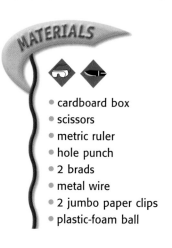

148

6 Use another brad to attach the third cardboard strip to the free end of the second strip. Now you have your mechanical arm. The brads form joints where the cardboard strips meet.

7 Straighten the wire, and slide it through the hole in one end of your mechanical arm. Bend about 3 cm of the wire in a 90° angle so that it will not slide back out of the hole.

8 Try to move the arm by holding the free ends of the cardboard and wire. The arm should bend and straighten at the joints. If the arm is hard to move, adjust the design. Consider loosening the brads, for example.

9 Now your mechanical arm needs a hand. Otherwise, it won't be able to pick things up! Straighten one paper clip, and slide it through the hole where you attached the wire in step 7. Bend one end of the paper clip to form a loop around the cardboard, and bend the other end to form a hook. You will use this hook to pick up things.

10 Bend a second paper clip into a U-shape. Stick the straight end of this paper clip into the foam ball. Leave the ball on your desk.

11 Move the arm so that you can lift the foam ball. The paper-clip hook on the arm will have to catch the paper clip on the ball.

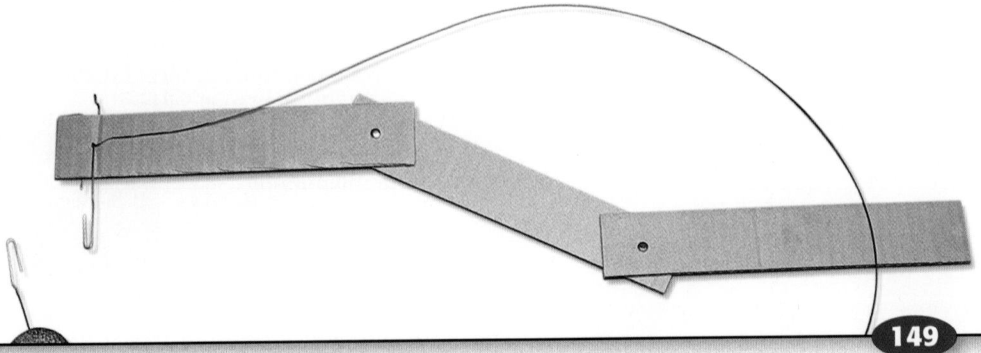

Analyze the Results

12 Did you have any trouble moving the arm in step 8? What changes did you make?

13 Did you have trouble picking up the foam ball? What might have made this step easier?

Draw Conclusions

14 What changes could you make to your mechanical arm that might make it easier to use?

15 How would a tool like this one help people work in space?

Going Further

Adjust the design for your mechanical arm. Can you find a way to lift anything other than the foam ball? For example, can you lift heavier objects or ones that do not have a loop attached? How?

Research the tools that astronauts use on space stations and on the space shuttle. How do their tools help them work in the conditions of space?

Answers

12. Answers will vary. Students may have loosened the paper brads.
13. Answers will vary. Altering the paper-clip loop on the ball or changing the shape of the hook on the arm could make the task easier.
14. Answers will vary. Students may suggest using different materials, changing the length of different arm segments, or mounting the arm on a secure base.
15. Answers will vary. This device could help astronauts manipulate objects outside a spacecraft without having to go on a spacewalk. Also, if the arm were mechanized, it could allow astronauts to move massive objects with precision.

Going Further

Answers will vary.

Datasheets for LabBook

Chapter Highlights

Vocabulary Definitions

Section 1

rocket a machine that uses escaping gas to move

NASA National Aeronautics and Space Administration; founded to combine all of the separate rocket-development teams in the United States

thrust the force that accelerates a rocket

orbital velocity the speed and direction a rocket must have in order to orbit the Earth

escape velocity the speed and direction a rocket must travel in order to completely break away from a planet's gravitational pull

Section 2

artificial satellite any human-made object placed in orbit around a body in space

low Earth orbit an orbit located a few hundred kilometers above the Earth's surface

geosynchronous orbit an orbit in which a satellite travels at a speed that matches the rotational speed of the Earth exactly, keeping the satellite positioned above the same spot on Earth at all times

Chapter Highlights

Section 1

Vocabulary

rocket *(p. 128)*
NASA *(p. 129)*
thrust *(p. 130)*
orbital velocity *(p. 131)*
escape velocity *(p. 131)*

Section Notes

- Two pioneers of rocketry were Konstantin Tsiolkovsky and Robert Goddard.
- Rockets work according to Newton's third law of motion—for every action there is an equal and opposite reaction.
- NASA was formed in 1958, combining rocket research from several programs. It was originally formed to compete with the Soviet Union's rocket program.

Labs

Water Rockets Save the Day! *(p. 168)*

Section 2

Vocabulary

artificial satellite *(p. 132)*
low Earth orbit *(p. 133)*
geosynchronous orbit *(p. 133)*

Section Notes

- The Soviet Union launched the first Earth-orbiting satellite in 1957. The first United States satellite went up in 1958.
- Low Earth orbits (LEOs) are located a few hundred kilometers above the Earth's surface. Satellites in geosynchronous orbits (GEOs) have an orbit period of 24 hours and remain over one spot.
- Satellite programs are used for weather observations, communications, mapping the Earth, and tracking ocean currents, crop growth, and urban development.
- One great legacy of the satellite program has been an increase in our awareness of the Earth's fragile environment.

Skills Check

Math Concepts

THE ROCKET EQUATION Suppose the mass of a certain rocket is 1,000 kg and the mass of the gas leaving the rocket is 100 kg. If the speed that the gas leaves the rocket is 50 m/s, the rocket will move at a speed of 5 m/s. Rearranging the rocket equation:

$$m_g \times v_g = m_r \times v_r$$

as $v_r = m_g \times v_g / m_r$

gives $$v_r = \frac{100 \text{ kg} \times 50 \text{ m/s}}{1{,}000 \text{ kg}} = 5 \text{ m/s}$$

Visual Understanding

GLOBAL COMMUNICATION As you saw on page 133, satellites can relay television, radio, and telephone signals around the world. Because they remain in GEO, these satellites are always above the same spot on Earth, letting them relay our signals without interruption.

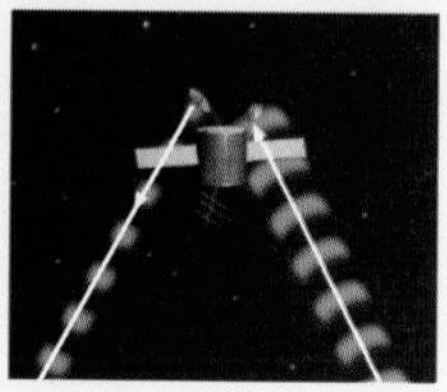

150

Lab and Activity Highlights

Reach for the Stars PG 148

Water Rockets Save the Day! PG 168

Datasheets for LabBook (blackline masters for these labs)

SECTION 3

Vocabulary

space probe *(p. 136)*

Section Notes

- Planetary exploration with space probes began with missions to the moon. The next targets of exploration were the inner planets: Venus, Mercury, and Mars.
- The United States has been the only country to explore the outer solar system, beginning with the Pioneer and Voyager missions.
- Space-probe science has given us information about how planets form and develop, helping us better understand our own planet Earth.

SECTION 4

Vocabulary

space shuttle *(p. 143)*

space station *(p. 144)*

Section Notes

- The great race to get a manned flight program underway and to reach the moon was politically motivated.

- The United States beat the Soviets to a manned moon landing with the Apollo moon flights in 1969.
- During the 1970s, the United States focused on developing the space shuttle. The Soviets focused on developing orbiting space stations.
- The United States, Russia, and 14 other international partners are currently developing the *International Space Station.*
- Because of scientific, economic, and even recreational reasons, humans may eventually live and work on other planets and moons.

internet**connect**

go.hrw.com — **GO TO:** go.hrw.com

Visit the **HRW** Web site for a variety of learning tools related to this chapter. Just type in the keyword:

KEYWORD: HSTEXP

sciLINKS NSTA — **GO TO:** www.scilinks.org

Visit the **National Science Teachers Association** on-line Web site for Internet resources related to this chapter. Just type in the ***sci*LINKS** number for more information about the topic:

TOPIC: Rocket Technology	***sci*LINKS NUMBER:** HSTE530
TOPIC: The History of NASA	***sci*LINKS NUMBER:** HSTE535
TOPIC: Artificial Satellites	***sci*LINKS NUMBER:** HSTE540
TOPIC: Space Probes	***sci*LINKS NUMBER:** HSTE545
TOPIC: Space Exploration and Space Stations	***sci*LINKS NUMBER:** HSTE550

151

VOCABULARY DEFINITIONS, *continued*

SECTION 3

space probe a vehicle that carries scientific instruments to planets or other bodies in space

SECTION 4

space shuttle a reusable vehicle that takes off like a rocket and lands like an airplane

space station a long-term orbiting platform from which other vehicles can be launched or scientific research can be carried out

Blackline masters of these Chapter Highlights can be found in the **Study Guide.**

Lab and Activity Highlights

LabBank

Whiz-Bang Demonstrations, Rocket Science

EcoLabs & Field Activities, There's a Space for Us

Inquiry Labs
- Crash Landing
- Space Fitness

Long-Term Projects & Research Ideas, Space Voyage

Chapter Review Answers

Using Vocabulary

1. Geosynchronous orbit (GEO) is 35,862 km above the Earth's surface. GEO enables satellites to orbit at a speed that matches the Earth's rotation. Low Earth orbit (LEO) is a few hundred kilometers above the Earth's surface. To remain in LEO, satellites must travel much faster than the Earth rotates.
2. A space probe is a vehicle that carries scientific instruments to planets or other bodies in space. It does not carry people. A space shuttle is a reusable vehicle that takes off like a rocket and lands like an airplane. It carries people and does not travel farther than Earth orbit.
3. An artificial satellite is any human-made object placed in orbit around a body in space. A moon is a natural satellite of a planet.
4. thrust
5. oxygen

Understanding Concepts

Multiple Choice

6. b
7. c
8. d
9. b
10. a
11. c
12. c
13. d
14. d
15. c

Concept Mapping Transparency 22

Blackline masters of this Chapter Review can be found in the **Study Guide.**

Chapter Review

USING VOCABULARY

For each pair of terms, explain the difference in their meaning:

1. geosynchronous orbit/low Earth orbit
2. space probe/space shuttle
3. artificial satellite/moon

To complete the following sentences, choose the correct term from each pair of terms listed below:

4. The force that accelerates a rocket is called __?__. (*escape velocity* or *thrust*)
5. Rockets need to have __?__ in order to burn their fuel. (*oxygen* or *nitrogen*)

UNDERSTANDING CONCEPTS

Multiple Choice

6. The father of modern rocketry is considered to be
   a. K. Tsiolkovsky. c. W. von Braun.
   b. R. Goddard. d. D. Eisenhower.
7. Rockets work according to Newton's
   a. first law of motion.
   b. second law of motion.
   c. third law of motion.
   d. law of universal gravitation.
8. The first artificial satellite to orbit the Earth was
   a. *Pioneer 4.* c. *Voyager 2.*
   b. *Explorer 1.* d. *Sputnik 1.*

9. Satellites are able to transfer TV signals across and between continents because satellites
   a. are located in LEOs.
   b. relay signals past the horizon.
   c. travel quickly around Earth.
   d. can be used during the day and night.
10. GEOs are better orbits for communications because satellites in GEO
    a. remain in position over one spot.
    b. are farther away from Earth's surface.
    c. do not revolve around the Earth.
    d. are only a few hundred kilometers high.
11. Which space probe discovered evidence of water at the moon's south pole?
    a. *Luna 9*
    b. *Viking 1*
    c. *Clementine*
    d. *Magellan*
12. When did humans first set foot on the moon?
    a. 1949 c. 1969
    b. 1959 d. 1979

13. Which one of these planets has not yet been visited by space probes?
    a. Mercury
    b. Neptune
    c. Mars
    d. Pluto
14. Of the following, which space probe is about to leave our solar system?
    a. *Galileo* c. *Mariner 10*
    b. *Magellan* d. *Pioneer 10*
15. Based on space-probe data, which of the following is the most likely place in our solar system to find liquid water?
    a. the moon c. Europa
    b. Mars d. Venus

Short Answer

16. Answers will vary. Sample answer: Newton's third law states that for every action, there is an equal reaction in the opposite direction. A rocket's combustion chamber contains gases that are under extreme pressure. As the gases escape through the rocket nozzle, the rocket reacts by moving in the opposite direction.
17. Answers will vary. One disadvantage of LEO is that a satellite cannot maintain constant communication with a ground station because it is orbiting faster than the Earth rotates.

Short Answer

16. Describe how Newton's third law of motion relates to the movement of rockets.

17. What is one disadvantage that objects in LEO have?

18. Why did the United States develop the space shuttle?

19. During which period were spy satellites first used?

Concept Mapping

20. Use the following terms to create a concept map: orbital velocity, thrust, LEO, artificial satellites, escape velocity, space probes, GEO, rockets.

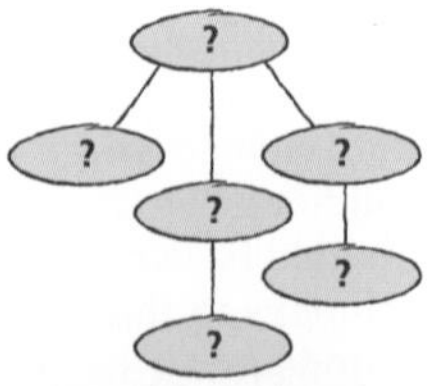

CRITICAL THINKING AND PROBLEM SOLVING

Write one or two sentences to answer the following questions:

21. What is the difference between speed and velocity?

22. Why must rockets that travel in outer space carry oxygen with them?

23. How will data from space probes help us understand the Earth's environment?

24. Why is it necessary for several nations to work together to create the *ISS*?

MATH IN SCIENCE

25. In order to escape Earth's gravity, a rocket must travel at least 11 km/s. This is pretty fast! If you could travel to the moon at this speed, how many hours would it take you to get there? (The moon is about 384,000 km away from Earth.) Round your answer to the nearest whole number.

INTERPRETING GRAPHICS

The map below was made using satellite data. It indicates the different amounts of chlorophyll in the ocean. Chlorophyll, in turn, identifies the presence of marine plankton. The blues and purples show the smallest amount of chlorophyll, and the reds and oranges show the most. Examine the map, and answer the questions that follow:

Chlorophyll Content

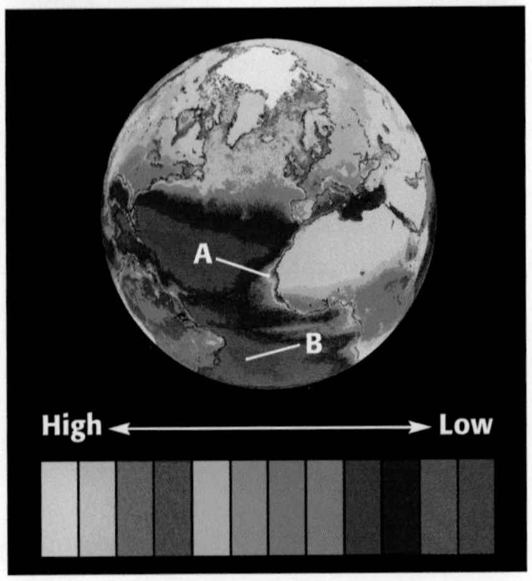

26. At which location, **A** or **B**, are more plankton concentrated?

27. What do you conclude about the conditions in which plankton prefer to live?

Reading Check-up

Take a minute to review your answers to the Pre-Reading Questions found at the bottom of page 126. Have your answers changed? If necessary, revise your answers based on what you have learned since you began this chapter.

153

18. Answers will vary. One reason the United States developed the space shuttle is that it is reusable.
19. Spy satellites were first used during the Cold War.

Concept Mapping

20. An answer to this exercise can be found at the front of this book.

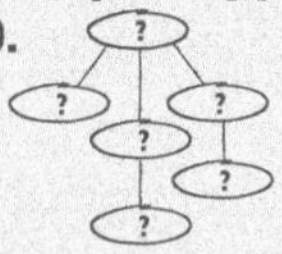

Critical Thinking and Problem Solving

21. Speed is a measure of how fast an object travels. Velocity is the speed and direction an object travels.
22. Rockets must carry oxygen with them because there is little or no oxygen in the Earth's upper atmosphere or in outer space. Without oxygen, rocket fuel cannot burn.
23. Answers will vary. Space probes enable us to study the atmosphere and surface of other bodies in the solar system. Scientists use this data to understand changes in Earth's environment.
24. Answers will vary. Building the *ISS* together gives different countries a common goal and encourages international cooperation. In addition, the cost of the *ISS* will be shared by many countries.

Math in Science

25. $\frac{384{,}000 \text{ km}}{11 \text{ km/s}} = 34{,}909 \text{ seconds}$

$34{,}909 \text{ s} \times \frac{1 \text{ min}}{60 \text{ s}} \times \frac{1 \text{ h}}{60 \text{ min}} =$
$9.7 \text{ h} = 10 \text{ hours}$

Interpreting Graphics

26. A
27. Answers will vary. Sample answer: Plankton populations tend to be concentrated in coastal waters. (Students may note that upwelling at continental margins provides the nutrients that plankton populations need in order to live.)

International Space Station

Teaching Strategy

Use the following questions to generate a discussion about the *International Space Station:*

1. In addition to scientific research, how could the space station be used? (Students might suggest that the station could be used as a refueling station for travel farther out into space. The station could be used for precision manufacturing because materials such as crystals grow with perfect symmetry in free fall.)
2. The space shuttle and other vehicles will transport materials to build the space station. What advantages and disadvantages will construction workers face while building a space station in space? (Every object will have to be tethered so that it does not float away. The construction will require special tools because workers will be in cumbersome spacesuits. Also, if a worker applies force to an object, he or she will be pushed in the opposite direction, so the workers will have to be securely anchored. One advantage is that it would take less energy to move massive objects.)

Lead a class discussion about the laws that might govern life in a space station. Who should determine the rules? Are there any laws unique to a space-station environment?

ACROSS THE SCIENCES

EARTH SCIENCE • LIFE SCIENCE

International Space Station

On a June day in 1995, the space shuttle *Atlantis* docked at the Russian space station, *Mir,* and picked up three passengers. These passengers, one from the United States and two from Russia, had completed a 3-month stay at the space station. This mission was the first in a series of missions to develop construction techniques for assembling the *International Space Station.* These missions are considered to be phase one of the process.

An International Place in Space

Sixteen nations plan to build the *International Space Station (ISS)* by the year 2004. These nations are the United States, Russia, Canada, Brazil, Japan, Denmark, Germany, France, Italy, Belgium, the Netherlands, Switzerland, the United Kingdom, Spain, Norway, and Sweden.

The *ISS* will be made up of cylindrical rooms called *modules.* Each of these components will be built on the ground and then assembled 274 km above Earth. The current plan calls for more than 40 space flights to carry the parts of the space station into orbit. Once the *ISS* is completed, a seven-member crew will be able to live and work there.

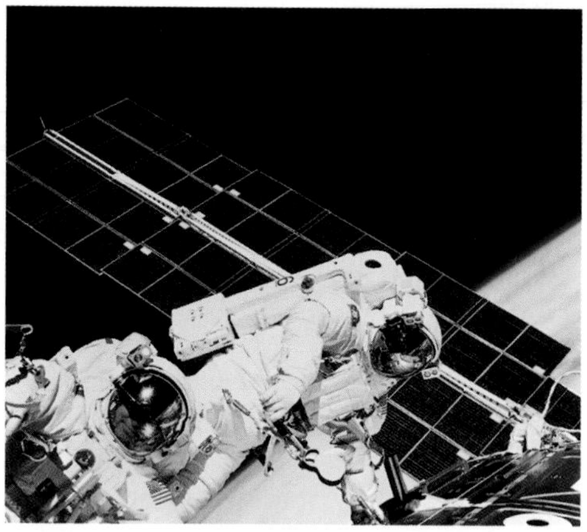

▲ *Parts of the* International Space Station *are being assembled in space.*

Life Aboard

One of the strange things about living in space is the reduced effect of gravity known as *free fall.* Everything inside the space station that is not fastened down, including the astronauts, will float! The designers of the *ISS*'s habitation module have come up with some intriguing solutions to this problem. For example, each astronaut will sleep in a sack similar to a sleeping bag that is fastened to the module. The sack will keep the astronauts from floating around while they sleep. Astronauts will shower with a hand-held nozzle that squirts water onto their body. Afterward, the water droplets will be vacuumed up so that they won't float around. Other problems being studied include how to prepare and serve food, how to design an effective toilet, and how to dispose of waste.

Ready to Go

Phase two began with the actual construction of the *ISS* in orbit. In November and December of 1998, two modules, *Zarya* and *Unity,* were launched into orbit. In early 2000, a three-person crew began living on board—the first of many crews expected to inhabit the *International Space Station.*

Address the Gravity of a Situation

► Create a sketch for a device that will help the space-station crew cope with free fall. Pick a problem to solve such as brushing teeth, getting exercise, or washing hair.

154

Answers to Address the Gravity of a Situation

As they create blueprints for a device, encourage students to be as creative and as detailed as they like. Suggest that students think about their daily lives and note a tool they use regularly. Have students consider how this tool would function in space.

Science Fiction

"Why I Left Harry's All-Night Hamburgers"

by Lawrence Watt-Evans

At 16, he needed a job. His dad was out of work and his family needed money. Right around the corner from his house was Harry's All-Night Hamburgers. With a little persistence, he talked Harry into giving him a job.

He worked from midnight to 7:30 A.M. so he could still go to school. He was the counterman, waiter, busboy, and janitor, all in one. Harry's was pretty quiet most nights, especially because the interstate was 8 mi away and nobody wanted to drive to Harry's. Most of the time, the customers were pretty normal.

There were some, though, who were unusual. For instance, one guy came in dressed for Arctic winter, even though it was April and it was 60°F outside. Then there were the folks who parked a very strange vehicle right out in the parking lot for anyone to see.

Pretty soon, the captivated waiter starts asking questions. What he learns startles and fascinates him. Soon he's thinking about leaving Harry's. Find out why by reading "Why I Left Harry's All-Night Hamburgers," by Lawrence Watt-Evans, in the *Holt Anthology of Science Fiction.*

155

Further Reading If you liked this story, check out more of Lawrence Watt-Evans's work, such as the following:

Crosstime Traffic, Del Rey Books, November 1992

Denner's Wreck, Avon, April 1988

Shining Steel, Avon, June 1986

Science Fiction

"Why I Left Harry's All-Night Hamburgers"

by Lawrence Watt-Evans

Flying saucers in the parking lot? Just how alien and strange are the late-night visitors to Harry's burger joint? And why does the teenager who works the night shift want to leave?

Teaching Strategy

Reading Level Students of all reading levels should find this story enjoyable. However, the class may benefit from a discussion of some of the concepts and themes introduced in the story.

Background

About the Author Lawrence Watt-Evans's memorable characters and stories have earned him high honors in the fields of science fiction and fantasy writing. Readers of *Isaac Asimov's Science Fiction Magazine* nominated "Why I Left Harry's All-Night Hamburgers" for the best short story of 1987. The next year that story earned Watt-Evans the Hugo Award and was nominated for the Nebula Award. Check out "Windwagon Smith and the Martians" and other stories in *Crosstime Traffic*.

Lawrence Watt-Evans currently lives in Maryland. He and his wife have two children and several pets, including a cat, a snake, and a hamster. You can learn more about Lawrence Watt-Evans by visiting his Web site, which is filled with illustrations from his book covers, notes on his own writing, and suggestions of his favorite works.

Exploring, inventing, and investigating are essential to the study of science. However, these activities can also be dangerous. To make sure that your experiments and explorations are safe, you must be aware of a variety of safety guidelines.

You have probably heard of the saying, "It is better to be safe than sorry." This is particularly true in a science classroom where experiments and explorations are being performed. Being uninformed and careless can result in serious injuries. Don't take chances with your own safety or with anyone else's.

Following are important guidelines for staying safe in the science classroom. Your teacher may also have safety guidelines and tips that are specific to your classroom and laboratory. Take the time to be safe.

Safety Rules!

Start Out Right

Always get your teacher's permission before attempting any laboratory exploration. Read the procedures carefully, and pay particular attention to safety information and caution statements. If you are unsure about what a safety symbol means, look it up or ask your teacher. You cannot be too careful when it comes to safety. If an accident does occur, inform your teacher immediately, regardless of how minor you think the accident is.

If you are instructed to note the odor of a substance, wave the fumes toward your nose with your hand. Never put your nose close to the source.

Safety Symbols

All of the experiments and investigations in this book and their related worksheets include important safety symbols to alert you to particular safety concerns. Become familiar with these symbols so that when you see them, you will know what they mean and what to do. It is important that you read this entire safety section to learn about specific dangers in the laboratory.

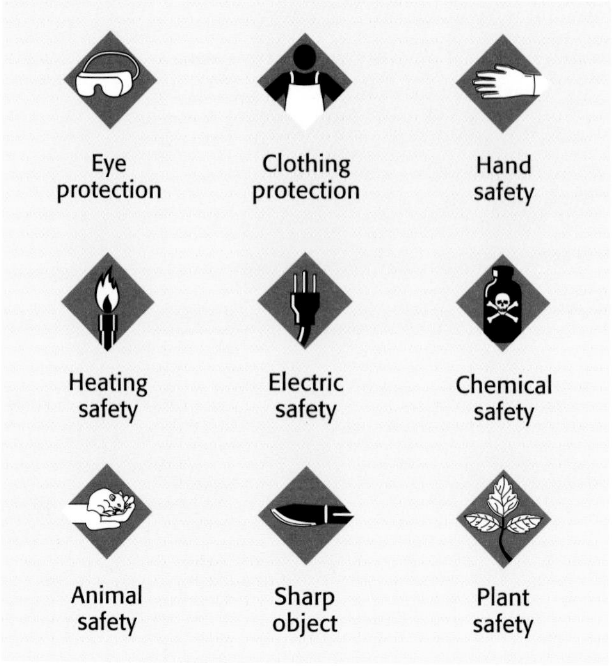

Eye Safety

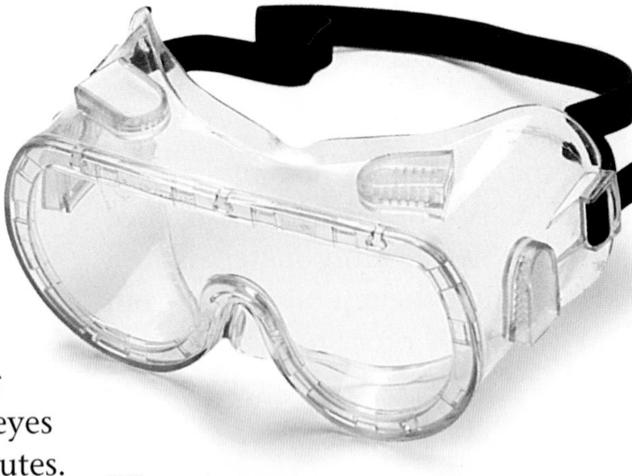

Wear safety goggles when working around chemicals, acids, bases, or any type of flame or heating device. Wear safety goggles any time there is even the slightest chance that harm could come to your eyes. If any substance gets into your eyes, notify your teacher immediately, and flush your eyes with running water for at least 15 minutes. Treat any unknown chemical as if it were a dangerous chemical. Never look directly into the sun. Doing so could cause permanent blindness.

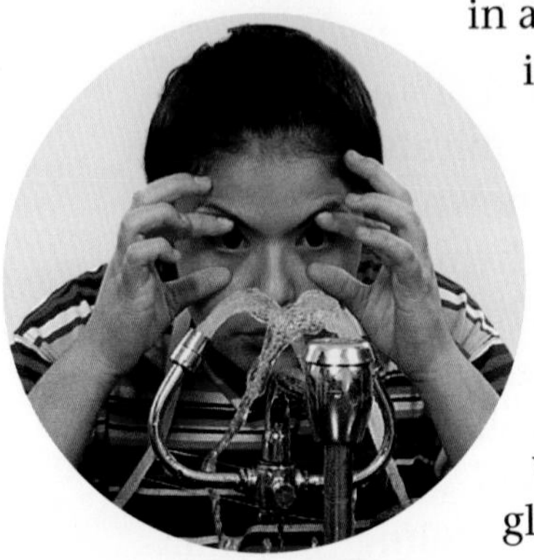

Avoid wearing contact lenses in a laboratory situation. Even if you are wearing safety goggles, chemicals can get between the contact lenses and your eyes. If your doctor requires that you wear contact lenses instead of glasses, wear eye-cup safety goggles in the lab.

Safety Equipment

Know the locations of the nearest fire alarms and any other safety equipment, such as fire blankets and eyewash fountains, as identified by your teacher, and know the procedures for using them.

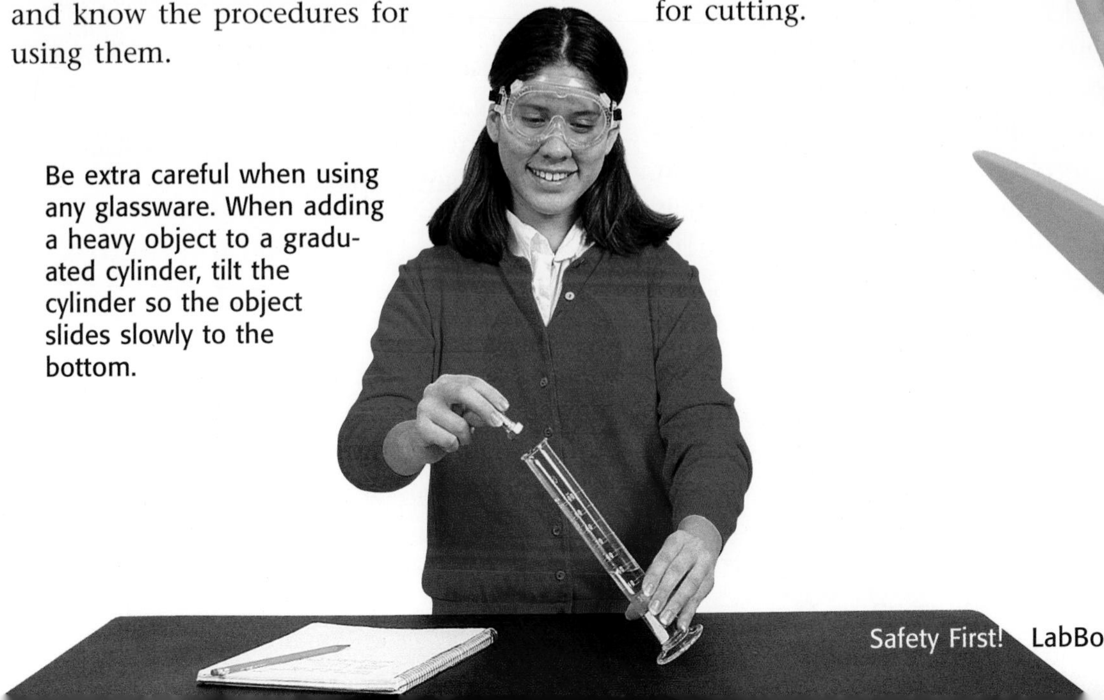

Be extra careful when using any glassware. When adding a heavy object to a graduated cylinder, tilt the cylinder so the object slides slowly to the bottom.

Neatness

Keep your work area free of all unnecessary books and papers. Tie back long hair, and secure loose sleeves or other loose articles of clothing, such as ties and bows. Remove dangling jewelry. Don't wear open-toed shoes or sandals in the laboratory. Never eat, drink, or apply cosmetics in a laboratory setting. Food, drink, and cosmetics can easily become contaminated with dangerous materials.

Certain hair products (such as aerosol hair spray) are flammable and should not be worn while working near an open flame. Avoid wearing hair spray or hair gel on lab days.

Sharp/Pointed Objects

Use knives and other sharp instruments with extreme care. Never cut objects while holding them in your hands. Place objects on a suitable work surface for cutting.

Heat

Wear safety goggles when using a heating device or a flame. Whenever possible, use an electric hot plate as a heat source instead of an open flame. When heating materials in a test tube, always angle the test tube away from yourself and others. In order to avoid burns, wear heat-resistant gloves whenever instructed to do so.

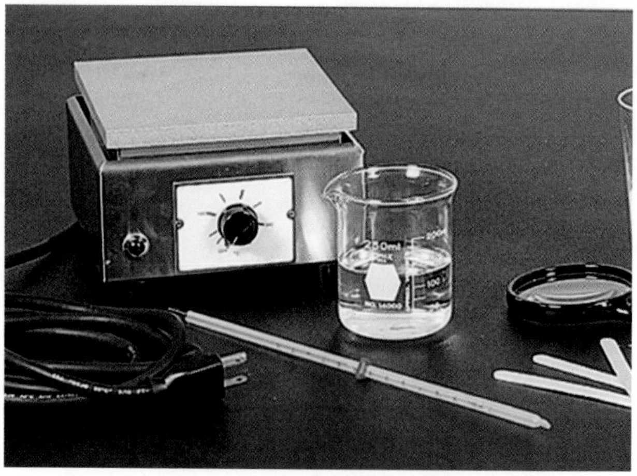

Electricity

Be careful with electrical cords. When using a microscope with a lamp, do not place the cord where it could trip someone. Do not let cords hang over a table edge in a way that could cause equipment to fall if the cord is accidentally pulled. Do not use equipment with damaged cords. Be sure your hands are dry and that the electrical equipment is in the "off" position before plugging it in. Turn off and unplug electrical equipment when you are finished.

Chemicals

Wear safety goggles when handling any potentially dangerous chemicals, acids, or bases. If a chemical is unknown, handle it as you would a dangerous chemical. Wear an apron and safety gloves when working with acids or bases or whenever you are told to do so. If a spill gets on your skin or clothing, rinse it off immediately with water for at least 5 minutes while calling to your teacher.

Never mix chemicals unless your teacher tells you to do so. Never taste, touch, or smell chemicals unless you are specifically directed to do so. Before working with a flammable liquid or gas, check for the presence of any source of flame, spark, or heat.

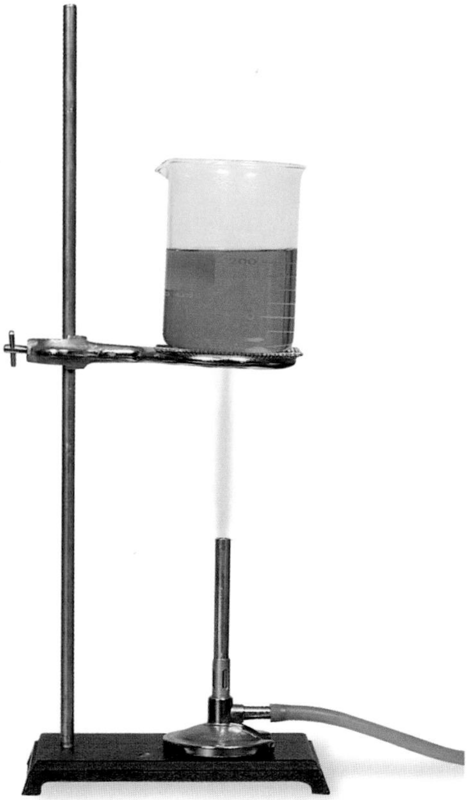

Animal Safety

Always obtain your teacher's permission before bringing any animal into the school building. Handle animals only as your teacher directs. Always treat animals carefully and with respect. Wash your hands thoroughly after handling any animal.

Plant Safety

Do not eat any part of a plant or plant seed used in the laboratory. Wash hands thoroughly after handling any part of a plant. When in nature, do not pick any wild plants unless your teacher instructs you to do so.

Glassware

Examine all glassware before use. Be sure that glassware is clean and free of chips and cracks. Report damaged glassware to your teacher. Glass containers used for heating should be made of heat-resistant glass.

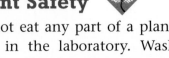

159

The Sun's Yearly Trip Through the Zodiac
Teacher's Notes

Time Required
Two 45-minute class periods

Lab Ratings
EASY → HARD

Teacher Prep 3
Student Set-Up 2
Concept Level 3
Clean Up 1

MATERIALS

The materials listed on the student pages are enough for a group of 12 students. However, you may choose to use this activity as a demonstration for the entire class.

Preparation Notes
One week before the activity, collect large cardboard boxes. Designate a large, clear area for the activity, such as a gym, cafeteria, playground, or large classroom. You may wish to get a basketball from the physical education instructor, or ask students to bring basketballs from home. Folding chairs work best for this activity because of their portability.

Review the terms *clockwise* and *counterclockwise* to ensure consistency of student results.

Using Scientific Methods

SKILL BUILDER

The Sun's Yearly Trip Through the Zodiac

During the course of a year, the sun appears to move through a circle of twelve constellations in the sky. The twelve constellations make up a "belt" in the sky called the *zodiac.* Each month, the sun appears to be in a different constellation. The ancient Babylonians developed a 12-month calendar based on the idea that the sun moved through this circle of constellations as it revolved around the Earth. They believed that the constellations of stars were fixed in position and that the sun and planets moved past the stars. Later, Copernicus developed a model of the solar system in which the Earth and the planets revolve around the sun. But how can Copernicus's model of the solar system be correct when the sun appears to move through the zodiac?

Materials
- 12 chairs
- 12 index cards
- roll of masking tape
- inflated ball
- large cardboard box

Ask a Question
1. If the sun is at the center of the solar system, why does it appear to move with respect to the stars in the sky?

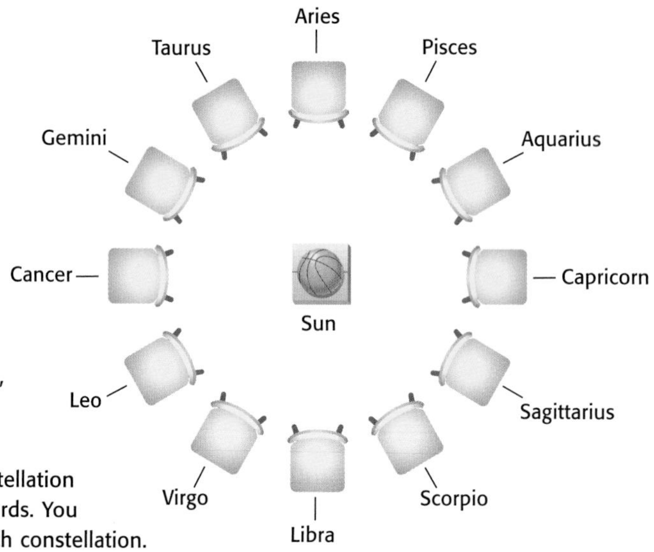

Conduct an Experiment
2. Set the chairs in a large circle so that the backs of the chairs all face the center of the circle. Make sure that the chairs are equally spaced, like the numbers on the face of a clock.
3. Write the name of each constellation in the zodiac on the index cards. You should have one card for each constellation.
4. Stand inside the circle with the masking tape and the index cards. Moving counterclockwise, attach the cards to the backs of the chairs in the following order: Aries, Taurus, Gemini, Cancer, Leo, Virgo, Libra, Scorpio, Sagittarius, Capricorn, Aquarius, and Pisces.
5. Use masking tape to label the ball "Sun."
6. Place the large closed box in the center of the circle. Set the roll of masking tape flat on top of the box.

Joseph W. Price
H.M. Browne Junior High
Washington, D.C.

7. Place the ball on top of the roll of masking tape so that the ball stays in place.

8. Stand inside of the circle of chairs. You will represent the Earth. As you move around the ball, you will model the Earth's orbit around the sun. Notice that even though only the "Earth" is moving, as seen from the Earth, the sun appears to move through the entire zodiac!

9. Stand in front of the chair labeled "Aries." Look at the ball representing the sun. Then look past the ball to the chair at the opposite side of the circle. Where in the zodiac does the sun appear to be?

10. Move to the next chair on your right (counterclockwise). Where does the sun appear to be? Is it in the same constellation? Explain your answer.

11. Repeat step 10 until you have observed the position of the sun from each chair in the circle.

Analyze the Results

12. Did the sun appear to move through the 12 constellations, even though the Earth was orbiting around the sun? How can you explain this?

Draw Conclusions

13. How does Copernicus's model of the solar system explain the apparent movement of the sun through the constellations of the zodiac?

Datasheets for LabBook

LabBook

Background

Begin the activity by asking students if they are familiar with the constellations of the Zodiac. Have they seen them depicted in a list or in a circle? How did the mythology of the Zodiac begin? (The 12 familiar signs of the Zodiac were adopted by the Babylonians about 3,000 years ago. The word *zodiac* means "circle," and the Babylonians thought that the sun and the planets moved in a circle through 12 fixed constellations in the night sky.)

Ask each student group to list as many Zodiac constellations as they can remember on the chalkboard. The constellations and their corresponding signs are as follows: Aries (the ram), Taurus (the bull), Gemini (the twins), Cancer (the crab), Leo (the lion), Virgo (the virgin), Libra (the scales), Scorpio (the scorpion), Sagittarius (the hunter), Capricorn (the mountain goat), Aquarius (the water bearer), and Pisces (the fish).

Answers

12. When students stand in front of a chair, the sun appears to be in the constellation opposite the chair. As they move outside the circle counterclockwise, the sun appears to shift through the constellations counterclockwise. As the Earth (the student) orbits the sun (the ball), the sun never appears in the same constellation because of the Earth's perspective relative to the fixed constellations.

13. In Copernicus' heliocentric model of the solar system, the Earth orbits the sun. As the Earth moves around the sun, the position of the sun in relation to the constellations changes.

LabBook

Through the Looking Glass
Teacher's Notes

Time Required

One 45-minute class period

Lab Ratings

EASY → HARD

Teacher Prep: 2

Student Set-Up: 3

Concept Level: 2

Clean Up: 1

MATERIALS

The materials listed on the student page are enough for a group of 2–3 students.

Safety Caution

Remind students to review all safety cautions and icons before beginning this lab activity. Students should never look at the sun through their telescopes. Caution students not to focus sunlight through their telescopes because it could start a fire.

Preparation Notes

One week before the activity, ask students to collect wrapping-paper and toilet-paper cardboard tubes to bring to class. Obtain two double-convex lenses for each group of students.

You may wish to experiment with the lenses before class to determine how far the paper must be to form an image. If you add another lens to the telescope, you can make the image right side up, but light is lost as it passes through the third lens.

Through the Looking Glass

SKILL BUILDER

Have you ever looked toward the horizon or up into the sky and wished you could see farther? Think a telescope might help? Astronomers use huge telescopes to study the universe. You can build your very own telescope to get a glimpse of what astronomers see with their incredible equipment.

Materials

- masking tape
- 2 convex lenses, 3 cm in diameter
- desk lamp
- sheet of construction paper
- metric ruler
- cardboard wrapping-paper tube
- cardboard toilet-paper tube
- scissors
- modeling clay

Procedure

1. Use modeling clay to form a base to hold one of the lenses upright on your desktop. When the lights are turned off, your teacher will turn on a lamp at the front of the classroom. Rotate your lens so that the light from the lamp passes through it.
2. Hold the construction paper so that the light passing through the lens lands on the paper. Slowly move the paper closer to or farther from the lens until you see the sharpest image of the light on the paper. Hold the paper in this position.
3. With the metric ruler, measure the distance between the lens and the paper. Record this distance in your ScienceLog.
4. How far is the paper from the lens? This distance, called the *image distance*, is how far the paper has to be from the lens in order for the image to be in focus.
5. Repeat steps 1–4 with the other lens.

162

CLASSROOM TESTED & APPROVED

Michael E. Kral
West Hardin Middle School
Cecilia, Kentucky

6. From one end of the long cardboard tube, measure and mark the image distance of the lens with the longer image distance. Place a mark 2 cm past this line toward the other end of the tube, and label the mark "cut."
7. From one end of the short cardboard tube, measure and mark the image distance of the lens with the shorter image distance. Place a mark 2 cm past this line toward the other end of the tube, and label the mark "cut."
8. Shorten the tubes by cutting along the marks labeled "cut."
9. Tape the lens with the longer image distance to one end of the longer tube. Tape the other lens to one end of the shorter tube. Slip one tube inside the other. Be sure the lenses are at each end of this new, longer tube.
10. Congratulations! You have just constructed a telescope! To use your telescope, look through the short tube (the eyepiece), and point the long end at various objects in the room. You can focus the telescope by adjusting its length. Are the images right side up, or upside down? Observe birds, insects, trees, or other outside objects. **Caution:** Never look directly at the sun! This could cause permanent blindness.

Analysis

11. Which type of telescope did you just construct—a refracting telescope or a reflecting telescope? What makes it one type and not the other?
12. Would upside-down images negatively affect astronomers looking at stars through their telescopes? Explain your answer.

LabBook

Background

Begin the activity by discussing the components of a telescope. Simple telescopes, like the one Galileo made, consist of two lenses and a tube. To provide a clear image, the tube should be as long as the sum of the image distances of the two lenses. Some students may have difficulty knowing when the image is in focus. Explain to these students that they should focus the light bulb's filament on the paper.

Answers

11. a refracting telescope; Refracting telescopes use lenses, while reflecting telescopes use mirrors and lenses.
12. Answers will vary. Accept all reasonable responses.

Datasheets for LabBook

LabBook

Why Do They Wander?
Teacher's Notes

Time Required
This activity will take approximately 30 minutes. But it may take as much as one 45-minute class period to instruct students on how to use a compass.

Lab Ratings
EASY → HARD

TEACHER PREP 2
STUDENT SET-UP 1
CONCEPT LEVEL 4
CLEAN UP 1

MATERIALS

The materials listed on the student page are enough for 1–2 students. The compasses, rulers, and colored pencils may be shared among several groups.

Safety Caution
Remind students to review all safety cautions and icons before beginning this lab activity.

Preparation Notes
Students may need instruction on how to use a drawing compass. You may need to demonstrate the proper use of a compass. This activity works best when students work individually or in pairs. Each group will need a compass, a piece of white paper, and a metric ruler. The compasses, rulers, and colored pencils may be shared among several groups.

Using Scientific Methods

MAKING MODELS

Why Do They Wander?

Before the discoveries of Nicholas Copernicus in the early 1500s, most people thought that the planets and the sun revolve around the Earth and that the Earth was the center of the solar system. But Copernicus observed that the sun is the center of the solar system and that all the planets, including Earth, revolve around the sun. He also explained a puzzling aspect of the movement of planets across the night sky.

If you watch a planet every night for several months, you'll notice that it appears to "wander" among the stars. While the stars remain in fixed positions relative to each other, the planets appear to move independently of the stars. First Mars travels to the left, then it goes back to the right a little, and finally it reverses direction and travels again to the left. No wonder the early Greeks called the planets wanderers!

In this lab you will make your own model of part of the solar system to find out how Copernicus's model of the solar system explained this zigzag motion of the planets.

Materials
- drawing compass
- white paper
- metric ruler
- colored pencils

Ask a Question
1. Why do the planets appear to move back and forth in the Earth's night sky?

Conduct an Experiment
2. Use the compass to draw a circle with a diameter of 9 cm on the paper. This circle will represent the orbit of the Earth around the sun. (Note: The orbits of the planets are actually slightly elliptical, but circles will work for this activity.)
3. Using the same center point, draw a circle with a diameter of 12 cm. This circle will represent the orbit of Mars.
4. Using a blue pencil, draw three parallel lines in a diagonal across one end of your paper, as shown at right. These lines will help you plot the path Mars appears to travel in Earth's night sky. Turn your paper so that the diagonal lines are at the top of the page.
5. Place 11 dots on your Earth orbit, as shown on the next page, and number them 1 through 11. These dots will represent Earth's position from month to month.

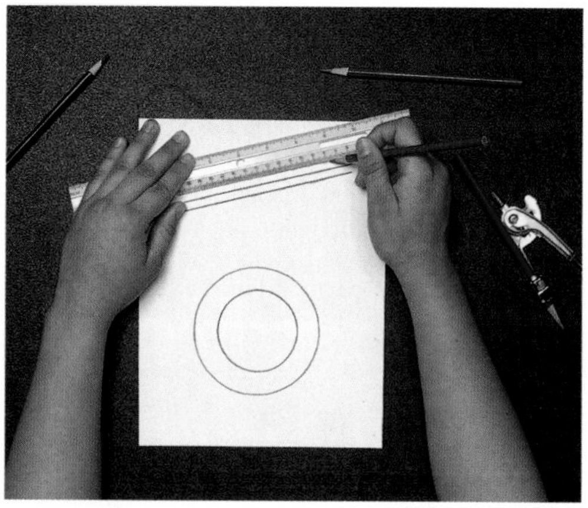

164

MISCONCEPTION ALERT

The apparent motion of Mars illustrated in this lab is called "retrograde motion." It should not be confused with retrograde orbit or retrograde rotation. In addition, this lab does not accurately portray the actual *positions* of Earth and Mars during their orbits, it merely shows how their relative positions change.

Joseph W. Price
H. M. Browne Junior High
Washington, D.C.

6. Now place 11 dots along the top of your Mars orbit, as shown below. Number the dots as shown. These dots will represent the position of Mars at the same time intervals. Notice that Mars travels slower than Earth.
7. Use a green line to connect the first dot on Earth's orbit to the first dot on Mars's orbit, and extend the line all the way to the first diagonal line at the top of your paper. Place a green dot where this green line meets the first blue diagonal line, and label the green dot *1*.
8. Now connect the second dot on Earth's orbit to the second dot on Mars's orbit, and extend the line all the way to the first diagonal at the top of your paper. Place a green dot where this line meets the first blue diagonal line, and label this dot *2*.
9. Continue drawing green lines from Earth's orbit through Mars's orbit and finally to the blue diagonal lines. Pay attention to the pattern of dots you are adding to the diagonal lines. When the direction of the dots changes, extend the green line to the next diagonal, and add the dots to that line instead.
10. When you are finished adding green lines, draw a red line to connect all the dots on the blue diagonal lines in the order you drew them.

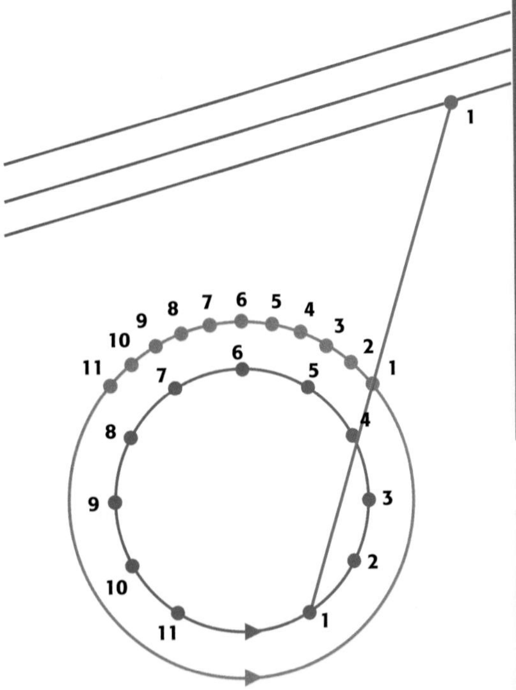

Analyze the Results

11. What do the green lines connecting points along Earth's orbit and Mars's orbit represent?
12. What does the red line connecting the dots along the diagonal lines look like? How can you explain this?

Draw Conclusions

13. What does this demonstration show about the motion of Mars?
14. Why do planets appear to move back and forth across the sky?
15. Were the Greeks justified in calling the planets wanderers? Explain.

LabBook

Answers

11. The lines connecting Earth's orbit and Mars's orbit represent the students' line of sight as they stand on Earth and look at Mars.
12. The line along the diagonals changed direction at the fifth and seventh points. This happened because Mars was behind Earth in its orbit. To a person on Earth, it would look as if Mars changed direction at those moments.
13. When Earth catches up to Mars, Mars appears to reverse its direction. As Earth passes Mars, Mars appears to revert to its original direction.
14. Planets appear to move back and forth because they travel around the sun at different speeds and at different distances. When the Earth overtakes a slower planet, such as Mars, that planet appears to move backwards in Earth's sky.
15. Answers may vary. Accept all well-supported responses. Although the planets do not actually wander, it does appear as if they do to people on Earth. Students may consider this enough justification for calling the planets wanderers.

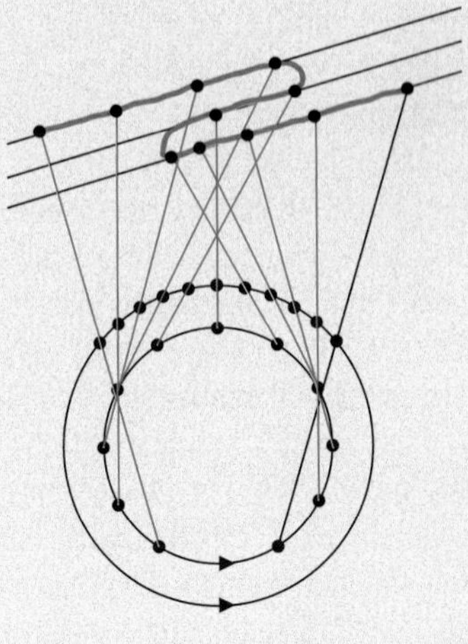

Lab Notes

Plan View Versus Sky View: It is important to note that the circles represent a plan view of part of the solar system, while the diagonal lines represent a view of the apparent motion of Mars in Earth's night sky. Students are asked to jump from line to line as they draw their dots in order to show them the apparent path of Mars in the sky.

Note on Scale: Notice that, according to the drawing, it appears that for less than half of its orbit, Mars travels more than a year of Earth's time. In fact, an Earth year is actually more than half of a Martian year. Mars's period of revolution is 1.88 Earth years. The drawing on this page is not to scale in this respect; if it were to scale, the wandering motion of the planets could not be depicted on one page.

Datasheets for LabBook

I See the Light!
Teacher's Notes

Time Required
One to two 45-minute class periods

Lab Ratings
EASY → HARD

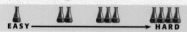

TEACHER PREP 2
STUDENT SET-UP 3
CONCEPT LEVEL 4
CLEAN UP 1

MATERIALS
The materials listed on the student page are enough for 1–2 students.

Safety Caution
Remind students to review all safety cautions and icons before beginning this lab activity. Remind students to be careful about traffic hazards around your school's flagpole.

Preparation Notes
Students may need an introduction to angles and the use of protractors. Be sure they understand how to use protractors *before* you perform this activity. Students may feel uneasy with the mathematics. Explain that astronomers use trigonometry, which is the measurement of triangles, to calculate distances to nearby stars. By using the TAN function on a calculator, the length of the unknown leg of the triangle formed by the sun, Earth, and a star can be found. If students are unfamiliar with the TAN function, they may prefer to use the table at right.

I See the Light!

SKILL BUILDER

How do you find the distance to an object you can't reach? You can do it by measuring something you can reach, finding a few angles, and using mathematics. In this activity, you'll practice measuring the distances of objects here on Earth. When you get used to it, you can take your skills to the stars!

Materials
- 16 × 16 cm piece of poster board
- metric ruler
- protractor
- scissors
- sharp pencil
- 30 cm string
- transparent tape
- meterstick
- metric measuring tape
- scientific calculator

Procedure
1. Draw a line 4 cm away from the edge of one side of the piece of poster board. Fold the poster board along this line.
2. Tape the protractor to the poster board with its flat edge against the fold, as shown in the photo below.
3. Use a sharp pencil to carefully punch a hole through the poster board along its folded edge at the center of the protractor.
4. Thread the string through the hole, and tape one end to the underside of the poster board. The other end should be long enough to hang off the far end of the poster board.
5. Carefully punch a second hole in the smaller area of the poster board halfway between its short sides. The hole should be directly above the first hole and should be large enough for the pencil to fit through. This is the viewing hole of your new parallax device. This device will allow you to measure the distance of faraway objects.

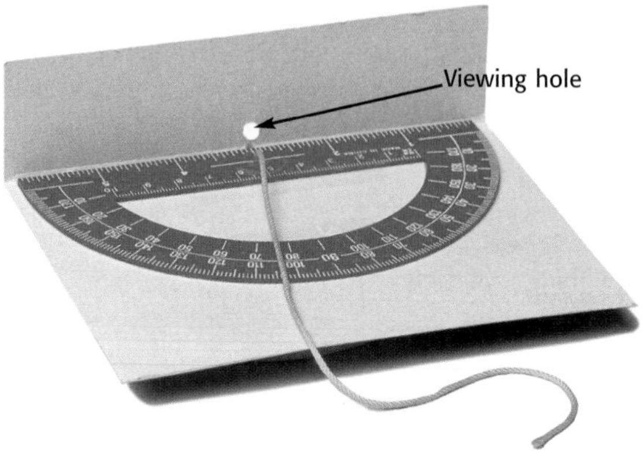

6. Find a location outside that is at least 50 steps away from a tall, narrow object, such as the school's flagpole or a tall tree. (This object will represent background stars.) Set the meterstick on the ground with one of its long edges facing the flagpole.
7. Ask your partner, who represents a nearby star, to take 10 steps toward the flagpole, starting at the left end of the meterstick. You will be the observer. When you stand at the left end of the meterstick, which represents the location of the sun, your partner's nose should be lined up with the flag pole.
8. Move to the other end of the meterstick, which represents the location of Earth. Does your partner appear to the left or right of the flagpole? Record your observations in your ScienceLog.
9. Hold the string so that it runs straight from the viewing hole to the 90° mark on the protractor. Using one eye, look through the viewing hole along the string and point the device at your partner's nose.

166

Angle	Tangent	Angle	Tangent
1°	0.0175	6°	0.1051
2°	0.0349	7°	0.1228
3°	0.0524	8°	0.1405
4°	0.0699	9°	0.1584
5°	0.0875	10°	0.1763

Susan Gorman
North Ridge Middle School
North Richmond Hills, Texas

10. Holding the device still, slowly move your head until you can see the flagpole through the viewing hole. Move the string so that it lines up between your eye and the flagpole. Make sure the string is taut, and hold it tightly against the protractor.

11. Read and record the angle made by the string and the string's original position at 90° (count the number of degrees between 90° and the string's new position).

12. Use the measuring tape to find and record the distance from the left end of the meterstick to your partner's nose.

13. Now find a place outside that is at least 100 steps away from the flagpole. Set the meterstick on the ground as before, and repeat steps 7–12.

Analysis

14. The angle you recorded in step 11 is called the *parallax angle.* The distance from one end of the meterstick to the other is called the *baseline.* With this angle and the length of your baseline, you can calculate the distance to your partner.

15. To calculate the distance (d) to your partner, use the following equation:

$$d = b/\tan A$$

In this equation, A is the parallax angle and b is the length of the baseline (1 m). (Tan A means the tangent of angle A, which you will learn more about in high school math classes.)

16. To find d, enter 1 (the length of your baseline in meters) into the calculator, press the "divide" key, enter the value of A (the parallax angle you recorded), then press the "tan" key. Finally, press the "equals" key.

17. Record this result in your ScienceLog. It is the distance in meters between the left end of the meterstick and your partner. You may want to use a table like the one shown at right.

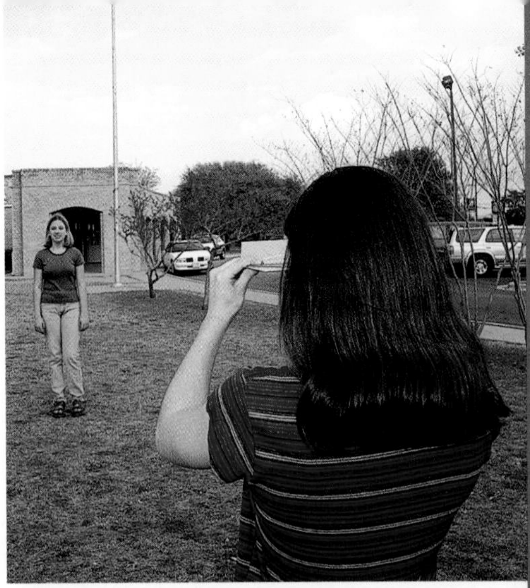

18. How close is this calculated distance to the distance you measured in step 12?

19. Repeat steps 15–17 using the angle you found when the flagpole was 100 steps away.

Conclusions

20. At which position, 50 steps or 100 steps from the flagpole, did your calculated distance better match the actual distance as measured in step 12?

21. What do you think would happen if you were even farther from the flagpole?

22. When astronomers use parallax, their "flagpole" is the very distant stars. How might this affect the accuracy of their parallax readings?

Distance by Parallax Versus Measuring Tape

	At 50 steps	At 100 steps
Parallax angle		
Distance (calculated)	DO NOT WRITE IN BOOK	
Distance (measured)		

Lab Notes

If the school's flagpole is not in a convenient spot, a tall tree or lamp post will work. If students have difficulty keeping the device still while moving their head, you might have them try steadying the device on a tripod or on the end of a meterstick.

Some students may have difficulty understanding the relationship between measuring stars with parallax and the parallax effects on measurements (e.g., reading a dial off to the side can give a different value). The viewing hole in the parallax device used in this activity reduces such errors. Thus, the parallax effect in this activity measures only faraway distances.

Students should realize that as the distance to a reference point (such as a flagpole or background stars) increases, the angle measured by the parallax device becomes closer to the actual parallax angle. Therefore, students should find that their calculation of the distance to their partner should be more accurate when they move 100 steps from the tree.

They should also realize that astronomers use the "fixed stars," which are essentially at optical infinity, as a reference.

Answers

18. Answers will vary but should approximate the actual distance given in meters.

19. Answers will vary due to differences in technique.

20. At 100 steps, the distance calculated should be closer to the distance measured.

21. Accuracy should increase.

22. Their calculations should be very close to the actual distance (if it could be measured).

Datasheets for LabBook

LabBook

Water Rockets Save the Day! Teacher's Notes

Time Required

Two 45-minute class periods

Lab Ratings

EASY → HARD

- Teacher Prep: 3
- Student Set-Up: 3
- Concept Level: 2
- Clean Up: 2

MATERIALS

The materials listed in this lab are enough for one student. Students can also work in groups of 3–4.

Safety Caution

Remind students to review all safety cautions and icons before beginning this lab activity. Make sure that students are several meters away from the launch site when the rockets are being launched.

Using Scientific Methods

DESIGN YOUR OWN

Water Rockets Save the Day!

Imagine that for the big Fourth of July celebration you and your friends had planned a full day of swimming, volleyball, and fireworks at the lake. You've just learned however, that the city passed a law that bans all fireworks within city limits. But you are not one to give up so easily on having fun. Last year at summer camp you learned how to build water rockets. And you kept the launcher in your garage all this time! With a little bit of creativity, you and your friends are going to celebrate with a splash!

Materials

- 2 L soda bottle with cap
- foam board
- modeling clay
- duct tape
- scissors
- water
- bucket, 5-gal
- rocket launcher
- watch or clock that indicates seconds

Ask a Question

1. How can I use water and a soda bottle to build a rocket?

Conduct an Experiment

2. Decide how you want your rocket to look. Draw a sketch in your ScienceLog.
3. Using only the materials listed, decide how to build your rocket. Describe your design in your ScienceLog. Keep in mind that you will need to leave the opening of your bottle clear. It will be placed over a rubber stopper on the rocket launcher.
4. Fins are often used to stabilize rockets. Do you want fins on your water rocket? Decide on the best shape for the fins, and then decide how many fins your rocket needs. Use the foam board to construct the fins.

Preparation Notes

Each student or group of students will need a 2 L soda bottle to construct their rocket. You can ask students a week or two ahead of time to save any 2 L soda bottles they have at home.

Water rockets require a launcher that you will need to make or purchase in advance. Launchers are the key to a successful and safe liftoff. They can be purchased at most hobby shops or from Science Kit®. You can expect to spend at least $20 for a launcher or launcher kit at a hobby shop. You need only one launcher for your class. When buying a launcher, make sure the launcher is compatible with your rocket bottle size.

If you wish to construct the launcher yourself, research one of the many water rocket Web sites on the Internet. This is a popular hobby, and good information on the subject is not hard to find.

Alyson Mike
East Valley Middle School
East Helena, Montana

5. Your rocket must be heavy enough to fly along a controlled pathway. Consider using clay in the body of your rocket to provide some additional weight and stability.
6. Pour water into your rocket until it is one-third to one-half full.
7. Your teacher will provide the launcher and assist you during blastoff. Attach your rocket to the launcher by placing its opening on the rubber stopper.
8. When the rocket is in place, clear the immediate area and begin pumping air into your rocket. Watch the pump gauge, and take note of how much pressure is needed for liftoff.
   Caution: Be sure to step back from the launch site. You should be several meters away from the bottle when you launch it.
9. Use the watch to time your rocket's flight. (How long was your rocket in the air?)
10. Make small changes in your rocket design that you think will improve the rocket's performance. Consider using different amounts of water and clay or experimenting with different fins. You may also want to compare your design with those of your classmates.

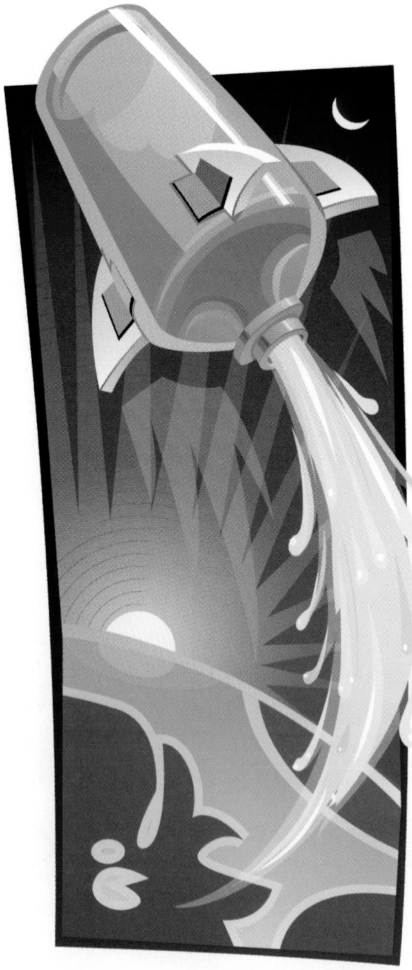

Analyze the Results

11. How did your rocket perform? If you used fins, do you think they helped your flight? Explain.
12. What do you think propelled your rocket? Use Newton's third law of motion to justify your answer.
13. How did the amount of water in your rocket affect the launch?

Newton's third law of motion: For every action there is an equal and opposite reaction.

Draw Conclusions

14. What modifications made your rocket fly for the longest time? How did the design help the rockets fly so far?
15. Which group's rockets were the most stable? How did the design help the rockets fly straight?
16. How can you improve your design to make your rocket perform even better?

LabBook

Answers

11. Answers will vary. Fins might help stabilize the rocket when it is in flight.
12. Answers will vary. Students should note that the water in the bottle was under pressure. When the rocket was released, the water escaped out of the opening. The bottle reacted by moving in the opposite direction—upward.
13. Answers will vary. Water is the propellant for the rocket. Pressurized air provides the force to launch the rocket. The amount of water in a rocket determines how much space air can occupy. The ideal rocket should expel all of the water at the maximum pressure.
14. Answers will vary. Modifying the fins, adjusting the water-to-air ratio, increasing the air pressure inside the rocket, and changing the amount of modeling clay used should affect the duration of the rocket's flight.
15. Answers will vary.
16. Answers will vary.

Datasheets for LabBook

Concept Mapping: A Way to Bring Ideas Together

What Is a Concept Map?

Have you ever tried to tell someone about a book or a chapter you've just read and found that you can remember only a few isolated words and ideas? Or maybe you've memorized facts for a test and then weeks later discovered you're not even sure what topics those facts covered.

In both cases, you may have understood the ideas or concepts by themselves but not in relation to one another. If you could somehow link the ideas together, you would probably understand them better and remember them longer. This is something a concept map can help you do. A concept map is a way to see how ideas or concepts fit together. It can help you see the "big picture."

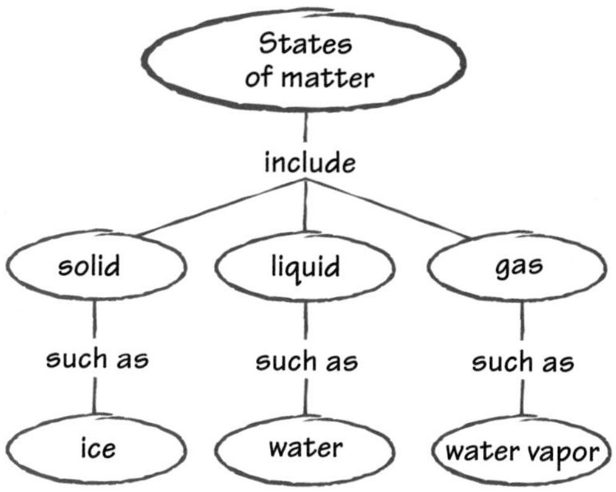

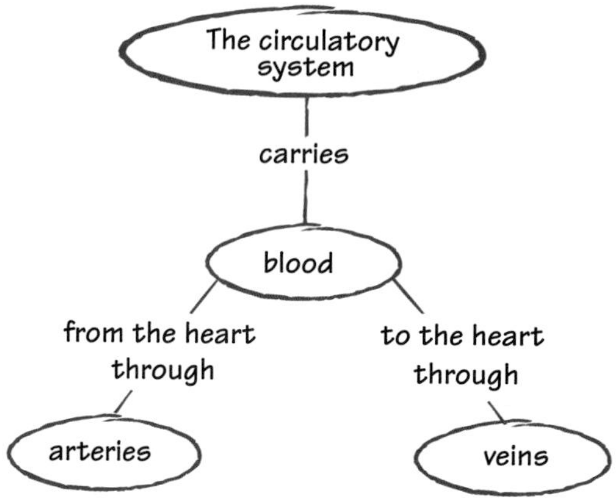

How to Make a Concept Map

1. **Make a list of the main ideas or concepts.**

   It might help to write each concept on its own slip of paper. This will make it easier to rearrange the concepts as many times as necessary to make sense of how the concepts are connected. After you've made a few concept maps this way, you can go directly from writing your list to actually making the map.

2. **Arrange the concepts in order from the most general to the most specific.**

   Put the most general concept at the top and circle it. Ask yourself, "How does this concept relate to the remaining concepts?" As you see the relationships, arrange the concepts in order from general to specific.

3. **Connect the related concepts with lines.**

4. **On each line, write an action word or short phrase that shows how the concepts are related.**

Look at the concept maps on this page, and then see if you can make one for the following terms:

plants, water, photosynthesis, carbon dioxide, sun's energy

One possible answer is provided at right, but don't look at it until you try the concept map yourself.

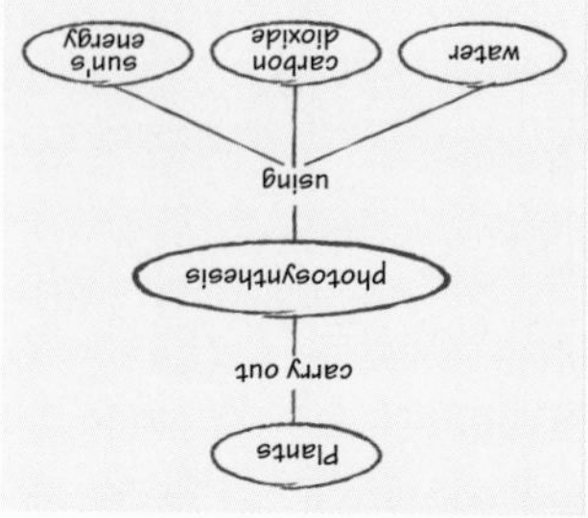

SI Measurement

The International System of Units, or SI, is the standard system of measurement used by many scientists. Using the same standards of measurement makes it easier for scientists to communicate with one another.

SI works by combining prefixes and base units. Each base unit can be used with different prefixes to define smaller and larger quantities. The table below lists common SI prefixes.

SI Prefixes

Prefix	Abbreviation	Factor	Example
kilo-	k	1,000	kilogram, 1 kg = 1,000 g
hecto-	h	100	hectoliter, 1 hL = 100 L
deka-	da	10	dekameter, 1 dam = 10 m
		1	meter, liter
deci-	d	0.1	decigram, 1 dg = 0.1 g
centi-	c	0.01	centimeter, 1 cm = 0.01 m
milli-	m	0.001	milliliter, 1 mL = 0.001 L
micro-	μ	0.000 001	micrometer, 1 μm = 0.000 001 m

SI Conversion Table

SI units	From SI to English	From English to SI
Length		
kilometer (km) = 1,000 m	1 km = 0.621 mi	1 mi = 1.609 km
meter (m) = 100 cm	1 m = 3.281 ft	1 ft = 0.305 m
centimeter (cm) = 0.01 m	1 cm = 0.394 in.	1 in. = 2.540 cm
millimeter (mm) = 0.001 m	1 mm = 0.039 in.	
micrometer (μm) = 0.000 001 m		
nanometer (nm) = 0.000 000 001 m		
Area		
square kilometer (km^2) = 100 hectares	1 km^2 = 0.386 mi^2	1 mi^2 = 2.590 km^2
hectare (ha) = 10,000 m^2	1 ha = 2.471 acres	1 acre = 0.405 ha
square meter (m^2) = 10,000 cm^2	1 m^2 = 10.765 ft^2	1 ft^2 = 0.093 m^2
square centimeter (cm^2) = 100 mm^2	1 cm^2 = 0.155 $in.^2$	1 $in.^2$ = 6.452 cm^2
Volume		
liter (L) = 1,000 mL = 1 dm^3	1 L = 1.057 fl qt	1 fl qt = 0.946 L
milliliter (mL) = 0.001 L = 1 cm^3	1 mL = 0.034 fl oz	1 fl oz = 29.575 mL
microliter (μL) = 0.000 001 L		
Mass		
kilogram (kg) = 1,000 g	1 kg = 2.205 lb	1 lb = 0.454 kg
gram (g) = 1,000 mg	1 g = 0.035 oz	1 oz = 28.349 g
milligram (mg) = 0.001 g		
microgram (μg) = 0.000 001 g		

171

Scientific Method

The series of steps that scientists use to answer questions and solve problems is often called the **scientific method.** The scientific method is not a rigid procedure. Scientists may use all of the steps or just some of the steps of the scientific method. They may even repeat some of the steps. The goal of the scientific method is to come up with reliable answers and solutions.

Six Steps of the Scientific Method

1 Ask a Question Good questions come from careful **observations.** You make observations by using your senses to gather information. Sometimes you may use instruments, such as microscopes and telescopes, to extend the range of your senses. As you observe the natural world, you will discover that you have many more questions than answers. These questions drive the scientific method.

Questions beginning with *what, why, how,* and *when* are very important in focusing an investigation, and they often lead to a hypothesis. (You will learn what a hypothesis is in the next step.) Here is an example of a question that could lead to further investigation.

Question: How does acid rain affect plant growth?

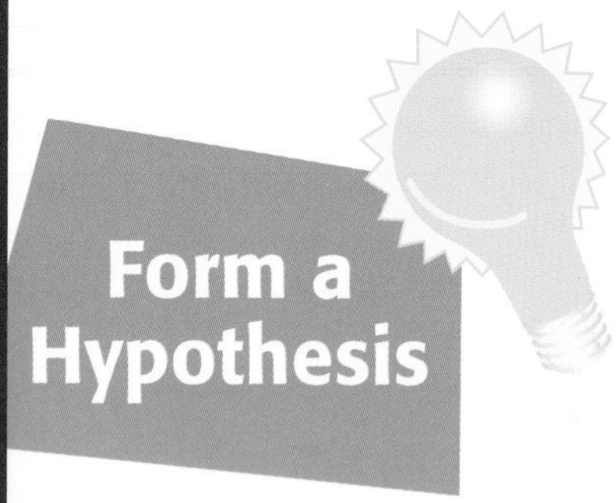

2 Form a Hypothesis After you come up with a question, you need to turn the question into a **hypothesis.** A hypothesis is a clear statement of what you expect the answer to your question to be. Your hypothesis will represent your best "educated guess" based on your observations and what you already know. A good hypothesis is testable. If observations and information cannot be gathered or if an experiment cannot be designed to test your hypothesis, it is untestable, and the investigation can go no further.

Here is a hypothesis that could be formed from the question, "How does acid rain affect plant growth?"

Hypothesis: Acid rain causes plants to grow more slowly.

Notice that the hypothesis provides some specifics that lead to methods of testing. The hypothesis can also lead to predictions. A **prediction** is what you think will be the outcome of your experiment or data collection. Predictions are usually stated in an "if . . . then" format. For example, **if** meat is kept at room temperature, **then** it will spoil faster than meat kept in the refrigerator. More than one prediction can be made for a single hypothesis. Here is a sample prediction for the hypothesis that acid rain causes plants to grow more slowly.

Prediction: If a plant is watered with only acid rain (which has a pH of 4), then the plant will grow at half its normal rate.

3 **Test the Hypothesis** After you have formed a hypothesis and made a prediction, you should test your hypothesis. There are different ways to do this. Perhaps the most familiar way is to conduct a **controlled experiment.** A controlled experiment tests only one factor at a time. A controlled experiment has a **control group** and one or more **experimental groups.** All the factors for the control and experimental groups are the same except for one factor, which is called the **variable.** By changing only one factor, you can see the results of just that one change.

Sometimes, the nature of an investigation makes a controlled experiment impossible. For example, dinosaurs have been extinct for millions of years, and the Earth's core is surrounded by thousands of meters of rock. It would be difficult, if not impossible, to conduct controlled experiments on such things. Under such circumstances, a hypothesis may be tested by making detailed observations. Taking measurements is one way of making observations.

4 **Analyze the Results** After you have completed your experiments, made your observations, and collected your data, you must analyze all the information you have gathered. Tables and graphs are often used in this step to organize the data.

5 **Draw Conclusions** Based on the analysis of your data, you should conclude whether or not your results support your hypothesis. If your hypothesis is supported, you (or others) might want to repeat the observations or experiments to verify your results. If your hypothesis is not supported by the data, you may have to check your procedure for errors. You may even have to reject your hypothesis and make a new one. If you cannot draw a conclusion from your results, you may have to try the investigation again or carry out further observations or experiments.

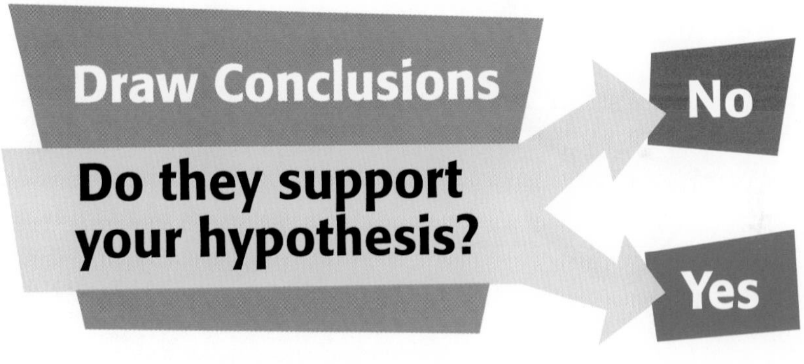

6 **Communicate Results** After any scientific investigation, you should report your results. By doing a written or oral report, you let others know what you have learned. They may want to repeat your investigation to see if they get the same results. Your report may even lead to another question, which in turn may lead to another investigation.

Scientific Method in Action

The scientific method is not a "straight line" of steps. It contains loops in which several steps may be repeated over and over again, while others may not be necessary. For example, sometimes scientists will find that testing one hypothesis raises new questions and new hypotheses to be tested. And sometimes, testing the hypothesis leads directly to a conclusion. Furthermore, the steps in the scientific method are not always used in the same order. Follow the steps in the diagram below, and see how many different directions the scientific method can take you.

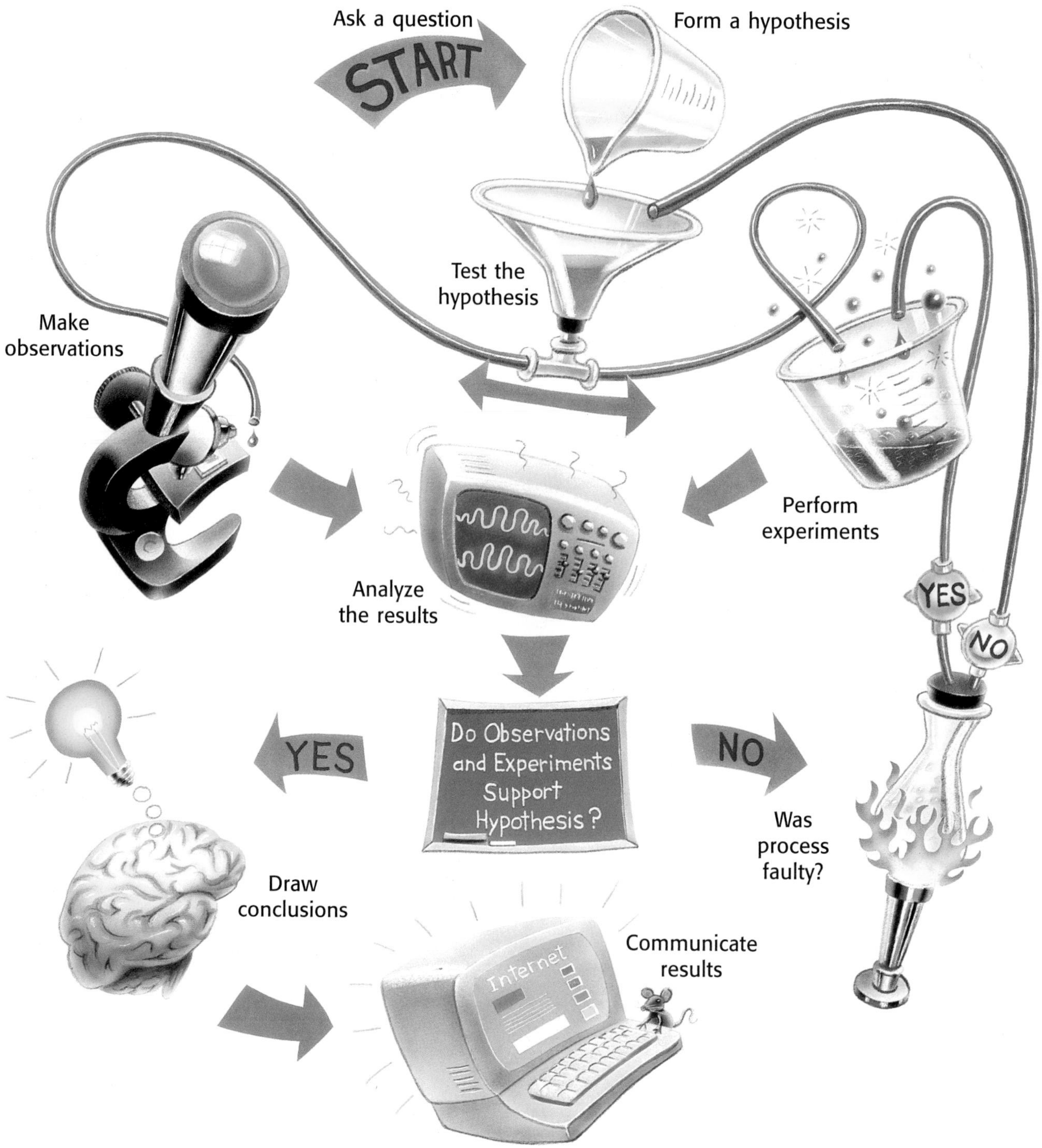

Making Charts and Graphs

Circle Graphs

A circle graph, or pie chart, shows how each group of data relates to all of the data. Each part of the circle represents a category of the data. The entire circle represents all of the data. For example, a biologist studying a hardwood forest in Wisconsin found that there were five different types of trees. The data table at right summarizes the biologist's findings.

Wisconsin Hardwood Trees

Type of tree	Number found
Oak	600
Maple	750
Beech	300
Birch	1,200
Hickory	150
Total	3,000

How to Make a Circle Graph

1. In order to make a circle graph of this data, first find the percentage of each type of tree. To do this, divide the number of individual trees by the total number of trees and multiply by 100.

$$\frac{600 \text{ oak}}{3{,}000 \text{ trees}} \times 100 = 20\%$$

$$\frac{750 \text{ maple}}{3{,}000 \text{ trees}} \times 100 = 25\%$$

$$\frac{300 \text{ beech}}{3{,}000 \text{ trees}} \times 100 = 10\%$$

$$\frac{1{,}200 \text{ birch}}{3{,}000 \text{ trees}} \times 100 = 40\%$$

$$\frac{150 \text{ hickory}}{3{,}000 \text{ trees}} \times 100 = 5\%$$

2. Now determine the size of the pie shapes that make up the chart. Do this by multiplying each percentage by 360°. Remember that a circle contains 360°.

$20\% \times 360° = 72°$ $25\% \times 360° = 90°$

$10\% \times 360° = 36°$ $40\% \times 360° = 144°$

$5\% \times 360° = 18°$

3. Then check that the sum of the percentages is 100 and the sum of the degrees is 360.

$$20\% + 25\% + 10\% + 40\% + 5\% = 100\%$$

$$72° + 90° + 36° + 144° + 18° = 360°$$

4. Use a compass to draw a circle and mark its center.

5. Then use a protractor to draw angles of 72°, 90°, 36°, 144°, and 18° in the circle.

6. Finally, label each part of the graph, and choose an appropriate title.

A Community of Wisconsin Hardwood Trees

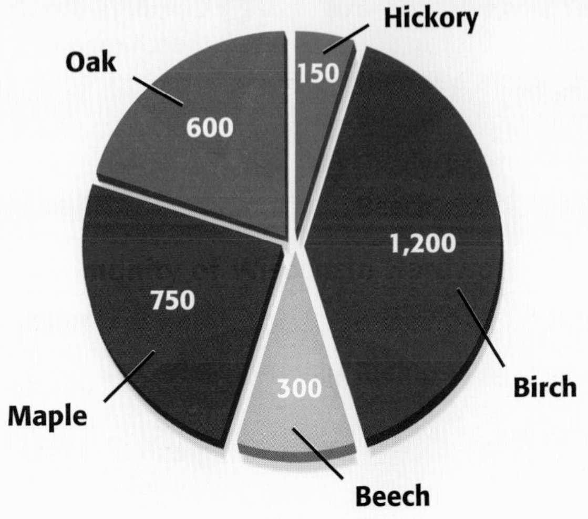

Line Graphs

Population of Appleton, 1900–2000	
Year	**Population**
1900	1,800
1920	2,500
1940	3,200
1960	3,900
1980	4,600
2000	5,300

Line graphs are most often used to demonstrate continuous change. For example, Mr. Smith's science class analyzed the population records for their hometown, Appleton, between 1900 and 2000. Examine the data at left.

Because the year and the population change, they are the *variables*. The population is determined by, or dependent on, the year. Therefore, the population is called the **dependent variable,** and the year is called the **independent variable.** Each set of data is called a **data pair.** To prepare a line graph, data pairs must first be organized in a table like the one at left.

How to Make a Line Graph

1. Place the independent variable along the horizontal (x) axis. Place the dependent variable along the vertical (y) axis.
2. Label the x-axis "Year" and the y-axis "Population." Look at your largest and smallest values for the population. Determine a scale for the y-axis that will provide enough space to show these values. You must use the same scale for the entire length of the axis. Find an appropriate scale for the x-axis too.
3. Choose reasonable starting points for each axis.
4. Plot the data pairs as accurately as possible.
5. Choose a title that accurately represents the data.

Population of Appleton, 1900–2000

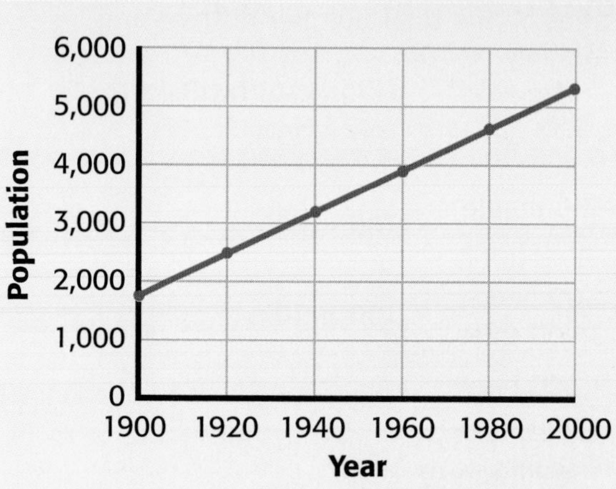

How to Determine Slope

Slope is the ratio of the change in the y-axis to the change in the x-axis, or "rise over run."

1. Choose two points on the line graph. For example, the population of Appleton in 2000 was 5,300 people. Therefore, you can define point a as (2000, 5,300). In 1900, the population was 1,800 people. Define point b as (1900, 1,800).
2. Find the change in the y-axis.
   (y at point a) − (y at point b)
   5,300 people − 1,800 people = 3,500 people
3. Find the change in the x-axis.
   (x at point a) − (x at point b)
   2000 − 1900 = 100 years
4. Calculate the slope of the graph by dividing the change in y by the change in x.

$$\text{slope} = \frac{\text{change in } y}{\text{change in } x}$$

$$\text{slope} = \frac{3{,}500 \text{ people}}{100 \text{ years}}$$

$$\text{slope} = 35 \text{ people per year}$$

In this example, the population in Appleton increased by a fixed amount each year. The graph of this data is a straight line. Therefore, the relationship is **linear.** When the graph of a set of data is not a straight line, the relationship is **nonlinear.**

Using Algebra to Determine Slope

The equation in step 4 may also be arranged to be:

$$y = kx$$

where y represents the change in the y-axis, k represents the slope, and x represents the change in the x-axis.

$$\text{slope} = \frac{\text{change in } y}{\text{change in } x}$$

$$k = \frac{y}{x}$$

$$k \times x = \frac{y \times x}{x}$$

$$kx = y$$

Bar Graphs

Bar graphs are used to demonstrate change that is not continuous. These graphs can be used to indicate trends when the data are taken over a long period of time. A meteorologist gathered the precipitation records at right for Hartford, Connecticut, for April 1–15, 1996, and used a bar graph to represent the data.

Precipitation in Hartford, Connecticut April 1–15, 1996

Date	Precipitation (cm)	Date	Precipitation (cm)
April 1	0.5	April 9	0.25
April 2	1.25	April 10	0.0
April 3	0.0	April 11	1.0
April 4	0.0	April 12	0.0
April 5	0.0	April 13	0.25
April 6	0.0	April 14	0.0
April 7	0.0	April 15	6.50
April 8	1.75		

How to Make a Bar Graph

1. Use an appropriate scale and a reasonable starting point for each axis.
2. Label the axes, and plot the data.
3. Choose a title that accurately represents the data.

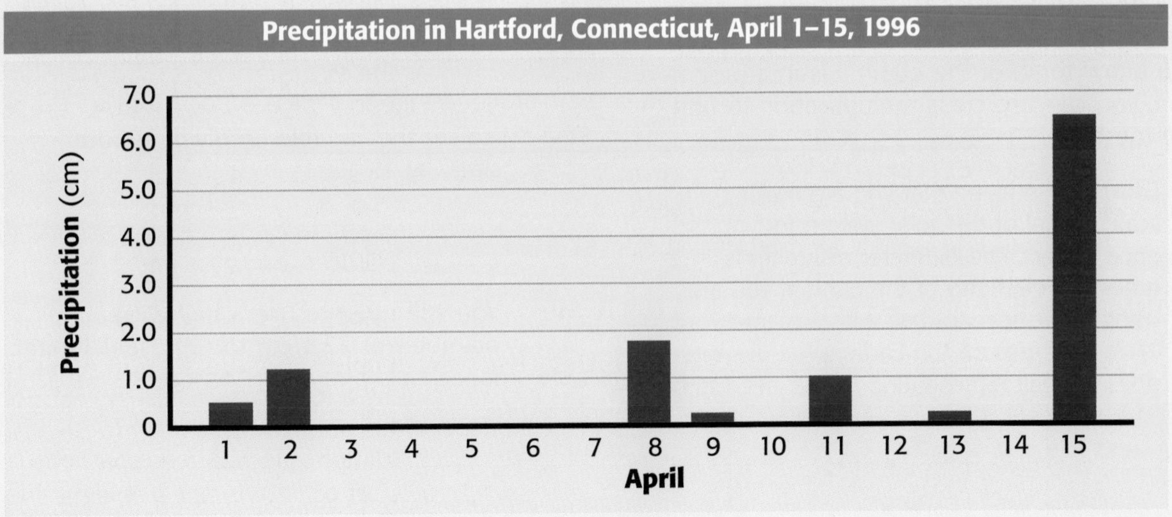

Appendix

Math Refresher

Science requires an understanding of many math concepts. The following pages will help you review some important math skills.

Averages

An **average,** or **mean,** simplifies a list of numbers into a single number that *approximates* their value.

Example: Find the average of the following set of numbers: 5, 4, 7, and 8.

Step 1: Find the sum.

$$5 + 4 + 7 + 8 = 24$$

Step 2: Divide the sum by the amount of numbers in your set. Because there are four numbers in this example, divide the sum by 4.

$$\frac{24}{4} = 6$$

The average, or mean, is **6.**

Ratios

A **ratio** is a comparison between numbers, and it is usually written as a fraction.

Example: Find the ratio of thermometers to students if you have 36 thermometers and 48 students in your class.

Step 1: Make the ratio.

$$\frac{36 \text{ thermometers}}{48 \text{ students}}$$

Step 2: Reduce the fraction to its simplest form.

$$\frac{36}{48} = \frac{36 \div 12}{48 \div 12} = \frac{3}{4}$$

The ratio of thermometers to students is **3 to 4,** or $\frac{3}{4}$. The ratio may also be written in the form 3:4.

Proportions

A **proportion** is an equation that states that two ratios are equal.

$$\frac{3}{1} = \frac{12}{4}$$

To solve a proportion, first multiply across the equal sign. This is called cross-multiplication. If you know three of the quantities in a proportion, you can use cross-multiplication to find the fourth.

Example: Imagine that you are making a scale model of the solar system for your science project. The diameter of Jupiter is 11.2 times the diameter of the Earth. If you are using a plastic-foam ball with a diameter of 2 cm to represent the Earth, what diameter does the ball representing Jupiter need to be?

$$\frac{11.2}{1} = \frac{x}{2 \text{ cm}}$$

Step 1: Cross-multiply.

$$\frac{11.2}{1} \times \frac{x}{2}$$

$$11.2 \times 2 = x \times 1$$

Step 2: Multiply.

$$22.4 = x \times 1$$

Step 3: Isolate the variable by dividing both sides by 1.

$$x = \frac{22.4}{1}$$

$$x = 22.4 \text{ cm}$$

You will need to use a ball with a diameter of **22.4 cm** to represent Jupiter.

Percentages

A **percentage** is a ratio of a given number to 100.

Example: What is 85 percent of 40?

Step 1: Rewrite the percentage by moving the decimal point two places to the left.

.85

Step 2: Multiply the decimal by the number you are calculating the percentage of.

$$0.85 \times 40 = 34$$

85 percent of 40 is **34.**

Decimals

To **add** or **subtract decimals,** line up the digits vertically so that the decimal points line up. Then add or subtract the columns from right to left, carrying or borrowing numbers as necessary.

Example: Add the following numbers: 3.1415 and 2.96.

Step 1: Line up the digits vertically so that the decimal points line up.

$$\begin{array}{r} 3.1415 \\ +\ \underline{2.96} \end{array}$$

Step 2: Add the columns from right to left, carrying when necessary.

$$\begin{array}{r} {\scriptstyle 1\ 1} \\ 3.1415 \\ +\ \underline{2.96} \\ 6.1015 \end{array}$$

The sum is **6.1015.**

Fractions

Numbers tell you how many; **fractions** tell you *how much of a whole.*

Example: Your class has 24 plants. Your teacher instructs you to put 5 in a shady spot. What fraction does this represent?

Step 1: Write a fraction with the total number of parts in the whole as the denominator.

$$\frac{?}{24}$$

Step 2: Write the number of parts of the whole being represented as the numerator.

$$\frac{5}{24}$$

$\mathbf{\frac{5}{24}}$ of the plants will be in the shade.

Reducing Fractions

It is usually best to express a fraction in simplest form. This is called *reducing* a fraction.

Example: Reduce the fraction $\frac{30}{45}$ to its simplest form.

Step 1: Find the largest whole number that will divide evenly into both the numerator and denominator. This number is called the greatest common factor (GCF).

factors of the numerator 30: 1, 2, 3, 5, 6, 10, **15,** 30

factors of the denominator 45: 1, 3, 5, 9, **15,** 45

Step 2: Divide both the numerator and the denominator by the GCF, which in this case is 15.

$$\frac{30}{45} = \frac{30 \div 15}{45 \div 15} = \frac{2}{3}$$

$\frac{30}{45}$ reduced to its simplest form is $\mathbf{\frac{2}{3}}$.

Adding and Subtracting Fractions

To **add** or **subtract fractions** that have the **same denominator,** simply add or subtract the numerators.

Examples:

$$\frac{3}{5} + \frac{1}{5} = ? \text{ and } \frac{3}{4} - \frac{1}{4} = ?$$

Step 1: Add or subtract the numerators.

$$\frac{3}{5} + \frac{1}{5} = \frac{4}{} \text{ and } \frac{3}{4} - \frac{1}{4} = \frac{2}{}$$

Step 2: Write the sum or difference over the denominator.

$$\frac{3}{5} + \frac{1}{5} = \frac{4}{5} \text{ and } \frac{3}{4} - \frac{1}{4} = \frac{2}{4}$$

Step 3: If necessary, reduce the fraction to its simplest form.

$\mathbf{\frac{4}{5}}$ cannot be reduced, and $\frac{2}{4} = \mathbf{\frac{1}{2}}$.

To **add** or **subtract fractions** that have **different denominators,** first find the least common denominator (LCD).

Examples:

$$\frac{1}{2} + \frac{1}{6} = ? \text{ and } \frac{3}{4} - \frac{2}{3} = ?$$

Step 1: Write the equivalent fractions with a common denominator.

$$\frac{3}{6} + \frac{1}{6} = ? \text{ and } \frac{9}{12} - \frac{8}{12} = ?$$

Step 2: Add or subtract.

$$\frac{3}{6} + \frac{1}{6} = \frac{4}{6} \text{ and } \frac{9}{12} - \frac{8}{12} = \frac{1}{12}$$

Step 3: If necessary, reduce the fraction to its simplest form.

$\frac{4}{6} = \mathbf{\frac{2}{3}}$, and $\mathbf{\frac{1}{12}}$ cannot be reduced.

Multiplying Fractions

To **multiply fractions,** multiply the numerators and the denominators together, and then reduce the fraction to its simplest form.

Example:

$$\frac{5}{9} \times \frac{7}{10} = ?$$

Step 1: Multiply the numerators and denominators.

$$\frac{5}{9} \times \frac{7}{10} = \frac{5 \times 7}{9 \times 10} = \frac{35}{90}$$

Step 2: Reduce.

$$\frac{35}{90} = \frac{35 \div 5}{90 \div 5} = \mathbf{\frac{7}{18}}$$

Dividing Fractions

To **divide fractions**, first rewrite the divisor (the number you divide *by*) upside down. This is called the reciprocal of the divisor. Then you can multiply and reduce if necessary.

Example:

$$\frac{5}{8} \div \frac{3}{2} = ?$$

Step 1: Rewrite the divisor as its reciprocal.

$$\frac{3}{2} \rightarrow \frac{2}{3}$$

Step 2: Multiply.

$$\frac{5}{8} \times \frac{2}{3} = \frac{5 \times 2}{8 \times 3} = \frac{10}{24}$$

Step 3: Reduce.

$$\frac{10}{24} = \frac{10 \div 2}{24 \div 2} = \mathbf{\frac{5}{12}}$$

Scientific Notation

Scientific notation is a short way of representing very large and very small numbers without writing all of the place-holding zeros.

Example: Write 653,000,000 in scientific notation.

Step 1: Write the number without the place-holding zeros.

653

Step 2: Place the decimal point after the first digit.

6.53

Step 3: Find the exponent by counting the number of places that you moved the decimal point.

6.53000000

The decimal point was moved eight places to the left. Therefore, the exponent of 10 is positive 8. Remember, if the decimal point had moved to the right, the exponent would be negative.

Step 4: Write the number in scientific notation.

$\mathbf{6.53 \times 10^8}$

Area

Area is the number of square units needed to cover the surface of an object.

Formulas:

Area of a square = side × side

Area of a rectangle = length × width

Area of a triangle $= \frac{1}{2} \times$ base × height

Examples: Find the areas.

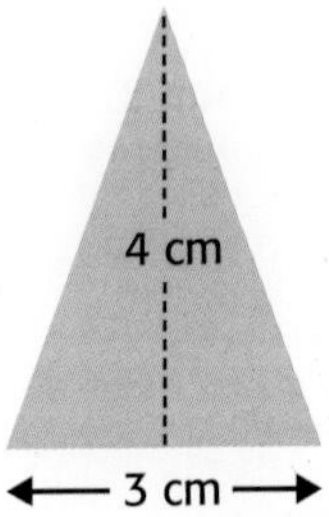

Triangle

Area $= \frac{1}{2} \times$ base × height

Area $= \frac{1}{2} \times 3 \text{ cm} \times 4 \text{ cm}$

Area = **6 cm^2**

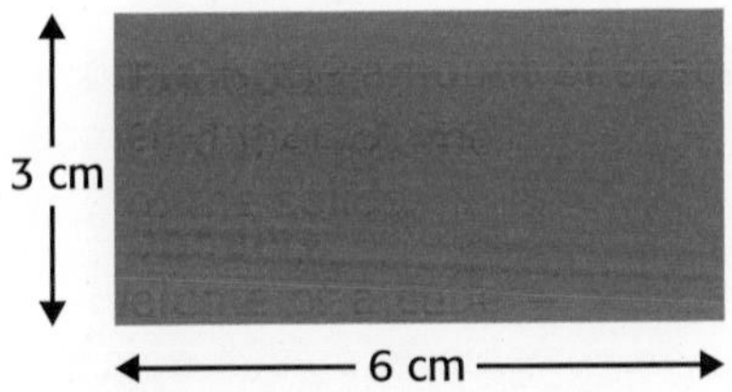

Rectangle

Area = length × width

Area = 6 cm × 3 cm

Area = **18 cm^2**

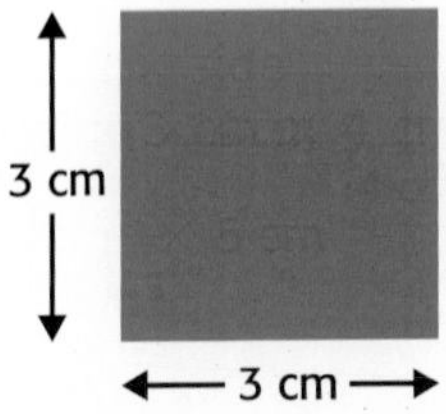

Square

Area = side × side

Area = 3 cm × 3 cm

Area = **9 cm^2**

Volume

Volume is the amount of space something occupies.

Formulas:

Volume of a cube = side × side × side

Volume of a prism = area of base × height

Examples:

Find the volume of the solids.

Cube

Volume = side × side × side

Volume = 4 cm × 4 cm × 4 cm

Volume = **64 cm^3**

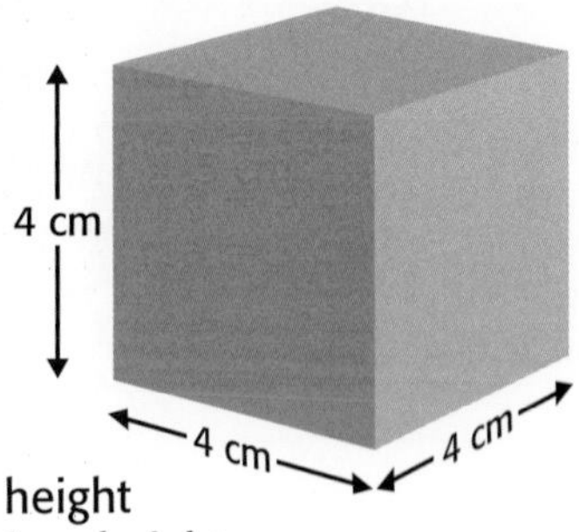

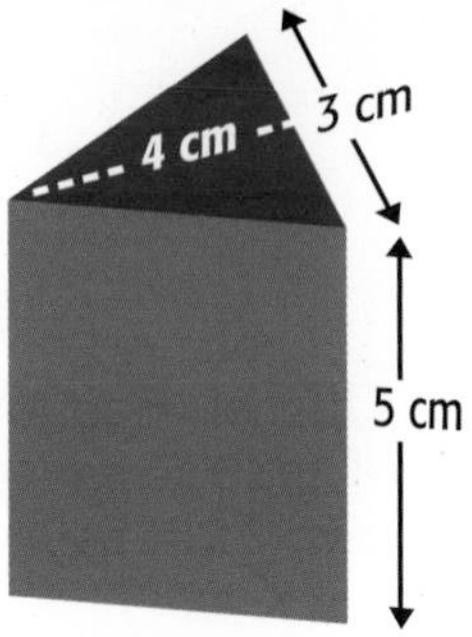

Prism

Volume = area of base × height

Volume = (area of triangle) × height

Volume $= \left(\frac{1}{2} \times 3 \text{ cm} \times 4 \text{ cm}\right) \times 5 \text{ cm}$

Volume = 6 cm^2 × 5 cm

Volume = **30 cm^3**

Periodic Table of the Elements

Each square on the table includes an element's name, chemical symbol, atomic number, and atomic mass.

Atomic number	6
Chemical symbol	C
Element name	Carbon
Atomic mass	12.0

The background color indicates the type of element. Carbon is a nonmetal.

The color of the chemical symbol indicates the physical state at room temperature. Carbon is a solid.

Background

- Metals
- Metalloids
- Nonmetals

Chemical Symbol

- Solid
- Liquid
- Gas

	Group 1	Group 2	Group 3	Group 4	Group 5	Group 6	Group 7	Group 8	Group 9
Period 1	1 H Hydrogen 1.0								
Period 2	3 Li Lithium 6.9	4 Be Beryllium 9.0							
Period 3	11 Na Sodium 23.0	12 Mg Magnesium 24.3							
Period 4	19 K Potassium 39.1	20 Ca Calcium 40.1	21 Sc Scandium 45.0	22 Ti Titanium 47.9	23 V Vanadium 50.9	24 Cr Chromium 52.0	25 Mn Manganese 54.9	26 Fe Iron 55.8	27 Co Cobalt 58.9
Period 5	37 Rb Rubidium 85.5	38 Sr Strontium 87.6	39 Y Yttrium 88.9	40 Zr Zirconium 91.2	41 Nb Niobium 92.9	42 Mo Molybdenum 95.9	43 Tc Technetium (97.9)	44 Ru Ruthenium 101.1	45 Rh Rhodium 102.9
Period 6	55 Cs Cesium 132.9	56 Ba Barium 137.3	57 La Lanthanum 138.9	72 Hf Hafnium 178.5	73 Ta Tantalum 180.9	74 W Tungsten 183.8	75 Re Rhenium 186.2	76 Os Osmium 190.2	77 Ir Iridium 192.2
Period 7	87 Fr Francium (223.0)	88 Ra Radium (226.0)	89 Ac Actinium (227.0)	104 Rf Rutherfordium (261.1)	105 Db Dubnium (262.1)	106 Sg Seaborgium (263.1)	107 Bh Bohrium (262.1)	108 Hs Hassium (265)	109 Mt Meitnerium (266)

A row of elements is called a period.

A column of elements is called a group or family.

Lanthanides	58 Ce Cerium 140.1	59 Pr Praseodymium 140.9	60 Nd Neodymium 144.2	61 Pm Promethium (144.9)	62 Sm Samarium 150.4
Actinides	90 Th Thorium 232.0	91 Pa Protactinium 231.0	92 U Uranium 238.0	93 Np Neptunium (237.0)	94 Pu Plutonium 244.1

These elements are placed below the table to allow the table to be narrower.

Group 10	Group 11	Group 12	Group 13	Group 14	Group 15	Group 16	Group 17	Group 18
								2 **He** Helium 4.0
			5 **B** Boron 10.8	6 **C** Carbon 12.0	7 **N** Nitrogen 14.0	8 **O** Oxygen 16.0	9 **F** Fluorine 19.0	10 **Ne** Neon 20.2
			13 **Al** Aluminum 27.0	14 **Si** Silicon 28.1	15 **P** Phosphorus 31.0	16 **S** Sulfur 32.1	17 **Cl** Chlorine 35.5	18 **Ar** Argon 39.9
28 **Ni** Nickel 58.7	29 **Cu** Copper 63.5	30 **Zn** Zinc 65.4	31 **Ga** Gallium 69.7	32 **Ge** Germanium 72.6	33 **As** Arsenic 74.9	34 **Se** Selenium 79.0	35 **Br** Bromine 79.9	36 **Kr** Krypton 83.8
46 **Pd** Palladium 106.4	47 **Ag** Silver 107.9	48 **Cd** Cadmium 112.4	49 **In** Indium 114.8	50 **Sn** Tin 118.7	51 **Sb** Antimony 121.8	52 **Te** Tellurium 127.6	53 **I** Iodine 126.9	54 **Xe** Xenon 131.3
78 **Pt** Platinum 195.1	79 **Au** Gold 197.0	80 **Hg** Mercury 200.6	81 **Tl** Thallium 204.4	82 **Pb** Lead 207.2	83 **Bi** Bismuth 209.0	84 **Po** Polonium (209.0)	85 **At** Astatine (210.0)	86 **Rn** Radon (222.0)
110 **Uun*** Ununnilium (271)	111 **Uuu*** Unununium (272)	112 **Uub*** Ununbium (277)		114 **Uuq*** Ununquadium (285)		116 **Uuh*** Ununhexium (289)		118 **Uuo*** Ununoctium (293)

This zigzag line reminds you where the metals, nonmetals, and metalloids are.

A number in parenthesis is the mass number of the most stable form of that element.

63 **Eu** Europium 152.0	64 **Gd** Gadolinium 157.3	65 **Tb** Terbium 158.9	66 **Dy** Dysprosium 162.5	67 **Ho** Holmium 164.9	68 **Er** Erbium 167.3	69 **Tm** Thulium 168.9	70 **Yb** Ytterbium 173.0	71 **Lu** Lutetium 175.0
95 **Am** Americium (243.1)	96 **Cm** Curium (247.1)	97 **Bk** Berkelium (247.1)	98 **Cf** Californium (251.1)	99 **Es** Einsteinium (252.1)	100 **Fm** Fermium (257.1)	101 **Md** Mendelevium (258.1)	102 **No** Nobelium (259.1)	103 **Lr** Lawrencium (262.1)

**The official names and symbols for the elements greater than 109 will eventually be approved by a committee of scientists.*

Physical Science Refresher

Atoms and Elements

Every object in the universe is made up of particles of some kind of matter. **Matter** is anything that takes up space and has mass. All matter is made up of elements. An **element** is a substance that cannot be separated into simpler components by ordinary chemical means. This is because each element consists of only one kind of atom. An **atom** is the smallest unit of an element that has all of the properties of that element.

Atomic Structure

Atoms are made up of small particles called subatomic particles. The three major types of subatomic particles are **electrons, protons,** and **neutrons.** Electrons have a negative electric charge, protons have a positive charge, and neutrons have no electric charge. The protons and neutrons are packed close to one another to form the **nucleus.** The protons give the nucleus a positive charge. Electrons are most likely to be found in regions around the nucleus called **electron clouds.** The negatively charged electrons are attracted to the positively charged nucleus. An atom may have several energy levels in which electrons are located.

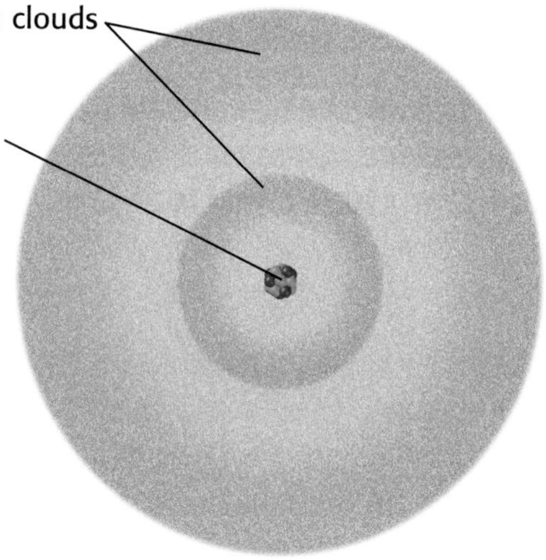

Atomic Number

To help in the identification of elements, scientists have assigned an **atomic number** to each kind of atom. The atomic number is the number of protons in the atom. Atoms with the same number of protons are all the same kind of element. In an uncharged, or electrically neutral, atom there are an equal number of protons and electrons. Therefore, the atomic number equals the number of electrons in an uncharged atom. The number of neutrons, however, can vary for a given element. Atoms of the same element that have different numbers of neutrons are called **isotopes.**

Periodic Table of the Elements

In the periodic table, the elements are arranged from left to right in order of increasing atomic number. Each element in the table is in a separate box. An atom of each element has one more electron and one more proton than an atom of the element to its left. Each horizontal row of the table is called a **period.** Changes in chemical properties of elements across a period correspond to changes in the electron arrangements of their atoms. Each vertical column of the table, known as a **group,** lists elements with similar properties. The elements in a group have similar chemical properties because their atoms have the same number of electrons in their outer energy level. For example, the elements helium, neon, argon, krypton, xenon, and radon all have similar properties and are known as the noble gases.

Molecules and Compounds

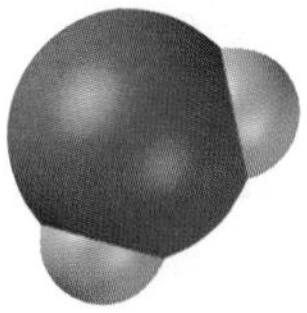

When two or more elements are joined chemically, the resulting substance is called a **compound.** A compound is a new substance with properties different from those of the elements that compose it. For example, water, H_2O, is a compound formed when hydrogen (H) and oxygen (O) combine. The smallest complete unit of a compound that has the properties of that compound is called a **molecule.** A chemical formula indicates the elements in a compound. It also indicates the relative number of atoms of each element present. The chemical formula for water is H_2O, which indicates that each water molecule consists of two atoms of hydrogen and one atom of oxygen. The subscript number is used after the symbol for an element to indicate how many atoms of that element are in a single molecule of the compound.

Acids, Bases, and pH

An ion is an atom or group of atoms that has an electric charge because it has lost or gained one or more electrons. When an acid, such as hydrochloric acid, HCl, is mixed with water, it separates into ions. An **acid** is a compound that produces hydrogen ions, H^+, in water. The hydrogen ions then combine with a water molecule to form a hydronium ion, H_3O^+. A **base,** on the other hand, is a substance that produces hydroxide ions, OH^-, in water.

To determine whether a solution is acidic or basic, scientists use pH. The **pH** is a measure of the hydronium ion concentration in a solution. The pH scale ranges from 0 to 14. The middle point, pH = 7, is neutral, neither acidic nor basic. Acids have a pH less than 7; bases have a pH greater than 7. The lower the number is, the more acidic the solution. The higher the number is, the more basic the solution.

Chemical Equations

A chemical reaction occurs when a chemical change takes place. (In a chemical change, new substances with new properties are formed.) A chemical equation is a useful way of describing a chemical reaction by means of chemical formulas. The equation indicates what substances react and what the products are. For example, when carbon and oxygen combine, they can form carbon dioxide. The equation for the reaction is as follows:

$$C + O_2 \rightarrow CO_2.$$

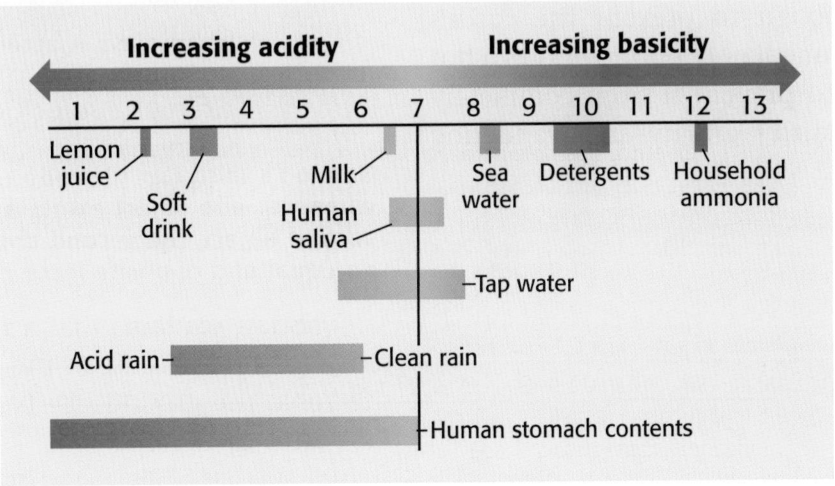

185

Physical Laws and Equations

Law of Conservation of Energy

The law of conservation of energy states that energy can be neither created nor destroyed.

The total amount of energy in a closed system is always the same. Energy can be changed from one form to another, but all the different forms of energy in a system always add up to the same total amount of energy, no matter how many energy conversions occur.

Law of Universal Gravitation

The law of universal gravitation states that all objects in the universe attract each other by a force called gravity. The size of the force depends on the masses of the objects and the distance between them.

The first part of the law explains why a bowling ball is much harder to lift than a table-tennis ball. Because the bowling ball has a much larger mass than the table-tennis ball, the amount of gravity between the Earth and the bowling ball is greater than the amount of gravity between the Earth and the table-tennis ball.

The second part of the law explains why a satellite can remain in orbit around the Earth. The satellite is carefully placed at a distance great enough to prevent the Earth's gravity from immediately pulling it down but small enough to prevent it from completely escaping the Earth's gravity and wandering off into space.

Newton's Laws of Motion

Newton's first law of motion states that an object at rest remains at rest and an object in motion remains in motion at constant speed and in a straight line unless acted on by an unbalanced force.

The first part of the law explains why a football will remain on a tee until it is kicked off or until a gust of wind blows it off.

The second part of the law explains why a bike's rider will continue moving forward after the bike tire runs into a crack in the sidewalk and the bike comes to an abrupt stop until gravity and the sidewalk stop the rider.

Newton's second law of motion states that the acceleration of an object depends on the mass of the object and the amount of force applied.

The first part of the law explains why the acceleration of a 4 kg bowling ball will be greater than the acceleration of a 6 kg bowling ball if the same force is applied to both.

The second part of the law explains why the acceleration of a bowling ball will be larger if a larger force is applied to it.

The relationship of acceleration (a) to mass (m) and force (F) can be expressed mathematically by the following equation:

$$\text{acceleration} = \frac{\textit{force}}{\textit{mass}} \quad \text{or} \quad a = \frac{F}{m}$$

This equation is often rearranged to the form:

$$\text{force} = \text{mass} \times \text{acceleration}$$

or

$$F = m \times a$$

Newton's third law of motion states that whenever one object exerts a force on a second object, the second object exerts an equal and opposite force on the first.

This law explains that a runner is able to move forward because of the equal and opposite force the ground exerts on the runner's foot after each step.

186

Useful Equations

Average speed

$$\textbf{Average speed} = \frac{\textbf{total distance}}{\textbf{total time}}$$

Example: A bicycle messenger traveled a distance of 136 km in 8 hours. What was the messenger's average speed?

$$\frac{136 \text{ km}}{8 \text{ h}} = 17 \text{ km/h}$$

The messenger's average speed was **17 km/h.**

Average acceleration

$$\textbf{Average acceleration} = \frac{\textbf{final velocity} - \textbf{starting velocity}}{\textbf{time it takes to change velocity}}$$

Example: Calculate the average acceleration of an Olympic 100 m dash sprinter who reaches a velocity of 15 m/s south at the finish line. The race was in a straight line and lasted 10 s.

$$\frac{15 \text{ m/s} - 0 \text{ m/s}}{10 \text{ s}} = 1.5 \text{ m/s/s}$$

The sprinter's average acceleration is **1.5 m/s/s south.**

Net force

Forces in the Same Direction

When forces are in the same direction, add the forces together to determine the net force.

Example: Calculate the net force on a stalled car that is being pushed by two people. One person is pushing with a force of 13 N northwest and the other person is pushing with a force of 8 N in the same direction.

$$13 \text{ N} + 8 \text{ N} = 21 \text{ N}$$

The net force is **21 N northwest.**

Forces in Opposite Directions

When forces are in opposite directions, subtract the smaller force from the larger force to determine the net force.

Net force (cont'd)

Example: Calculate the net force on a rope that is being pulled on each end. One person is pulling on one end of the rope with a force of 12 N south. Another person is pulling on the opposite end of the rope with a force of 7 N north.

$$12 \text{ N} - 7 \text{ N} = 5 \text{ N}$$

The net force is **5 N south.**

Density

$$\textbf{Density} = \frac{\textbf{mass}}{\textbf{volume}}$$

Example: Calculate the density of a sponge with a mass of 10 g and a volume of 40 mL.

$$\frac{10 \text{ g}}{40 \text{ mL}} = 0.25 \text{ g/mL}$$

The density of the sponge is **0.25 g/mL.**

Pressure

Pressure is the force exerted over a given area. The SI unit for pressure is the pascal, which is abbreviated Pa.

$$\textbf{Pressure} = \frac{\textbf{force}}{\textbf{area}}$$

Example: Calculate the pressure of the air in a soccer ball if the air exerts a force of 10 N over an area of 0.5 m^2.

$$\text{Pressure} = \frac{10 \text{ N}}{0.5 \text{ m}^2} = 20 \text{ N/m}^2 = 20 \text{ Pa}$$

The pressure of the air inside of the soccer ball is **20 Pa.**

Concentration

$$\textbf{Concentration} = \frac{\textbf{mass of solute}}{\textbf{volume of solvent}}$$

Example: Calculate the concentration of a solution in which 10 g of sugar is dissolved in 125 mL of water.

$$\frac{10 \text{ g of sugar}}{125 \text{ mL of water}} = 0.08 \text{ g/mL}$$

The concentration of this solution is **0.08 g/mL.**

Properties of Common Minerals

	Mineral	Color	Luster	Streak	Hardness
Silicate Minerals	**Beryl**	deep green, pink, white, bluish green, or light yellow	vitreous	none	7.5–8
	Chlorite	green	vitreous to pearly	pale green	2–2.5
	Garnet	green or red	vitreous	none	6.5–7.5
	Hornblende	dark green, brown, or black	vitreous or silky	none	5–6
	Muscovite	colorless, gray, or brown	vitreous or pearly	white	2–2.5
	Olivine	olive green	vitreous	none	6.5–7
	Orthoclase	colorless, white, pink, or other colors	vitreous to pearly	white or none	6
	Plagioclase	blue gray to white	vitreous	white	6
	Quartz	colorless or white; any color when not pure	vitreous or waxy	white or none	7
Nonsilicate Minerals	**Native Elements**				
	Copper	copper-red	metallic	copper-red	2.5–3
	Diamond	pale yellow or colorless	vitreous	none	10
	Graphite	black to gray	submetallic	black	1–2
	Carbonates				
	Aragonite	colorless, white, or pale yellow	vitreous	white	3.5–4
	Calcite	colorless or white to tan	vitreous	white	3
	Halides				
	Fluorite	light green, yellow, purple, bluish green, or other colors	vitreous	none	4
	Halite	colorless or gray	vitreous	white	2.5–3
	Oxides				
	Hematite	reddish brown to black	metallic to earthy	red to red-brown	5.6–6.5
	Magnetite	iron black	metallic	black	5–6
	Sulfates				
	Anhydrite	colorless, bluish, or violet	vitreous to pearly	white	3–3.5
	Gypsum	white, pink, gray, or colorless	vitreous, pearly, or silky	white	1–2.5
	Sulfides				
	Galena	lead gray	metallic	lead gray to black	2.5
	Pyrite	brassy yellow	metallic	greenish, brownish, or black	6–6.5

Density (g/cm³)	Cleavage, Fracture, Special Properties	Common Uses
2.6–2.8	1 cleavage direction; irregular fracture; some varieties fluoresce in ultraviolet light	gemstones, ore of the metal beryllium
2.6–3.3	1 cleavage direction; irregular fracture	
4.2	no cleavage; conchoidal to splintery fracture	gemstones, abrasives
3.2	2 cleavage directions; hackly to splintery fracture	
2.7–3	1 cleavage direction; irregular fracture	electrical insulation, wallpaper, fireproofing material, lubricant
3.2–3.3	no cleavage; conchoidal fracture	gemstones, casting
2.6	2 cleavage directions; irregular fracture	porcelain
2.6–2.7	2 cleavage directions; irregular fracture	ceramics
2.6	no cleavage; conchoidal fracture	gemstones, concrete, glass, porcelain, sandpaper, lenses
8.9	no cleavage; hackly fracture	wiring, brass, bronze, coins
3.5	4 cleavage directions; irregular to conchoidal fracture	gemstones, drilling
2.3	1 cleavage direction; irregular fracture	pencils, paints, lubricants, batteries
2.95	2 cleavage directions; irregular fracture; reacts with hydrochloric acid	minor source of barium
2.7	3 cleavage directions; irregular fracture; reacts with weak acid, double refraction	cements, soil conditioner, whitewash, construction materials
3.2	4 cleavage directions; irregular fracture; some varieties fluoresce or double refract	hydrochloric acid, steel, glass, fiberglass, pottery, enamel
2.2	3 cleavage directions; splintery to conchoidal fracture; salty taste	tanning hides, fertilizer, salting icy roads, food preservation
5.25	no cleavage; splintery fracture; magnetic when heated	iron ore for steel, gemstones, pigments
5.2	2 cleavage directions; splintery fracture; magnetic	iron ore
2.89–2.98	3 cleavage directions; conchoidal to splintery fracture	soil conditioner, sulfuric acid
2.2–2.4	3 cleavage directions; conchoidal to splintery fracture	plaster of Paris, wallboard, soil conditioner
7.4–7.6	3 cleavage directions; irregular fracture	batteries, paints
5	no cleavage; conchoidal to splintery fracture	dyes, inks, gemstones

Sky Maps

Spring

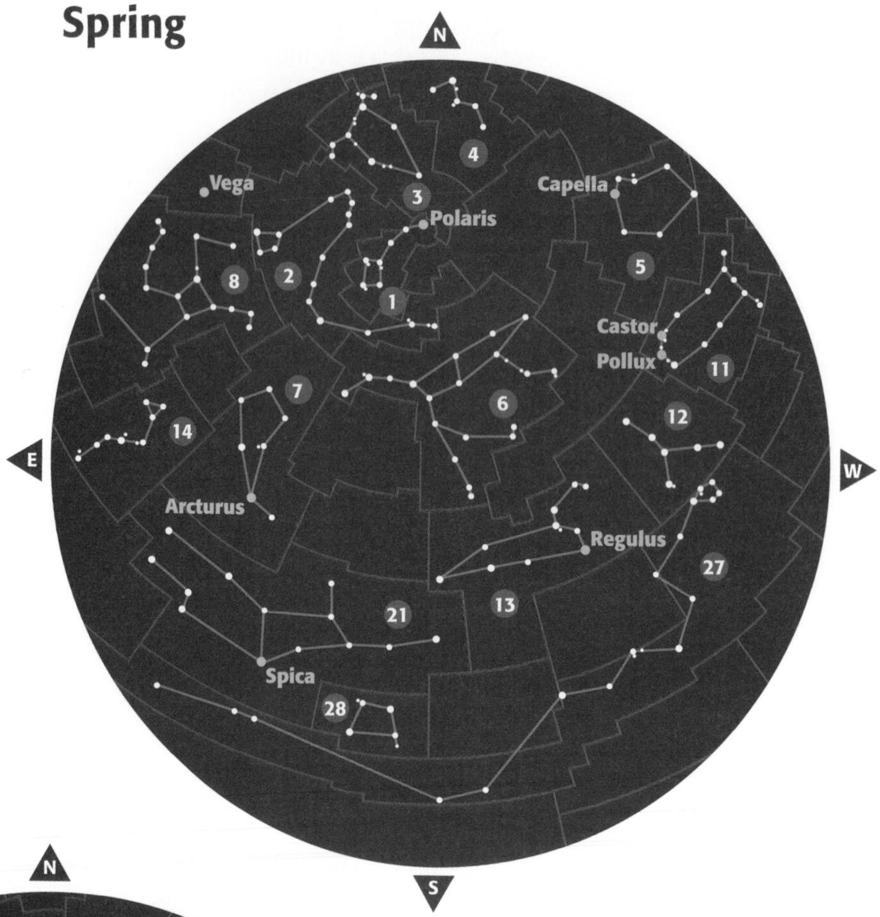

Summer

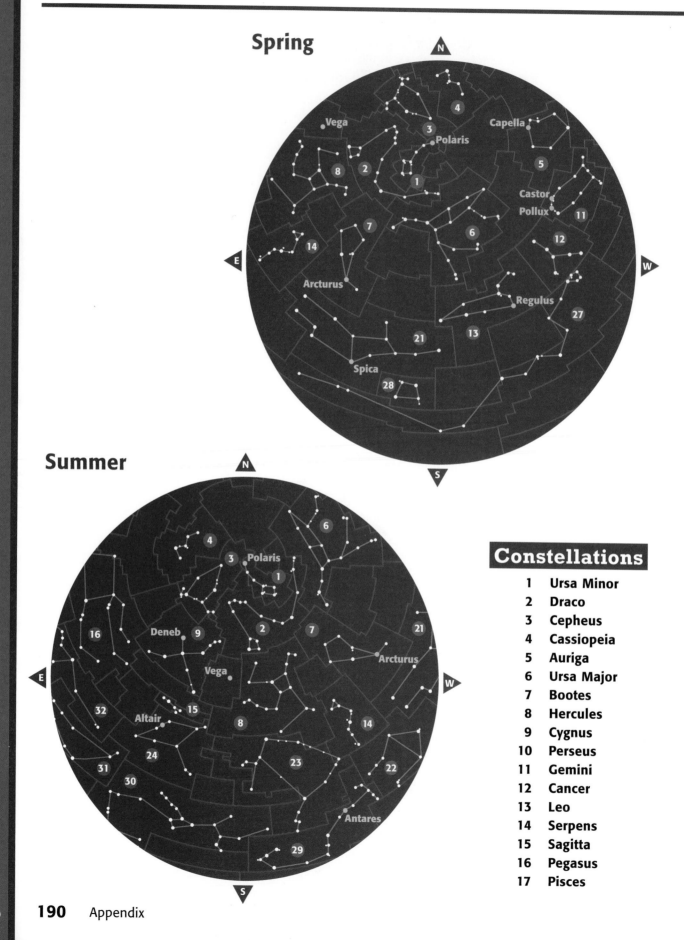

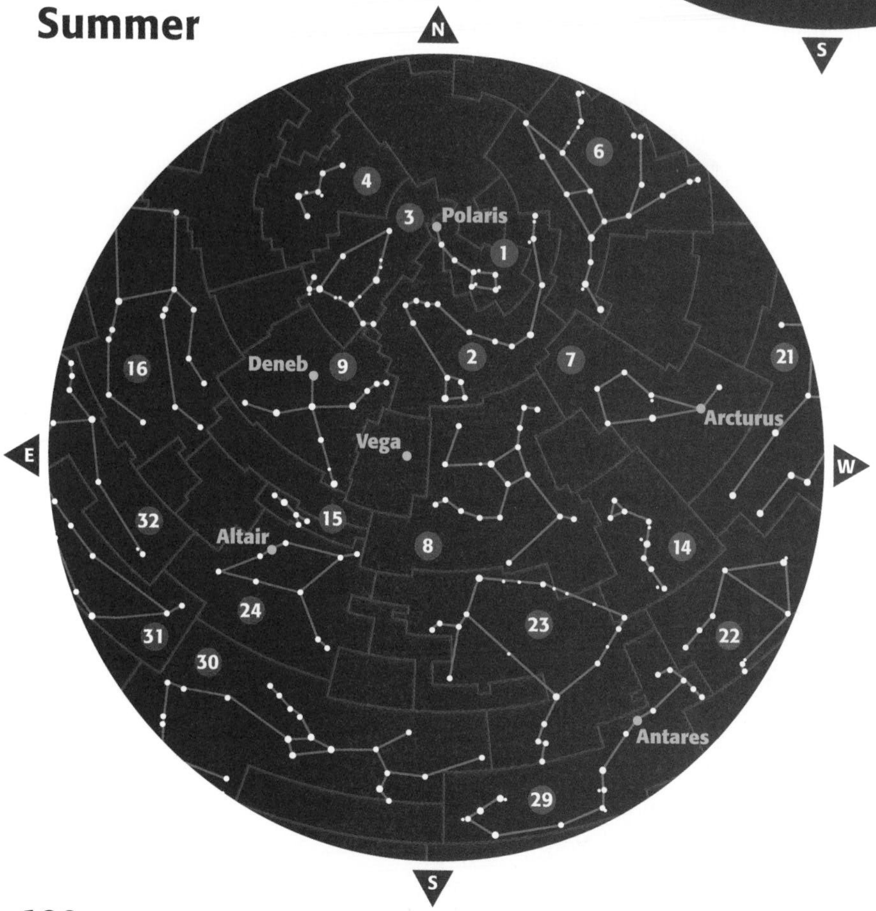

Constellations

1 **Ursa Minor**
2 **Draco**
3 **Cepheus**
4 **Cassiopeia**
5 **Auriga**
6 **Ursa Major**
7 **Bootes**
8 **Hercules**
9 **Cygnus**
10 **Perseus**
11 **Gemini**
12 **Cancer**
13 **Leo**
14 **Serpens**
15 **Sagitta**
16 **Pegasus**
17 **Pisces**

Autumn

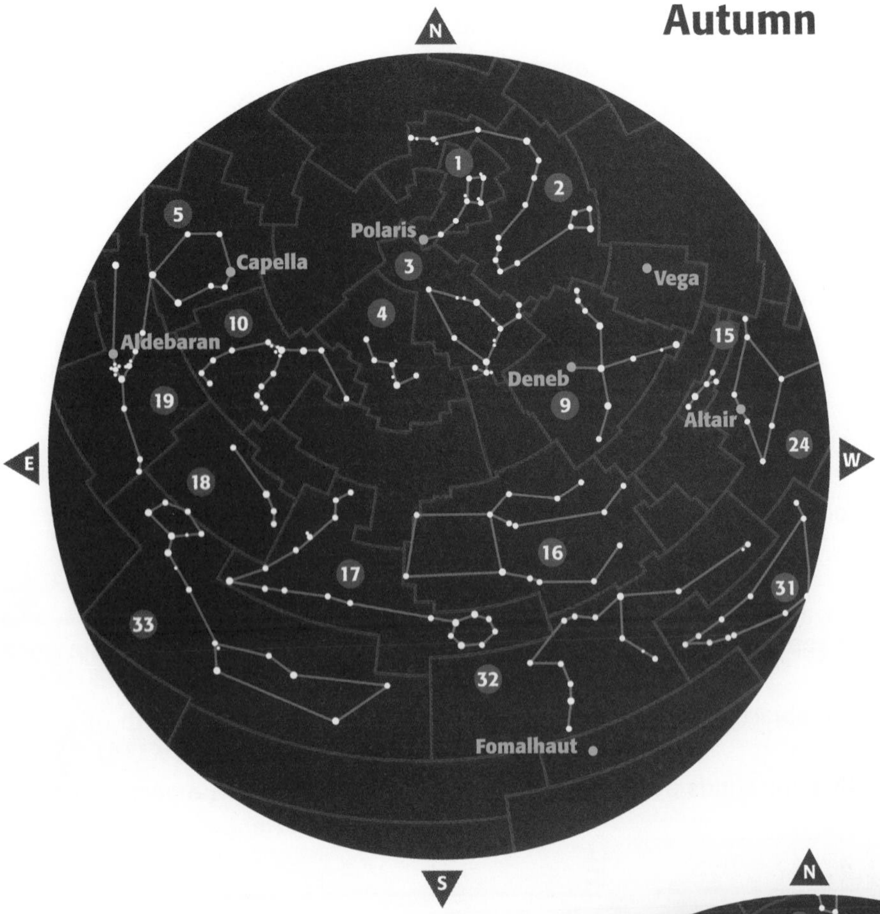

Winter

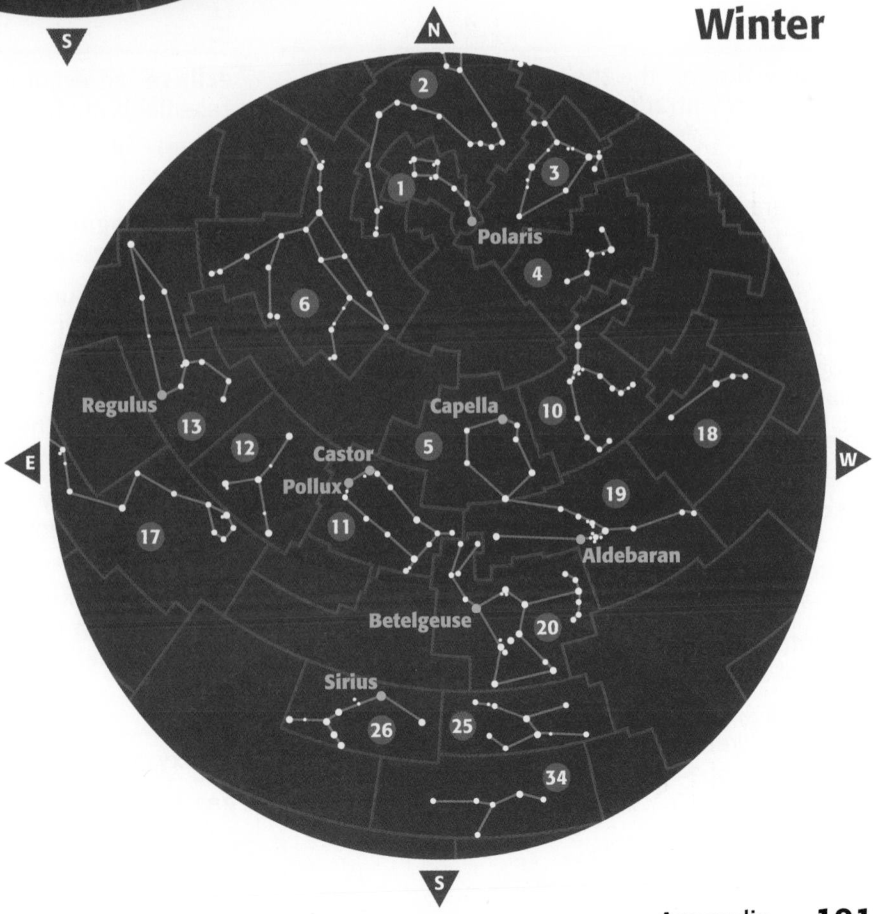

Constellations

18 **Aries**
19 **Taurus**
20 **Orion**
21 **Virgo**
22 **Libra**
23 **Ophiuchus**
24 **Aquila**
25 **Lepus**
26 **Canis Major**
27 **Hydra**
28 **Corvus**
29 **Scorpius**
30 **Sagittarius**
31 **Capricornus**
32 **Aquarius**
33 **Cetus**
34 **Columba**

Glossary

A

absolute magnitude the actual brightness of a star (102)

altitude in astronomy, the angle between an object in the sky and the horizon (13)

annular (AN yoo luhr) **eclipse** a solar eclipse during which the outer ring of the sun can be seen around the moon (78)

apparent magnitude how bright a light appears to an observer (102)

artificial satellite any human-made object placed in orbit around a body in space (132)

asteroid a small, rocky body that revolves around the sun (85)

asteroid belt the region of the solar system most asteroids occupy; roughly between the orbits of Mars and Jupiter (85)

astronomical unit (AU) the average distance between the Earth and the sun, or approximately 150,000,000 km (40, 64)

astronomy the study of all physical objects beyond Earth (4)

atmosphere a mixture of gases that surrounds a planet, such as Earth (50)

B

big bang theory the theory that states the universe began with a tremendous explosion (114)

black hole an object with more than three solar masses squeezed into a ball only 10 km across whose gravity is so strong that not even light can escape (109)

C

calendar a system for organizing time; most calendars organize time within a single unit called a year (4)

celestial equator imaginary circle created by extending Earth's equator into space (14)

chromosphere (KROH muh SFIR) a thin region of the sun's atmosphere between the corona and the photosphere; too faint to see unless there is a total solar eclipse (43)

circumpolar stars stars that can be seen at all times of the year and all times of the night (14)

comet a small body of ice, rock, and cosmic dust loosely packed together that gives off gas and dust in the form of a tail as it passes close to the sun (50, 83)

constellation a section of the sky that contains a recognizable star pattern (11)

convective zone a region of the sun where gases circulate in convection currents, bringing the sun's energy to the surface (43)

core the central, spherical part of the Earth below the mantle (49); *also* the center of the sun where the sun's energy is produced (43)

corona the sun's outer atmosphere, which can extend outward a distance equal to 10–12 times the diameter of the sun (43)

cosmic background radiation radiation left over from the big bang that fills all of space (115)

cosmology the study of the origin and future of the universe (114)

crust the thin, outermost layer of the Earth, or the uppermost part of the lithosphere (49)

D

day the time required for the Earth to rotate once on its axis (4)

declination a measure of how far north or south an object is from the celestial equator (14)

density the amount of matter in a given space; mass per unit volume (189)

E

eclipse an event in which the shadow of one celestial body falls on another (78)

ecliptic the apparent path the sun takes across the celestial sphere (14)

electromagnetic spectrum all the wavelengths of electromagnetic radiation (21)

element a pure substance that cannot be separated or broken down into simpler substances by ordinary chemical means (186)

ellipse a closed curve in which the sum of the distances from the edge of the curve to two points inside the ellipse is always the same (40)

elliptical galaxy a spherical or elongated galaxy with a bright center and very little dust and gas (111)

escape velocity the speed and direction a rocket must travel in order to completely break away from a planet's gravitational pull (131)

G

galaxy a large grouping of stars in space (110)

gas giants the large, gaseous planets of the outer solar system (70)

geosynchronous orbit an orbit in which a satellite travels at a speed that matches the rotational speed of the Earth exactly, keeping the satellite positioned above the same spot on Earth at all times (133)

globular cluster a group of older stars that looks like a ball of stars (112)

greenhouse effect the natural heating process of a planet, such as the Earth, by which gases in the atmosphere trap thermal energy (66)

H

horizon the line where the sky and the Earth appear to meet (13)

H-R diagram Hertzsprung-Russell diagram; a graph that shows the relationship between a star's surface temperature and its absolute magnitude (105)

hypothesis a possible explanation or answer to a question (174)

I

irregular galaxy a galaxy that does not fit into any other category; one with an irregular shape (111)

K

Kuiper (KIE per) **Belt** the region of the solar system outside the orbit of Neptune that is occupied by small, icy, cometlike bodies (84)

L

leap year a year in which an extra day is added to the calendar (5)

light-minute a unit of length equal to the distance light travels in space in 1 minute, or 18,000,000 km (64)

light-year a unit of length equal to the distance that light travels through space in 1 year (15, 103)

low Earth orbit an orbit located a few hundred kilometers above the Earth's surface (133)

lunar eclipse an event in which the shadow of the Earth falls on the moon (78)

M

main sequence a diagonal pattern of stars on the H-R diagram (106)

mantle the layer of the Earth between the crust and the core (49)

mass the amount of matter that something is made of; its value does not change with the object's location (34)

meteor a streak of light caused when a meteoroid or comet dust burns up in the Earth's atmosphere before it reaches the ground (86)

meteorite a meteoroid that reaches the Earth's surface without burning up completely (86)

meteoroid a very small, rocky body that revolves around the sun (50, 86)

month roughly the amount of time required for the moon to orbit the Earth once (4)

moon a natural satellite of a planet (75)

N

NASA National Aeronautics and Space Administration; founded to combine all of the separate rocket-development teams in the United States (129)

nebula (NEB yuh luh) a large cloud of dust and gas in interstellar space; the location of star formation (34, 112)

neutron star a star in which all the particles have become neutrons; the collapsed remains of a supernova (109)

nuclear fusion the process by which two or more nuclei with small masses join together, or fuse, to form a larger, more massive nucleus, along with the production of energy (45)

O

observation any use of the senses to gather information (174)

Oort (ort) **cloud** a spherical region of space that surrounds the solar system in which distant comets revolve around the sun (84)

open cluster a group of stars that are usually located along the spiral disk of a galaxy (112)

orbit the elliptical path a body takes as it travels around another body in space; the motion itself (39)

orbital velocity the speed and direction a rocket must have in order to orbit the Earth (131)

P

parallax an apparent shift in the position of an object when viewed from different locations (103)

period of revolution the time it takes for one body to make one complete orbit, or *revolution,* around another body in space (39, 65)

period of rotation the time it takes for an object to rotate once (65)

phases the different appearances of the moon due to varying amounts of sunlight on the side of the moon that faces the Earth; results from the changing relative positions of the moon, Earth, and the sun (77)

photosphere the layer of the sun at which point the gases get thick enough to see; the surface of the sun (43)

planetesimal (PLAN i TES i muhl) the tiny building blocks of the planets that formed as dust particles stuck together and grew in size (36)

plate tectonics the theory that the Earth's lithosphere is divided into tectonic plates that move around on top of the asthenosphere (53)

prograde rotation the counterclockwise spin of a planet or moon as seen from above the planet's north pole (66)

pulsar a spinning neutron star that emits rapid pulses of light (109)

Q

quasar (KWAY ZAHR) a "quasi-stellar" object; a starlike source of light that is extremely far away; one of the most powerful sources of energy in the universe (113)

R

radiation energy transferred as waves or particles (115)

radiative zone a very dense region of the sun in which the atoms are so closely packed that light can take millions of years to pass through (43)

red giant a star that expands and cools once it runs out of hydrogen fuel (107)

reflecting telescope a telescope that uses curved mirrors to gather and focus light (19)

refracting telescope a telescope that uses a set of lenses to gather and focus light (19)

remote sensing gathering information about something without actually being nearby (134)

retrograde orbit the clockwise revolution of a satellite around a planet as seen from above the north pole of the planet (82)

retrograde rotation the clockwise spin of a planet or moon as seen from above the planet's or moon's north pole (66)

revolution the elliptical motion of a body as it orbits another body in space (39, 65)

right ascension a measure of how far east an object is from the point at which the sun appears on the first day of spring (14)

rocket a machine that uses escaping gas to move (128)

rotation the spinning motion of a body on its axis (39, 65)

S

satellite a natural or artificial body that revolves around a planet (75)

scientific method a series of steps that scientists use to answer questions and solve problems (174)

solar eclipse an event in which the shadow of the moon falls on the Earth's surface (78)

solar energy energy from the sun (44)

solar nebula the nebula that formed into the solar system (35)

solar system the system composed of the sun (a star) and the planets and other bodies that travel around the sun (34)

space probe a vehicle that carries scientific instruments to planets or other bodies in space (136)

space shuttle a reusable vehicle that takes off like a rocket and lands like an airplane (143)

space station a long-term orbiting platform from which other vehicles can be launched or scientific research can be carried out (144)

spectrum the rainbow of colors produced when white light passes through a prism or spectrograph (98)

spiral galaxy a galaxy with a bulge in the center and very distinctive spiral arms (110)

sunspot an area on the photosphere of the sun that is cooler than surrounding areas, showing up as a dark spot (47)

supernova the death of a large star by explosion (108)

surface gravity the percentage of your Earth weight you would experience on another planet; the weight you would experience on another planet (65)

T

telescope an instrument that collects electromagnetic radiation from the sky and concentrates it for better observation (18)

temperature a measure of how hot (or cold) something is (35)

terrestrial planets the small, dense, rocky planets of the inner solar system (65)

thrust the force that accelerates a rocket (130)

V

volume the amount of space that something occupies or the amount of space that something contains (183)

W

white dwarf a small, hot star near the end of its life; the leftover center of an old star (106)

Y

year the time required for the Earth to orbit the sun once (4)

Z

zenith an imaginary point in the sky directly above an observer on Earth (13)

Index

A **boldface** number refers to an illustration on that page.

A

B

C

D

E

F

G

H

I

J

K

L

M

N

O

Credits

Abbreviations used: (t) top, (c) center, (b) bottom, (l) left, (r) right, (bkgd) background

ILLUSTRATIONS

All work, unless otherwise noted, contributed by Holt, Rinehart & Winston.

Scope and Sequence: T11, Paul DiMare, T13, Dan Stuckenschneider/Uhl Studios, Inc.

Chapter One: Page 5(t), Nenad Jakesevic; 8, Dan McGeehan/Koralick Associates; 11, Stephen Durke/Washington Artists; 12(c), Sidney Jablonski; 13(cl), Stephen Durke/Washington Artists; 14(t), Sidney Jablonski; 15(b), Stephen Durke/Washington Artists; 17, Paul DiMare; 19, Uhl Studios, Inc.

Chapter Two: Page 35(c), Stephen Durke/Washington Artists; 36-37, Paul DiMare; 39(c), Sidney Jablonski; 40(t), Mark Heine; 40(br), Sidney Jablonski; 42(c), Sidney Jablonski; 43(br), Uhl Studios, Inc.; 44, Marty Roper/Planet Rep; 45(c), Marty Roper/Planet Rep; 45(b), Stephen Durke/Washington Artists; 46, Stephen Durke/Washington Artists; 47(b), Sidney Jablonski; 49, Uhl Studios, Inc.; 50(bl), Paul DiMare; 51(tr), Paul DiMare; 53(br), Uhl Studios, Inc.

Chapter Three: Page 64(b), Sidney Jablonski; 65(tr), Sidney Jablonski; 70(tl), Sidney Jablonski; 72(b), Sidney Jablonski; 73(tr), Dan McGeehan/Koralick Associates; 74(cl), Paul DiMare; 76, Stephen Durke/Washington Artists; 77(c), Sidney Jablonski; 78(c), Paul DiMare; 79(c), Paul DiMare; 84(tl), Stephen Durke/Washington Artists; 84(br), Paul DiMare; 85, Craig Attebery/Jeff Lavaty Artist Agent; 90(br), Sidney Jablonski; 91(cl), Stephen Durke/Washington Artists.

Chapter Four: Page 99(c), Stephen Durke/Washington Artists; 100(tl), Stephen Durke/Washington Artists; 103(c), Sidney Jablonski; 104(tl), Sidney Jablonski; 104(c), Stephen Durke/Washington Artists; 106-107, Stephen Durke/Washington Artists; 115(br), Craig Attebery/Jeff Lavaty Artist Agent; 117(r), Craig Attebery/Jeff Lavaty Artist Agent; 123(cr), Sidney Jablonski.

Chapter Five: Page 129(b), Stephen Durke/Washington Artists; 130(l), John Huxtable/Black Creative; 133(tr), Stephen Durke/Washington Artists; 136, Stephen Durke/Washington Artists; 137, Stephen Durke/Washington Artists; 138, Stephen Durke/Washington Artists; 139(b), Craig Attebery/Jeff Lavaty Artist Agent; 139(tr), Stephen Durke/Washington Artists; 139(br), Stephen Durke/Washington Artists; 141(tl), Paul DiMare; 147(c), Paul DiMare.

Appendix: Page 172(c), Terry Guyer; 174 (b) Mark Mille/Sharon Langley; 184, Kristy Sprott; 185, Kristy Sprott; 190-191, Sidney Jablonski.

PHOTOGRAPHY

Cover and Title Page: David Nunuk/Science Photo Library/ Photo Researchers, Inc.

Sam Dudgeon/HRW Photo: Page viii-1, 156, 157(bc), 158(tr), 158(cl), 158(br), 159(tl), 164, 166, 167.

Table of Contents: iv(tl), Daniel Schaefer/HRW Photo; iv(cl), A. J. Copley/Visuals Unlimited; iv(bl), NASA/TSADO/Tom Stack & Associates; v(tr), George Holton/Photo Researchers, Inc.; v(cr), Stephen Durke/Washington Artists; v(b), Sam Dudgeon/HRW Photo; vi(tl), NASA; vi(bl), NASA; vii(tl), Anglo-Australian Telescope Board; vii(cl), X-Ray Astronomy Group, Leicester University/Science Photo Library/Photo Resesarchers, Inc.; vii(bl), John Sanford/Astrostock.

Scope and Sequence: T8(l), Lee F. Snyder/Photo Researchers, Inc.; T8(r), Stephen Dalton/Photo Researchers, Inc.; T10, E. R. Degginger/Color-Pic, Inc., T12(l), Rob Matheson/The Stock Market

Master Materials List: T25(br), Image ©2001 PhotoDisc

Chapter One: pp. 2-3 Roger Ressmeyer/CORBIS; 3 HRW Photo; 4, George Holton/Photo Researchers, Inc.; 6(tl), J. McKim Mallville/University of Colorado; 6(cl), Telegraph Colour Library/FPG; 7(tr), Tha British Library Picture Library; 7(br), David L. Brown/Tom Stack & Associates; 9(tr), The Bridgeman Art Library; 9(bl), Scala/Art Resource; 10, Roger Ressmeyer/Corbis; 13(br), Peter Van Steen/HRW Photo; 13(bkgd), Johnny Johnson/Index Stock; 14(bl), A.J. Copley/Visuals Unlimited; 16(tl), Jim Cummings/FPG International/PNI; 16(cl), Mike Yamashita/Woodfin Camp/PNI; 16(c, br), NASA; 17(tr), Jerry Lodriguss/Photo Researchers, Inc.; 17(cr), Tony & Daphne Hallas/Science Photo Library/Photo Researchers, Inc.; 18(bl-bkgd), David Nunuk/Science Photo Library/Photo Researchers, Inc.; 18(br-bkgd), Jerry Lodriguss; 18(bl, br), Peter Van Steen/HRW Photo; 20(tl), Simon Fraser/Science Photo Library/Photo Researchers, Inc.; 20(b), NASA; 20(inset), Roger Ressmeyer/Corbis Images; 21(keyboard), Chuck O'Rear/Woodfin Camp & Associates, Inc.; 21(sunburn), Andy Christiansen/HRW Photo; 21(x-ray), David M. Dennis/Tom Stack & Associates; 21(head), Michael Scott/Stone; 22(all NASA except bl), David Parker/Science Photo Library/Photo Researchers, Inc.; 23(tr), Larry Mulvehill/Photo Researchers, Inc.; 23(cr), Harvard-Smithsonian Center for Astrophysics; 25 Sam Dudgeon/HRW Photo; 26(c), George Holton/Photo Researchers, Inc.; 27(cr), Daniel Schaefer/HRW Photo; 28, Jerry Lodriguss/Photo Researchers, Inc.; 30, NASA; 31, Benjamin Shearn/FPG.

Chapter Two: pp. 32-33 David Malin/Anglo-Australian Observatory; 32 Roger Ressmeyer/CORBIS; 33 HRW Photo; 34, David Malin/Anglo-Australian Observatory/Royal Observatory, Edinburgh; 38(tl), Royal Observatory, Edinberg/AATB/Science Photo Library/Photo Researchers, Inc; 38(insets), NASA/Liaison Agency; 41(br), Michael Freeman/Bruce Coleman; 47, John Bova/Photo Researchers, Inc; 48, Earth Imaging/Stone; 51(bl), SuperStock; 52(bl), Breck P. Kent/Animals Animals/Earth Scenes; 52(br), John Reader/Science Photo Library/Photo Researchers, Inc; 54 Courtesy NASA; 55 Sam Dudgeon/HRW Photo; 58, NASA/TSADO/Tom Stack& Associates; 59, John T. Whatmough/JTW Incorporated; 60(bl), NSO/NASA; 61, Dean Congerngs/National Geographic Society Image Collection.

Chapter Three: pp. 62-63 Lynette Cook/Science Photo Library/Photo Researchers, Inc.; 63 HRW Photo; 64(l), Hulton Getty/Liaison Agency; 64(tr), NASA; 65, NASA/Mark S. Robinson; 66(tl), NASA; 66(bl), Mark Marten/NASA/Science Source/Photo Researchers, Inc.; 67(tr), Frans Lanting/Minden Pictures; 67(br), 68(c) NASA; 68(tl), World Perspective/Stone; 68-69(b), NASA; 69(cr), NASA; 70, NASA/Peter Arnold, Inc.; 71(all), 72(tl), 73, 74(tl), 75(l, br), NASA; 77(all), John Bova/Photo Researchers, Inc.; 78(bl), Fred Espenak; 79(tr), Jerry Lodriguss/Photo Researchers, Inc.; 80(all), 81(tr), NASA; 81(br), USGS/Science Photo Library/Photo Researchers, Inc.; 82, World Perspectives/Stone; 83(cl), Bob Yen/Liaison Agency; 83(br), Bill & Sally Fletcher/Tom Stack & Associates; 85(tr), NASA/Science Photo Library/Photo Researchers, Inc.; 86(bc), Breck P. Kent/Animals Animals/Earth Scenes; 86(bl), E.R. Degginger/Bruce Coleman Inc.; 86(br), Ken Nichols/Institute of Meteorites; 86(cl), Dennis Wilson/Science Photo Library/Photo Researhers, Inc.; 87, NASA; 88, Victoria Smith/HRW Photo; 90, 92(bl), NASA; 92(tr), Ken Nichols/Institute of Meteorites.

Chapter Four: pp. 96-97 Jean-Charles/Cuillandre/Canada-France-Hawaii Telescope/Science Photo Library/Photo Researchers; 96 Courtesy NASA; 97 HRW Photo; 98(tc), Phil Degginger/Color-Pic, Inc.; 98(bl), John Sanford/Astrostock; 98(tr), E. R. Degginger/Color-Pic, Inc.; 100(cr), Allan Morton/Science Photo Library/Photo Researchers, Inc.; 101, Magrath Photography/Science Photo Library/Photo Researchers, Inc.; 102, Andre Gallant/Image Bank; 105(c), Astrophysics Library, Princeton University; 108(br), Dr. Christopher Burrows, ESA/STScl/NASA; 108(cl, bl), Anglo-Australian Telescope Board; 109, David Hardy/Science Photo Library/Photo Researchers Inc.; 110, Bill & Sally Fletcher/Tom Stack & Associates; 111(bl), Dennis Di Cicco/Peter Arnold, Inc.; 111(tr), David Malin/Anglo-Australian Observatory; 112(tl), I M House/Stone; 112(br), Bill & Sally Fletcher/Tom Stack & Associates; 112(bl), Jerry Lodriguss/Photo Researchers, Inc; 113, NASA/CXC/Smithsonian Astrophysical Observatory; 115(tr), Pictures Unlimited, Inc; 118 Sam Dudgeon/HRW Photo; 119, John Sanford/Astrostock; 120(c), John Sanford/Astrostock; 121, I M House/Stone; 122(bl), NASA; 122(tr), David Nunuk/Science Photo Library/Photo Researchers Inc; 124(all), NASA; 125(tl), The Open University.

Chapter Five: pp. 126-127, Smithsonian Institution/Lockheed Corporation/Courtesy of Ft. Worth Museum of Science and History; 127, HRW Photo; 128(tr), Gustav Dore/Hulton Getty/Liaison Agency; 128(bl), NASA; 129(tr), Hulton Getty Images/Liaison Agency; 132(cr), Brian Parker/Tom Stack & Associates; 132(b), NASA; 133(br), Hesler, Chester, Jentoff-Nilsen/ NASA Goddard Lab of Atmospheres & Nielsen, U. of Hawaii; 134, Aerial Images, Inc. and SOVIN-FORMSPUTNIK; 135(tr, cr), EROS Data Center/USGS; 136(tr), NASA; 136(bkgr), Jim Ballard/Stone; 136(br), TSADO/JPL/Tom Stack & Associates; 137(br), NASA/Liaison Agency; 137 (bkgd), Jim Ballard/Stone; 138(c), NASA; 138(bl), JPL/NASA/Liaison Agency; 138(bkgd), 139(bkgd), Jim Ballard/Stone; 140(tl, bl), JPL/NASA; 142, SuperStock; 143(tr, b), 144, NASA; 145(tr), NASA/Science Photo Library/Photo Researchers, Inc.; 145(bl), 146 NASA; 148 NASA/Stone; 149 Sam Dudgeon/HRW Photo; 150(c), Hesler, Chester, Jentoff-Nilsen/ NASA Goddard Lab of Atmospheres & Nielsen, U. of Hawaii; 151(c), 152(bl), NASA; 152(cr), Zvi Har'El/Jules Vern; 153, Dr. Gene Feldman, NASA GSFC/Photo Researchers, Inc. .

LabBook/Appendix: "LabBook Header", "L", Corbis Images; "a", Letraset Phototone; "b", and "B", HRW; "o", and "k", images ©2001 PhotoDisc/HRW; Page 157(tr), John Langford/HRW Photo; 157(cl), Michelle Bridwell/HRW Photo; 157(br), Image ©2001 PhotoDisc, Inc./HRW; 158(bl), Stephanie Morris/HRW Photo; 159(tr), Jana Birchum/HRW Photo; 159 (b), Peter Van Steen/HRW Photo; 161, 162, 163, Peter Van Steen/HRW Photo; 168, Jeff Hunter/The Image Bank; 173(tr), Peter Van Steen/HRW Photo.

Feature Borders: Unless otherwise noted below, all images copyright ©2001 PhotoDisc/HRW. "Across the Sciences" 154, all images by HRW; "Careers" 125, sand bkgd and Saturn, Corbis Images; DNA, Morgan Cain & Associates; scuba gear, ©1997 Radlund & Associates for Artville; "Eye on the Environment" 31, clouds and sea in bkgd, HRW Photo; bkgd grass, red eyed frog, Corbis Images; hawks, pelican, Animals Animals/Earth Scenes; rat, Visuals Unlimited/John Grelach; endangered flower, Dan Suzio/Photo Researchers, Inc.; "Scientific Debate" 61, 94, Sam Dudgeon/HRW Photo; "Science Fiction" 95, 155, saucers, Ian Christopher/Greg Geisler;book, HRW; bkgd, Stock Illustration Source; "Science Technology and Society" 30, 60, robot, Greg Geisler; "Weird Science" 124, mite, David Burder/Tony Stone; atom balls, J/B Woolsey Associates; walking stick, turtle, EclectiCollection.

Self-Check Answers

Chapter 1—Observing the Sky

Page 9: Ptolemy and Tycho Brahe thought that the universe was Earth-centered. Copernicus and Galileo thought the universe was sun-centered.

Page 12: No, the object is within the boundaries of the constellation.

Chapter 2—Formation of the Solar System

Page 35: The balance between pressure and gravity keeps a nebula from collapsing.

Page 37: The giant gas planets were massive enough for their gravity to attract hydrogen and helium.

Page 48: The Earth has enough mass that gravitational pressure crushed and melted rocks during its formation. The force of gravity pulled this material toward the center, forming a sphere. Asteroids are not massive enough for their interiors to be crushed or melted.

Chapter 3—A Family of Planets

Page 81: The surface of Titan is much colder than the surface of the Earth.

Chapter 4—The Universe Beyond

Page 102: The two stars would have the same apparent magnitude.

Chapter 5—Exploring Space

Page 133: It requires much less fuel to reach LEO.